INTRODUCTION

Welcome to the world of digital publishing ~ the book you now hold in your hand, while unchanged from the original **1969** edition, was printed using the latest state of the art digital technology. The advent of print-on-demand has forever changed the publishing process, never has information been so accessible and it is our hope that this book serves your informational needs for years to come. If this is your first exposure to digital publishing, we hope that you are pleased with the results. Many more titles of interest to the classic automobile and motorcycle enthusiast, collector and restorer are available via our website at **www.VelocePress.com.** We hope that you find this title as interesting as we do.

NOTE FROM THE PUBLISHER

The information presented is true and complete to the best of our knowledge. All recommendations are made without any guarantees on the part of the author or the publisher, who also disclaim all liability incurred with the use of this information.

TRADEMARKS

We recognize that some words, model names and designations, for example, mentioned herein are the property of the trademark holder. We use them for identification purposes only. This is not an official publication.

INFORMATION ON THE USE OF THIS PUBLICATION

This manual is an invaluable resource for the classic **Porsche 912** enthusiast and a must have for owners interested in performing their own maintenance. However, in today's information age we are constantly subject to changes in common practice, new technology, availability of improved materials and increased awareness of chemical toxicity. As such, it is advised that the user consult with an experienced professional prior to undertaking any procedure described herein. While every care has been taken to ensure correctness of information, it is obviously not possible to guarantee complete freedom from errors or omissions or to accept liability arising from such errors or omissions. Therefore, any individual that uses the information contained within, or elects to perform or participate in do-it-yourself repairs or modifications acknowledges that there is a risk factor involved and that the publisher or its associates cannot be held responsible for personal injury or property damage resulting from the use of the information or the outcome of such procedures.

It is important that the reader recognizes that any instructions may refer to either the right-hand or left-hand sides of the vehicle or the components and that the directions are followed carefully. One final word of advice, this publication is intended to be used as a reference guide, and when in doubt the reader should consult with a qualified expert.

PORSCHE 912

HANDBOOK AND SERVICE MANUAL

by
David Vincent
Technical Editor

With Assistance From
Lee Price and Dick Lovell

Published in 1969 by

FLOYD CLYMER PUBLICATIONS
World's Largest Publisher of Books Relating to Automobiles, Motorcycles, Motor Racing, and Americana
222 NO. VIRGIL AVENUE, LOS ANGELES, CALIFORNIA 90004

ANNOUNCEMENT

THE DYNAMIC DR. FERDINAND PORSCHE
AND HIS UNUSUAL MOTOR CARS

In every field of endeavor seldom does one man dominate his profession as did Dr. Ferdinand Porsche in the automotive field. Not because Dr. Porsche designed cars that were to outsell all others or designed the cars that changed basic thinking of automotive design and construction, but because of the uniqueness of cars that were his ideals.

Long before Volkswagen or Porsche cars were heard of, Dr. Porsche, who was born in 1875 in Maffersdorf, Austria, was designing unique automobiles in Austria. He developed the Electromobile Car, carrying the name Porsche-Lohner-Chaise. A gas engine powered the generator, which was a source of power for electric motors mounted in each of the four wheels. This was only one of the many revolutionary ideas that Dr. Porsche was to develop in the years to follow.

In 1906 he became technical director of the firm that manufactured the famed Austro-Daimler. In 1907 he designed light engines suitable for airplanes and industrial use. In the spring of 1923 he joined the factory of Daimler-Benz as Technical Director and Member of the Board. His outstanding engineering ability had much to do with the development of these famous cars.

Later on he designed the Auto-Union and these rear-engined racing cars were highly successful against Mercedes-Benz, Alfa Romeo and all other makes of racing cars.

When he designed the Volkswagen few ever dreamed that it would reach the tremendous popularity that it enjoys today. Dr. Porsche stuck with certain basic ideas in which he strongly believed, such as the rear engine, air cooling, and torsion bar suspension. While many of his other ideas became popular, these three basic engineering features have revised the thinking of many automotive manufacturers throughout the world.

He later founded his own company to manufacture the Porsche Sports Car — which now enjoys a fine sale throughout the world to customers who enjoy owning and driving a thoroughly different type of motor car. Using the basic Volkswagen engine, Porsche engineers, through special tuning of this engine, developed one of the outstanding performance cars of the world. The remarkable ability of the Porsche to operate at sustained high speeds over treacherous road racing courses has been one of the outstanding characteristics of this car.

Fortunately, Dr. Porsche had a son who was intensely interested in continuing the good work and honorable business principles and manufacturing techniques established by his father. Ferry Porsche, along with his sons Ferdinand III and Peter, is to be commended for the businesslike way in which this company has continued building a fine reputation.

We thank Ferry Porsche and his excellent organization for all the technical and press information that they have supplied to Clymer Publications during their period of existence.

It is not suggested that the owner attempt to do major repairs or service work that may require special factory tools. To the owner whose car needs proper care and important work, we suggest he take it to an authorized Porsche dealer, who has factory-trained mechanics and the necessary special tools to properly do the job. Responsible Porsche dealers and distributors are located throughout the world, and the Porsche owner is assured of good service wherever he or she may reside.

We are proud to present the Porsche 912 Handbook and Service Manual, a new concept for us in arrangement, accuracy and usefulness to the Porsche enthusiast. The book includes exhaustive research into the latest changes and specifications incorporated into the 900 Porsche series. Our advisors are competition oriented and highly experienced Porsche technicians — ideal for a manual on the "race proven" Porsche breed. They have viewed this work from both the standpoint of accuracy and usefulness, especially to the reader with limited knowledge of Porsche products.

Many charts are included in the appendix of this book to aid in easy conversion of measurements. For added convenience the torque wrench settings are listed in both foot or inch/pounds and also in meter/kilogram/pounds or centimeter/kilogram/pounds, while the temperature readings are given in both Fahrenheit and Centigrade.

Aside from the main repair operations found in this manual, the reader will find the descriptive paragraphs, the cautions, warnings, and other notes to be both helpful and to contain necessary information. I hope that the Porsche owner will receive as much satisfaction from this Handbook as we have gained in being able to publish it.

Floyd Clymer

CONTENTS

SUBJECT	PAGE
Porsche Personalities	D
Family Tree	E
General Notes	J
Lubrication And Maintenance Service	K
Braking System	1
Disc Brake	1
Handbrake	8
Master Cylinder	14
Front Suspension	19
Steering	29
Rear Suspension	37
Wheel Alignment	48
Body	58
Repairs	58
Heating And Ventilation	65
Transmission And Differential	68
Transmission	68
Differential	81
Transmission Overhaul	94
Clutch	121
Electrical System	127
Fuses	127
Wiring Diagram	142
Power Generation And Ignition	143
Generator And Regulator	143
Ignition System	149
Fuel System	158
Carburetors	158
Fuel Pump	168
Exhaust Emission Control System	177
Engine	184
Description	184
Engine Removal And Replacement	186
Engine Disassembly And Reassembly	188
Cooling System	189
Exhaust System	194
Lubrication System	194
Cylinder Head Servicing	200
Servicing Valves	203
Cylinder And Piston Servicing	208
Crankcase/Crankshaft/Camshaft	212
Engine Specifications	222
Data	235
Driver's Manual	240

PORSCHE PERSONALITIES

EDITOR'S NOTE: We would like to thank Dick Lovell and Lee Price for their assistance in the preparation of this Handbook and Service Manual.

Dick Lovell

This car is one of the few Porsche 912 models competing in SCCA National Races. It is owned and maintained by Dick Lovell, 38, of Van Nuys, California. Up until June, 1969, Dennis Harrison, a SCCA National Champion, piloted the car to 4 wins and 2 second places in 8 E-Production races. Three first places were garnered at Santa Barbara, while the fourth was taken at Willow Springs. They copped the second places at Santa Barbara and Riverside.

All engine and suspension work is done by Dick, who owns Performance Products, Van Nuys (Los Angeles), an independent supplier of Porsche parts, tools, and accessories. He equipped the above car with a rollcage, vented brake discs, magnesium wheels, adjustable sway bars and shock absorbers front and rear, forged aluminum pistons, and his own exhaust system and velocity stacks. Dick is now building a Porsche 911 for C-Production events.

Dick acquired his first Porsche in 1957 and has since owned over 17, including two 911 models and three racing Porsches. He is a member of Porsche Club of America and a past board member of Porsche Owners Club. A former sales engineer, Dick formed his company in 1963 and has since enlarged it with a racing division so he now offers engine and suspension building and competition parts besides his regular lines.

Lee Price

Lee Price, 34, of Arleta, California, has served as a Porsche tuneup technician for Century Motor Sales, Alhambra, California, since 1966. He is now service manager for newly created Century West Porsche-Audi of Alhambra. Through to the end of the 1969 racing season he prepared the Porsche owned by Century and driven by Merwin Ink for participation in California Club SCCA E-Production Class racing events. With this car they took second place in regional points for E-Production.

Previous to this Lee prepared for West Coast competition both the Porsche 906 prototype and the Porsche 911 Trans-American under-2-liter class cars owned and driven by Fred Baker. In 1967 Baker won the Laguna Seca and placed second in the Riverside and Kent-Washington events with the 906 prototype. In 1968 Baker placed second at the Riverside Trans-American with the 911. This car was acquired by Century, where Lee is preparing it for the 1970 racing season in C-Production.

Lee himself has raced jalopies, motorcycles, modified sportsmen, and midgets, starting back in his home town of Dayton, Ohio, where he first joined Volkswagen-Porsche in 1955. Moving to the West Coast in 1957, Lee rejoined Volkswagen-Porsche, and has served with them ever since in many capacities, including management. He also continued his motor sport sideline at such Southern California tracks as Bakersfield, Ascot Park, and El Cajon. He prepared his own motorcycle, besides assisting with preparation of some of the URA midgets he piloted and various sports cars (used in SCCA events) for other drivers.

FAMILY TREE

Every Porsche owner who has taken delivery on a shiny new car knows the thrill of the first few hours of possession . . . the minute examination of detail, re-exploring of features and most of all, digesting the maintenance manual. It is probably the restrained but prideful statement of background in the preface to this little handbook which firmly convinces the Porsche buyer that he has a singular automobile. Aside from the other considerations of beauty, finish, design or performance — that may have brought him to the purchase of the Porsche, the owner can take jusitfiable satisfaction from knowing that his car is the product of a unique organization. And, the enthusiast who feels that competition breeds competence knows he has an **able** tool at his command.

The Dr. Ing. h.c.F. Porsche K.G. of Stuttgart-Zuffenhausen, Germany, a development center without precedent in the annals of automobile and engine designing, has, for some 30 years, been engaged as an independent research and development bureau with the aim of advancing the automobile and its engine. Many productions of this firm have acquired fame and reputation of international significance.

The latest creation, the Porsche Type 912 sports touring car is a product of the long experience of our construction staff and has been developed by the pick of our developing department. It has established itself an unrivalled record for performance in the fastest European class.

The Porsche torsion-bar suspension, the engine and transmission in one unit in the rear, the low center of gravity and the steering arrangement have been adopted in principle from the Auto-Union racing car, another famous Porsche creation.

The beautifully designed body is an improved version of the service-tested Auto-Union world record car which had been designed on the results of months of wind tunnel testing.

The air-cooled engine, the torsion resistant frame and the sturdy wheel suspension are backed by the abundant experience gained by the Volkswagen which was subjected to severest trials during the war in climates ranging from the glowing heat of North Africa to the ice and snow of the far north, under the worst possible conditions in regard to terrain and temperature.

With the knowledge gained from this unique background we are in a position to offer our clientele a supreme combination of speed, driving safety and high quality workmanship.

. . . this car has been produced in limited quantity for discriminating drivers.

So goes the factory introduction in the manual issued with the first export models of the 912 . . . and there is no reason to change a word except to add that American victories in racing have also produced an "unrivalled record".

Two references in the above paragraphs catch the eye more than any other: Auto-Union and Volkswagen.

To have been the 'father' of one of the world's fastest and most renowned Grand Prix automobiles and one of the world's most 'practical' and use-tested sedans is a unique achievement for one man. To begin with, most automobiles are the product of many minds, but there is no doubt that these two designs, so widely separated in application, were the brain-children of that singular person; Dr. Ferdinand Porsche.

The Porsche story, at least many parts of it, is probably quite familiar to owners of the cars that bear his name, but, since the qualities that induced us to buy the vehicle in the first place are so typical of and dependent on the prior designs, we should examine this background at least briefly. Pride of ownership too, if nothing else, dictates that we should be adequately informed on a car that has such an ancestry.

Dr. Porsche was born in Austria and reached maturity at a time of great industrial development; the late 1890's. As a young man he was fascinated by electricity which, at the turn of the century, occupied the same relative position as 'electronics' in the mid-fifties. His first designs for Lohner in 1900 were of electric-powered automobiles, driven by individual motors in the wheel hubs with a power source of an engine generator in the chassis. This principle is basically employed today by the "Diesel" locomotives at the head of freight and passenger trains.

The automobile, in a relatively infantile state as far as production went in 1905 (when Porsche joined the Austro-Daimler firm), had already been exposed to nearly all the concepts that we find in a 'modern' car. Since that time we have benefited mainly from 'improvements,' but Porsche managed to come up with several innovations in the next few years that can be tabbed as original, culminating in the designs for the 'Peoples Car' and the 'P-Wagen'.

Having established his own engineering firm in 1930 at Stuttgart, Porsche speculated on a couple of ideas that he had toyed with while heading the design staffs at Daimler-Benz (now Mercedes as we know it) and Steyr, an Austrian automotive concern.

The 'P-Wagen' was a pure and simple race car: A Grand Prix machine to compete in the then new Formula 1 which placed a weight limitation of 750 kg. (approximately 1,650 lbs.) on the car without fuel, water, oil or tires, but no ceiling on displacement. This type of restriction was made to order for Porsche who had long been an advocate of the use of light alloys, aluminum and magnesium and formed-steel shapes that provided strength without excess weight.

THE AUTO-UNION G.P. CAR

About this time the German government decided to encourage national participation in GP racing by offering a $200,000 subsidy to firms who competed successfully in such events. Auto-Union, a newly-organized concern made up of the independent marques, Horch, Audi, DKW and Wanderer, enticed by this bonus and convinced that race-bred publicity would be good for sales, bought Dr. Porsche's design for the competition machine and retained his services. Thus the 'P-Wagen' (which it was at first called) became the Auto-Union A-Type.

The Auto-Union record during the 750 kg. formula period is outstanding. Victories in the French GP, German

Above — The V-16 cylinder 6000 cc supercharged Auto Union racing car. Driver Rosemeyer is cornering during 1936 German Grand Prix.

Left — Dr. Ferdinand Porsche, famous German engineer who designed the Auto Union Racing cars and the Volkswagen.

The 1937 6000 cc V-16 cylinder Auto Union Race Car engine. Photo taken during world's speed records and after the "Internationales Eifelrennen" in 1937.

GP (2), Swiss GP (2), Italian GP (3), Belgian GP, Tunis GP, Eifel GP and the Vanderbilt Cup Race plus innumerable hill climbs attest to the soundness of Porsche's design and the thoroughness with which the cars were prepared. In fact, the 'tryout' of the first model produced a new world record for 100 miles (134.46 mph) on the Avus track near Berlin.

The car, regarded as highly unconventional, placed the engine at the rear, used transverse torsion bars to suspend the front wheels, employed the swing axle principle and made much use of light alloys. Its 16 cylinder powerplant developed 295 bhp at 4500 rpm and the car was capable of close to 200 mph. Modified and developed, with various bodies, the Auto-Union eventually attained speeds of nearly 270 mph. In photos taken at Montlhery, France, where the Auto-Unions made their debut in 1934, there is a historic shot showing Dr. Porsche with the team manager and driver Hans Stuck. Clearly evident in the photograph is the torsion bar suspension with twin trailing arms identical to your present Porsche. The only difference is that friction shock absorbers were used at that time in place of the later hydraulics.

One outstanding difference, of course, was the use of a supercharged V-16 water cooled engine at the rear rather than an air cooled type. The engine, of 4.3 litres displacement, used a single camshaft to operate valves in both banks of cylinders in a highly developed and weight-saving arrangement of rocker arms and pushrods.

As Dennis May says in his article TURNABOUT TORNADOS in the July, 1958 **Sports Cars Illustrated;** "The fewness and simplicity of the modifications to the original concept that proved necessary during the life of the 750 kilogram formula are their own testimony to Porsche's remarkable foresight. So far as the running gear was concerned, they amounted to little more than the substitution of longitudinal torsion bars for the original transverse leaf spring at the back and revisions to the shock absorbers. In the engine department, a three-stage growth in swept volume was achieved without altering the original cylinder centers. The first of these increases marked the A to B transition, brought the capacity to 4950 cc and the power to 340 bhp at 4700 rpm. The C type successor, operative during 1936/37, displaced 6000 cc, developed 520 horses at 5000 rpm. Finally there was the 6300 cc R-Type, prepared for records, which gave 545 bhp at 5000."

So, in competition with the worlds finest machines through six strenuous Grand Prix seasons, (and actually halted only by the outbreak of World War II) Dr. Porsche's winning race car was refined basically by merely adding cubic inches to the engine. A remarkable bit of foresight, indeed.

THE PEOPLE'S CAR

That the production Porsche is based on the concepts employed in this car — and other race-bred vehicles — is probably a large part of the reason that it gives such a feeling of assurance on the road. The other side of the coin is equally intriguing. Given the leeway, any successful competition car builder can put a race car on the road in dress suitable for town and country. But, to make it untemperamental, long-lived and demanding no special service is another story. And, here is where the Volkswagen or 'People's Car' comes in.

As far back as 1930 Dr. Porsche was trying to promote interest in a cheap, light, easily made and maintained sedan that could be used anywhere in the world. The visionary Doctor, knowing that export was life blood to Germany, wanted to build a car that could be sold in Africa, South America and the north of Europe where water, strangely enough, is sometimes more of a problem than gasoline. His design called for an air-cooled engine, transmission/differential integral with it, and swing axle/torsion bar suspension.

The first attempt to market the car was made by the German motorcycle firm of Zundapp, whose familiarity with air cooled power plants made them a natural choice. The depression and other factors, however, did not let this effort get off the ground and it was not until after NSU had given it a whirl and Hitler seized upon this ideal to extract extra **Reichmarks** from his minions that further progress was made. Then, the political shenanigans of the Nazi government prevented any big realization of the premise.

There is no need to go into the VW story which is a modern industrial drama with few counterparts, but, just as Auto-Union found it necessary to make substantially no changes in their race cars except for power requirements, so has VW found it practical to stand by Dr. Porsche's original concept.

More remarkable foresight.

The Porsche, too, first of all his designs in a 50 year career to bear his name, is a sort of 'timeless' vehicle. The familiar shape and mechanical aspects of the Porsche coupe bear more than a little resemblance to the modified streamlined Volkswagen prepared 20 years ago for a projected Berlin-to-Rome race which was never held due to the war. Though this cannot be tagged as the direct antecedent of current series cars, its 40 hp hopped up VW 1100 cc engine reminds us that the maintenance manual states that the Porsche power unit is "an improved Volkswagen engine".

PORSCHE #1

Porsche #1 was actually built in 1947 by Dr. Porsche's son, Ferry, who had been actively assisting his father since the early 1930's. The Porsche firm, an engineering consulting service then operating out of Gmuend, Austria, had gotten re-established after the war with a design for a Grand Prix car for Cisitalia. This Italian concern commissioned the firm to produce the racer and the young members of the organization used most of the money to get the elder Porsche out of France where he had been jailed by the eager French as an enemy alien. Aside from the fact that it too made use of the torsion bar suspension and other design ideas from the Auto-Union, the Cisitalia need not enter into Porsche history. Although tremendous in potential it never reached the track and we have plenty of other experimental models that did.

The number one car was a roadster that looks a great deal like the present day 'D' or Speedster. It had the engine ahead of the rear axle but otherwise was built along the same lines as the cars being produced 13 years later. A VW mill, again modified to put out about 40 hp, was employed.

It took only two years to progress to the point where a production model could be offered to the public. Unveiled at the Geneva automobile show in 1949, the tiny streamlined coupe was an instant hit and a most controversial subject. Between the first "speedster" and the '356' coupe were about fifty hand-built aluminum bodied models. The show car and succeeeding series models had a steel body by Reutter. Aluminum has since been used in racing coupes and, of course, the Spyder. Now the ultra-streamlined Porsche Series 900 body, designed by Ferry Porsche, is obviously a continuation of the Porsche heritage. It, too, uses a steel body.

In another two years the Porsche name was synonymous with class victories in sports car racing all over Europe. The drivers took to the little coupe in such numbers that by 1952 the Porsche factory, now moved to Stuttgart-Zuffenhausen, was turning out six units a day and foreign trade had become a reality. Factory-sponsored cars had won the 1100 cc class at Le Mans in both 1951 and 1952 and three record cars had established 17 international marks at Montlhery. The 1100 cc coupe averaged 100.72 mph for 1,000 kilometers (621 mi.) the 1500 cc coupe averaged 98.95 for 3,000 miles (!) and

Unusual, one-off Glockler-Porsche coupe had pleasing lines

the Glockler-Porsche went 500 km. at 116.88.

The mention of Glockler brings up a name closely associated with Porsche during those early days and a person whose enthusiasm and efforts led to a greater participation by Porsche in competition.

Walter Glockler, a VW dealer in Frankfurt, grabbed onto an early Porsche 1100 cc engine and tweaked it up to 58 hp output on alcohol, stuffed it in a tube frame and surrounded the chassis with a light body of his own manufacture which kept the Porsche family resemblance. With this car he promptly went out and waxed everything in sight. He copped the 1950 German Championship, then sold the car to fellow driver Kathrein who repeated in 1951. In 1952 the Glockler-Porsche was in the hands of a young man named Brendel who also cleaned up and took the 1100 cc title. Glockler had moved up to the 1500 class when Porsche brought out that engine and his new machine (practically a dead-ringer for the first Spyder) won him the 1951 1500 cc German Championship and was used to set the records referred to above. This car was sold to Max Hoffman, Porsche Distributor in New York, who drove it rather capably. Glockler then built a

Porsche 1.5 litre

coupe version of the car that competed notably in races and rallies in Europe, then found its way to the U.S. where it finally was destroyed in a highway accident that took the life of young Tom Shipman, a promising actor and sports car enthusiast.

Glockler stood aside to let the factory carry racing development with the advent of the Spyder and particularly the Type 547 engine, but it can legitimately be said that he inspired the Spyder and the Speedster which, rather than the coupe so popular in Europe, captured America.

With the advent of the 1500 cc Formula 2, Porsche decided to enter into single seater racing, especially as the forthcoming Formula 1 would be limited to that capacity. The first experiments were with a streamlined single seater version of the well-known sports car which ran at Rheims and then at The Monaco GP of 1960 where a Formula 2 event was held concurrently with the Grand Prix. Successes and failures produced a mixed bax for Porsche that year.

In 1961, with the new Formula 1 in force, great things were awaited from Porsche but the Farrari opposition was too strong. Dan Gurney put up many brilliant performances and finished second in the French, Italian and USA Grand Prix. He also finished second at Syracuse and third at Solitude and Modena. Bonnier, the other works driver, was second at Solitude, Karlskoga and Modena, with a third place at Zeltweg.

In 1962, with the flat-eight engine developed to a higher state, and relying principally on Dan Gurney and Jo Bonnier to carry colors, Porsche was in the thick of contention at nearly every event. Gurney finally managed to win Porsche's first Grand Prix — the French at Rouen. Gurney also put up a great show at the Nurburgring in the German GP, setting fastest practice lap and leading the race for a time. A broken battery mount slowed him, however, and he finished third.

A discussion of the Spyder is not within the confines of this chapter and, since the Carrera is a hybrid, it will not be considered as an extension of the line historically. The new 912 is definitely an offspring of the pushrod engines.

So, we have a car with remarkably little history in its tremendous "history". It is safe to say that the Porsche works has succeeded within very close limits in the projects it has undertaken and has produced cars with a high degree of integrity. They are sound, well found and need only a master, as the seagoing saying has it. Now that yours has a master, lets see what adventures lie ahead.

356 B Porsche 1600 Roadster

356 B Porsche 1600 Coupe

GENERAL NOTES

DRIVER'S MANUAL CAUTION: On page 240 will be found a reprint of the DRIVER'S MANUAL issued with each Porsche Type 912. When using the information contained therein, please note that the balance of this publication has been authenticated for use by either the non-technician or professional mechanic, and has been updated to conform with the latest American service techniques. The DRIVER'S MANUAL has page numbering following the original publication's index which will be found on page 280 of this book (page 93 of the DRIVER'S MANUAL).

DRIVING CAUTION: When shifting gears, do not speed shift or power shift EVEN ONCE, because transmission synchromesh brake bands will be holding the synchro ring out, and it will be difficult for the shifting sleeve to depress the synchro ring to engage into gear. When this happens, it causes excessive wear on the synchro ring and the shift sleeve. Symptoms: The transmission will not engage into that gear without grinding.

DRIVING CAUTION: Should the red ignition warning light stay on after the engine is started or come on while the engine is running, investigate the cause immediately (the same applies to the oil pressure indicator). The red light not only serves as a check on the generator, but also on the fan belt and cooling fan. Should the belt break, not only will the generator and fan remain stationary, but the engine and oil cooler will overheat. It is wise to carry a spare fan belt and an adjustable wrench.

WARNING: A very common problem is for the cable connector AT THE STARTER SOLENOID (observed from under the vehicle) to come loose, in which case the battery will not receive the output of the generator, even though the red ignition warning light WILL STAY OUT. This connector joins one cable from the voltage regulator and a separate cable from the battery to the starter solenoid.

HOT WEATHER CAUTION: Check battery water level every 30 days.

EMERGENCY STARTING CAUTION: DO NOT push start a 900 Series Porsche with another car as the rear bumpers are of light metal and some body panel repairs will surely be needed. It is possible to start the car by hand pushing, or towing with a 10 ft. or longer cable, chain, or heavy rope attached to the center towhook located just forward of the front suspension. If the car has stalled because of a weak battery, it is possible to connect cables between the Porsche's battery and another 12-volt car battery to start the engine. Make sure the plus terminal is connected to the plus terminal on the other battery, and the minus to the minus terminal. For more emergency starting procedures see the GENERATING SYSTEM TESTS and IGNITION TROUBLE-SHOOTING in the POWER GENERATION AND IGNITION chapter, the STARTER TROUBLE CHART in the ELECTRICAL SYSTEM chapter, and finally the CARBURETOR SERVICE DIAGNOSIS chart in FUEL SYSTEM chapter.

CAUTION: Brake fluid level in the reservoir must be checked at regular intervals and replenished if necessary. Due to the relatively large cylinder cross-section of the brake calipers, the brake fluid level decreases much faster with continuing brake pad wear than is the case in braking systems employing brake drums.

CAUTION: Brake fluid attacks the paint finish. If brake fluid should spill on it, wash paint immediately with water. Brake fluid pumped out during the bleeding operation may be contaminated and should not be reused.

NOTE: To preserve ALL body rubber components (weatherstripping, gaskets, etc.) that are exposed to the elements, wipe ordinary drugstore variety glycerine into the rubber once every three months. This will even seal up old cracks and give rubber a new life.

NOTE: Procedure for setting Cylinder No. 1 to TDC: With the engine completely assembled and the valve covers off, use a wrench on the crankshaft pulley nut to rotate the engine clockwise (which is normal direction of engine rotation) until No. 1 Cylinder intake valve goes down and returns (opens and closes). Continue turning the crankshaft in the same direction until the "OT" (TDC) mark on the crankshaft pulley is lined up with the mark on the crankcase. This locates the TDC of the No. 1 Cylinder.

VEHICLE STORAGE CAUTION: If the vehicle is to be stored many months, it would be best to have it completely lubricated and the oil topped up beforehand, the carburetor drained, and the least amount of gas in the tank possible. Placing the car up on blocks will keep the tires from developing deflation cracks and out-of-round tires. It also helps to increase tire pressure to 50 pounds since there will be some air leakage. To save the battery, be sure to disconnect at least the ground cable, but preferably disconnect both cables. If possible, charge the battery once a month to prevent deterioration of the plates. First, the battery should be discharged prior to each third charging at a rate of 2 to 4 amperes until the low limit of 1.75 volts per cell has been reached. After that, the battery should be fully recharged with a trickle of about 4 amperes.

LUBRICATION AND MAINTENANCE SERVICE

LUBRICATION

NOTE: In general, the car should be driven only one block prior to servicing. Allow the oil to empty until it drips instead of pours, and while this is going on (or before replacing oil), the oil filter should be changed and the oil screen cleaned. Normal replacement period for the filter is 6,000 miles (every second oil change); however, in dusty climates change the oil and filter more frequently. Be sure not to get engine too warm if tuning engine or adjusting valves.

CHANGING OIL FILTER

Replace cartridge with a new one when it becomes contaminated; normal service period is every 6,000 mi. (10,000 km). Warm up engine beforehand.

1. Remove filter cover retaining bolt, then pull off cover.
2. Lift out filter cartridge with a slight turn. Hold it in a waste rag to contain oil drips.

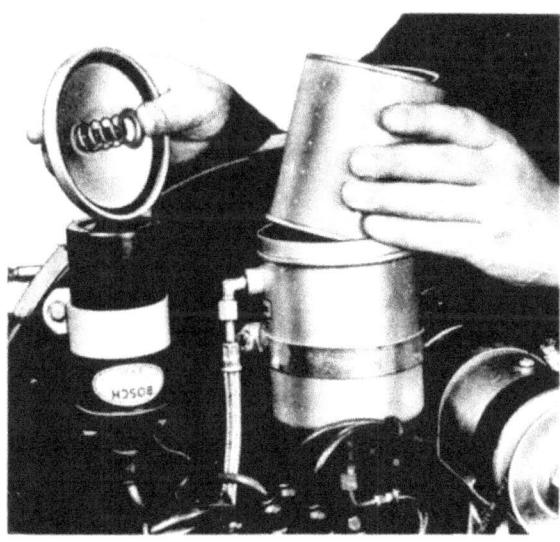

3. Use a suction pump to remove old oil from filter housing.
4. Use a lint-free cloth or paper to clean out the filter housing.
5. Insert a new filter cartridge, turning it slightly.
6. Place a new gasket into the housing cover, position the cover on the housing, depress, then tighten the bolt.
7. Check the engine oil level after filling crankcase.
8. Allow engine to idle for a few moments, then check the filter housing body and oil line connections for leakage.
9. Recheck engine oil level, then replenish engine oil to the top mark on the oil dipstick.

DRAINING ENGINE OIL AND SERVICING OIL STRAINER

Removal

1. Place suitable container under oil drain plug, then remove plug.
   NOTE: Engine should be warmed up slightly beforehand.
2. Remove hex nuts, then remove oil strainer cover, holding it in waste rags to catch oil drips.
3. Remove oil strainer and gaskets (see illustration).

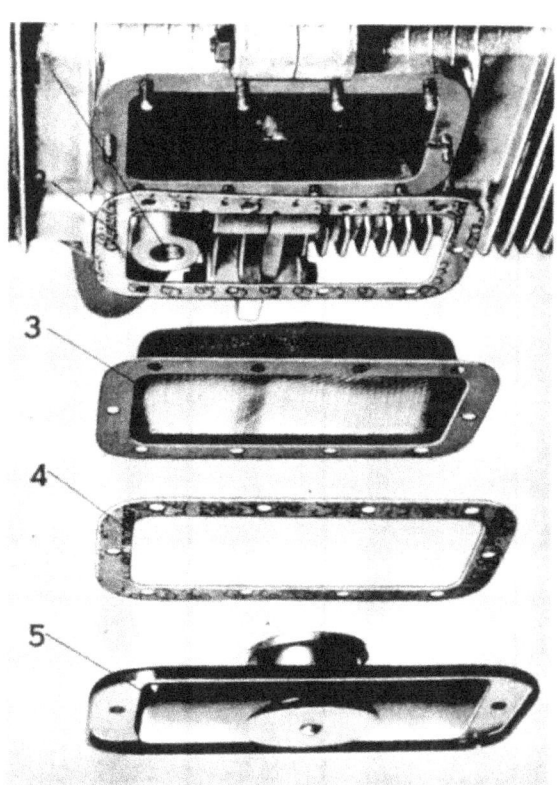

1 Oil drain plug
2 Gasket
3 Oil strainer
4 Gasket
5 Oil strainer cover with magnetic filtering element

LUBRICATION SCHEDULE

3,000 to 3,600 mi.	6,000 to 6,600 mi.	Service required
●	●	Change engine oil and clean filter magnets. At least twice a year: before the cold and warm season. HD oil, SAE 30 in summer, SAE 20 in winter
	●	Change oil filter cartridge.
●	●	Clean oil strainer.
●	●	Change transmission oil. Approx. 2.5 liters (2.6 US qts) SAE 90 hypoid gear lubricant
●	●	Lubricate door and lid hinges

Installation

To install plug and oil strainer, reverse the above procedure, noting the following points:

1. After oil has had time to drain sufficiently so as to remove most sediment, replace the oil drain plug, then tighten snugly to 18 ft. lb. (2,5 mkp).
2. Check the oil suction tube for proper positioning.
3. Clean the oil strainer and remove any gasket fragments, then place new gaskets on both sides of the strainer.
4. Replace oil strainer, making sure that the orifice in the strainer has a close fit around the oil suction tube.
5. Clean the oil strainer cover of any old oil and gasket remnants, then straighten out any bends or warps in the cover to prevent leaks.
6. Clean the magnetic filtering element.
7. Snug up the hex retaining nuts when replacing the cover, but do not overtighten (especially with thick gaskets), as this may cause cover warpage.
8. Fill the crankcase with $3\frac{1}{2}$ qt (or $4\frac{1}{2}$ qt. with new filter) of the appropriate weight of oil, run engine, then check oil level with dipstick, topping up if necessary.

NOTE: A magnetic oil filtering element is an integral part of the oil strainer cover to provide better oil filtration. As shown in both illustrations, the element is located in the center of the oil strainer cover with the oil suction tube inserted through it. The oil first passes through the oil screen and then flows through the magnetic filtering element.

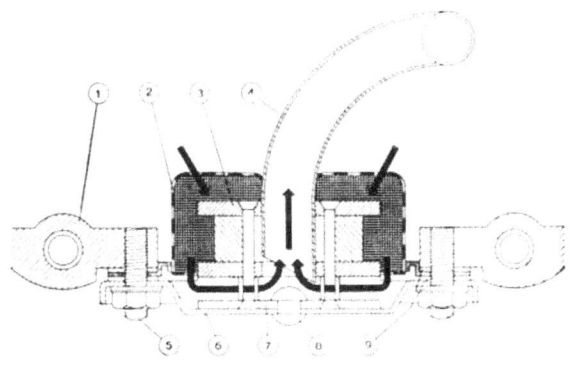

1 Crankcase
2 Oil strainer
3 Magnetic filter
4 Oil suction tube
5 Stud
6 Oil strainer cover
7 Disc
8 Rivet
9 Gasket

CHANGING OR ADDING TRANSMISSION FLUID

Car should be driven beforehand to warm up transmission fluid and to stir up sediment so it will drain.

1. Place suitable container under oil drain plug (on the driver's side, bottom), then remove oil drain plug with a 19 mm wrench.
2. After old oil has completely drained, snug up drain plug.
3. See LUBRICATION SCHEDULE. Use a 19 mm wrench to remove fill plug (driver's side, top, middle of the transmission), and fill to edge of hole.
4. Be sure to snug up fill plug.

LUBRICATION POINTS

NOTE: There are no undercarriage lubrication points whatsoever. Inspect tie rod and ball joint dust seals for damage or cracks, and replace parts as available, but DO NOT add any lubrication, even to rubber. On door and compartment lid hinges, use a light household oil or silicone lubricant.

NOTE: To preserve ALL body rubber components (weatherstripping, gaskets, etc.) that are exposed to the elements, wipe ordinary drugstore variety glycerine into the rubber once every three months. This will even seal up old cracks and give rubber a new life.

MAINTENANCE SERVICE

NOTE: The following items are a fuller explanation of services outlined in the MAINTENANCE SERVICE SCHEDULE chart. Items should be followed in sequence for (a) allowing the engine to cool down before setting valve adjustment, (b) ignition timing (1966–1967 models), (c) ease of service on a hoist (first, all the way up, then waist level after muffler check, and finally on the floor for torquing wheel nuts) and, (d) correct sequence for engine adjustments (allowing engine to cool down or heat up as required by adjustment).

CHECKING EXHAUST SYSTEM

With engine running and vehicle raised, check muffler for leaks and engine flanges for black carbon streaks indicating a leak. If uncertain about a particular area, hold a rag over the end of the exhaust pipe. This higher pressure will cause black carbon and smoke to blow out of any leaks present. Replace as necessary.

CHECKING TIRES

Check the tires for tears, imbedded foreign matter, uneven wear, or bumps caused by wheel unbalance, bad shocks, or misalignment. Normally Porsches wear rear tires faster than front tires, and these rear tires

MAINTENANCE SERVICE SCHEDULE

3,000 to 3,600 mi.	6,000 to 6,600 mi.	SERVICE REQUIRED*
✓	✓	Inspect muffler, service as necessary.
✓	✓	Check tires for wear, safety, and correct pressure.
✓	✓	Inspect brake system, fill reservoir as necessary.
✓	✓	Inspect foot brakes and hand brakes, note condition of the linings.
	✓	Inspect tie rod and ball joint dust seals for cracks, replace as available.
	✓	Check rack and pinion steering mechanism, then check shock absorbers.
	✓	Check front wheel bearings for play.
✓	✓	Adjust clutch pedal free play.
	✓	Check battery level, fill as necessary. Clean terminals and cover as necessary.
✓	✓	Inspect wiper blades and fill washer reservoir.
✓	✓	Adjust door striker plates, lubricate latches.
	✓	Check all electrical systems (lights, horn, wipers, warning lights and compartment lights).
	✓	Fan belt checked and adjusted.
	✓	Clean, gap, and test spark plugs or replace.
	✓	Adjust valve clearance. Replace valve cover gasket if necessary.
	✓	Check compression (individual cylinder readings shouldn't vary over 25 psi).
	✓	Contact points adjusted and ignition timing set (timing set ONLY with cool engine).
	✓	Check E.E.C. System air pump oil level (if so equipped).
	✓	Adjust idle, then balance carburetors.
	✓	Inspect air filters and clean screen if screen type air cleaner. Reinstall air cleaners.
	✓	Test wheel nut torque, make sure all even.
✓	✓	Check front-end height (adjust torsion bar if necessary).
	✓	Road Test**
	✓	Adjust idle mixture control screws and adjust idle speed.
	✓	Adjust throttle positioner.

*This procedure is listed in proper order for (a) allowing the engine to cool down before setting valve adjustment, (b) ignition timing (1966-'67 models), (c) ease of service on the hoist and, (d) correct sequence. Do not adjust throttle positioner or idle volume control screws unless engine is at OPERATING TEMPERATURE. See LUBRICATION for additional information.

**Check car for performance and also until the engine oil temperature gauge needle is in the operating range. This is necessary so the next two procedures can be done with the engine at the correct temperature; proceed with them immediately after road test.

are worn more on the inside. Only rotate tires when there is improper wear, and also have alignment checked. Bumps are from unbalanced wheels and worn shocks. Tire pressure should be checked every 2—3 weeks since they come equipped with natural rubber tubes which tend to lose air. Tires should be inflated to 30 lb. front, 32 lb. rear. These pressures give maximum tire life, maximum comfort, and maximum roadability.

CHECKING BRAKES

Inspect the brake system for cracked hoses, dented lines, leakage around the drums, calipers and fins. Replace any fluid loss in the reservoir with fresh, clean 70 R-1 S.A.E. specification fluid. Never use any Girling fluids since they will not mix with the original fluid. Caliper brake system is self-adjusting.

CHECKING FOOT BRAKES

Caliper brakes are self-adjusting, but if pedal goes to the floor, first check the fluid level in the reservoir. If it is empty, refill reservoir and bleed the whole braking system, using the instructions in the BRAKING SYSTEM chapter. If the pedal still goes to the floor, replace master cylinder with a new one (dealership recommendation is that new master cylinders are worth the small amount over the price of a rebuilding kit) using the instructions in the BRAKING SYSTEM chapter. If there is the smell of braking fluid in the car, look for a leak from the master cylinder or the connecting lines, and correct as necessary. To check brake pads, look through openings. If pads look thin, remove the wheel and inspect the brake pads for wear, and see if calipers are leaking. To check pad thickness, remove and measure with (preferably) a micrometer, using the dimensions in the BRAKING SYSTEM chapter. Replace as necessary.

CHECKING HAND BRAKES

Pull up on hand brake, counting the number of notches (clicks) until brakes are set. If more than eight notches are passed, adjust the rear brake shoes correctly as described in the BRAKING SYSTEM chapter, recheck, then adjust cable length as necessary. After adjustment, hand brakes should hold on the fourth notch.

FRONT AND REAR SUSPENSIONS

Inspect the front suspension tie rod and ball joint dust seals for damage and cracks, replace parts as available. On the rear axles, make sure the LOBRO half-axle dust boot is intact. Replace if necessary, being sure to repack it with grease. The full procedure is in the REAR SUSPENSION chapter.

CHECKING STEERING

With the car on a hoist or front wheels off ground, push on front or back of tire. It should feel only slightly stiff, and the steering wheel should turn immediately when the wheel begins to move. If not, adjust rack-and-pinion as described under STEERING.

CHECKING SHOCK ABSORBERS

The usual bouncing-on-the-bumper method will not work to test the shock absorbers on a Porsche, and poor riding qualities can also be attributed to weak torsion bars, misalignment, soft tires, etc. The only sure test is to look for oil streaks on the shock absorbers, and if oil is present, remove the shocks and test as described in the FRONT SUSPENSION and REAR SUSPENSION chapters.

CHECKING FRONT WHEEL BEARINGS

Experienced mechanics can check a wheel bearing by shaking the tire, but for the uninitiated this procedure is better: Remove the dust covers, then you should be JUST able to move the steel thrust washer sideways using a screwdriver. This shows that there is the correct amount of preload on the bearing. If the bearing thrust washer is loose enough to move by finger, or too tight to turn with the screwdriver, then readjust according to instructions in the FRONT SUSPENSION chapter.

CAUTION: If you wash bearing in gasoline or solvent, first THOROUGHLY DRY with compressed air (but do not spin bearings). Then repack with fresh grease. If the bearings are not dried, the grease will not adhere to the bearings, resulting in quick failure.

CHECKING CLUTCH ADJUSTMENT

There are threads at both ends of the clutch cable, allowing adjustment at either the clutch control lever in the transmission housing or at the clutch pedal. The following adjustment (if needed) should be carefully made, since insufficient clearance will result in clutch slippage followed by burnt linings. Correct pedal free travel is ¾ to 1 in. (20 to 25 mm) from resting point of pedal to point of resistance.

NOTE: On 1967 and later models, reach behind pedal and pull up. There should be ¾ in. play. Use the following adjustment procedure.

Adjusting At The Clutch Control Lever

1. After raising the car, loosen the lock nut at the clutch lever clevis (see illustration).
2. Turn adjusting screw to adjust clutch free travel.
3. Tighten lock nut when adjustment has been made.

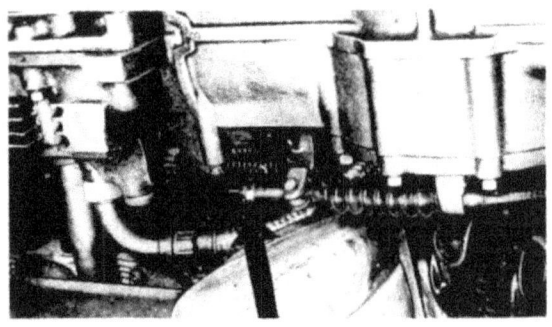

BATTERY CARE

Make sure all cells are filled to the split rings. Replace any lost fluids with distilled water. To inhibit corrosion around the terminals, remove any white powder with a water and baking soda solution, replace connectors, THEN coat terminals with chassis lubrication grease.

WINDSHIELD WIPERS AND WASHER

Check wiper blades for hardening, cracking or splitting. Replace as necessary. The electrically-powered window washer should be filled with water to which has been added window washer solvent with antifreeze.

DOOR STRIKER PLATE ALIGNMENT

If a door is dragging when it is opened, check the alignment of the door with the surrounding body metal when the door is closed. Check the gaps around the edges, but also check whether the metal is flush with the body panels. Move the striker plate so this alignment is accomplished. Lubricate latches.

ELECTRICAL SYSTEMS

Test all road lights, including turn signals (both ways), high and low beams, parking lights, tail lights, license plate light, backup lights, stop lights, and warning flasher system. Check horn, wipers, electrical washer, and any accessories. Check interior lights, instrument panel lights, and front luggage compartment light. Corrections, if necessary, are outlined in the ELECTRICAL SYSTEM chapter.

CHECKING AND ADJUSTING FAN BELT

Since the fan belt is considerably stressed at high speed and during downshifts, it needs to be frequently checked and adjusted to perform properly. The function of the fan belt is to drive the generator and air blower; loose fan belts can result in belt slippage, causing the engine to run hot. On the other hand, an over-tight belt leads to belt failure and possibly, premature wear of the generator bearings.

Checking

Contamination: Should a fan belt be freshly contaminated with oil during engine-compartment servicing, remove the belt and wash it in soap or detergent, then thoroughly rinse in clear water (or, better yet, install a new belt). Should a belt be contaminated with oil and then run for some time, it is generally no longer serviceable and must be replaced.

Adjustment: When correctly adjusted, the fan belt can be deflected by ⅝ to ¾ in. (15-20 mm) under slight thumb pressure applied midway between both fan belt pulleys. The belt should not show any signs of wear such as frayed edges or split sides. Adjust or replace belts as necessary (see illustration).

Adjusting Fan Belt Tension

1. Use a 36 mm wrench to remove the generator pulley nut. To lock the pullley in place during this process, insert a screwdriver into the recess in the inner edge of the pulley and brace it against the top bolt protruding from the generator housing (see illustration).
2. Remove outer pulley half, then adjust belt tension by adding or removing spacers between the two pulley halves. Adding spacers decreases belt tension, while removing spacers increases the tension. Replace retaining nut to test belt tension; it should yield by ⅝ to ¾ in. (15 to 20 mm) under light thumb pressure. If the belt has stretched or worn to such a degree that only one spacer remains between the pulleys at correct belt tension, it should be replaced since the condition will result in insufficient cooling due to decreased impeller speeds. In addition, it should be noted that the belt does not ride at the pulley root, i.e., on the pulley spacers (see illustration).

3. Those spacers not used between the two pulley halves should be placed on the shaft between the outer pulley half and the nut so they will be retained for later (see previous illustration).

CAUTION: After replacing the fan belt with a new one, check it for proper tension after driving about 30–60 miles (50–100 km) since the belt will stretch quickly while first being used. Failure to do this could result in engine damage. Also, do not attempt to remove the fan belt with a screwdriver without loosening the generator pulley as the belt and pulley could both sustain damage.

TESTING SPARK PLUGS

If there is a spark plug tester available (at a 3,000 mile servicing), plugs that hold their spark past 90 lb. pressure can be filed, gapped, and reinstalled. It is recommended that plugs used for over 6,000 miles be automatically replaced.

CHECKING VALVE CLEARANCE

Summary

Adjust valves when engine is cold (allow to cool overnight, if possible), or otherwise tolerances will be changed due to heat expansion. Tight or loose valves will cause the following problems:

Insufficient clearance: Decreased power and rough running; valves overheating, warping, or burning; carburetor flashback (which may cause a carburetor fire); and valve timing off.

Excessive clearance: Valve noise, excessive wear, valve timing off, decreased power and rough running.

The best sequence for adjustment is cylinders. 1, 2, 3, and 4 while rotating the crankshaft counterclockwise. Prior to adjusting, position the piston in Cyl. 1 on top dead center (TDC) on the compression stroke, since both valves are closed at this point.

To set Cylinder No. 1 to TDC (assuming the engine is completely assembled and the valve covers are off), use a wrench on the crankshaft pulley nut to rotate the engine clockwise (which is normal direction of engine rotation) until No. 1 Cylinder intake valve goes down and returns (opens and closes). Continue turning the crankshaft in the same direction until the "OT" (TDC) mark on the crankshaft pulley is lined up with the crankcase mark. This locates the TDC of Cylinder No. 1.

Checking And Adjusting

1. Pull wire clips downward to release both valve rocker covers, then remove covers (engine cold).
2. Remove distributor cap, then turn the crankshaft counterclockwise (if this hasn't been done previously) — using a box wrench on the crankshaft pulley, if necessary — until the "OT" mark on the pulley has lined up with the mark on the crankcase and the distributor rotor is pointing toward a notch machined into the distributor housing (see illustration). That is Cylinder No. 1.
3. Check valve clearance at Cyl. 1, using the following settings:

Valve clearance in a cold engine

Intake . . . . .004 in. (0,10 mm)
Exhaust . . . . .006 in. (0,15 mm)

4. If adjustment is necessary, loosen the lock nut on the adjusting screw, leave wrench on the nut, then adjust the clearance by turning the screw while simultaneously checking the clearance with a feeler gauge (see illustration).

5. Hold the adjusting screw in position when tightening the lock nut, then recheck the clearance (it may have been inadvertently changed in the tightening process).
6. Clean off gasket and mating surface on cylinder head, or if gasket compressed or damaged, scrape old gasket off valve rocker cover and glue a new gasket into place with gasket compound.
7. Replace valve rocker cover, center it, then clip into place. Check spring for fit and tighten if necessary.

CYLINDER COMPRESSION TEST

Before conducting this test, the valves must be adjusted and the throttle must be held completely open. The limits for the 912 engine are 170 psi to 140 psi. However, the difference between the highest compression and lowest compression cylinders cannot vary by more than 25 psi.

For example, if cylinders 1, 2, 3, and 4 were tested and were shown to give 155 lb., 165 lb., 140 lb., and 150 lb. readings respectively, the engine would still be serviceable. However, if the No. 3 (140 psi) cylinder were to drop to a lower reading, the engine would need to be repaired.

CONTACT POINTS AND IGNITION TIMING

This procedure is outlined under POWER GENERATION AND IGNITION SYSTEM. Be sure to clean out the points with a lint-free cloth after filing to remove metal particles. File only minimally.

EEC SYSTEM

Aside from the throttle valve compensator, checks to the Exhaust Emission Control System (EEC System) are relatively simple. Make sure there is the proper amount of oil in the air pump reservoir (see EXHAUST EMISSION CONTROL SYSTEM chapter for this check), then check all hoses and connections for cracks and sealing. The throttle valve compensator is the last item adjusted following engine settings.

ADJUSTING IDLE

See ADJUSTING IDLE SPEED under FUEL SYSTEM to balance the carburetors. Leave the idle speed (for the time being) around 800 rpm (adjust with idle speed screws, both the same amount, in or out, if necessary). Adjust throttle pedal travel limiter.

AIR FILTER

There are 4 types of air filters used, all of the dry element variety. The wire filter may be washed in gasoline or solvent. The paper elements can usually be cleaned by "bouncing" them on the floor from ankle level. Be sure the element lands flat on the rubber gasket. If this doesn't produce any appreciable cleaning of the element, it is time to renew it. Renewal period depends on the dust content of the air — there is no mileage figure one can depend upon, but elements generally last for several years in an urban environment. Reinstall air cleaners prior to road-testing (warming) the vehicle and making final adjustments. See the FUEL SYSTEM chapter for more information.

WHEEL NUTS

Lower car to ground. If car is new to you, or a wheel has been removed in the last 12,000 miles, torque all wheel lug nuts to 90–94 ft. lb.

ROAD TEST

Bring the oil temperature gauge needle into the operating range by DRIVING the vehicle. Check the performance, steering, braking action, and ride.

ADJUSTING IDLE MIXTURE AND SPEED

Adjust the idle speed to 1,000–1,100 rpm (1966–'67 models), 900–950 rpm (1968 models), as described in ADJUSTING IDLE SPEED in the FUEL SYSTEM chapter, using a portable multi-range tachometer. Adjust the idle mixture screws (using the same set of instructions), then recheck the idle speed and readjust if necessary.

ADJUST THROTTLE POSITIONER

On cars equipped with an exhaust Emission Control System (EEC System), check and adjust the throttle valve compensator. The engine should operate at 2200 rpm when the compensator is fully closed, and then adjust the time delay action as close to 3 seconds as possible, since there is a possibility the throttle linkage could hang up with a longer delay (refer to TESTING THROTTLE VALVE COMPENSATOR in the EXHAUST EMISSION CONTROL SYSTEM chapter).

MEMO

DECIMAL EQUIVALENTS

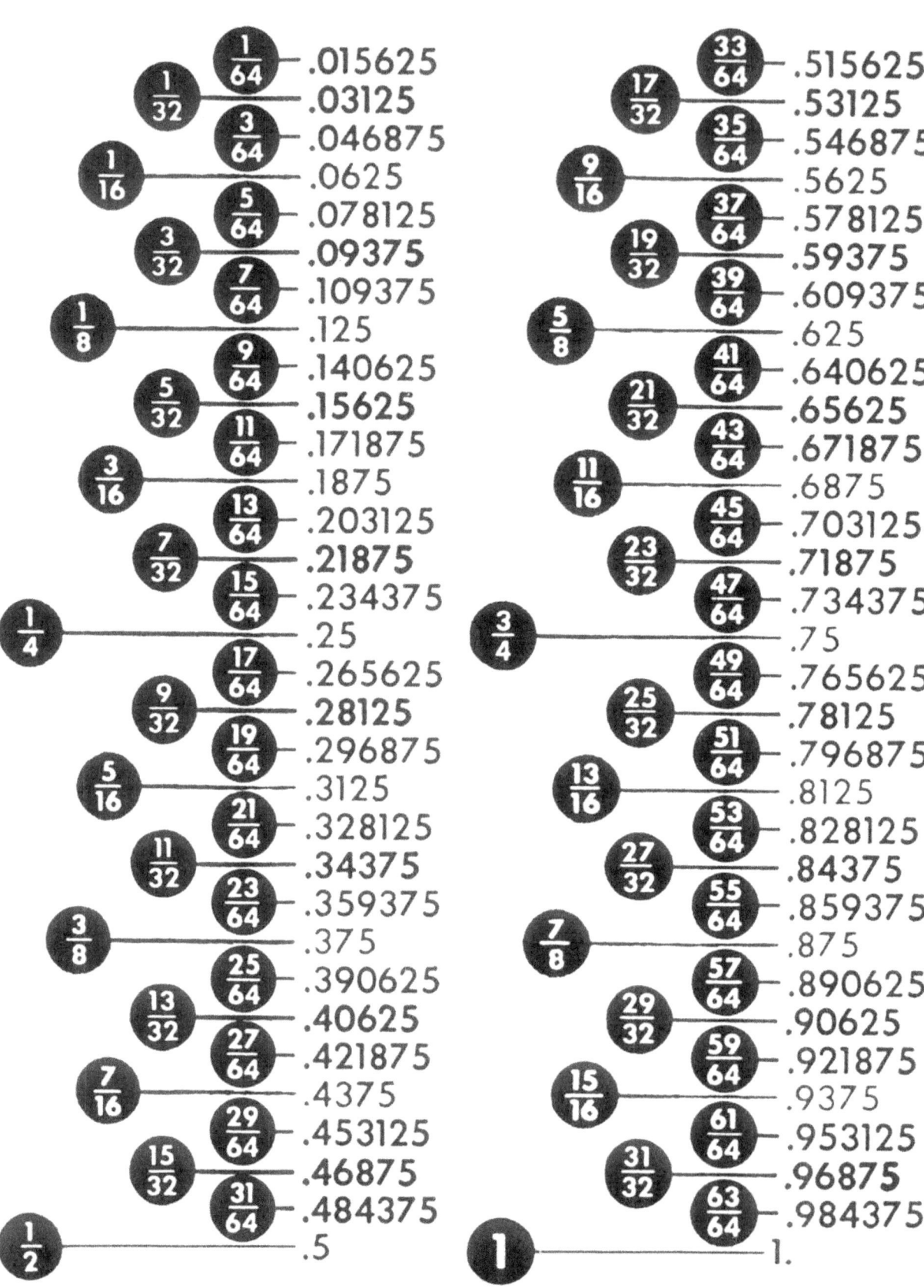

BRAKING SYSTEM

DISC BRAKE DESCRIPTION

The ATE disc brake (Dunlop licensed) is of a very simple design and consists of a flat disc, or rotor, and a brake caliper assembly (see illustration). The front wheel disc is attached to the wheel hub by appropriate bolts and is centered on the hub collar. The rear wheel disc is also attached by the hub collar. However, the main load is carried by the wheel lugs rather than by the two countersunk screws.

In both cases, the brake caliper straddles the disc. Two bolts attach the caliper to its carrier flange at the shock absorber strut at the front, and the axle guiding arm at the rear. The caliper base housing and the caliper cover housing are bolted together by four bolts, thus forming the caliper assembly. Each caliper assembly half (base and cover) has a brake cylinder with piston; piston sealing is by means of an O-ring embedded in a groove machined into the cylinder wall.

Dust boots have been provided to protect the brake cylinders and pistons against contamination by road dirt, dust, or moisture. The dust boot is secured to the housing collar by a clamping ring, and to the piston through snap fit in a groove provided for that purpose. Each brake pad segment (brake pad with base plate) has axial freedom in its slot in the housing and is guided by two retaining pins which are secured by pin retainers. A cross-spring, located under the retaining pins and exerting pressure upon the brake pad segments, ensures that the segments do not rattle and also serve as a brake pad wear indicator. The brake disc is protected against coarse dirt and direct water spray by an inboard mounted disc shroud.

NOTE: When spraying the underbody with undercoating or other corrosion preventatives, make sure that the brake disc assemblies are covered. Note also, that the brake calipers differ in size for front and rear wheels and are thus not interchangeable. The cylinder

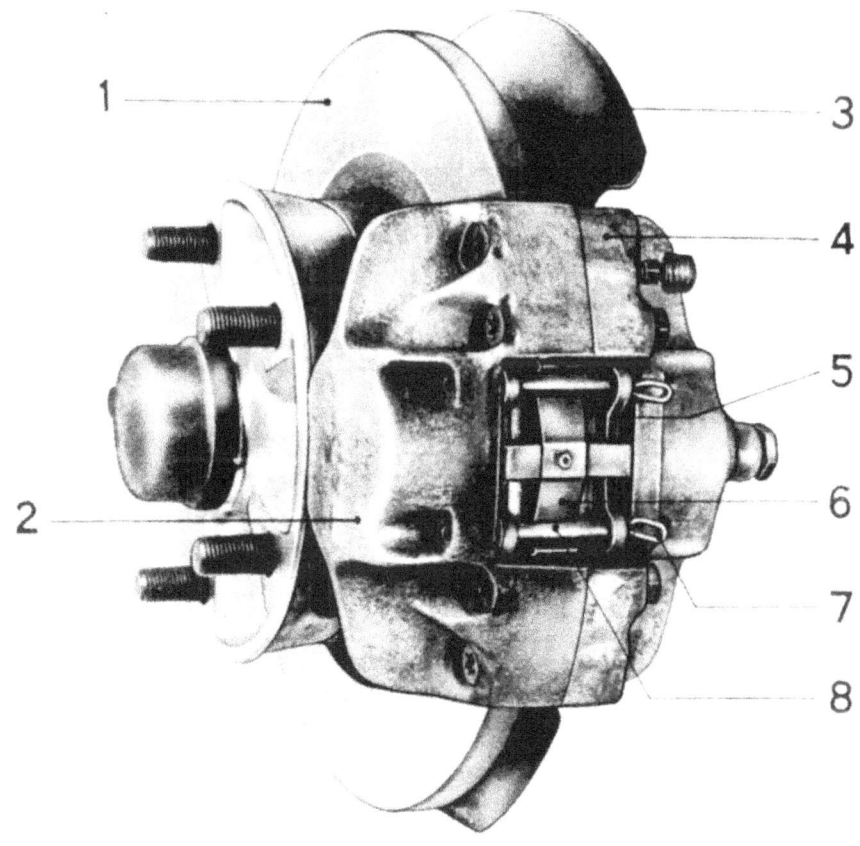

1 Brake disc
2 Caliper cover
3 Disc shroud
4 Caliper base housing
5 Brake pad segment
6 Cross-spring
7 Pin retainer
8 Retaining pin

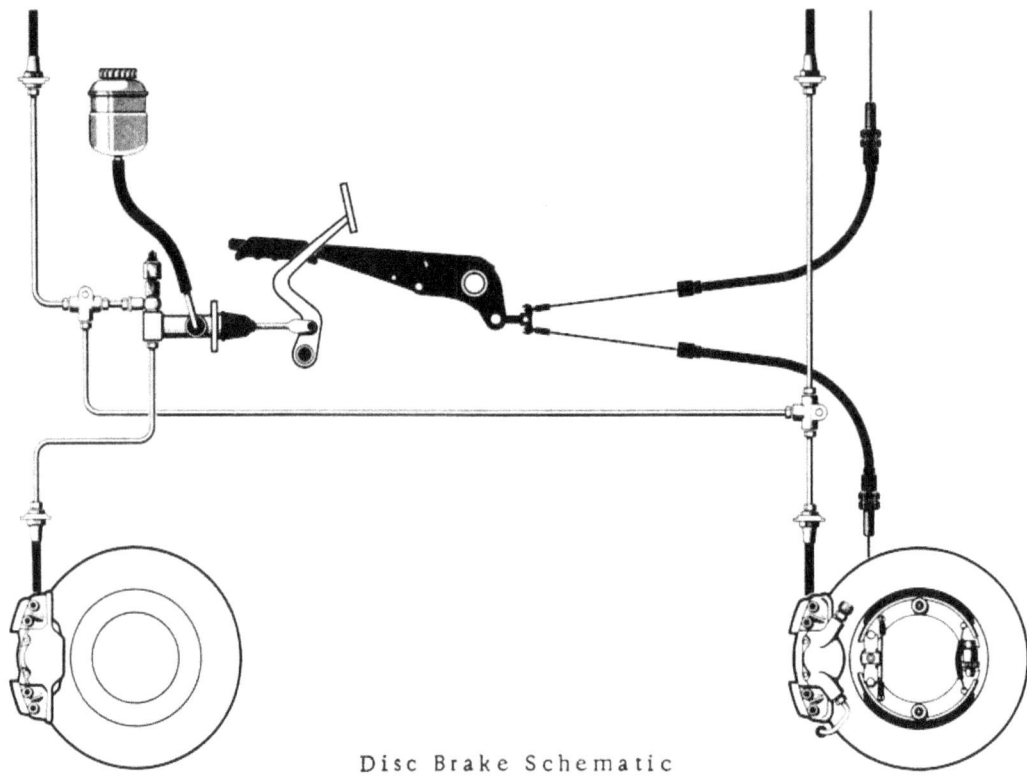

Disc Brake Schematic

diameter is 1.890 in. (48 mm) for front wheels, 1.378 in. (35 mm) for rear wheels.

The brake pads of the disc brakes require no adjustment (hand brake components excepted) since this happens automatically. The self-adjusting device is contained within the pistons in the brake calipers; it includes an arresting element, which in connection with a stud in both the caliper base housing and its cover, performs the automatic pad adjustment. The self-adjusting device, together with the inherent pad clearance it provides, cannot be changed or repaired. In the event of malfunctions it is necessary to replace the complete piston assembly.

Damaged disc surfaces may be redressed, although the removal of base metal must not exceed .02 in. (0,5 mm) per disc side, whereby the coarseness depth of the finished surface must be less than .0024 in. (0,06 mm). The permissible disc thickness variation at the braking surface is .0012 in. (0,03 mm) and must be kept within this limit or otherwise the brakes will have a tendency to chatter. In addition, when reconditioning brake discs, the lateral runout must not exceed .0020 in. (0,05 mm); this measurement should be made as close to the outer edge of the rim as possible.

The front wheel disc diameter is 11.1 in. (282 mm). The rear wheel disc diameter is 11.2 in. (285 mm). When new, the front wheel discs have a thickness of .500 to .492 in. (12,7 to 12,5 mm), rear discs .394 to .386 in. (10,0 to 9,8 mm) or .413 to .406 in. (10,5 to 10,3 mm).

The effective braking area per wheel is front 8.14 sq. in. (52,5 cm^2), rear 6.20 sq. in. (40,0 cm^2). Total effective braking area is 28.68 sq. in. (185,0 cm^2).

CAUTION: The brake disc must be dressed symmetrically only, i.e., equally on both sides. Recondition brake discs only when absolutely necessary. Brake thickness wear limit when worn symmetrically is .43 (11,0 mm) in front, and .33 in. (8,5 mm) in the rear.

COMPETITION EQUIPMENT

Competition Modification

For competition driving or the like, when brakes will be heavily worn, it is best to remove the disc shrouds to facilitate better cooling and, thus, extend brake pad life.

ATE Disc Brakes With Ventilated Discs

Type 911 S and E vehicles and all those equipped with the sportomatic transmission have been fitted with the disc brakes with the ventilated (slotted) discs. Lower brake disc operating temperatures are possible because of the cooling air channels cast into the discs in a radial arrangement. As a result, brake pad wear is lessened and the resistance to brake fading or formation of steam bubbles further increased. For competition driving of Porsche Series 900 vehicles not so equipped, this equipment may be added using the instructions in this chapter.

Since the ventilated discs are thicker, the brake calipers have been provided with an intermediate plate .287 in. (7,3 mm) thick in the front wheel calipers, and .417 in. (10,6 mm) thick in the rear wheel calipers. The brake caliper size remains the same for both the front and rear wheels. However, the diameter of the wheel brake cylinder in the rear wheel caliper now is 1.496 in. (38 mm). Following are deviations from the previous ATE disc brake description:

Disc Perimeter Diameter:

Front: 11.12 in—11.11 in. (282,5—282,2 mm)
Rear: 11.26 in.—11.25 in. (286—285,7 mm)

Disc Thickness (new):

Front: }
Rear: }   .787 in.—.780 in. (20—19,8 mm)

NOTE: When installing the rear wheel brake calipers, it is absolutely necessary to install the intermediate plate, Part No. 901.352.817.00 between the brake caliper and the rear axle control arm. The dust cap shield in the front wheel caliper has been discontinued. Vehicles that are continually used in low speed traffic and travel over dusty or muddy road surfaces may show an accumulation of dirt in the disc ventilation air channels to the point of plugging. Therefore, it is advisable to occasionally clear the disc channels with a water hose when the car is being washed. Other than the items mentioned below, the instructions for servicing these units remain the same.

Surface dressing: Recondition the brake discs only when absolutely necessary. The example below is of a disc that should NOT be dressed.

However, if the grooves in the disc have sharp edges as shown in the illustration below, the disc requires dressing. A dressing also is necessary when the brake disc shows excessive lateral runout or excessive thickness variations.

Dressing data: Brake surface of the brake disc may be dressed down to a maximum of .028 in. (0,7 mm) per disc side, to a disc thickness of .732 in. (18,6 mm). The coarseness depth can only be up to a maximum of .0002 in. (.006 mm). Deviation in brake disc thickness up to a maximum of .001 in. (0,03 mm). Brake disc lateral runout up to .002 in. (0,05 mm) when measured .4 in. (10 mm) below the brake disc outer periphery.

CAUTION: The brake discs may be dressed symmetrically only, that is evenly on both sides, as shown by arrows in the following illustration, which shows brake disc areas. See the table for Specification Value "a" for determining brake disc dressing symmetry and disc thickness wear limit. The wear limit in the brake thickness is .04 in. (1 mm) per disc side (when worn symmetrically, .71 in. (18 mm).

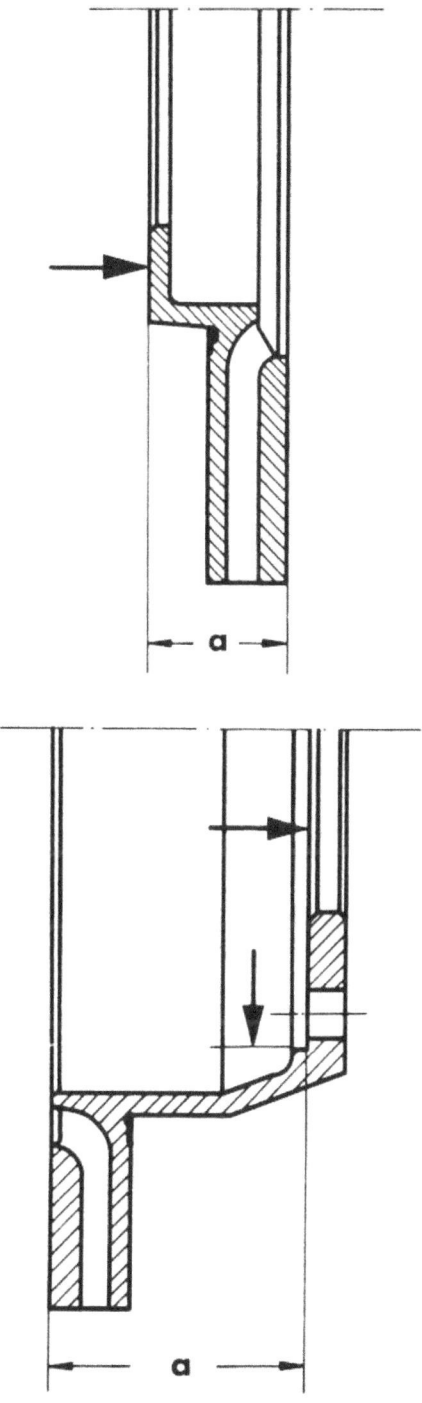

CAUTION: The above dressing and wear limits apply as long as the minimum brake pad thickness of .08 in. (2 mm) is not disregarded since otherwise brake malfunctions could occur (this is the purpose of the cross-spring).

Brake Disc Type	Location	Specification Value "a"	New-Disc Thickness
Solid disc	Front	1.378" ± .004" (35 ± 0.1 mm)	.5" - .008" (12.7 - 0.2 mm)
Solid disc	Rear	2.441" - .004" (62 ± 0.1 mm) 2.451" - .004" (62.25 ± 0.1 mm)	.394" - .008" (10.0 -0.2 mm) .413" - .008" (10.5 -0.2 mm)
Ventilated disc	Front	1.378" ± .004" (35 ± 0.1 mm)	.787" - .008" (20.0 - 0.2 mm)
Ventilated disc	Rear	2.559" - .004" (65 ± 0.1 mm)	.787 - .008" (20.0 - 0.2 mm)

Unbalance: Only balanced discs are supplied. Balancing is effected by inserting special clips into the disc ventilating channels. Do not remove the clips already in place (see illustration).

BRAKE PAD SERVICE

General Information

Brake pad wear is influenced, among other things, by driving habits and road conditions. Accelerated brake pad wear may be expected when driving on wet and dirty roads (winter-serviced) as well as through hard use of the brakes (high-temperature conditions). The thickness of the brake pads must be visually inspected in the course of all servicing operations.

Clearance must be in evidence between the cross-spring and the brake pad segment (see illustration). The wear limit has been reached when the brake pad segment touches the cross-spring or when the pad lining has worn to a thickness of .079 in. (2 mm).

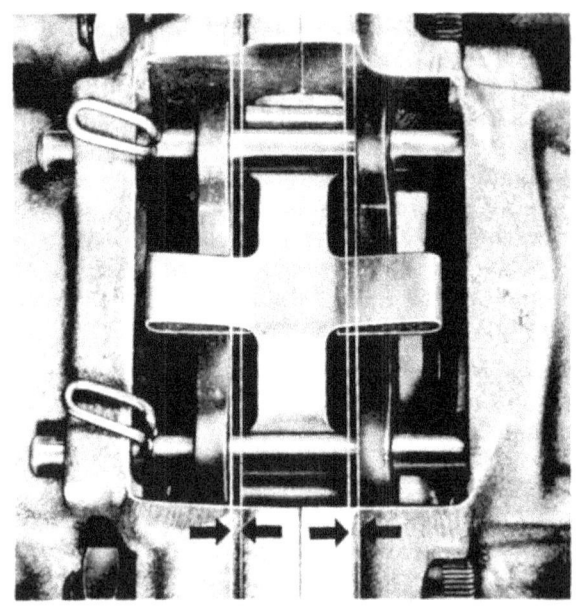

The installed thickness of the brake pad segment (lining supporting plate) is about .590 in. (15 mm). The pads installed in front and rear wheel brakes are of different size, and thus, are not interchangeable. The pads are marked on the lining plate. The proper brake pad type may be determined by consulting the Porsche spare parts catalogue.

Prior to the onset of the cold season, it is recommended that the competition pads be replaced by pads designed for normal driving. Only Porsche-approved brake pads may be installed. The front and rear wheel pairs must always be equipped with one type of brake pad. Although it is permissible to replace individual brake pads, it is suggested that at least all pads of a given axle (wheel pair) be replaced at any one time.

CAUTION: Used brake pads should be marked prior to removal from the calipers to ensure that they are reinstalled in the same position. The original position of the brake pads should not be changed by switching them from one place to another.

Changing Brake Pads

1. Place car on stands and remove wheels.
2. Withdraw pin retainers (see illustration).

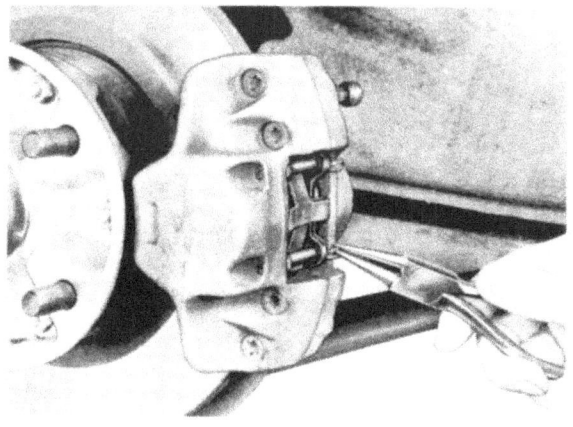

3. Push retaining pins towards the car while depressing the cross-spring (see illustration).

4. Mark original position of brake pads which are still usable.
5. Withdraw brake pad segments with the aid of the P 86 remover.

CAUTION: Do not insert the attaching dowels of the remover too deeply since this could engage into the cover shield and make pad withdrawal impossible.

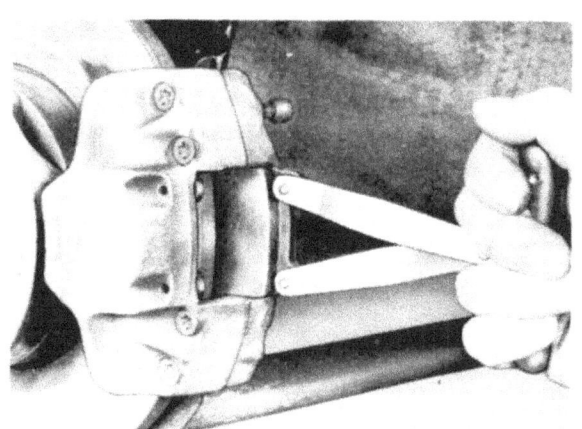

6. Push pistons fully back with the aid of the P 83 piston depressor. If not available, a hardwood block may be used instead. Do not use other tools due to the possibility of damaging the piston or brake (see illustration).

CAUTION: During this operation, fluid displaced by the pistons will cause the fluid level in the master cylinder to rise, and it may be necessary to siphon off some of the fluid to prevent it from overflowing. Use the siphon exclusively for brake fluid.

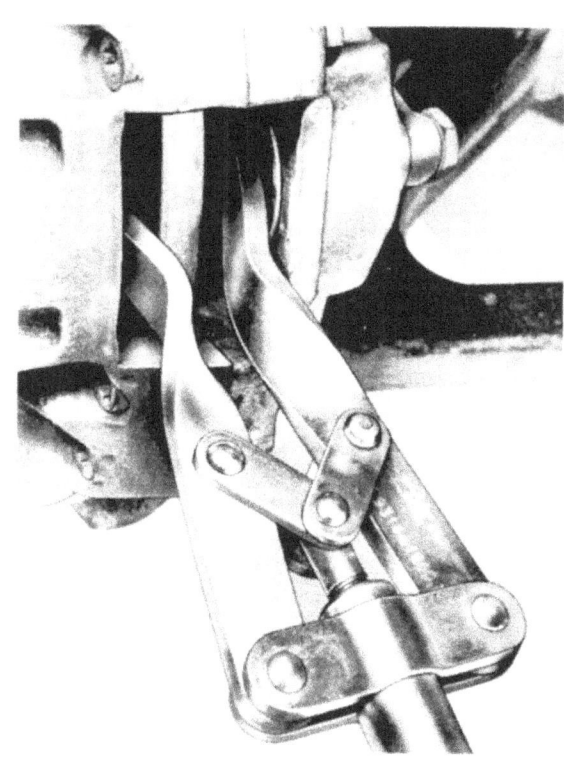

7. Clean the brake pad contact surfaces in their slots in the calipers; do not use mineral solvents or sharp-edged tools. Alcohol may be used if necessary.
8. Check dust boots and clamping rings for damage, and replace hard or porous boots.
9. Clean brake discs with fine emery cloth and smooth any evident disc wear ridge (top and bottom).
10. Install new brake pads in the caliper slots, together with retaining pins, cross-spring, and pin retainers; check pin retainers and if worn or deformed in any way, replace. The brake pads must hang free in their caliper slots without binding.
11. Repeat these procedures at the other brake calipers.

CAUTION: Before driving the car, repeatedly depress the brake pedal as far as possible to force the brake pistons into their proper positions. While doing this, repeatedly check the hydraulic fluid level in the master cylinder, replenishing when necessary.

Conditioning the Brake Pads

An inherent characteristic of factory-new brake pads is to fade once during the conditioning period of about 125 miles (200 km). This phenomena does not reoccur thereafter. During this period, the brake should not be used hard and severe application of the brakes should not be practiced from high speeds unless an emergency situation should be faced. New brake pads should be conditioned through moderate pedal pressure at reasonable intervals. It is only after this conditioning period that the brakes reach their effectiveness.

BLEEDING BRAKE SYSTEM

Bleed the braking system whenever the pedal travel is abnormally long or the brakes pull to one side. After every service operation during which any hydraulic line has to be disconnected (except the line connecting the brake master cylinder with the fluid reservoir), the entire brake system must be bled.

If the brake system has been fully drained for any reason, such as complete brake system overhaul, it may be necessary to rebleed the system subsequent to the road test. The pedal free travel will always remain the same due to the automatically adjusted brake pads, providing that the system is properly bled; pedal travel to brake actuation is approximately 30 to 50 percent of total pedal travel.

CAUTION: When any hydraulic connection is detached, the brake fluid will drain from the reservoir by flowing through the resupply port in the master cylinder. Such draining can, however, be prevented by slightly depressing the brake pedal with a pedal depressor, thus blocking the flow with the repositioned piston in the master cylinder.

Manually Bleeding Brake System

This operation must be carried out by two mechanics. Bleeding is started at the farthermost point from the master cylinder (applies to cars with left-hand drive).

    a. Left rear wheel; first outer bleeder valve, then inner bleeder valve.
    b. Right rear wheel; first outer bleeder valve, then inner bleeder valve.
    c. Right front wheel.
    d. Left front wheel.

NOTE: A fully drained system should first be filled with disc brake hydraulic fluid. Next, open the bleeder valve by about ½ to ¾ turns, depress the brake pedal, close the bleeder valve, then release the brake pedal. This sequence is to be repeated until the hydraulic brake fluid begins to spill from the bleeder valve. Repeat the procedure with all bleeder valves, then proceed with the actual bleeding of the system.

1. Remove the dust cover from the bleeder valve and install the bleeder hose.
2. Place the free end of the bleeder hose into a glass container with enough brake fluid to completely submerge the hose end.
3. Repeatedly depress the brake pedal in quick succession (pumping) until a slight pressure become evident, then hold the pedal under pressure while opening the bleeder valve by about ½ to ¾ turn, and quickly

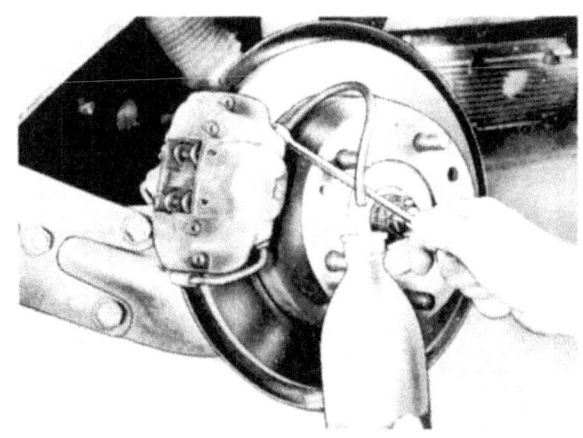

depress the pedal to the floor. Before releasing the pedal, always close the bleeder valve first, then allow the pedal to return slowly. Repeat this procedure until no air bubbles come out through the bleeder hose submerged in the brake fluid in the container.
4. Withdraw the bleeder hose from the bleeder valve and replace the dust cap.
5. Bleed the system at all other bleeder valves in the above outlined sequence. Make sure that the brake fluid reservoir does not run dry at any time since this would allow new air to enter the system.

CAUTION: Brake fluid attacks the paint finish. If brake fluid should spill on it, wash paint immediately with water. Brake fluid pumped out during the bleeding operation may be contaminated and should not be reused.

6. Check the effectiveness of the bleeding operation by depressing the brake pedal.
7. Refill the brake fluid reservoir up to its proper level of about .8 in. (2 cm) below the top ridge of the reservoir.

CAUTION: Brake fluid level in the reservoir must be checked at regular intervals and replenished if necessary. Due to the relatively large cylinder cross-section of the brake calipers, the brake fluid level decreases much faster with continuing brake pad wear than is the case in braking systems employing brake drums.

NOTE: Although there is no special brake fluid necessary for the system, it has been found that disc brake fluids are better than drum brake fluids. For competition work, brake fluid with higher boiling points may be used. It should be remembered, however, that the expected improvement can be realized only if the system is refilled with fresh brake fluid prior to each competition event.

REMOVING AND INSTALLING FRONT WHEEL BRAKES

Removal

1. Place car on stands and remove wheels.

2. Remove brake pads as previously described.
3. Detach hydraulic line at banjo connection in brake caliper.

NOTE: First, use a prop to slightly depress the brake pedal and lock it in that position. This will keep the brake fluid from draining out of the master cylinder fluid reservoir.

4. Remove caliper retaining bolts, then withdraw the caliper and shield (see illustration).

5. Remove grease cap from front wheel hub by prying evenly on all sides (see illustration).

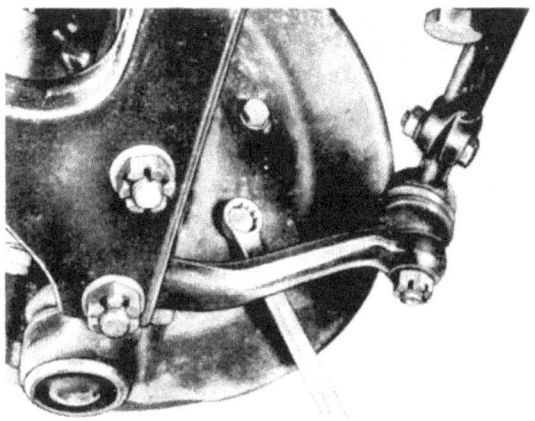

6. Loosen Allen bolt in wheel bearing clamping nut and withdraw bearing washer (see illustration).

7. While holding the brake disc with both hands at two opposite points, pull it off with a strong yank (fully-seated disc should be removed with a puller. Never hit the disc with a hammer or a mallet).

8. Remove retaining bolts from disc shroud and withdraw shroud (see illustration).

9. Remove retaining bolts from brake carrier and withdraw carrier (see illustration).

10. Mark brake disc and wheel hub, remove attaching bolts, and detach disc from hub (see illustration).

Installation

This procedure is a reversal of the removal and dismantling process. Note the following instruction:

1. Clean all parts of dirt and grease contamination.
2. Join disc and hub so that markers match.
3. Torque bolts attaching disc to hub to 17 ft. lb. (2,3 mkp).
4. Check wheel bearings, spacer, and seal for their condition, and replace any worn parts.
5. Install both bearings with about 1.6 oz (50 cm^3 or 45 g) lithium multipurpose grease.
6. Use new safety strips for brake carrier retaining bolts, and tighten bolts to 34 ft. lb. (4,7 mkp).
7. Tighten shroud retaining bolts to 18 ft. lb. (2,5 mkp).
8. Ensure proper wheel bearing adjustment (see FRONT SUSPENSION chapter).
9. The brake disc lateral runout must not exceed .008 in. (0,2 mm). Check disc for lateral runout with the P 87 gauge as described later in this chapter.
10. Using new spring washers, torque (front) caliper retaining bolts to 51 ft. lb. (7 mkp).
11. Install all brake pads in their original positions as previously described.
12. Bleed brake system as previously described.

CAUTION: Before driving the car, repeatedly depress the brake pedal as far as possible to force the brake pistons into their proper positions. While doing this, repeatedly check the hydraulic fluid level in the master cylinder, replenishing when necessary.

HANDBRAKE DESCRIPTION

The handbrake is of the duo-servo type and provides

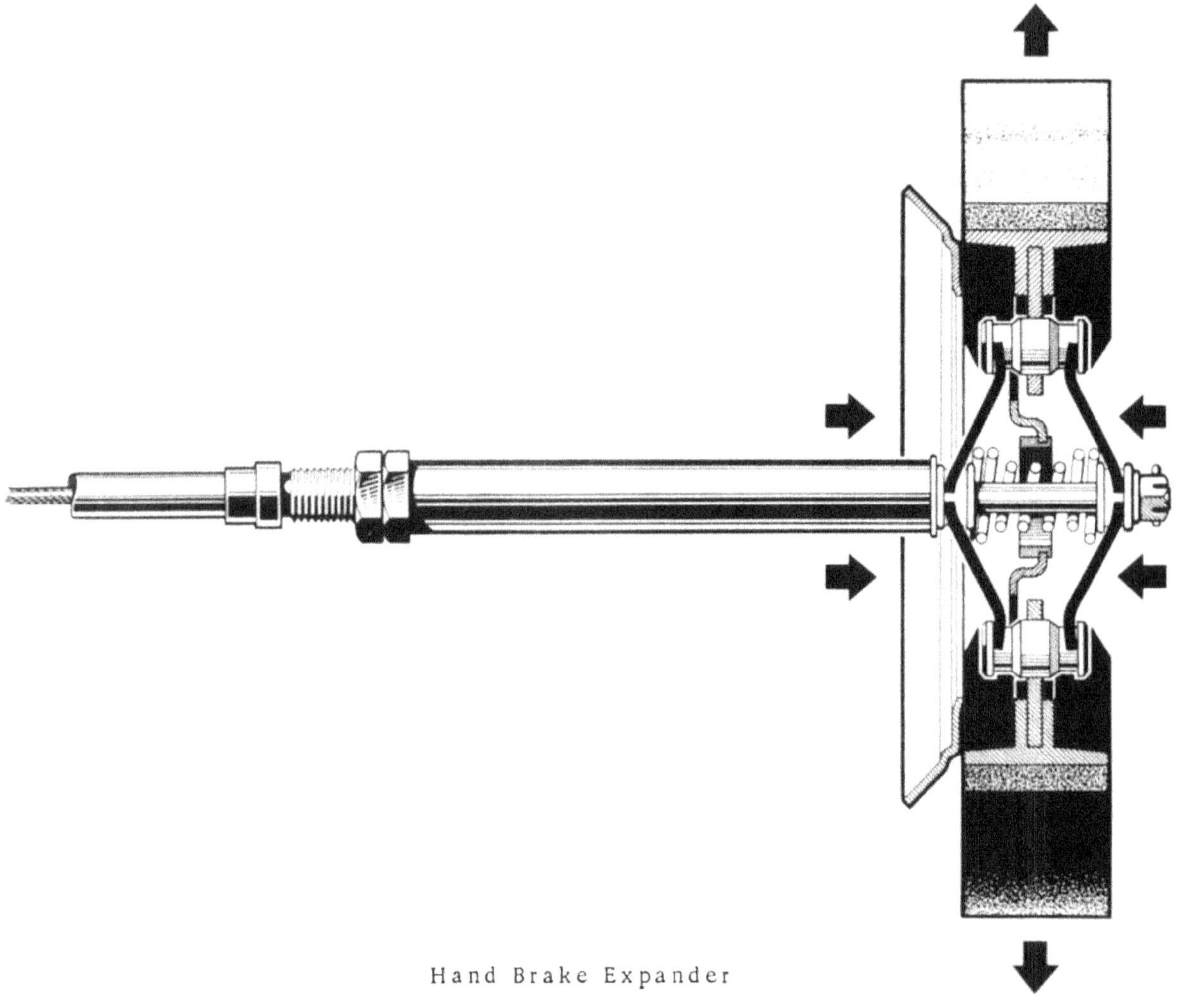

Hand Brake Expander

Rear Wheel Brake
Cross-sectional View

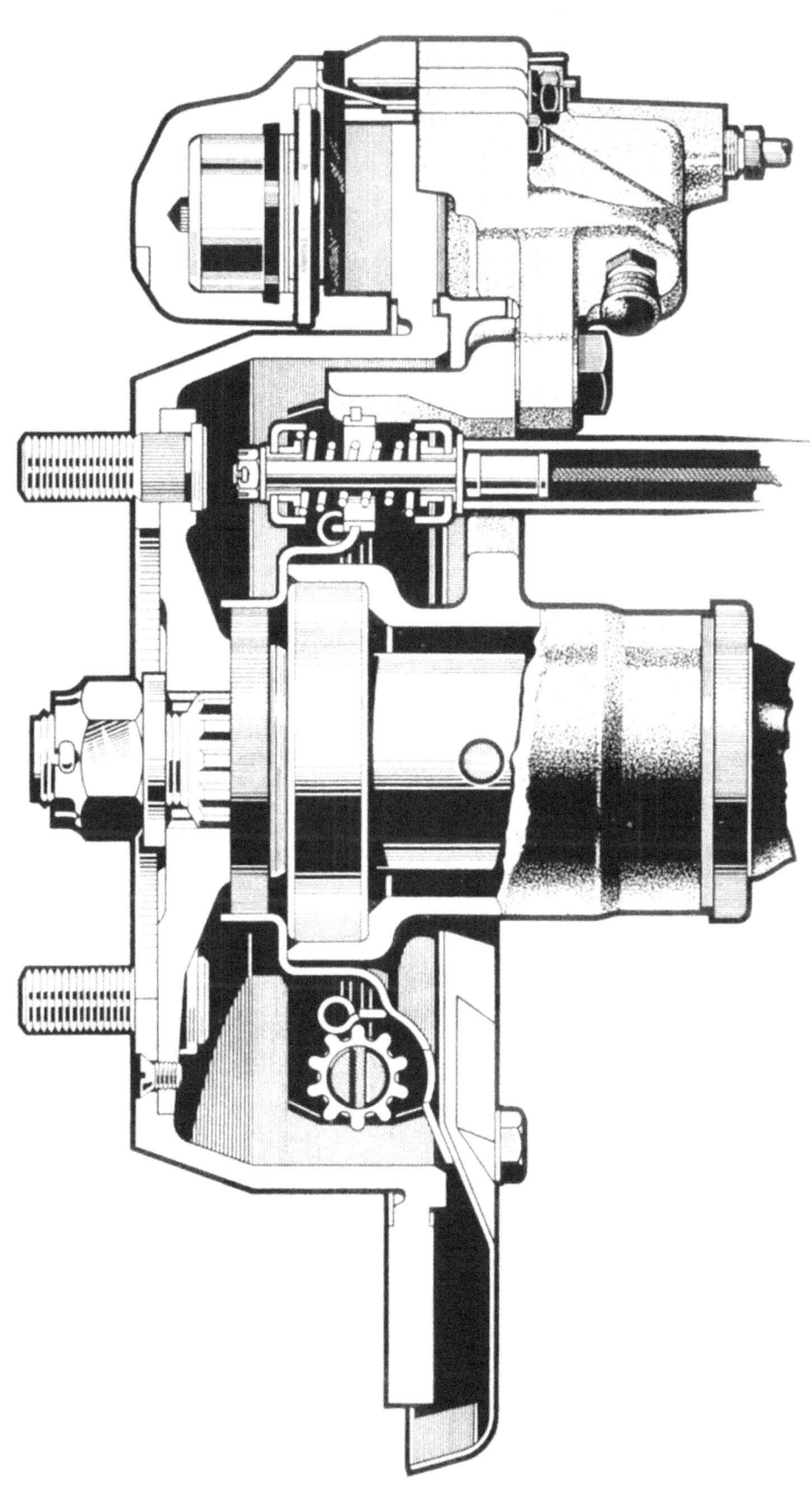

a good braking effect through the application of the self-energizing effect. The pot-shaped part of the rear wheel discs serves as a brake drum so that both are in one unit. The linings are bonded to the shoes, and only Porsche-approved linings should be used. Handbrake action is to the rear wheels only, and is applied mechanically. The handbrake and the foot brake are two completely separate systems.

When the handbrake is set, two brake shoes in each rear wheel expand against the brake drum contained within the rear brake discs through force transmitted over brake cables and mechanical expanders. Forward or rearward rotation of the wheels creates a self-energizing effect by the advancing primary shoe. Therefore, the floating adjusting assembly is both the anchoring point for the shoes and increases the braking force. Consequently, the secondary shoe receives sufficient braking pressure, the braking effectiveness being equally good in both directions of rotation.

The drum diameter for the handbrake is 7.087 in. (180 mm), the width of the brake lining is 1.26 in. (32 mm), and the total effective braking area of the handbrake is 32.55 sq. in. (210 cm^2).

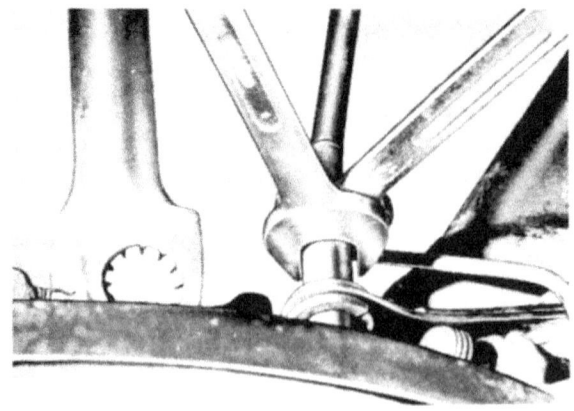

HANDBRAKE ADJUSTMENT

Adjustment

1. Place car on stands and remove rear wheels.
2. Release handbrake and push brake pads of rear disc brakes back so that the discs rotate freely.
3. Loosen cable conduit adjusting nuts so that cables are not under tension (see illustration).
4. Insert screwdriver into opening in drum of rear brake disc assembly and turn handbrake adjusting sprocket until tight, i.e., so that the brake disc can no longer be turned by hand (see illustration).
5. Repeat the adjusting procedure on the opposite rear brake.
6. Adjust handbrake cable tension by turning nuts at the cable conduit so as to remove the cable slack.
7. Pull tunnel cover and handbrake lever boot up at the rear and check the position of the cable equalizer by looking through the two inspection holes in the handbrake bracket. The equalizer must be exactly across

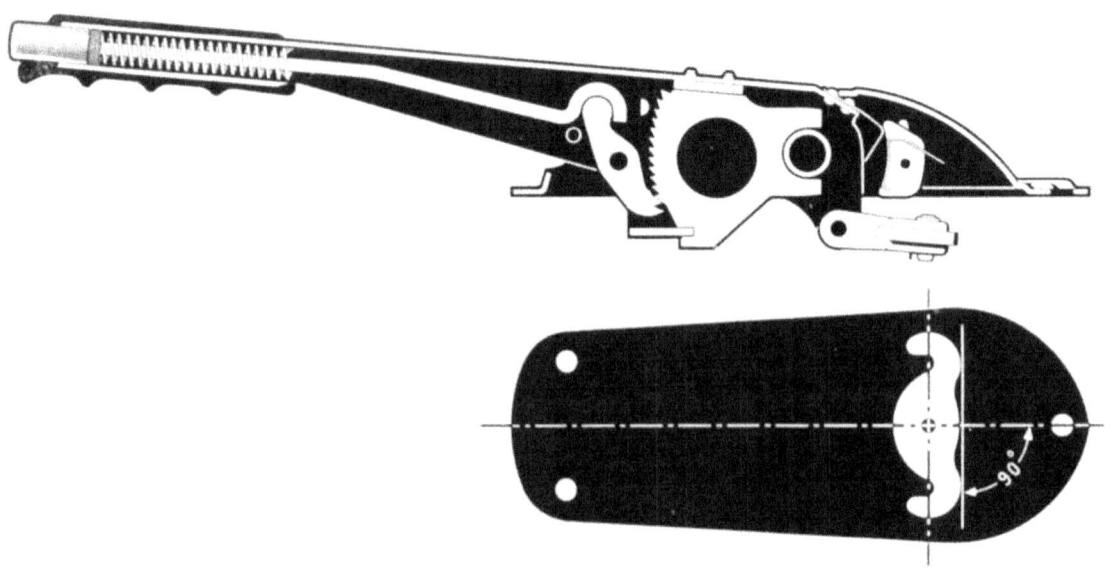

Cross - section of Handbrake Lever with Cable Equalizer

the car's long axis when the handbrake is pulled up. If necessary, reposition the equalizer by loosening or tightening the cable conduit adjusting nut (see this and previous illustration).

8. Tighten lock nuts at the conduit adjusting nuts.
9. Back off adjusting sprocket in each wheel by about 4-5 teeth so that the brake disc can turn freely.
10. Check clearance of handbrake at the handbrake lever. The lever should have a slight clearance, although the handbrake should be set when the lever is pulled up by 4 teeth of the ratchet.

HANDBRAKE LAMP SWITCH CONTACT BLOCK ADJUSTMENT

1. Pull tunnel cover and handbrake lever boot up at the rear.
2. Pull handbrake up until it is hooked on the first tooth of the ratchet, loosen fillister screw of the contact block by one to two turns, then move the contact block to the position where the control lamp just lights up (see illustration).
3. Tighten fillister screw of contact block and check the proper functioning of the handbrake control lamp.

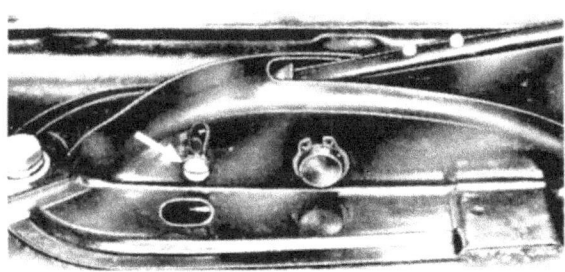

REMOVING AND INSTALLING REAR WHEEL BRAKES

Removal

1. Place car on stands and remove wheels.
2. Remove brake pads as previously described.
3. Remove disc shroud retaining bolts and withdraw shrouds.
4. Detach hydraulic line from caliper.

   NOTE: First, use a prop to slightly depress the brake pedal and lock it in that position. This will keep the brake fluid from draining out of the master cylinder fluid reservoir.

5. Remove caliper retaining bolts and withdraw the caliper.

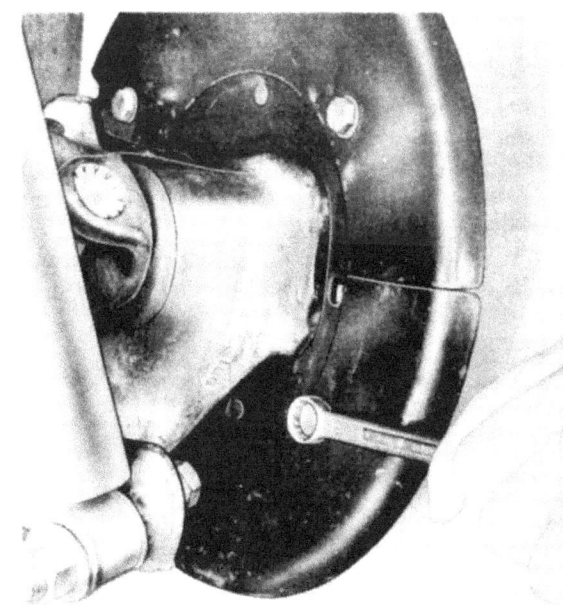

6. Remove countersunk screws from brake disc and detach disc (see illustration).

7. Remove cotter pin and castellated nut from brake cable and pull cable out towards the car (see illustration).
8. Remove mechanical expander and ring.
9. Remove spring retainer disc from holddown pin in upper brake shoe while pulling the brake shoe outward (withdraw spring by turning, pull the pin out through the back).
10. Raise upper brake shoe with a screwdriver, withdraw adjusting assembly, and unhook spring.

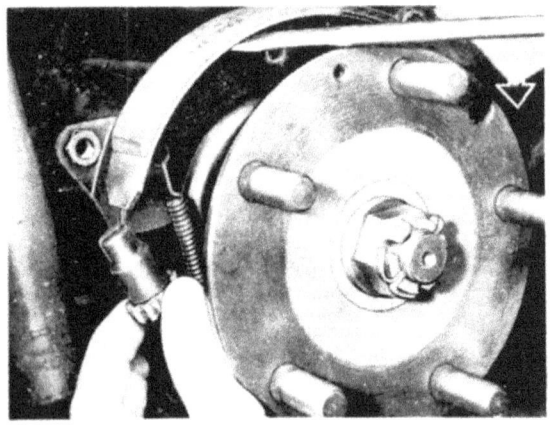

11. Remove spring retainer disc from holddown pin in lower shoe and withdraw spring and pin.
12. Remove both shoes by moving them towards the front of the car, then unhook the special return spring.

Installation

Reverse the above order to install. Note the following instructions:

1. Clean all parts, and replace worn or oily brake linings with Porsche-approved linings.
2. Insert brake cable from behind and slide inner part of expander onto cable.

NOTE: Be sure to install the washer between the spacer tube and the expander.

3. The return spring coils must be oriented towards the axle center when it is installed (see illustration).

4. After installing shoes, raise the upper shoe with a screwdriver and insert the handbrake adjusting assembly so that the adjusting sprocket is down in the right brake and up in the left brake.
5. After installing second return spring, turn adjusting nut in cable conduit all the way back. Then install spring, second expander half, washer, and castellated nut; tighten castellated nut until one of its slots clears the cotter pin orifice, then install a new cotter pin.

NOTE: Recheck expander assembly for proper seating in the shoes.

6. The brake disc must not have lateral runout in excess of .008 in. (0,2 mm), using procedure that follows.
7. Using new spring washers, torque (rear) caliper bolts to 43.5 ft. lb. (6 mkp).
8. Install all brake pads in their original locations.
9. Bleed brake system according to previous instructions.
10. Adjust handbrake as outlined earlier in this chapter.

REMOVING AND INSTALLING HANDBRAKE CARRIER PLATE

Removal

1. Follow steps (1) through (7) in previous procedure on removing rear wheel brakes.
2. Remove cotter pin from half-axle castellated nut and remove nut with special tools P 42a, P 36b, P 44a, and P 296 or equivalent (see illustration).

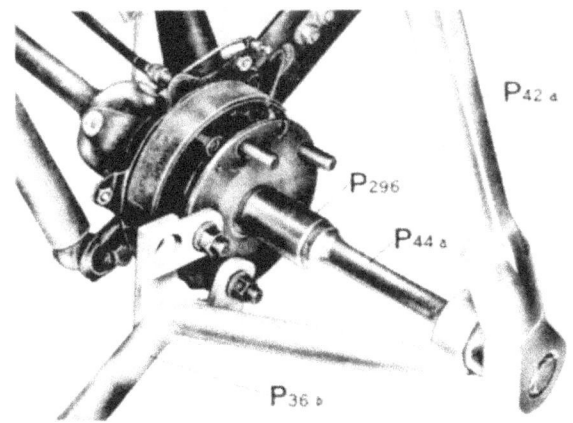

3. Remove half-axle Allen retaining bolts at the universal joint, then drive out the axle and remove.
4. Drive out the rear hub with special tool P 297 or equivalent (see illustration).

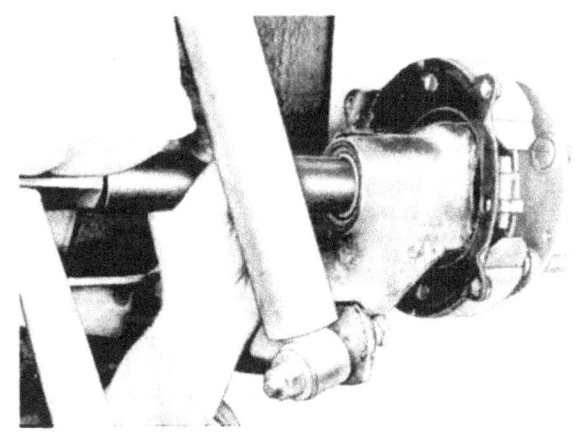

5. Remove the brake carrier plate retaining bolts, then withdraw the carrier plate (see illustration).

Installation

Reverse the above order to install. Note the following instructions:

1. Replace oil seal in brake carrier plate if necessary, using special tool P 294.
2. Clean all parts, then pack multipurpose lithium grease into ballbearing and rollerbearing.
3. Use a new O-ring, placing it into position with a little grease; ensure that O-ring is in its proper position (see illustration).

4. Torque brake carrier plate retaining bolts to 18 ft. lb. (2,5 mkp).
5. Torque castellated nut of half axle to 217–253 ft. lb. (30–35 mkp).
6. Torque Allen bolts of half-axle flange to 34 ft. lb. 4,7 mkp).
7. Using new spring washers, torque (rear) caliper retaining bolts to 43.4 ft. lb. 6 mkp).
8. Install all brake pads in their original positions.
9. Bleed brake system according to previous instructions.
10. Adjust handbrake as outlined earlier in this chapter.

BRAKE DISC LATERAL RUNOUT TEST

Front Units

1. Remove brake pads segments as previously described.
2. Adjust front wheel bearing clearance according to previous instructions.

3. Attach gauge P 87 with retaining pins, align, and tighten wing nut, with wing nut pointing down. Adapt a dial indicator for this purpose if the special gauge is not available (see illustration).

4. Install dial gauge and tighten retaining screw.
5. Push feeler pin onto gauge and fasten with a slight preload. The feeler point should ride on the disc about 10-15 mm below the outer circumference of the disc.

NOTE: In critical cases, the lateral runout should be checked on both sides of the disc, whereby the gauge should be turned around by 180°. Maximum permissible runout is .008 in. (0,2 mm).

6. Brake discs showing excessive runout (laterally) should be dressed or replaced (see BRAKE DISC DESCRIPTION).
7. Install brake pad segments as previously described.

Rear Units

1. Install gauge holder or equivalent as previously outlined (see illustration).

2. Using wheel nuts, tighten brake disc to wheel hub. To prevent disc warpage, machined steel discs should be placed under the wheel nuts. Torque wheel nuts to 72 ft. lb. (10 mkp) in a cross pattern.

NOTE: Permissible lateral runout is .008 in. (0,2 mm) maximum.

3. Brake discs showing excessive lateral runout should be dressed or replaced (see BRAKE DISC DESCRIPTION).
4. Install brake pad segments as previously described.

MASTER CYLINDER DESCRIPTION

When the foot brake is applied, the piston in the brake master cylinder is forced forward, transmitting hydraulic pressure to the brake cylinders in the calipers through hydraulic lines. The hydraulic pressure acts on the piston in the brake calipers, squeezing the brake pad segments against both sides of the rotating discs and creating the friction required for braking. The amount of braking force is determined by the amount of pedal pressure.

The brake master cylinder has a purging check valve which ensures a complete negation of pressure in the hydraulic system. Contrary to the normal designs, the check valve cone has a small purging passage of .276 in. (0,7 mm) diameter which also permits quick re-pumping under rapid pedal actuation, such as when refilling or bleeding the system without using a filling or bleeding tank. The hydraulic fluid reservoir is located below the forward luggage compartment (see illustrations).

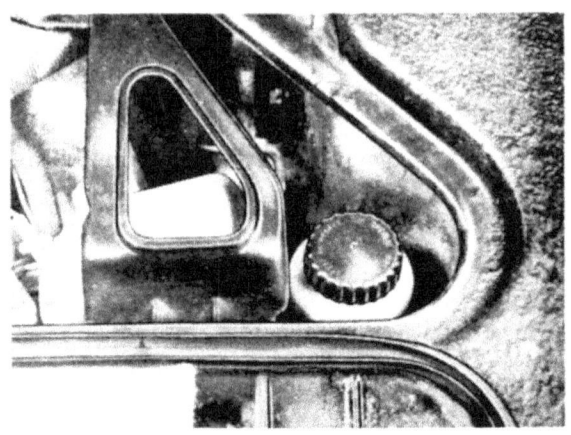

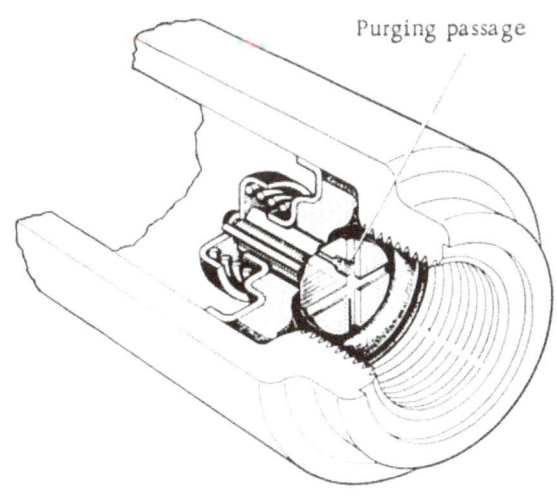

CAUTION: This brake master cylinder is not interchangeable with brake master cylinders utilized in drum-type brake systems. For this reason the brake master cylinder bears an identifying plastic band which reads "This cylinder has a special check valve," or in German "Zylinder hat Spezialbodenventil." The master cylinder has a bore diameter of .750 in. (19,05 mm).

REMOVING AND INSTALLING MASTER BRAKE CYLINDER

1. Place car on stand.
2. Detach accelerator pedal from pressure rod by pulling pedal back, then detach left-front floormat and remove.
3. Remove floorboard retaining nut and withdraw floorboard (see illustration).

4. Withdraw rubber boot from brake master cylinder.
5. Drain brake fluid reservoir with a siphon.
6. Remove retaining nuts and bolts from bottom shield and withdraw shield (see illustration).

7. Detach hydraulic lines and stop-light switch wires from the master brake cylinder (see illustration).

8. Loosen hose clamp at hose connecting fluid reservoir with the master cylinder, then withdraw the hose.
9. Remove retaining nuts from master cylinder mounting flange, then remove master cylinder.

Installation

Reverse the above order to install. Note the following instructions:

1. Properly position the piston rod while installing the master cylinder. Also, seal the flange with sealing compound to prevent water entering the passenger compartment.
2. Place new spring washers under the retaining hex nuts and tighten to 18 ft. lb. (2,5 mkp).
3. Provide a clearance of about .04 in. (1 mm) between the piston rod and the piston in the master cylinder. Loosen the lock nut and turn the rod for adjustment, then tighten lock nut (see illustration).
4. Check for possible restrictions in fluid reservoir cap venting passage.
5. Refill system with new brake fluid.
6. Bleed brake system as previously described.
7. Check brake lights.
8. Install bottom shield and tighten retaining nuts to 47 ft. lb. (6,5 mkp).

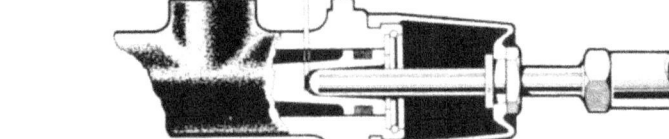

RECONDITIONING MASTER CYLINDER

Disassembly

1. Fasten master cylinder in a vise with jaw covers. Do not overtighten.
2. Withdraw lock ring with a small screwdriver (see illustration).

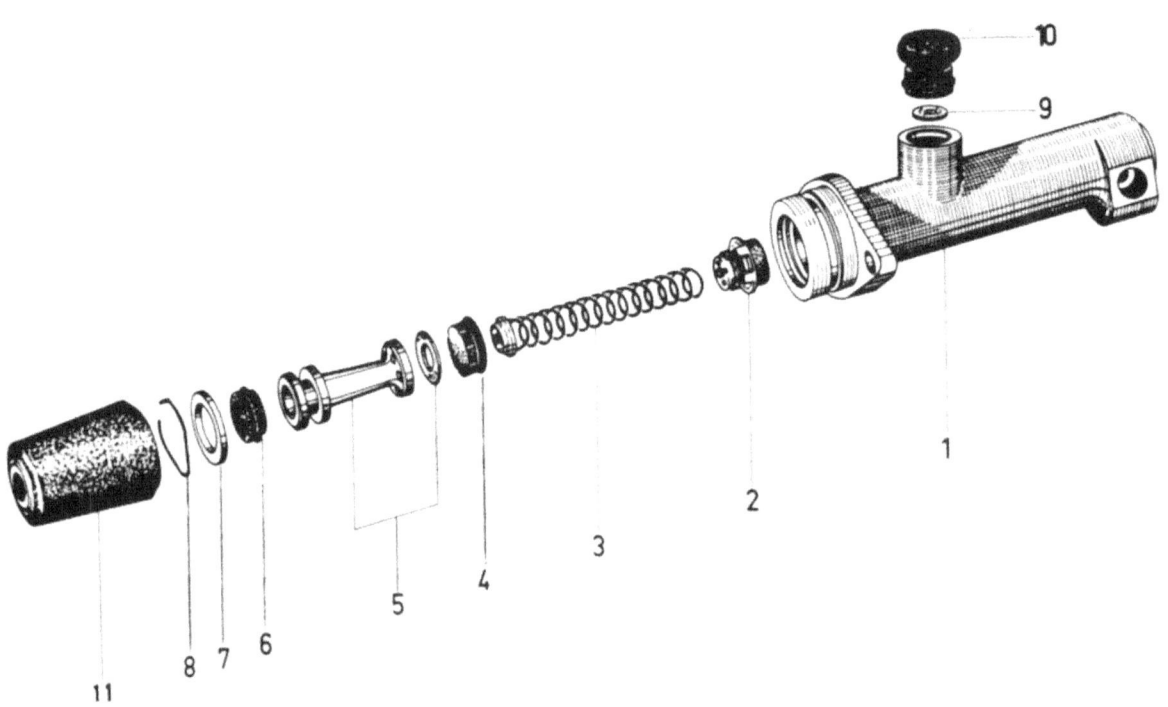

1 Housing	4 Primary piston cup	7 Piston stop plate	10 Rubber grommet
2 Special check valve	5 Piston with washer	8 Lock ring	11 Rubber boot
3 Spring	6 Secondary piston cup	9 Washer	

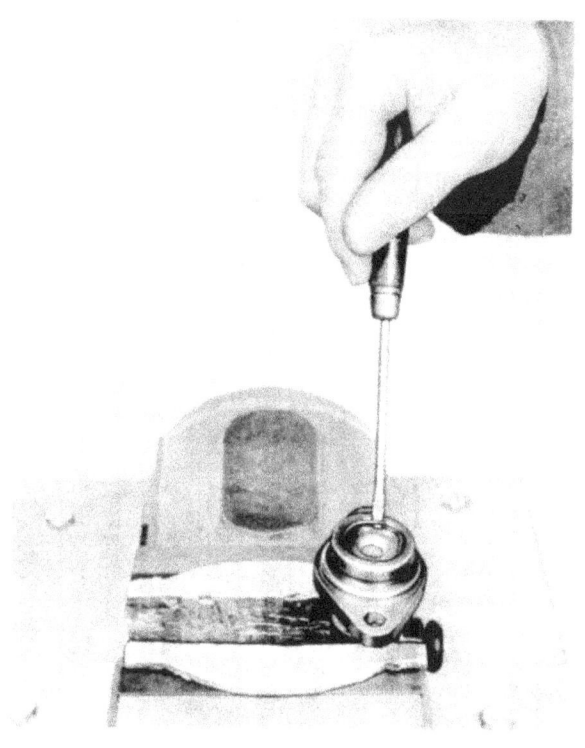

3. Withdraw piston stop plate, then piston with secondary piston cup and washer.
4. Apply light air pressure of about 15 psi (1 atm) (DO NOT use high pressure air hose) to blow out the primary piston cup, then remove spring and check-valve.

Reassembly

Reverse the above order to install. Note the following instructions:

1. Use denatured alcohol to clean all parts.
2. Check parts for wear. The cylinder intake passage must be free of dirt or other obstructions such as burrs, or deep scratches. Replace the assembly if the clean and dry piston does not move in the cylinder with suction drag when moved either way. Check the purging passage for possible obstructions.
3. Lightly coat the cylinder bore, piston surface, and piston cups with a good brand of brake cylinder lubricant.
4. See previous illustration for order of assembly.

NOTE: Be sure to install the piston washer.

5. Ensure good seating of the lock ring.

Torque Values for Disc Brake Fasteners

	mkp	lbs/ft
Nut, master cylinder mounting flange (M 8)	2.5	18.0
Nut, bottom shield (M 16 x 1.5)	6.5	47.0
Bolt, bottom shield (M 10)	4.7	34.0
Nut, attaching brake disc to wheel hub (M 8)	2.3	16.6
Bolt, brake carrier (M 10)	4.7	34.0
Bolt, disc shroud (M 8)	2.5	18.0
Bolt, front wheel caliper (M 12 x 1.5)	7.0	50.6
Bolt, rear wheel caliper (M 10)	6.0	43.4
Bolt, brake carrier plate (M 8)	2.5	18.0
Castellated nut, on half-axle (M 20 x 1.5)	30-35	217-253
Allen bolt, half-axle flange (M 10)	4.7	34.0
Allen bolt, front wheel caliper (M 8 - 10 K)	3.4	24.6
Allen bolt, rear wheel caliper (M 6 - 12 K)	1.8	13.0
Hollow bolt, hydraulic line banjo-connector	2.0	14.5
Wheel nuts	13.0	94.0

DISC BRAKE MALFUNCTIONS AND CORRECTIVE ACTION

Maximum brake disc thickness variation = 0.03 mm (.0012")

Maximum lateral runout (brake disc installed) = 0.2 mm (.008")

Malfunction	Use prescribed brake pads (+)	Clean dirt from brake pad slots (++)	Check dust covers	Check 20° piston step down (+++)	Replace brake pads	Recondition oil-saturated brake	Replace cross-spring	Adjust wheel bearing clearance	Check disc and caliper mounting, check alignment of mating parts	Check lateral runout or thickness variation of discs	Check disc shrouds	Clean corrosion from brake cylinders	Check piston progressor (piston seal)	Repair leak in brake system	Clogged purging passage, rectify pressure condition in disc brakes	Bleed brake system
Uneven brake pad wear	x	x	x								x	x	x			
Slanted brake pad wear		x	x		x	x	x			x	x	x				
Stuck brake pads		x			x											
Brake pad does not back off from disc (overheated brakes)		x			x	x				x	x	x			x	
Brake pulls to one side	x	x	x	x							x					
Brake squeaks or chatters	x	x	x		x	x	x	x								
Excessive pedal free travel	x							x	x	x			x	x		x
Stuck pistons in calipers		x							x			x	x			
Rapid loss of brake fluid in fluid reservoir														x		
Pulsating sensation in brake pedal								x	x	x						
Poor braking effect on wet pavement											x					

+   Use special brake pads for racing, possibly remove disc shrouds

++   Dress brake pads, possibly recondition brake disc surfaces

+++   Overworked or overstressed brake pads may become noisy

FRONT SUSPENSION

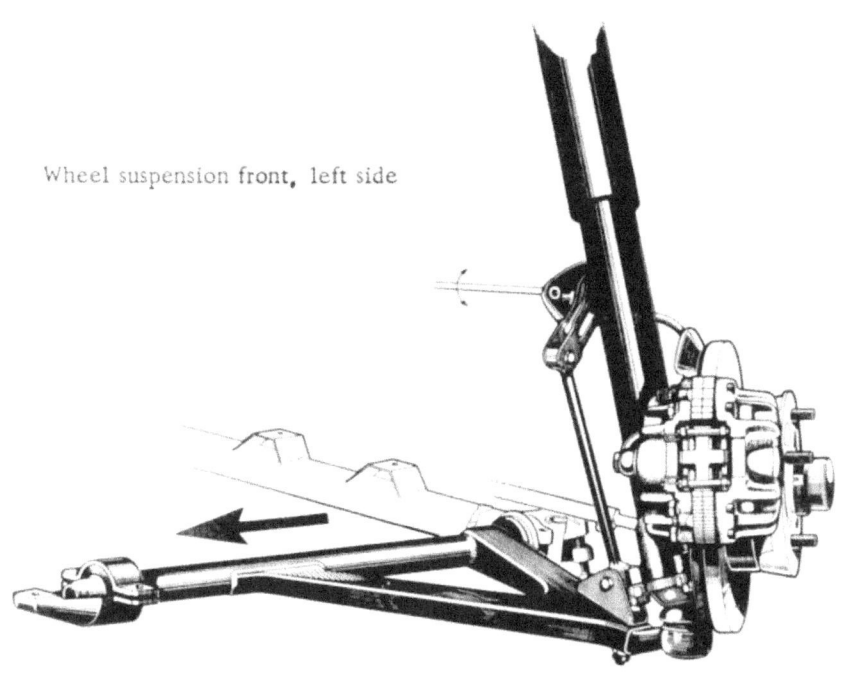

Wheel suspension front, left side

DESCRIPTION

Each front wheel is suspended with the shock absorber strut mounted in a permanently lubricated ball joint, and has a transverse control arm attached to a reinforcing crossmember.

Front wheel springing is effected through an adjustable, longitudinal torsion bar at each wheel. Complementing the springing is a progressively-acting rubber buffer installed in each of the two double-action hydraulic shock absorber struts. The cornering qualities are further enhanced by a transverse stabilizer which is connected to the suspension component of both front wheels through levers and shackles.

LUBRICATION AND MAINTENANCE DESCRIPTION

Lubrication

The front suspension has no lubrication points, although it is necessary to properly refill the front wheel bearings with new grease when repairs are being made.

Maintenance

All front axle joints are permanently lubricated and require no attention. To maintain the good road handling qualities and mechanical safety of the vehicle, it is necessary to carry out the periodic inspections prescribed in the maintenance schedule, including checking and adjusting the front wheel bearings, checking the wheel nuts for tightness, and checking and correcting tire pressure.

REMOVING AND INSTALLING FRONT WHEEL BEARINGS

Removal

1. Place car on stands and remove wheel(s), then unscrew hydraulic line gland nut from brake caliper; use pedal prop to hold brake pedal down slightly to keep hydraulic fluid from running out of the fluid reservoir.
2. Remove brake pads and caliper retaining bolts, then remove entire caliper assembly (see BRAKING SYSTEM).

ARRANGEMENT OF FRONT WHEEL BEARINGS

Cross - sectional View

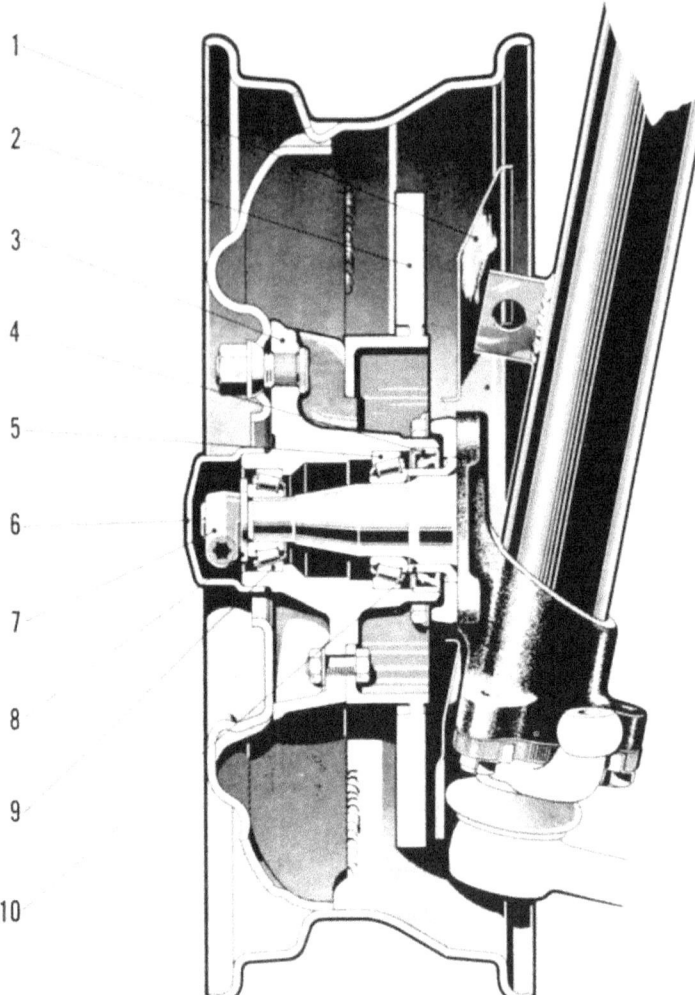

1. Cover shroud
2. Brake disc
3. Front wheel hub
4. Seal
5. Tapered roller bearing
6. Grease cap
7. Clamping nut
8. Washer
9. Tapered roller bearing
10. Distance ring

3. Remove grease cap from front wheel hub by prying evenly on all sides (see illustration).

4. Loosen Allen bolt in wheel bearing clamping nut and withdraw bearing washer (see illustration).

5. Remove wheel hub with brake disc and bearings.
6. Using a shop press, press wheel bearings out; depending on the type of press used, it may become necessary to remove the brake disc from the wheel hub.
   a. Mark brake disc and wheel hub, remove disc retaining bolts, then remove wheel hub.
   b. Heat wheel hub to 250–300°F. (120–150°C.).
   c. Press out inner tapered roller bearing and seal on a shop press (see illustration).

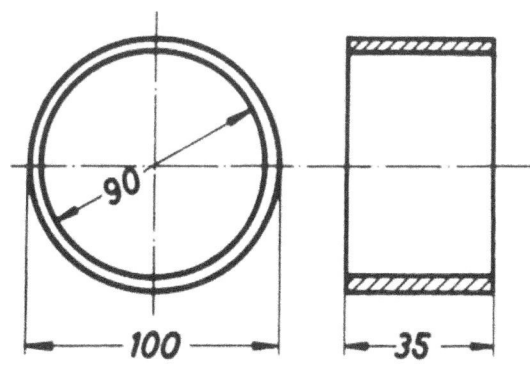

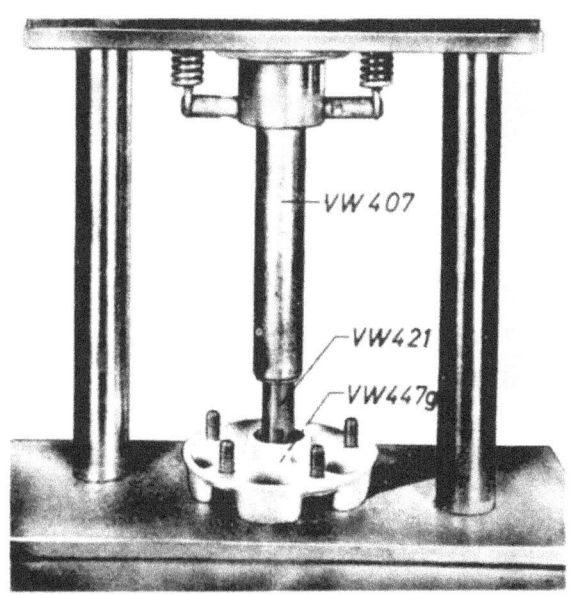

d. Press out outer race of the outer tapered roller bearing on a shop press (see illustration). Use spacer No. 1 (see illustration), which can be made using the metric dimensions.

Installation

Note the following points when installing front wheel bearings:

Tapered roller bearings of various brands (SKF, FAG, and Timken) are installed during assembly at the factory. Therefore, new bearing parts, such as the outer race, inner race, and roller are interchangeable within a given brand, but care must be taken that the complete bearing consists of one-brand parts.

1. Thoroughly clean both tapered roller bearings and check for wear or damage, replace if necessary.
2. Heat wheel hub to 250–300°F. (120–150°C.).
3. Press in the outer race of the inner roller bearing on a shop press using spacer No. 1 (see previous illustrations).
4. Insert the inner race into the inner tapered roller bearing and press oil seal in with the help of special tools VW 410, VW 433, Spacer No. 1, and VW 401 until the oil seal is flush with the wheel hub housing.
5. Press in the outer race of the outer tapered roller bearing (see illustration).

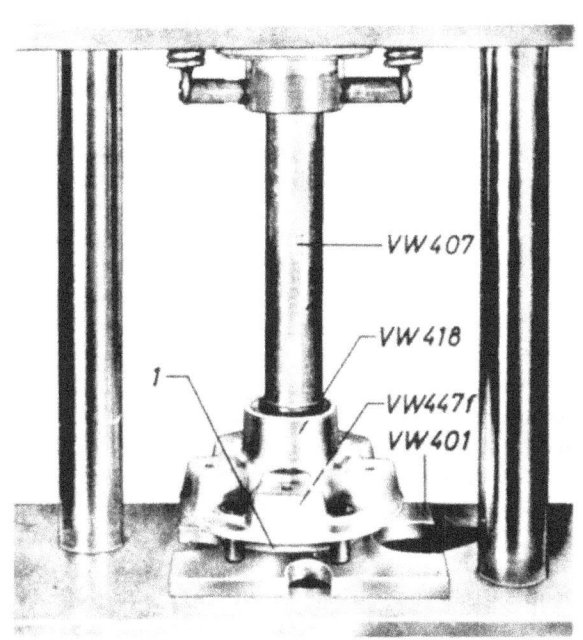

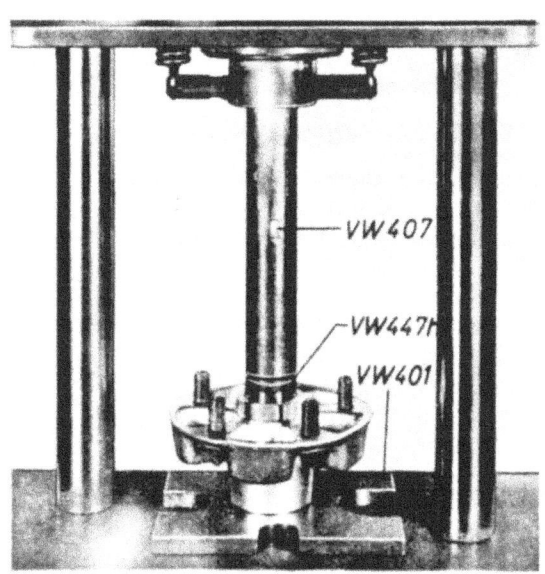

6. Place brake disc on the wheel hub so that the markings line up.
7. Torque brake disc/wheel hub retaining bolts to 16.6 ft. lb. (2,3 mkp). Make certain that the bolts are installed from inside to outside so that bolt heads come to rest against the brake disc; place new spring washers under the nuts.
8. Fill wheel hub with 3 cu. in. or 1½ oz. (50 cc or 45 g) of multipurpose lithium grease, and also coat the bearings well with grease. Fill the space between both sealing lips of the oil seal with grease, also, to prevent the outer sealing lip from running dry.
9. Adjust the front wheel bearings as follows:
   a. Lightly tighten the clamping nut about 11 ft. lb. (about 1,5 mkp) while turning the wheel or hub to seat the tapered rollers in their races.
   b. Loosen the clamping nut so that the thrust washers can be moved sideways under light pressure of a screwdriver yet no bearing play is felt when shaking the wheel hub axially.

NOTE: The screwdriver should not be pressed against the hub for this purpose but held free for better feel.

FRONT SHOCKABSORBER STRUT

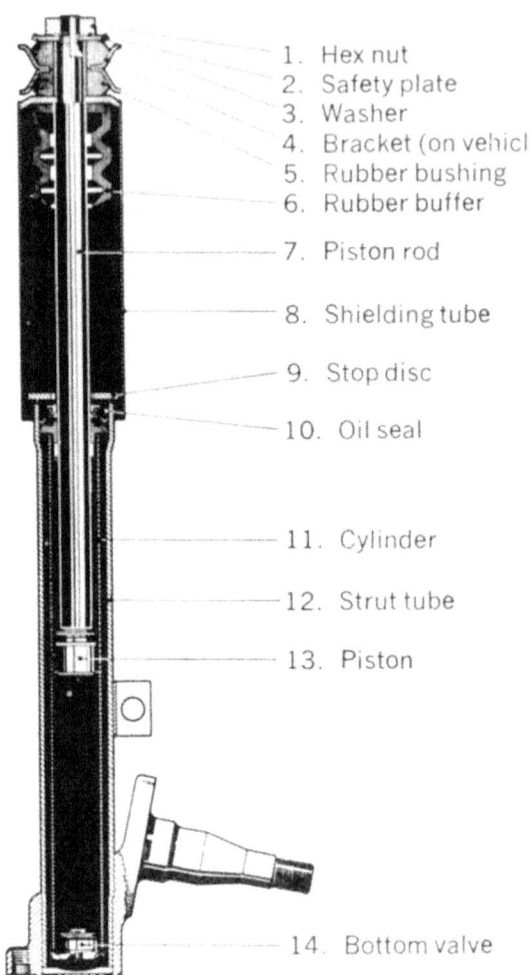

1. Hex nut
2. Safety plate
3. Washer
4. Bracket (on vehicle)
5. Rubber bushing
6. Rubber buffer
7. Piston rod
8. Shielding tube
9. Stop disc
10. Oil seal
11. Cylinder
12. Strut tube
13. Piston
14. Bottom valve

   c. Torque Allen bolt in clamping nut to 18 ft. lb. (2,5 mkp), making sure that the clamping nut remains in the adjusted position. Recheck adjustment by moving the thrust washer, readjust if necessary.
   d. Lightly coat the clamping nut and thrust washer with lithium grease. Install grease cap with the aid of a plastic hammer or similar tool.

NOTE: DO NOT fill cap with grease.

10. Install brake caliper retaining bolts with spring washers and torque to 50.6 ft. lb. (7,0 mkp).
11. Torque gland nut of brake line at brake caliper to 14.5 ft. lb. (2,0 mkp).

REMOVING AND INSTALLING SHOCK ABSORBER STRUT

NOTE: Rather than perform the complete procedure that follows, when merely replacing a shock absorber strut that has too much free travel (is worn out), the reader may instead us a "Koni Insert", Koni Part No. 1394 (front), 1738 (rear), that will fit either the standard "Boge" or the adjustable Koni shock absorber strut member. In this way, the advantages of having adjustability is added to the Boge standard without having to replace the whole spindle-control arm assembly. The insert installation only requires that the upper portion of the shock absorber strut be removed, and the stop disc be unscrewed (see procedure and illustration). The insert is then screwed in and adjusted. The rest of the installation is similar to the procedure following. For strictly competition use, Koni "Double Adjustable" shock absorber struts (available on special order) may be installed. These allow adjustment for both rebound and jounce. In any case, shock absorbers should be replaced in pairs, both fronts together and both rears together.

Removal

1. Raise car and remove wheels.
2. Unscrew cover shroud retaining bolts and remove shroud (see illustration).

3. Remove hydraulic line from brake caliper, then remove brake caliper using previous procedure under REMOVING AND INSTALLING WHEEL BEARINGS.
4. Detach brake line from brake hose supporting bracket, pull out hose, then withdraw line together with the retaining spring.
5. Remove grease cap and front wheel hub as previously described under REMOVING AND INSTALLING WHEEL BEARINGS.
6. Unlock and remove brake carrier retaining bolts, then withdraw carrier.
7. Unlock and remove ball stud castellated nut, then withdraw ball joint from steering arm using special tool VW 266h (see illustration).

8. Unlock and remove castellated nuts from bolts on underside of transverse control arm, then pull out the bolts.
9. Unlock and remove hex nut at top of shock absorber strut, then remove strut (see illustration).

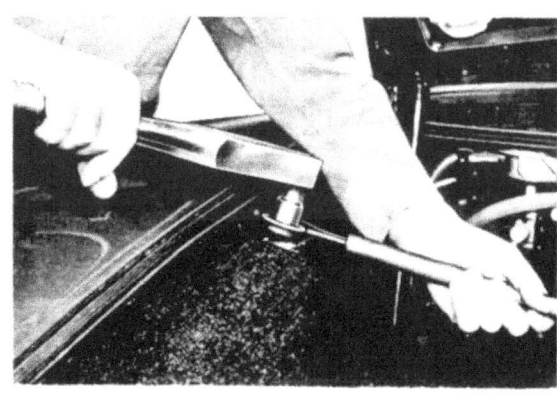

Dismantling

1. Mount shock absorber strut in a bench vise with protective jaw covers.
2. Remove shielding tube and withdraw rubber buffer.
3. Unlock and remove steering lever hex bolts, then remove steering lever and ball joint assembly, taking care not to lose the bushing (see illustration).

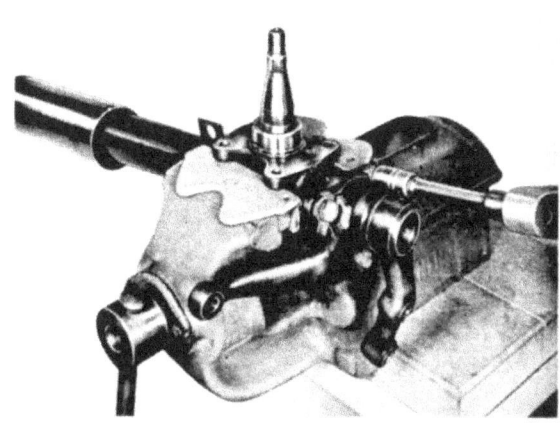

4. Mount steering lever and ball joint assembly in a bench vise, then unlock and remove the castellated nut on the ball joint.
5. Press the ball joint out of its seat in the steering lever using the shop press or a suitable puller (see illustration).

6. Drive distance ring off wheel spindle, striking with drift punch at different locations. Remove only if necessary (see illustration).

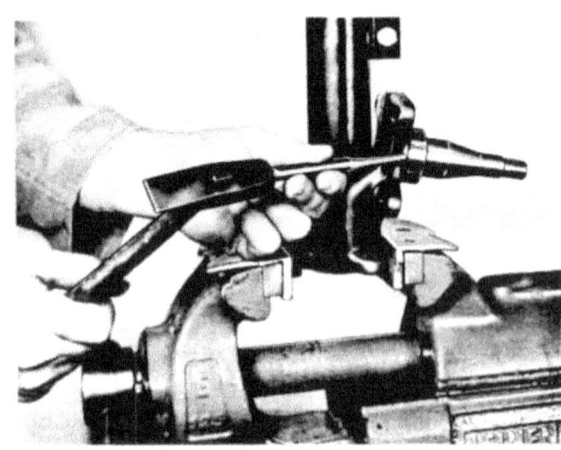

Inspection

1. The shock absorber strut and wheel spindle assembly can be properly checked for bends and misalignment on special tool P 286, which is used for the standard-version and Koni adjustable shock absorber strut. The distance ring on the spindle must be in place (see illustrations).

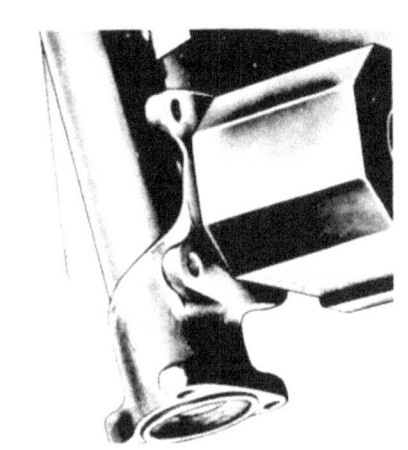

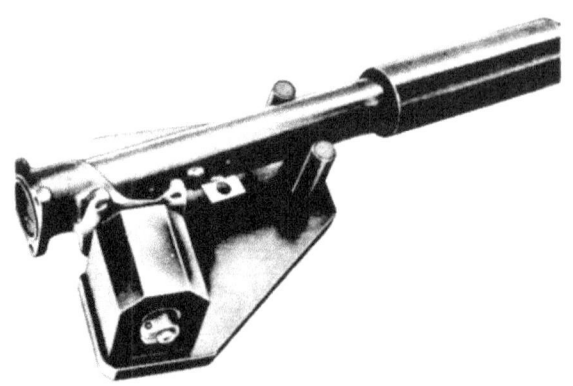

2. Check the shock absorber strut for hydraulic action and possible leaks.
   a. Visually inspect the strut for possible oil deposits. If the strut is covered with oily dirt, replace strut.
   b. Mount the shock absorber strut in a bench vise, keeping it in a vertically upright position. Pump the strut a few times to fill its cylinder with oil, then check it for free travel through quick movement in the opposite direction. If the free travel is unusually long, replace the strut.

3. Check ball joint. A slight drag must be perceptible at the ball stud when it is being moved. If the ball stud can be moved freely and axial play is in evidence, replace the ball joint. Check the rubber dust cover and replace it if defective.

Adjusting the Koni Shock Absorber Strut

The rebound damping can be adjusted on cars fitted with Koni adjustable shock absorber struts. Type 912 vehicles are fitted with shock absorber struts adjusted to the softest setting: Type 911 vehicles have shock absorber struts set one turn harder (360° to the right). Should it become necessary through weakening of the action to readjust the shock absorber damping action, follow these instructions:

1. Mount the shock absorber strut in a vise, positioning it vertically with the plunger rod pointing up, and gripping it at the steering lever attaching flange (see illustration).
   a. When adjusting the shock absorber in the vehicle, first raise the front of the car and remove both wheels.
   b. Unlock the hex nut at the top of the strut and remove the nut while supporting the transverse control arm with a shop jack.
2. Press plunger rod and shielding tube fully down and turn plunger rod to the left, without forcing, until the adjusting lug engages the mating recess in the bottom valve (see previous and following illustrations).
3. Mark the engagement point of the adjusting lug on the shielding tube and the shock absorber body.
4. Turn the shielding tube farther to the left to determine if an adjustment has been made (harder setting) and if so, by how much.

5. Starting from the original position, turn the tube one-half or more turns to the right until the desired damping action has been reached (see illustration). Pull plunger rod up again to disengage the adjusting components.

NOTE: Maximum adjustment is 2¼ turns.

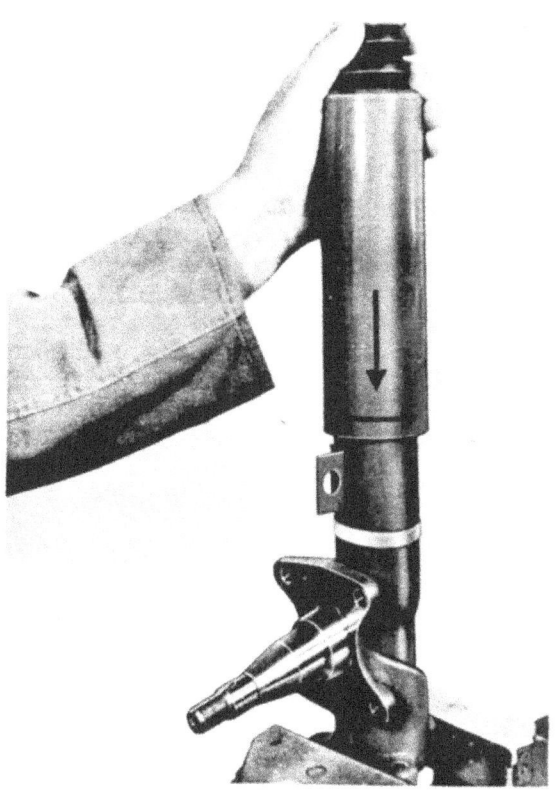

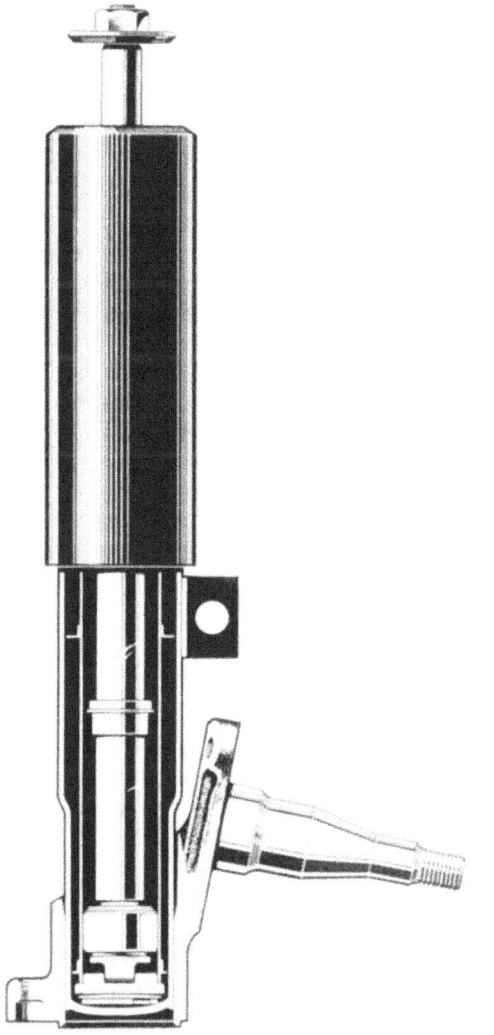

6. Make certain that the left and right shock absorber struts are adjusted to an equal degree. The degree of damping can easily be felt by "pumping" the plunger rod.

7. If work is performed on an installed strut, torque hex nut at top of strut to 58 ft. lb. (8,0 mkp). Use a new safety plate and note that the safety plate tab should be pointing up at time of installation (see previous illustration).

Assembling and Installing Shock Absorber Strut

This procedure is a reversal of the removal and dismantling process. Note the following instructions:

1. If distance ring was removed or renewed, first install O-ring between the distance ring and wheel spindle to prevent rust.
2. Heat distance ring to about 300°F. (150°C.) and push it into place (see previous illustration).
3. Prior to installation of new ball joints, fill the rubber boot with 0.2 oz. (6,5 g) of multi-purpose MoS_2 grease. The tapered end of the ball stud must, however, be free of grease.
4. Install ball stud castellated nut and torque to 32.5 ft. lb. (4,5 mkp). If the cotter pin orifice appears above

the top of the castellated nut, place a spacer under the nut (see previous illustration).
5. Install steering lever attaching hex bolts and torque to 34 ft. lb. (4,7 mkp); use new safety plates (see previous illustration).
6. Install rubber buffer dry, without lubricants.
7. Install hex nut on the shock absorber strut and torque to 58 ft. lb. (8,0 mkp); use a new safety plate and make sure that its lip points up (see previous illustration).
8. Install castellated nuts in transverse control arm and torque to 54 ft. lb. (7,5 mkp); use washers, secure with cotter pins.
9. Install castellated nut on tie rod ball stud, then torque to 32.5 ft. lb. (4,5 mkp) and secure with cotter pin.
10. Install brake carrier retaining bolts and torque to 34 ft. lb. (4,7 mkp); use new safety plates.
11. Install front wheel bearings and adjust, then install brake caliper and brake line according to instructions under REMOVING AND INSTALLING WHEEL BEARINGS.
12. Torque cover shroud retaining bolts to 18 ft. lb. (2,5 mkp) (see previous illustration).
13. Bleed brake system as shown in BRAKE SYSTEM chapter.
14. Check wheel alignment as described in WHEEL ALIGNMENT chapter.

STABILIZER SERVICING

NOTE: The stabilizer bar on the 900 Series Porsche comes in sizes 12, 13, 14, 15, and 16 mm, with the 13 mm size being the normal diameter of the bar, and 16 mm being the competition size. The extra thick competition size stabilizer bar (anti-sway bar) will reduce wheel lift and side sway. Some 1968 Porsche models are not equipped with stabilizer bars, and these cars will require mounting hardware if the bars are to be fitted.

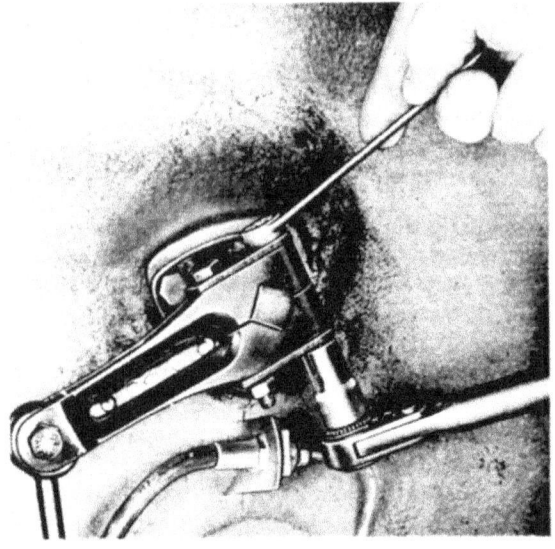

Removal

1. Loosen stabilizer lever clamping bolts, then withdraw lever (see illustration).
2. Remove bush support retaining bolts, squirt some penetrating oil or other rust solvent onto the bush support and rubber bush, then pry both parts loose with two large screwdrivers and remove (see illustration).

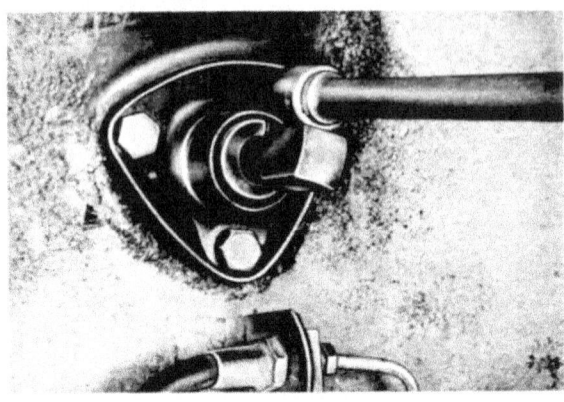

3. Remove both support retaining bolts on the other side and pull out stabilizer together with bush and support.
4. Use a shop press to remove the stabilizer from its support or the rubber bush. Penetrating oil may aid removal.
5. Remove shackle attaching bolt (below), then remove shackle with stabilizer lever.

Checking and Replacement

1. Visually check the rubber grommets in the stabilizer shackle for wear and replace if necessary.
2. To replace stabilizer, reverse the removal procedure, noting the following:
   a. Treat the stabilizer and rubber bush with glycerine paste or similar rubber lubricant.
   b. Lightly tighten both bush supports, center the stabilizer, then torque the hex bolts to 18 ft. lb. (2,5 mkp) (see previous illustration).
   c. Position each stabilizer lever on the square end of the stabilizer so that the stabilizer end protrudes about .004 in. (0,1 mm) beyond it (see illustration).
   d. Torque nuts of the shackle retaining bolts to 18 ft. lb. (2,5 mkp).

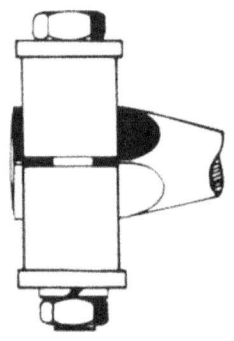

TORSION BAR SERVICING

Removal

1. Remove undershield by removing bolts and nuts (see illustration).

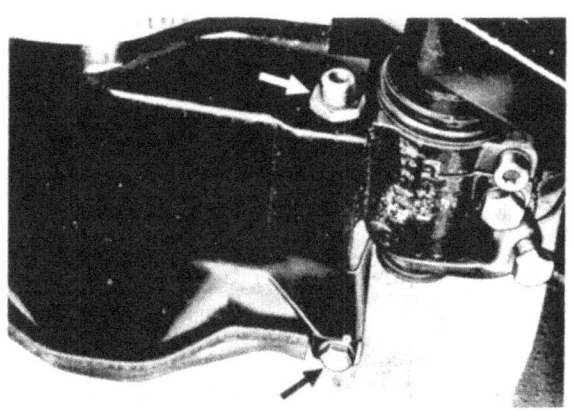

2. Turn the torsion bar adjusting screw back (see illustration).

3. Remove retaining bolts from the control arm bushing bracket, then remove the bracket and the bracket cap (see illustration).

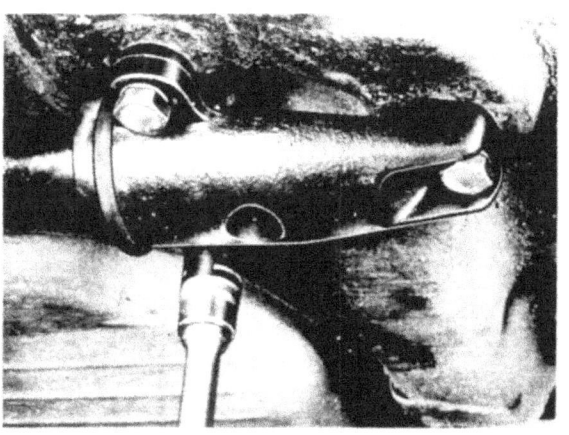

4. Remove both torsion bar dust caps and the locking ring in the forward part of the transverse control arm (see illustration).

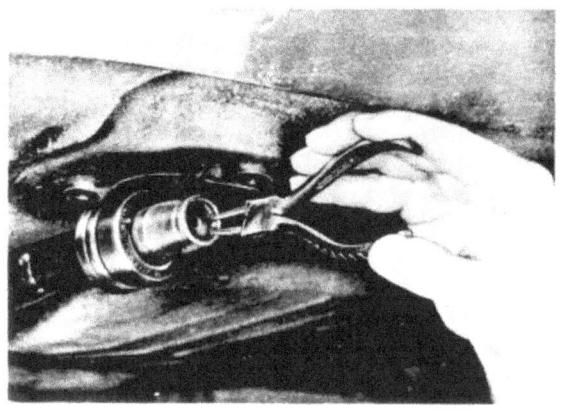

5. Drive the torsion bar forward out of the transverse control arm using an appropriate driver.

6. Drive the torsion bar adjusting lever rearward and out of the transverse control arm.

CAUTION: Do not damage the torsion bar splines during these operations.

7. Check torsion bar for damage to splines or protective paint, especially for rust, and replace bar if necessary.

Installation

To install, reverse the above instructions, noting the following:

1. Lightly coat the torsion bar with Lithium grease, taking special care when greasing the splines, then install the torsion bar by inserting it into the forward end of the control arm. Be sure to install the lock ring and the dust cap.

CAUTION: The torsion bars are pre-stressed in manufacture, so ensure that the right and left bars are not switched before installation. To aid identification, each bar is stamped with an "L" for left side or an "R" for right side. The identifying letter is stamped on the end. (see illustration).

2. Install the bracket cap as indicated in the illustration, being sure the two matching faces are together.

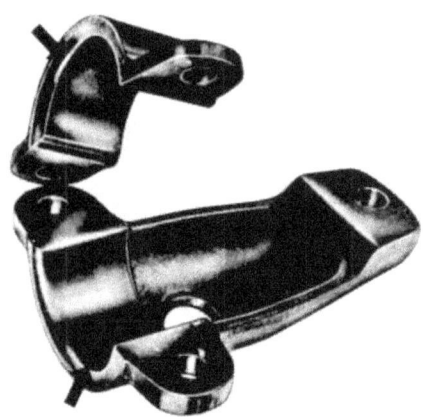

3. Before installing, coat the rubber bushing with glycerine lubricant and make sure the rubber bushing is not pinched along the sides between the bracket cap and the bracket while tightening. To aid installation, lightly tighten the forward bolt first, then install the rear bolts. Torque these bolts to 34 ft. lb. (4,7 mkp) (see previous illustration).
4. Install the torsion bar adjusting lever into the reinforcing crossmember as follows:
   a. With the shock strut pushed down to the stop in the shock strut (this is with the shock strut attached to the transverse control arm at a stage of decompression) insert the torsion bar adjusting lever, with the adjusting screw turned all the way back, into the reinforcing crossmember and onto the splined torsion bar end, leaving as little clearance at the lever adjusting point as possible (see illustration).

   b. Be sure to coat the lever with graphite grease prior to installation into the support arm.
   c. Slightly tighten the adjusting screw.
   d. Install the lock ring and dust cover.
5. Adjust the height of the front end and check the wheel alignment according to instructions in the WHEEL ALIGNMENT chapter.

IMPORTANT

Torque values for front axle nuts and bolts are to be found near the end of the STEERING chapter.

STEERING

DESCRIPTION

The steering is of the rack-and-pinion type. The steering rack rides in a replaceable bushing installed at each outer end of the housing. A floating pinion carrier, located in the housing, supports the pinion which turns in two ball bearings. The steering pinion presses against the steering rack through a pressure block, spring, and adjusting nut. This results in play-free steering action. A certain amount of torque drag in the steering pinion is obtained through the steering adjustment nut in the housing.

The steering gear assembly requires no maintenance, and is filled with a special, permanent lubricant at the time of manufacture.

ADJUSTING STEERING GEAR

NOTE: The steering gear adjusting methods vary according to the type of steering rack pressure block.

Method No. 1

Method No. 1 applies to steel pressure blocks with DELRIN (plastic) contact surface. External distinguishing features on the steering housing are: Steering gear with dust boot (see illustration).

1. Remove hex retaining bolts from base plate and withdraw plate (see illustration).
2. Tighten adjusting nut to seating contact; the base plate may be used as a wrench in that the plate is placed on the adjusting nut allowing the pins in the plate to engage the teeth in the nut.

Side-section View

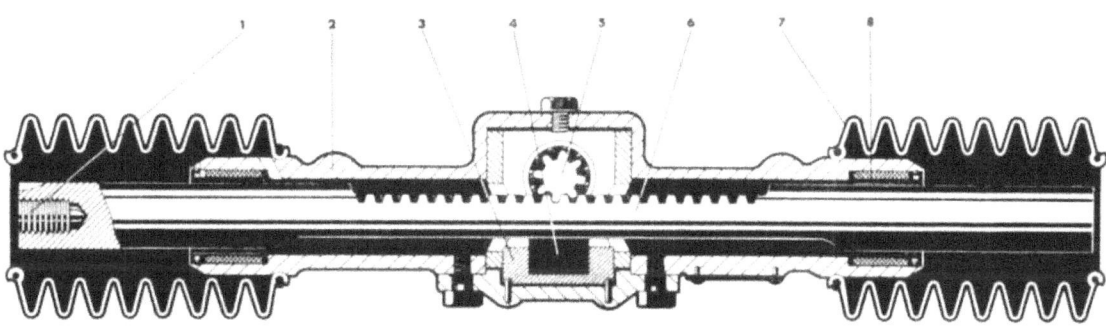

| 1 Thread for tie rod joint | 3 Adjusting nut | 5 Steering pinion | 7 Rubber boot |
| 2 Housing | 4 Pressure block | 6 Steering rack | 8 Bushing |

Cross-section View

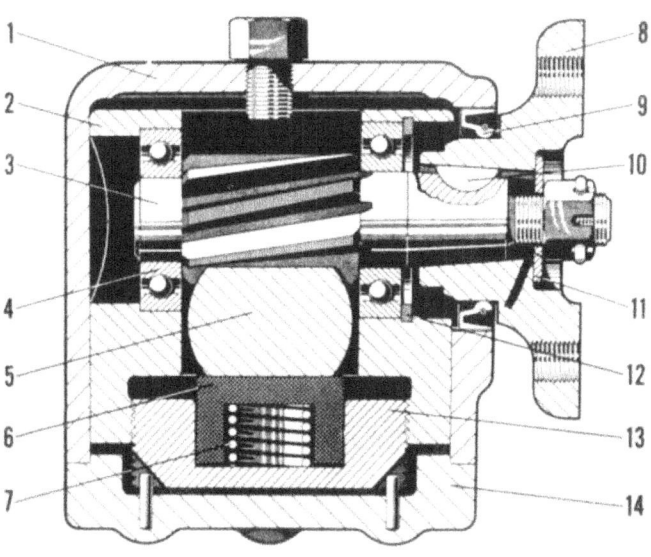

1 Housing
2 Pinion carrier
3 Steering pinion
4 Ball bearing
5 Steering rack
6 Pressure block
7 Spring
8 Thrust plate
9 Oil seal
10 Woodruff key
11 Spacer
12 Lock ring
13 Adjusting nut
14 Base plate

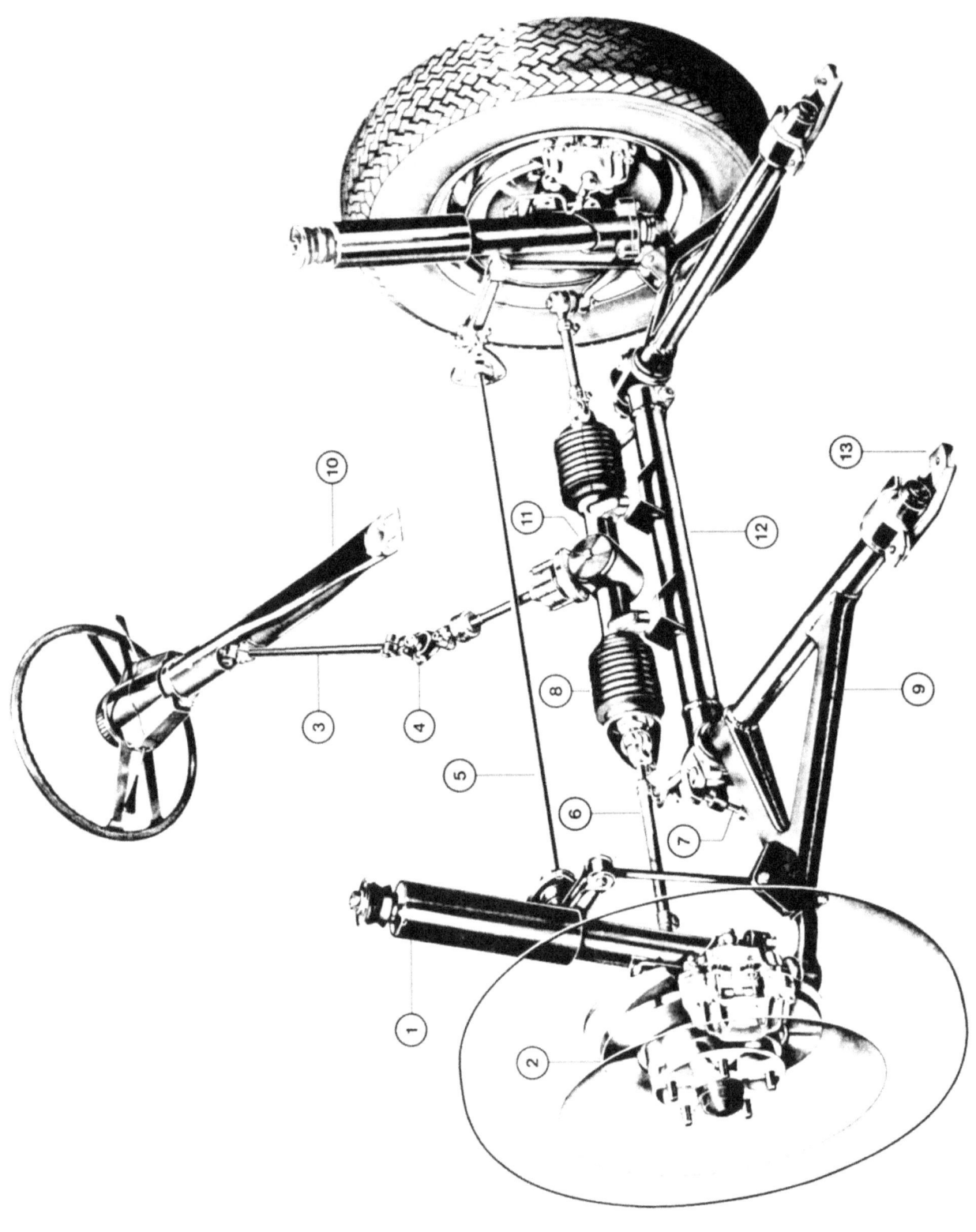

1 Shockabsorber strut
2 Brake disc
3 Steering intermediate shaft
4 Universal joint
5 Stabilizer
6 Steering tie rod
7 Adjusting screw
8 Bellows
9 Transverse control arm
10 Steering Post
11 Steering gear assembly
12 Reinforcing crossmember
13 Bearing support

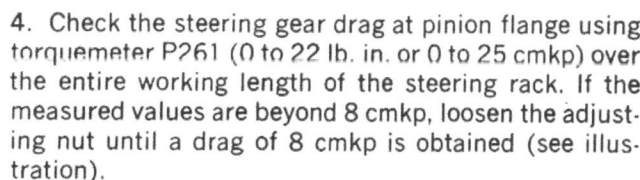

4. Check the steering gear drag at pinion flange using torquemeter P261 (0 to 22 lb. in. or 0 to 25 cmkp) over the entire working length of the steering rack. If the measured values are beyond 8 cmkp, loosen the adjusting nut until a drag of 8 cmkp is obtained (see illustration).

NOTE: It is possible that after backing the nut off by three teeth a drag of not less than 4 cmkp will be noted; in such cases the adjusting nut should not be re-tightened.

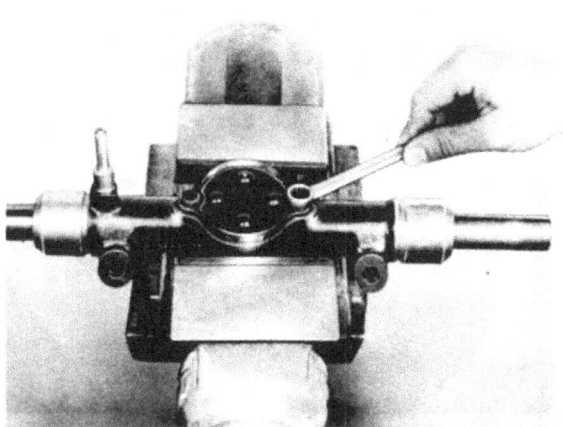

5. The maximum steering adjustment is as follows:
   a. Adjustment nut backed off by three teeth from its point of contact.
   b. A maximum drag of 8 cmkp at the pinion flange with tie rods and steering damper disconnected. Remove bolt(s) from damper end(s).
   c. A maximum drag of 10 cmkp at the steering shaft or steering wheel retaining nut with tie rods and steering damper disconnected. The steering damper is disconnected by removing bolt(s) from damper end(s). See REMOVING AND INSTALLING STEERING HOUSING and REMOVING AND INSTALLING STEERING WHEEL for other procedures (see illustration).

3. Back the nut off by three teeth (see illustration).

6. Install base plate and paper gasket, torque hex bolts to 16 ft. lb. (2,2 mkp).

WARNING: When installing the base plate, the four pins in the plate must easily fit into the teeth of the adjusting nut; if necessary move the nut slightly.

Method No. 2

Method No. 2 applies to DELRIN (plastic) pressure blocks. The external distinguishing feature on the steering housing is that there is no dust seat boot (see illustration).

REMOVING AND INSTALLING STEERING WHEEL

Removal

1. Disconnect battery.
2. Push in, then turn horn button to left and withdraw (see illustration).

1. Remove hex retaining bolts from base plate and withdraw plate.
2. Tighten adjusting nut so that a drag of maximum 8 cmkp is obtained over the entire working length of the steering rack, measured with the torquemeter P 261 at the pinion flange.

3. Pull out contact pin.
4. Unscrew steering wheel retaining nut.
5. Mark relative position of steering wheel and steering upper shaft and withdraw steering wheel, noting bearing support ring and spring.

Installation

Note the following points during reassembly:

1. Place spring and support ring onto steering wheel hub (see illustration).

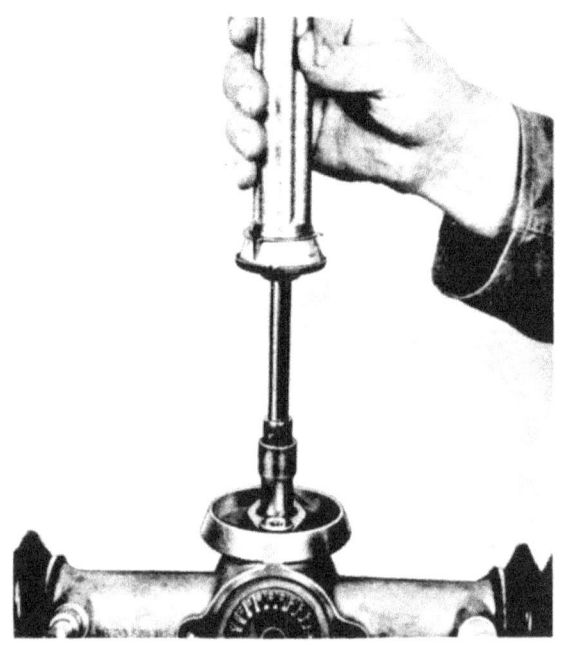

3. The maximum steering adjustment is as follows:
   a. A maximum drag of 8 cmkp at the pinion flange with tie rods and steering damper disconnected. Remove bolt(s) from damper end(s). See REMOVING AND INSTALLING STEERING HOUSING for other procedure (see previous illustration).
   b. A maximum drag of 10 cmkp at the steering shaft or steering wheel retaining nut, with tie rods and steering damper disconnected. The steering damper is disconnected by removing bolt(s) from damper end(s). See REMOVING AND INSTALLING STEERING WHEEL for other procedure (see previous illustration).
4. Install base plate and paper gasket, then torque hex bolts to 16 ft. lb. (2,2 mkp).

WARNING: When installing the base plate, the four pins in the plate must fit easily into the teeth of the adjusting nut; if necessary move the nut slightly.

2. Install steering wheel, with road wheels in straight ahead position, so that the return striker points to the left towards the blinker switch, and the steering wheel spokes are in a horizontal position; or place wheel according to markings made at time of disassembly.
3. Torque steering wheel retaining nut to 58 ft. lb. (8,0

mkp); insert spring washer under nut.
4. Check blinker return striker for proper functioning.
5. Lightly lubricate horn contact ring.
6. Insert contact pin, position horn button and depress, then turn it right to lock.

REMOVING AND INSTALLING STEERING HOUSING

Removal

1. Remove front compartment carpeting, detach heating duct of auxiliary heater from the steering post and lay duct to the side.
2. Open access door and remove intermediate shaft cover. Pry up on one of the two prongs in the spring clip with a small screwdriver to aid removal (see illustration).

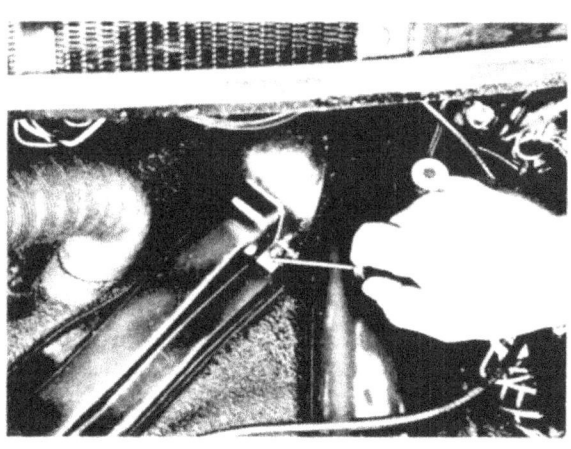

3. Remove the three heater fuel pump retaining bolts and lay the pump aside (see illustration).

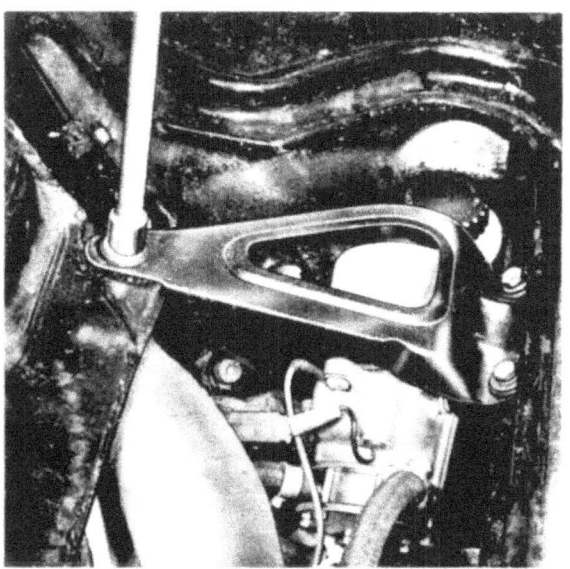

4. Remove cotter pin from lower hex bolt of the universal joint, loosen castellated nut, and pull universal joint off the steering shaft.
5. Remove Allen bolts from steering shaft bushing cap, remove cap, then pull out bushing and dust boot (see illustration).

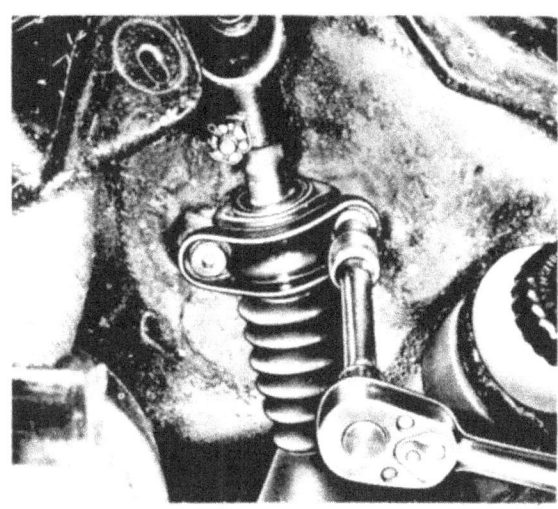

6. Unlock and remove steering coupling retaining bolts (see illustration).

7. Unscrew undershield retaining bolts and nuts, then remove undershield (see illustration).

8. Unlock and remove tie rod ball joint retaining nut, detach joint from tie rod with special tool VW 266h or a similar tool (see illustration).

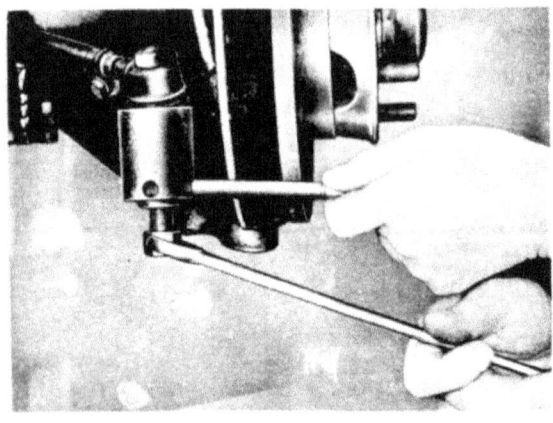

9. Unscrew steering housing retaining bolts (see illustration).

10. Remove right reinforcing crossmember brace (see illustration).

11. Withdraw, to the right, the entire steering housing assembly.
12. Unlock and remove the bolt from the tie rod yoke, then remove the tie rod.

Installation

Note the following instructions during installation:

1. Check tie rods for damage or deformation.
2. Check tie rod ball joints for serviceable conditions; when moving the ball stud, slight friction must be felt. If the ball stud can be moved freely and axial play is detectable, the ball joint will have to be replaced.
3. Coat the yoke bolt with MoS_2 paste, install, and torque to 34 ft. lb. (4,7 mkp).
4. Install crossmember reinforcing brace without binding. Torque hex nuts to 47 ft. lb. (6,5 mkp) and hex bolts to 34 ft. lb. (4,7 mkp) (see previous illustration).
5. Using new lockwashers, install and torque steering housing retaining bolts to 34 ft. lb. (4,7 mkp) (see previous illustration).
6. Torque tie rod ball joint castellated nuts to 32.5 ft. lb. (4,5 mkp), then secure with cotter pin.
7. Torque Allen bolts for cap of steering bushing to 18 ft. lb. (2,5 mkp).
8. Install steering coupling retaining bolts, using new safety washers, and torque to 18 ft. lb. (2,5 mkp).

REMOVING AND REPLACING SILENTBLOC EYEBOLTS

WARNING: The Silentbloc eyebolts must be installed in a precise position to ensure free movement of the steering components and exact guiding of the tie rods (see illustration).

Removal

1. Unlock safety washer at the eyebolt lock nut, place steering housing into special tool P 285 (steering gear adjustment gauge) or mount in a bench vise with protective vise jaw inserts, then loosen the eyebolt locknut (see illustration).

Torque Values for Front Axle Bolts and Nuts

Ball joint castellated nut (M 12x1,5)	4,5 mkp (32,5 lb/ft)
Steering lever hex bolts (M 10)	4,7 mkp (34,0 lb/ft)
Shockabsorber hex nut (M 14x1,5)	8,0 mkp (57,9 lb/ft)
Transverse control arm castellated nut (M 12x1,5)	7,5 mkp (54,2 lb/ft)
Tie rod ball stud castellated nut (M 10x1)	4,5 mkp (32,5 lb/ft)
Brake carrier retaining bolt (M 10)	4,7 mkp (34,0 lb/ft)
Brake caliper retaining bolt (M 12x1,5)	7,0 mkp (50,6 lb/ft)
Brake caliper banjo bolt (brake line)	2,0 mkp (14,4 lb/ft)
Brake disc shroud hex bolts (M 8)	2,5 mkp (18,1 lb/ft)
Brake disc hex bolts (M 8)	2,3 mkp (16,6 lb/ft)
Clamping nut Allen bolt (wheel bearing M 7)	2,5 mkp (18,1 lb/ft)
Flanblock-mounting Allen bolt (M 10)	4,7 mkp (34,0 lb/ft)
Bearing carrier hex bolts (M 10)	4,7 mkp (34,0 lb/ft)
Reinforcing crossmember hex bolt (M 12x1,5)	9,0 mkp (65,1 lb/ft)
Hex bolt for reinforcing crossmember brace (M 10)	4,7 mkp (34,0 lb/ft)
Hex nut for reinforcing crossmember brace (M 16x1,5)	6,5 mkp (47,0 lb/ft)
Bush support hex bolts (Stabilizer-M8)	2,5 mkp (18,1 lb/ft)
Stabilizer lever hex bolts (M 8)	2,5 mkp (18,1 lb/ft)
Bolt for tie rod yoke (M 10)	4,7 mkp (34,0 lb/ft)
Steering housing hex bolts (M 10)	4,7 mkp (34,o lb/ft)
Allen bolts for lower shaft bearing cap (M 8)	2,5 mkp (18,1 lb/ft)
Steering coupling hex bolts (M 8)	2,5 mkp (18,1 lb/ft)
Eyebolt lock nut (M 16x1,5)	6,5 mkp (47,0 lb/ft)
Castellated nut for steering pinion flange (M 8)	2,5 mkp (18,1 lb/ft)
Hex bolts for steering housing base plate (M 8)	2,2 mkp (15,9 lb/ft)
Steering wheel hex nut (M 18x1,5)	8,0 mkp (57,9 lb/ft)
Allen bolt for switch assembly clamp (M 8x1)	2,5 mkp (18,1 lb/ft)
Steering post hex bolts (M 8)	2,5 mkp (18,1 lb/ft)
Universal joint hex bolts (M 8)	3,5 mkp (25,3 lb/ft)
Allen bolts for steering post extension	2,5 mkp (18,1 lb/ft)
Wheel nuts	13,0 mkp (94,0 lb/ft)
Hex bolts for splined universal joints (M 8)	2,5 mkp (18,1 lb/ft)

2. Unscrew eyebolt, then remove stop plate and bellows.

Inspection

Visually check the Silentbloc for wear and replace if necessary.

Replacement

1. Install both bellows on steering gear housing.

2. Apply a coat of gasket paste (such as Teroson-Atmosit) to the eyebolt threads, steering rack end flanks, and both sides of the stop plate and safety washer, then install the eyebolts.

3. Mount the steering housing in special tool P 285, set eyebolts accordingly, tighten hex nuts with a SW 41 box wrench or equivalent, then torque to about 47 ft. lb. 6,5 mkp).

4. Secure eyebolt locknut.

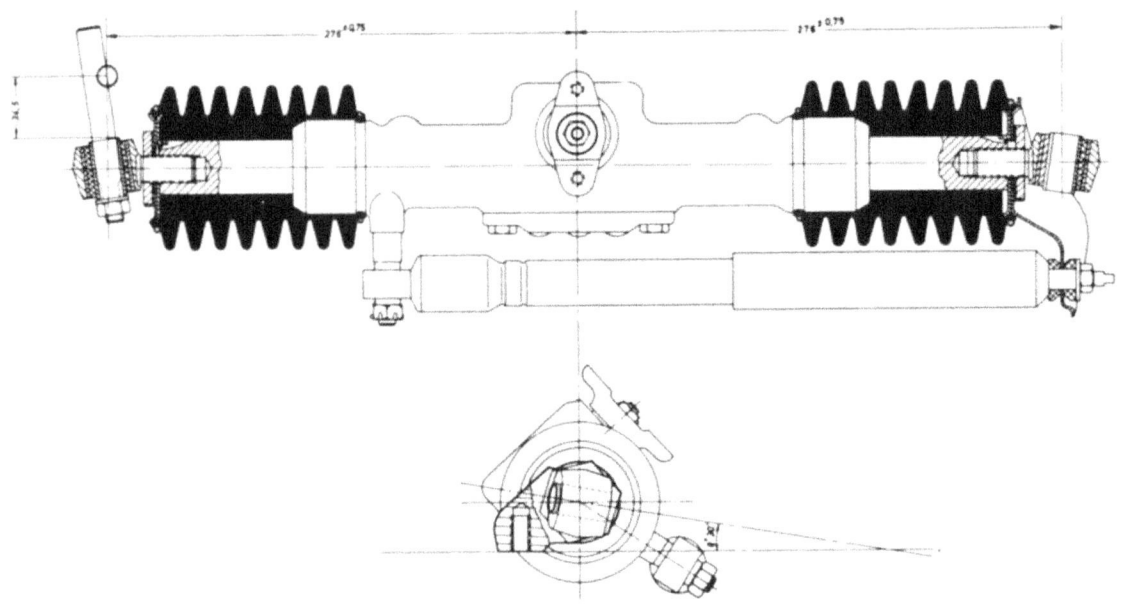

REAR SUSPENSION

DESCRIPTION

Both rear wheels are guided by triangulated control arms and are driven through double-jointed half-axles. Each wheel is independently suspended, with springing provided by a round transverse torsion bar on each side. Also, a telescopic shock absorber with a progressively acting rubber buffer inside supplements the springing of each wheel.

Since the torsion bar splines are in a vernier arrangement, both torsion bars can be adjusted to close specifications. Other adjustments are an eccenter bolt in the control arm to permit fine adjustment of the camber, and another eccenter bolt for adjusting the wheel tracking (see illustrations). None of the joints require lubrication.

SERVICING SHOCK ABSORBER

Removal

1. Shock absorber stress must be relieved to remove shock absorber, so it is best to allow the vehicle to stand on its wheels. Raise the car on a ramp lift or place it over a pit.
2. Remove rubber cap from shock absorber top and remove self-locking nut, holding plunger rod with vise-grip pliers if necessary (see illustration).
3. Remove the shock absorber retaining bolt, then remove the shock absorber (see illustration). Remove grommet, cover tube and rubber buffer.

Inspection

1. Check exterior of shock absorber for deposits of oily dirt. If the whole shock absorber is covered with oily dirt, the shock absorber is leaking and will have to be replaced.
2. To check the free travel of the shock absorber plunger rod, mount the shock absorber vertically in a

1 = Camber eccenter

2 = Tracking eccenter

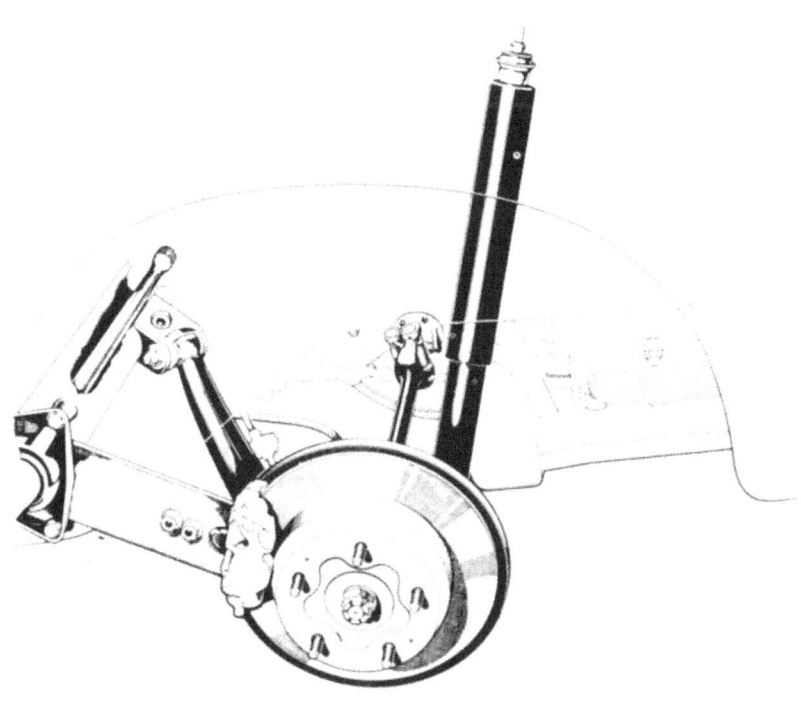

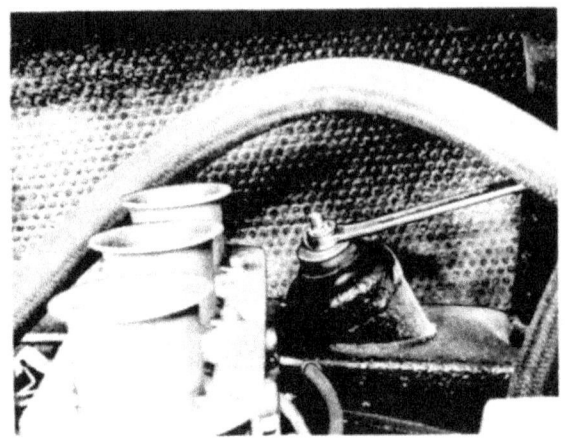

vise with the plunger rod up. Then push the plunger rod repeatedly in and out to bring the fluid into the cylinder and determine the free travel of the plunger rod by short counter strokes. If the free travel is excessive, replace the shock absorber.

3. Check the rubber buffer and replace when necessary (see illustration).

4. If car is equipped with Koni adjustable shock absorbers, adjust using the procedure outlined in the FRONT SUSPENSION chapter.

Replacement

To replace, reverse the removal procedure, noting the following:

1. Ensure that the stop disc (Item 9 of above illustration and illustration following) grooves face the shock absorber plunger since otherwise the hydraulic shock absorber fluid will be siphoned out.

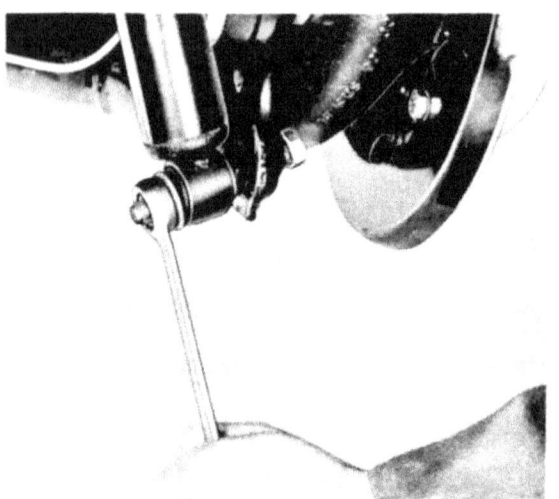

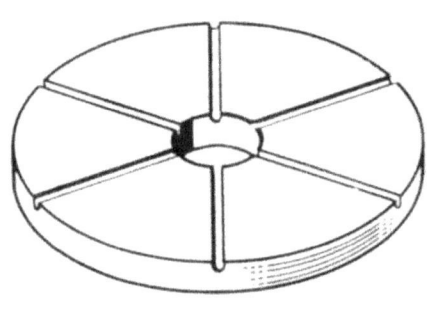

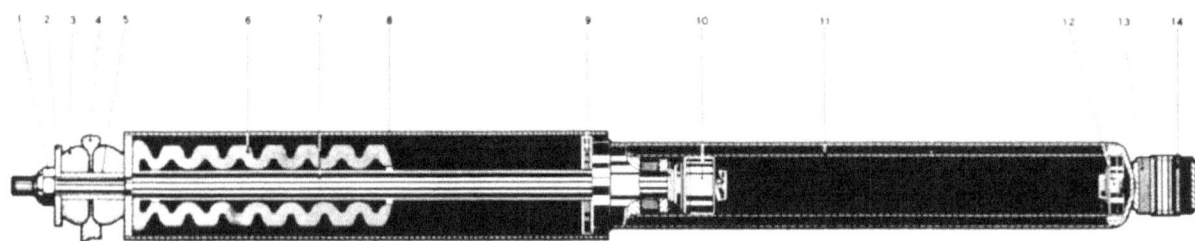

Rear Shockabsorber

1 Self-locking nut
2 Washer
3 Grommets
4 Seat in vehicle
5 Grommet bushing
6 Rubber buffer
7 Plunger rod

8 Cover tube
9 Stop disc
10 Plunger
11 Cylinder
12 Check valve
13 Grommet
14 Grommet bushing

Rear Wheel Cross-section

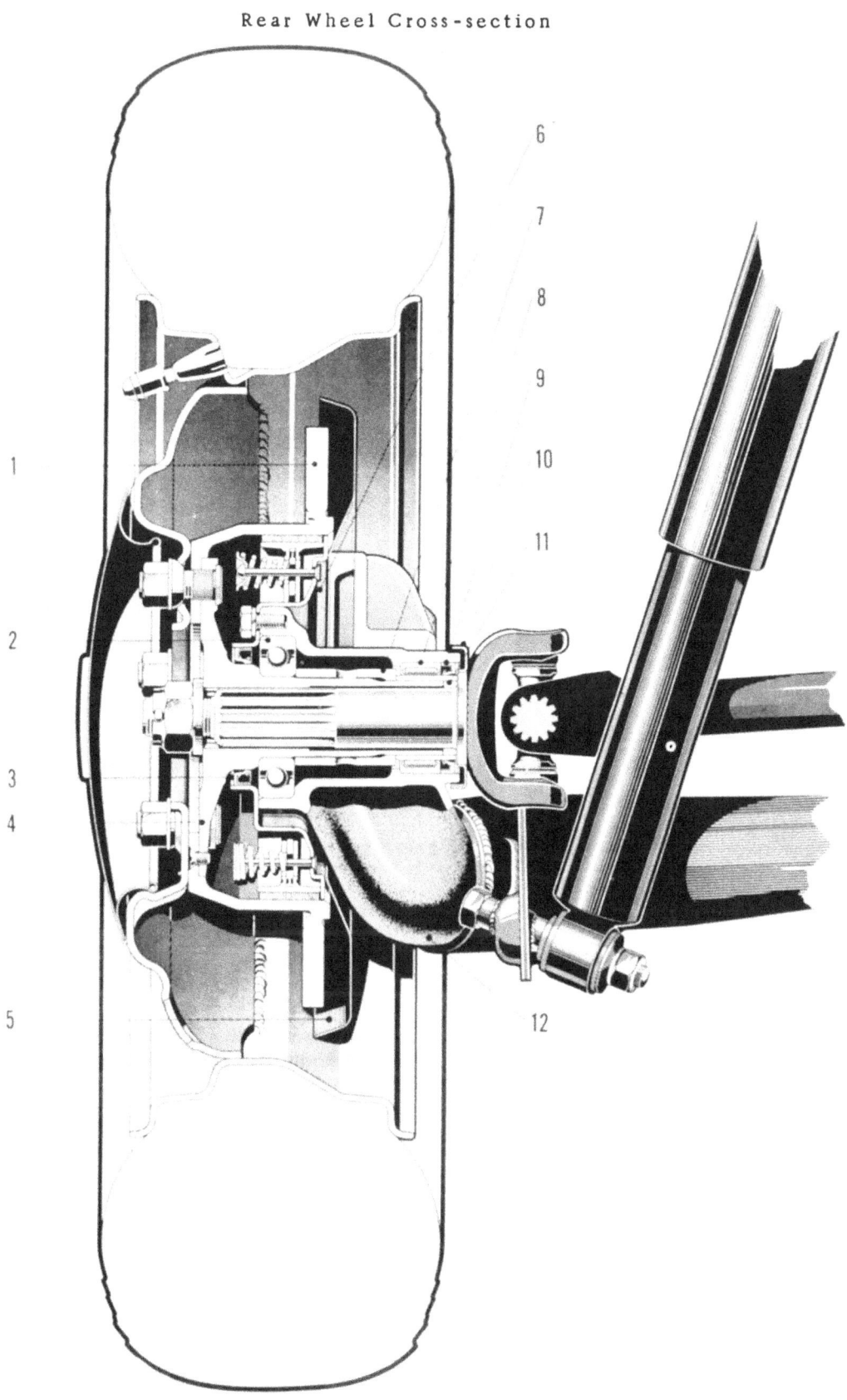

1 Brake disc, rear
2 Ballbearing
3 Oil seal
4 Rear wheel hub
5 Disc shroud
6 Brake carrier plate
7 Spacer tube
8 Rollerbearing
9 Oil seal
10 Dust cap
11 Gasket ring
12 Control arm, left

2. Install the rubber buffer dry, without using any lubricants.
3. Tighten the shock absorber retaining bolt to 54 ft. lb. (7,5 mkp).

REMOVING AND REPLACING REAR WHEEL CONTROL ARM

Removal

1. Follow steps (1) through (7) of REMOVING AND INSTALLING REAR WHEEL BRAKES in the BRAKING SYSTEM chapter. If brake pads can be forced away from the disc to allow removal of caliper, there is no need to remove the pads (they will fall out anyway).
2. Remove cotter key from the castellated nut in the half-axle, then remove the nut with the aid of special tools P 42a, P 36b, P 444a, and P 296 (see illustration), or use an equivalent setup.

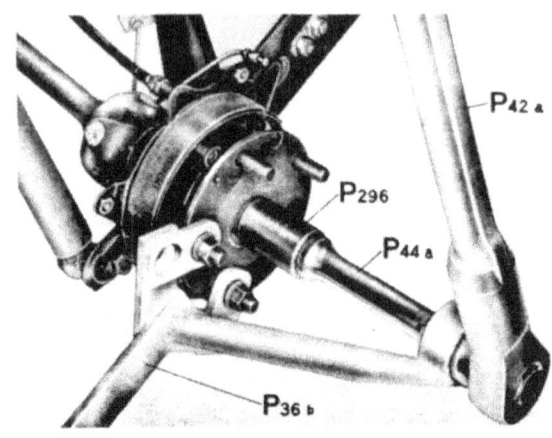

3. Remove Allen bolts from the half-axle flange, then knock the half-axle from its seat and remove (see illustration).

4. Drive the rear hub out with special tool P 297 or equivalent (see illustration).

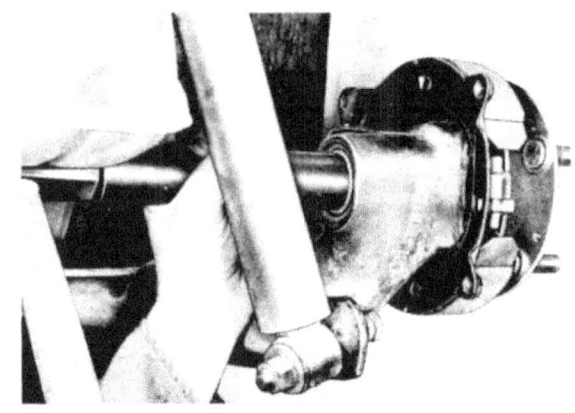

5. Remove retaining bolts from the brake carrier plate and withdraw the plate (see illustration).

6. Raise radius arm with the aid of special tool P 289 or equivalent (see illustration).

7. Remove shock absorber lower retaining nut, then remove nuts of the control arm retaining bolts and eccenter bolts and withdraw the bolts (see illustration).

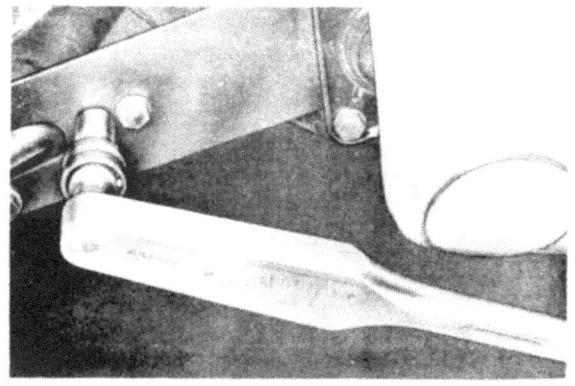

2. Tighten retaining bolts to 65 ft. lb. (9 mkp) (see illustration).
3. The camber eccenter should be torqued to 36 ft. lb. (5 mkp), and the tracking eccenter to 43 ft. lb. (6 mkp) (see illustration).
4. Tighten shock absorber retaining bolt to 54 ft. lb. (7,5 mkp).
5. Use a new O-ring and place it into the groove with a little grease. Ensure that the O-ring is well seated.

8. Detach brake hose from control arm.
9. Remove the self-locking nut of the control arm mounting bolt and drive the bolt out with the aid of a punch. At the same time move the control arm slightly so that the bolt can clear the transmission housing, then remove the control arm. If necessary, slightly loosen the transmission carrier retaining bolts, remove the control arm bolt, then remove the control arm (see illustration).

6. Tighten the brake carrier plate retaining bolts to 18 ft. lb. (2,5 mkp).
7. Screw the castellated nut onto the hand brake cable stub until the nut clears the cotter pin hole, then secure the nut with a new cotter pin.

CAUTION: Check the mechanical expander for proper seating.

8. Push a new gasket onto the half-axle stub.
9. Use a plastic mallet or similar tool to drive the rear wheel hub into place all the way to stop. Supporting the hub flange, drive the inner roller bearing ring into place.
10. Tighten the Allen bolts of the half-axle flange to the specified torque value as described in REMOVING AND REPLACING REAR HALF-AXLES.
11. Tighten castellated nut of half-axle to 217–253 ft. lb. (30–35 mkp).
12. Tighten the rear caliper retaining bolts to 43 ft. lb. (6 mkp).
13. Tighten disc shroud retaining bolts to 18 ft. lb. (2,5 mkp).
14. Adjust rear wheel tracking and camber as described in the WHEEL ALIGNMENT chapter.

Replacement

To replace the control arm, reverse the previous procedures and the procedures used from the BRAKING SYSTEM (being sure to refer to the installation notes), noting the following instructions:

1. Slide the hex bolt (M 14 x 1,5) from inside to outside while simultaneously moving the control arm to make the insertion easier.

WARNING: A washer must be placed under the bolt head as well as under the nut. The hex bolt may be tightened only after the car has been placed on its wheels since otherwise the twisting capability of the Flanblocks (bearing) would be exceeded. Torque nut to 87 ft. lb. (12 mkp) (see illustration).

REMOVING AND REPLACING REAR HALF-AXLES

Description

Porsche models are being equipped with NADELLA

half-axles (shafts) (Spare Part No. 901.332.025.02), and LOBRO half-axles (Spare Part No. 901.332.026.10), on an alternating basis.

CAUTION: Vehicles equipped with the ZF Multiple Disc Self-Locking Differential are originally equipped with NADELLA half-axles (see illustration). However, the replacement part involves an adapter for the differential ring gear with a new mounting for the new half-axle design. NADELLAs have been discontinued.

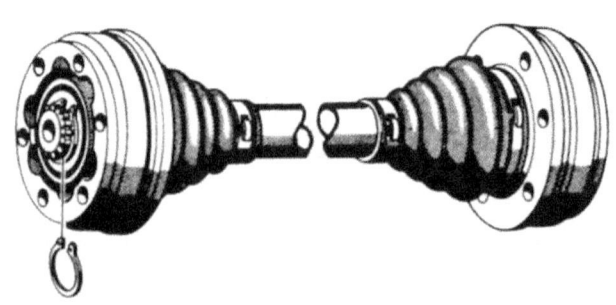

Removal

Remove as outlined in REMOVING AND REPLACING REAR WHEEL CONTROL ARM.

Checking

Check universal joints on half-axles for play. If the universal joints are worn, the entire half-axle will have to be replaced.

Replacement

1. Place a new gasket ring on the half-axle stub, lightly oil the splines, then insert the stub into the wheel hub.
2. Tighten the Allen bolts in the half-axle flange to the following torque:

NADELLA half-axle . . . . **34 ft. lb. (4,7 mkp)**
LOBRO half-axle . . . . **31 ft. lb. (4,3 mkp)**

CAUTION: The Schnorr washer for the Allen bolt on the LOBRO half-axle must face the base plate with the hollow side. The LOBRO half-axle must also be fastened with only the Allen bolts M 8 x 45 DIN 912 — 12 K, Spare Part No. 900.067.073.01 (minimum tensile strength of 120 kp/mm^2). These bolts bear markings 130—140 or 12 K, respectively, on the head or the side. The flange surfaces of the half-axle must be free of grease at the time of installation.

3. Tighten the half-axle castellated nut to 217 to 253 ft. lb. (30 to 35 mkp), then secure nut with a new cotter pin.

REPLACING LOBRO HALF-AXLE DUST BOOT

1. Remove the hose clamps from the dust boot.
2. Remove the lock ring and withdraw the universal joint and wire retainer from the half-axle splines (see illustration).

3. Remove the dust boot, clean all parts, then insert a new dust boot on the half-axle and slide the wire retainer and universal joint onto the half-axle. Secure with the lock ring.
4. Fill the universal joint with about 2½ oz. (70 gm) of Mo S$_2$ multipurpose grease. Apply as much grease as possible to the universal joint and the dust boot inside, then place the remainder inside the flange area.
5. Clean all the grease from the contact surface of the large end of the dust boot and its counterpart flange, then glue the dust boot into place with gasket compound (EC 750 M — 2 G 51) or equivalent. Suggested supplier is the Minnesota Mining & Manufacturing Co.
6. To aid in installation, the hose clamp bands may be drilled with two holes of .078 in. (2 mm) diameter each (see illustration).

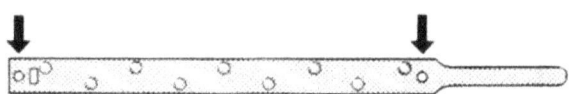

7. Tighten the hose clamp bands with round nose pliers, bend the end over and tap down with a light hammer (see illustration).

REMOVING AND REPLACING TORSION BAR

Removal

1. Raise car, remove rear wheels, then raise radius arm with special tool P 289 or equivalent (see illustration).

2. Remove shock absorber lower attaching bolt.
3. Remove control arm retaining bolts and adjusting eccenter bolts (see illustration).

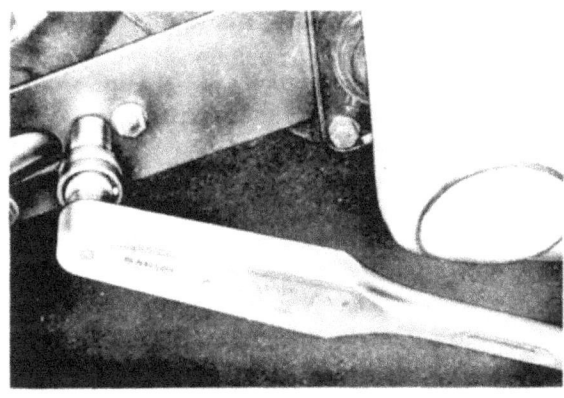

4. Remove retaining bolts from radius arm cover, then withdraw the single spacer (see illustration).
5. Pry the radius arm cover off, using two large screwdrivers.
6. Remove the radius arm tensioner, special tool P 289 or equivalent.
7. Remove the body plug in the side of the body, then remove the radius arm.
8. Withdraw the torsion bar.

CAUTION: Be careful not to damage the torsion bar protective paint since this would allow corrosion to set in, possibly resulting in the formation of a fatigue crack in the torsion bar. The inner end of a broken torsion bar may be removed from its seat by removing the other torsion bar and pushing through with a suitable steel rod.

Checking

1. Check the torsion bar for damage in the splines and

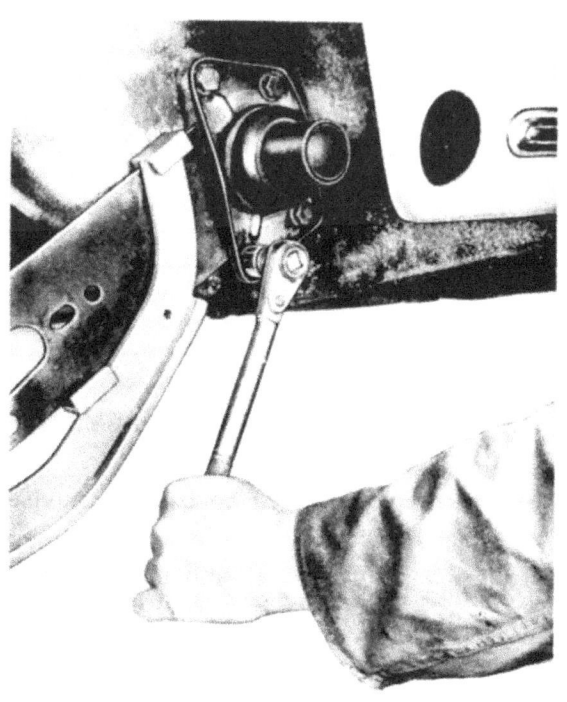

the protective coating. Especially look for evidence of rust formation, and replace a suspicious-looking torsion bar.
2. Check the rubber support of the torsion bar for wear, replacing if necessary.

Replacement

Reverse the removal procedure, noting the following:

1. Lightly coat the torsion bar with multipurpose lithium grease, carefully filling all grooves in the splines.

CAUTION: The torsion bars are prestressed in manufacture and the right and left bars therefore must not be interchanged. The torsion bar ends are stamped with an R and an L for right and left sides, respectively, to aid in identification (see illustration).

2. Adjust torsion bar as outlined following.
3. Coat the rubber support of the torsion bar with rubber preserving glycerine paste, such as "Conti-Fix Assembly Paste."
4. Place the radius arm cover in position, then start the three accessible bolts into their threads.
5. Raise the radius arm with special tool P 289 or equivalent until the spacer and the fourth bolt can be installed.

6. Torque the retaining bolts of the radius arm cover to 34 ft. lb. (4,7 mkp).
7. Torque the attaching bolts of the control arm, and the adjusting eccenter bolts, to 65 ft. lb. (9 mkp).
8. The camber eccenter should be torqued to 36 ft. lb. (5 mkp), and the tracking eccenter to 43 ft. lb. (6 mkp).
9. Torque the shock absorber retaining bolt to 54 ft. lb. (7,5 mkp).
10. Adjust the rear wheel camber and tracking as described in the WHEEL ALIGNMENT chapter.

SERVICING LATER RADIUS ARMS

The above procedure can be used to service the radius arms.

Beginning with the chassis serial numbers that follow, Type 911, 911 S, and 912 vehicles are equipped with radius arms that have rubber bushings vulcanized into place (see illustration):

   Type 911 S. from Chassis Serial No. 305 101 S
   Type 911 ...from Chassis Serial No. 307 325
   Type 912 ...from Chassis Serial No. 354 938

The new radius arms can only be installed in vehicles built since the above chassis serial numbers since the radius arm seats in the transverse support tubes had to be enlarged to accommodate the new arms. The installation procedure and adjustment specifications remain unchanged.

TORSION BAR ADJUSTMENT

Description

The exact adjustment of the torsion bar is made by measuring the angle of the radius arm in relation to the horizontal plane of the car (with radius arm hanging free). To measure the horizontal plane of the car, the special tool VW 261, a clinometer, is used. This is placed onto the lower edge of the door cavity in the body.

To achieve the specified values in the rear wheel camber adjustment, it is important to have the adjusted angle of the radius arm the same on both sides of the car. If the radius arm has been adjusted on one side, the other side should be checked also, and its setting adjusted if necessary. The adjusted radius arm angle of a free hanging radius arm (all axle components removed) is:

Type 912 (coupe & targa) .... **33°**
Type 911 & 911S (coupe & targa) .... **36°**

Adjustment

1. Place the torsion bar into the transverse tube with the inner end splines first.
2. Slip the radius arm onto the outer end splines in approximately the correct position.
3. Place special tool VW 261 onto the lower edge of the door cavity in the body (see illustration).

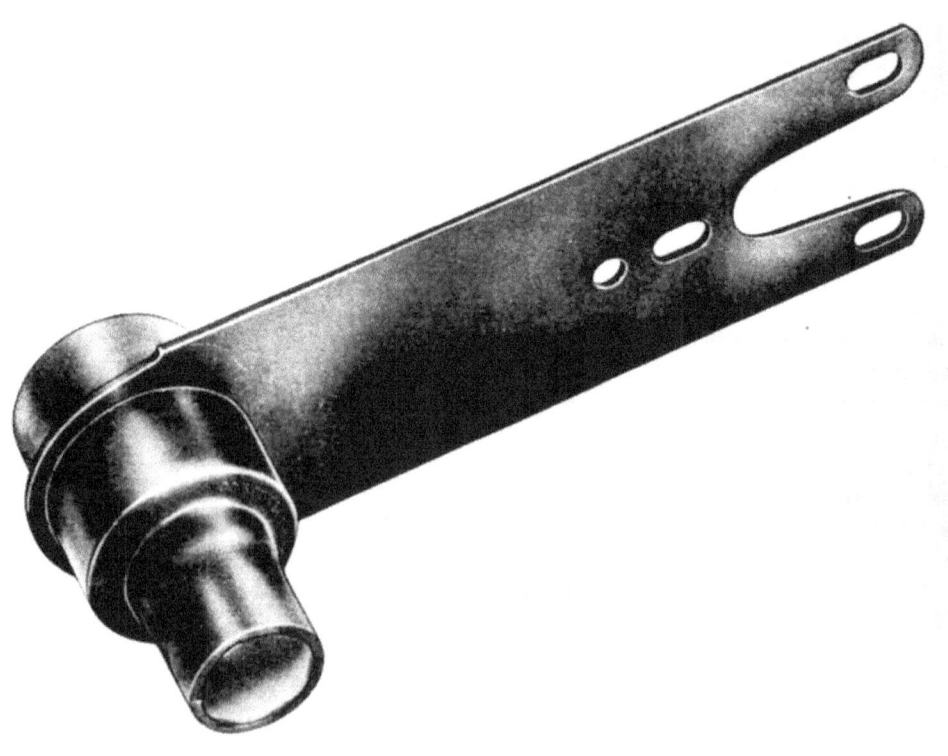

4. Adjust the clinometer so that the bubble in the glass tube marked AXLE HOUSING/ANGLE is centered.
5. Reset the glass tube carrier by the value specified for the car.
6. Place the clinometer onto the free-hanging radius arm and check the adjustment of the arm (see illustration).

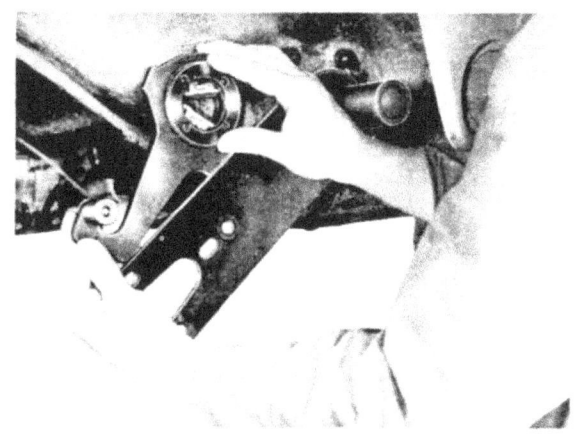

7. If necessary, adjust the radius arm, as noted under MEASUREMENTS.

Measurements

An error of one graduation mark on the glass tube shown by the air bubble equals an error in adjustment by 50' (minutes: 60 minutes equals one degree). In this case, the torsion bar and radius arm must be reset in their splined seats by one spline each, both moving towards each other. Note that the torsion bar needs to be moved in the same direction in which the glass tube carrier would have to be moved to bring the bubble into the center position.

The torsion bar adjustment variations are made possible through the spline arrangement in both ends of the torsion bar. On the inner end of the torsion bar there are 40 splines, while there are 44 splines on the outer end. This arrangement acts as a vernier for adjusting the radius arm angle. If the torsion bar is reset by one spline at its inner end, a 9° change is made. If the radius arm is reset by one spline at the outer end of the torsion bar, a change of 8°10' is made. This results in the smallest possible change of 50' in the radius arm adjustment. The closest possible degree of adjustment should be made using this add-and-take procedure.

Completing Adjustment

Adjust rear wheel tracking and camber as described in the WHEEL ALIGNMENT chapter.

REAR STABILIZER SERVICING

Description

A rear stabilizer of .63 in. (16 mm) diameter is installed in Type 911S vehicles as standard equipment, and can be adapted to all other 900 Series cars as competition equipment. Instructions for this adaptation come with the kit, but we warn the reader that the procedure involves exacting welding using templates as guides. However, the increased stability and road contact during hard cornering and high speed curves should be well worth the effort. The stabilizer joints are service-free (see illustration).

Removal

1. Press the upper eye of the stabilizer shackle off the supporting ballstud in the transverse control arm using a large screwdriver.
2. Remove the bracket cap retaining bolts and remove the stabilizer with bracket caps.

TORQUE VALUES FOR REAR AXLE FASTENERS

Hex bolt for rear axle control arm (M 14 x 1.5 - 10K)	12.0	(86.8)
Hex bolts for radius arm (M 12 x 1.5 - 10K with 8G nut)	9.0	(65.1)
Camber eccenter bolts for radius arm (M 12 x 1.5 - 10K with 8G nut)	6.0	(43.4)
Tracking eccenter bolts for radius arm (M 12 x 1.5 - 10K with 8G nut)	5.0	(36.2)
Hex bolt for shockabsorber (M 12 x 1.5)	7.5	(54.2)
Castellated nut of rear half shaft	30-35	(217-253)
Allen bolts for NADELLA half shaft flange (M 10 - 8G)	4.7	(34.0)
Allen bolts for LÖBRO half shaft flange (M 8 - 12K)	4.3	(31.1)
Hex bolts for radius arm cover (M 10)	4.7	(34.0)
Wheel nuts	13.0	(94.0)

Checking and Replacing

1. Check the rubber bushings and mounting grommets for wear, and replace faulty parts.
2. Lightly lubricate the shackle mounting grommets and press into the shackles using a vise.
3. DO NOT lubricate rubber bushings when installing.
4. See illustration for proper positioning of the shackles. The grommet openings must point inward.
5. Lightly lubricate the upper shackle grommets with MoS$_2$ multipurpose grease, then press them onto their supporting ballstuds with a large screwdriver.

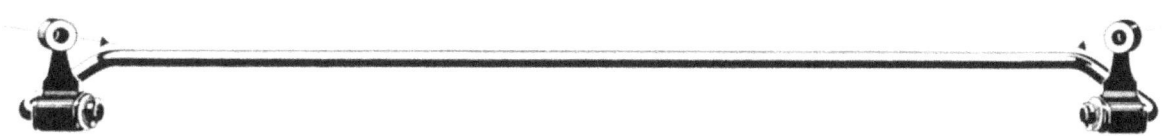

WHEEL ALIGNMENT

DESCRIPTION

A wheel alignment device, any of those in current use, is necessary for checking the wheel alignment. Since the various devices have their own measuring techniques, the actual wheel alignment procedure has been omitted and this outline confined to information dealing with adjustments and permissible tolerances.

The roadholding and cornering qualities of the car are greatly influenced by wheel alignment and vehicle height adjustment. Considerable deviations from established specifications with regard to tracking, caster, camber, vehicle height, and cornering angle differential will have a negative effect upon the proper roadholding properties and will also result in abnormally high tire wear.

In order to determine the condition of wheel alignment, the following factors must be observed:

1. Tires must be properly inflated and must be equally worn.
2. Wheel rims must have lateral or vertical runout within the permissible tolerances.
3. The empty weight of the vehicle must meet specifications, in other words, road-ready including a full fuel tank and a spare tire (properly located).
4. All moving components of the steering and suspension must have proper mechanical clearance.

Toe-In: In this condition, the distance between the horizontal wheel centers is smaller in front of the wheels and larger at the rear. Wheel camber and rolling resistance of the front wheels cause each wheel to have a tendency to run outward from the direction of travel. To counteract this outward force, it is necessary to establish a toe-in value of such proportion as to prevent a toe-out condition at speed, taking into account all the outward forces and mechanical clearances existing in the steering components (see SPECIFICATIONS).

Cornering Angle Differential: The front wheels track in parallel. That is, the steering trapeze formed by the front axle and steering components is so designed that no significant angular difference is created between the right and left wheels; any existing cornering angle differential will be the sum of the toe-in value plus the mechanical clearance in the steering components. Contrary to the normally used tracking angle geometry, the parallel-tracking layout has a tendency to toe-in (see SPECIFICATIONS).

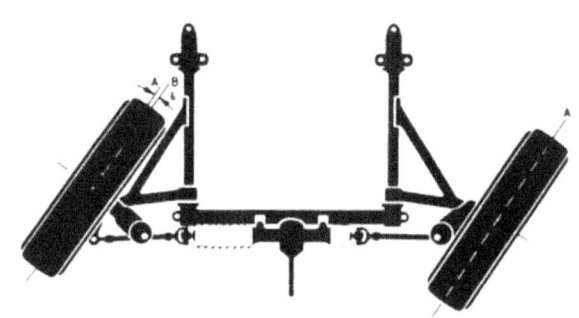

A' = Parallel to A
B = Wheel plane
δ = Angle differential

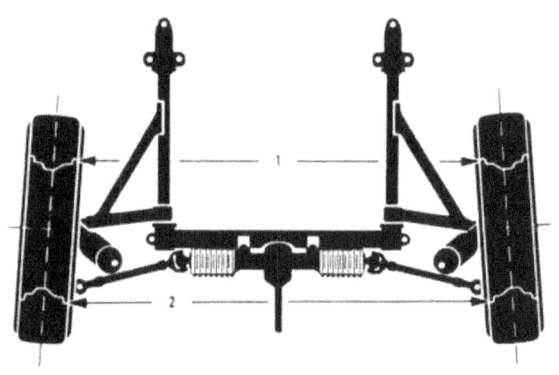

Value 1 is smaller than Value 2

Camber and Steering Axis Inclination: Camber is the angular difference between the wheel plane and the vertical plane with the root established at the wheel's point of contact with the ground. Steering axis inclination is the angular difference between the center line of the suspension strut and the vertical plane. The angular values of camber and steering axis inclination are calculated to place the point of contact of the tire and the center line of the suspension strut at the most favorable point where the rolling radius values of the cornering wheel are kept as small as possible yet, simultaneously, road shock transfer to the steering components is at its minimum (see SPECIFICATIONS).

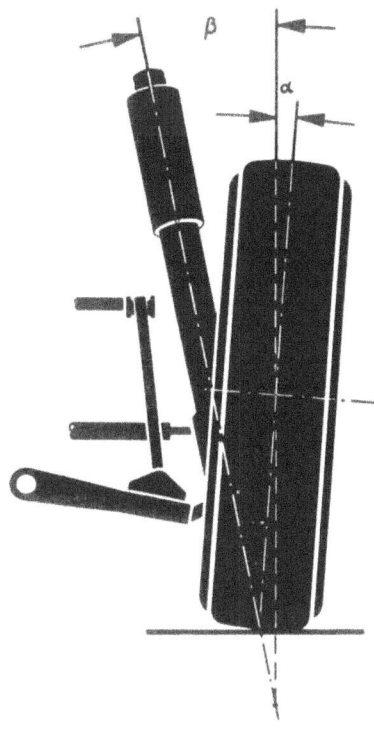

a = Camber angle
ß = Steering axis inclination

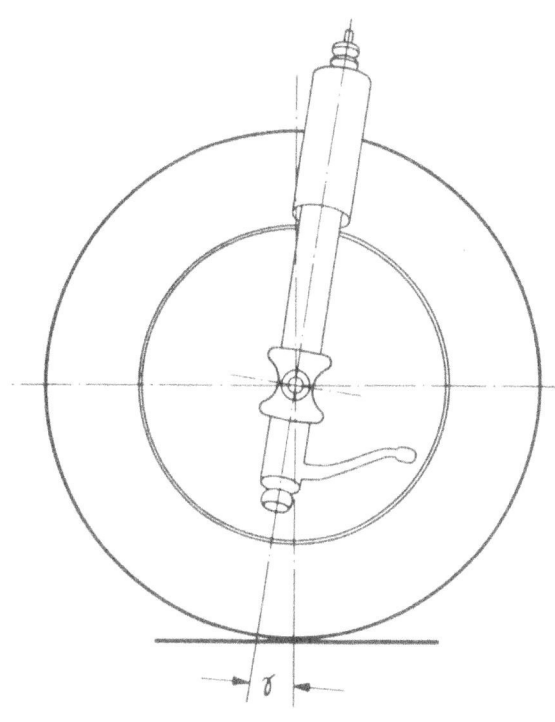

γ = Caster

Caster: Front wheel caster is created by positioning the upper part of the suspension strut to the rear of the wheel center so that the center line of the suspension strut meets the ground ahead of the wheel's point of contact. This causes a pulling force to be exerted upon the moving wheel, maintaining a forward direction of travel (see SPECIFICATIONS).

ADJUSTING VEHICLE HEIGHT

An exact height adjustment provides the necessary basis for the accomplishment of a wheel alignment check. Be sure the car has been prepared as outlined in DESCRIPTION, then drive the vehicle onto the alignment ramp or level floor. The vehicle must remain on its wheels.

Front Axle Height Adjustment

1. Mark the dead center on the dust covers of the front wheel hubs.
2. To set the suspension at the proper attitude, depress the front of the car several times by pushing down on the front bumper guards and allowing the body to come up by itself on the rebound.

3. Measure the vertical distance between the front wheel center and a level part of the ramp or floor (see dimension "a" in SPECIFICATIONS).

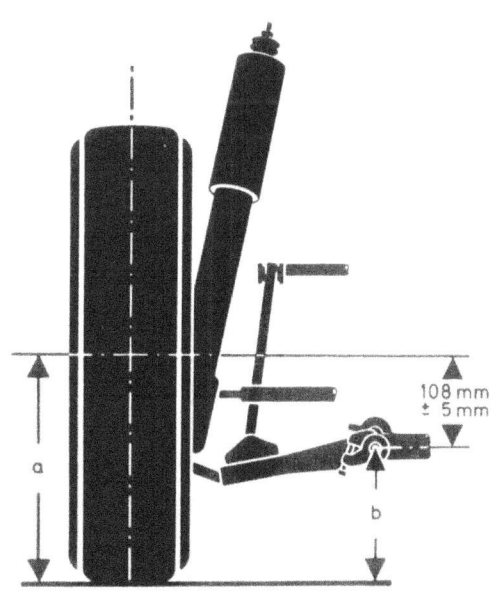

4. Value "a" minus 4¼ in. (108 mm) equals value "b". A height marker adjusted to value "b" can be effectively used for taking measurements at the torsion bar center (see illustration).
5. Remove the torsion bar dust cover at the adjusting lever to gain access to the torsion bar centering mark which should be used as a reference point.
6. Loosen or tighten the torsion bar adjusting screw until value "b" is obtained at the torsion bar center.
7. Push down on the front of the car once more, allow it to come up by itself, and recheck the height of both sides for value "b", then correct if necessary.

NOTE: Even though a ±5 mm deviation is permitted for value "b" on either side, the difference in height between the right and left sides must not be more than 5 mm. See example below:

Example: Value "a" = 315 mm
                   − 108 mm
          Value "b" = 207 mm ± 5 mm
                    (= 202 to 212 mm)

Based on the above example where value b measures 207 mm with permissible deviations anywhere between 202 and 212 mm, the following adjustment possibilities can be accomplished:

a. If value "b" on the left side is 202 mm (= 207 minus 5), then value "b" on the right side can be 202 to 207 mm (up to minus 5 mm difference).
b. If value "b" on the left side is 207 mm (= 207 ± 0), then value "b" on the right side can be 202 to 212 mm (up to ± 5 mm difference).
c. If value "b" on the left side is 212 mm (= 207 plus 5), then value "b" on the right side can be 212 to 207 mm (up to minus 5 mm difference).

8. If proper suspension adjustment values cannot be achieved, then check the height adjustment of the front suspension and correct if necessary.

Rear Axle Height Adjustment

1. To set the suspension at the proper attitude, depress the rear of the car several times by pushing down on the rear bumper guards and allowing the body to come up by itself on the rebound.
2. Measure the vertical distance between the rear wheel center and level part of the alignment ramp or the floor (see dimension "a" in illustration in SPECIFICATIONS).
3. Value "a" plus 12 mm equals value "b"; however, value "b" cannot be measured since the torsion bar is off center within its rubber bushing mounting.
4. Value "b" less bushing-cover radius (½ diameter) equals value "b1".
5. Measure the height of the vehicle (value "b1") with the help of a height marker or a similar device. The actual value "b1" should not differ from the calculated value "b1" (items 3 and 4, above) by more than ± 5 mm; in addition, the height difference between the right and left side should not be more than 8 mm.

Example: Value "a" = 315 mm
                   + 12 mm
          Value "b" = 327 mm
                     Value "b" = 327 mm
          − Bushing-cover radius = 30 mm
                    Value "b1" = 297 mm

The permissible tolerance for Value "b1" then, is as follows:

a. If value "b1" on the left side is 292 mm (297 minus 5), then value "b1" on the right side can be 292 to 300 mm (up to plus 8 mm difference).
b. If value "b1" on the left side is 302 mm (297 plus 5), then value "b1" on the right side can be 294 to 302 mm (up to minus 8 mm difference).

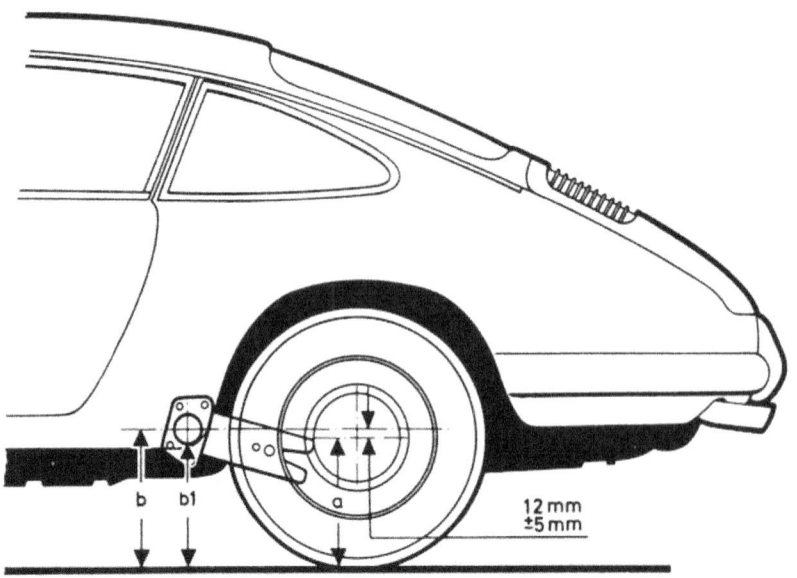

6. If the proper suspension adjustment values cannot be achieved, then check the rear torsion bar adjustment and correct it if necessary.

WHEEL ALIGNMENT CHECK

Front Wheel Alignment

Adjusting toe-in: Toe-in much be adjusted with the steering mechanism in its midmost position since otherwise the wheel turning angle will not be the same on both sides, resulting in unequal turning circle.
1. Turn the steering wheel to lock, applying slight pressure to feel the stop in the steering box.
2. Holding the steering wheel against the stop, note the position of the lower spoke in the steering wheel in relation to the switch panel (see illustration). Mark this spoke with chalk as shown.

3. Turn the steering wheel in the opposite direction to lock, and note dimension "a" at the unmarked lower spoke (see illustration).

4. If dimension "a" differs on one side from that on the other, the steering wheel will have to be removed and appropriately reset (see STEERING chapter).
5. Set the steering wheel to its midmost position. Using an optical wheel aginment device, adjust the left and right tie rods to bring each road wheel to a 20' (minute: 60 minutes = one degree) toe-in. Wheels should be pressed with a preload of 33 lb. (15 kp).

Cornering Angle Differential

Cornering angle differential exceeding the specifications cannot be eliminated through tie rod adjustment. Deviations falling within limits indicated on the measurement data card are tolerable (see at the back of this chapter). Excessive error will most likely be due to deformed steering arms, tie rods, or steering knuckle at the suspension strut.

CASTER AND CAMBER ADJUSTMENT

NOTE: Caster and camber cannot be adjusted on vehicles up to Chassis Serial No. 302.694, as well as Chassis No. 302.736 and 302.805. Should vehicles in the above categories show error in excess of limits shown on the vehicle measurement data card (see at the back of this chapter), it will be necessary to check the suspension components as well as the suspension strut supporting points for possible deformation or wear.

Adjusting Camber

1. Pull back enough luggage compartment carpeting to facilitate access to the three retaining screws of the shock absorber strut-position adjustment.
2. Scrape and clean off the sealing compound from the pressure plates and the movable dish ring, using tar solvent.
3. Mark the position of the single-hole and two-hole plates, loosen the retaining screws with special tool P 291 or equivalent (see illustration).

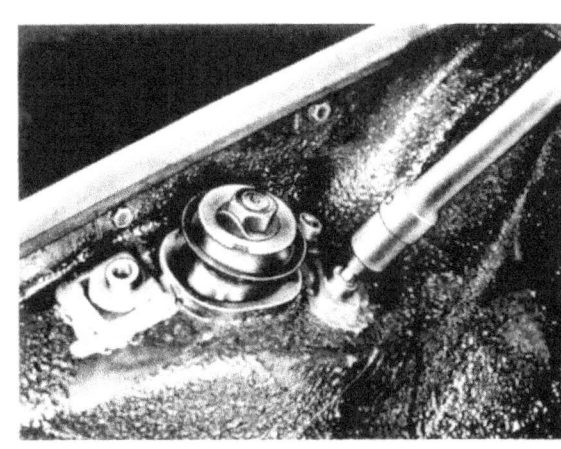

4. Reset the movable dish ring together with the suspension strut end across the direction of travel to obtain the desired camber adjustment; resetting the dish ring by 1 mm equals a 6' (minute) change in suspension strut attitude.

CAUTION: Resetting the dish ring along the direction of travel (forward or back) affects the caster adjustment.

5. Torque the retaining screws with special tool P 291 to 34 ft. lb. (4,7 mkp).
6. Reseal the surfaces around the pressure plates and the dish ring with non-hardening sealer such as National Kleber 670 or equivalent, then refasten the carpet with an appropriate adhesive.

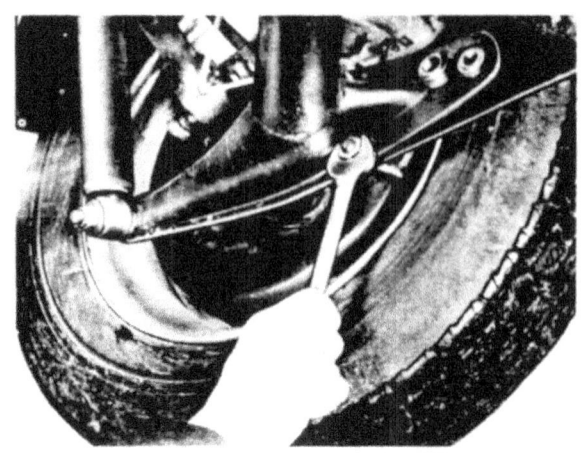

Adjusting Caster

CAUTION: Use the instructions dealing with the camber adjustment to adjust the caster. Reset the dish ring and suspension strut in the longitudinal direction (forward or back in the direction of travel); transverse resetting will affect the camber adjustment.

NOTE: When using optical alignment devices which have no provision for taking direct readings of caster values, caster angle can be determined from the overall camber differential taken at 20° left turn and 20° right turn, then multiplied by a factor of 1.5.

Example: Left Wheel
Caster at 20° left turn = + 3°
Caster at   right turn = − 2°
(on right wheel 20° turn adjusted)
Overall camber angle differential = 5°
Total camber angle differential of 5° x
1.5 = 7.5° caster.

Rear Wheel Alignment

IMPORTANT: A mandatory prerequisite for obtaining permissible camber values at the rear wheels is proper adjustment of the torsion bars. Then the rear wheel camber and tracking is adjusted with built in eccenters. The camber adjusting eccenter allows smaller camber corrections than is possible to achieve through the torsion bar adjustment.

1 = Camber eccenter
2 = Tracking eccenter

Adjusting Rear Camber and Tracking

1. Loosen the retaining-bolt nuts and eccenter-bolt nuts at the rear axle flange (see illustration).
2. Turn the tracking and camber eccenters so that the required adjustment values are obtained on the optical alignment device (see illustration).

CAUTION: When installing the eccenters or when adjusting the camber or tracking, note the following:

3. It is possible that prior to adjustment requiring considerable tracking angle changes, the position of the camber eccenter happens to be in the extreme right or left end of the oblong cavity in the radius arm; in such cases the eccenter should be turned around by 180° to prevent binding.
4. The camber eccenter must always point down at the time of installation to prevent binding when camber and tracking angle adjustments are made.
5. Tighten eccenter retaining nuts.

NOTE: On 900 Series vehicles being set up for competition, only 1¼ degrees negative camber on the rear suspension is recommended. With the wider tires now being run, there is not enough road contact with more decamber.

MEASUREMENT DATA CARD

Prior to 1968 Models

The permissible adjustment values have been indicated on this measurement data card by way of small triangles to provide a concisely compiled reference data for quick evaluation of measurements made on wheel alignment measuring devices.

The latest wheel alignment data, effective with the 1968 models, may also be applied to earlier versions of both 912 and 911 Types for better directional stability and more even rear tire wear.

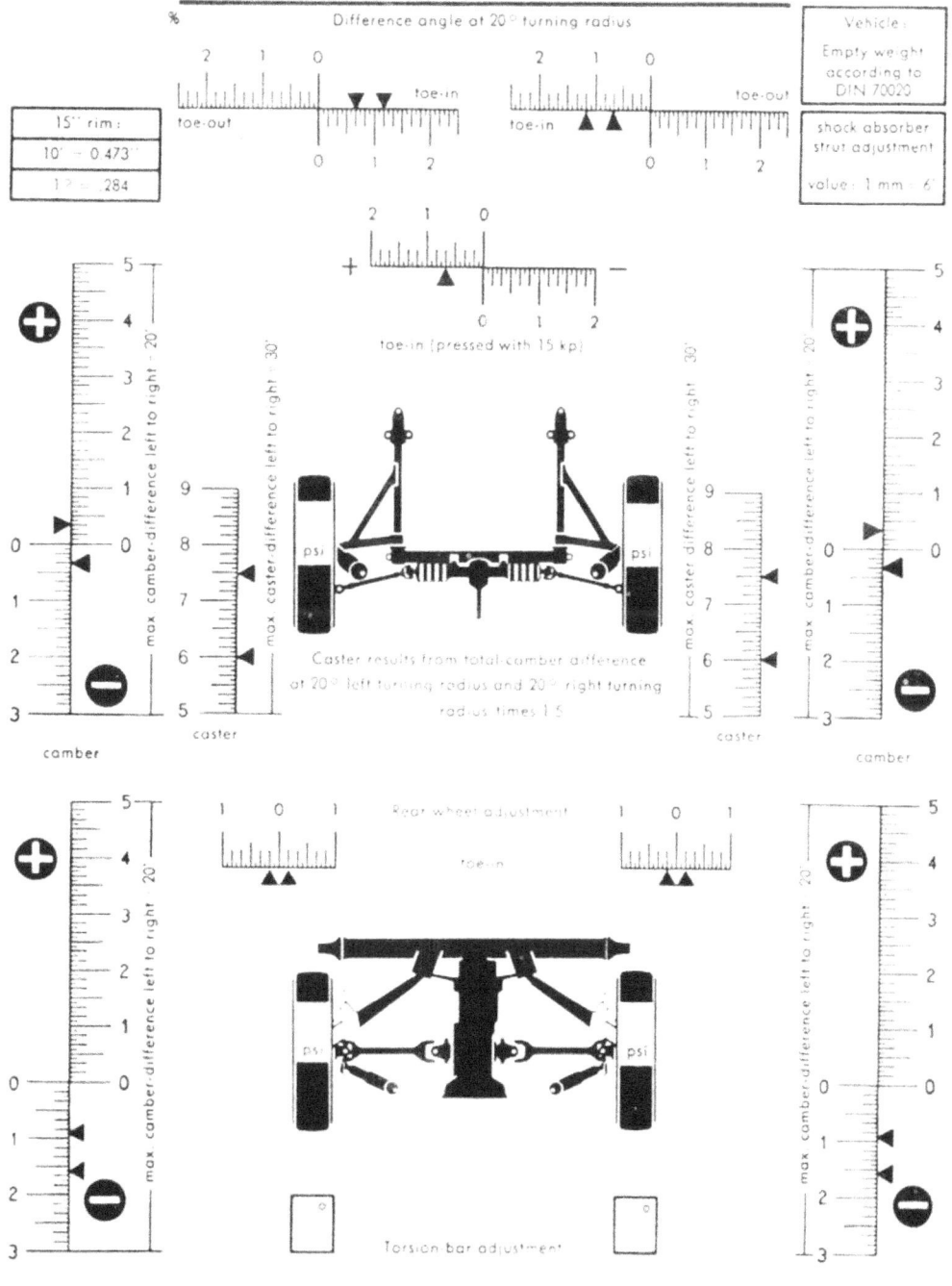

WHEEL ALIGNMENT DATA CARD

(From 1968 models on)

The latest wheel alignment data, effective with the 1968 models, may also be applied to earlier versions of both 912 and 911 Types for better directional stability and more even rear tire wear.

The permissible adjustment values have been indicated on this measurement data card by way of small triangles to provide a concisely compiled reference data for quick evaluation of measurements made on wheel alignment measuring devices.

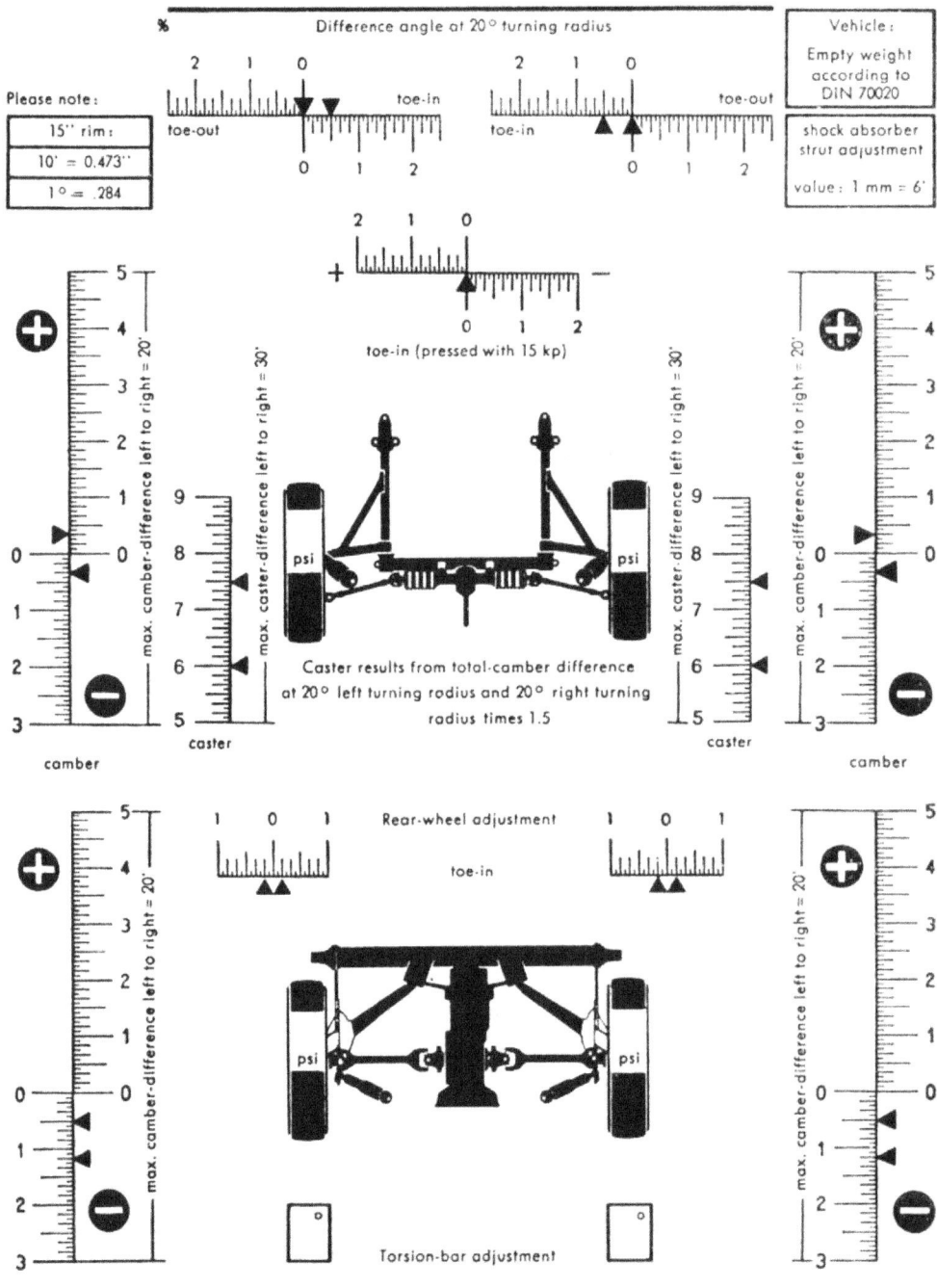

TOLERANCES AND ADJUSTMENT SPECIFICATIONS

(Type 911 vehicle in no-load condition, Empty Weight = DIN 70020)

Item	Nominal Value and Tolerances	Maximum Deviation left to right	
Front Axle Height adjustment: Rear center of front axle torsion bar lower than front wheel center	108 mm (4.25 in.) ± 5 mm (.2 in.)	5 mm (.2 in.)	
Toe-in (pressed, preload 15 kp or 33 lbs) Total left plus right wheel Value 1 is smaller than value 2	+ 40' From model '68 on 0°	none	
Angle differential in 20° turn (with toe-in bias) A' = Parallel to A δ = Angle differential	40' to 1° 10' From model '68 on 0° to 30'	Corrections possible only through replacement of steering arms	

Item	Nominal Value and Tolerances	Maximum Deviation left to right	
Front wheel camber (in straight-ahead road wheel attitude) α = Camber angle	$0 \pm 20'$	20'	
Caster γ = Caster	$6° 45' \pm 45'$	30'	

Item	Nominal Value and Tolerances	Maximum Deviation left to right	
Rear Axle Height adjustment: Center of transverse carrier above rear wheel center	12 mm (.47 in.) ± 5 mm (.2 in.)	8 mm (.32 in.)	
Radius arm adjustment Type 911 Type 912 From model '68 on Type 911 (all) Type 912	36° 33° 39° 36°	-- -- --	
Toe-in, per wheel	0' ± 10'	--	
Camber	1° 15' negative ± 20' From model '68 on 50' negative ± 20'	20' 20'	

57

BODY

DESCRIPTION

Rigidity and strength are assured by the monocoque construction of the Porsche body. It is made by welding — not bolting — the all-steel body to the chassis to form a unitized assembly. The frame side members are made of light, thin-wall box sections of high rigidity. Each section is painstakingly smoothed by hand and fitted into place before welding. The total unit is strong and free from rattles. The center tunnel accommodates the transmission shift linkage, all control cables, and electrical wires. The sharply-tapered hood affords excellent visibility and, combined with the rounded windshield and roof, as well as the falling rear contours, provides the proper aerodynamic effect.

The targa convertible naturally has the above features, but adds the safety of a roll bar as an integral part of the design. This streamlined, stainless steel band-sheathed bar actually adds strength to the unitized body, while protecting the open passenger compartment in the event of a roll-over.

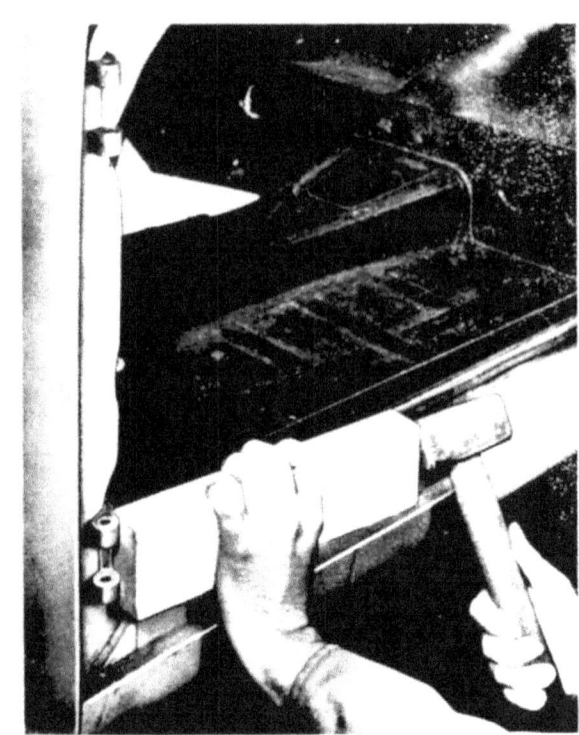

DOOR REPLACEMENT AND SERVICING

Description

The doors are supported by the forward door posts by means of concealed hinges. Opening the doors from inside and outside is by means of pushbuttons or door-pulls, depending on the model. Both doors can be locked from the outside. Adjustable door hinges and lock striker plates permit realignment of each door in the body shell. The door travel is limited by a travel stop. The doors are sealed by weatherstrip installed over the entire circumference of the door frame.

Fitting Door Shell

1. Bolt door shell to hinge post. Tighten only one of the three attaching bolts to make the resetting of the hinge possible when the front fender is being installed.
2. Adjust door for height and gap as follows:

   a. The door height should be adjusted according to the height of the doorstep sill.
   b. The gap at this point should be about $9/64$ to $11/64$ in. (3,5 to 4,5 mm). Proper door gap can be achieved by realigning the hinge post.
   c. To widen the gap, realign the hinge post by hitting the hinge with a hammer (see illustration).

3. If considerable realignment of the hinge is required remove the door; remove the hinge pins with special tool P 290 (see illustration).

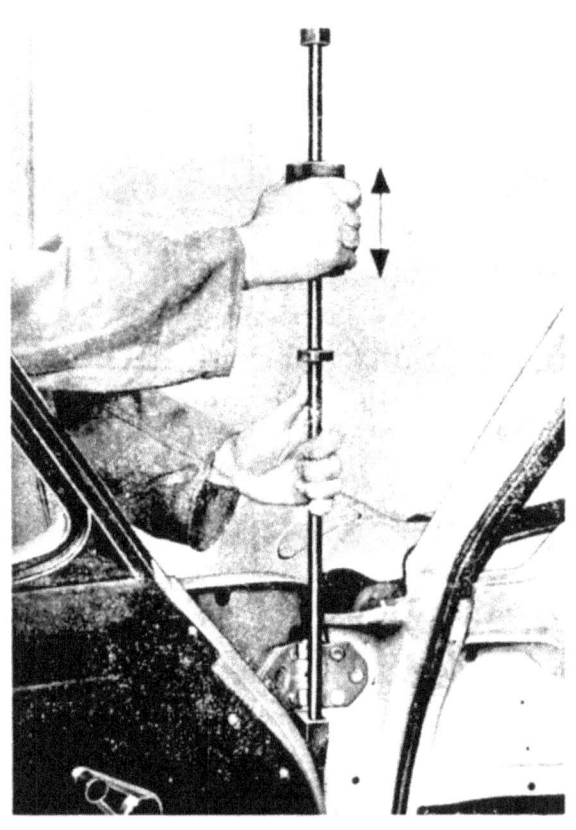

4. Check both hinge halves with a straight edge to determine in-line alignment (see illustration).

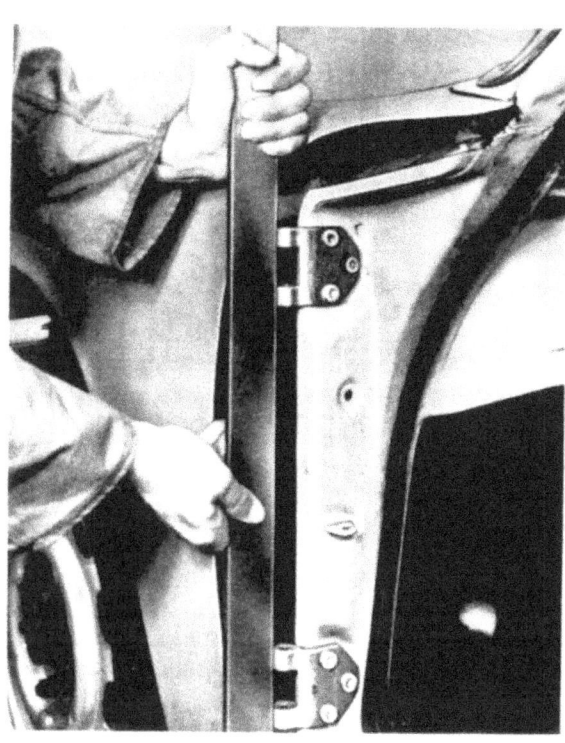

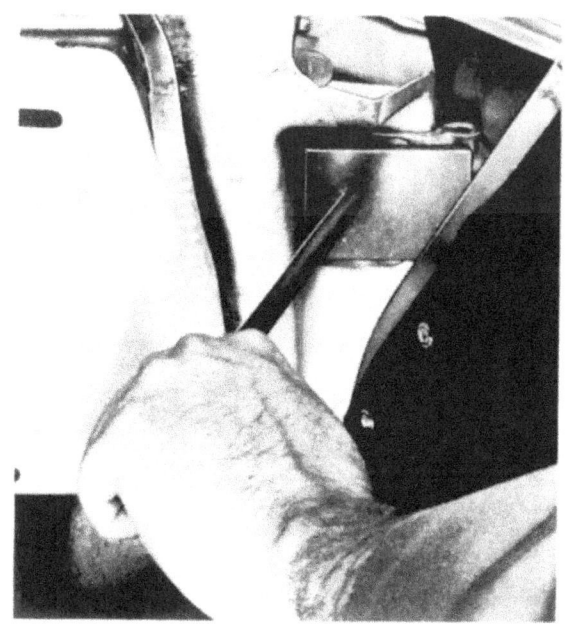

6. Check the door flange with either special tool P 1000 or a tool that can be easily made in the shop. The distance to the door should be 9 mm (see illustration). Dimensions for the tool are in millimeters (see illustration).

5. The door can be reset outward using a tool that can be easily made in the shop (see illustration). Dimensions for the tool are in millimeters (see illustration).

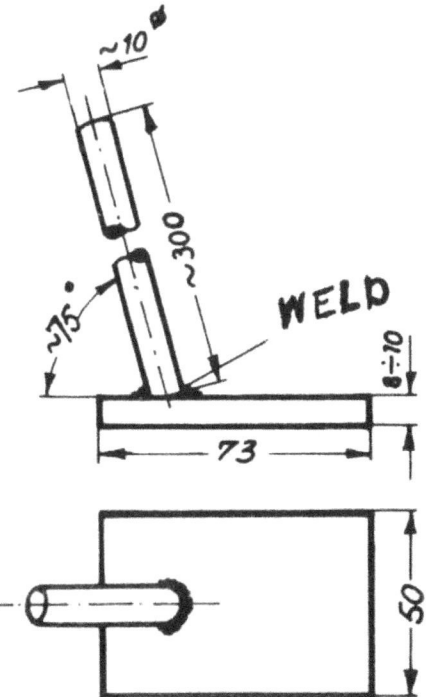

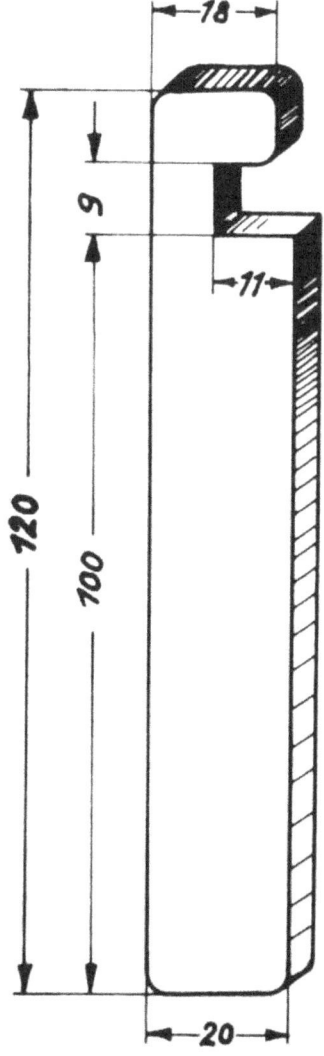

Material:
strip steel of
8 - 10 mm thickness

59

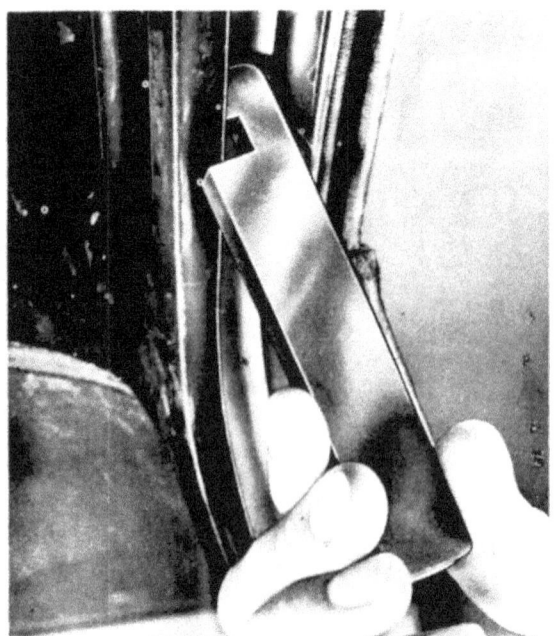

NOTE: The door shell is purposefully not welded at the points shown (see illustration). This makes it possible to twist the shell of the door, if necessary, at time of fitting it into the body. Once the door has been fitted, the points shown must be welded. In addition, a terminal piece must be cut for the front and rear upper door edge.

INSTALLING DOOR SHELL FITTINGS

Glass Description

The windshield is of laminated glass and has a convex contour with rounded sides. It is mounted in a rubber channel which also supports the decorative aluminum molding. The door windows are of tempered glass (Sekurit) and can be fully lowered by hand cranks. The window glass is supported by chromed brass frames which are lined with a combination of rubber channel and velvet.

Equipping Door Shell

IMPORTANT: The hinges should be greased heavily, otherwise the hinge pin will tend to rotate, causing the door to squeak when opened.

1. Install door lock and linkage; there are two variations, the new one having a through pin instead of the two short pins (see illustration). The fault of the old lock was that if two persons attempted to open a door simultaneously from the inside and outside when the door was locked, the mechanical parts could miss one another, causing the lock to jam (see illustration). Therefore, it is best to install the new lock assembly.
2. When a new lock is being installed in an old door, be aware of the following:

   a. The present door version accommodates the lock in a position offset by 6°. Since the door button in

the outside door handle (lock cylinder) is the same for all doors, the door button pressure receiving plate in the new lock is of a steeper angle.

b. Thus, if a lock with a steeper angled receiving plate is being installed, the door button actuating finger has to be replaced with one of a special version.

c. When installing an extended pressure pin, it should be noted that it must not rest against the lock since the possibility would then exist that the door would open by itself when driving over very rough surfaces.

3. Insert the window cranking mechanism and lightly tighten the four Allen bolts.

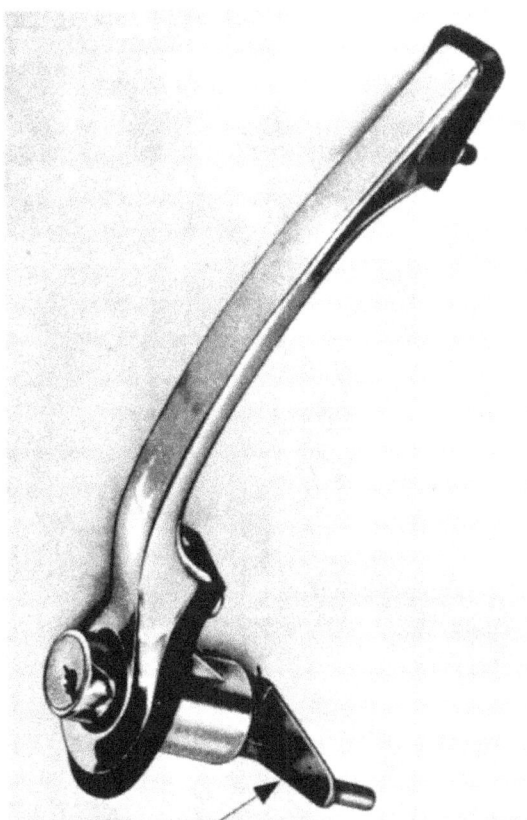

NOTE: There are two cranking mechanism versions, the older version having rollers and the new version having plastic sliders. These two versions are not readily interchangeable. When installing the window cranking mechanism, the bolts should be secured with both washers and lock washers since the frame may loosen through road shock. To prevent window rattles, install the new version of the cranking mechanism, frame and elevating rails into older models.

4. Place the window mechanism into the full up position and push the window pane with the caulked elevating rail into the cranking mechanism forward from the rear. Assemble parts belonging only to one version of the cranking mechanism, frame, and elevating rail rather than trying to combine them.

5. Crank the window to half height, then insert the frame into the door by pushing it in from above. The glass slides in velvet pile inside the window frame. Adjust window frame so there is no stiffness or binding, then tighten the retaining screws according to the following sequence (see illustration).

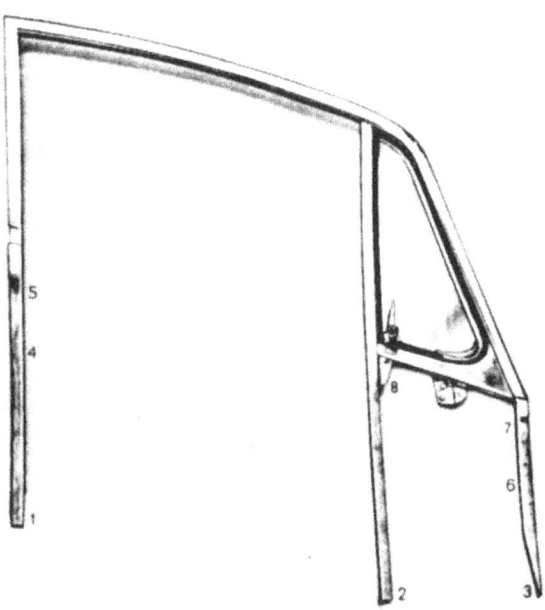

NOTE: Two screws of uneven length are used to fasten the window frame to the rear of the door. The shorter screw is installed in the upper position (see illustration).

6. The first models of the Type 911 cars were equipped with hollow-profile weatherstrip. When the weatherstrip is to be replaced on one of these cars, there is a choice of either a thicker rubber strip or the new type weatherstrip. When using the thicker weatherstrip, adjust the window frame (using a gauge) to a gap of 12 mm: or 9 mm with the new type weatherstrip. Tighten all 6 bolts holding the frame.

7. Use a good brand of rubber weatherstrip cement to fasten the weatherstrip into place.

8. Install the outside door handle, then install the door travel limiter.
9. Install rubber strip in the window well covering rail and cut to size. Fasten the covering rail with attaching clips.
10. Place a strip of pliable rubber putty under the ends of the chrome trim in the upper edge of the door, then secure the trim. The putty prevents wind noise.
11. Align the glass by cranking the window fully up and then tightening the bolts.
12. Lubricate the door lock and window cranking mechanism, then check for ease of movement.
13. Cement the cranking mechanism travel stops into place.
14. On the older model cranking mechanisms only, cement a 5/16 in. (8 mm) thick piece of foam rubber about 2 x 2 in. (50 x 50 mm), between the glass elevating rail and the cranking mechanism. This prevents friction between the elevating rail and cranking mechanism.
15. Cement 1/4 in. (6 mm) thick felt liners to sheetmetal under the lock remote control rods.
16. Make a water-tight cover by cementing heavy oiled paper (leatherette) over the access holes on the interior side of the door (see illustration).

17. Fasten the door panel to the door by sliding the attaching clips into the rubber receptacles.
18. Use sheetmetal screws to further secure the door panel. Be sure to place a screw at each end of the door pocket to keep it from ripping.
19. The armrests are installed as follows:
   a. Stand the armrest up and secure with an Allen bolt at the back end. The leatherette should first be punched through, but the door panel board already has the necessary holes.
   b. Place the armrest into its normal position, then install the two additional Allen bolts.
   c. Fasten the handgrip with 2 bolts installed under the ornamental strip. There is no grip on the driver's side.
   d. Guide the pushbutton of the remote control at the armrest forward from the rear and press into the center of the nipple. Should the pushbutton bind in its hole, remove the button and enlarge the hole with a file.
20. Fasten the ornamental strip to the window frame with the preinstalled velvet liner, using the snap nut and the sheetmetal screw at the rear, and the sheetmetal screw at the front.
21. Install the safety lock button, then install the window crank handle with the ring. The crank should be in an offset down position when the window is up.
22. Close all openings in the door with rubber caps. Recheck door for fitting in frame with gauge P 1001 as illustrated. Check gap with a tool that can be made as illustrated. All dimensions are in millimeters.
23. Align lock plate with lock.

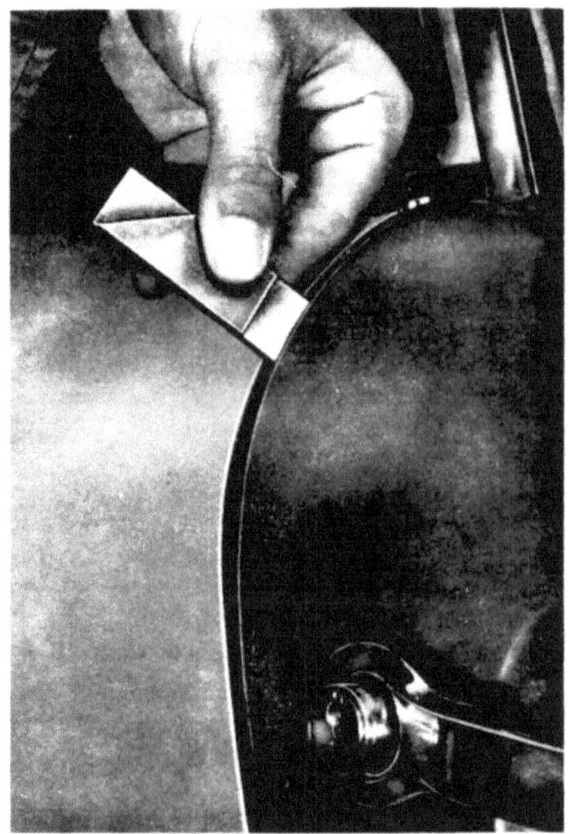

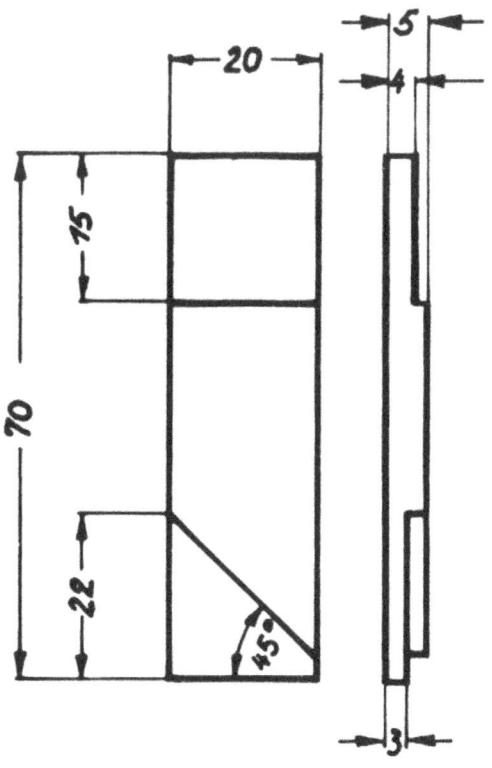

INSTALLING LIDS

Description

The front and rear lids are attached to concealed hinges. Gas cushioned props keep each lid in any desired position. Both lids are opened from the passenger compartment by means of control knobs. The front lid is secured by a safety latch in addition to the lock. Each lid opens automatically should the control cable break, thus preventing a lock-out.

Luggage Compartment Lid

1. Install lid hinges and gas prop. Be sure the piston rod of the gas prop is down.
2. Install the front lid lock and adjust roughly, then tension the lock spring with a piece of wire.
3. Install the front lid, then adjust the gap between the top edge and the windshield center piece of the body to 4 to 5 mm.
4. Adjust lid to a 1 to 1,5 mm gap between the wheelhouse and the lid edge. The lid height should be adjusted once the fenders are installed (if necessary).
5. To adjust the lid height, install spacers under the lid hinges. When spacers are placed under the forward end of the hinge, the lid is lowered, when placed under the rear of the hinge, the lid is raised (see illustration).

Engine Compartment Lid

1. Install the lid hinges and the gas prop, with the gas prop piston rod attached to the lid frame.
2. Adjust the lid on the hinges so the following gaps are achieved:
    a. The gap between the upper edge of the lid and the body should be 3,5 to 4,5 mm.
    b. The side gap should be about 2,5 to 3,5 mm per side.
    c. The bottom gap depends upon the height of the fenders, with the lower edge of the lid flush with the fender edges.
3. Should the lid gap be too wide despite careful fitting (especially following body repairs), narrow the gap with body solder or by stretching the lid edge.
4. Install the lid lock and the control cable. Make sure the lock bolt slams into the proper position.

REPLACING FRONT FENDERS

1. Fit the fuel filler cover into place prior to installing the left front fender.
2. Fit the Terostat body sealer strip under the fender mounting flange.
3. Fit the snap nuts in the fender.
4. Hold the fender in place and install the attaching bolts without tightening (to allow adjustment). As the fender is guided in, bring the cable conduit for the filler cover release into place. Do not yet install the fender seal strip since it may be necessary to apply body solder to certain areas. As a result, the gap between the fender

and the door, at the top edge, will be wider by 1 mm for the time being.

5. Tighten the fender in the sequence shown (see illustration).

6. Once the fender fits exactly, drill two 4 mm holes through the fender attaching flange and the forward body panel; place steel rivets into these holes and braze the heads to the forward body panel (or else use Pop-Rivets). This provides for easy reassembly when the fenders are removed for painting and then reinstalled.

REPLACING BUMPERS

NOTE: If necessary, new bumpers as well as the rear shield must be replaced before painting.

Front

1. Straighten the surface below the forward lid edge, which is important for obtaining an even gap between the bumper and the lid.
2. Fit the front bumper without the use of the rubber strip. Check the distance to the blinker housing, reworking as necessary.
3. Fit the blinker lens into the housing.
4. Adjust the holder at the body forward section and bumper so that a good degree of tension is created at reassembly. Bend the holder in the direction of the arrow (see illustration).

5. Install a bumper reinforcement into Types 911 and 911 S bodies. To do this, apply a thick coat of epoxy cement to the weight piece, then slide it into the bumper.
6. Attach the bumper braces to the front bumper, placing braces deep as possible to obtain as much preload tension as possible.
7. Glue the sealing rubber to the body front section.
8. Install the front bumpers.

Rear

1. Fit the bumper side pieces, then straighten the attaching tabs.
2. Fit the bumper center piece. Insert the bumper horns and adjust to equal height. The gap between the bumper and the horn is obtained by filing.
3. Remove the fitted parts, then glue the sealing rubber strip and cut the edges off.
4. Install the bumper parts, then the bumper horns. Cover the hole with plastic caps.

SIDE WINDOW INSTALLATION

1. Fit the cover strip at the bottom; if necessary, use a file to enlarge the holes.
2. Place Terostat strip under the cover strip.
3. Secure strip with Quicklock nuts.
4. Place the Terostat strip under the vertical window mounts.
5. Insert the window and tighten securely.

HEATING AND VENTILATION

Description

Hot air is guided through air ducts located in the frame side members and forward door posts. Air outlets for heating the passenger compartment are located in the frame side members adjacent to the front seats. The hot air flow can be regulated by means of sliding gates. The defrosting of the windshield is through two defroster nozzles located under the instrument panel. Defrosting of the rear window in the coupe is through a perforated pipe located beneath the rear window. On late models the ventilation system has been improved to include a three-stage electric blower to mix fresh and warm air and the ducting of the air stream from top to bottom. On coupes with electrically heated rear windows, the air ducts have been eliminated at this point. On the targa models, "gills" in the roll bar provide the air outlets for ventilation.

The entire fresh air supply enters through slots in the engine compartment lid (1) (refer to illustration). being drawn in by the cooling air blower (2). The air blower forces the cooling air over the cylinders (3) where it is preheated, and on to the lower air ducts. When the heater is not used, the air flows directly outside. When the heater control lever (15) is moved back, this turns on the heater. In this case, the air flows through a heat jacket into connecting hoses (8), ducting pipes (9), and silencers (10), into the passenger compartment. The hot air is distributed in the passenger compartment as follows:

1. Windshield defrosting nozzles (11).
2. Rear window defrosting nozzles (12).
3. Leg area outlets through sliding gates (13) located adjacent to the front seats.

In addition to this. outside ventilating air may be introduced into the passenger compartment through the ventilating inlet (14) in front of the windshield. This system operates from a separate control and is completely independent of the heating system (see illustration).

A thermostatically-controlled system warms the engine compartment when the heater is on. The warm air enters the engine compartment through outlets (5) to prevent carburetor icing and undercooling of the engine.

When the heater control lever (15) is moved back to operate the system, air gate flaps are moved in the gate assembly (8) through a cable connection. Should the cable break, the two flaps shut automatically and the hot air is permitted to flow outside (see illustration). Other heater controls are the two sliding gates (13) in the heater outlets located in the forward leg

Functional View of the Heating System

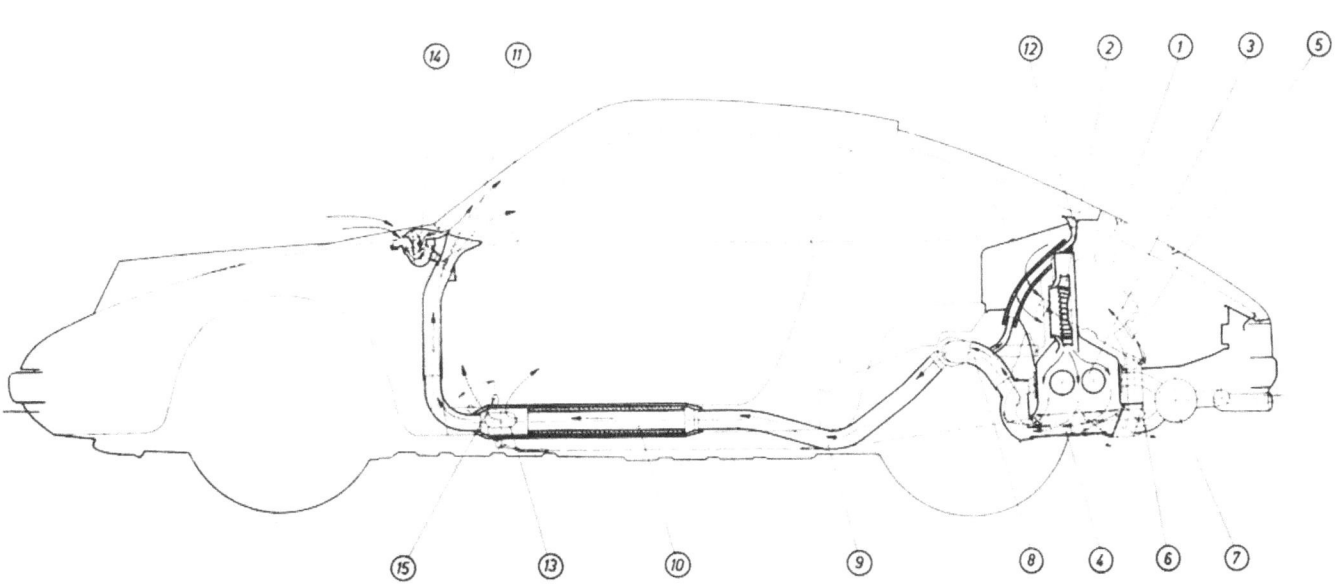

area, along the right and left sides adjacent to the front seats. When the gate is moved forward, the flow of air at this point is cut off, diverting the entire flow to the defroster nozzles (11) and (12) (see illustration).

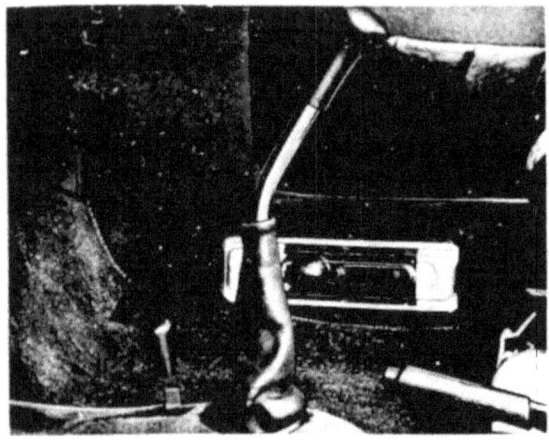

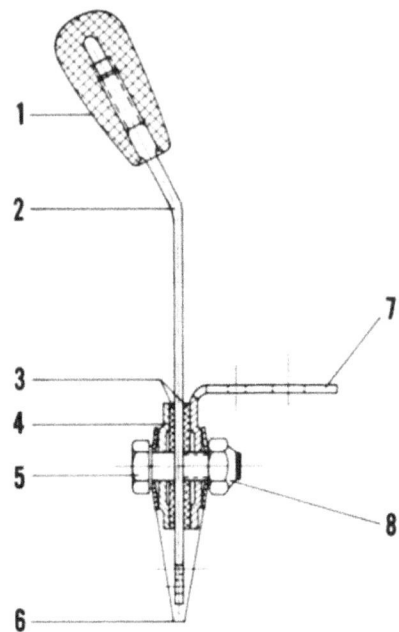

1 Control lever grip
2 Control lever (left hand drive cars)
3 Friction discs
4 Pressure disc
5 Hex bolt
6 Diaphragm spring
7 Supporting bracket
8 Self-locking nut

SERVICING HEATER CONTROL LEVER

Removal

1. Refer to illustration. Hold head of hex bolt in a vise or with vise-grip pliers, then remove self-locking nut.
2. Remove components one by one.

Reassembly

1. Hold head of hex bolt in a vise or with vise-grip pliers.
2. Refer to previous illustration. Replace components in the order shown, then replace nut.
3. Torque nut to 3.5 ft. lb. (50 cmkp), then turn back one complete turn (360°).
4. Refer to following illustration. Adjust to proper friction, which should be 22 ± 2½ ft. lb. (10 ± 1 mkp), measured with a spring scale attached to the lever through the upper hole at 90° and pulled to the lever pivot center. If setting is too weak, tighten nut; if setting is too tight, loosen nut.

SERVICING HEATER CONTROL CABLE

Removal

1. Disconnect cable ends from levers on the air gate assemblies (see illustration).

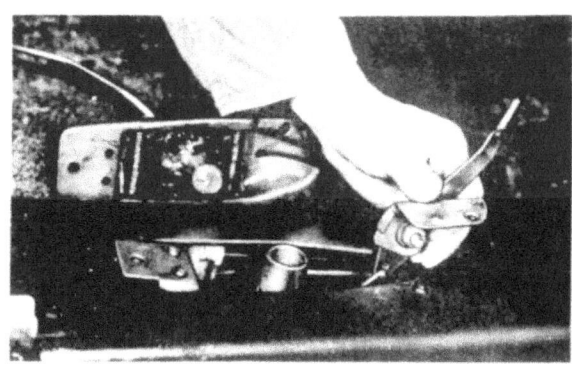

2. Remove cover from center tunnel.
3. Remove the three retaining bolts holding the shift lever base.
4. Remove the two bolts holding the shift rod carrier (see illustration).

Replacement

NOTE: The cable connects to the larger bottom hole on the heater control assembly. The smaller upper hole is for models used in Germany and Sweden, which have a different heating arrangement.

1. Thread the straight end of the control cable through the proper (bottom) hole in the control lever and pull through to the bent end.
2. Insert both ends of the control cable into the conduit tube, making sure the cables do not cross.
3. With the heater control lever properly positioned, install the shift lever base over the lever (see illustration).

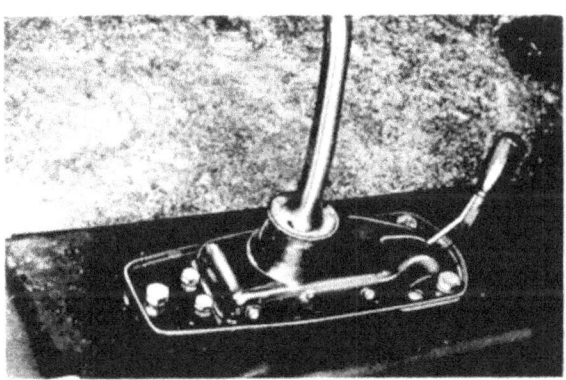

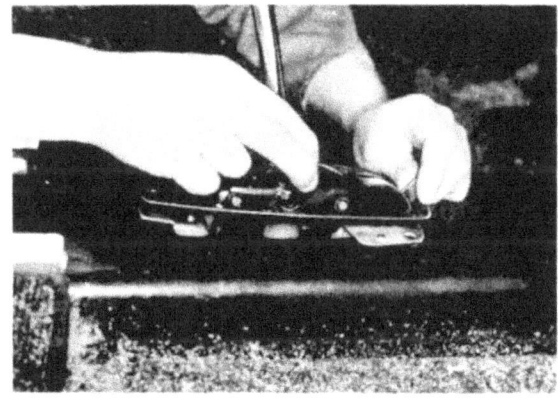

5. Pull out the shift lever assembly.
6. Pull the heater control assembly slightly away from the tunnel, then pull the control cable out (see illustration).

4. Be sure to align the base plate of the control lever, then insert bolts and tighten uniformly.
5. Move the control lever fully forward into the OFF position, then attach the cable ends to the connecting levers at the air gate assemblies. Check that the heater flaps work in unison, opening and closing fully.

TRANSMISSION AND DIFFERENTIAL

TRANSMISSION

DESCRIPTION

NOTE: This section deals with the 5-speed transmission. Procedures for the 4-speed transmission are identical with the obvious exception.

Summary

The transmission and differential, contained in one housing, is bolted to the engine and forms a unified power transmission assembly located at the rear of the vehicle. The assembly is mounted in rubber on supports attached to the forward part of the transmission and rear of the engine. The total unit must be removed or installed only as an assembly.

Transmission Housing

The housing, which is a tunnel-type case, is made of die-cast aluminum alloy. A cast iron insert is cast into the center web of the case to support the bearings.

Transmission

The transmission has five forward speeds and one reverse. A servo-lock synchronization is incorporated in all forward speeds. The forward speed gears and gear II of the reserve gear twin cluster are in constant mesh. Silent operation is achieved through the use of helical gears. The 4th and 5th speed gears on the input shaft are arranged as free-wheeling gears; due to this arrangement, the two gears remain stationary in the neutral gear speed, resulting in less gear noise at idling.

Gear Ratios

Due to the 5-speed transmission, it was possible to provide close ratios between the gears, thus achieving excellent acceleration and top speed characteristics. The individual gear ratios are shown in the accompanying diagrams. These diagrams are handy references showing the relative engine RPM, vehicle speed and gear ratios.

Example: With engine RPM (left vertical column at 5,000, a third speed gear ratio of 23:28, effective vehicle speed is 69 MPH (bisecting lines of the horizontal 5,000 RPM line and the third speed diagonal). Similar readings can be made at any place on the diagram.

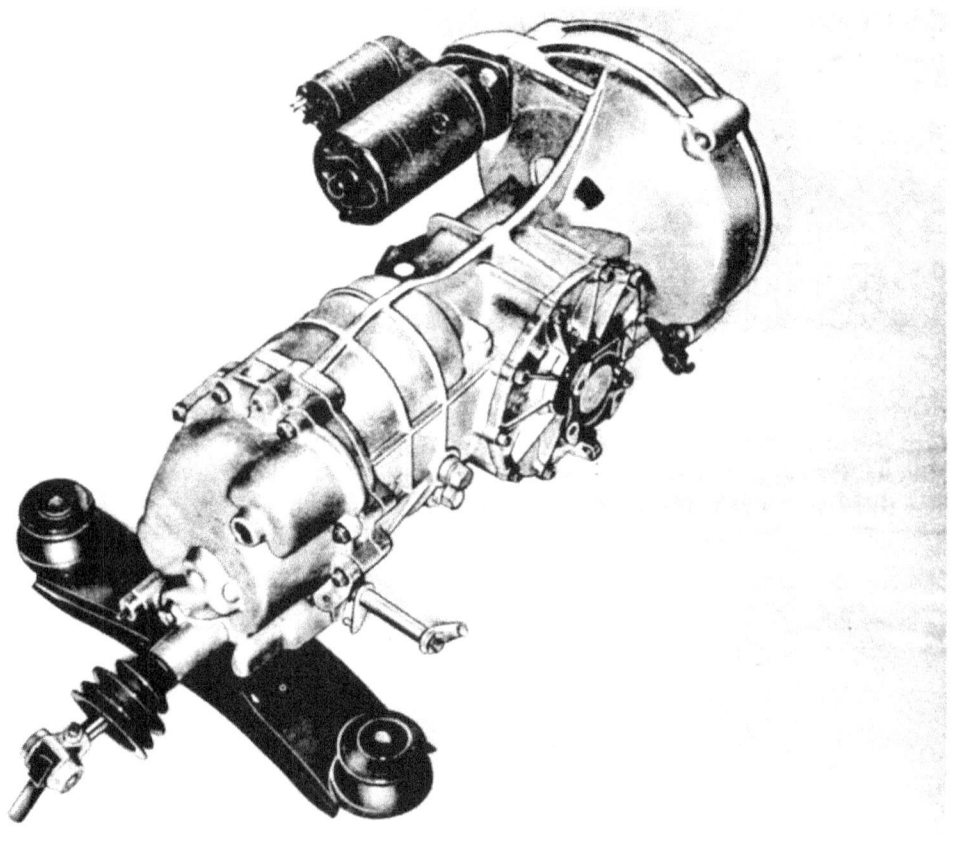

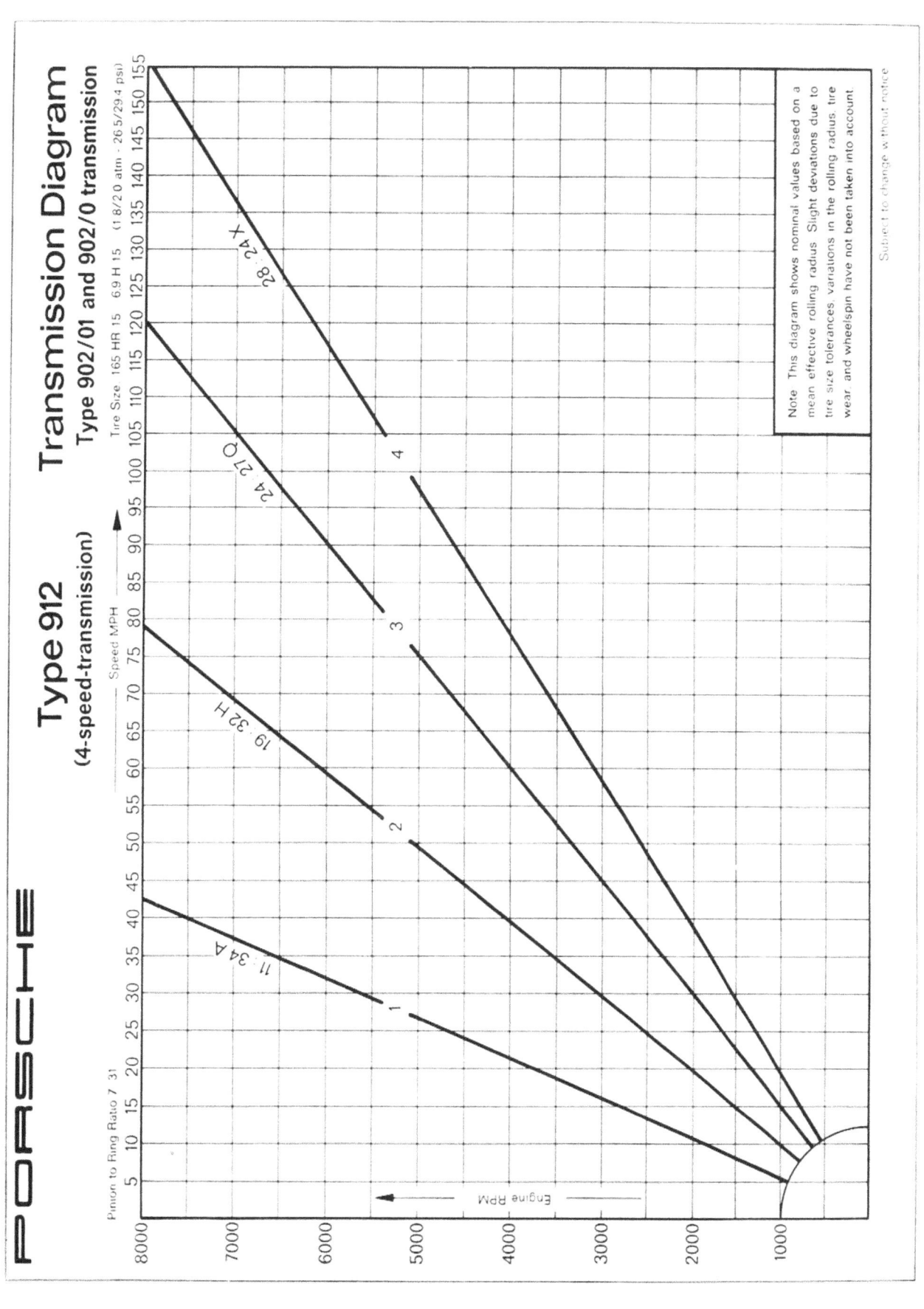

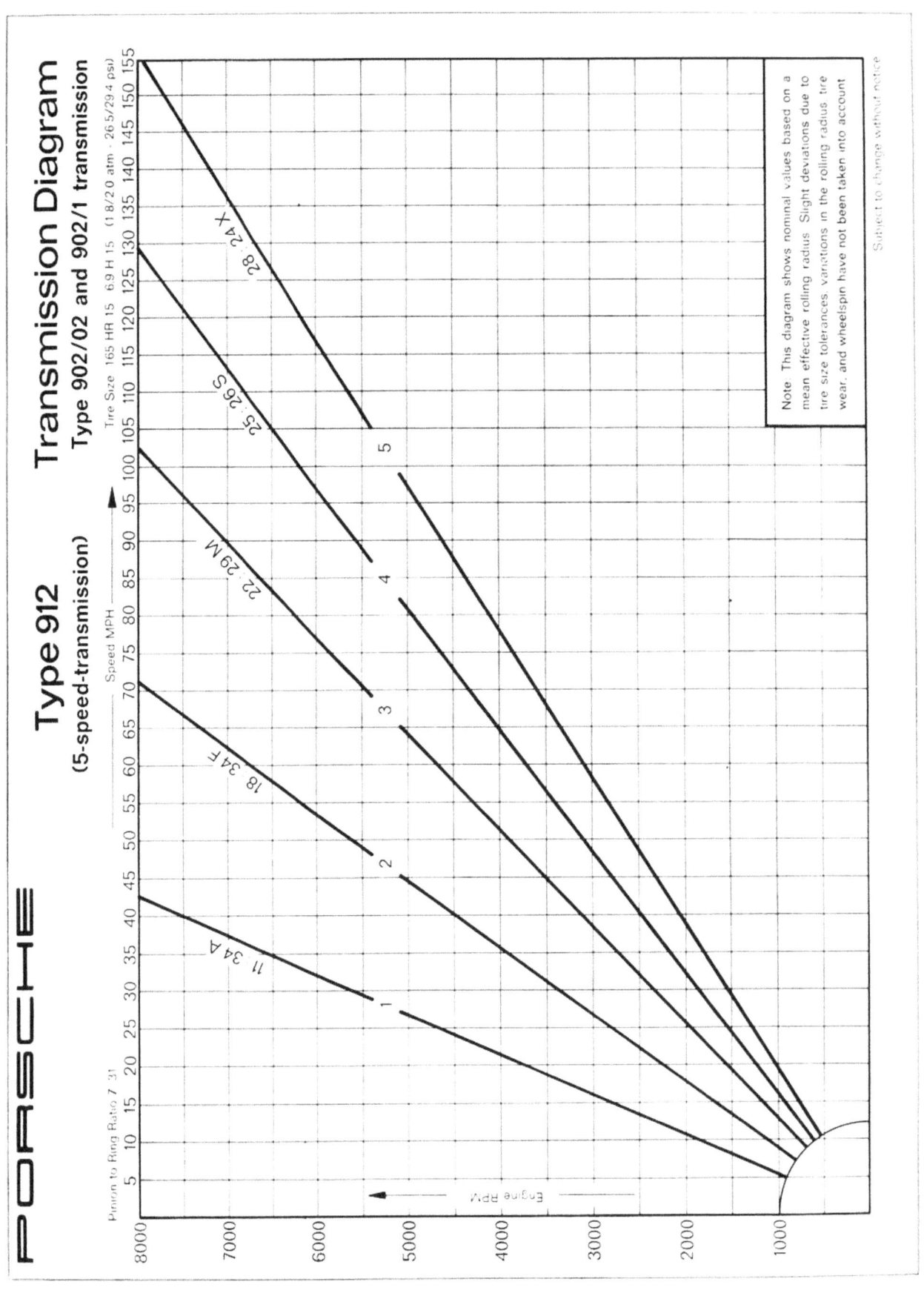

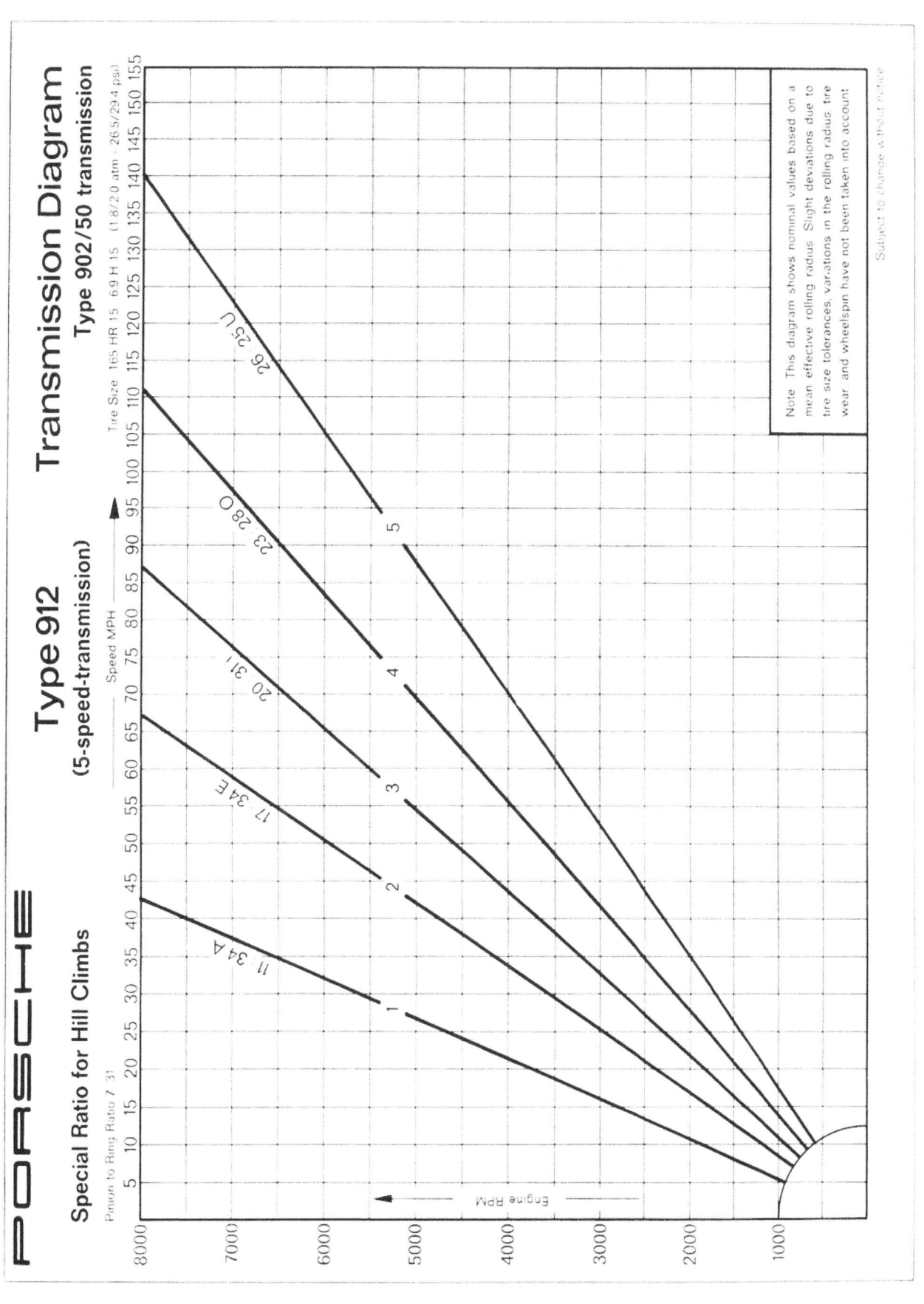

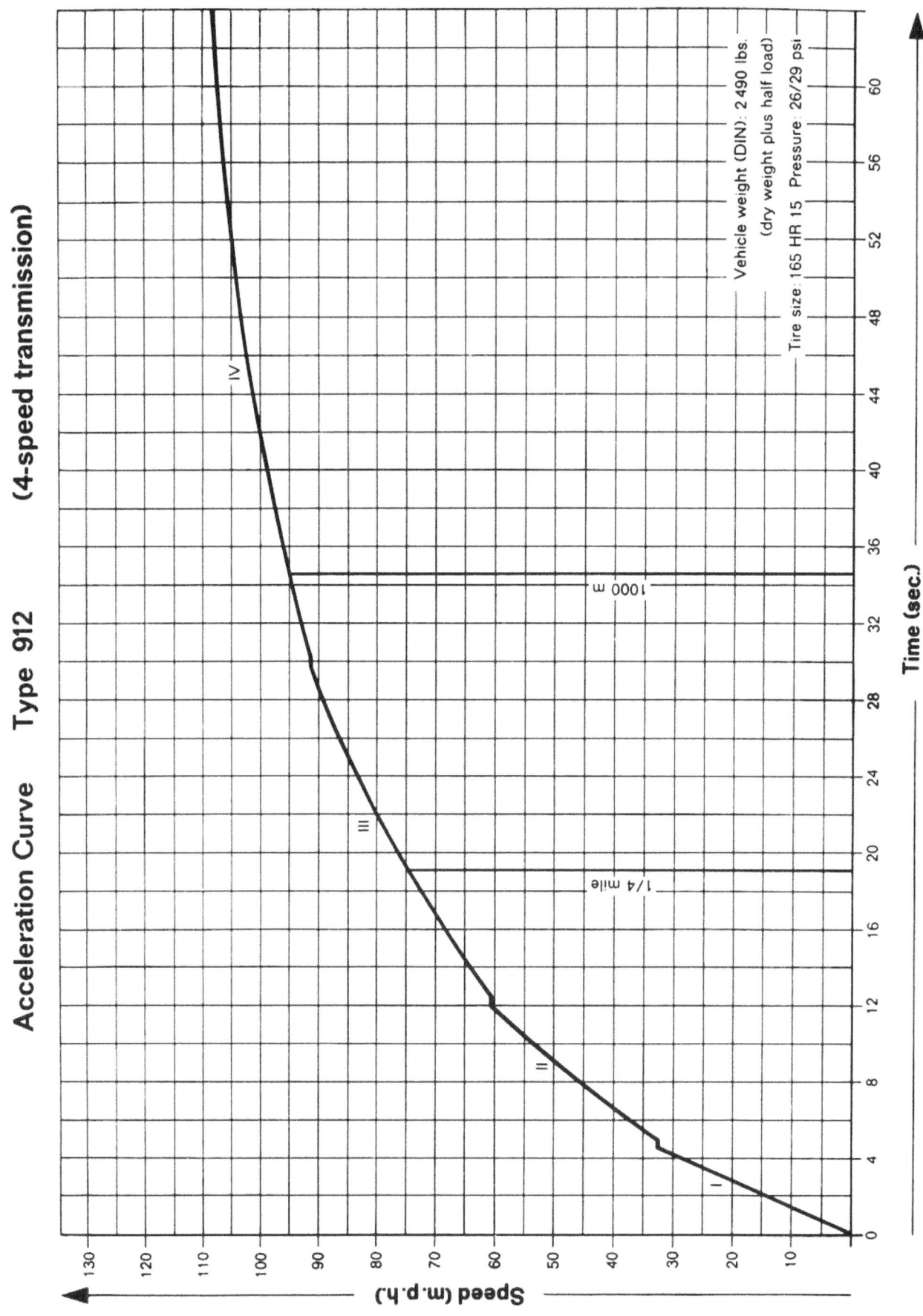

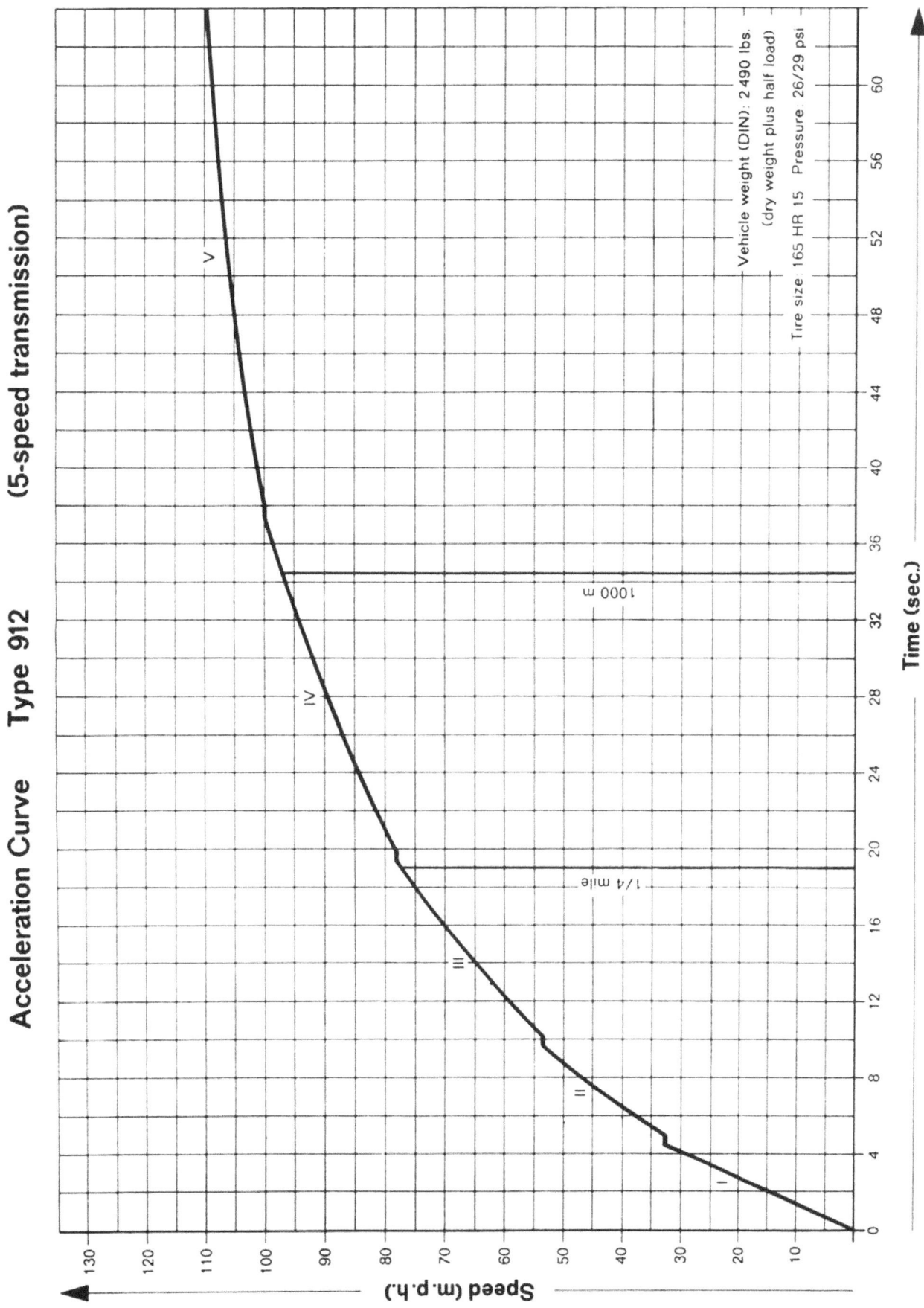

Pinion Shaft Cross-section

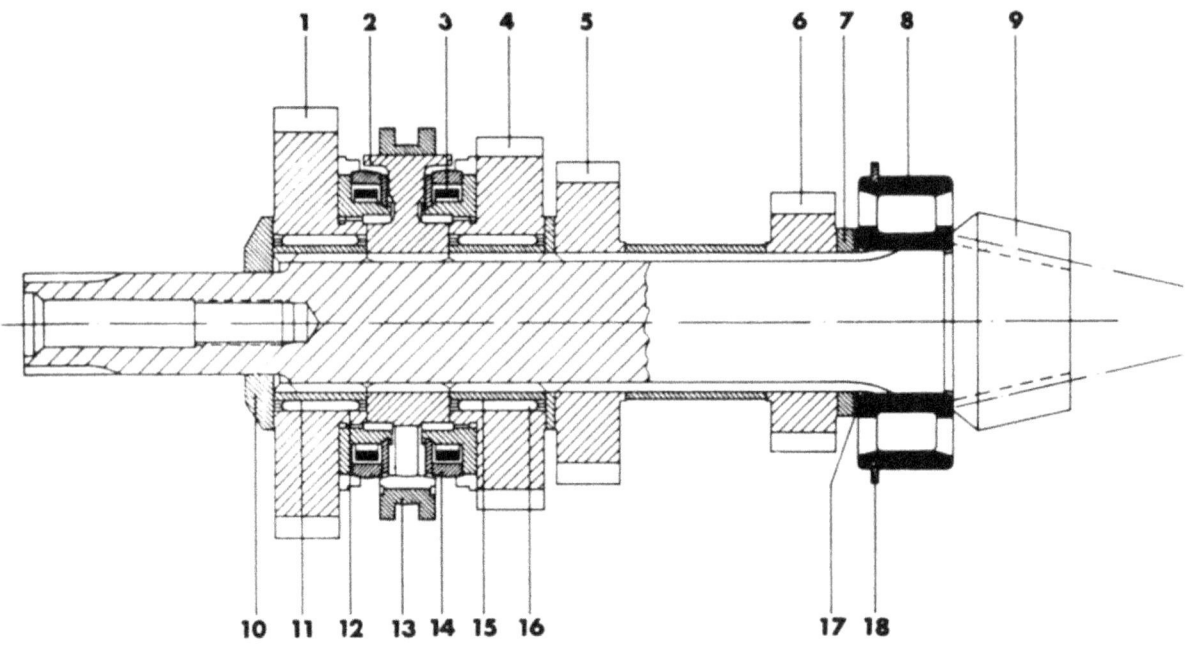

1 Gear II for 2nd speed (free-wheeling)
2 Spider
3 Brake band
4 Gear II for 3rd speed (free-wheeling)
5 Gear II for 4th speed (fixed)
6 Gear II for 5th speed (fixed)
7 Spacer
8 Roller bearing
9 Pinion shaft

10 Thrust washer (6.6. mm thickness)
11 Needle bearing inner race (gear speeds 2 thru 5)
12 Needle bearing cage (gear speeds 1 thru 5)
13 Sliding sleeve
14 Synchronizing ring
15 Needle bearing inner race
16 Needle bearing cage
17 Spacers
18 Retaining ring

Exploded View of Pinion Shaft Components

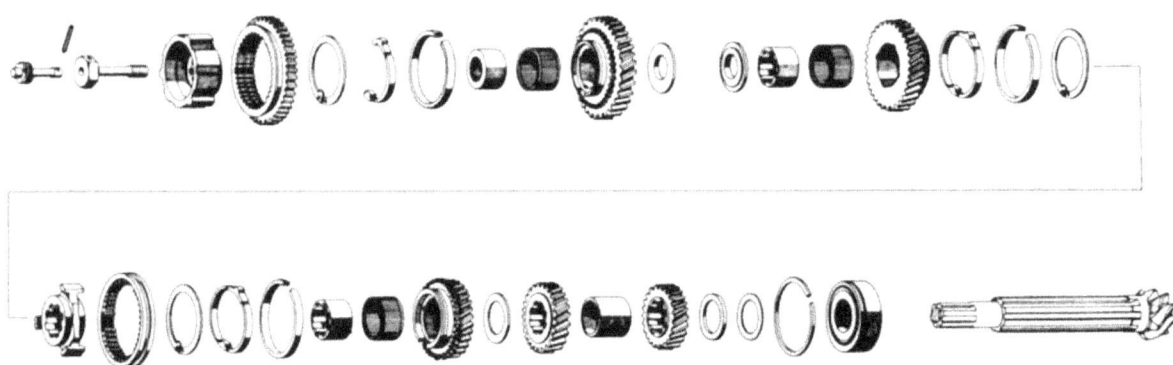

Pinion Shaft Cross-section (4-speed transmission)

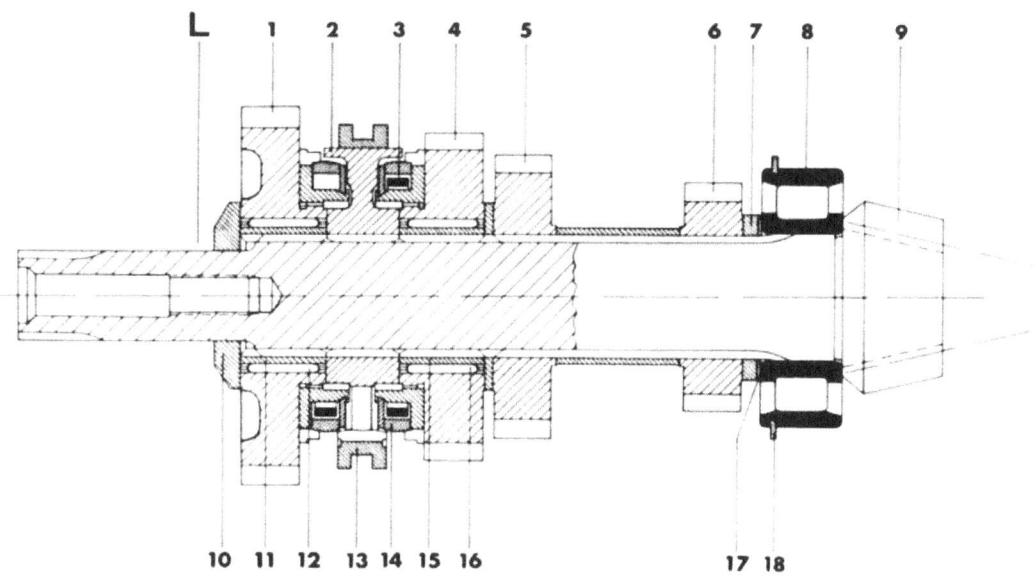

- L Four-point ballbearing
- 1 Gear II for 1st speed (Freewheeling)
- 2 Spider
- 3 Brake band
- 4 Gear II for 2nd speed (Freewheeling)
- 5 Gear II for 3rd speed (Fixed)
- 6 Gear II for 4th speed (Fixed)
- 7 Spacer
- 8 Roller bearing
- 9 Pinion shaft
- 10 Thrust washer (6.6 mm thickness)
- 11 Needle bearing inner race (gear speeds 1 thru 4)
- 12 Needle bearing cage (gear speeds 1 thru 4)
- 13 Sliding sleeve
- 14 Synchronizing ring
- 15 Needle bearing inner race
- 16 Needle bearing cage
- 17 Spacers
- 18 Retaining ring

Exploded View of Pinion Shaft (4-speed transmission)

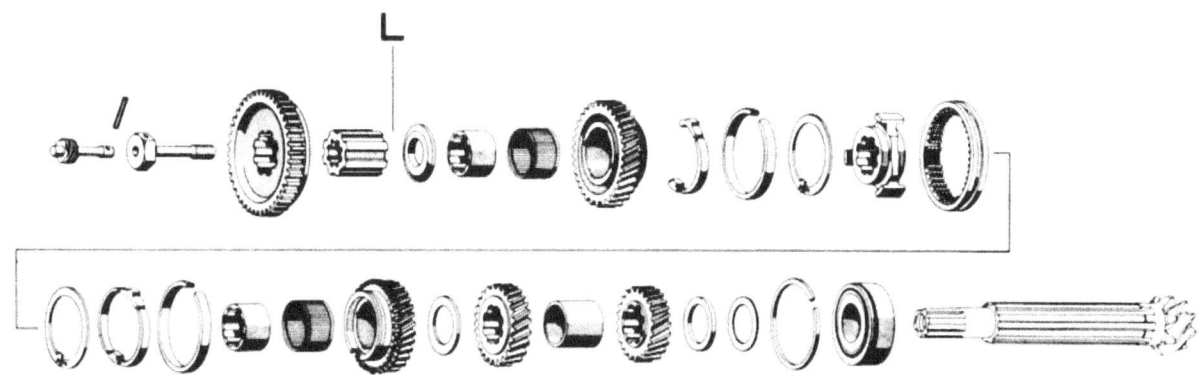

Cross-sectional View of Input Shaft

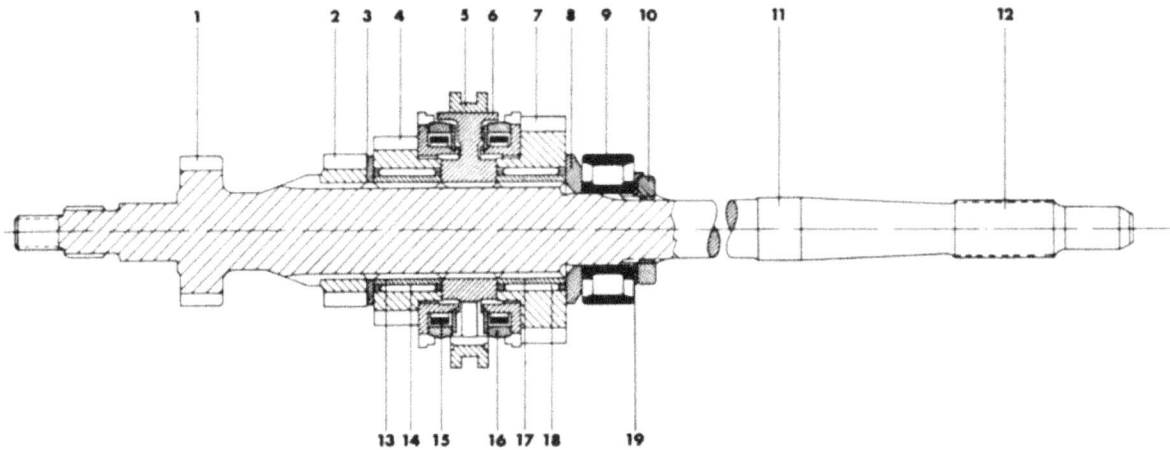

1 Input shaft (with Gear I for 2nd speed)
2 Gear I of 3rd speed (fixed)
3 Thrust washer
4 Gear I of 4th speed (free-wheeling)
5 Sliding sleeve
6 Spider
7 Gear I of 5th speed (free-wheeling)
8 Thrust washer (5.9 mm thickness)
9 Roller bearing
10 Hex nut
11 Oil seal race
12 Splined end for clutch plate
13 Needle bearing inner race
14 Needle bearing cage
15 Brake band
16 Synchronizing ring
17 Needle bearing inner race
18 Needle bearing cage
19 Nut lock plate

Exploded View of Input Shaft

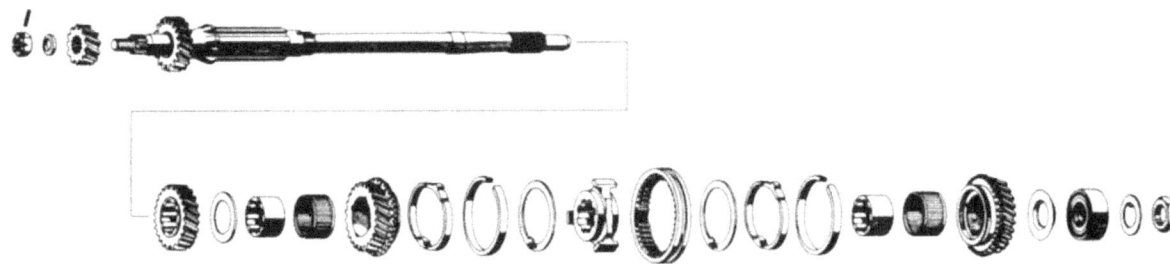

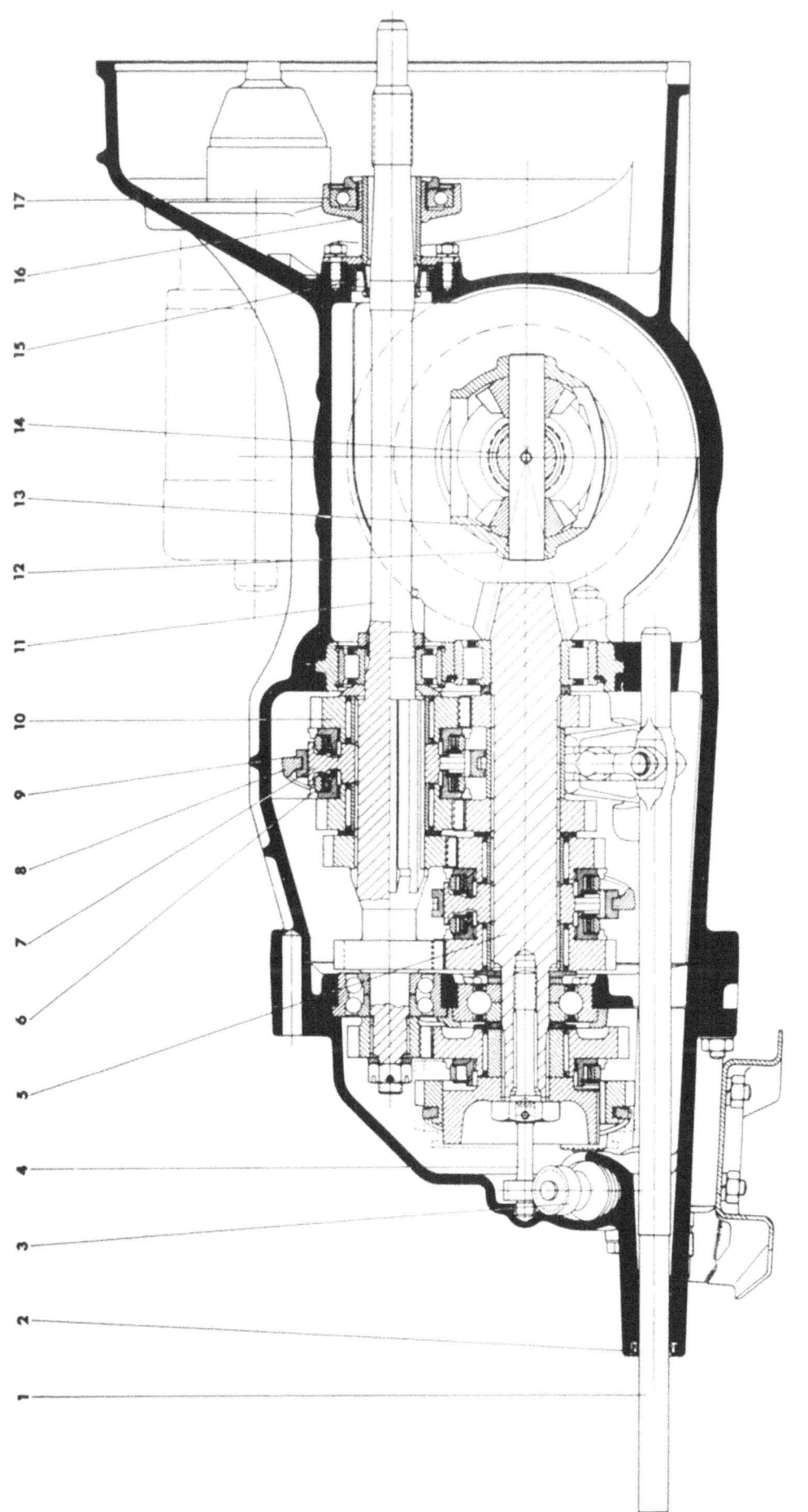

CROSS-SECTION VIEW OF TRANSMISSION AND DIFFERENTIAL

1 Shift rod
2 Oil seal
3 Tachometer drive
4 Gear shaft
5 Pinion shaft
6 Synchronizing ring
7 Spider
8 Shift fork
9 Sliding sleeve
10 Gear 1, 5th speed
11 Input shaft
12 Differential carrier
13 Bevel spider gear
14 Side gear shaft
15 Oil seal
16 and 17 Clutch throwout bearing

Function of the Synchromesh in Shifting Gears.

Gear shifting is performed by the floor-mounted gearshift lever through a shift rod leading to the transmission through the chassis center tunnel. The reverse gear engages by sliding a gear into reverse speed position. The forward speeds are engaged through the servo-lock synchromesh units. The servo-thrust force in the synchromesh units varies according to the prevailing friction. This means that the greater the difference in the gears' speed, the more friction is created. The synchromesh units permit a rapid synchronization of the given gears with the minimal application of force at the gearshift lever.

Lubrication

The transmission has an oil capacity of about 5 U.S. pints (2,5 liters). The transmission oil should be changed as indicated in the LUBRICATION SCHEDULE. The oil must be of the prescribed specifications. When changing the transmission oil, refill fully as noted above.

TRANSMISSION REMOVAL AND INSTALLATION

Refer to ENGINE chapter for removal and installation procedure. Both the engine and transmission must be removed as a unit.

NOTE: The differential can be removed without removing the engine/transmission assembly. However, if the work requires adjustments or replacement of parts, it would be helpful to remove the transmission/engine from the vehicle.

GEARSHIFT KNOB REMOVAL AND INSTALLATION

NOTE: Previous to March 21, 1967, vehicles left the factory with gearshift knobs which had a gearshift pattern imprint for either 4 or 5 speed transmission, whichever was installed in the car. These knobs were threaded onto the shaft. Such knobs on vehicles leaving the factory since the above date are pressed onto the gearshift lever and are held against turning or moving vertically with an internal lock ring. The removal or installation procedure for the latter knob follows:

Removal

1. Make a tool to remove knob as detailed in diagram below. Use steel that is about 6 mm thick, and bevel all edges. Dimensions are in millimeters.

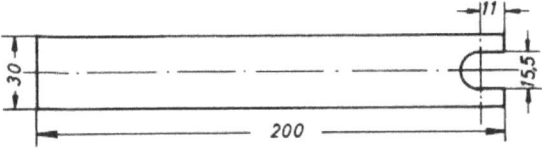

2. Shift into low gear and drive the knob off the shaft with the tool (see illustration).
3. Pull internal locking ring out of the knob with a suitable hook.

Installation

1. Press new internal locking ring into gearshift knob, using a suitable driver, until the ring seats in place.
2. Mark travel depth of knob onto the shaft to ensure that the knob will be pushed in all the way.
3. Shift into third gear. Place knob onto shaft, positioning the pattern imprint properly, then drive the knob into place with a block of soft material that has a hollow cut into it, such as special tool 299 (see illustration).

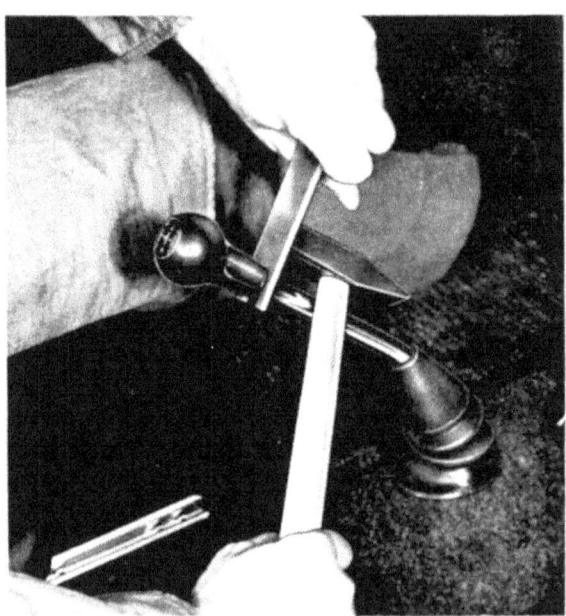

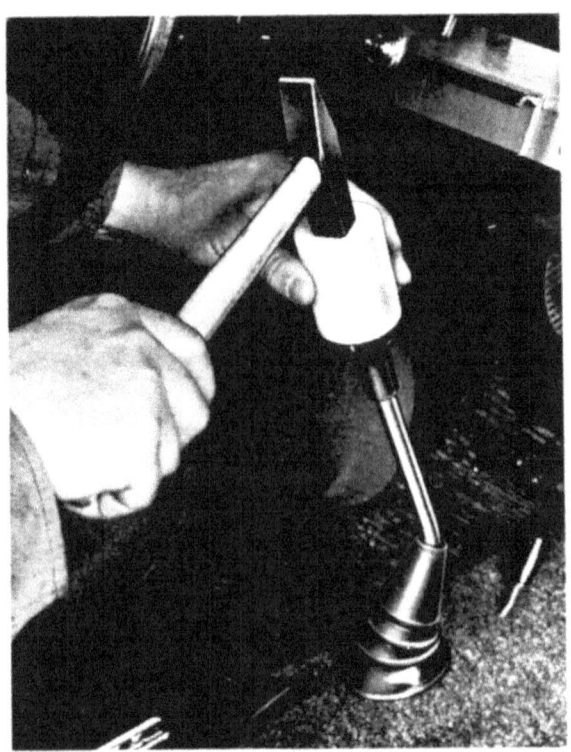

GEARSHIFT LINKAGE ADJUSTMENT

1. Remove retaining screws from cover in rear of center tunnel and withdraw cover (see illustration).

2. Remove dust boot from board flange in body and push forward over the gearshift rod.
3. Loosen hex bolt in shift rod clamp (see illustration).

4. Move selector shaft of internal shift lever in transmission all the way to stop while in the neutral position.
5. With the transmission in neutral, move the gearshift lever to the right (facing from driver's seat) to stop.
6. Tighten hex bolt of clamp to 18 ft. lb. (2,5 mkp). Be sure serrated washer is under the hex nut.
7. Check adjustment by shifting all gears. Gearshift linkage play should be the same amount in all directions.

GEARSHIFT LINKAGE REMOVAL AND INSTALLATION

Removal

NOTE: If gearshift rod must be removed, the engine and transmission must first be removed to allow access.

1. Remove both front seats.
2. Remove gearshift knob as previously described, then remove heater knob, dust boot, and tunnel carpeting.

3. Remove M8 and M6 gearshift base retaining bolts (front and back) and withdraw base (see illustration).

4. Perform steps (1) through (3) under GEARSHIFT LINKAGE ADJUSTMENT, then drive shift rod off coupling.
5. Withdraw shift rod clamp and dust boot from shift rod.
6. Remove safety wire from square-head tapered screw in shift rod joint, loosen the screw, then slide the shift rod off its base (see illustration).

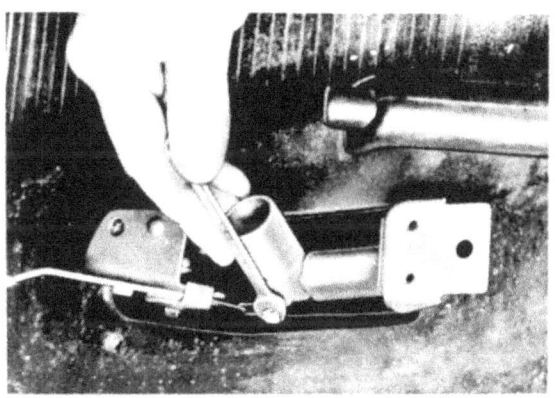

7. Slide shift rod joint off shift rod.
8. Remove safety wire from square-head tapered screw, loosen screw, then withdraw shift rod coupling.

Installation

To install, reverse the above procedure, noting the following:

1. Install the shift rod by sliding it in from the rear while the engine and transmission are out of the vehicle.
2. Tighten the square-head tapered screw securely, then fasten with safety wire. Tighten to a torque of 11 ft. lb. (1,5 mkp).
3. Place shift rod clamp and dust boot onto shift rod before attaching the rod to the shift rod coupling.

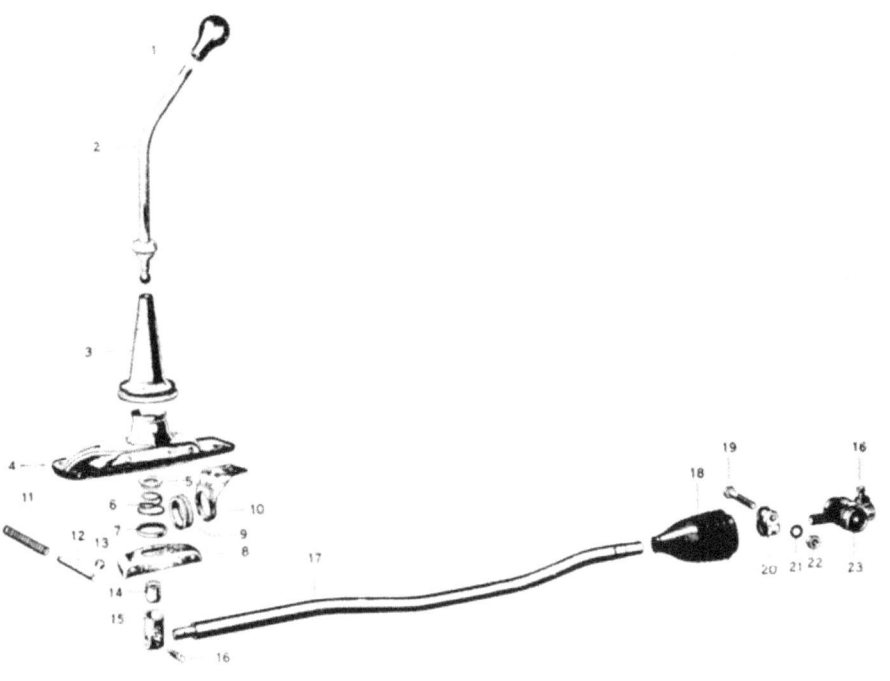

1	Gearshift knob
2	Gearshift lever
3	Dust boot
4	Gearshift base
5	Spring seat
6	Gearshift spring
7	Spring seat
8	Gearshift stop plate
9	Guide bushing
10	Guide bracket
11	Stop plate thrust spring
12	Guide pin
13	Retainer
14	Ball socket
15	Shift rod joint
16	Tapered screw
17	Shift rod
18	Dust boot
19	Hex bolt
20	Clamp
21	Serrated washer
22	Hex nut
23	Shift rod coupling

GEARSHIFT LINKAGE

4. Use lithium multipurpose grease to coat the inside surface of the shift rod joint as well as the area of the guide bracket.
5. Tighten the M8 hex bolts of the gearshift base to 18 ft. lb. (2,5 mkp).
6. Tighten M6 hex bolts which secure the shift rod guide bracket to 7,2 ft. lb. (1 mkp).
7. Adjust gearshift linkage as previously described.

SERVICING GEARSHIFT BASE

Disassembly

1. Remove plastic ball socket from gearshift lever with the help of a screwdriver.
2. Hold gearshift lever base in a vise (with protective vise jaw covers) and remove both pin retainers (see illustration).
3. Push one pin out about half-way, being sure the spring does not jump out. Place the end of a screwdriver behind the unsupported end of the spring, cover the gearshift base with a cloth to catch the spring, then force the spring out of its seat (see illustration).
4. Repeat the above operation with the other spring.
5. Remove the gearshift stop plate.
6. Remove the spring seat and the spring of the gearshift lever together with the plastic spring seat.
7. Withdraw the gearshift lever.
8. Clean all parts, then inspect for wear or damage, replacing parts as they are needed.

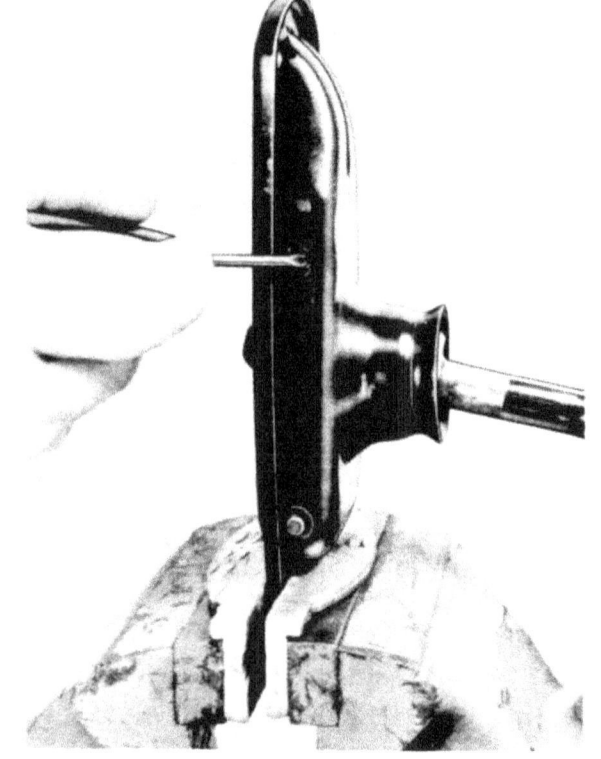

Reassembly

To reassemble, reverse the above procedure, noting the following:

1. Place plastic spring seat onto the shift lever spring so that the plastic seat snaps into the spring.
2. Use lithium multipurpose grease to coat the lower

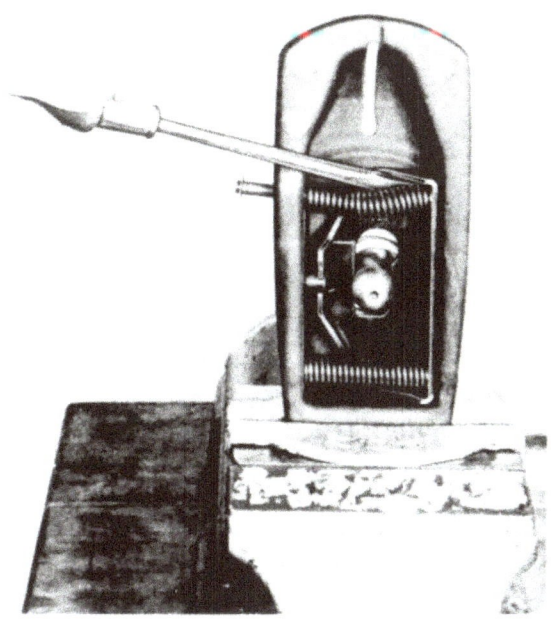 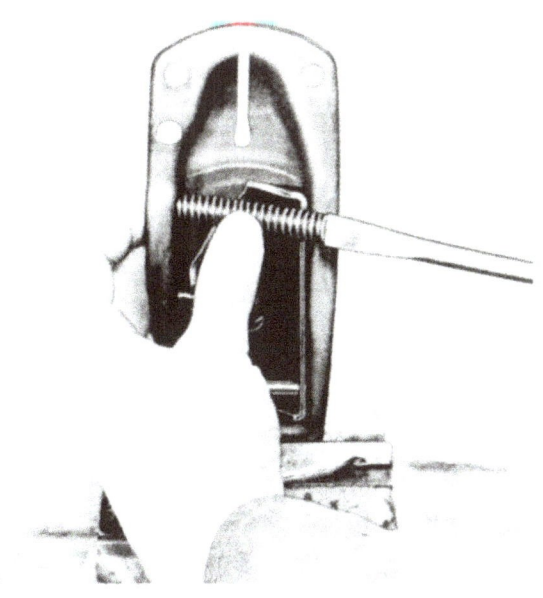

part of the gearshift lever well, then insert the lever into the gearshift base.

3. Place a pin retainer on each of the two pins which guide the gearshift stop plate.

4. Modify a screwdriver for mounting the thrust springs as shown in the diagram.

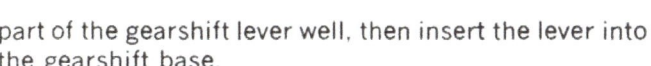

a = 12 mm (approx. 1/2 inch)
b = 6 mm (approx. 1/4 inch)

5. Mount the thrust springs as follows:

   a. Install the gearshift stop plate in the gearshift base by installing one guide pin.

   b. Place the second guide pin and retainer in position at an angle, then slip the spring on.

   c. Use the modified screwdriver to press the thrust spring into position (see illustration).

   CAUTION: In this position, the spring could jump out.

   d. Push the pin guide through and install the pin retainer.

   e. Repeat the above operation to install the other thrust spring.

6. Use lithium multipurpose grease to coat the springs as well as the ball end of the shift rod, then use a hammer to install the plastic ball socket.

DIFFERENTIAL

STANDARD DIFFERENTIAL DESCRIPTION

The power is transmitted to the rear wheels through a spiral bevel gear differential with bevel spider gears, and two double-joint half-axles. Quiet operation and long service of the rear axle is contigent upon the exact adjustment of the ring and pinion gears. When the vehicle is turned, the outside wheel covers a longer distance than the inside wheel, resulting in differing axle speeds. The purpose of the differential is to make up for the varying axle speeds and ensure that driving torque is evenly distributed between both rear wheels. The ring and pinion gear ratio is 1:4.428 (7:31).

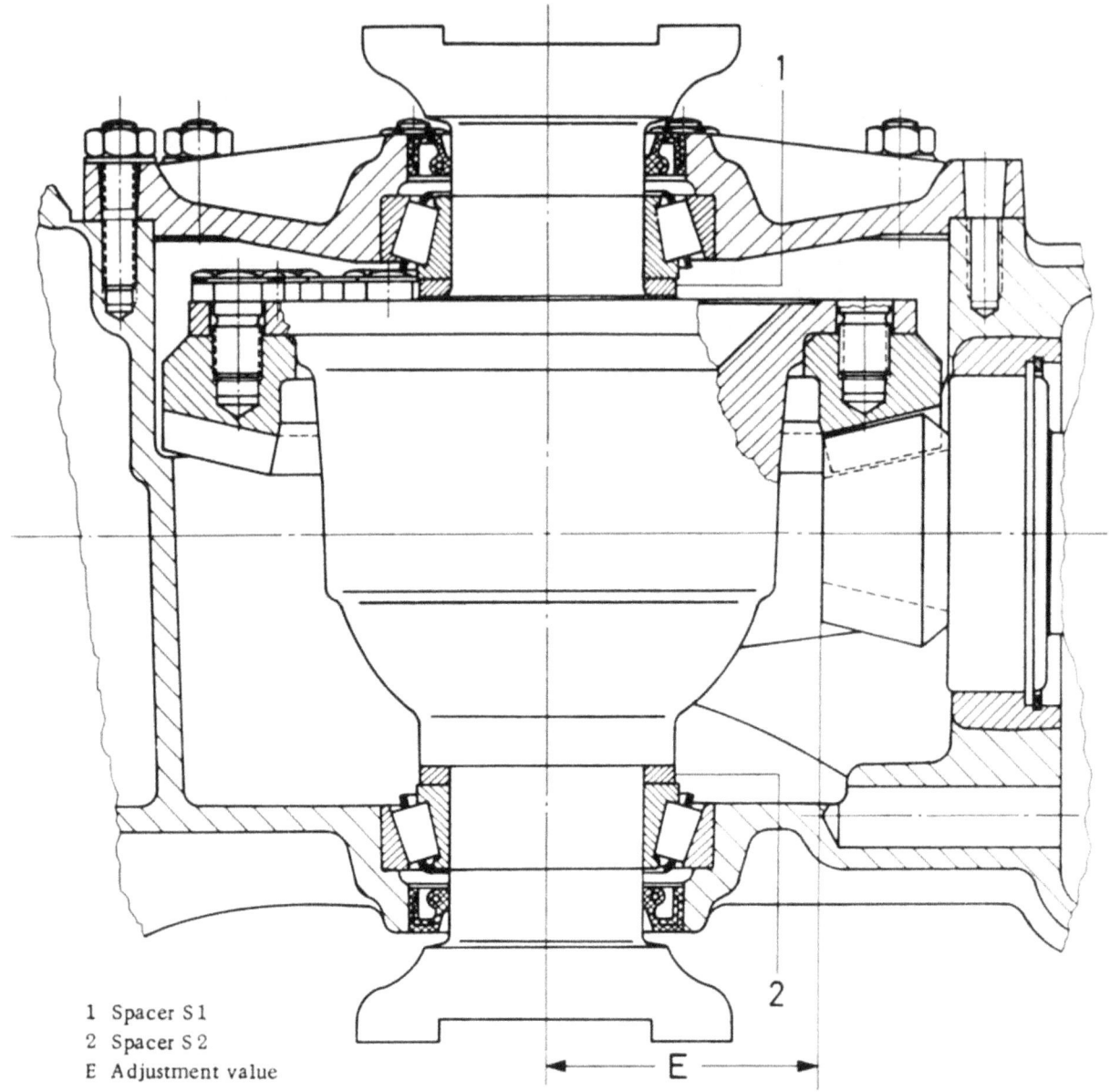

1 Spacer S 1
2 Spacer S 2
E Adjustment value

ZF MULTIPLE DISC SELF-LOCKING DIFFERENTIAL DESCRIPTION

The self-locking effect is achieved through internal friction in the differential, created by two multiple disc retarders arranged symmetrically on both sides of the differential. In comparison, the conventional differential will transmit the torque to the wheel which is easiest to turn. When the car is raised off the ground, it is very easy to hold one of the two driving wheels from rotating, in which case the other wheel spins faster. In the self-locking differential, this path of least resistance is eliminated to a great degree. The driving torque is also improved.

This additional torque is caused by the fact that the torque transmitted to the differential does not transfer directly onto the spider shafts, as is the case with conventional differentials, but over the two side gear rings which cannot rotate but are free to slide axially in the differential carrier. The contact ramps of the spider shafts, and their counterparts in the side gear rings, are slanted.

The driving force resulting from the transfer of torque forces the side gears apart, thus exerting additional pressure to the preloaded friction discs. Since the friction plates are mechanically fixed on the side gears through the use of splines, the axle shafts become semi-locked to the differential unit, thus eliminating the possibility of one-sided wheelspin. Two advantages are combined in the ZF self-locking differential:

1. A constant locking effect prevails in the differential since the friction discs are axially preloaded. The advantage of this arrangement is that the locking effect imposed upon both axles is present at all times; for instance, when one of the two driving wheels should have little traction in a given moment, one-sided wheel-spin can be avoided.

2. A torque-governed locking effect is obtained through the axial thrust of the slanted spider shafts, which always remain proportionate to the induced torque.

Therefore, the locking action varies according to the engine torque changes, including the increased torque in the individual gears. This is especially advantageous in hard cross-country driving when great torque forces are to be transmitted. Also, this virtue definitely improves the road handling qualities of high-powered passenger cars driven at high speeds.

The ZF self-locking differential, Part No. 904.332.053.00, is factory preset to an effectiveness of 50%. The accompanying exploded view shows the arrangement of the friction discs and plates.

On March 6, 1967, cars started leaving the factory with a modified ZF self-locking differential. This version has the advantage of a selection of either 50% or 75% effectiveness, depending on how the discs and plates are arranged. See the accompanying illustrations for the two arrangements in discs and plates.

Compared with conventional units, the ZF self-locking differentials offer the following advantages to improve road handling qualities:

1. Elimination of wheelspin by one wheel when starting or driving over surfaces which provide poor traction on one side.
2. Greatly reduced tendency of one wheel to spin when passing over bumps in the road surface.
3. Elimination of skidding dangers at high speed due to uneven traction on both sides, which is especially true in high-performance vehicles.
4. In fast cornering, the wheel on the inside of the curve bears a much smaller load due to the effect of centrifugal forces and could spin were it not controlled by a limited-slip differential.
5. When a powerful vehicle travels at high speed on a smooth, rain-wetted surface, traction may become uneven at both wheels as a result of the "hydroplaning" effect. The self-locking differential prevents a one-sided wheelspin in such cases.

REMOVING AND REPLACING DIFFERENTIAL

WARNING: This procedure is only to be used when the standard differential unit is removed and then replaced WITHOUT DISASSEMBLY, or when the ZF Self-Locking Differential is ONLY removed to have the effectiveness changed from 50% to 75% or vice-versa. Should parts need to be replaced, the problem of adjusting gear backlash will have to be confronted. This type of adjustment, along with other internal transmission repairs, should ONLY be done by an experienced and properly equipped transmission rebuilder. The following TRANSMISSION OVERHAUL part of this chapter outlines these repairs. In the meantime, use extreme caution when carrying out the following procedure, noting the number and location of spacers and gaskets, and being sure that parts are not switched side-for-side.

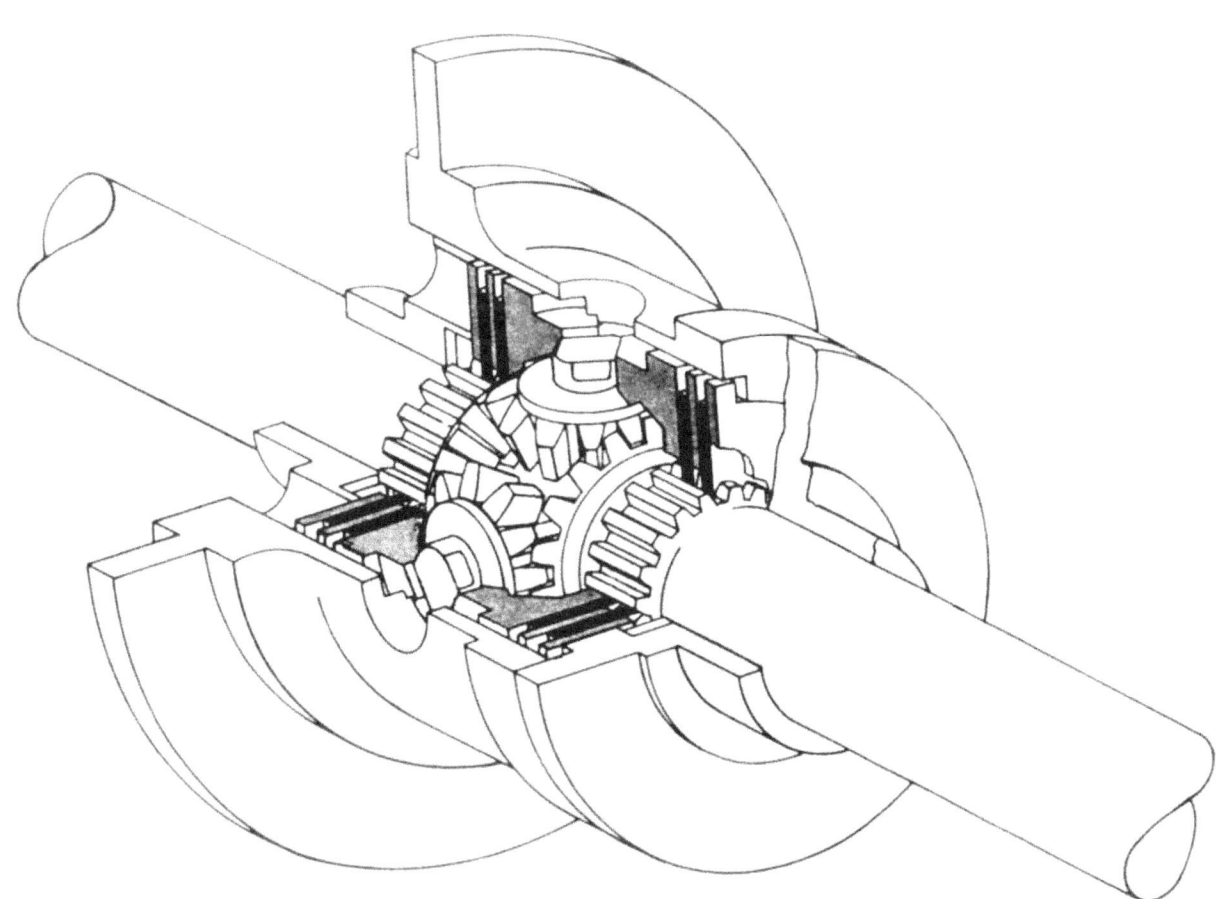

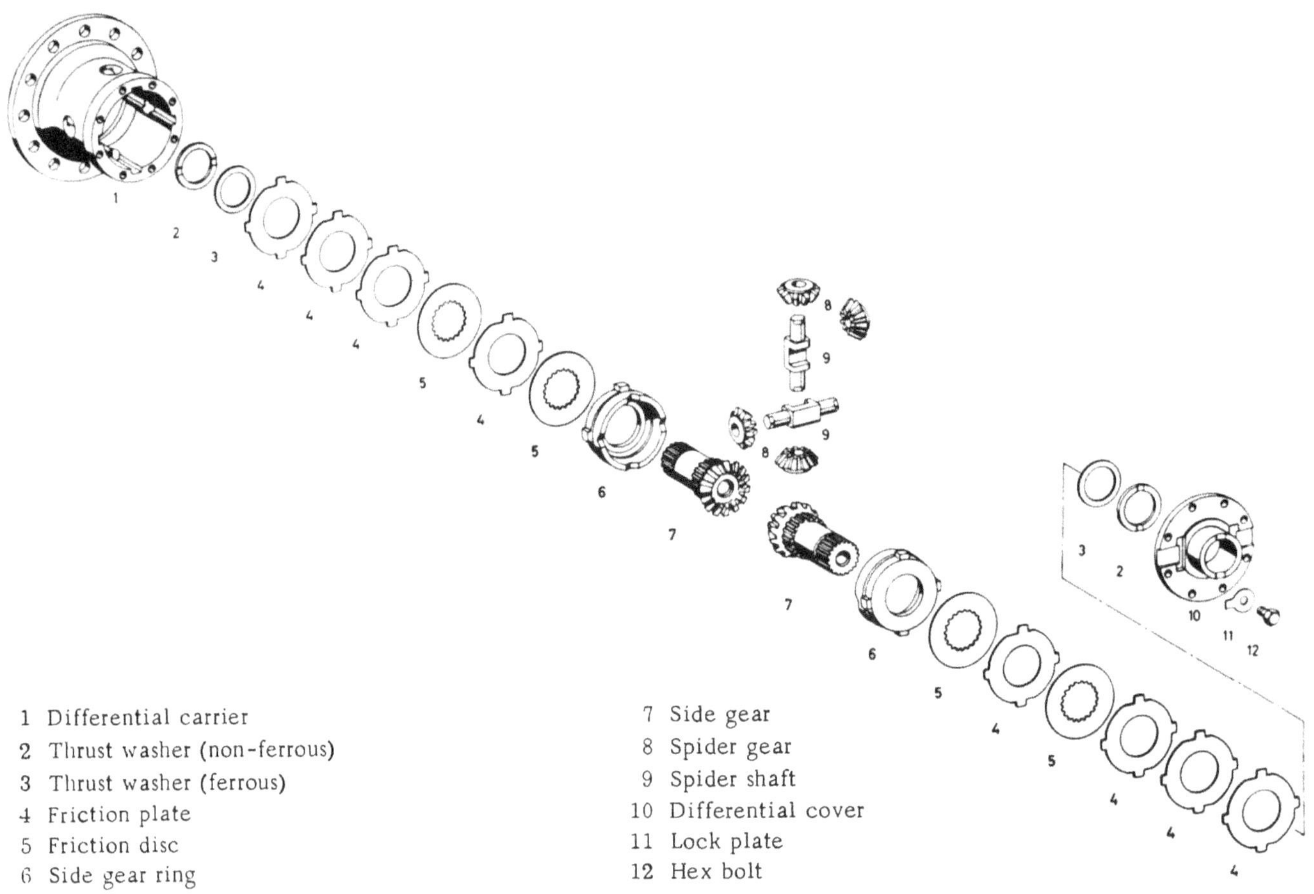

Exploded View of the ZF Multiple Disc Self Locking Differential

1. Differential carrier
2. Thrust washer (non-ferrous)
3. Thrust washer (ferrous)
4. Friction plate
5. Friction disc
6. Side gear ring
7. Side gear
8. Spider gear
9. Spider shaft
10. Differential cover
11. Lock plate
12. Hex bolt

Removal

NOTE: The differential can be removed without removing the engine/transmission assembly. However, if the work involves adjustments or replacement of parts, it is best to remove the whole assembly. In this case, see ENGINE chapter for removal procedure. Otherwise, follow this procedure:

1. Detach both rear axle half-shafts at the differential flanges.
2. Detach the clutch cable and the rear throttle linkage.
3. Remove transmission oil drain plug and drain oil.
4. Remove caps from the universal joint mounting flanges using two screwdrivers (see illustration).

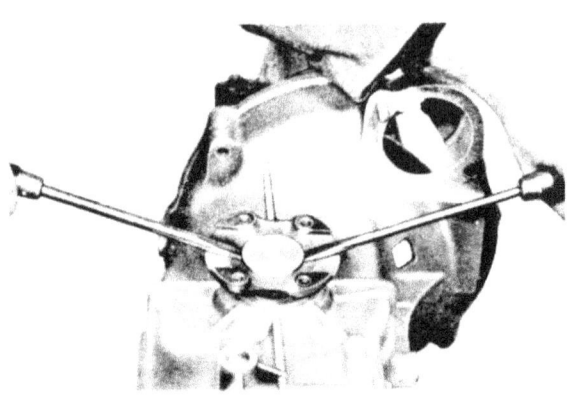

5. Remove stretchbolts from flanges and withdraw flanges (shift into 5th gear for this operation by turning the inner shift rod clockwise to stop, then pulling outward; block input shaft with special tool P 37 or equivalent) (see illustration).

6. Remove side cover retaining nuts and withdraw differential unit, being sure not to lose any gaskets or spacers (see illustration).

Exploded View of the ZF Multiple Disc Self Locking Differential

From manufacture date of 6 Mar 67

50 % anti-slip effectiveness

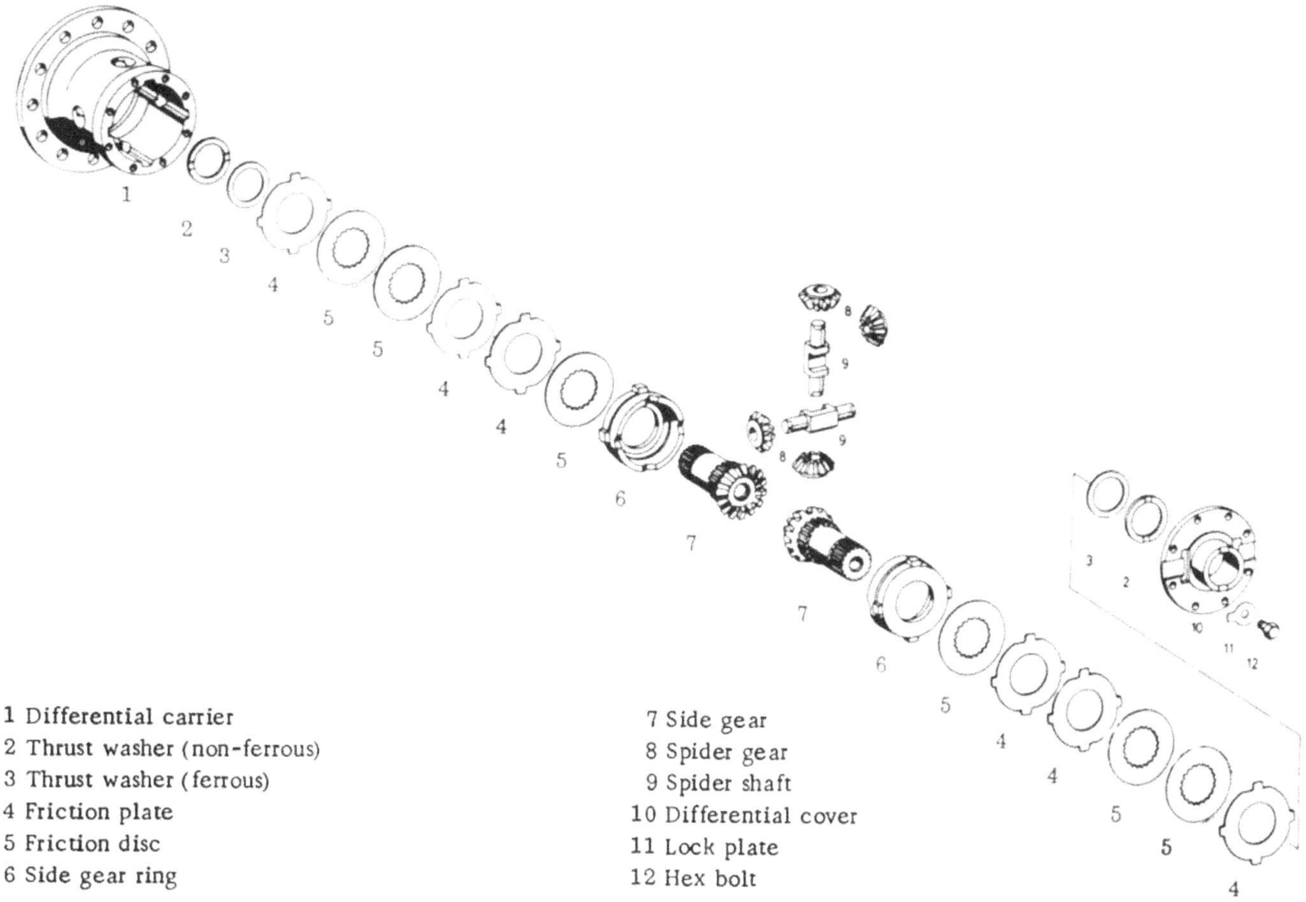

1 Differential carrier
2 Thrust washer (non-ferrous)
3 Thrust washer (ferrous)
4 Friction plate
5 Friction disc
6 Side gear ring
7 Side gear
8 Spider gear
9 Spider shaft
10 Differential cover
11 Lock plate
12 Hex bolt

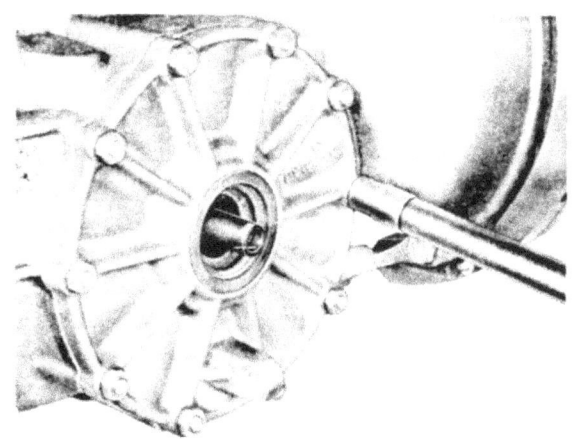

Checking Standard Differential

1. Check differential carrier for signs of wear at the seats of side and spider gears, and side bearings.
2. Inspect side and spider gears for condition of gear teeth and especially signs of wear at the spherical seats.
3. Check spider gear shaft and side gear splines as well as axle joint flanges for signs of wear.
4. Check side bearings for wear or damage. If these need servicing, they must be replaced together with the bearing outer races in the housing or side cover.

WARNING: Should any of the above components prove faulty, they should be replaced. However, this means the total dimensions of the differential unit may be changed, necessitating a gear backlash adjustment. It is suggested that the total repair should be carried out by a Porsche-trained mechanic, or as described in the TRANSMISSION OVERHAUL section on page 94.

Replacement

1. Replace differential unit in exactly the reverse order, being sure to use the same spacers and gaskets (gaskets are a certain thickness).
2. Replace the side cover and nuts, torque nuts to 18 ft. lb. (2,5 mkp).
3. Replace flange and torque to 80–87 ft. lb. (11–12 mkp), after blocking the pinion shaft through a stretch-bolt and special tool P 259 (see illustration).

Exploded View of the ZF Multiple Disc Self Locking Differential
75 % anti-slip effectiveness

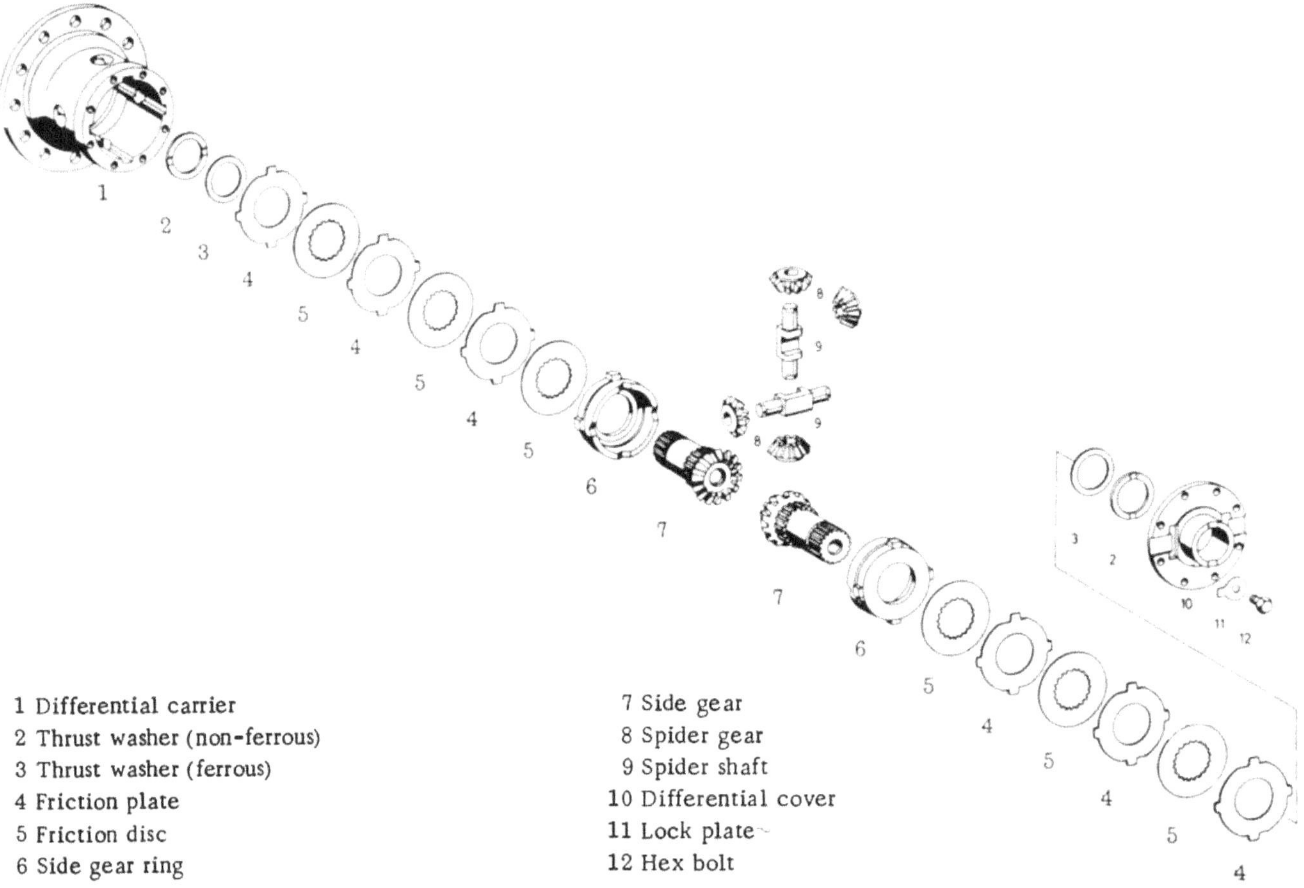

1 Differential carrier
2 Thrust washer (non-ferrous)
3 Thrust washer (ferrous)
4 Friction plate
5 Friction disc
6 Side gear ring
7 Side gear
8 Spider gear
9 Spider shaft
10 Differential cover
11 Lock plate
12 Hex bolt

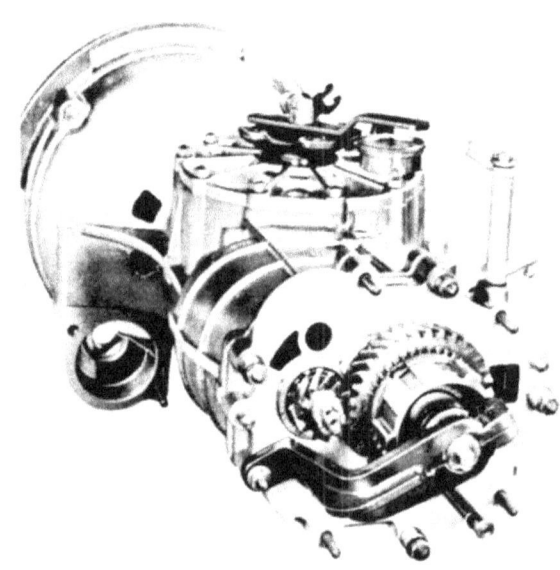

4. The remainder of the procedure is a reversal of the removal procedure, being sure to torque the Allen bolts on the NADELLA half-axle flange to 34 ft. lb. (4,7 mkp) or LOBRO to 31 ft. lb. (4,3 mkp).

NOTE: On the LOBRO, the Schnorr washer for the Allen bolt must face the base plate with the hollow side.

SERVICING ZF SELF-LOCKING DIFFERENTIAL

NOTE: The ZF Self-Locking Differential can only be installed with NADELLA half-axles or a later substitute.

1. Unlock safety plate tabs, remove retaining bolts from cover and remove cover (see illustration).

2. Remove thrust washers, friction plates and discs, then side gear ring and side gear (see illustration).

3. Withdraw spider gears and spider shafts from the differential carrier (see illustration).

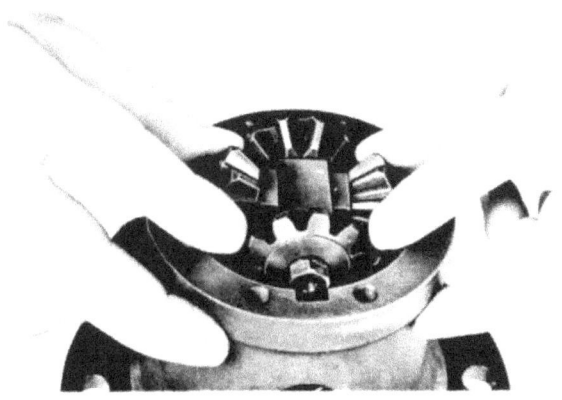

4. Remove the second gear side, side gear ring, multiple disc retarder, and thrust washers from the differential carrier (see illustration).

NOTE: Observe the sequential location of the retarder discs and plates; the original sequence must not be disarranged, unless the effectiveness is being changed from 50% to 75% on units manufactured after March 6, 1967.

Inspection

1. **Differential Carriers:** Check thrust surface of thrust washers for wear or grooving. Check friction plate locating grooves in the differential carrier for wear.
2. **Differential Cover:** Check thrust surface of thrust washers for wear or grooving.
3. **Side Gear Ring:** The locating tabs and thrust surfaces should not be obviously worn or grooved. The side gear rings must move freely in the differential carrier.
4. **Side Gears:** Thrust surfaces for thrust washers should not be excessively worn. The friction discs must move freely on the side gear splines.
5. **Thrust Washers:** Check thrust washers for wear.
6. **Friction Discs and Plates:** Check the plates for wear. The guide tabs of the friction plates and the inner teeth of the friction discs must not be worn or peened.

Reassembly

1. Coat all contact surfaces of the friction discs and plates, side gear rings, and spider shafts with Molykotepaste 'G', or LM 348, prior to reassembly.
2. The entire retarder assembly, including the side gear rings and spider shafts, must be checked for installation length under a pressure load of about 220 lb. (100 kp) whereby distance 'a' (see illustration) must be achieved, max. 3.240 in. to min. 3.213 in. (max. 82,3 mm to min. 81,6 mm). The tolerance between maximum and minimum includes the maximum permissible wear of all parts. The determination of length can be accomplished out of the differential carrier by placing the parts in a shop press. If the values cannot be reached, determine which parts are worn and replace these with new. Wear can occur at the following parts; the friction discs or plates, the side gear rings, and the slanted ramps of the spider shafts.
3. Place the differential carrier so that the large opening faces up. Place the non-ferrous thrust washer (see No. 2 of the exploded view) into the differential carrier with the machined recess facing down. Place the ferrous thrust washer (see No. 3 of the exploded view) on top of the non-ferrous washer (see illustration).

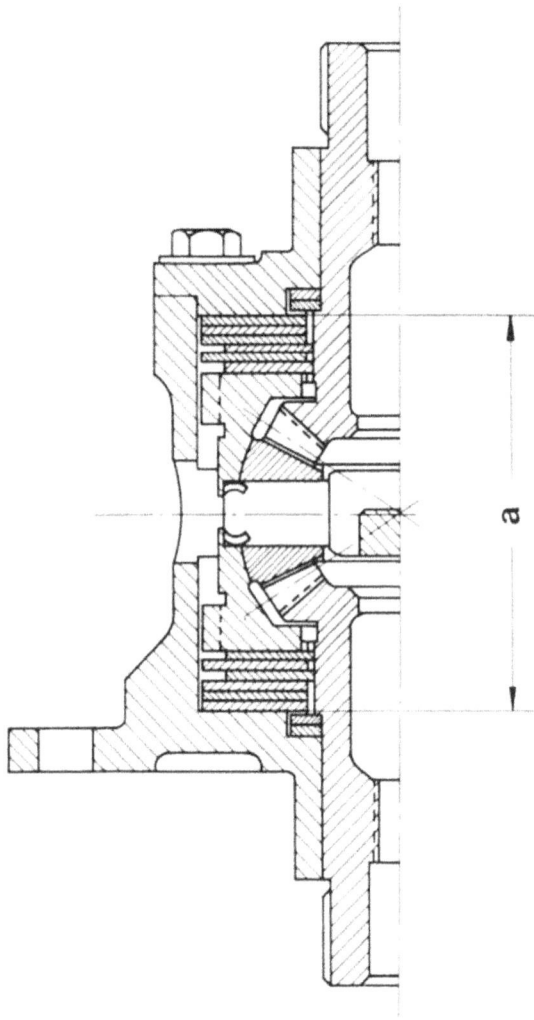

a = max. 82.3 mm to min. 81.6 mm

4. Place the friction discs and plates into the differential carrier in the same sequence as noted during disassembly (a friction plate is placed at the differential carrier as well as at the differential cover) (see illustration).

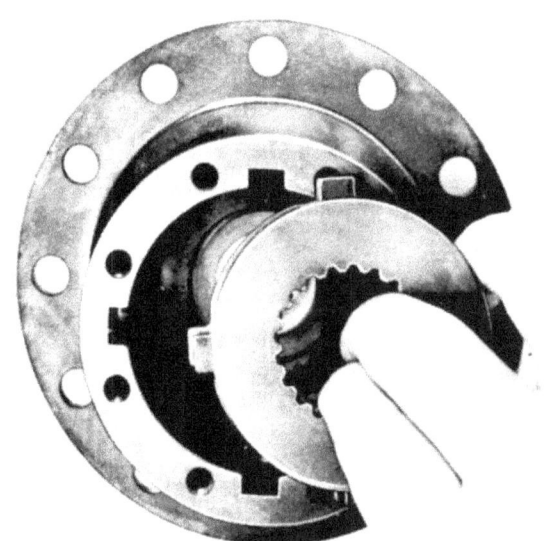

5. Some differentials are equipped with a preloaded friction disc and plate assembly. On these check the following:

   a. The undulated friction plates (shown in No. 4 of the exploded view) should be placed next to the differential carrier and the differential cover.

   b. The plate undulation should be so arranged that a free space exists between the oil groove in the base of the differential carrier or the differential cover, respectively, and the mating friction plate (see illustration).

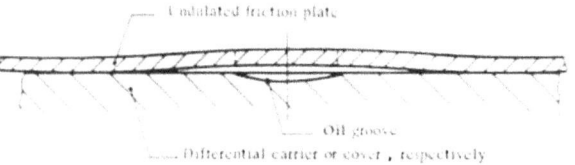

6. Special attention must be devoted to the proper positioning of the friction discs and plates, since otherwise the self-locking effectiveness may be inadvertently changed (see cross-sectional view accompanying Step No. 2 in this procedure). Place one side gear ring onto the friction plates and discs (see illustration).

7. Insert one side gear so that the outer splines of the side gear engage into the inner teeth of the friction discs (see illustration).

8. Place two spider gears onto each spider shaft. Place the spider shafts across each other and insert them into their seats in the differential carrier (see illustration).

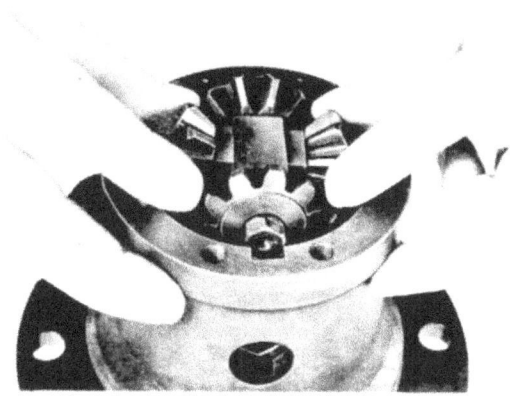

9. Place the second side gear onto the four spider gears and place the second side gear ring on top (see illustration).

10. Insert the second set of friction discs and plates (see Step No. 5 again) (see illustration).

11. Place the ferrous thrust washer (see No. 3 of the exploded view), then the non-ferrous thrust washer (see No. 2 of the exploded view), with the machined groove facing up, onto the side gear (see illustration).

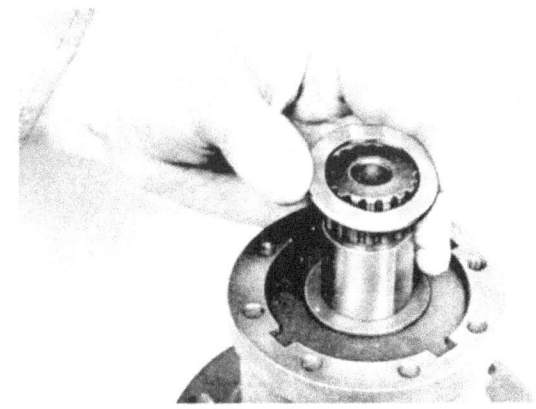

12. Place differential cover on differential carrier, insert retaining bolts together with safety plates. Torque bolts to 18 ft. lb. (2,5 mkp), then secure bolts with safety plates.

Testing

The unit, with bolts completely torqued, must turn freely with a torque of 7 to 11 ft. lb. (1 to 1,5 mkp) without binding at any one point. Moderate noises may occur, especially when driving through sharp curves under power. The noise is inherent to the design and will not result in damage to the differential. The noises are caused by mechanical operation of the parts such as friction between the thrust surfaces of the friction discs and plates.

SERVICING INPUT SHAFT OIL SEAL

NOTE: The input shaft oil seal can be replaced without having to disassemble the transmission. The engine/transmission assembly must be removed from the vehicle, then the transmission must be removed from the engine.

Removal

1. Loosen the cylinder screw in the clutch release lever, detach spring, then remove the release lever along with the throwout bearing (see illustration).

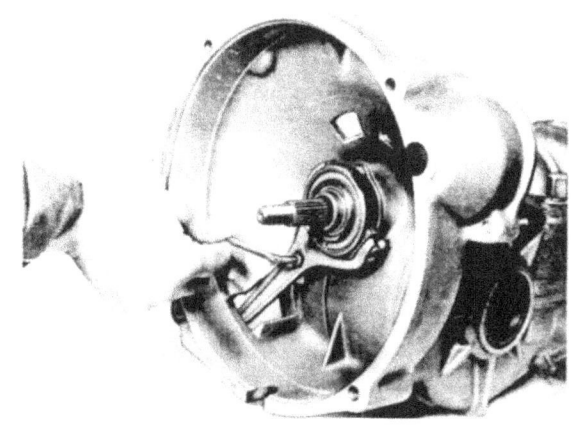

2. Remove the hex nuts from the throwout bearing guide, then remove the guide (see illustration).

3. Remove the defective oil seal with an appropriate tool, possibly with a medium-size screwdriver.

WARNING: Do not damage bore or contact surface.

Replacement

1. Thinly coat the outer circumference of the oil seal with Aviation Permatex No. 3 gasket compound. Use oil to coat the oil seal race on the shaft and the sealing part of the seal.
2. Push the oil seal onto the input shaft and drive into the housing with special tool VW 244b or equivalent (see illustration).

NOTE: Push the oil seal gently to keep the inner spring from leaving its seat.

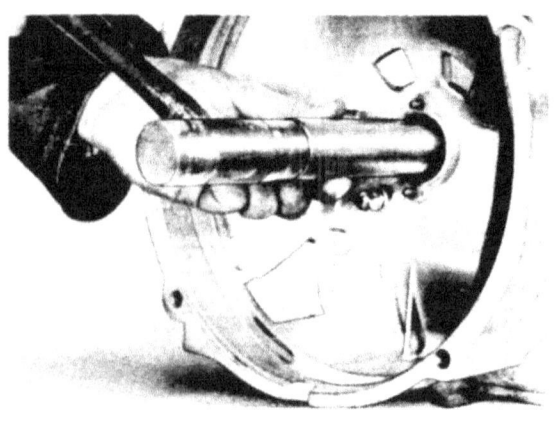

SPEEDOMETER DRIVE SERVICING

Description

The speedometer is driven by the transmission pinion shaft over a drive pinion, connecting shaft, and elbow drive. These are all situated in the transmission front cover. A retaining pin holds the drive pinion to the pinion shaft stretchbolt (see illustration).

Removal

NOTE: The entire elbow drive and connecting shaft can be removed with the transmission installed in the vehicle, provided that the transmission is propped up and the transmission support is removed from the housing. However, should the gear shaft need servicing, the transmission (along with the engine), must be removed from the vehicle, and the transmission housing cover withdrawn from the transmission. See ENGINE chapter and SERVICING TRANSMISSION FRONT COVER in this chapter.

1. Remove transmission support.
2. Remove speedometer drive set screw and withdraw elbow drive (see illustration).

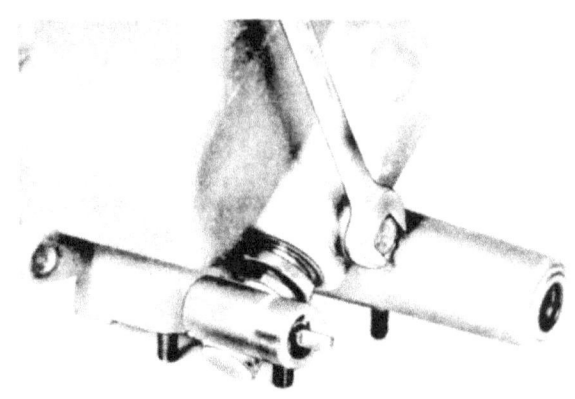

3. If speedometer pinion shaft must be removed, proceed as follows:

   a. Remove transmission housing front cover (see NOTE above).
   b. Remove pinion shaft stretchbolt with special tool P 251 or equivalent, after putting transmission in gear, and blocking input shaft with special tool P 37 or equivalent.
   c. Drive out retaining pin from stretchbolt.

Tachometer Drive Components

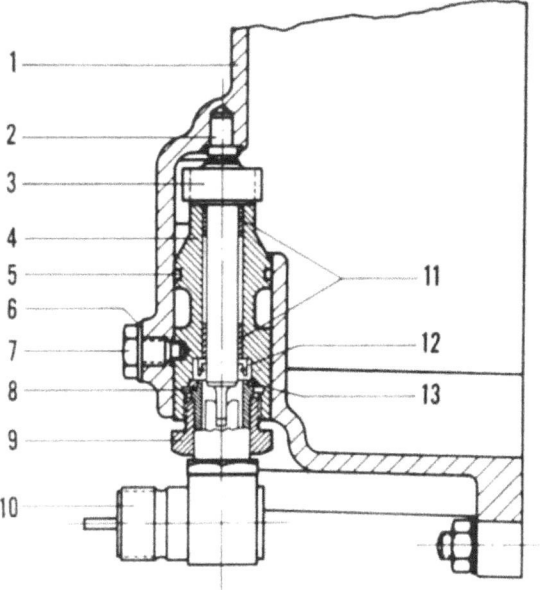

1 Front cover of transmission
2 Thrust stud
3 Connecting shaft
4 Guide bushing
5 O-ring
6 Spring ring
7 Hex bolt (set screw)
8 Elbow drive jacket
9 Coupling nut
10 Elbow drive
11 Support bushings
12 Oil seal
13 Centering disc

Disassembly

1. Using a vise with soft-metal jaw covers, clamp guide bushing tightly and remove coupling nut, then pull out elbow drive and centering disc (see illustration).

2. Withdraw connecting shaft from guide bushing.
3. The support bushings of the connecting shaft and the oil seal can be withdrawn with a suitable tool, if necessary.

Reassembly

To reassemble, reverse the above procedure, noting the following:

1. Thoroughly clean all parts, check for wear or damage, and replace as necessary.
2. Tighten coupling nut connecting elbow with guide bushing; make sure that the two parts are so oriented that the set screw orifice and the connecting end of the speedometer drive point in the same direction (see previous illustration).
3. Insert complete drive assembly, including connecting shaft, into transmission cover. Make sure the set screw orifice lines up with that in the cover (see illustration). Check O-ring, replace if necessary, then install set screw and washer, torque to 18 ft. lb. (2,5 mkp).

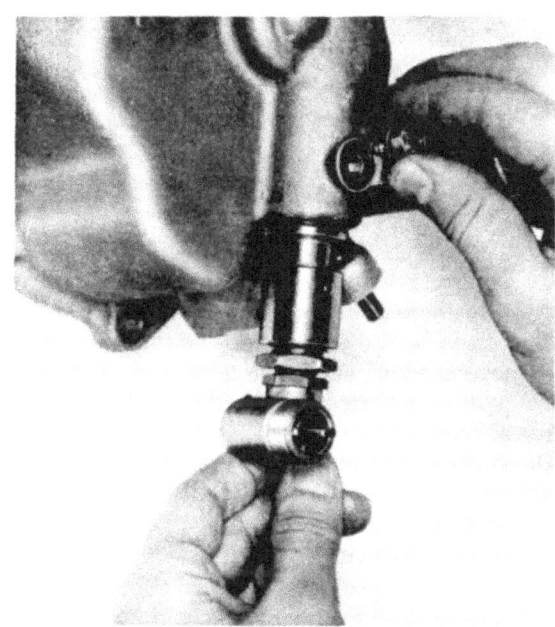

4. Ensure that the gear shaft bushing and the thrust stud of the connecting shaft have been installed in the cover.
5. If the pinion shaft stretchbolt has been loosened, it must be tightened with special tools P 251 and P 37 or equivalent to 79 to 86 ft. lb. (11 to 12 mkp).
6. Install front cover on the transmission.

SERVICING TRANSMISSION FRONT COVER

NOTE: The transmission front cover can only be serviced after the engine/transmission combination has been removed from the vehicle.

Disassembly

1. Remove transmission support.
2. Remove cover retaining nuts, then withdraw cover.

   NOTE: As cover is withdrawn, parts of the reverse gear can fall out (see illustration).

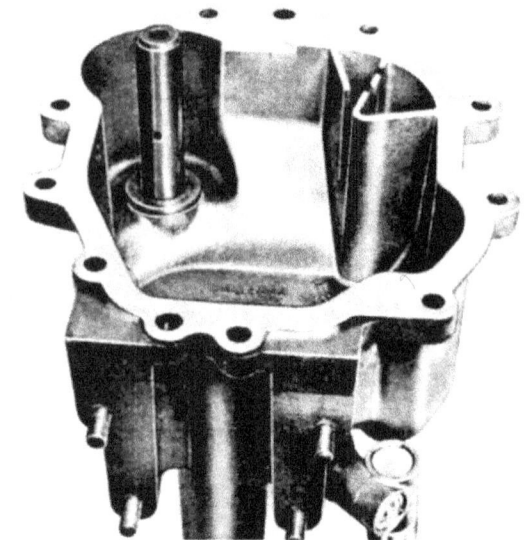

3. Remove cover gasket, reverse speed gear and loose bearing parts from transmission, noting their position.
4. Remove speedometer drive lock screw and pull out elbow drive (see illustration in SPEEDOMETER DRIVE SERVICING).
5. Drive out retaining pin for reverse gear shaft, then heat the cover to about 248°F. (120°C.) and drive the shaft inward to remove.
6. Press the thrust washer (bronze) off reverse gear shaft.

Reassembly

1. Check oil seal of inner shaft rod and replace if necessary.
2. Check reverse gear, shaft, thrust washers, and needle bearings for wear, replace these if necessary (note mating numbers).
3. Heat cover to about 248°F. (120°C.), then install reverse gear shaft, making sure that the oil passage in the shaft points down (see illustration).
4. Drive in retaining pin.
5. Heat bronze thrust washer to about 248°F. (120°C.) and push it onto reverse gear shaft until firmly seated against the cover. The washer must seat well against the cover in order to prevent a reduction of axial play of the reverse gear.
6. Install bearing cages and spacer bushing (see illustration).

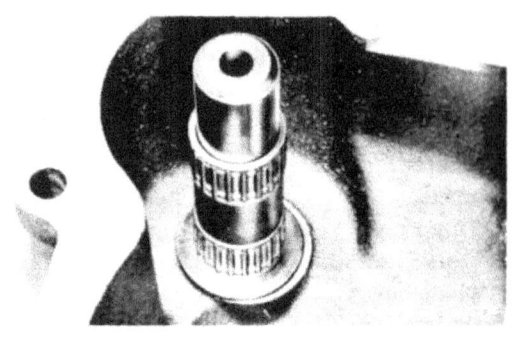

7. Install reverse gear, axial thrust needle bearing, and thrust washer (see illustration).

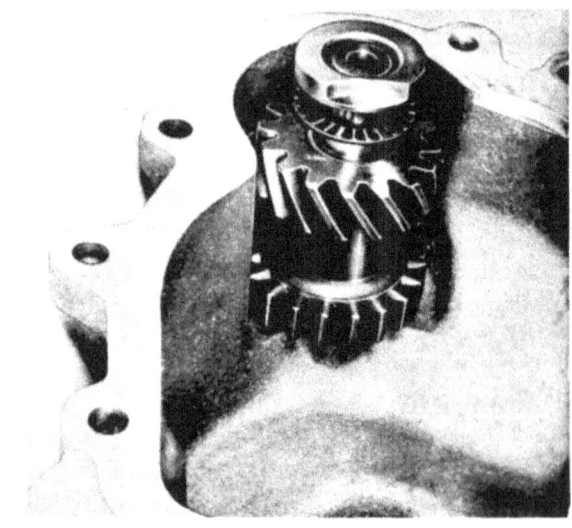

8. Insert speedometer elbow drive into cover, making certain that the orifice for the set screw lines up with that in the cover (see illustration). Check O-ring, replacing if necessary, then install set screw and washer, tightening to 18 ft. lb. (2,5 mkp).
9. Place a new 0,2 mm thick paper gasket onto the intermediate plate.
10. Install the front housing cover.

NOTE: To bring the helical reverse gear past the sliding gear of reverse and 1st speed, pull the reverse gear and its axial thrust washer as far to the end of the shaft as possible (outwards). The machined recess in the thrust washer must align with the outer collar of the pinion shaft ball bearing (see illustration under Point No. 2 of DISASSEMBLY).

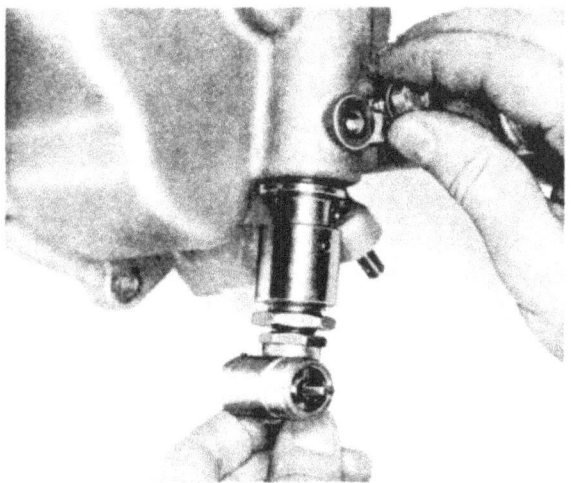

11. Tighten cover retaining nuts to 18 ft. lb. (2,5 mkp), then install transmission support (see illustration).

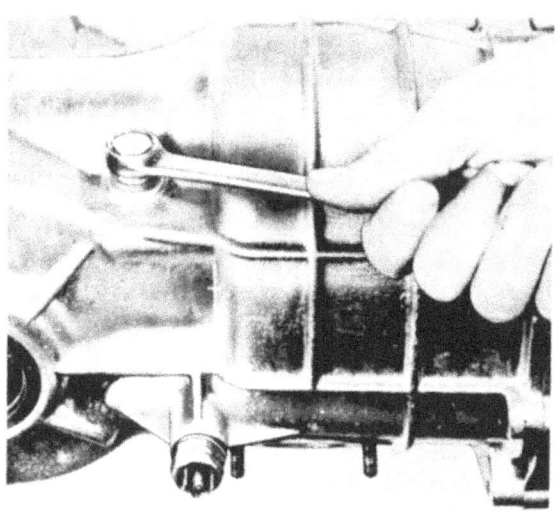

Replacement

1. Clean breather.
2. Screw breather in while noting the proper position of the vent bore (see illustration).

NOTE: If the breather were to point in the wrong direction, oil could spill through it.

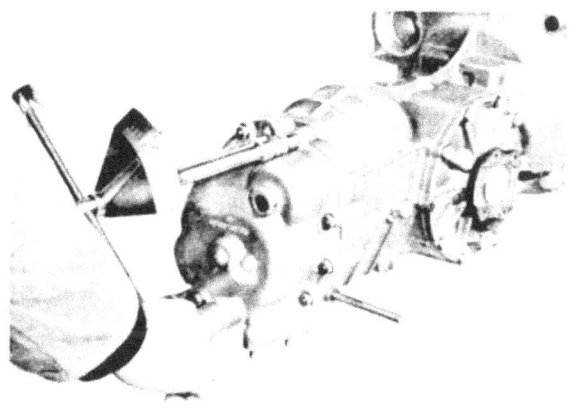

REPLACING TRANSMISSION BREATHER

NOTE: Transmission ventilation through a labyrinth in the housing front cover and a small breather pipe has been replaced, beginning with transmission No. 100 100, by a breather screwed into the differential section of the transmission housing. When replacing front cover on transmission preceding transmission No. 100 100, make sure that the new cover has the venting provision; if not, install a breather into the transmission housing.

Removal

NOTE: The breather can be removed from an assembled or disassembled transmission simply by unscrewing it (see illustration).

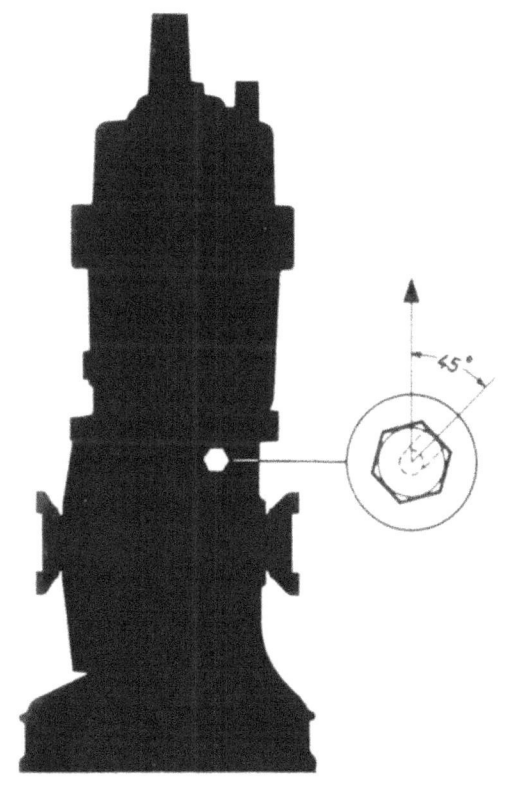

SERVICING BACKUP LIGHT SWITCH

NOTE: Information on servicing the backup light switch can be found in the ELECTRICAL SYSTEM chapter. The switch is mounted in the transmission housing.

TRANSMISSION OVERHAUL

WARNING: The following operations should ONLY be accomplished by a mechanic experienced with transmission rebuilding and properly equipped with the necessary tools and measuring instruments. Included are the differential pinion and ring gear backlash adjustment procedures.

DESCRIPTION

All transmission castings are interchangeable and can be individually replaced if damage or wear is confined to the individual pieces. All gears are equipped with synchromesh, with the exception of reverse. When replacing the transmission housing, it will be necessary to determine the differential side bearing preload and readjust the pinion and ring gear backlash. When replacing the intermediate plate or the four-point ball bearing of the pinion shaft, check the pinion shaft adjustment. These procedures will be found within this part of the chapter.

TRANSMISSION DISASSEMBLY

With the transmission mounted on a suitable stand with the starter motor removed, follow the procedures under REMOVING AND REPLACING DIFFERENTIAL and SERVICING TRANSMISSION FRONT COVER as previously described, then proceed as follows:

1. Remove retaining screw of selector fork (First and Reverse gears), then remove gear and selector fork (see illustration).

2. Remove stretchbolt from pinion shaft using special tool P 251 or equivalent (transmission engaged in Fifth gear and pinion shaft blocked with Special Tool P 37) (see illustration).

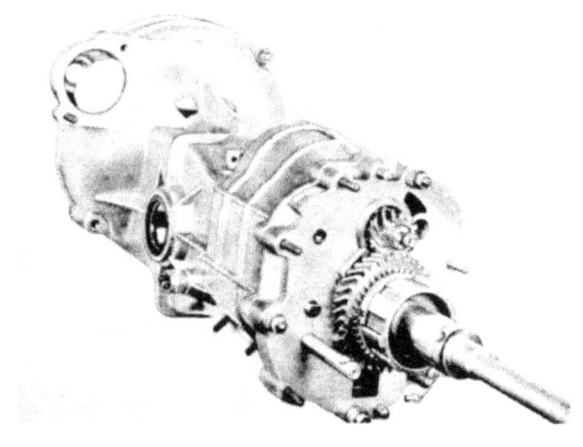

3. Remove roll pin from castle nut on input shaft using a punch. Remove castle nut and First speed gear (see illustration).

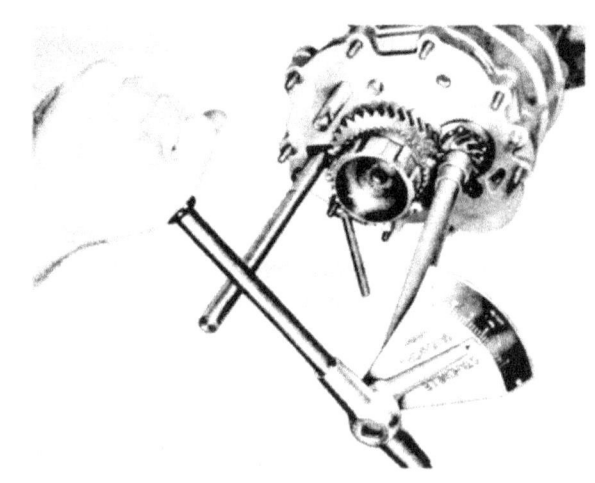

4. Shift into neutral. Remove retaining nuts from plate of inner shift rod guide fork and withdraw the guide fork (see illustration).

5. Pull out inner shift rod through the rear access hole. Using a screwdriver inserted into the guide fork orifice, shift into Fifth gear and remove the intermediate plate with gear clusters (tap plate lightly with a plastic mallet if plate does not come out by hand).

WARNING: Check gasket thickness for reassembly. The gear clusters can ONLY be inserted or removed from the housing when the transmission is in the Fifth gear position.

6. Mount intermediate plate with gear clusters in a vise equipped with soft, unworn jaw protectors.
7. Withdraw spider wheel of the First and Reverse speed using two screwdrivers (see illustration).

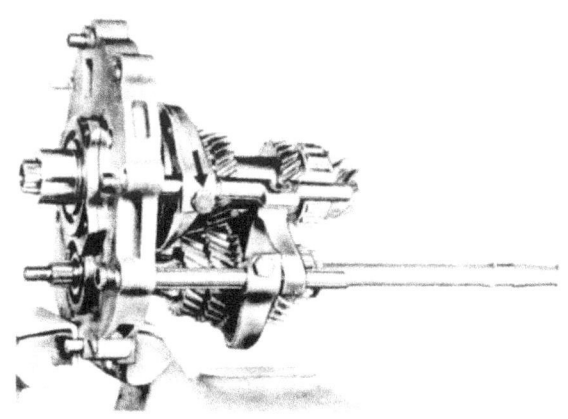

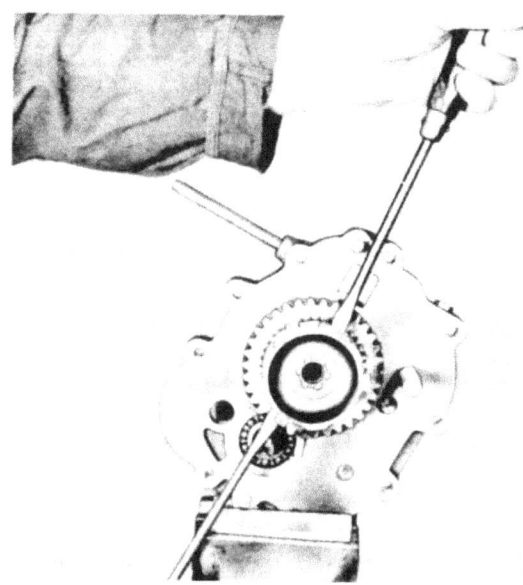

8. Remove Gear 2 of First speed, then remove needle bearing cage.
9. Shift into neutral, unscrew selector shaft detent plug and pull out spring (see illustration).

10. Withdraw selector shaft of First and Reverse gear, together with detent ball.
11. Remove retaining screw of selector fork for Second and Third gear, remove selector shaft, selector fork, and detent.
12. Remove retaining screw of selector fork for Fourth and Fifth gear, remove selector shaft, selector fork, and detent ball.

NOTE: Mark selector forks for Second and Third, and Fourth and Fifth gears to prevent any slip-ups during assembly.

13. Remove detent ball, spring, and detent, following arrangement in illustration.

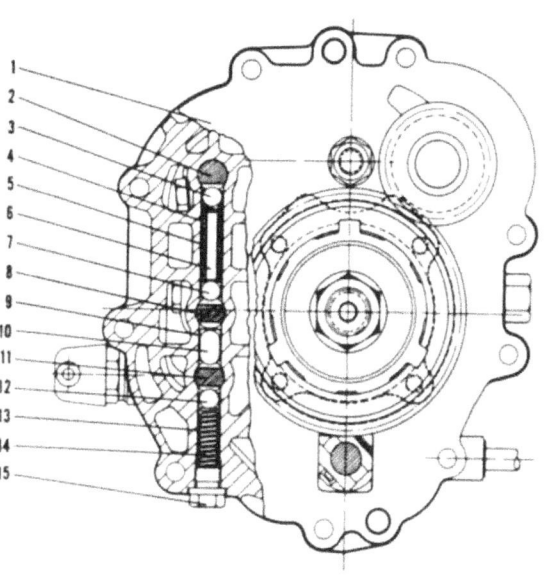

ARRANGEMENT OF DETENT COMPONENTS

1. Intermediate plate
2. Selector shaft of 4th and 5th speed
3. Ball
4. Detent bushing
5. Detent spring of 2nd thru 5th speed
6. Detent pin
7. Ball
8. Selector shaft of 2nd and 3rd speed
9. Detent bushing
10. Detent pin
11. Selector shaft of 1st and reverse speed
12. Ball
13. Detent bushing
14. Detent spring (reverse speed)
15. Cap screw

14. Drive aligning dowels in plate back and remove throttle linkage to allow plate to rest flat on a press.
15. Press out input and pinion shafts, together, from the intermediate plate using press adapter P 253 and VW tool 407 or equivalent (see illustration).

WARNING: It is possible for the ball bearings to fall out of the double-row offset ballbearing.

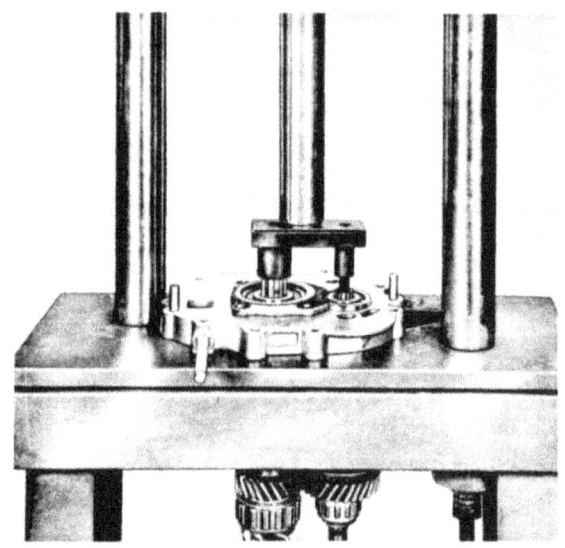

15. If necessary, disassemble intermediate plate as described under SERVICING INTERMEDIATE PLATE. Be sure to readjust the ring and pinion if the intermediate plate has to be replaced.
16. Remove from case center web both spring retainers of the input shaft bearing and the front retainer of the pinion shaft using a small screwdriver (see illustration).

Reassembly

To reassemble, reverse the previous procedure, noting the following instructions:

1. Clean the transmission housing and check for wear, external damage, and cracks. It is advisable to have the housing magnafluxed, especially if the transmission is to be used in competition. If there was a damaged drive pinion or ring gear (such as breakage), check if the bearing bores in the case center web show any damage; if necessary, replace housing.
2. Check input shaft for runout as described under REBUILDING INPUT SHAFT further in this chapter.
3. Check roller bearings of the input shaft and pinion shaft for wear or damage, replacing as necessary.
4. Install appropriate spring retainer into the outer bearing race of the pinion shaft roller bearing, being sure to position retainers as illustrated.

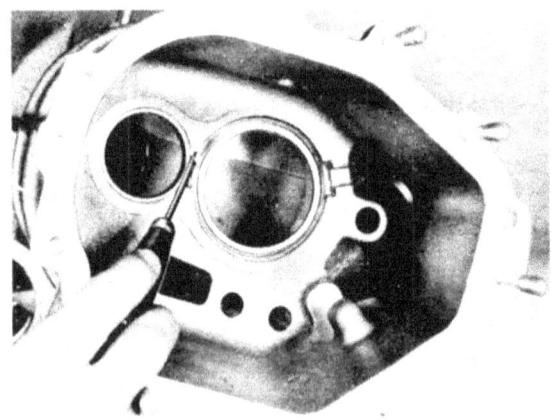

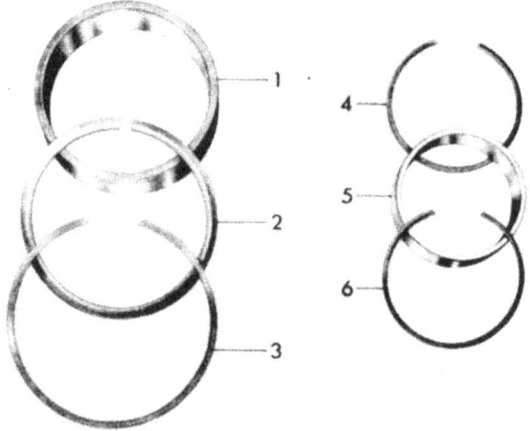

17. Heat the housing to about 248°F. (120°C.), then using special tool P 254 and a plastic hammer, tap out both bearing races (one at a time) (see illustration). If necessary, remove the input shaft oil seal as discussed under SERVICING INPUT SHAFT OIL SEAL in the previous section of this chapter.

1 Pinion shaft roller bearing outer race
2 Spring retainer (mounted onto outer race)
3 Spring retainer
4 Spring retainer
5 Outer race of pinion shaft roller bearing
6 Spring retainer

5. Place the rear spring retainer of the input shaft roller bearing into the bearing bore, positioning it at a slant, then guide it into its groove with a small screwdriver (see illustration).

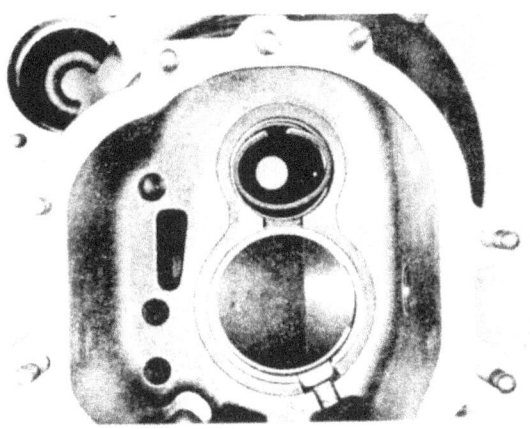

6. Heat housing to about 248°F. (120°C.), install outer race of the input shaft roller bearing in its seat with Special Tool P 254, then hold in place with the spring retainer (see illustration).

7. Install the outer race of the pinion shaft roller bearing, with the spring retainer mounted on the race, in its seat using Special Tool P 254, then hold in place with front spring retainer (see illustration).

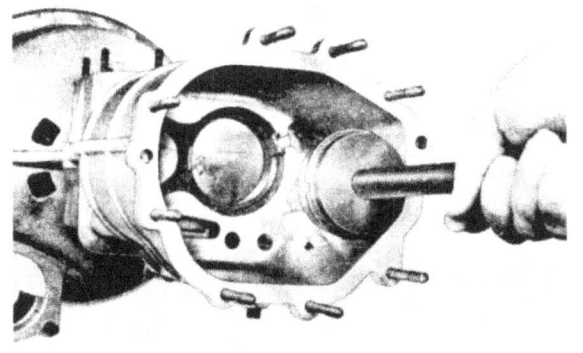

8. Install input shaft oil seal as discussed under SERVICING INPUT SHAFT OIL SEAL in the previous section of this chapter.

9. Place the assembled intermediate plate onto the bearing inner race halves of the input and pinion shaft, then mount other halves of the bearing inner race with an appropriate pipe tool. Be sure the mating numbers match, and that the inner race half of the pinion shaft bearing, marked "X", is mounted on the outer side of the plate as illustrated.

10. Insert the intermediate plate with input and pinion shaft gear clusters, lightly tighten in a cross-sequence at four housing studs by using spacer bushings. Be sure the Fifth gear is engaged.

11. Install the gear of First speed on the input shaft, then insert spacer and torque castellated nut to 43 to 47 ft. lb. (6,0 to 6,5 mkp). Use Special Tool P 37 or equivalent to install, then secure castellated nut with spiral pin (see illustration).

12. Place the thrust washer over the pinion shaft with the small collar facing the bearing, then guide the needle bearing race into place with a suitable pipe tool (see illustration).

97

13. Install needle bearing and Gear II of First speed, then install the spider wheel of First and Reverse speed.
14. Lubricate the pressure seat of the pinion shaft stretchbolt (bolt has an extension for speedometer take-off), then torque to 80 to 86 ft. lb. (11 to 12 mkp) with special Tool P 251 while blocking input shaft with Special Tool P 37 or equivalent (see illustration).

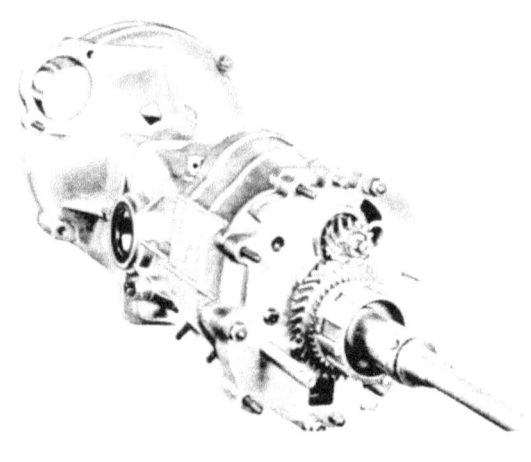

15. Place intermediate plate, with shafts and gear clusters installed, into a vise with jaw protectors (see illustration).

NOTE: The following procedures (16) through (22) must be performed in sequence.

16. Secure the shift arm on the selector shaft with a roll pin, then place the selector fork of the Fourth and Fifth speed onto the respective sliding sleeve. Push Fourth and Fifth speed selector shaft through until it enters its bore in the intermediate plate, then slightly tighten the fork retaining screw, being sure the spring washer is in place (see illustration).

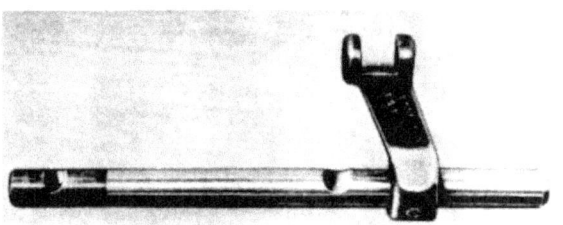

17. Using the previous illustration showing the arrangement of the detent components, insert the detent pin into the long spring with some grease, then place into the detent bore (the one that connects the selector shaft bores) one ball, detent pin with long spring for detents of speeds Two through Five, then one more ball.
18. Place the selector fork of Second and Third speed onto the respective sliding sleeve and push the Second and Third speed selector shaft through until it enters its bore in the intermediate plate; for this operation, the selector shaft of the Fourth and Fifth speed must be in neutral position and the detent ball of the Second and Third speed pushed down. Slightly tighten the fork retaining screw, being sure the lock washer is in place.
19. Move the Second and Third Speed selector shaft into neutral, then insert detent.
20. Install the selector shaft of First and Reverse gear, insert detent ball and short spring, then tighten the cap screw to 18 ft. lb. (2,5 mkp).
21. Slide the selector fork and the sliding gear for First and Reverse speed together onto the spider wheel and selector shaft, then slightly tighten the fork retaining screw with washer, using the previous illustration showing the proper arrangement of the detent components.
22. Check the springs of the detent mechanism, replace if necessary. The free length of the spring for the Reverse and First speed is 29,2 mm, minimum 28,2 mm, while the spring for Second through Fifth speed is 38,5 mm, minimum 37,3 mm.

IMPORTANT: If a new intermediate plate is being installed, or the three detent bushings have been removed, be sure to readjust the ring and pinion gears and follow instructions under SERVICING INTERMEDIATE PLATE.

23. Adjust the selector fork of First and Reverse gears. Press the assembled Reverse twin gear (with bearings and shaft) against the intermediate plate to check that there is a clearance of 1 mm between the reverse gear and the sliding gear when transmission is in neutral. As

you check, eliminate any free-play factor there may be between the selector fork and the sliding gear by pushing the sliding gear in the car's direction of travel, while at the same time, making sure that during actual operating conditions the sliding gear does not strike the reverse gear (see illustration). Adjust clearance if necessary.

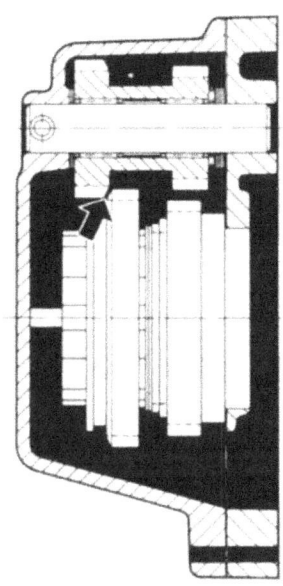

26. To adjust, make sure the sliding sleeve is positioned in the exact center in relation to both synchronizing rings when in neutral. After shift test, check this adjustment and relocate the sliding sleeve into correct position, if necessary, since smooth and effective gear synchronization will otherwise not be possible.

27. Tighten the selector fork retaining screws to 18 ft. lb. (2,5 mkp), making sure that the selector shaft actuating tabs on Fourth and Fifth speed shaft have a side clearance of 2 to 3 mm in relation to those of Second and Third speed (see illustration).

24. Tighten the selector fork retaining screw to 18 ft. lb. (2,5 mkp), making sure that the selector shaft actuating tabs on First and Reverse speed shaft have a side clearance of 2 to 3 mm in relation to those of Second and Third speed (see illustration).

28. Put together the inner shift rod, ensuring that the tapered bore in the rod points in the same direction as as the inner shift rod. Press the retaining pin in and secure with a cotter pin (see illustration).

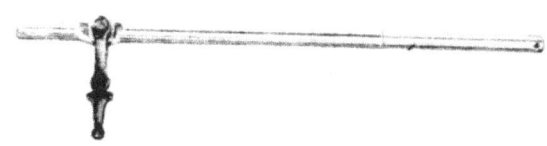

25. Install the Special Tool P 260 on the selector shafts and adjust the selector forks of speeds Four/Five and Two/Three (see illustration).

IMPORTANT: Install the inner shift rod at the same time as the gear cluster assembly is installed; it is best to insert the shift rod into the housing first (see illustration).

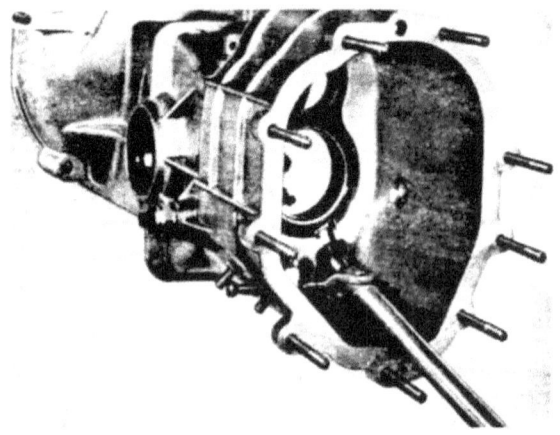

29. Install the intermediate plate with the gear clusters and gaskets which have been adjusted at the time of the pinion and ring gear adjustment (shift gears into Fifth speed).

WARNING: Be careful when guiding the gear assembly into the case so that the input shaft oil seal is not damaged.

30. Shift the gears into neutral position, then guide the shift rod into proper position at the selector shaft tabs and into the rear rod bore (see illustration).

31. Install the guide fork of the inner shift rod using a new gasket, ensuring that the inner shift rod enters the guide fork (see illustration).

32. See SERVICING TRANSMISSION FRONT COVER in the previous section of this chapter for remainder of the procedure.

REBUILDING PINION SHAFT

Disassembly

1. Press the pinion shaft from the gears using hydraulic press VW 400F and Special Tools P 255, VW 401, and VW 412 or equivalent (see illustration).

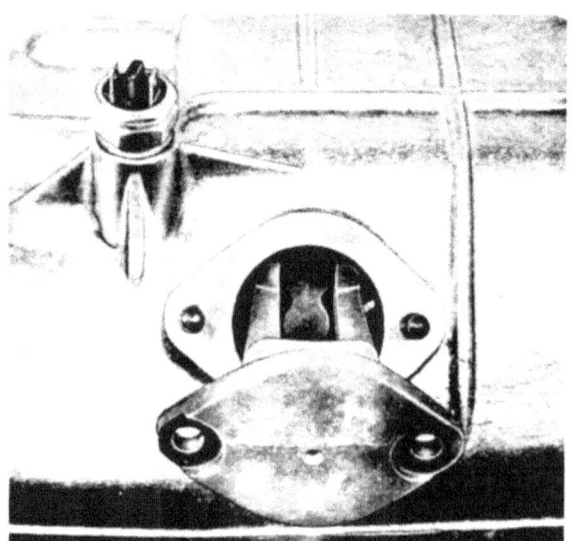

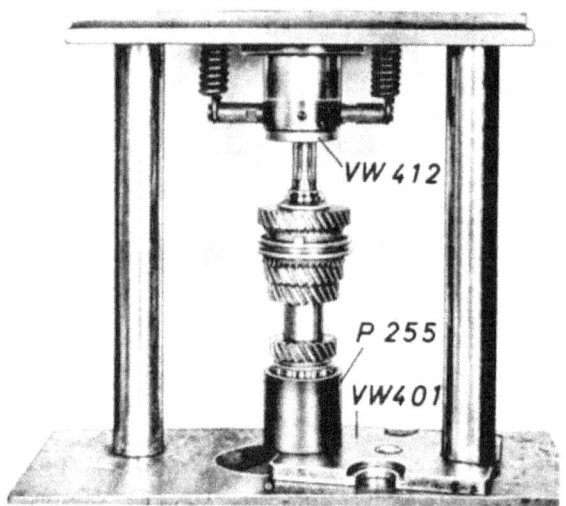

2. Remove all the pinion shaft components, such as the gear and bearings, keeping them in order for easier replacement. See previous exploded view showing the arrangement of the parts. Be sure to mark the needle bearing cages so as to avoid misplacing them during reassembly.

WARNING: Note the number and thickness of the spacers (for pinion and ring gear adjustment) between the roller bearing and thick spacer, so that reassembly can be possibly accomplished without the necessity of recomputing the spacer thickness.

Inspection

1. Inspect the pinion shaft and, especially, the splines for wear or damage, noting the mating identification numbers.
2. Check the roller bearing and four-point ball bearing, replacing parts as necessary. Be sure to note the mating numbers.
3. Check the gears for wear or damage, replace as necessary. Be sure to note the mating numbers.
4. Check all the synchromesh components for wear.

Checking Pinion Shaft Spacer Thickness

1. Determine the adjustment value E from the blueprint value R = 63.50 by adding or subtracting the value of the machined deviation "r" which is marked on the pinion face. See illustration and example below:

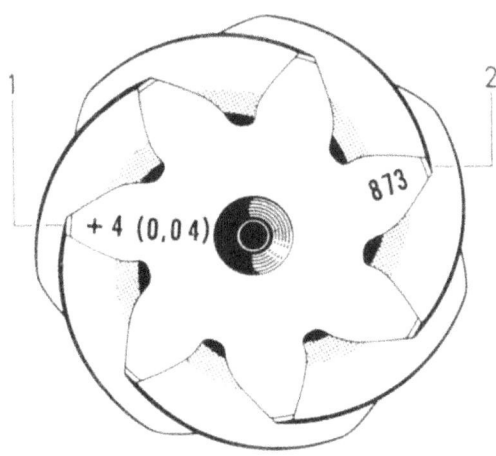

1 Deviation r shown in plus (+) or minus (−) values:
 +4 = in 1/100 mm
 +0.04 = in mm
2 Mating identification number

Example:

If the machined deviation r is shown as +4 or +0.04, proceed as follows:

R	(blueprint value)	63.50 mm
r	(machined deviation)	0.04 mm
E	(adjustment value)	63.54 mm

2. A so-called basic approximation value (based on averages) of 64.70 mm makes it possible to predetermine the spacer thickness required, i.e. the difference between the adjustment value E and the approximation value (64,70 mm) indicates the spacer thickness needed. See example below, which is related to the previous example:

Example:
When the adjustment value E is 63.54 mm, compute as follows:

Approximation value	64.70 mm
Less E (adjustment value)	63.54 mm
Difference	1.16 mm

1.16 mm = required thickness of spacers

3. The spacers are available in thicknesses of 0,25, 0,30, and 0,40 mm. The 0,10 and 0,15 mm spacers should no longer be used. To do this, be sure to round off the values (up or down) to the nearest 0,05 mm. In the preceding example, the requirement would be three 0,30 mm and one 0,25 mm spacers.

NOTE: REBUILDING PINION SHAFT continues after SYNCHROMESH procedures with ASSEMBLING PINION SHAFT.

SNYCHROMESH

Functional Description

NOTE: The following description deals with the mechanical process that takes place when the shifts are made with the transmission at a standstill.

When a gear is shifted at this point, the selector fork moves the sliding sleeve from its neutral position towards the selected gear and proceeds to engage it with the toothed engagement ring of the selected gear. As this happens, the synchronizing ring is compressed within the sliding sleeve and, upon completion of the move, snaps to rest within the machined groove on the inner race of the sliding sleeve, locking itself in that position.

NOTE: The following description deals with the mechanical process that takes place when the shifts are made while the vehicle is in motion.

Conditions are completely different when the gears are shifted as the vehicle is in motion. The purpose of the synchromesh units is to equalize the speeds of the input shaft or pinion shaft and the respective gear on a given shaft; this is made possible through the use of a mechanical clutch, i.e. the synchromesh unit. This clutch must be able not only to synchronize the gear speeds through friction, but also keep the sliding sleeve from clashing with the toothed ring on the selected gear (clutch carrier) as long as the gears run at unequal speeds. When shifting gears, the engine clutch must be fully disengaged since the clutch plate is part of the mass to be synchronized and must be accelerated or decelerated, as the case may be.

When the driver shifts a gear while the vehicle is moving, the selector fork guides the sliding sleeve off the synchronizing ring of the engaged gear, through the neutral position, and on to the point of contact between the internal teeth of the sliding sleeve and the beveled edge of the synchronizing ring of the next gear. As this contact is made, friction created by the unequal gear speeds drags the synchronizing ring to one side, against the brake band energizer. The floating brake band energizer thus slides against a brake band whose other end rests against the brake band stop.

Since the brake band stop keeps the brake band from sliding around from the pressure of the band energizer, the brake band is forced outward against the inner race of the synchronizing ring, causing it to expand within the sliding sleeve. Consequently, there is an instantaneous increase of friction between the synchronizing ring and the inner race of the sliding sleeve which further increases the force exerted upon the brake band and, in turn, upon the synchronizing ring. As described, the synchronizing effect is thus received from the self-energized thrust exerted by the brake band upon the synchronizing ring.

Because of the previous action, the gear about to be engaged is forced to assume the speed of the sliding sleeve. As long as there is a difference in speed between the sliding sleeve and the gear-coupled synchronizing ring, the energized brake band prevents a further compression of the synchronizing ring, preventing the engagement of the sliding sleeve with the teeth in the clutch carrier.

As the speeds between the sliding sleeve and the gear become more equal, the friction between the synchronizing faces also decreases. When the speeds between the two parts equalize, the servo-thrust components return to normal and now, it becomes possible to compress the synchronizing ring in its diameter and move the sliding sleeve fully onto the synchronizing ring. Then, the synchronizing ring snaps into the groove machined in the inner race of the sliding sleeve and locks itself in that position. For this reason, it is no longer necessary to incorporate a locking device in the selector shaft.

Identical synchromesh components are located on all forward speeds of the transmission. As any gear is slowed down, the friction force resulting at the synchronizing ring acts directly onto the gear through the brake band energizer and its tab. Due to its slanted tab, the brake band energizer exerts pressure, through its longer end, against the inner face of the synchronizing ring. This small force is sufficient to ensure an easy engagement of the lower gear while still preventing a gear clash.

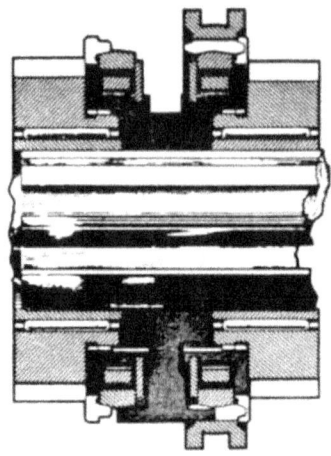

During a static transmission gearshift, it is necessary to overcome only the static resistance created by the spring tension of the synchronizing ring as it is compressed in its diameter by the sliding sleeve.

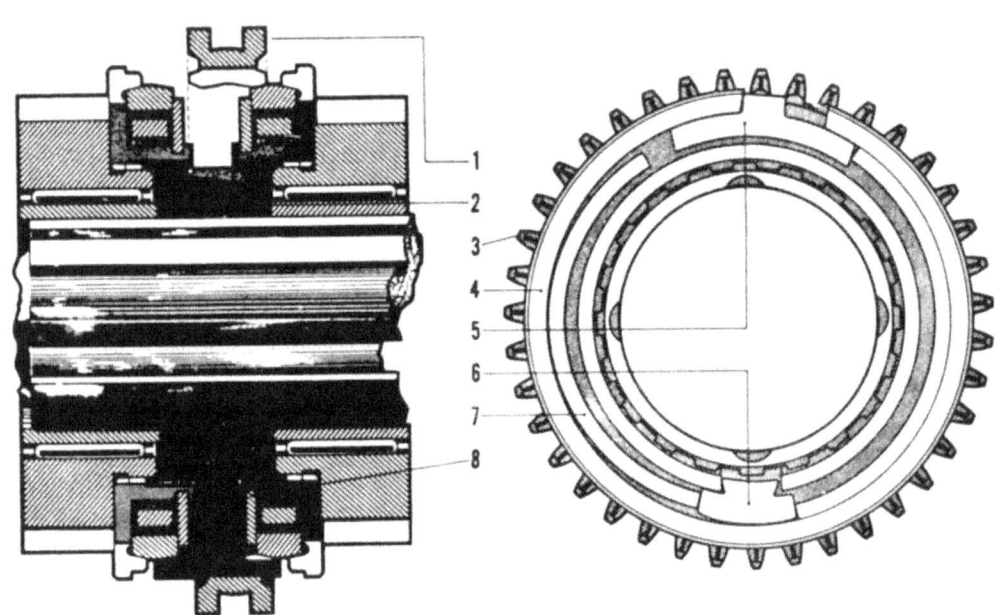

1 Sliding sleeve
2 Spider
3 Clutch carrier
4 Synchronizing ring
5 Brake band energizer
6 Brake band stop
7 Brake band
8 Retaining ring

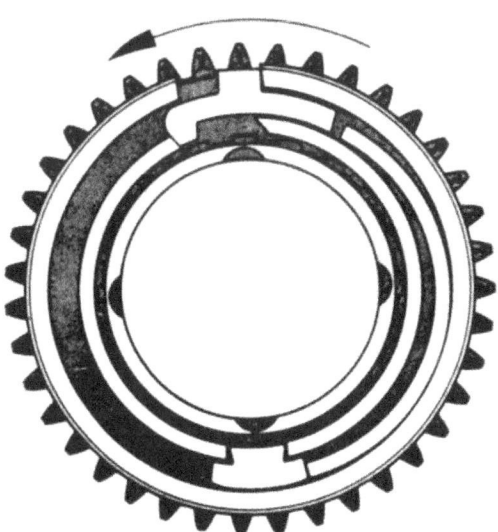

There is a tab on the brake band energizer for First gear which rests in a recess machined into the clutch carrier; also, only one brake band is utilized. The engine idle speed is very low when compared with revolutions prevailing at operating speeds. When the engine clutch is disengaged prior to shifting into low speed at standstill, the clutch plate stops within a short time following disengagement. To further shorten the engine clutch stopping time and enable the driver to quickly shift into low gear without gear clash, it is necessary to provide a synchronizing device for this purpose; in this case, the synchromesh unit acts as a brake.

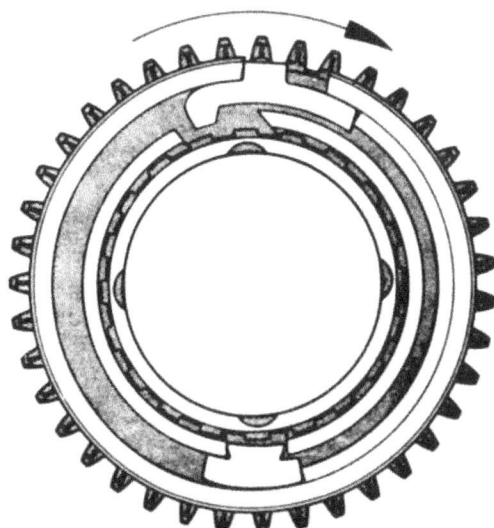

When a shift is made from Second to First gear with the vehicle in motion, the First gear must be accelerated to match its counterpart. For this purpose, a normal brake band has been provided on the respective synchromesh side to ensure the same synchronization as on all other gears.

The sliding sleeve makes friction contact with the synchronizing ring on its tapered part of the inner race. Besides this, the toothed race engages with corresponding teeth in the gear-coupled clutch carrier of the selected gear providing a firm mechanical connection. The inside race contour, in addition to the tapered outer edges, includes a machined groove in its center which has the purpose of locking the sliding sleeve onto the synchronizing ring once the respective shift has been completed; for this reason it is no longer necessary to incorporate a locking device in the selector shaft.

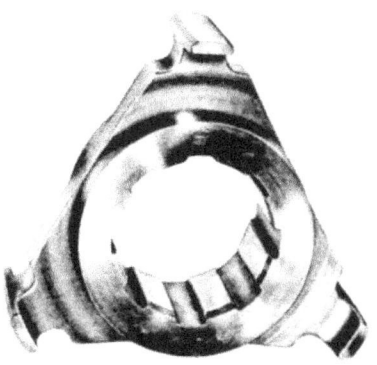

The three-pronged spider carries the sliding sleeve and transmits the engine torque; the sliding sleeve is free to move forwards or backwards to engage or disengage a given gear.

The gear-coupled clutch carrier is the actual gear coupler connecting the gear with the sliding sleeve. The synchronizing ring and the servo-thrust components are contained within the clutch carrier. The First gear clutch carrier has two slots machined into the body and located opposite one another; the slanted slot provides for the brake band energizer. The retaining ring tab must never be positioned within the slanted slot since it belongs in the slot of the brake band stop.

The synchronizing ring is a split spring with two beveled outer edges. One beveled edge is the synchronizing friction face, while the other edge completes the contour to mate with the machined inner groove within the inside race of the sliding sleeve provided for locking the sliding sleeve on the synchronizing ring when the shift has been completed.

The brake band energizer is acted upon by one end of the synchronizing ring. In turn, the energizer transmits this pressure to the brake band.

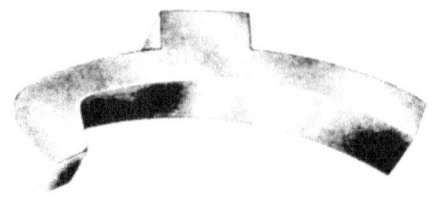

This modified brake band energizer with the actuating tab is used only on the first gear synchronizer.

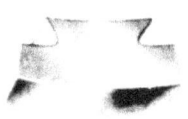

The brake band stop is contained within the slot machined into the clutch carrier and is mechanically connected with the respective gear, transmitting the friction forces (moment of friction) from the synchronizing components to the clutch carrier.

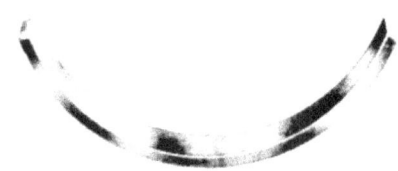

The brake band receives the synchronizing force, or thrust, exerted by the synchronizing ring against the brake band energizer. This force is in turn transmitted to the brake band, forcing it outward against the inner face of the synchronizing ring.

The retaining ring contains the synchronizing ring and the synchromesh components in the clutch carrier.

Synchromesh Disassembly

1. Remove synchronizing ring retainer from clutch carrier using needle nose pliers.
2. Use solvent to clean all parts.
3. Inspect all parts for wear or damage. If the synchronizing was no longer operational, install a new synchronizing ring.

Synchromesh Reassembly

1. Place the synchronizing ring into the clutch carrier, then insert the brake band energizer, brake band stop, and brake bands (see illustration).

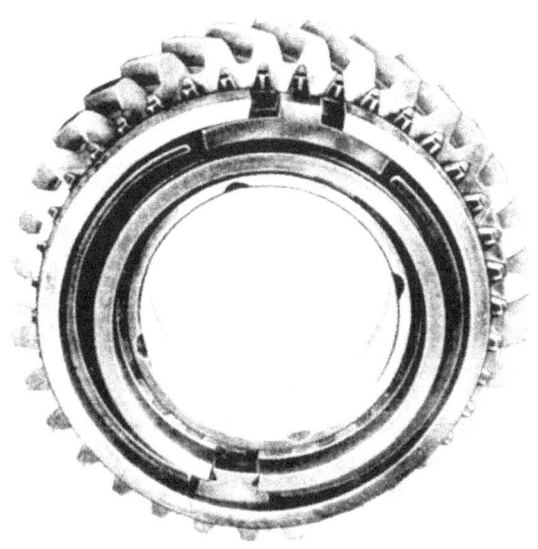

2. When assembling the First speed synchronization, make sure that only one brake band is installed. The band should be positioned exactly as illustrated.

3. Use needle-nose pliers to install the synchronizing ring retainer (see illustration).
Check the installed synchronizing ring for installed diameter (76,30 mm ± 0,18 mm).

Assembling Pinion Shaft

NOTE: All pinion shaft parts are to be dry-assembled so that no oil covers the seating surfaces. Illustrations showing the pinion shaft cross-section and an exploded view of the pinion shaft components (both Five and Four speed) will be found in the preceding section of this chapter. The ring gear and pinion are identified with matching numbers as illustrated under PINION SHAFT AND RING GEAR ADJUSTMENT later in this chapter section. It is essential that these numbers match when the components are assembled.

IMPORTANT: The pinion shaft components must be assembled in the sequence outlined below. Be sure that the roller bearing inner race, together with the cage and rollers, is facing in the proper direction, i.e., the two-piece roller cage must face with its attached ring towards the transmission gears (see illustration).

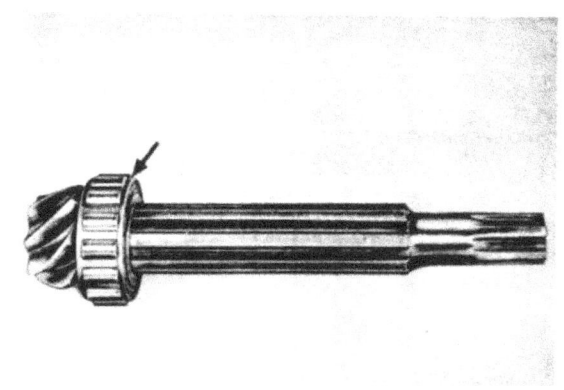

1. Install roller bearing using hydraulic press VW 400F, VW 401, and VW 407 (see illustration).

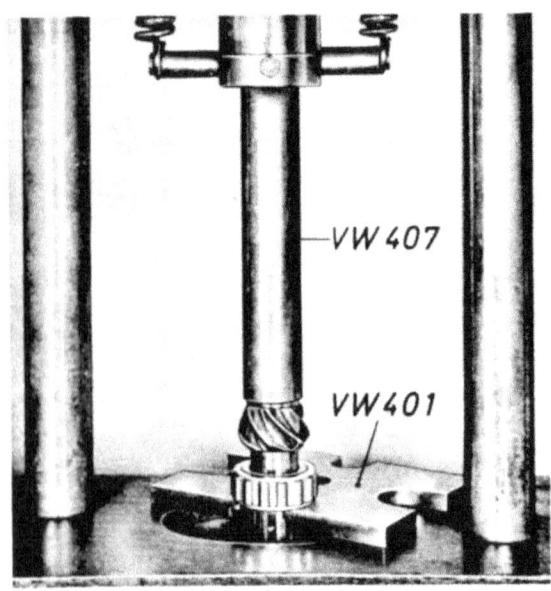

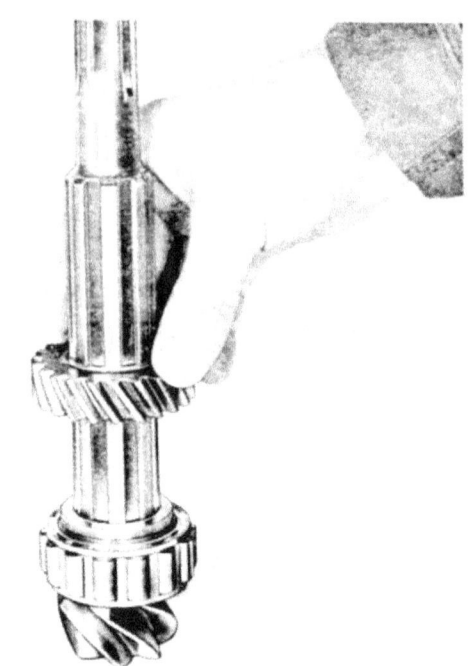

2. Either reinstall the same thickness and number of spacers as was removed (considering whether parts replacement may have changed the thickness required), or install the thickness and number of spacers computed from the CHECKING PINION SHAFT SPACER THICKNESS between the roller bearing and the thick spacer, then install the thick spacer (see illustration).

4. Slide spacer bushing on shaft, then follow with Gear II of Fourth speed, small collar facing down against the bushing.

5. Slide the thrust washer and roller bearing inner race onto shaft (see illustration).

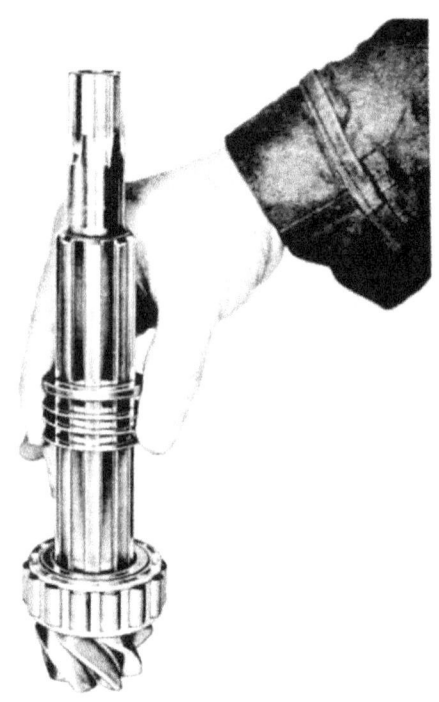

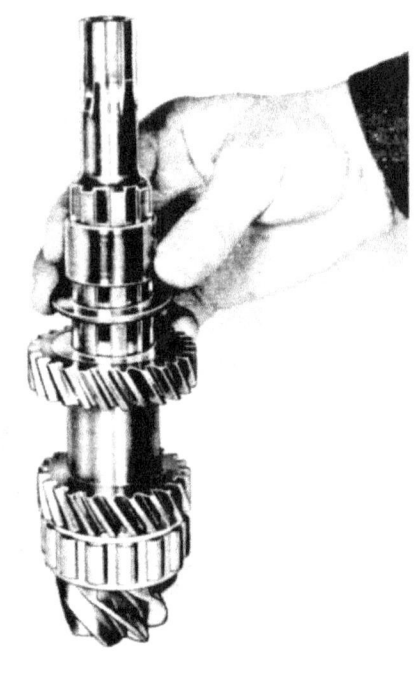

3. Slide Gear II of the Fifth speed on the shaft, small collar facing upward (see illustration).

6. Install needle bearing cage, Gear II of Third speed, and spider (see illustration).

WARNING: Used needle bearing cages must be reinstalled with the same gear.

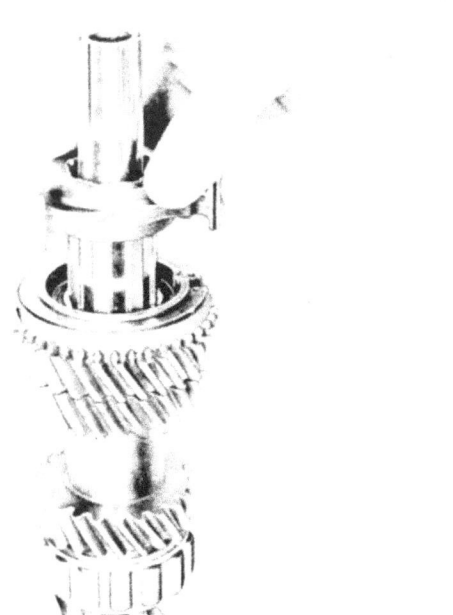

7. Install needle bearing inner race, needle bearing cage, and sliding sleeve (see illustration). Install Gear II of Second speed.

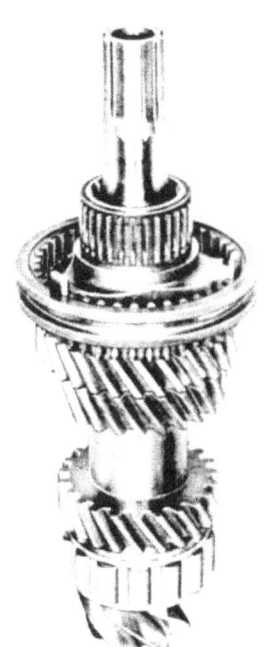

8. Install beveled thrust washer with plain face towards the needle bearing, then follow with the small spacer (see illustration). After transmission No. 100 407, a single, beveled thrust washer of 6.6 mm thickness replaces both parts.

9. With an appropriate pipe tool, press onto the shaft the bearing inner race half which shows only the mating number (without the letter "X").

REBUILDING INPUT SHAFT

NOTE: The differential may remain installed in the transmission housing if ONLY the input shaft is being serviced. Note the thickness of the paper gaskets between the housing and the intermediate plate when removing.

Removal

Follow instructions under TRANSMISSION DISASSEMBLY for complete procedure.

Disassembly

1. Drive back the plate locking tabs at the hex nut.
2. Use a vise to hold Special Tool P 256, insert input shaft into receptacle, then remove retaining nut with Special Tool P 252 (see illustration).

3. Using a 400F hydraulic press or equivalent, press roller bearing off input shaft with VW 401 and VW 402 (see illustration).

5. Check Gear I of Second speed for wear or damage. Replace the input shaft (see mating numbers in illustration) if wear or damage is advanced.

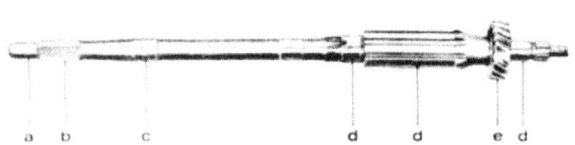

6. Examine all synchromesh parts for wear or damage.
7. Check all gears for wear or damage (noting mating numbers), replacing as necessary.
8. Check double-row ball bearing and the roller bearing for damage or wear, (noting mating numbers), replacing as necessary.
9. To check input shaft for runout, remove the double-row ball bearing from the intermediate plate and the outer roller bearing race from the case; spare bearings can also be used. Be sure the input shaft is assembled and the hex nut (M24 x 1,5), is tight since it may bring about a certain degree of runout. Place the assembled input shaft on V-blocks as illustrated, then check for runout at the flywheel bushing journal. The maximum allowable runout is 0,1 mm.

4. Remove all input shaft components, being sure to mark needle bearing cages to avoid slip-ups when reinstalling them.
5. Drive the inner half of the ball bearing race slightly away from its seat with a drift or similar tool, then pull off with a puller (see illustration).

IMPORTANT: Be careful not to damage Gear I of Second speed.

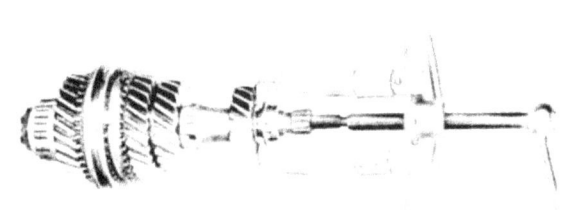

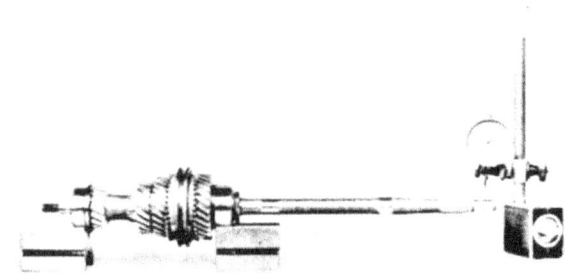

Inspection

After cleaning parts, check for wear and damage as follows:

1. Check the stub fitting into the flywheel gland bushing for traces of wear.
2. Check the clutch plate seating splines for radial play or wear.
3. Check the oil seal race for wear.
4. Check the bearing and gear seats for wear or damage.

10. Excessive runout up to 0,3 mm can be corrected on the press VW 400F using tools VW 405 and VW 406 or equivalent.

Reassembly

Dry-assemble all input shaft components to keep oil from coating the contact surfaces. To reassemble, reverse the preceding instructions, noting the following points.

1. Slide Gear I of Third speed onto input shaft with small collar facing the flange on the shaft (see illustration).

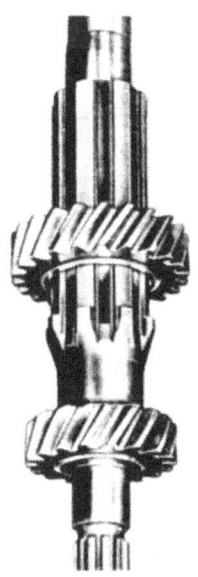

2. Slip the thrust washer and the needle bearing inner race onto the shaft (see illustration).

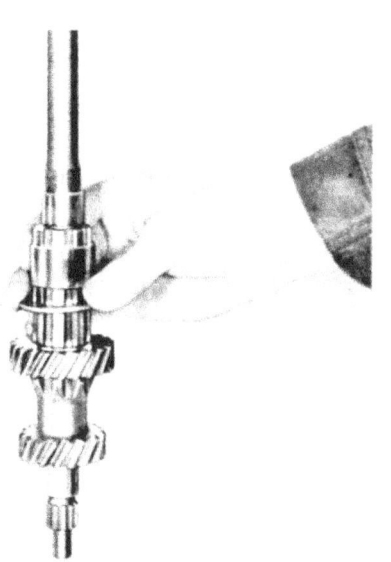

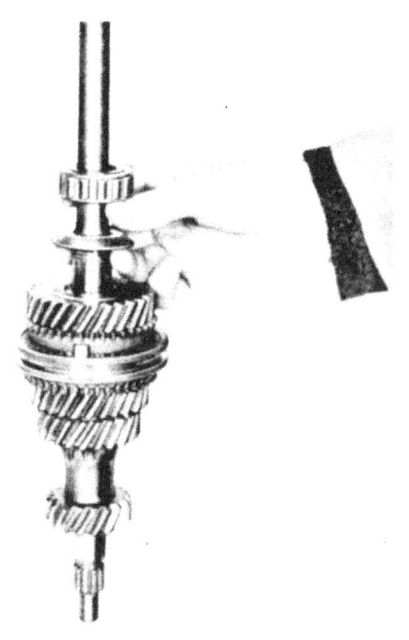

3. Install the needle bearing cage, Gear I of Fourth speed, and spider (see illustration).

WARNING: Used needle bearing cages have to be reinstalled with the same gear.

4. Slip the sliding sleeve, the needle bearing inner race, needle cage, then Gear I of Fifth speed onto the shaft.
5. Slip the beveled thrust washer (5,9 mm thickness) and the roller bearing (with the cage cover ring facing towards the clutch plate splines) onto the shaft (see illustration).

6. Use hydraulic press VW 400F or equivalent to press the roller bearing onto the shaft with Special Tools VW 401, VW 409, and pipe piece 1 (20 x 3,5 mm, 25 mm long). Be sure not to damage the input shaft threads (see illustration).
7. Install a new nut locking plate, making sure the guide tab of the plate fits into the shaft groove and under the inner race of the roller bearing (see illustration).
8. Lubricate the threads and seat of the hex nut, then install the nut with the spherical part up.
9. Tighten the hex nut to 72 to 86 ft. lb. (10 to 12 mkp)

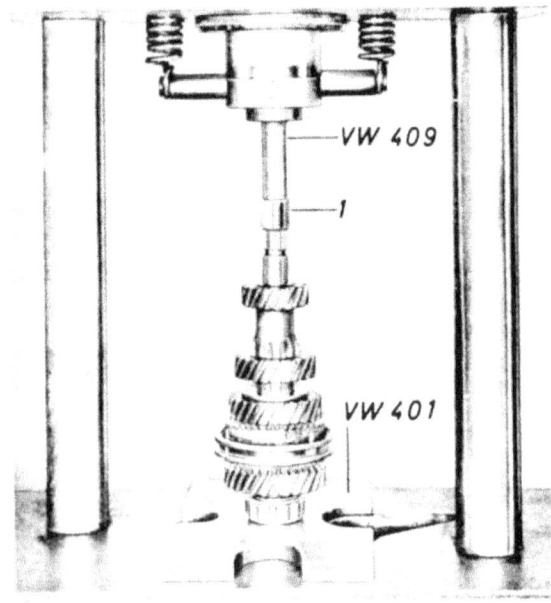

SERVICING INTERMEDIATE PLATE

Check the intermediate plate, the bearing brace plate, and the bearings for wear or damage; service as follows:

Disassembly

1. Bend back the bolt locking tabs, unscrew the bolts, then remove bearing brace plate (see illustration).

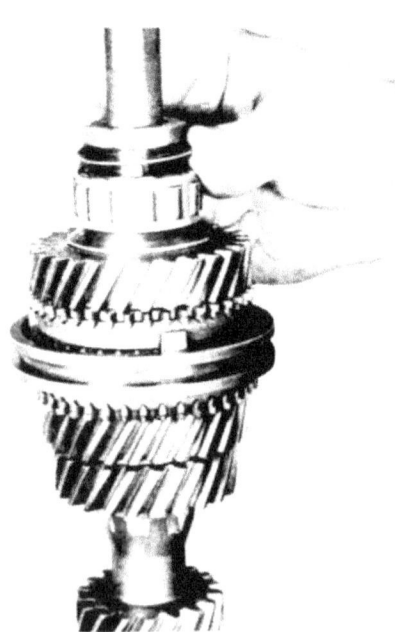

2. Heat the intermediate plate to about 250°F. (120°C.), then press out the four-point ball bearing and the double-row ball bearing with appropriate tools.
3. Drive the dowel pins out of the intermediate plate, then (if necessary), remove the detent bushing with Special Tool P 66a (see illustration).

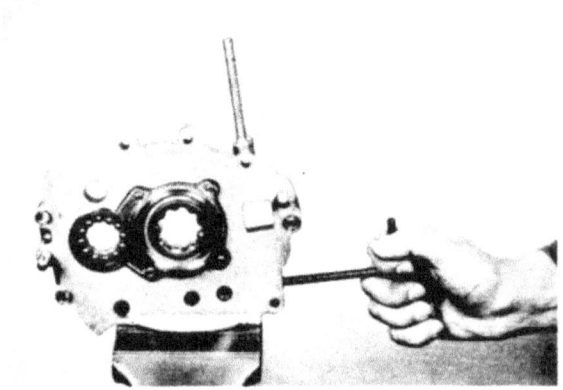

with Special Tools P 256 and P 252 (see illustration).
10. Bend the lock plate edge to hold the hex nut, then press the inner race half of the ball bearing onto the shaft (note mating numbers).

Reassembly

1. Clean all parts, check for wear, then replace as necessary.
2. Heat the intermediate plate to about 250°F. (120°C.), then insert the four-point ball bearing and the double row ball bearing so the race flange seats well on the intermediate plate (see illustration); grease and insert into the bearing any loose bearing balls.

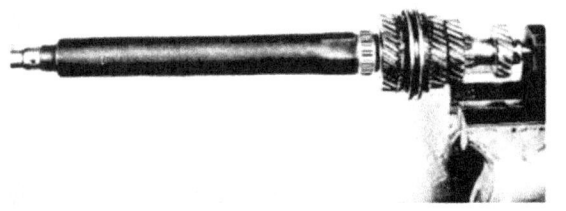

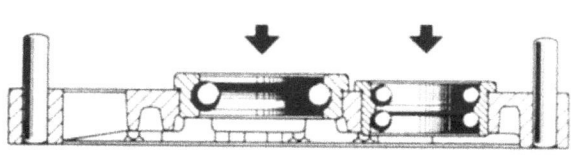

3. Position the bearing brace plate as shown in the illustration. Insert the retaining bolts and lock plates, tighten the nuts to 18 ft. lb. (2,5 mkp), then lock in place by bending the tabs (check for proper lock plate positioning).

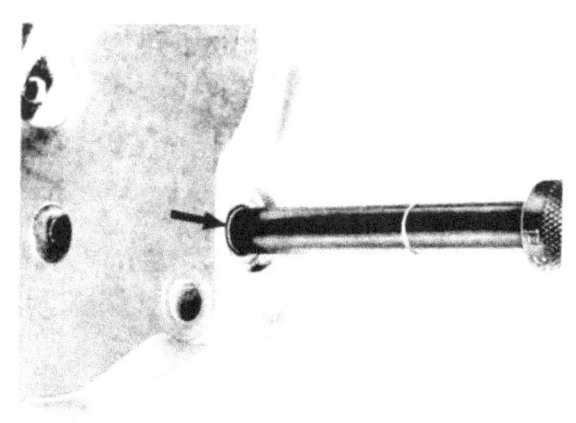

REBUILDING DIFFERENTIAL

NOTE: See REMOVING AND REPLACING DIFFERENTIAL in the previous section of this chapter, then proceed as follows. Note the spacer thickness (beneath the side bearings) to aid in proper reassembly.

Disassembly

1. Remove the differential side bearings with a puller and special tool P 263 or equivalent (see illustration).

4. Use Special Tool P 262 to install detent bushings as follows:

   a. Drive the long bushing to collar of driver, P 262.
   b. Drive the short bushing to the second mark on the driver.
   c. Drive the middle-length bushing to the first mark on the driver, P 262 (see illustration).

WARNING: Ensure that none of the three bushings protrude into the selector shaft bores. Detent bushing arrangement is shown in a previous illustration.

2. Remove the shaft retaining pin with special tool P 257/2 (see illustration).
3. Remove the spider gear shaft using a driver, then remove the side gear shaft (see illustration).
4. Turn the spider gears to the side and remove through the openings in the differential carrier, then remove the differential side gears through the larger, oval opening in the differential carrier.
5. Bend back the bolt locking tabs, unscrew the bolts, then remove the ring gear (see illustration).

2. Inspect the side and spider gears for the condition of the gear teeth and especially for signs of wear at the spherical seats; replace parts as necessary.

3. Check the spider gear shaft and side gear splines as well as axle joint flanges for signs of wear; replace as necessary.

4. Examine side bearings for wear or damage. If necessary, replace together with bearing outer races in housing or side cover.

NOTE: Up to transmission No. 100 268, axial preload for the differential side bearings was determined by diaphragm springs. Gear backlash was, and still is, adjusted with Spacer S1 located under the side bearing on the ring gear side.

WARNING: To obtain the proper diaphragm spring effect, the inner race of the side bearing must be free to move sideways on the carrier trunnion when the springs are installed. When replacing a differential carrier designed for use with diaphragm springs with a new part, the springs can no longer be used since the design is different. The new carrier should be installed with Spacers S1 and S2 placed beneath the side bearings; use instructions following under REASSEMBLY. Differential carriers which still have the necessary trunnion length for use with diaphragm springs but also have been modified for use with spacers alone, have to be assembled with a 5 mm spacer ring under the S2 Spacer.

Reassembly

To reassemble, reverse the previous instructions, noting the following:

1. Use MoS_2 compound to coat the seats of the side and spider gears, then insert the side gears through oval openings in the carrier and position with the aid of axle flanges.

2. Place the spider gears through the opening in the differential carrier and position opposite each other so that the shaft will pass through; it may be necessary to reset the gears in teeth to align with the shaft.

Examination

1. After cleaning differential parts, check the carrier for signs of wear at the seats of the side and spider gears; then at the side bearings. Replace carrier if necessary.

3. Rotate the spider gears until their bores align with those in the carrier, then insert the side gear shaft. Drive the spider gear shaft in, orienting the roll pin bore towards the axles (see illustration).

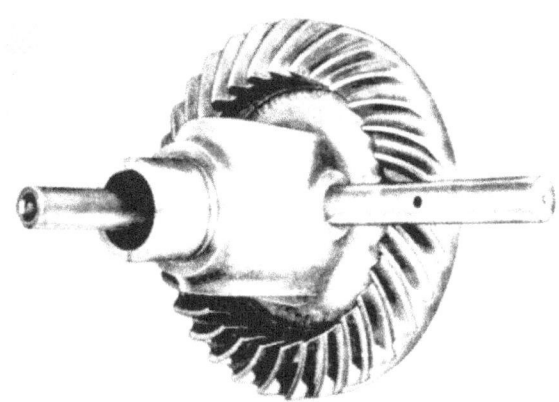

4. Insert the roll pin in Special Tool P 257/1 and drive it into place, in the side and the spider gear pins, to its stop (with axle flanges removed prior to assembly).

7. Assuming that spacer thickness has been recorded or calculated, place the appropriate spacers onto the trunnions and install the side bearings with Special Tool P 264 (see illustration).

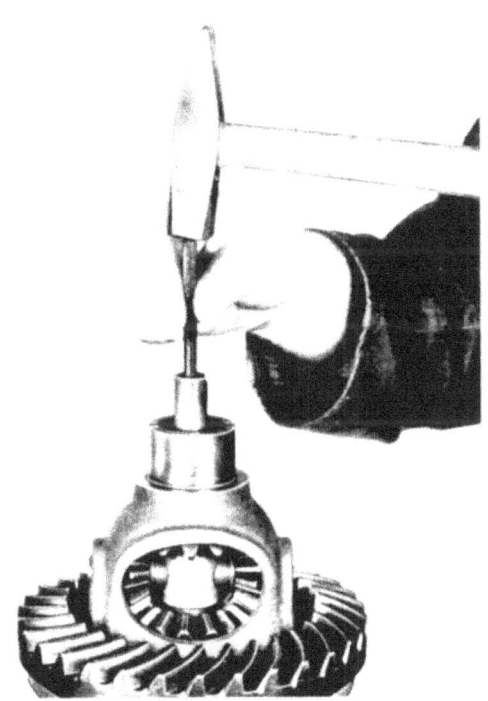

5. Place the ring gear onto the differential carrier flange, then tighten the hex bolts to 69 to 72 ft. lb. (9,5 to 10 mkp) (see illustration).

6. Insert the bolt locking plates into grooves in the bolt heads, then squeeze the open ends with pliers to firmly connect the plates with the bolt heads. Lock the bolts by bending the plates down on one flank of each bolt as illustrated.

8. To install the outer races of the side bearings, heat the transmission housing or the cover to about 250°F. (120°C.), then install the outer races with an appropriate tool.

IMPORTANT: The ring gear must be readjusted whenever a new differential carrier is installed. See **RING GEAR ADJUSTMENT** and **RING GEAR BACKLASH ADJUSTMENT** instructions following.

PINION SHAFT AND RING GEAR ADJUSTMENT

Description

Proper adjustment of the pinion shaft and ring gear is necessary for quiet operation and long service of the rear axle drive. These parts are mated at the factory, then checked on special test devices for best contact patterns and minimal noise in both directions of rotation.

The position for minimal noise is found by moving the pinion shaft axially while keeping the ring gear within tolerances of prescribed gear backlash of 0,12 and 0,18 mm. The deviation from the designed adjustment position (blueprint value R) is found and then etched into the pinion face (see illustration). Every pinion and ring gear set is marked with mating numbers and can be replaced as a set only.

CAUTION: BE SURE to exercise meticulous care and cleanliness in all these adjustments, since dirt can alter the readings of measuring instruments. The location of the spacers is shown in the illustration on Page 82.

RING GEAR ADJUSTMENT

NOTE: This procedure determines the spacer thickness for ring gear adjustment. To determine ring gear backlash, see procedure following.

1. Ensure that the side bearing outer races are well seated in the transmission housing or cover.
2. Install on the ring gear side of the utilized differential carrier a 3,5 mm thick spacer (S1), and a 3,0 mm spacer (S2) on the other side, placing the spacers under the side bearings (install side bearings with Special Tool P 264) (see illustration).

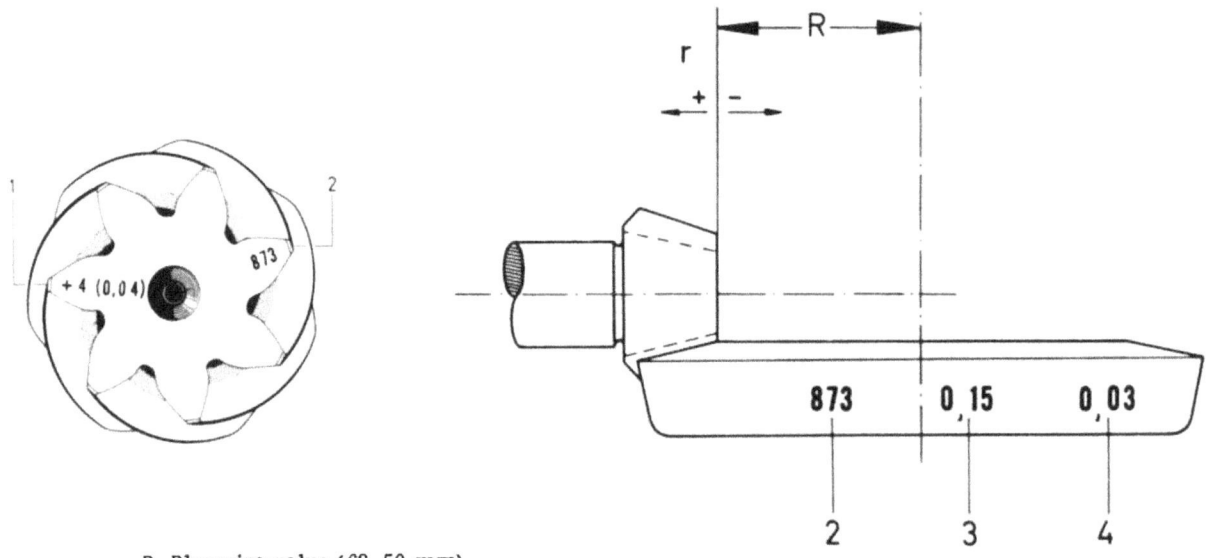

R Blueprint value (63,50 mm)
r Deviation from R plus (+) or minus (-) shown in 1/100 mm (+4) or in mm (+0,04)
1 Deviation r
2 Mating number
3 Gear backlash
4 Deviation from T-value in plus (+) or minus (-) (indicated in mm)

3. Place the differential with side bearings into the transmission housing. Set housing cover (without oil seal) together with a 0,20 mm thick gasket onto the housing.

4. Place two nuts across from each other, then slightly tighten down housing cover against the side bearing. Check the gap between the cover and gasket with a feeler gauge. The nominal value for side bearing preload is about .006 in., (0,15 mm) (see illustration).

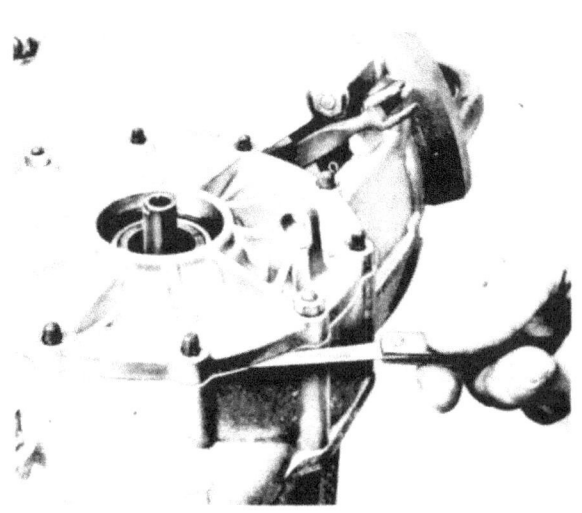

5. Select the ring gear side spacer (S1) of a thickness permitting a preload clearance of .006 in. (0,15 mm); mount the spacer using Special Tools P 263 and P 264 or equivalent.

Example:

Clearance determined with feeler gauge   0,40 mm
Minus desired preload clearance   0,15 mm
The installed 3,5 mm spacer (S 1) to be replaced with one 0,25 mm thinner, i.e., 3,25 mm

6. Tighten the housing side cover with a 0,20 mm gasket in place. Torque the nuts EQUALLY to 18 ft. lb. (2,5 mkp) to obtain the necessary reading.

7. Insert the axle flange, place the thrust washer on bolt, then tighten the stretchbolt slightly.

8. Measure the drag of the installed differential with Special Tool P 261.

NOTE: Be sure the pinion shaft is not engaged and the axle flange oil seal in the housing side cover is removed when measuring differential drag, or otherwise additional drag will be created.

9. The differential drag should be between 15.6 and 20.8 in. lb. (18 and 24 cmkp) when the side bearing is properly preloaded. If the above value has not been obtained, replace the spacer with one of proper thickness (see illustration).

10. Remove the differential, remove both side bearings, then measure the thickness of all spacers using a micrometer and measuring each spacer at four different locations. The total thickness of all spacers shows spacer thickness for the ring gear adjustment.

11. To prepare for the actual adjustment of the pinion and ring gear, Spacer S1 should be 0,1 mm thinner than one-half of the spacer total, and Spacer S2 should be 0,1 mm thicker. Follow example below:

Example:

Total thickness of spacers $S1 + S2 = 6,25$ mm

Thickness of spacer S 1 $(\frac{6,25 \text{ mm}}{2})$ = 3,125 mm
                                                 − 0,100 mm
                                                 3,025 mm

Thickness of spacer S 2 $(\frac{6,25 \text{ mm}}{2})$ = 3,125 mm
                                                + 0,100 mm
                                                 3,225 mm

NOTE: The spacers are available in increments of 0,10 mm from 2,5 mm to 3,5 mm. Adjustments to the nearest 0,05 mm are possible by using a 0,25 mm washer. The calculated thickness of spacers required should be rounded off to match the actual (available) spacer thickness, making sure that the rounding-off does not alter the value of the total spacers required (S1 + S2). See example following for procedure:

Example:

Calculated spacer thickness
$S1 + S2 = 3,025 + 3,225 = 6,25$ mm
Rounded-off spacer thickness of
$S1 + S2 = 3,0 + 3,25 = 6,25$ mm

10. As a check, measure the spacer thickness at four points of each spacer with a micrometer. Permissible thickness variation is 0.02 mm. Be sure to remove any burrs from spacers BEFORE taking this measurement.

PINION SHAFT ADJUSTMENT

NOTE: See page 114 for illustration showing the pinion gear face.

Description

Determine the adjustment value E from the known blueprint value R (63,50), plus or minus deviation "r" which is etched into the pinion face (see previous illustration). The shaft has been approximately preadjusted at the time of reassembly with the placement of the correct spacers.

Procedure

1. Insert the preassembled intermediate plate, with gears and selector shafts, into transmission housing, omitting the paper gasket. Place the spacer bushings onto 4 opposing housing studs and tighten the nuts in a cross-wise manner, torquing them to 80 to 86 ft. lb. (11 to 12 mkp). Only after fully torquing nuts should measurements be taken.

2. Place the dummy carrier P 258 onto the gauge setting plate and fasten the dial gauge to a preload of 1 mm (small pointer to 1, larger pointer to 0) (see illustration).

3. Install the dummy carrier P 258, with side bearings, into the transmission housing. Make sure that the dummy carrier is under an axial preload of about 0,1 mm when the side cover has been installed. In no case should the dummy carrier be free to move axially when the measurements are being taken.

NOTE: Use differential spacers to install the dummy carrier so as to eliminate axial play.

4. Carefully turn the dummy carrier until the gauge sensor pin comes to right angles with the face of the pinion. It is at this point that the gauge should show the highest reading, which should be noted. Note the notch in the flank of the dummy carrier. This shows the location of the gauge sensor pin (see illustration).

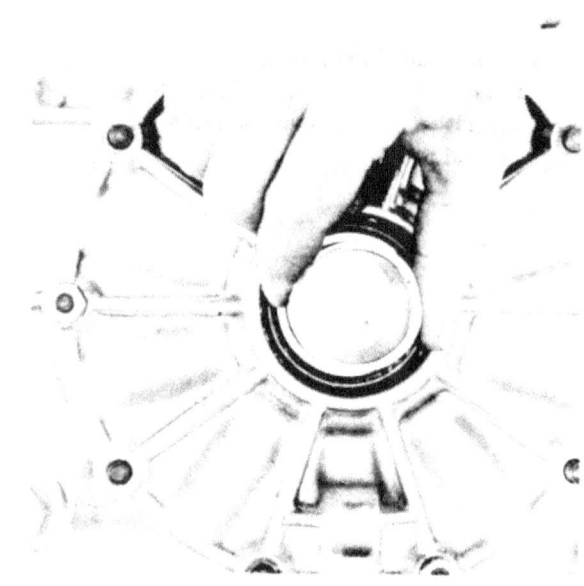

5. The distance from the center axis of the dummy carrier to its resting base at the setting plate is indicated on the side of the dummy carrier as actual value, for example 53,98. The distance from the calibrating surface of the setting plate to the resting base for the dummy carrier is indicated on the side of the gauge setting plate, for example 9,52. Both values added together represent the value to which the gauge has been set. See example following:

Example: Actual value of dummy carrier	53.98
Actual value of setting plate	9.52
Actual adjustment value:	63.50

6. If the gauge reading differs, in clockwise direction, from the adjusted value of, for example, 63,50 mm, then the distance is smaller than 63,50 mm and the shortage must be deducted from the value of 63,50 mm. See example following:

Example:

If the small pointer is between 1 and 2, the large one at 0.24 mm:

Gauge adjustment	63.50 mm
Minus measured value	0.24 mm
Distance to face of pinion	63.26 mm

Adjustment value E (as example)	63.54 mm
Minus distance to face of pinion	63.26 mm
Thickness of paper gaskets	0.28 mm

7. Thus the pinion shaft must be moved away from the ring gear center by 0,28 mm. This is done by inserting paper gaskets of 0,3 mm thickness; second digit decimal fractions are rounded off as follows: 3 and up are changed to 5, while 7 and up are changed to 10.

8. If the gauge reading differs, in counterclockwise direction, from the adjusted value of 63,50 mm, then the distance is larger than 63,50 and that excess must be added to the value of 63,50. See example following:

Example:

If the small pointer is between 1 and 0, the large one at 0.08 mm:

Gauge adjustment	63.50 mm
Plus measured value	+ 0.08 mm
Distance to face of pinion	63.58 mm
Adjustment value E (as example)	63.68 mm
Minus distance to face of pinion	− 63.58 mm
Thickness of paper gaskets	0.10 mm

NOTE: It is permissible to install paper gaskets in thicknesses of 0,10 to 0,50 mm between the housing and the intermediate plate. If this amount is inadequate for obtaining proper adjustment, disassemble the pinion shaft again and change the adjustment shims appropriately. Paper gaskets are available in thicknesses of 0,1, 0,15, and 0,2 mm.

9. Prior to the installation of the paper gaskets, the adjustment value E must be checked again; deviations of ± 0,03 mm are permissible. It is not required to check the gear contact pattern again.

RING GEAR BACKLASH ADJUSTMENT

With the preassembled intermediate plate with gears and selector shafts together with the paper gaskets (proper thickness found at the time of pinion shaft adjustment) inserted into the transmission housing, proceed as follows:

1. Place the spacer bushings onto 4 opposing studs in the housing and tighten, then torque the pinion shaft stretchbolt to 80 to 86 ft. lb. (11 to 12 mkp) before making the following measurements.

2. Install in the transmission housing the differential unit together with the side bearings and spacers (proper thickness found previously in the RING GEAR ADJUSTMENT procedure for Spacers S1 and S2).

3. Install the side cover with a 0,20 mm paper gasket. When tightening the side cover retaining nuts, continuously check to ensure that a certain side play exists. In no case is it permissible to allow the pinion and ring gear to jam or bind. Torque nuts to 18 ft. lb. (2.5 mkp).

4. Use Special Tool P 259 to block pinion shaft through stretchbolt. See illustration on page 86.

5. Place the dial gauge onto a holder, then tighten the holder lock screw and holder retaining bolt (installed into the differential shaft) so that the gauge sensor pin comes into contact with the base of the clutch conduit bracket (see illustration).

6. Carefully move the dial gauge from stop to stop and record the amount of gear backlash.

7. Repeat the measurement at every 90° of ring gear rotation. The values must not differ by more than 0,05 mm between each point.

IMPORTANT: The exact amount of gear backlash is etched into the ring gear as illustrated on page 114. A gear backlash of 0,12 to 0,18 mm is permissible.

8. Special Tools P 263 and P 264 can replace Spacers S1 and S2 until the correct axial (flank) play has been obtained. Be especially careful to ensure that the total spacer thickness is not changed.

9. Check the axle flange oil seals and replace if necessary.

Transmission tolerances

Measuring Point	Fitted tolerances (when new in mm)	Wear limit in mm	
1. Blacklash between gears I and II 1st speed 2nd speed 3rd speed 4th speed 5th speed	0.06 - 0.12 (0.0023" - 0.0047")	0.22 (0.0086")	
2. Loose wheels on drive shaft and first motion shaft 1st speed 2nd speed 3rd speed end play 4th speed	0.3 - 0.4 (0.011" - 0.015") 0.2 - 0.3 0.2 - 0.3 0.2 - 0.3 (0.007" - 0.011")	0.5 (0.019") 0.4 0.4 0.4 (0.015")	
3. Selector shafts a) Radial play in the guides	0.095 - (0.0037") 0.156 (0.0061")	0.4 (0.015")	
b)	-	0.10 (0.0039")	

Measuring Point	Fitted tolerance (when new) in mm	Wear limit in mm	
4. Selector fork in operating sleeve			
1st and reverse speed	0.1 - 0.3	0.5	
2nd and 3rd speed	0.1 - 0.3	0.5	
4th and 5th speed	0.1 - 0.3 (0.003" - 0.011")	0.5 (0.019")	
End play			
5. Synchronizing rings			
1st speed			
2nd speed		in accordance with local wear of molybdenum layer a)	
3rd speed			
4th speed			
5th speed			
Outer diameter fitted	76.12 - (2.996") 76.48		
6. First motion shaft			
a) Run out on guide pin	max. 0.1 (0.003")	max. 0.1 (0.003") (align)	
b) Radial play in bushing of banjo bolt on engine	0.145 - (0.0057") 0.231 (0.0090")	0.3 (0.011")	

Torque tightening figures for screws and nuts on the transmission

M 8	Hexagon nuts on transmission housing:	2.5 mkp (18.08 lb.ft.)
M 6	Hexagon nuts on guide tube:	1.0 mkp (7.23 lb.ft.)
M 6	Socket head screw for withdrawal fork:	1.0 mkp (7.23 lb.ft.)
M 8	Hexagon bolt with pin (angular drive):	2.5 mkp (18.08 lb.ft.)
M 12	drain plug on intermediate plate :	2.5 mkp (18.08 lb.ft.)
M 24	oil filter plug:	2.0 - 2.5 mkp (14.46 -18.08 lb.ft.)
M 24	magnetic oil drain plug:	2.0 - 2.5 mkp (14.46 - 18.08 lb.ft.)
	Hexagon bolt for clamping plate of intermediate plate:	2.5 mkp (18.08 lb.ft.)
M 24	Hexagon nut on first motion shaft:	10 - 12 mkp (72.33 - 86.79 lb.ft.)
M 12	Crown nut on first motion shaft:	6.0 - 6.5 mkp (43.39 - 47.01 lb.ft.)
M 14	crown nut on first motion shaft (reinforced type):	9.0 - 11.0 mkp (65.09 - 79.56 lb.ft.)
M 12	expansion screw or drive shaft:	11-12 mkp (79.56 - 86.79 lb.ft.)
M 8	Hexagon bolt of selector forks:	2.5 mkp (18.08 lb.ft.)
M 12	Hexagon bolts for securing crown wheel:	9.5 - 10.0 mkp (68.71 - 72.33 lb.ft.)
M 10	expansion screw for joint flange of differential:	4.5 - 5.0 mkp (32.54 - 36.16 lb.ft.)
M 8	ball pin for withdrawal fork:	2.1 - 2.3 mkp (15.18 - 16.63 lb.ft.)

CLUTCH

NOTE: Whenever work has been done on the clutch system, the clutch pedal travel must be checked, and if necessary, corrected. This is necessary since the diaphragm spring clutch requires an exactly limited clutch pedal travel.

DESCRIPTION

Porsche 900 Series vehicles use a dry single plate clutch in the flywheel between the engine and transmission. The spring cushioned clutch disc uses friction lining on both sides. The disc rides on the splined input shaft and can be displaced axially.

The diaphragm spring is housed in the flywheel and occupies a central position on the clutch. When the clutch is engaged, the clutch disc is held against the flywheel by the pressure plate from the pressure of the diaphragm spring. This provides a mechanical lock between the engine and transmission.

The withdrawal fork is located in the transmission housing together with a throwout bearing mounted centrally in the bearing. The throwout bearing is permanently lubricated and requires no service.

An adjustable cable connects the clutch pedal to the withdrawal fork and throwout bearing. Upon depressing the clutch pedal, the throwout bearing is forced against the segments of the diaphragm spring, displacing it axially, which in turn relieves pressure from the pressure plate and thus, from the clutch disc, resulting in a broken connection between the engine and tranmission (see illustration).

Clutch maintenance is limited to adjustment of the clutch pedal clearance as described in the MAINTENANCE SERVICE chapter, and also to the adjustment of the clutch pedal travel limiter following repair operations, in this chapter. See CLUTCH FAULT TRACING CHART in this chapter and TOLERANCES AND WEAR LIMITS in the ENGINE chapter for more information.

CLUTCH CABLE REMOVAL AND REPLACEMENT

Removal

1. Fold back the rubber mat or carpeting located in front of the passenger seat, then raise the rubber tunnel cover from the center tunnel and fold back.
2. Loosen the locknut of the clevis in the threaded portion of the clutch cable, disengage the retaining spring from the clevis pin, and remove the pin (see illustration).
3. Remove the clevis pin and lock nut from the threaded cable end, then pull out the clutch cable from the rear.

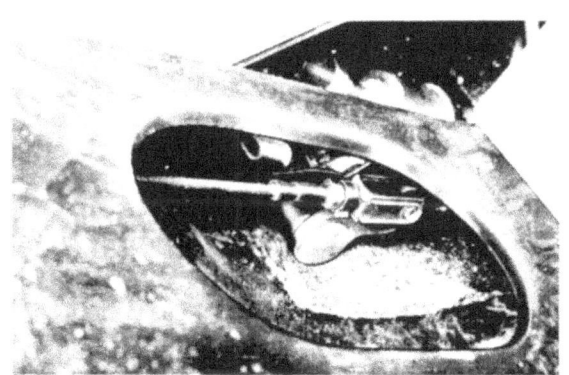

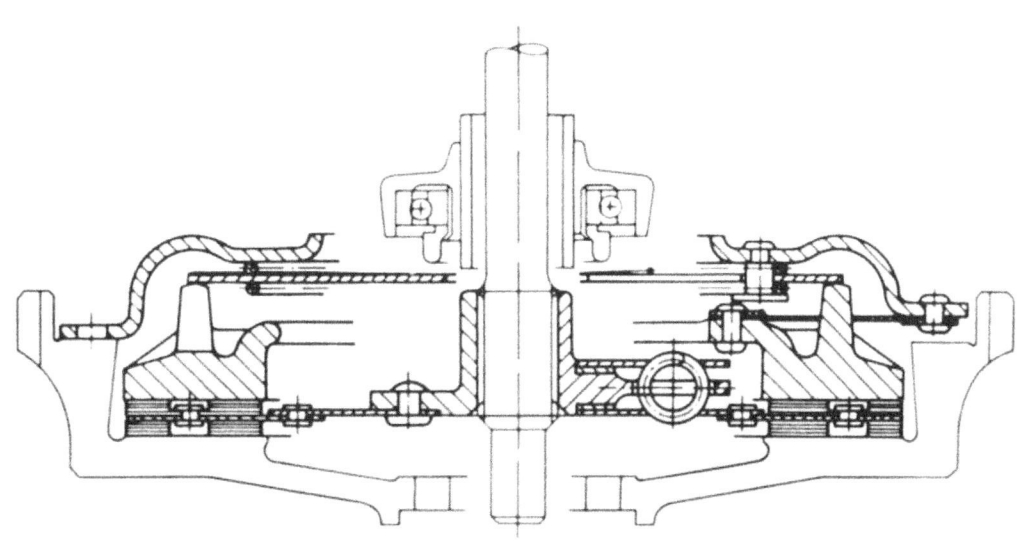

4. Remove the lock nut and adjusting nut from the threaded rear part of the cable.

Replacement

NOTE: Prior to replacing cable, check the cable cover tube and bellows for condition, renew if necessary.

1. Coat the cable with MoS_2 multipurpose grease and slide into the cable cover from the rear.
2. Reattach and reset the clutch clearance, then see CLUTCH PEDAL TRAVEL LIMITER ADJUSTMENT in this chapter.

CLUTCH REMOVAL AND REPLACEMENT

Engine/transmission unit must be removed from car first. See ENGINE chapter.

Removal

1. After carefully removing transmission from engine, loosen the clutch retaining bolts, slackening each by one or two turns at a time and switching in a cross sequence until the spring pressure is relieved, to avoid distortion of the spring housing (see illustration).

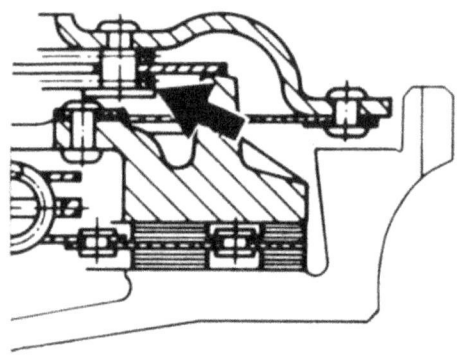

2. Withdraw the clutch assembly, then the clutch disc.

Checking Clutch Assembly

1. Clean the entire assembly, then check the diaphragm spring segment ends for running marks from the throwout bearing. If running marks are deeper than .011 in. (.3 mm), replace clutch assembly.
2. Check the contact surface of the pressure plate for cracks, burn marks and wear. Check surface as illustrated. If the inward deflection is over .011 in. (.3 mm), replace clutch assembly.
3. Check the spring connections between the pressure plate and the cover for cracks and check the rivet attachments for tightness. Should the rivets be loose or damaged, renew clutch assembly.
4. The diaphragm spring is mounted in the cover between two wire rings with a rivet connection. Should there be visible wear on the rivet head or wire ring (see illustration), the clutch assembly should be renewed.

5. Lightly coat the diaphragm spring between the wire rings with MoS_2 multipurpose grease before refitting the clutch.
6. Check the throwout bearing for wear and true rotation, replacing if necessary. Then check the withdrawal fork seat in the transmission housing for wear and good seating, repair if defective.

Checking The Clutch Disc

1. The flexible clutch disc is riveted to undulating spring leaves. The individual leaves curve from side to side to provide a cushioning effect in the clutch disc. It is essential for the proper functioning of the clutch that the offset positions of all leaves are evenly balanced.
2. The clutch disc should slide freely on the splined input shaft but it must not show evidence of radial play.
3. Inspect the clutch linings for oil coating, scorching, tearing or other wear. Visible formation of cracks in the lining surface between the rivets can be disregarded, but all the previous faults are grounds for clutch replacement.
4. If the clutch disc has no visible faults, check it for thickness of the lining as follows:

(Check the distance between the friction surfaces of the clutch disc on a disc with riveted linings).

Thickness in tension = .362 ± .007 in (9,2 ± 0,2)
Wear limit = .314 — .307 in. (8 — 7,8 mm)
See illustration :
Distance A without tension = .397 — .015 in. (10,1 — 0,4 mm)

5. Check the clutch disc for runout at the linings; permissible runout is .024 in. (0,6 mm) (see illustration).

4. Place the 10K hexagon bolts with circlips into their holes, then evenly tighten them one or two turns at a time in a cross sequence to prevent distortion of the cover. Torque all bolts to 25 ft. lb. (3,5 mkp).

5. With the transmission attached to the engine, pull the clutch release lever in the direction of travel. The distance between the lever and the transmission housing must be not less than 4/5 in. (20 mm) (see illustration).

SERVICING CLUTCH THROWOUT BEARING

NOTE: Several changes were incorporated in clutch throwout bearing assemblies. Refer to the cautionary notes to determine type of bearing used and its part number.

Removal

1. Remove engine/transmission assembly as previously described in the ENGINE chapter.
2. Loosen Allen bolt in the clutch release fork.
3. Unhook the spring and pull out the throwout bearing and the release fork.

Replacing

1. Fill the bushing in the gland nut at the flywheel with a small amount of graphite grease or MoS₂ multipurpose grease (2 cc).
2. Fit the clutch disc with an arbor or a shortened clutch sliding shaft so that it is exactly central in the flywheel.
3. Push the clutch assembly onto the aligning dowels in the flywheel. Should the flywheel not be provided with dowel pins, align the clutch assembly with the help of the P 219 locating arbor or similar device (see illustration).

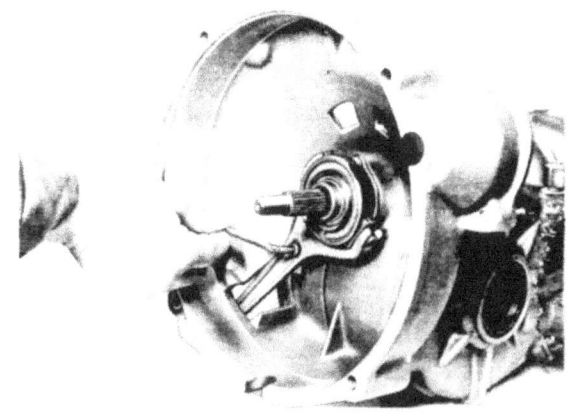

Checking

The throwout bearing is service free. DO NOT wash it in cleaning solvent or any other liquid, instead merely wipe it with a clean rag, or else the original grease content will be dissipated. Replace any throwout bearing which is dirty inside or is noisy.

Clutch fault tracing chart

Malfunction	Possible Cause	Remedy
1. Noisy clutch: when disengaging and driving away	a. Worn bushing in flywheel gland nut	a. Install new bushing and fill with 2 cc graphite grease
when disengaging	b. Excessively worn throwout bearing	b. Install new throwout bearing, ensure proper clutch free play
at acceleration or deceleration	c. Loose or damaged torsion damper in clutch disc	c. Install new clutch disc
2. Clutch chatters:	a. Loose cable conduit	a. Preload cable conduit
	b. Unsatisfactory action of undulated cushioning segments between disc linings	b. Install new clutch disc
	c. Transmission and engine not firm in support	c. Tighten attaching bolts and nuts. Replace engine and transmission support if damaged
3. Clutch drags:	a. Excessive clutch free play	a. Adjust clutch free play to 20-25 mm pedal travel
	b. Whipping clutch plate or transmission input shaft	b. Straighten or replace clutch disc or input shaft
	c. Clutch disc cushioning segments excessively tensioned	c. Install new clutch disc
	d. Transmission input shaft too tight in flywheel gland nut	d. Ream bushing in gland nut to specifications
	e. Insufficient clutch pedal travel	e. Check clutch pedal travel and adjust travel limiter.
4. Clutch slips:	a. Clutch free play too small, diminishing with clutch disc wear	a. Adjust clutch free play to 20-25 mm at clutch pedal
	b. Oiled or worn clutch disc linings	b. Install new clutch disc, if necessary replace oil seals at transmission or engine
	c. Weak diaphragm spring	c. Install new clutch assembly

Replacement

1. Coat all rubbing surfaces with multipurpose MoS₂ grease.
2. Torque Allen bolt in release fork to 7 ft. lb. (1 mkp).

CAUTION: Along with the introduction of the modified clutch release with live throwout bearing, the return spring, Part No. 901.116.731.01, is no longer needed. The modified clutch release may be recognized through a spring located on the clutch pedal shaft where it pushes the clutch pedal towards the floorboard, that is, the clutch pedal free travel can be checked by pulling the clutch pedal away from the floorboard.

NOTE: The later clutch throwout bearing, Part No. 901.116.081.11, is being installed beginning with the following dates:

Vehicle Type 912	From Jan. 12, 1967
Vehicle Type 911	From Jan. 12, 1967
Vehicle Type 911 S	From first vehicle

This part must only be used in conjunction with both plastic guides, Part No. 901.116.825.11. The bearing must be in free suspension in the release fork; if necessary, the plastic guides should be dressed with fine crocus cloth (see illustration). This assembly replaces the previous throwout bearing completely and is installed without further modification.

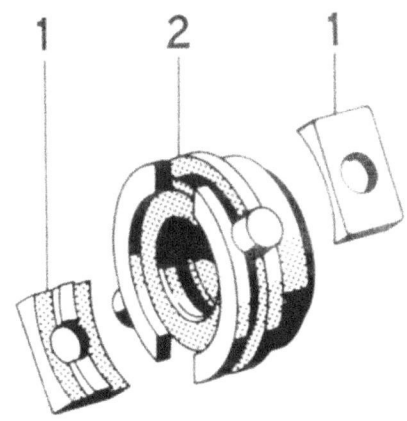

1 Plastic guide
2 Clutch throwout bearing

SERVICING THE CLUTCH WITHDRAWAL FORK BALL PIN

Removal

1. Remove the engine/transmission assembly as previously described in the ENGINE chapter, then carefully disconnect the transmission from the engine.
2. Loosen the Allen bolt in the clutch release fork.
3. Unhook the spring and pull out the throwout bearing and the release fork (see previous illustration).

WARNING: Do not wash the throwout bearing in cleaning solvent or any other liquid, instead merely wipe it with a clean rag, or else the original grease content will be dissipated. Replace any throwout bearing which is dirty inside or is noisy.

4. Unscrew the ball pin and remove it together with the sealing washer (see illustration).

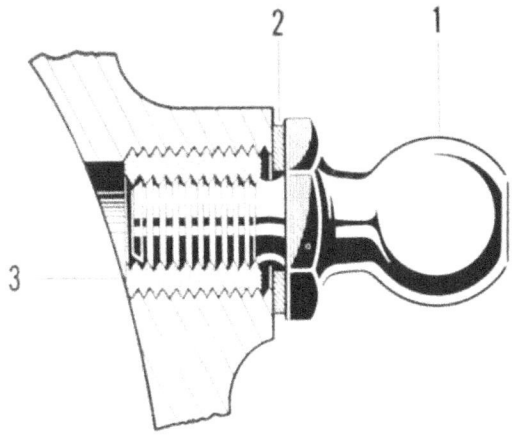

1 Ball pin
2 Sealing washer
3 Threaded insert

Checking

Examine ball pin and bush for visbile wear and replace if necessary.

NOTE: Up to Transmission No. 102082 or 222706, the ball pin was cemented in place into the transmission housing (see illustration).

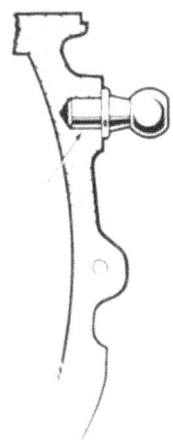

Replacement

1. Torque the ball pin and the sealing washer to 15 to 17 ft. lb. (2,1 to 2,3 mkp).
2. Apply multipurpose MoS₂ grease into the bushing for the ball pin and all sliding surfaces of the clutch thrust bearing.
3. Torque the Allen bolt of the withdrawal fork to 7 ft. lb. (1 mkp).

CLUTCH PEDAL TRAVEL LIMITER ADJUSTMENT

NOTE: Whenever work has been done on the clutch system, the clutch pedal travel must be checked, and if necessary, corrected. This is necessary since the diaphragm spring clutch requires an exactly limited clutch pedal travel.

Checking

1. Bring the transmission to operating temperature.
2. Depress the clutch pedal to stop. At this point it should be possible (after a quick pause between clutch pedal depression and gearshift movement) to SILENTLY engage reverse gear.
3. If this is not the case, adjust as follows, then recheck as described above.

Adjusting

The pedal limiter is secured with two 3 mm Allen head bolts in slot holes to permit adjustment.

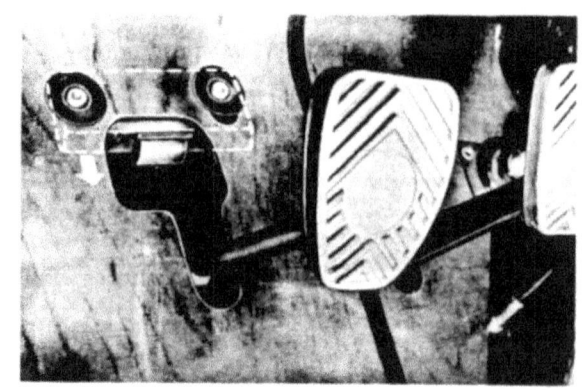

1. Loosen the rubber mat or carpeting and fold back.
2. Loosen both limiter retaining bolts with a 3 mm Allen-head wrench.
3. Slide the limiter up or down, as required, then tighten the limiter retaining bolts (see illustration).
4. Recheck the clutching-shifting action as described above, readjust pedal limiter until action is perfect.

ELECTRICAL SYSTEM

NOTE: Generating and ignition systems are covered in the POWER GENERATION AND IGNITION chapter further on in this manual.

NOTE: With few exceptions, repairs in the electrical system are confined to the replacement of worn or defective parts and the repair of the wiring system. In general, damaged wiring removed from the system should be replaced by wire of the same cross-section. BOSCH components should be replaced or serviced by BOSCH service whenever possible.

FUSES

The fuse box is located under the luggage compartment mat. Fuses are removed by opening plastic top and applying pressure against the retaining clamps. When a fuse burns out, investigate the cause rather than simply replacing the fuse. Note the accompanying chart for fuse location. It is advisable to carry a small supply of 8/15 and 25/40 ampere fuses in the car at all times.

1 High beam, left
2 High beam, right
  High beam indicator
3 Low beam, left
4 Low beam, right
5 Parking lamp, left
6 Parking lamp, right
7 License plate lamp and luggage compartment lamp
8 Fog lamps
9 Windshield wipers and washer
10 Auxiliary combustion heater
11 Interior light, cigar lighter, electric clock
12 Stop lights, blinkers, backup light

BATTERY

Description

The six-cell, 12 volt, 45 Ah battery acts as a cushion and reservoir for the electrical energy in the vehicle. It is located within the luggage compartment under the front lid. The negative terminal is connected to ground.

Testing

Use a voltmeter with a parallel wired resistance of 80 to 100 amps to test the battery. The voltage of a given cell must not drop below 1.6 volts during the test periods of 10-15 seconds each. Should the voltage drop below 1.6 volts, then the cell is defective or dead. Normal voltage is 2 volts. The voltage of the individual cells should not vary by more than 0.2 volts.

Servicing

Be sure that battery anchors are tight at all times, and that the battery terminals and wire clamps are clean. The terminals should be greased with vaseline or some other corrosion-preventing grease to keep the resistance low. Cable clamps which have corroded and cannot be lifted off the battery terminals must be removed with a puller. Spilled electrolyte must be immediately neutralized with a soda solution to prevent damage to fabrics and painted surfaces.

ROAD LIGHTS

Description

The two headlights are mounted in the front fenders and have high and low beams in each. Parking lights are accommodated in the front directional blinker housings. The parking lights and headlights are switched on through a switch on the instrument panel, next to the ignition switch. The headlights are dimmed with the blinker/dimmer/headlight flasher switch located on the steering post below the steering wheel. The flasher relay switch is located under the left floorboard. This unit reduces the current load on the headlights. A blue headlight control light in the tachometer dial goes on when the high beams are turned on.

The two tail lights go on with the headlights. Tail lights are combined with stop lights and directional blinkers. Two small lights illuminate the rear license plate.

The stop and tail lights use a common bulb for each side. The green turn signal control lights are situated within the tachometer dial. The turn signal pulse switch is located in the luggage compartment under the mat next

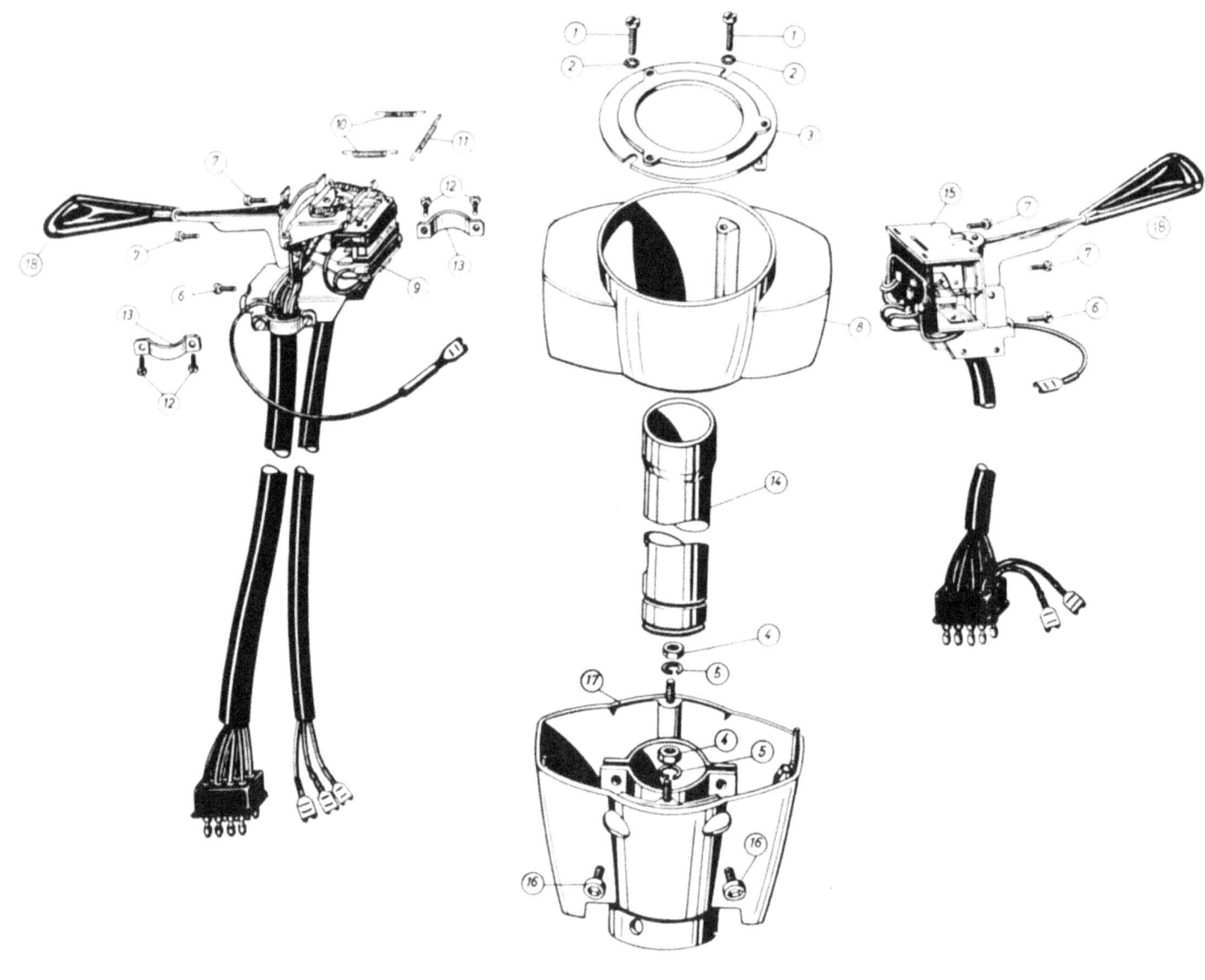

COMBINED BLINKER, DIMMER, AND HEADLAMP FLASHER SWITCH

1 ... Fillister screw
2 ... Serrated lock washer
3 ... Contact ring
4 ... Hex nut
5 ... Lock washer
6 ... Fillister screw
7 ... Round head countersunk screw
8 ... Upper housing assembly
9 ... Combination switch

10 ... Spring
11 ... Spring
12 ... Fillister screw
13 ... Clamp
14 ... Steering post extension
15 ... Wiper and washer switch
16 ... Allen bolt
17 ... Lower housing assembly
18 ... Lever knob

to the steering post support. A three-prong connector holds the switch in place, allowing easy removal. A magnetic switch interrupts the ground connection of the turn signal control light whenever one of the bulbs becomes inoperative to indicate this condition; this indicator works, naturally, only so long as the control light is in working order.

The stop lights are controlled by a switch mounted in the brake master cylinder. These go on when the foot brake is depressed. The backup lights go on when the reverse gear is engaged; the lights are located in the tail light housing, the switch is in the side of the transmission housing. The backup light switch is actuated through the respective positioning of the internal shift rod within the transmission when reverse gear is engaged, thus moving a contact pin which switches on the backup light.

Foreign Sealed-Beam Regulations

Cars equipped for export to America are equipped with sealed-beam headlights instead of the asymmetric-type headlights with bulbs. However, the sealed-beams are not approved for use on public roads in some European countries; at the time of this printing, the following countries prohibited the use of sealed-beam lights:

France, Holland, Italy, Sweden, and Germany

In the sealed-beam headlight, the double-filament bulb is replaced by a sealed unit which encompasses the reflector, lamp lens, and the filaments. When a filament fails, the entire unit must be replaced. The sealed-beam unit cannot be installed into normal headlight housings; installation is only possible by using special housings.

When driving the American-equipped export car in any of the above listed countries (such as when one takes delivery of the car in Europe and later has it shipped to America), the sealed-beam unit must be replaced with a so-called "sealed-beam substitute" (SB-substitute). This unit has the same shape as the regular sealed-beam unit, but it consists of only the headlight lens and reflector. In the center of the reflector is an opening for the placement of the normal double-filament bulb of the asymmetric type. When the car is returned to America, the substitutes must be replaced with regular sealed-beam units. The cable connector fits both the sealed-beam unit and the filament bulb, whichever is used.

Servicing Combined Blinker, Dimmer, and Flasher Switch

1. Remove steering wheel as outlined in the STEERING chapter.
2. Detach all wire connections from the combination switch.
3. Remove the screws from the horn contact ring, detach the wire, then remove the ring.
4. Remove the upper housing assembly retaining nuts and pull the assembly upward to remove. Lead wires and connectors should be withdrawn through the hole provided for that purpose.
5. Remove the three retaining screws which secure the combination switch and remove switch.
6. To install, reverse the above order, being sure that all wires are properly connected.

Blinker Switch Return Spring Servicing

Performs steps (1) and (3) above, then unhook return spring and install new spring. Replace horn contact ring and steering wheel.

Servicing Road Light Bulbs (except headlights)

1. Remove light unit retaining screws and remove unit.
2. Using a screwdriver, lift the plastic holder at the cut-off corner and withdraw holder.
3. On a bayonet lock bulb, push the bulb into the holder and turn it to the left, then pull bulb straight out.
4. Install a new bulb by lining up contact pins with their respective slots, pushing bulbs into their holders, then turning bulb 90° to the right until the socket pins have engaged their seat.
5. Place the holder into the lamp unit and push lightly in so it snaps into place.
6. Install light unit, then tighten retaining screws.
7. Check light for proper functioning.

NOTE: Handle glass bulb with a soft paper or clean towel to keep it free of grease.

Servicing License Plate Light

1. Remove both screws that hold the license plate light assembly to the engine compartment lid and withdraw the light assembly.
2. Replace the bulb, keeping it free of dirt and grease, then replace the assembly.

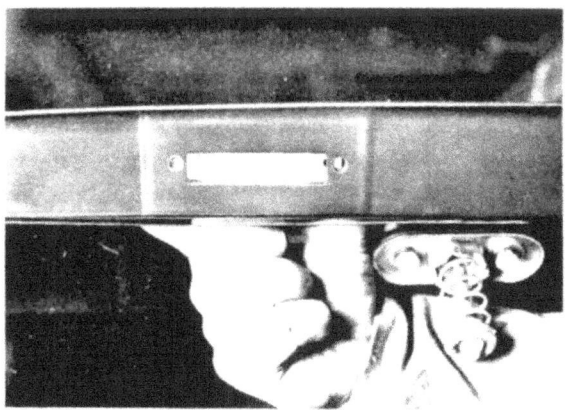

Servicing Backup Light Switch

NOTE: The backup light switch is actuated by the transmission selector shaft of 1st and reverse gear over an actuating pin. When reverse is selected, a slanted tab pushes the actuating pin outward and actuates the switch. The transmission need not be removed from the vehicle for this operation.

1. Withdraw the cover cap from the switch and pull the connecting wires off the terminals.

2. Unscrew the switch from the housing, then withdraw the actuating pin.
3. To replace, insert the actuating pin, with the installed retaining ring. Be sure the longer, rounded end is facing into the bore guide in the transmission housing (see illustration).

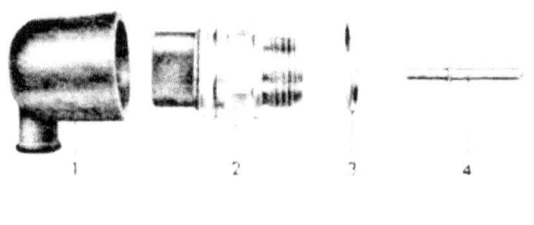

1 Cover cap
2 Backup light switch
3 Gasket
4 Actuating pin with spring retainer

4. Screw the switch in and make sure that the gasket is well seated.

Servicing Sealed-Beam Headlights

1. Loosen Phillips screw in the lower center of the lamp rim and withdraw rim and lens.
2. Withdraw cable connector.
3. Remove clips holding sealed-beam unit in place, then withdraw sealed beam unit.
4. Reverse the above procedure to install, being sure sealed-beam unit is upright and aligned.
5. Check lights for proper functioning.

Servicing Headlight Lens

1. Unscrew Phillips screw in the lower center of the lamp rim, then withdraw rim and lens.
2. Remove clips holding sealed-beam unit in place, then withdraw sealed-beam unit.
3. Unscrew adjusting screws fully (on lamp rim), then remove reflector.
4. Using a screwdriver, remove lens retainers from rim.
5. Take out lens or glass remnants.
6. Place rubber sealing ring onto new headlight lens and place lens into the lamp rim so that the BOSCH inscription is upright, or the wedge-shaped asymmetric low beam outlet in the lens is on the left side when looking in the direction of travel.
7. Replace retaining ring with reflector, check if the sealing ring between the lens holder and retaining ring is well positioned.
8. Install sealed-beam unit, then adjust headlights.

Testing Headlight Voltage

1. Remove headlight unit.
2. Connect a voltmeter to the two terminals (yellow and brown, or white and brown), and switch on the headlights.
3. The voltage should read 12 to 12.5 volts when the engine is running at about 2,000 rpm and the headlights are switched on.
4. If the voltage reading is not as above, perform the following tests:
   a. Check battery terminals for proper attachment and oxidation.
   b. Check regulator connections for tightness.
   c. Check slip-on connections in light switch for tightness.
   d. Check electrical conductivity at both ends of the fuse box, including the fuse, for oxidation and firm seating.
   e. Check the wire connections at the sealed-beam connector.
5. If the voltage is still not 12 to 12.5 volts, check the voltage after installing a new sealed-beam unit. Aged units with weakened filaments can cause a voltage drop.
6. If the voltage is still not up to requirements, then the defect probably lies in the battery, generator, or voltage regulator.

HAZARD WARNING LIGHTS

Description

The warning light system consists of the main parts listed below which may be had in kit form, as No. 901.612.901.00:
1. 1 Hazard light push-pull switch with control lamp.
2. 1 Relay switch.
3. 1 Flasher unit.
4. 1 Light fuse.

The switch is mounted on the instrument panel above the radio compartment cover. The relay switch and flasher unit are mounted under the left floorboard (below the pedals) next to the headlight signal flasher relay. The fuse holder for the hazard light system is located under the luggage compartment carpeting, next to the main fuse box. The necessary wire connections are included in the wire loom of all cars regardless of whether or not these leave the plant with the hazard light system installed.

Operation

The hazard light system is switched on by pulling out the switch knob, at which time a red control light goes on to indicate that the system is in operation. With the switch in the ON position, the regular directional signal system is switched off through the hazard light relay switch. A label attached to the hazard light switch serves as a reminder against misuse of the system.

Installation or Servicing

1. Install switch in the center hole (prefabricated) above the radio compartment cover in the instrument panel.
2. Install hazard light relay switch and flasher unit under the floorboard next to the headlight signal flasher relay.
3. Connect wires with fuse by following the wiring diagram and the color code.

WIRING DIAGRAM FOR HAZARD WARNING LIGHT SYSTEM

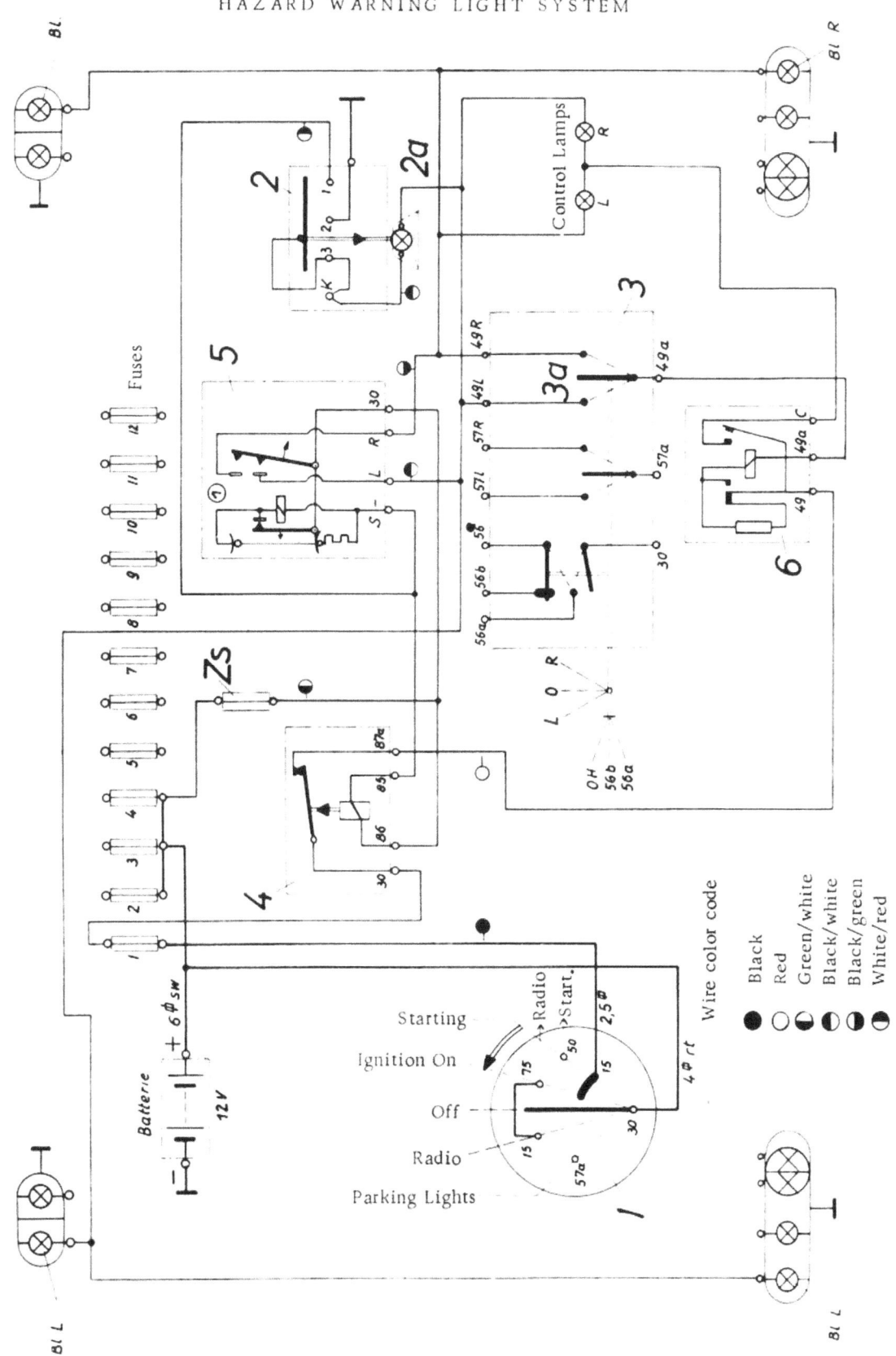

INSTRUMENTS AND INTERIOR LIGHTS

Description

The tachometer is transistorized; electrical pulses eminating from the ignition system pass through a transistorized converter and are fed into an electric counter in the tachometer unit.

The speedometer, odometer, and trip mileage counter are driven by means of a cable drive from a gear in the transmission. The speedometer indication is effected through the application of eddy currents. A disc-shaped magnet rotates within a closely-spaced aluminum shell. The shell is connected to the speedometer needle. A spiral spring counterbalances the force to return the needle. As the car moves and thus, the driving cable rotates, both the eddy currents and the spring maintain an equilibrium. This causes the speedometer to show the given speed at which the vehicle is moving.

The odometer drive consists of a triple reduction gear. The odometer has a five-digit counter. The trip mileage counter can be reset to zero with a knob on the instrument panel.

The fuel level is indicated by means of a fuel gauge which is connected to an electrical sending unit in the fuel tank. In addition, the gauge has a low fuel warning light.

The oil temperature gauge and the pressure gauge are electrically connected to their sending units in the crankcase. The oil level gauge is connected to its sending unit in the oil tank.

Instrument lights go on when road lights are turned on, and instrument light brightness can be varied with the light switch knob by turning it to the desired position.

The interior lights are located above the doors. The lights can be turned on or off by tilting the entire lens left or right. In the same manner, the lights can be set for courtesy operation together with the opening doors via a door contact switch located in the forward door post. The cigar lighter in the instrument panel can also be used for plugging in a hand light or other accessories. A light in the luggage compartment goes on automatically when the lid is raised.

Removing and Installing Instruments

NOTE: Disconnect battery to prevent shorts. Connecting terminals of all instruments are accessible from the luggage compartment upon removal of the carpeting.

1. Detach all cables from the instrument that is to be removed.
2. In the case of the speedometer, also remove the cable knurled nut and withdraw the cable and housing.
3. Remove the small knurled nuts which secure the instrument, withdraw the retaining clamp, and carefully remove the instrument from the passenger compartment side.
4. Reverse the above order to install new or repaired instruments.

Servicing Instrument Lights (control and illumination)

1. Loosen luggage compartment carpeting retainers and pull carpeting forward.

2. Pull out the respective lamp socket from a defective component.

CAUTION: Do not remove lamp socket by pulling on the wiring.

3. Remove bulb from socket, then replace with new bulb of the same type.
4. Reverse the above order to install.

Servicing Fuel Gauge Sender Unit

1. Loosen luggage compartment carpeting retainers and fold back carpeting.
2. Withdraw multiple-pin socket.
3. Unscrew sender retaining bolts and remove sender unit.
4. Reverse the above order to install, checking the gasket for condition and proper seating.

Servicing Door Contact Switch

1. Remove rubber cap from switch, which is found on the forward door post (see illustration).
2. Unscrew contact switch with a 12 mm box wrench, then detach wire.
3. Connect a new switch to wire and reinstall switch.

Replacing Interior Light Bulb

1. Gently press the lamp base out with a screwdriver, always applying force at the rear part of the base, toward the car's front end (see illustration).
2. Make sure that the bulb holding clamps are sufficiently tensioned to firmly hold the new 10 W cartridge bulb in place.
3. Install unit by pressing into place.

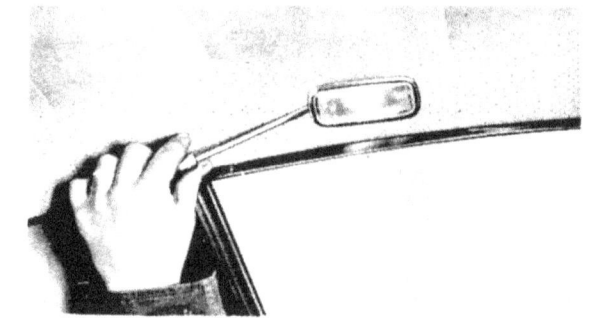

Replacing Luggage Compartment Bulb

1. Remove the glass lens on the lower part of the lid.
2. Replace the 4 W cartridge bulb which is held in clamp contacts.
3. Replace glass lens.

WINDSHIELD WIPER AND WASHER

Description

The windshield wiper motor and actuating linkage are located just in front of the instrument units. The motor is controlled by a four-position wiper/washer switch. The windshield wiper linkage joints are service-free. The wiper blades should make even contact with the windshield and move equally far on both sides. Worn blades should be replaced to prevent streaking of the glass.

The electrical windshield washer pump is located in the forward luggage compartment next to the windshield washer reservoir (later type).

NOTE: Up to Chassis Serial No. 302,695 the windshield washer reservoir was installed in a recess alongside the luggage compartment floor. The windshield washer pump was installed in the right rear part of the luggage compartment under the carpeting (early type).

Removing and Replacing Wiper Motor With Linkage

1. Remove the forward ventilating case after removing the retaining clip and air duct (see illustration).

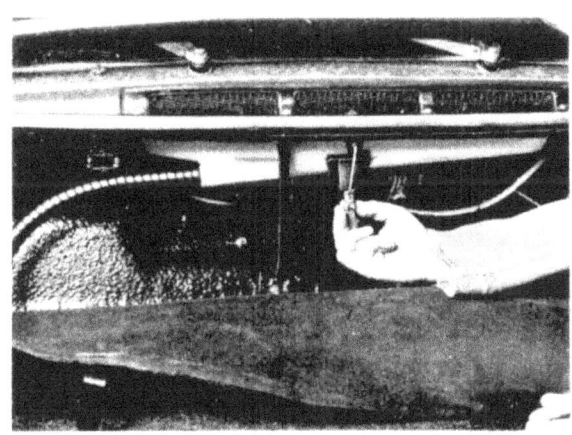

2. Detach the five wire terminals from the wiper motor.
3. Remove the wiper arms by depressing clip and wedging with screwdriver.
4. Remove rubber discs located beneath the wiper arms and unscrew retaining hex nuts (see illustration).
5. Withdraw wiper motor downward, together with linkage.
6. When replacing the wiper system, check for proper placement of connecting wires and free movement of the linkage.

Removing & Replacing Windshield Washer System (early type)

1. Pump the reservoir completely dry, remove cap and hose, then remove reservoir by turning it.
2. Remove washer pump by detaching cables, then remove suction and pressure hoses.
3. Loosen plastic retaining straps from pump and pull the pump out.
4. To replace both units, reverse above procedures.

Removing & Replacing Windshield Washer System (later type)

1. Remove both slotted screws which secure the reservoir, then withdraw the reservoir.
2. Detach the wires and loosen the plastic retaining straps from the pump, then withdraw the pump.
3. To replace both units, reverse the above procedure.

HORNS

The signal horns are shock-mounted under both front fenders. See STEERING chapter for horn button servicing.

Servicing

1. Detach snap-on wire connectors.
2. Remove horn retaining nut, then withdraw horn.
3. When replacing the horn, make sure that it does not make contact with the body.

STARTER DESCRIPTION

An 8/10 HP, 12 volt, solenoid-operated started is used. The starter is controlled by the ignition/starter switch on the instrument panel. This DC motor provides a considerable amount of torque needed for turning the crankshaft at speeds needed for starting the engine, and with enough force to overcome the initial resistance on the compression stroke. The starter has a helical spline drive with a

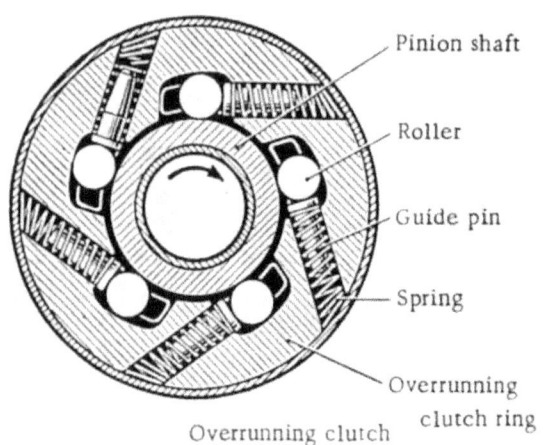

self-releasing pinion (BOSCH Type EB). To obtain the necessary torque from a starter and battery of proportionately acceptable size, the starter drives the starter ring on the flywheel with a small pinion. The gear teeth in the starter ring and starter pinion are beveled on one side to make engagement smoother.

REMOVING AND REPLACING STARTER

Removal

1. Disconnect battery ground strap.
2. Detach battery and alternator cables from terminal 30 at the starter.
3. Detach control wire (to ignition switch) from terminal 50 at the starter.
4. Unscrew flanging bolts and remove starter.

NOTE: If the starter gear on the flywheel shows unusual traces of wear, the starter ring will have to be replaced. When reinstalling, make sure that the terminals are clean and properly tightened.

Replacement

Reverse the removal procedure, noting the following terminal numbers:

1. Battery ground strap.
2. Generator and battery cables at the starter solenoid.
3. Control wire to ignition switch.

REMOVING AND REPLACING STARTER SOLENOID

Removal

1. Detach wire strand from solenoid (see illustration).
2. Remove retaining bolts of solenoid from the drive housing.
3. Pull starter pinion out a bit and remove solenoid switch.

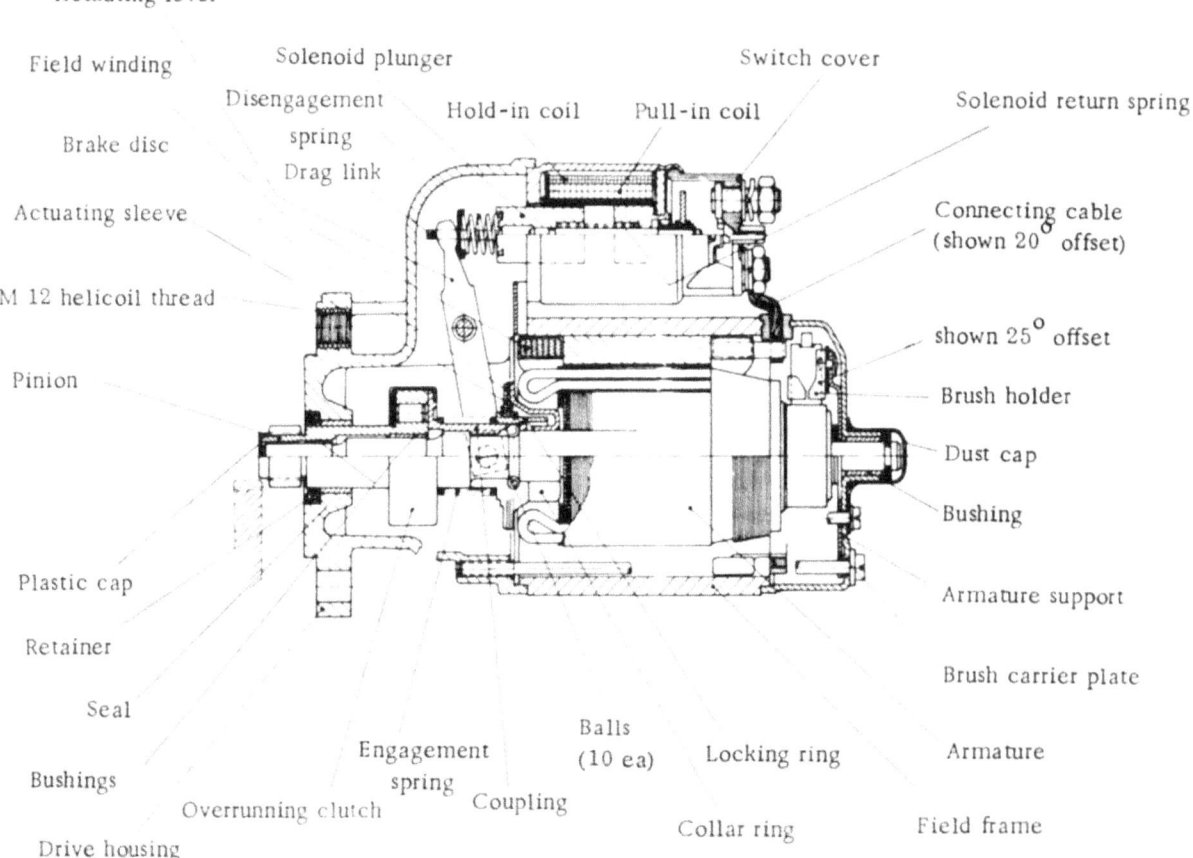

Replacement

Reverse the removal procedure, noting the following points:

1. Defective solenoids should be replaced with new units. It is advisable to install a new solenoid during engine overhaul. Do not attempt to readjust the solenoid.
2. Hold the cable terminals with pliers when tightening the cable retaining nuts in the solenoid. Tighten the nuts only moderately tight since it is possible to twist the solenoid switch contacts.
3. Pull the starter pinion forward so that the connecting end of the actuating lever moves closer to the solenoid mounting flange, and insert the connecting end of the solenoid plunger into the receptacle in the actuating lever.
4. When installing a new solenoid switch, adjust the connecting end of the solenoid plunger so that the distance from the hole center in the plunger clevis to the switch mounting flange is 1.276 in. ± .004 in. (32,4 ± 0,1 mm) when the plunger is in position.
5. To check engagement operation, connect solenoid so the switch pulls up (don't make motor turn needlessly). When the switch pulls up, travel of the solenoid plunger must be .394 in. ± .008 in. (10 ± 0,2 mm). Of that, .118 in. (3 mm) is engagement reserve.

BRUSH AND COMMUTATOR SERVICING

1. Remove starter dust cover.
2. Brushes which completely disappear into the holders so that the connecting strand touches the holder are worn out. Also, brushes that have become oily or have a loose connecting strand should be replaced with new ones of the same type.
3. When installing the new brushes, make sure that the connecting strands are free so as to prevent their binding in the holder. If one brush is worn down, it is best to install a whole new set.
4. Check brush springs for tension (see TECHNICAL DATA). Slacked or annealed springs must be replaced.
5. If the commutator is oily or dirty, it can be cleaned with a clean cloth wrapped around a wooden stick and wetted in gasoline. Be sure to keep gasoline and dirt out of the bearing.
6. If the commutator is scored or uneven, it should be redressed on a lathe.

STARTER SERVICING

Disassembly

1. Remove dust cover, lock ring, and spacers, being sure not to loose the O-rings. Detach connecting strand from the solenoid (see illustration).
2. Remove solenoid retaining screws. Withdraw solenoid from drive housing, at the same time unhooking the solenoid plunger from the actuating lever.
3. Remove through bolts and commutator support.
4. Withdraw the brushes from their holders. Note that the plus-brushes are soldered to the winding, and the minus-brushes to the brush holders (see illustration).

5. Remove the brush carrier plate, noting the location of the insulating washer and metal disc (see illustration).

6. Take field frame off drive housing, noting the sealing rubber and metal plate. Remove the stud bolt from the drive housing (see illustration).
7. Remove armature and actuating lever from the drive housing.

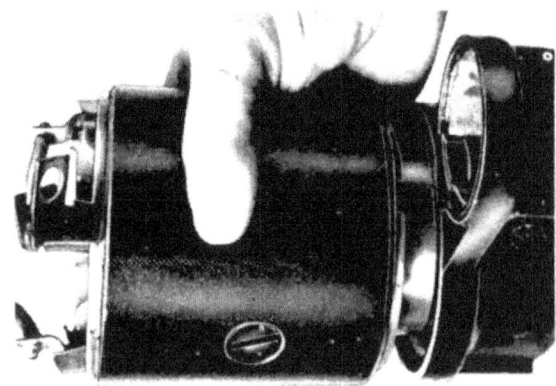

on the armature shaft. The actuating lever and linkage must not rub or bind anywhere. Bent actuating levers must be replaced (see illustration for a good part).

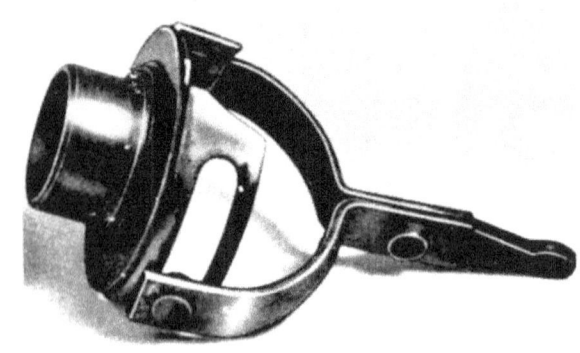

2. Replace brake disc, if necessary.
3. Field coil must not be scorched or have its solder melted, nor must it protrude past the pole shoes. Check the coil for continuity. Closely inspect connecting joints (see illustration).

8. Place armature in a vise. Press actuating sleeve against the overrunning clutch and take it off the armature shaft, noting the location of the locking balls (see illustration).

4. Test brush carrier plate and field coil for shorting to ground. Use a test voltage of 40 volts AC (see illustration).
5. Test armature for shorts to ground, using the same voltage as above (see illustration).

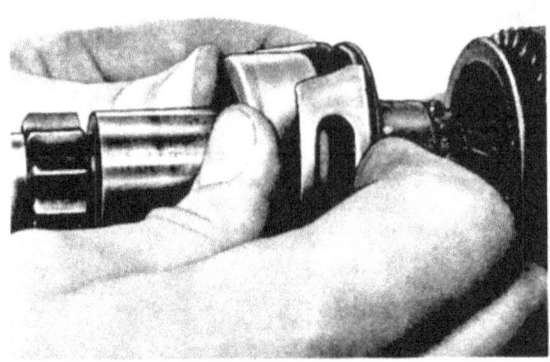

Cleaning

1. Clean all parts (except armature or overrunning clutch) in cleaning solvent and blow out with air.
2. Replace bearing bushings.

Inspecting and Servicing Parts

1. The mechanical engagement parts must slide freely

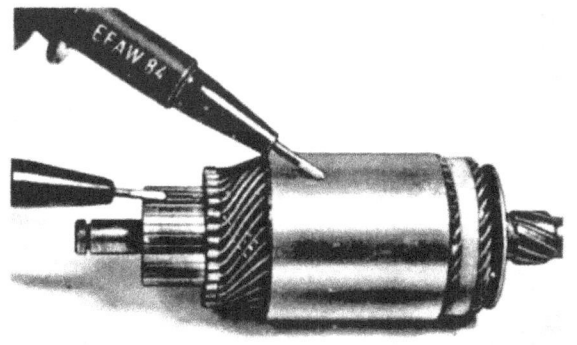

NOTE: A ground short will occur when the armature core comes in contact with the winding or when carbon dust has entered the assembly (direct or indirect short to ground). The best method to test the armature is with a test lamp by connecting one lead to the metal core of the armature and the other to the commutator. The test lamp should not light.

6. Commutator specifications should agree to the following: Maximum permissible runout should be .002 in. (0,05 mm), and minimum diameter should be 1.319 in. (33,5 mm). If necessary, remove insulating mica to a depth of about .031 in. (0,8 mm) with a commutator file, working with care around the segments and soldered points (see illustration).

7. The brushes must move freely in the holders. If the brushes are dirty, broken or unsoldered, replace the whole set.

8. Replace worn or unserviceable bearing bushings in the drive housing, using proper drivers for pressing the bushings in or out. The bushing must be flush on the inside. Peen with care.

9. When replacing the sintered metal bushing and the sealing ring, replace the rivets with screws and peen the screw ends. Use four M4 x 10 Fillister screws, four spring washers, and four suitable nuts (see illustration).

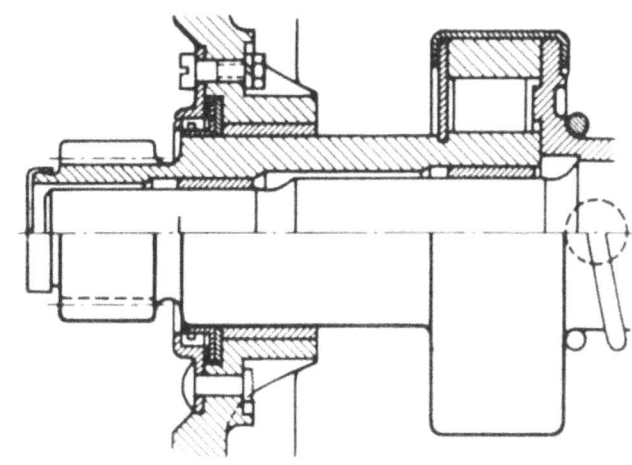

10. Center the sealing ring with an aligning mandrel (see illustration).

Reassembly

1. Place balls into locking ring with grease (such as Ft 2 v 3) (see illustration).

2. Place armature in a vise. Push overrunning clutch with actuating sleeve and brake disc onto the armature shaft until the balls engage the groove in the shaft (see illustration).

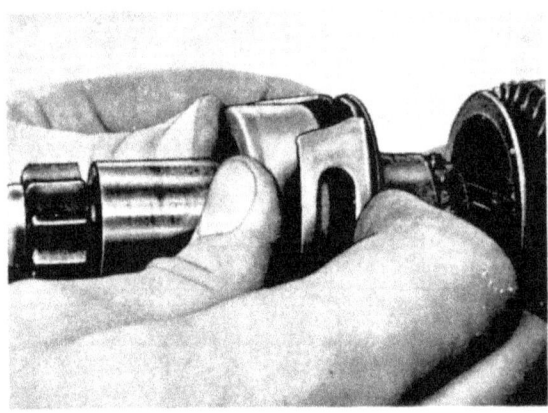

3. Make sure the pinion and overrunning clutch are properly seated on the armature shaft. The mechanical engagement parts must move freely on the armature when released (see illustration).

4. Push armature together with the actuating lever into the drive housing.
5. Screw pivot stud of actuating lever into drive housing. Tab of profiled rubber must seat in the cutout within the field frame (see illustration).

6. Push the field frame over the armature. Do not forget the steel shims and insulating washer on the commutator side.
7. Place the brush carrier plate onto the commutator shaft. Brush pressure should be 40.6—47.6 oz. (1150—1350 p). Note the placement of the twist notch in the plate (see illustration).

8. Make sure that the rubber grommet for the connecting strand fits properly as the dust cover is installed. The ground connections between the brush carrier plate and cover, as well as between the cover and housing, must be bare (see illustration).

9. Install spacer discs and lock ring. Axial play of armature should be .004—.006 in. (0,1—0,15 mm) (see illustration).

10. Bolt cap of commutator bearing in place. Connect the solenoid plunger and bolt solenoid switch to drive housing. Connect terminal of winding to solenoid switch (see illustration).

RADIO

The car's radio should perform well under relatively poor conditions. The major problems encountered are:

1. Signal strength (antenna input) is very low due to the short length of the antenna.
2. The ignition system, generator, and windshield wiper motor are a more or less constant source of static or interference.

The latter problem causes the most trouble. For this reason then, it is of great importance that the vehicle is kept free of interference generators, especially in the case of FM reception. Loose ground connections, for one, are a common source of static noise. When installing a radio in the car, much care should be devoted to checking the ground connections. Normally, radio noise suppressors are selected by the set manufacturer and may be found in the radio accessory lists.

If a test drive should reveal that the radio reception still suffers from static or other interference, despite the installation of suppressors, the entire system should be rechecked, including all ground connections. If further corrections should be necessary, use the services of a radio shop which will have the necessary testing equipment on hand.

NOTE: The maximum suppressor condenser capacity between the generator terminal D+ and ground is 3.0 mfd, and at the regulator terminal D+ it is 0.3 mfd, since otherwise the contacts will burn.

BULB CHART

All bulbs 12 volts

Qty	Nomenclature	Wattage
2	Twin filiament headlamp bulbs	45/40 W
2	Sealed beam inserts (US made)	50/40 W
4	Cartridge bulbs for parking and license plate lamps	4 W
2	Cartridge bulbs for parking lamps (Italy)	3 W
4	Single filiament bulbs for directional blinkers	18 W
4	Single filiament bulbs for directional blinkers (Italy)	15 W
(6)	Single filiament bulbs for directional blinkers and backup lights (USA)	32 cp
(2)	Twin filiament bulbs for stop and tail lights (USA)	32/4 cp
2	Twin filiament bulbs for stop and tail lights	18/5 W
2	Single filiament bulbs for backup lights	25 W
2	Cartridge bulbs for interior lights	10 W
1	Single filiament bulb for luggage compartment light	5 W
16	Bulbs for instrument illumination and control lamps	2 W
(2)	Single filiament bulbs for parking lights (USA)	2 cp

STARTER TROUBLE CHART

Symptom	Cause	Remedy
Starter does not turn when starter switch is actuated:	Switch the lights on for testing: a. Lights do not burn: Wire connecting or ground broken; dead battery. b. Lights burn but go dim or off when starter switch is turned on: Excessive resistance due to loose or corroded connections. c. Lights burn but slowly grow dim when starter is engaged: Low battery. d. Lights burn brightly. Jump-wire Terminal 30 with 50 at starter: starter runs. Connection 50 to starter switch broken; connection 30 to light switch broken; ignition/starter switch defective. e. Lights burn brightly, solenoid working Battery cable from Terminal 30 at the starter should be detached and connected to the contact bolt of the connecting strip -- starter runs. Solenoid contacts worn or dirty.	a. Check battery cables and connections. Check battery charge, recharge if necessary. b. Clean battery terminals and clamps. Make sure that electrical connections between battery, starter, and ground are adequate. c. Charge battery. d. Eliminate defect, replace defective parts. e. Replace solenoid.
Starter does not turn when battery cable is placed directly onto the contact bolt of the connecting strip; starter turns too slow or can't turn crankshaft:	a. The brushes are sticking. b. Worn brushes. c. Insufficient spring tension; brushes not making contact. d. Dirty commutator. e. Scored or scorched commutator. f. Defective armature or field coils.	a. Clean brushes and holders in the brush carrier. b. Replace brushes. c. Replace springs. d. Clean commutator. e. Overhaul starter. f. Overhaul starter.
Starter engages and pulls, but engine does not turn or turns only intermittently; pinion does not disengage:	a. Dead battery. b. Excessive resistance due to loose or corroded connections. c. Brushes are sticking. d. Worn out brushes. e. Dirty commutator. f. Scored or scorched commutator. g. Defective starter or field coils.	a. Charge battery. b. Clean battery terminals and clamps, tighten connections. c. Clean brushes and brush holders. d. Replace brushes. e. Clean the commutator. f. Overhaul starter. g. Overhaul starter.
Starter engages and pulls, but engine does not turn or turns only intermittently.	a. Defective pinion. b. Defective starter ring in flywheel.	a. Replace pinion. b. Dress starter ring, replace flywheel if necessary.
Pinion does not disengage:	a. Dirty or defective pinion or helical spline shaft. b. Defective solenoid switch.	a. Overhaul starter. b. Replace solenoid.

STARTER

TECHNICAL DATA

EB 12 V, 0.8 HP

Minimum voltage for solenoid actuation	7 volts
Specifications:	
Brush pressure	$42.3 {}^{+5.29}_{-1.76}$ oz ($1200 {}^{+150}_{-50}$ p)
Armature axial play	.004 - .006" (0.10 - 0.15 mm)
Overrun torque of clutch	1.56 - 2.17 in-lb (1.8-2.5 kpcm)
Brake torque	3.04 - 4.34 in-lb (3.5-5.0 kpcm)

NOTE: Later data is found at the end of the POWER GENERATION AND IGNITION chapter.

Lubricants

Lubrication prior to or during the reassembly.

Lubricants (BOSCH)	Lubricating Points	Dosage
Ft 2 v 3	Engagement Parts Coupling shaft, coil springs, locking ring, surfaces of the guide pan for the actuating lever pin, discs, and 10 greased balls.	Grease well
Ft 2 v 3	Armature Shaft Pinion running surface, helical spline shaft, commutator bearing	Grease lightly
Ol 1 v 13	Shaft Bushing Bushings in drive housing and commutator support	Oil well
Ft 2 v 3	Actuating Lever Pivot stud, studs in coupling	Grease lightly
Ft 2 v 3	Thrust Washers -on commutator side of armature	Grease lightly
Ft 2 v 3	Solenoid Switch Pivot, spring, spring pan at the actuating lever receptacle	Grease lightly

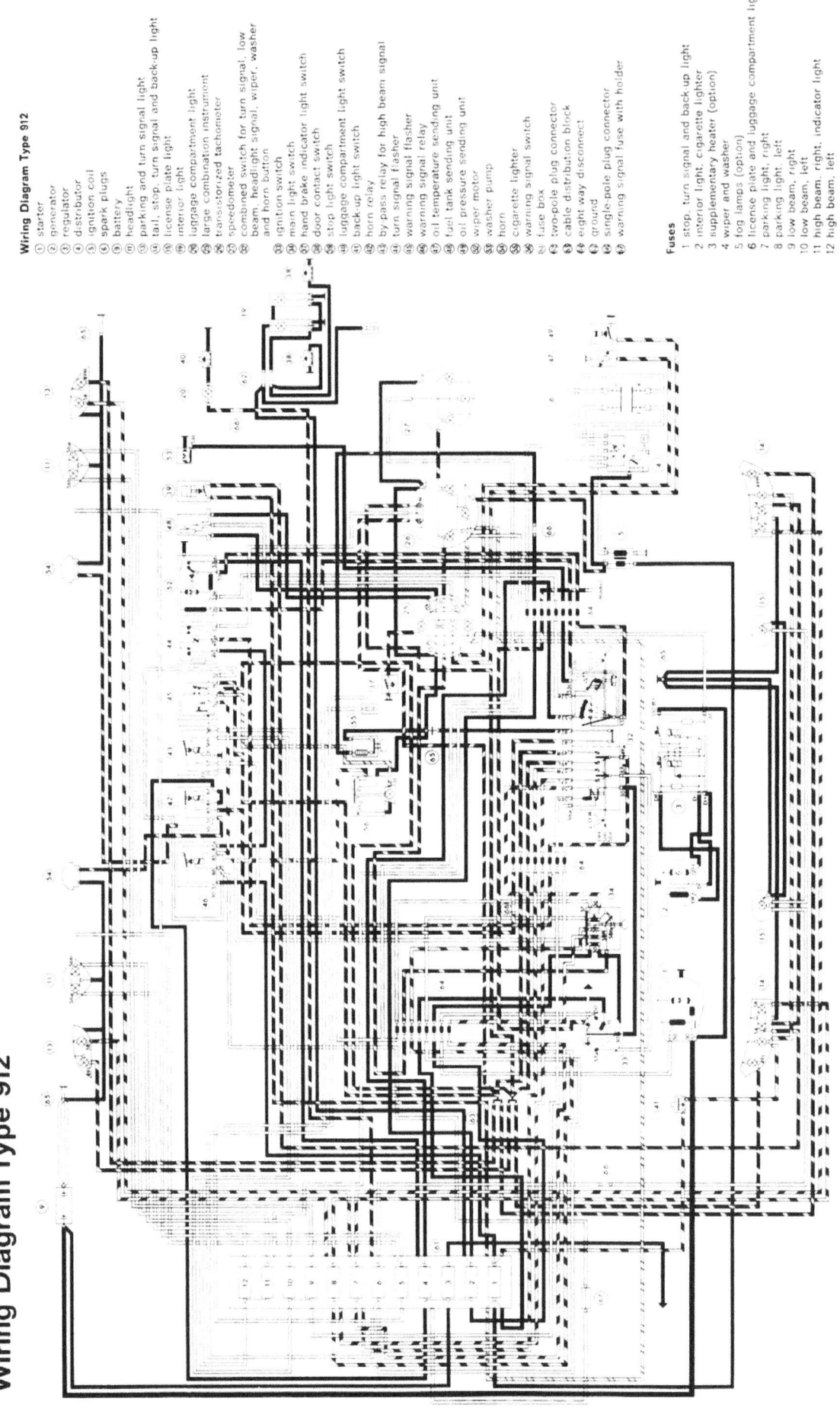

POWER GENERATION AND IGNITION

WARNING: Should the red ignition warning light stay on after the engine is started or while the engine is running, investigate the cause immediately. The light not only serves as a check on the generator, but also on the fan belt and cooling fan. Should the belt break, not only will be generator and fan remain stationary, but the engine and oil cooler will overheat.

WARNING: A very common problem is for the cable connector AT THE STARTER SOLENOID (observed from under the vehicle) to come loose, in which case the battery will not receive the output of the generator, even though the red ignition warning light WILL STAY OUT. This connector joins one cable from the voltage regulator and a separate cable from the battery to the starter solenoid.

NOTE: Data is at the end of this chapter. The wiring diagram is located at the end of the ELECTRICAL SYSTEM chapter. See the same chapter for other electrical system components.

GENERATOR AND REGULATOR

DESCRIPTION

The generator and regulator combination supplies power to all the electrical units in the vehicle and keeps the battery in a state of charge. The generator is driven by the engine through a V-belt. The variode-limited regulator (which uses a semiconductor) controls the voltage output. Generator output varies according to the loading of the generator by the current consuming units or by the varying speed of the engine. This "toggle" regulator has a sloping characteristic curve, varied by a control winding.

With this system, the DC shunt-wound generator operates at about the same level of voltage output no matter what the input speed and loading. The electro-magnetic high-speed regulator keeps the voltage output independent, and also prevents overloading of the battery. An electro-magntic switch switches the generator on automatically and at low speeds disconnects it from the battery so that discharge of the battery through the generator is prevented. Regulator and switch are combined to form a regulator switch, and the regulator has a definite output limitation.

The variode regulator has on the voltage regulator unit a second winding. This control winding is connected on one side to the switch contact, while on the other side it is connected to D+ via the variode (see generator/regulator wiring diagram). When current flows through the main current lead a potential drop arises between D+ and the switch contact. When the output limit of the generator is reached, the variode semiconductor becomes conductive as a result of the potential drop. This causes a current flow in the control winding, and this in turn strengthens the magnetic field on the voltage regulator unit, causing a reduction in generator potential. Thus the generator is protected against overload.

The generator is made up of the pole housing with the pole shoes and the exciter coils connected in series. These coils consist of a large number of windings of insulated copper wire. Between the pole shoes rotates the armature, an iron core onto which are imbedded the windings (armature conductors) of the armature coil and on whose shaft is also fitted the commutator (current reversal switch) from which the induced generator potential is collected by the carbon brushes. These are pressed against the commutator under uniform spring pressure and are located in box-shaped brush holders (see illustration). The armature rotates in the bearing cap (drive bearing and commutator bearing, and is also the shaft for the cooling system fan. The voltage regulator is mounted on the engine compartment wall.

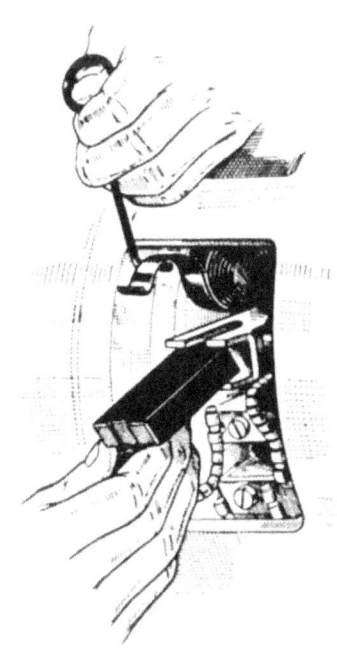

GENERATOR MAINTENANCE

1. Check the carbon brushes for wear and free travel every 6,000 mi. (10,000 km). Brushes can be examined after removal of the cover strap, and should be replaced if worn. Do not oil brushes (see previous illustration).
2. Normally the ball bearings should be replaced at the same time as the brushes.

WARNING LIGHT SERVICING

Description

The red ignition warning light is connected between terminal D+ and 61 of the generator regulator switch and lights up in the combination instrument on the instrument panel when the ignition is switched on. After starting the engine, the light should go out as soon as the increasing charge voltage of the generator equals the battery voltage. The light not only serves as a check on the generator, but also on the fan belt and cooling fan. Should the belt break, not only will the generator and fan remain stationary, but the oil cooler and engine will overheat.

Checking

1. As the ignition switch is turned, the red ignition warning light should come on. Leave switch in this position.
2. Remove generator cable from terminal D+ on the regulator. The light should go out.
3. If light stays on, the cable is shorting to ground. Check cable and correct problem, then reconnect to terminal D+/61.

Servicing Bulb

1. Remove luggage compartment carpeting from area of dashboard.

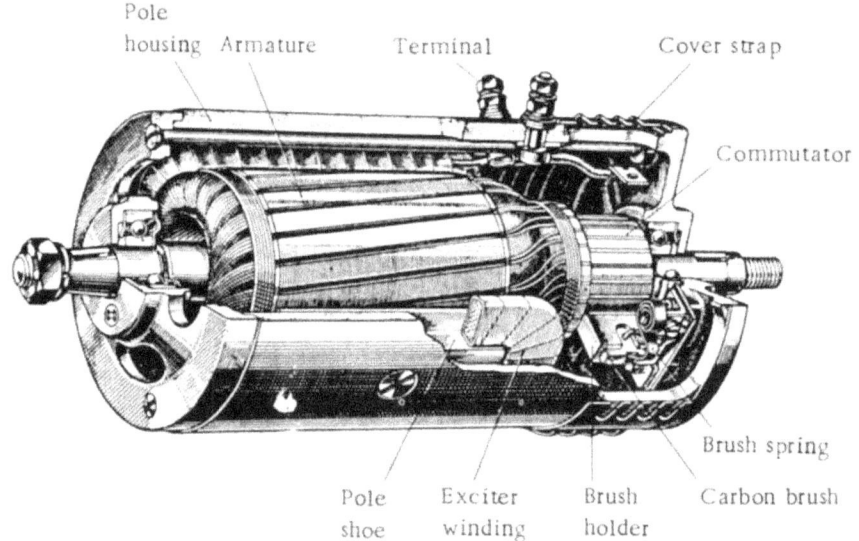

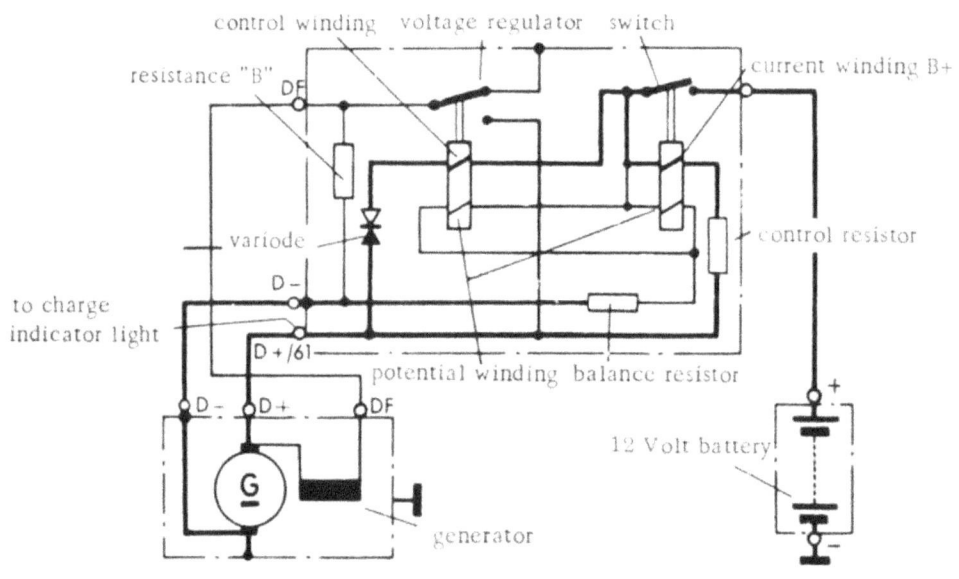

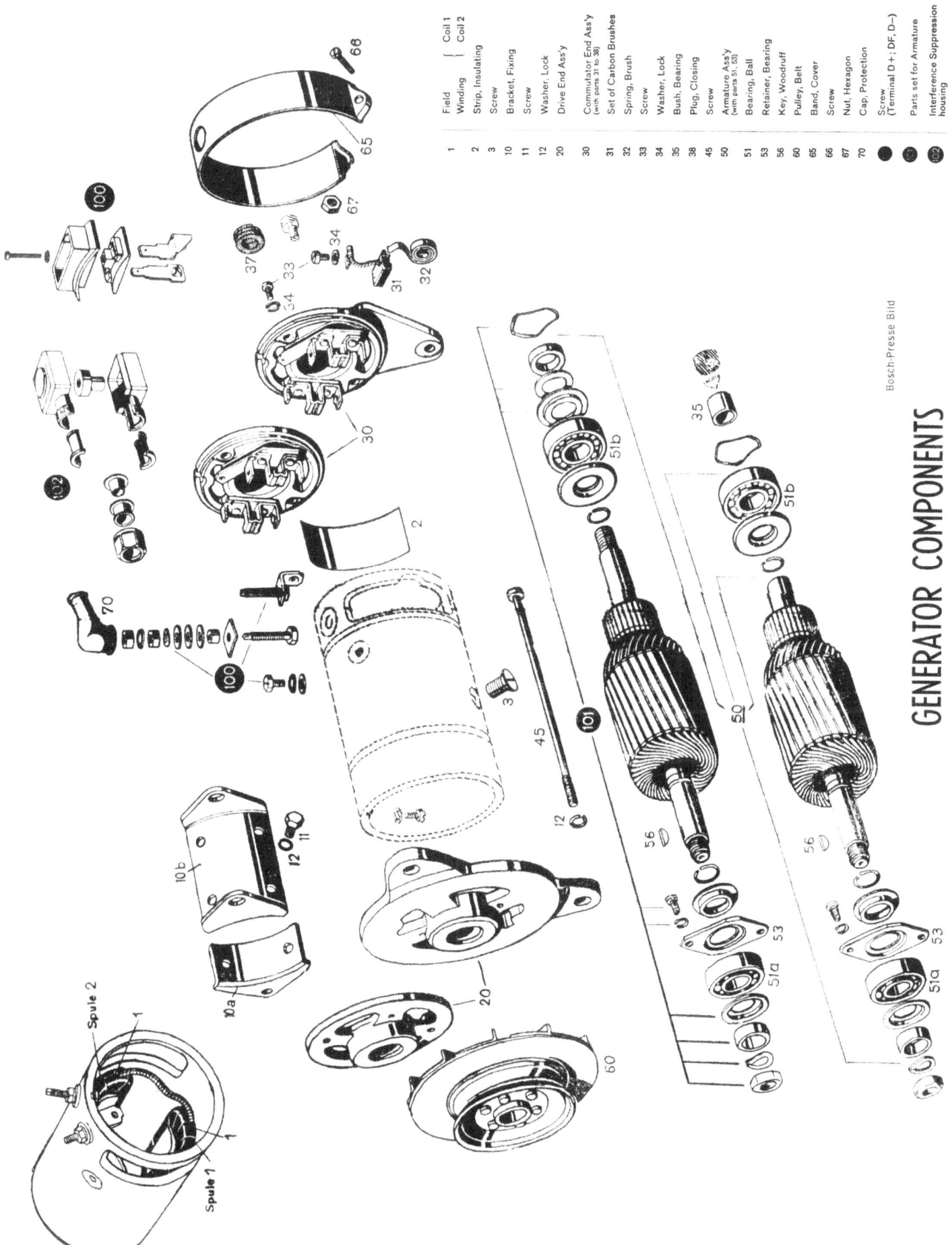

2. Pull out bulb holder (be sure it is correct bulb by looking through opening to see the lens coloring).
3. Push bulb slightly into holder, rotate slightly, then withdraw.
4. Fit new bulb in reverse order.

GENERATING SYSTEM TESTS

Description

Even if the ignition warning light operates in a normal manner (see previous outline), other symptoms can warn of a defective system. Among the problems encountered are:

a. Battery needing excessive fillings.
b. Weak or variable headlight illumination (especially noticeable when starting at night).
c. Car starts slowly or not at all.

Before starting any tests, check the condition and tension of the fan belt. Next check the electrical wiring for shorts or breaks. If a full test is deemed necessary, the following instruments will be necessary:

a. One 0–20 Volt range voltmeter.
b. One 10–0–60 Amp. range ammeter.
c. One 500 Watt nominal capacity adjustable load resistor.

Test 1: Regulator Voltage No Load

1. Remove battery lead from terminal B+ on the regulator and temporarily insulate cable shoe. The positive lead of the voltmeter is then connected to terminal D+/61 and the negative lead to ground (see illustration).
2. Start the engine and run the generator up to double the rated speed. If the voltmeter does not show the correct regulator voltage (see ELECTRICAL DATA at the back of this chapter), the generator and regulator will have to be overhauled.

Test 2: Regulator Voltage On Load

1. Connect instrument to regulator as previously described, except the ammeter should be connected in series with the adjustable load resistor between terminal B+ on the regulator and ground.
2. Start engine, increase speed up to generator test speed (see ELECTRICAL DATA), and keep constant. Adjust resistor until the ammeter indicates the corresponding test voltage.
3. At this setting the voltmeter should indicate 12 V at the minimum. If such is not the case, the generator must be removed and repaired.

Test 3: Variode Current Value

1. Connect instruments as described in Test 2 and run generator at double the nominal speed.
2. Using the adjustable resistor, increase load up to the maximum capacity of the generator (see ELECTRICAL DATA). With any further increase of load the voltage must drop.
3. If the voltage drops at lower loads or loading just above the recommended value, replace the regulator.

Test 4: Reverse Current Switch

1. Check the condition of the battery. It must be at half-charge or more (specific gravity of electrolyte min. 1,230 g/cm^3).
2. Set at the normal "switch on voltage".
3. Connect instruments as in Test 2, except the voltmeter positive should be connected to B+ 61 on the voltage regulator. Set the adjustable resistor to nominal capacity.
4. Start the engine and gradually increase the speed. The voltage should gradually increase. When the switch is open, no current should flow. When the switch is closed, the indicated voltage will fall and the ammeter will begin to rise. The maximum reading before the pointer starts to fall back again will give the switch on voltage. This reading should be at least 12 V.
5. If reading is below 12 V, adjust the switch or replace the regulator.

Test 5: Switch Opening

1. Check battery as in Test 4.
2. Remove insulation (if necessary) from generator lead B+ and connect to negative lead of ammeter. Connect positive lead of ammeter to terminal B+ on the regulator (see illustration).

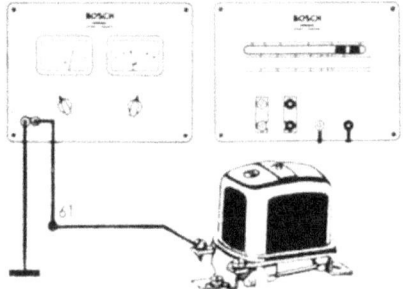

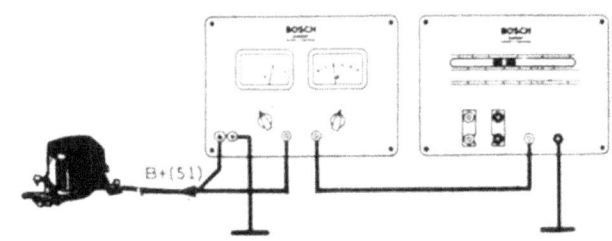

3. Increase engine speed until the ammeter indicates charging current. The engine speed should then be slowly reduced and thus the ammeter needle will pass the 0 mark and will indicate a negative value. The maximum negaitve reading of the ammeter indicates the reverse current necessary for interruption of the connection between the generator and the battery (see ELECTRICAL DATA).
4. Should the contacts open whilst the ammeter indicates a charge, there is a short circuit in the relay winding. In this case, replace the regulator. With engine at operating temperature, the slow running should be set so that the ammeter falls back to 0 during engine idle. If such is not the case, either have the regulator adjusted by Bosch Service or replace it.

SERVICING VOLTAGE REGULATOR

Removal

1. Disconnect battery.
2. Remove regulator leads, label wires for replacement.
3. Unscrew mounting bolts and remove regulator.

Replacement

1. Before replacing voltage regulator, be sure there is no short to ground in the field coils of the generator.
2. Remount regulator and replace leads (use wiring diagram on the regulator housing as a guide).
3. Polarize generator as outlined under REMOVING AND INSTALLING GENERATOR.
4. If the power generation system fails to operate correctly after replacing the regulator, either the generator or the wiring system is out of order. Recheck or have Bosch Service conduct their own tests.

CHECKING GENERATOR

NOTE: These checks can be carried out with the generator in place in the vehicle. This will often cure the more frequent and minor complaints.

1. Remove generator cover strap.
2. Check carbon brushes for wear and free travel in the brush holder guides. Should the top of the brush be below the top of the brush holder, renew the brush since it has worn down too far. Also replace brushes which have become heavily oiled. To eliminate extra expense (to save the armature from total ruination), skim the commutator on a lathe at the same time, unless the repair is an emergency situation.
3. Should the commutator be oily or greasy, clean it with a clean cloth which has been soaked in clean gasoline or solvent. Turn the shaft.

WARNING: Be sure not to get any dirt into the ball bearing while cleaning the commutator. Allow any solvent or gasoline to evaporate completely before starting the engine to minimize fire hazard.

4. Check the pressure springs for correct tension (see ELECTRICAL DATA). A small spring scale can be utilized. Replace both springs if one is found to be defective.
5. If the commutator surface has become uneven as a result of running in of the brushes or has burn spots, it will be necessary to:

   a. Normally, remove the generator from the vehicle and skim the commutator on a lathe.
   b. Emergency, hold a loop of crocus cloth (never emery cloth) against the commutator and turn the shaft by hand (loosen fan belt).

REMOVING AND INSTALLING GENERATOR

CAUTION: Before replacing the fan belt, be sure to polarize the generator so no damage is caused to the regulator and the charging is correct. Do this by connecting the battery lead for 5 to 15 seconds to the terminal 61/D+ on the regulator. The generator must now start to run as an electric motor, i.e. in the direction of rotation of the engine.

Removal

1. Disconnect the cable at the generator.
2. Detach the fan belt.
3. Remove the strip clamping the generator to the generator bracket.
4. Unscrew the bolts on the generator bracket.
5. Unscrew the four bolts on the fan cover (support the generator), then remove the generator and the bracket.

Installation

To install, reverse the removal procedure, noting the previous CAUTION and the following:

1. Renew the paper gasket between the generator bracket and the crankcase if necessary.
2. Reconnect all cables, using wiring diagram on the regulator housing or the one at the back of the ELECTRICAL SYSTEM chapter.

SERVICING GENERATOR

Disassembly

1. Remove fan belt pulley and cooling impeller (see COOLING SYSTEM in the ENGINE chapter).
2. Unscrew the field coil connection from the brush holder of the positive brush.
3. Unscrew both generator housing bolts.
4. Disassemble generator housing, removing armature carefully.
5. Remove ball bearings, then wipe all individual parts with a clean cloth, finally blowing through with compressed air (do not spin bearings). If there is the least wear, or if brushes are also being replaced, renew the bearings.

GENERATOR FAULTS AND THEIR ELIMINATION

FAULT	CAUSE	REMEDY
Warning light does not come on when ignition is switched on	a. Battery flat	a. Charge up battery
	b. Battery defective	b. Renew battery
	c. Bulb burned out	c. Renew bulb
	d. Battery terminal corroded or loose	d. Clean connections and if necessary tighten up
	e. Cable loose or broken	e. Tighten cable or repair
	f. Ignition switch defective	f. Renew ignition switch
	g. Generator brushes are not running on commutator	g. Free carbon brushes or renew or replace pressure springs. Do not oil carbon brushes!
Ignition warning light does not go out when engine speed rises or flickers, glows	a. V-belt loose or defective	a. Tighten or renew belt
	b. Regulator switch defective	b. Exchange regulator switch
	c. Charging lead loose or broken	c. Check cables and connections
	d. Generator defective	d. Check generator
	e. Ignition switch lead has bad connection	e. Tighten connections
Ignition warning light only goes out at high engine speeds	a. Generator defective	a. Check generator, repair
	b. Regulator switch defective	b. Exchange regulator switch
Ignition warning light continues to burn after ignition switched off	a. Short to earth in cable or warning light	a. Eliminate earth short

Testing Field Coils

Both field coils should be checked for open circuit, ground and winding shorts.

1. Test a field coil for open circuit by connecting its ends with a 12 V test light in series with the battery. The test light will not light up if there is an open circuit.
2. Repeat the above test on the other field coil.
3. Check for shorts in the winding by connecting the ohmmeter across the ends of each coil and comparing the reading with the ELECTRICAL DATA at the end of this chapter. An alternate test is to connect a 12 V battery in series with an ammeter to the coil ends. Compare the current intensity at the coils. If the difference in current consumption is greater than 0.5 Amps, the coil with the higher reading has a short circuit.
4. Check the coils for short circuit to ground by connecting a 40 V test lamp to one end of the field coil and to the generator housing. The test light should not light up (see illustration).

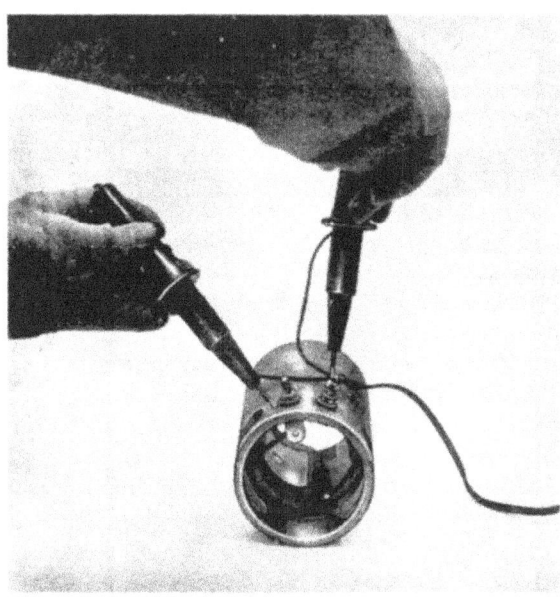

5. The field coils should also be checked for satisfactory electrical and mechanical contact with each other.

Testing Armature

NOTE: Test for open circuits as well as for winding and ground shorts, since in many cases defects are not externally visible.

1. Burn spots between two segments of the commutator indicate an open circuit. Open circuits can also be measured with a sensitive resistance measuring bridge.
2. Melted soldered connections can also indicate short circuits between the windings. The best test is to use the instrument consisting of an AC magnet with jaws (usually called a "growler"). A piece of thin steel sheet metal is hand-held on top of the armature, and the armature slowly rotated about its axis. If there is a short circuit, the sheet metal will vibrate violently at 2 or more places around the circumference of the armature.
3. A short to ground will occur if the armature core is shorted to the winding or if carbon dust has penetrated into the winding. The test should be carried out with a test light of 40 V between the armature iron and commutator. The test light should not light up.
4. If the commutator is oval or rough as a result of burn spots or grooves (from running-in of the carbon brushes), skim it on a lathe to depth of the low spot, then polish with fine crocus cloth. Be sure to remove all metal from between commutator bars, and use a commutator saw (break a used hacksaw blade at an angle and sharpen the broken edge) to recess the insulators about 0.3—0.5 mm from the contact face of the commutator.

Reassembly

To assemble generator, reverse the disassembly procedure, noting the following points:

1. Following previous tests, check other cable connection points and brushes.
2. Check ball bearings for wear and damage, replace if necessary. In an emergency situation, wipe bearings with a clean cloth, then blow through with compressed air (do not spin). Pack bearings with Bosch grease Ft 1 V 33, or some other BALL BEARING grease, unless new prepacked bearings are being installed.
3. Be sure leads are properly connected to brush holders.

IGNITION SYSTEM

DESCRIPTION

A 12 V battery ignition system is used, with the spark advanced centrifugally. All components and method of operation are similar to the great majority of 4-cylinder engines.

Battery current flows through a contact breaker in the distributor which sends it on in the form of electrical pulses to the primary winding of the coil. This induces a high tension voltage of about 20,000 V, with low amperage of a few mA, in the secondary coil. The coil is filled with oil to allow better heat dissipation.

This high voltage flows to the distributor, which controls the current flow to the individual spark plugs. The ignition timing advance at varying engine speeds is performed by a built-in centrifugal spark advance mechanism. Radio interference suppression is provided.

The cast distributor housing is shaped like a pot, and

it accommodates the breaker point plate with the point carrier and breaker points, the centrifugal spark advance mechanism, and the distributor rotor and cover.

The supporting neck of the distributor housing is mounted in an orifice in the crankcase. The neck is hollow and accommodates the distributor drive shaft which is driven by a gear mounted on the crankshaft. The contact breaker plate supports the breaker arm and fixed breaker support. Each of the breaker components has a wolfram contact point brazed on. **Contact breaker gap in open position should be .016 in. (0,4 mm)** and is adjusted with an eccentric screw. The actual distributor consists of the rotor atop the cam and the distributor cover.

IGNITION TROUBLESHOOTING

NOTE: This is only an emergency checkout procedure to determine whether the ignition system is preventing engine operation, and which components may be at fault. It is not intended as a substitute for a thorough analysis which can only be accomplished with proper knowledge and sensitive instruments. Use a non-conducting cable holder when testing for spark, and do not "ground" yourself.

1. Check all high tension cables between the distributor cap and the coil and spark plugs for proper seating and damage. If engine still doesn't run, pull the coil cable out of the distributor cap and hold it about ¼ in. (5—7 mm) from a grounding point; when the engine is cranked, a spark should jump between the cable and ground. If a strong spark is given off, the primary and secondary coil windings are in working order; if there is no spark, continue with tests (2), (3), and (4).
2. Connect a 12 V test light between Terminal 1 at the distributor and a grounding point. Switch the ignition on and crank the engine. If the test light goes on and off, the primary coil winding is in working order.
3. If the test light burns continuously while the engine is being cranked, check in the distributor to see if the breaker point gap is too wide, or if oil, grease, dirt or similar obstruction has become lodged between the breaker points.
4. If the test light does not illuminate at all when the engine is being cranked, then the primary coil winding is broken or the points do not open fully (also check that the test light actually works). Check the condition and opening of the points (inside the distributor body), and also for loose cable connections, broken terminal ends, and grounding distributor wire. If possible, substitute another 12 V coil.
5. Check the inside of the distributor cap for condensation, corrosion, electrical scorching, and black tracks (cracks) between cable connectors (electrodes or contacts).
6. Check spark plug connectors for water condensation and current conductivity (hold each cable ¼ in. from a grounding point and crank engine: a strong spark should jump across). Remove the spark plugs, check against chart under SPARK PLUGS, and readjust electrode gap if necessary.

7. If the malfunction has not been found by now, check the ignition timing as described further on in this chapter. If the timing is in order, conclude that the ignition system is not the cause of the malfunction and check the fuel system, using the CARBURETOR SERVICE DIAGNOSIS chart as a troubleshooting guide.

SERVICING BREAKER POINTS

Checking

Due to their high state of tuning, Porsche engines are very sensitive to ignition malfunctions. It is wise to give the ignition system regular service and promptly correct any malfunctions. The breaker points are subject to erosion and normally do erode. They should, therefore, be lightly filed and cleaned with a lint-free cloth when pitting is in evidence so as to prevent further ignition system breakdown. If, after filing, the points are still improperly mated, they should be replaced, since they are burned instead of just eroded. Also replace the condensor, since this has caused electrode burning.

Replacement

1. With distributor cap and rotor removed, loosen the nut of the screw which secures the leaf spring of the breaker arm.
2. Remove the lock ring from the breaker arm pivot stud.
3. Remove breaker arm, then remove retaining screw from fixed contact support (anvil) and remove support.
4. Reinstall breaker points in reverse order, then adjust gap.
5. Slightly grease the pivot and cam with the special grease used for this purpose (usually provided in the breaker point package in a capsule).

Adjustment

1. Remove distributor cap and rotor.
2. Turn crankshaft by placing a wrench on crankshaft pulley nut until a cam lobe in the distributor fully lifts the breaker point arm.
3. Check the breaker point gap with a feeler gauge; the gap should be not less than .010 in. (0,25 mm), and ideally .016 in. (0,4 mm).
4. Check dwell angle with an engine tester; dwell angle should be 50° ± 3°.
5. Dwell angle can be corrected by changing the breaker point gap. To do this, first loosen the set screw in the fixed contact support, then adjust with the eccenter screw. Keep resetting the breaker gap until the dwell angle is correct.
6. Retighten the set screw in the fixed contact support.

NOTE: Subsequent to the adjustment of the dwell angle, always check the ignition timing since changes in dwell angle adjustment affect timing. Ignition timing should be adjusted each time points are adjusted.

CHECKING CONDENSER

A defective condenser will show itself by poor engine performance, difficult starting, and excessive distributor contact erosion. Check the condenser on an electronic engine test instrument. In any case, if the condenser is suspect, it is best to replace it immediately and with every point change.

CHECKING ROTOR AND DISTRIBUTOR CAP

The rotor as well as the electrodes in the distributor cap are subject to erosion since the high voltage pulses continuously cross between them when the engine is running. Should the insulating qualities of the distributor cap or rotor be impaired due to small cracks (through which the high tension voltage may escape to ground), the ignition system can be expected to malfunction. This condition is known as "tracking", and shows up as a black line on the bakelite.

A spring-loaded carbon contact in the distributor cap conducts the high-tension voltage to the rotating rotor. From there, the current jumps across a .026 in. (0,7 mm) wide gap, in proper sequence, from the moving to the stationary electrodes.

The distributor cap must be properly ventilated to prevent damage by the ozone created inside. The distributor cap should be kept clean, inside and out, to prevent arcing and current losses.

TESTING AUTOMATIC IGNITION ADVANCE/RETARD

Description

The automatic ignition advance/retard operation works on the centrifugal principle. The centrifugal governor is fitted in the ignition housing below the contact breaker plate. On a plate connected to the distributor spindle two arms with weights of different sizes are located so that the arms are free to rotate. They are pulled inwards by two coil springs. As the engine speed rises, the centrifugal force pushes the weights further outwards, which in turn advances the contact breaker cam. The shape of the distributor advance curve (see accompanying illustration), is governed by the differing weights of the centrifugal weights and by special design of the carrier arms.

Checking

A superficial check of the centrifugal governor is accomplished by removing the distributor cap, then spinning the distributor shaft in a clockwise direction. When released, the distributor arm must spring back to the stop at its starting point.

Instrument Testing

An exact test of the advance curve is only possible with a distributor tester or an electronic engine test instrument. If the ignition advance is functioning satisfactorily, the amount of advance should be within the tolerance limit of the ignition advance curve illustrated. The tolerance is the amount between the two curves. This works out to 15—16 degrees total (maximum) advance of the distributor, or 32 degrees at the crankshaft plus the 5 degrees initial advance or a total (maximum) of 37 degrees advance at the crankshaft pulley.

If measurement is carried out wtih an engine test instrument, further marks must be made around the periphery of the fan belt pulley. The diameter of the fan belt pulley is 145 mm. The linear measurement for $5°$ will therefore be 6,15 mm and this can be marked out on the pulley (using a caliper) working from the TDC mark.

SETTING IGNITION TIMING

IMPORTANT: Before adjusting timing, the contact breaker point gap must always be checked and corrected if necessary. Make it a matter of principle with the highly-tuned Porsche engine to only adjust the ignition timing with a stroboscope (timing light) with the engine running (1968-'69 models).

1. Connect engine to instrument.
2. Note that the fan belt pulley has a notch on its outer edge to indicate the TDC of the No. 1 cylinder.
3. Depending on the year of the car, use either of the following procedures:
    a. On 1966-1967 cars, use a 12-volt trouble shooting light and set ignition to $3°$ before TDC by rotating the crankshaft pulley clockwise until the light goes on. At this point the timing mark should be at $3°$ before TDC.
    b. On 1968-'69 cars, run the engine at 950 (± 50) rpm, and hold at this setting. Set the ignition timing, using the stroboscope, to $3°$ after TDC.
4. Adjust the ignition timing by first slackening the clamp bolt at the foot of the distributor so the distributor housing can be barely rotated by hand, then with the engine shut down or running (depending on year), rotate the distributor housing until the correct setting is indicated.
5. Retighten the clamp bolt at the foot of the distributor carefully so as not to disturb distributor setting, then recheck setting.

TESTING IGNITION COIL

It is best to use an electronic tester to diagnose an ignition coil since in many cases the malfunction occurs in warm coils at high pulse frequency. When such test equipment is not available, a superficial test can be carried out as described under IGNITION TROUBLE-SHOOTING. The test can be made even more valid after the engine has heated up for some time, and the wire is removed while the engine is running.

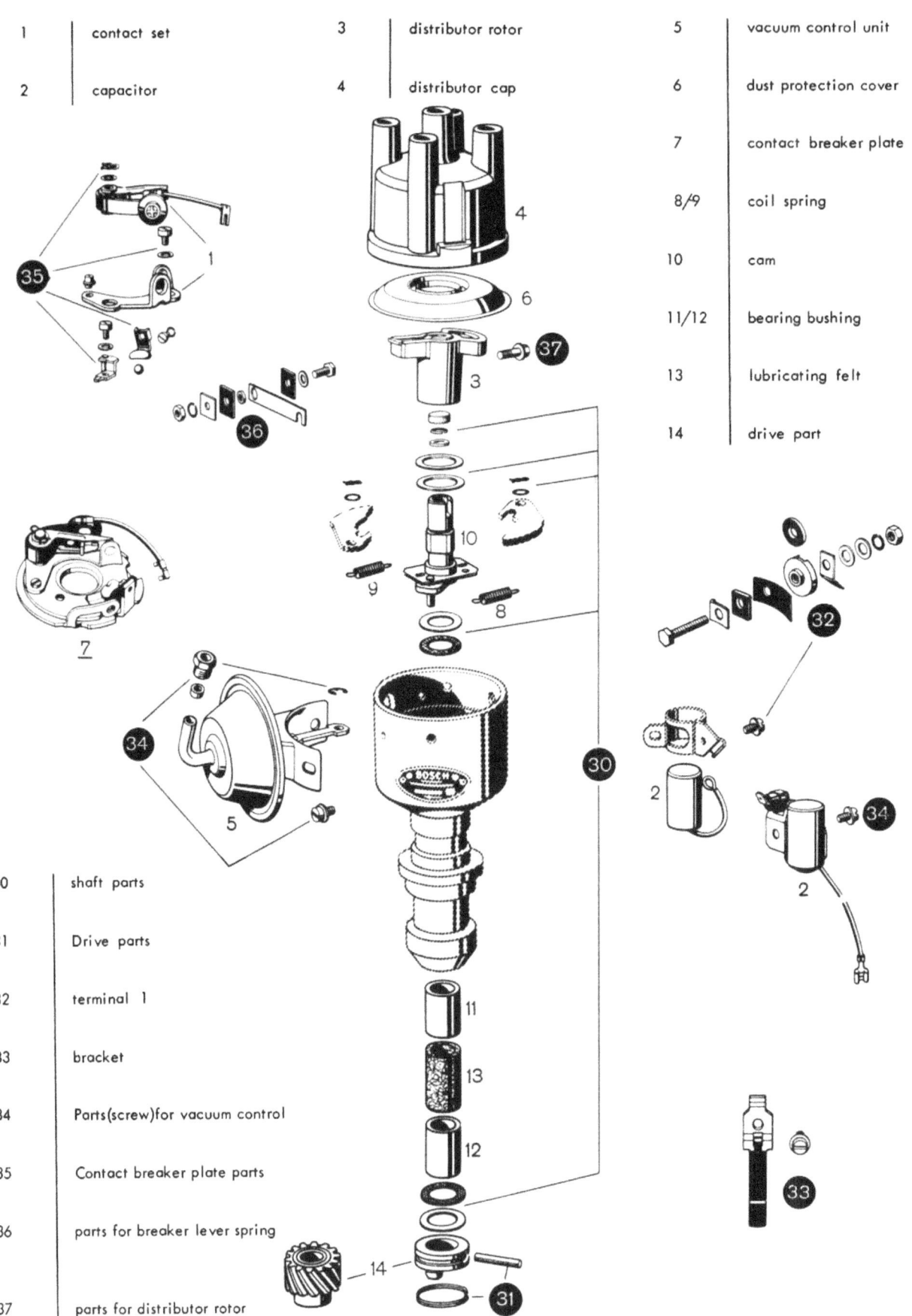

Late model Bosch distributor (typical)

1	contact set	3	distributor rotor	5	vacuum control unit
2	capacitor	4	distributor cap	6	dust protection cover
				7	contact breaker plate
				8/9	coil spring
				10	cam
				11/12	bearing bushing
				13	lubricating felt
				14	drive part

30	shaft parts
31	Drive parts
32	terminal 1
33	bracket
34	Parts(screw) for vacuum control
35	Contact breaker plate parts
36	parts for breaker lever spring
37	parts for distributor rotor

Bosch-Presse Bild

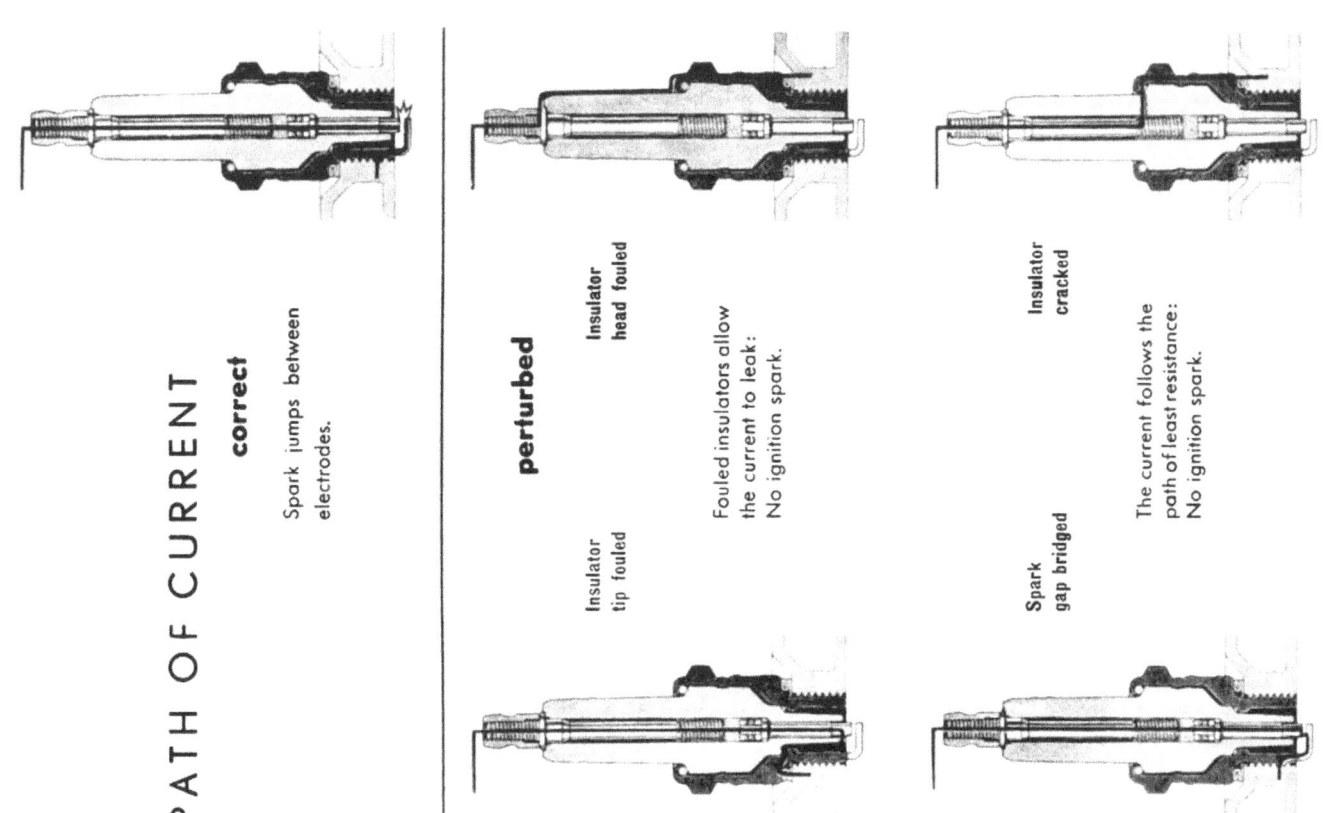

IGNITION ADVANCE CURVE FOR BOSCH DISTRIBUTOR

Type 0 231 129 022   J FR 4 (R)

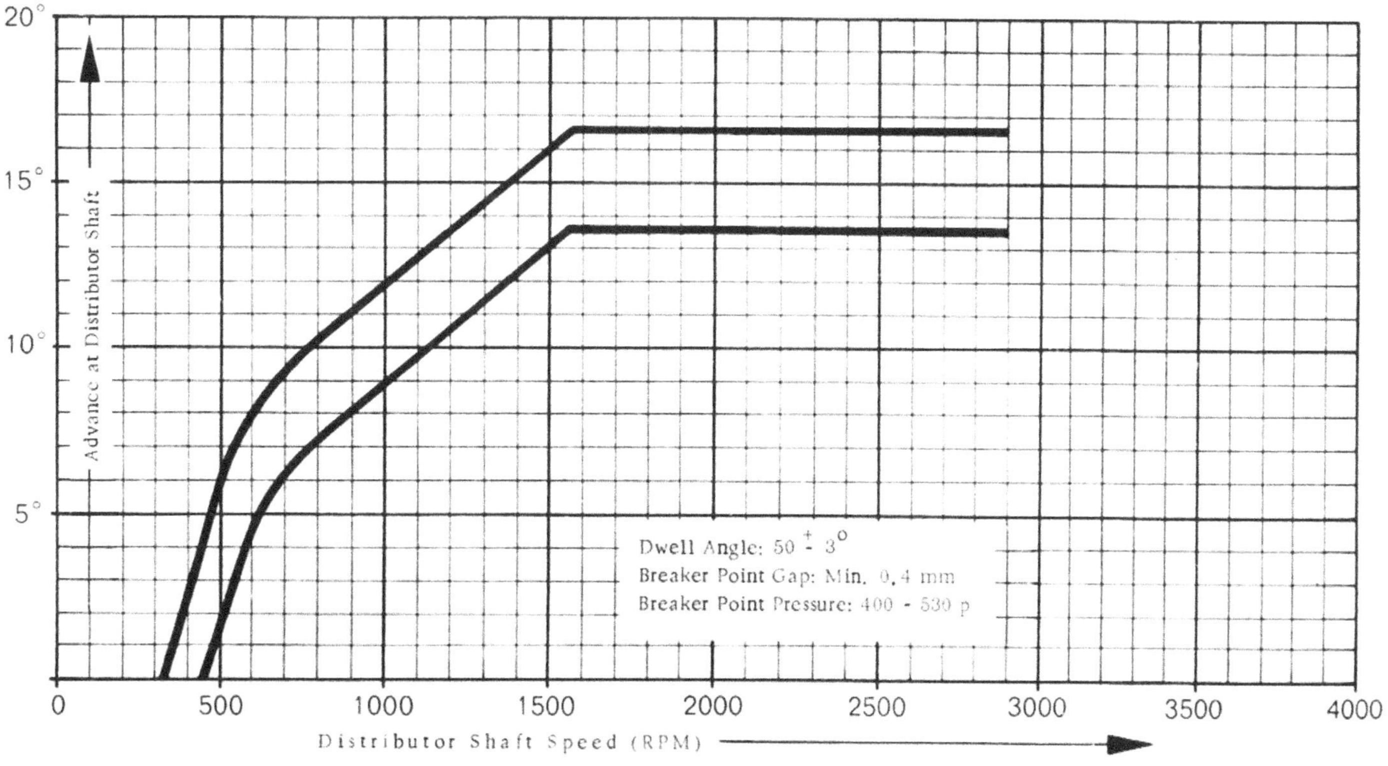

Dwell Angle: $50 \pm 3°$
Breaker Point Gap: Min. 0.4 mm
Breaker Point Pressure: 400 - 530 p

The Sparking Plug Face

without tetraethyl lead added to the fuel

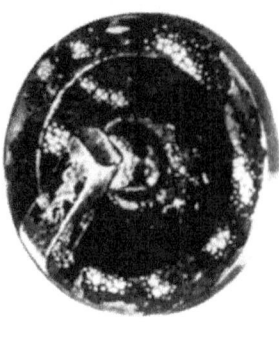

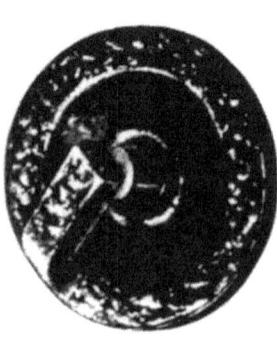

Plug overheated
Plug having too low a calorific value; adjustment of carburettor too low; ignition too far advanced.

Plug in normal condition
Proper choice of plug; carburettor correctly adjusted.

with tetraethyl lead added to the fuel as an anti-knock agent
to improve the octane number

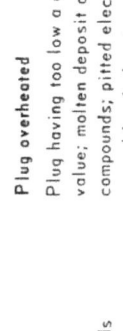

Plug in normal condition
after a long period of operation or when fuel with a high lead content is used
Heavy deposit of powdery lead compounds coloured a greyish yellow to brown. Carburettor correctly adjusted.

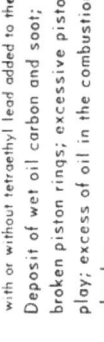

Plug overheated
Plug having too low a calorific value; molten deposit of lead compounds; pitted electrodes; enamel beads forming on the insulator.

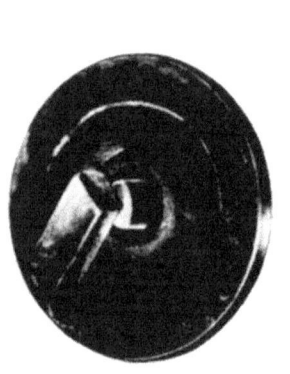

Plug fouled by soot
with or without tetraethyl lead added to the fuel
Velvety, dull black soot deposit; fuel-air mixture too rich; carburettor jet too wide; insufficient air.

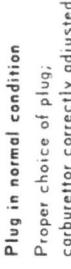

Plug fouled by oil
with or without tetraethyl lead added to the fuel
Deposit of wet oil carbon and soot; broken piston rings; excessive piston play; excess of oil in the combustion chamber.

ROBERT BOSCH GMBH STUTTGART

SERVICING SPARK PLUGS

Description

The spark plugs have the function of introducing the high-voltage ignition current in insulated form into the engine combustion chamber and to induce combustion of the compressed fuel/air mixture by means of the sparks bridging its electrodes. Use only those spark plugs listed on the following chart, or better yet, check with the friendly neighborhood Porsche dealership for the best type of spark plug currently available for individual uses.

(As of March 1967)

Maker	Type	Electrode gap
Bosch	W 225 T 7	0.6 - 0.7
Bosch	W 200 T 35	0.6 - 0.7
Beru	P 225/14	0.6 - 0.7

Checking Plugs

Remove the plugs during each servicing period of 6,000 mi. (10,000 km) or sooner, and check for appearance (using the accompanying plug appearance chart), electrode gap and satisfactory function. With a little experience, the operating condition of the engine and carburetor setting can be read from the appearance of the spark plugs. Be sure to warm up the engine thoroughly, then shut it off immediately WITHOUT IDLING. Remove plugs without touching electrodes and place in order. This way an accurate reading can be made on each cylinder. The construction of the plug determines the electrode gap which must be maintained for the plug in question. When replacing the plug, use a new washer, even when the old plug is being reused. Torque in plug until the washer is heard to "crush." Porsche dealerships normally replace the plugs every 6,000 miles.

SERVICING DISTRIBUTOR

Removal

1. Remove distributor cap.
2. Using a wrench on the crankshaft pulley nut, set Cylinder No. 1 to TDC (see NOTE under SERVICING DISTRIBUTOR PINION SHAFT). To be sure of position, note the following when removing or replacing distributor:

   a. In this position, the central slot in the head of the distributor drive shaft should be at right angles to the longitudinal axis (direction of travel) of the engine.
   b. The smaller segment of the drive shaft head should point towards the fan belt pulley (rear of engine). Therefore, place the shaft offset lug so that the offset is toward the rear of the vehicle, then lower into place.

3. Undo leads at the distributor (see illustration).

4. Loosen 10 mm hex nut and bolt at the distributor clamp.
5. Remove distributor.

WARNING: Do not turn engine over since setting will be lost.

Replacement

Replacement is the reverse of the removal procedure, being sure the shaft is aligned as described previously before replacing distributor. Be sure the spring is in place on the end of the distributor pinion shaft.

SERVICING DISTRIBUTOR PINION SHAFT

NOTE: Procedure for setting Cylinder No. 1 to TDC: With the engine completely assembled and the valve covers off, use a wrench on the crankshaft pulley nut to rotate the engine clockwise (which is normal direction of engine rotation) until No. 1 Cylinder intake valve goes down and returns (opens and closes). Continue turning the crankshaft in the same direction until the "OT" (TDC) mark on the crankshaft pulley is lined up with the mark on the crankcase. This locates the TDC of the No. 1 Cylinder.

Removal

With distributor removed as previously described, proceed as follows:

1. Remove the distributor pinion shaft, using one of the following methods:

   a. Remove fuel pump, insulating flange, gaskets, and actuating plunger as described in the FUEL SYSTEM chapter, then withdraw pinion shaft by pushing up and turning to the left through the orifice of the fuel pump receiving flange.
   b. Remove fuel pump, then guide a strong bar

magnet into the hole until it adheres to the shaft, then withdraw both while turning the magnet to the left and also shaking it to release the shaft from the gear and bearing.

CAUTION: In either of the above cases, be careful that the distributor pinion shaft thrust washer does not adhere to the shaft and then drop into the crankcase interior. To remove washer, place a metal rod into the crankcase interior, then withdraw thrust washer with a suitable hook (see illustration). If washer is dropped into crankcase interior, use a magnet or remove timing gear cover to remove washer, since washer could cause damage if it remained loose inside. Reverse the procedure above to replace washer.

2. Withdraw spring from pinion shaft.

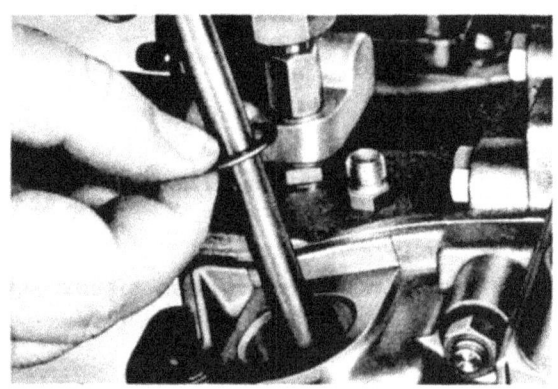

Installation

To install distributor pinion shaft, reverse the removal procedure, noting the following points:

1. Inspect fuel pump cam and shaft pinion for wear. If pinion shows traces of wear, install new pinion shaft as well as distributor drive gear (bronze) on crankshaft.
2. Inspect thrust washer at base of pinion shaft for wear, replace if necessary, heeding previous CAUTION to use a rod to guide washer into place so washer does not fall into crankcase interior.
3. Replace shaft using REPLACEMENT under SERVICING DISTRIBUTOR as a guide to proper gear alignment (see illustration).

NOTE: As shaft is inserted, it will rotate clockwise about 20°. With pinion shaft fully down, the slot will be angled toward the lock pin bolt that holds the No. 4 Main Bearing into place.

4. Insert the spring into pinion shaft with the help of a thin screwdriver or a welding rod (see illustration).

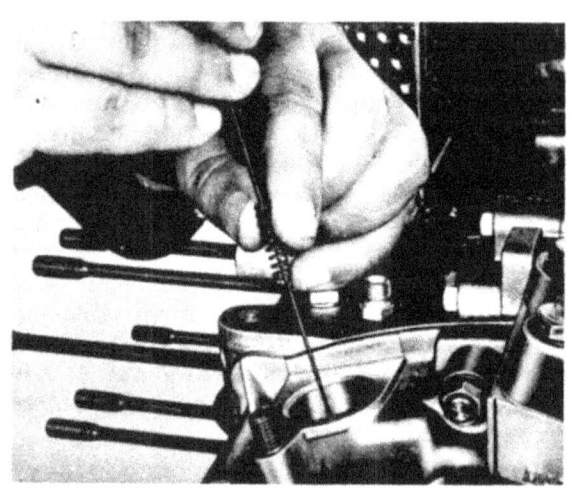

5. Install distributor as previously described.

ELECTRICAL DATA

Generator BOSCH shunt wound	0101 206 113
Load setting for output test	300/2500 rpm (generator armature)
Speed at rated voltage	1850 - 2050 rpm (generator armature)
Field coil resistance	3.5 Ohm
Carbon brush spring pressure	450 - 600 g
Regulator (BOSCH)	0190 350 014
Switch-on voltage	12.4 - 13.1 V
Reverse current	2 - 7.5 A
Switch contact gap (at rest)	Main contact 0.5 - 1.2 mm
Regulator voltage at idling speed	no load: 13.5 - 14.5 V on load: 12.8 - 13.8 V
Magnet gap voltage regulator	Closed min.: 0.2 mm open: 0.8 - 1.3 mm
Contact gap voltage regulator	0.25 - 0.4 mm
Starter (BOSCH)	0001212002
Free running test	11.5 V 33 - 50 A at 6400 - 7900 rpm
Load test	9 V 160 - 200 A at 1100 - 1400 rpm
Short circuit test	6 V 250 - 300 A
Carbon brush spring pressure	$1200 ^{+130}_{-50}$ p
Distributor (BOSCH)	0231 129022
Contact breaker gap	min. 0.3 mm
Centrifugal advance, degrees at engine speed	Commences at 5 - 14 ... 1000 29 - 34 ... 3000 30 - 35 ... 3100 13 - 19 ... 1250 21 - 26 ... 2000
Closing angle	47 - 53°
Contact pressure	400 - 530 p
Condenser	0.27 - 0.32 Microfarad
Ignition coil (BOSCH)	0221 102 016
Spark on tester with ionised spark gap	14 mm, 1.4 A Primary current Primary resistance 3.1 - 3.6 Ohm
Spark plugs	Electrode gap 0.6 - 0.7 mm
Battery	12 V 45 Ah

FUEL SYSTEM

CARBURETORS

DESCRIPTION

The major components of the fuel system are: the fuel tank, located under the luggage compartment in the front of the car, with a capacity of 16.4 U.S. gallons (62 liters), with 1.8 U.S. gallons (7 liters) in reserve, and a filler opening in the left fender; the fuel supply line through the frame tunnel to the cam-actuated fuel pump (operated off a cam machined into the distributor pinion shaft); and one double-throat downdraft carburetor with an accelerating pump for each bank of two cylinders, equipped with air cleaners or induction silencers to remove dust and dirt from the induction air.

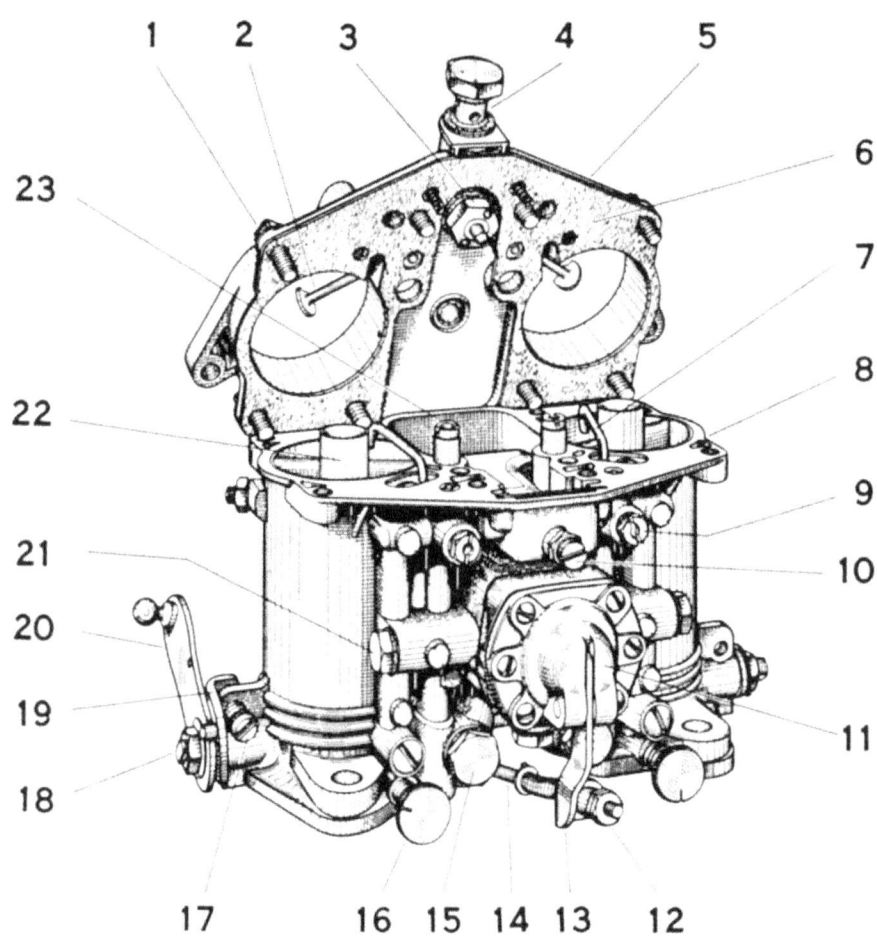

1 Cover retaining screws
2 Power enrichment nozzle
3 Float needle valve
4 Fuel line connector
5 Carburetor cover
6 Cover gasket
7 Accelerating pump nozzle
8 Carburetor body
9 Idle jet
10 Float level adjustment
11 Accelerating pump
12 Accelerating pump adjustment
13 Accelerating pump lever
14 Accelerating pump rod
15 Main jet carrier with jet
16 Idle mixture adjustment
17 Idle speed adjustment
18 Throttle shaft
19 Throttle return stop
20 Throttle arm
21 Accelerating pump jet
22 Preatomizer
23 Air correction jet

The carburetors are Solex 40 P II, which gives the engine 2 double-throat downdraft carburetors. Each induction throat measures 1.575 in. (40 mm) in diameter. Since the carburetors are located very close to the combustion chambers, cold starting enrichment devices are not necessary. The main body and cover, with a gasket between the two, makes up the basic components. The main body contains the two induction barrels, each having an independent idle and power metering system. The throttle shaft, which passes through both barrels, controls both throttle valves and carries a throttle return stop and throttle arm. Later models have an adjustment screw located between the barrels to change the pitch between the two throttle valve plates. Exploded views of early and later model carburetors can be found further on in this chapter.

The accelerating pump, located on the broad side of the carburetor, is actuated through an adjustable rod and feeds fuel to both induction throats (see illustration). The float chamber is located between both induction throats, and serves both at the same time. The fuel level in the float chamber is regulated through the buoyancy of the float, i.e., the float tang opens or closes the float needle valve. An externally located screw (see illustration) can be used to adjust the height of the intermediate swivel joint to change the float level. This makes it possible to quickly adjust the float level for the particular grade of gasoline used. The fuel level may be checked by removing the plug from the inspection port.

SCHEMATIC VIEW OF CARBURETOR

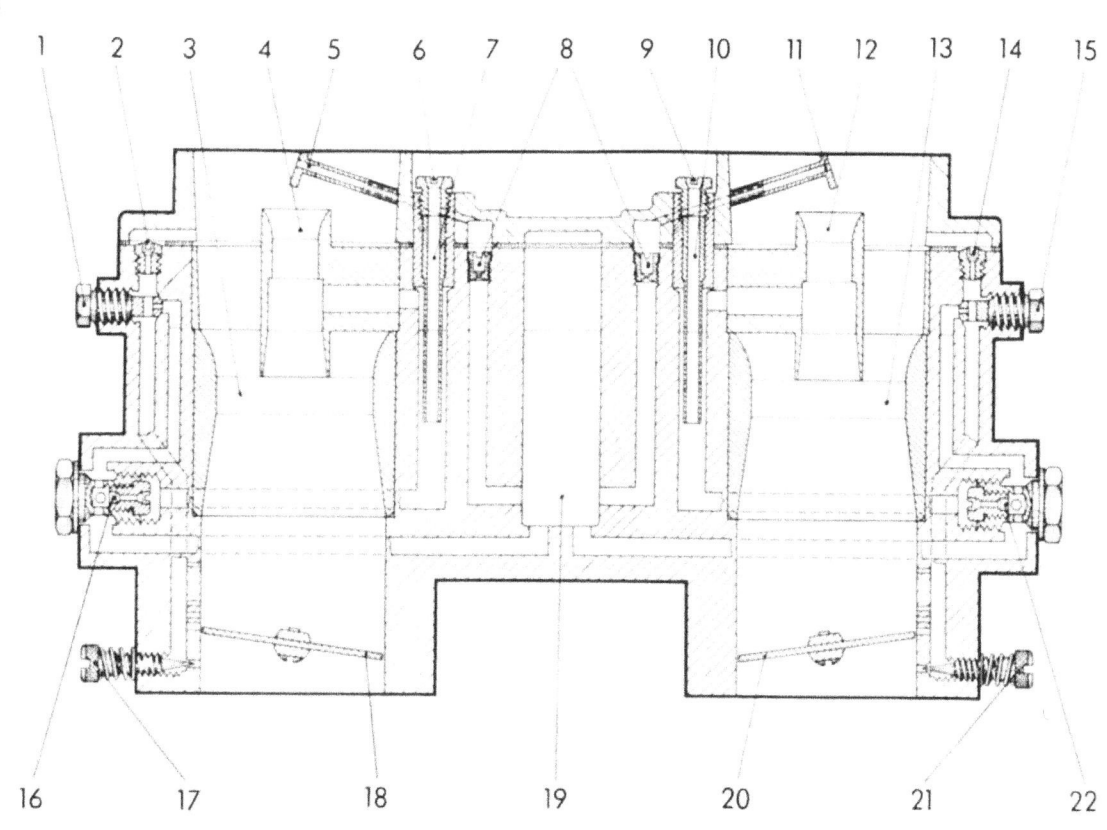

1 Idle metering jet
2 Idle air bleed
3 Venturi
4 Preatomizer
5 Power enrichment nozzle
6 Air correction jet
7 Emulsioning tube
8 Power enrichment jets
9 Air correction jet
10 Emulsioning tube
11 Power enrcihment nozzle
12 Preatomizer
13 Venturi
14 Idle air bleed
15 Idle metering jet
16 Main jet carrier
17 Idle mixture adjustment
18 Throttle valve
19 Float chamber
20 Throttle valve
21 Idle mixture adjustment
22 Main jet carrier

The carburetor cover contains the fuel inlet, the float chamber vent, and the float needle valve (the latter is accessible from the interior). Also, the cover accommodates two power enrichment nozzles, which are press-fit into the cover.

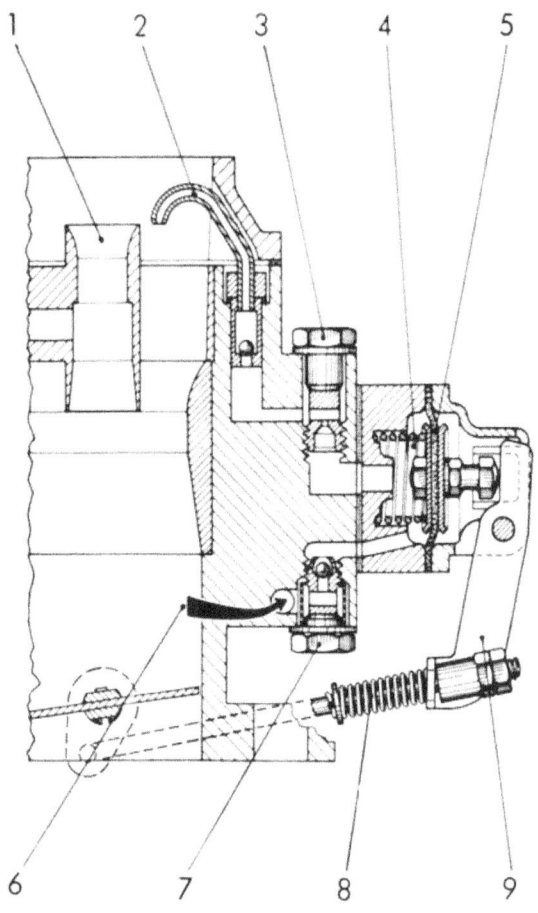

1 Preatomizer
2 Accelerating pump nozzle
3 Accelerating pump jet
4 Pump diaphragm spring
5 Pump diaphragm
6 Fuel passage, float chamber to check valve
7 Check valve with return flow port
8 Pump rod spring
9 Pump arm

IMPORTANT: The main jet size is of great importance when operating the vehicle at varying altitudes. Apply the following rule-of-thumb: change the main jet size by 6 percent for each 3,280 ft. (1,000 m) of altitude variation. As an example, the normal jet size for a 1966—'67 Porsche at an altitude of 1,300 ft. (400 m) is 0115; proper jet size for an altitude of 4,600 ft. (1,400 m) is 0112.5. For use outside of the U.S., see a

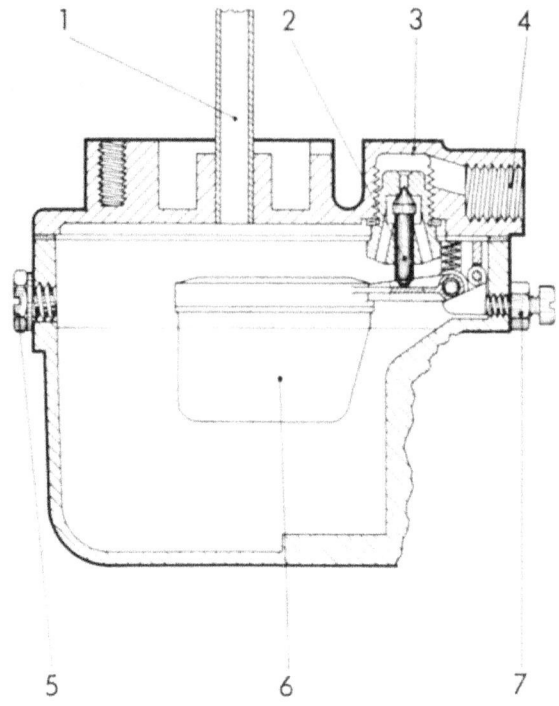

1 Float chamber vent
2 Float needle valve
3 Carburetor cover
4 Threads for fuel line connector
5 Inspection port plug
6 Float
7 Float level adjusting screw

local dealership for their recommendation. On 1968 and later Porsche's, use an 0125 jet size. See CARBURETOR SPECIFICATIONS chart at the back of this chapter for more information.

SERVICING AIR CLEANERS

Removal

1. Disconnect carburetor heating hose (see illustration).

2. Unsnap all four fasteners at the lower part of the air cleaner housing.
3. Disconnect crankcase breather hose from the air cleaner housing.
4. Depending on the type of air cleaner housing used, either withdraw the housing upward or remove the five retaining bolts at the forward air duct box and remove the box.
5. Remove the cartridge (Knecht-Filter).
6. Remove the retaining bolts from the air cleaner base plate (if necessary).

Replacement

To replace the air cleaner, reverse the order of the removal procedure. Make sure the gasket sealing surfaces are clean, and if necessary, replace the cartridge (see MAINTENANCE SERVICE for cleaning procedure) and square plastic foam gasket (if it is damaged).

ADJUSTING IDLE SPEED

CAUTION: If vehicle is equipped with an Exhaust Emission Control (EEC) System, the final idle mixture control screw adjustment is ¼ TURN BACKWARD from the point where the idle speed slows. If vehicle is NOT equipped with EEC, the final idle mixture control screw adjustment is ½ TURN BACKWARD from the point where the idle speed slows. A portable, multi-range tachometer should be used, especially with EEC equipped vehicles, since the idle speed slows minimally. On EEC equipped vehicles, a throttle valve compensator is used, and this must be checked and adjusted following idle speed adjustment since the compensator is affected by manifold vacuum. See TESTING THROTTLE VALVE COMPENSATOR in the EXHAUST EMISSION CONTROL SYSTEM chapter.

NOTE: To accomplish this adjustment, Special Tool P 227, Carburetor Synchronizer or "Unisyn", is necessary. Be sure to follow steps in sequence.

Synchronizing Carburetor Throats

1. Remove idle mixture adjusting screws and check if the cone tips are clean and in good condition. Renew if at all doubtful. Replace each one all the way in until it just touches (turning very slowly so as not to damage cone tips), then turn out 1½ to 2 turns.

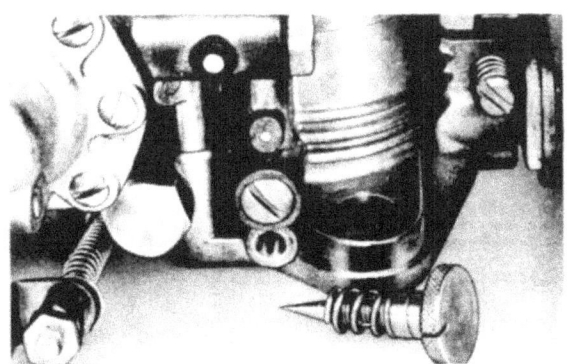

2. Remove air cleaners (see SERVICING AIR CLEANERS procedure). Check the injection quantity of the carburetors (see ACCELERATION PUMP DELIVERY procedure following).
3. Start the engine. Disconnect both throttle control linkages from the throttle cross-shaft arms.
4. Check the tachometer. If the engine is idling above 900 rpm, adjust the idle speed screws to lower it. If the idling speed is below 900 rpm, leave it alone.
5. Place the carburetor synchronizer ("Unisyn") on the rear throat of the left carburetor (serving cylinder No. 4) and adjust the glass tube to a vertical position.

NOTE: The left rear throat will serve as the "master" for the other three throats.

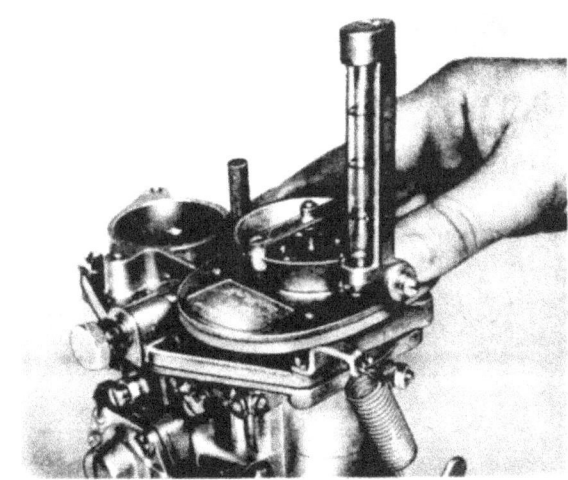

6. Turn the adjusting disc in the synchronizer until the indicator bubble in the glass comes to about half-way between the top and bottom of the glass. This sets the synchronizer for the particular engine and it should not be reset for taking subsequent readings (except as noted).
7. Place the synchronizer in the right carburetor rear throat (serving cylinder No. 2). The indicator bubble should move up to the same position in the glass tube as previously noted. Should the reading differ from the left rear throat, adjust the idle speed screw until the bubble reaches the same level as the left rear throat.
8. Place carburetor synchronizer back on the left carburetor as before. If the bubble has moved higher, readjust the bubble to the center with the disc (do this on the left rear throat only). If, on the other hand, the idle speed has increased above 900 rpm, adjust the idle speed screw so the bubble is centered in the glass (do this on the left rear carburetor only).
9. Check the right rear carburetor with the carburetor synchronizer. If necessary only, adjust with the idle speed screw to match the bubble level of the left rear throat.
10. Reconnect the right control linkage to the throttle control arm.

11. Check the relationship of the left throttle linkage to the ball on the throttle control arm.

12. If there is not an exact relationship between the ball and socket, adjust the rod to align to the ball, then connect the arm.

NOTE: In other words, connect arm so there is no preload or binding. Make sure all parts of the linkage, including the cross-shaft, are lubricated. Ball joint lock nuts must be properly tightened.

13. Place the carburetor synchronizer in the front throat of the left carburetor. The bubble should become centered in the glass tube. Should the reading differ from the left rear throat, follow either of these procedures:

  a. On 1966–'67 cars, there is no adjustment to cure this problem. If there is a great discrepancy, have the carburetor throttle valve reworked by a qualified Porsche dealership technician.

  b. On 1968–'69 cars, an adjusting screw is found beside the accelerating pump rod between the throats of the carburetors near the mounting flange (see throttle shaft in exploded view under SERVICING CARBURETOR). Use a small screwdriver to adjust the screw. Turn the screw in to raise the synchronizer bubble, out to lower the bubble.

NOTE: Adjust 1 carburetor at a time. When the front is adjusted to the rear throat of the left carburetor, raise the rpm to 3,000 for a few seconds, release, then recheck the whole adjustment on that one carburetor.

14. Place the synchronizer onto the rear throat of the right carburetor in the same manner. Change the disc adjustment in the gauge only to place the bubble in the exact center. This is the only time the disc is changed when it is not on the left rear throat. Check the front throat of the right carburetor as described under step 13. Once synchronized, both front throats are left alone.

15. If idle speed has risen to 900 rpm or above because of these adjustments, (which is the usual case), lower to 800 rpm by using the carburetor synchronizer, starting with the left rear throat and adjusting the idle control screw out slightly, then proceed to the right rear throat and bring the level of the carburetor synchronizer bubble to the same level as the left by using the idle speed adjusting screw ONLY.

NOTE: Do not change the disc in the carburetor synchronizer when it is on any throat except the left rear (as noted).

16. Place the synchronizer on the left rear throat and bring the bubble back to the center of the glass tube by adjusting the disc, then recheck the right rear throat for the same level. If the bubble level differs, adjust only with the idle speed screw.

NOTE: Once it has been established that the carburetor synchronizer is at the same level on both rear carburetors and that the rpm is around 800, the carburetors should be considered completely synchronized. It is possible that the previous procedure may have to be redone several times to get the necessary results.

17. Check the throttle pedal travel limiter, readjust if necessary. When the throttle pedal rests against the pedal limiter in the floorboard, the carburetor control levers must be about .004 in. (1 mm) from their travel stop. Adjust throttle pedal limiter if necessary.

18. Replace the air cleaners (see SERVICING AIR CLEANERS procedure).

19. The engine must now be brought up to the correct temperature for the remaining adjustments. To do this, bring the oil temperature gauge needle into the operating range by DRIVING the car. Check the performance of the engine (acceleration and deceleration).

Adjusting Idle Volume And Speed

1. Using portable tachometer (if available), bring idle speed to about 900 rpm by **EVENLY ADJUSTING THE IDLE SPEED SCREWS.**

2. See the CAUTION at the beginning of adjusting idle speed procedure. Follow any convenient sequence to adjust the idle mixture screws. First, with the idle speed set at about 900 rpm, turn the selected idle mixture adjustment screw in slowly until the idle speed recorded on the tachometer slows slightly. On 1966–'67 cars the lag is quite obvious; turn the screw **BACKWARD (OUT) ABOUT ½ TURN.** On EEC models there is little lag, so watch the tachometer; turn screw **BACKWARD (OUT) ABOUT ¼ TURN.** Repeat on the remaining three throats.

NOTE: After adjustment of each idle mixture control screw, readjust idle to 1,000 rpm (1966–'67 models), 900 rpm (EEC cars) with idle speed adjustment screw before going on to next idle mixture control screw adjustment. For maximum idle smoothness, and to maintain proper performance, repeat steps (1) and (2) again, since the air velocity has changed with the idle adjustment. For even a finer adjustment, repeat steps (1) and (2) once more.

NOTE: In no case should the screws be left in a fully-turned-in position. If this is the case, the idle circuit is plugged and the carburetor should be boiled out.

CAUTION – FINAL IDLE ADJUSTMENT: Once idle mixture adjustment screws and all other controls have been completely adjusted on the fuel system, raise the rpm to 3,000 for a few seconds, then let the engine return to idle speed. Idle speed on a 1966–'67 Porsche should be between 1,000–1,100 rpm, EEC models should be between 900–950 rpm. If not, adjust by **EVENLY ADJUSTING THE IDLE SPEED SCREWS.**

IMPORTANT: If the car is a 1968 EEC equipped model, be sure to adjust the throttle positioner following all these adjustments. Refer to TESTING THROTTLE VALVE COMPENSATOR in the EXHAUST EMISSION CONTROL SYSTEM chapter.

ACCELERATION PUMP DELIVERY

NOTE: This procedure is generally conducted with the carburetors mounted on the engine and the air filters removed, although it can be done on a bench-

mounted carburetor. Performance in the zero to 30 mph range is much affected by the volume of charge delivered by the acceleration pump. The amount discharged at each two strokes should be 0,45 cc (7.3 minums) during the warm season, 0,55 cc during mild winter, and 0,65 cc (10.6 minums) in below zero weather. Both carburetors should deliver an identical amount as closely as can be determined. Special Tool P 25a, a calibrated vial with a handle, can be used, or seal the small end of a common glass eyedropper by holding it in a gas stove flame for a few minutes. Then take another dropper and put 5 drops of ethyl gas (which is red and easy to see) into the first dropper. With a file, scribe a line at this level. This is 0,35 cc. Add 3 drops to get 0,55 cc and scribe another line. For the warm season reading, the level should be halfway between the two marks, for mild winter the level should be at the top mark, and for below zero weather the level should be the same amount above the top mark. The average dropper is too long for this purpose, so cut it off with a glass cutter or hot wire to about ¾ in. above the top mark, then loop a piece of wire around it for a handle and you have your own "Calibrated Vial P 25a".

1. Run engine to fill float chamber with fuel, or (if necessary), fill chamber manually.
2. Stop engine, remove both air cleaners.
3. Work throttle arm until stream from pump injection nozzle becomes steady.
4. Hold Calibrated Vial P 25a at the tip of the nozzle and push the throttle arm down and hold for a few seconds TWO times from stop to stop (see illustration).

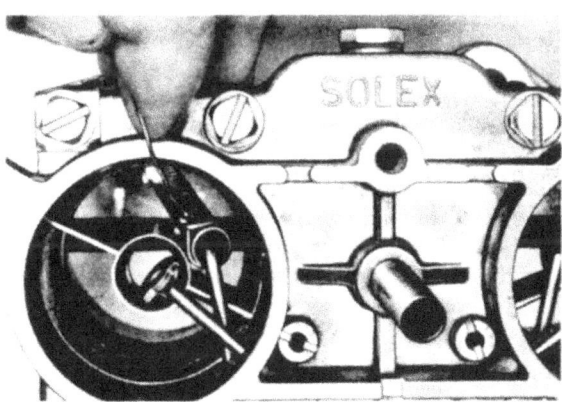

5. Check injection quantity, empty the calibrated vial, then repeat the procedure on the second injection nozzle. See the previous NOTE for the correct injection quantity for each nozzle.
6. If required, readjust the injection quantity by resetting the adjusting nut on the pump rod. If adjustment is not possible due to lack of threads, insert a spacer between the pump arm and the nut. Clockwise lengthens the stroke, counterclockwise shortens it.

IMPORTANT: Fuel squirting from the pump nozzle should not strike the preatomizer nor the venturi, and must pass through the slit between the carburetor wall and the throttle valve (see illustration). Should it be necessary to bend the injection nozzle, make sure that its tip remains at the correct height (check it against another nozzle). The pump jet does not affect the injection quantity. Changes in size of the pump jet affect only the duration of injection since the jet size controls the flow only in respect to flow duration. Injection quantity as well as the moment of injection must be identical in all carburetor throats.

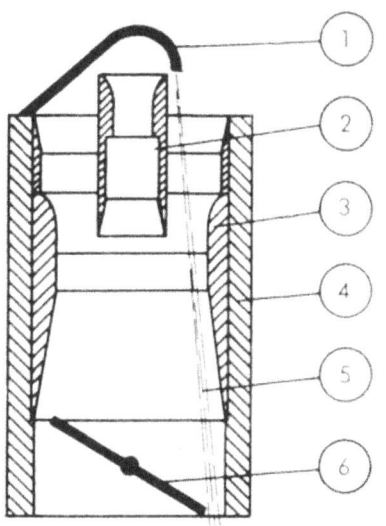

1 Injection nozzle   4 Carburetor body
2 Preatomizer   5 Squirting fuel
3 Venturi   6 Throttle valve

CARBURETOR FLOAT LEVEL TEST

NOTE: Special Tool P 78 Float Level Gauge is useful but NOT required for this test. Make sure the vehicle is on a level base. This test is necessary only after a carburetor boil out; it may help when there are flat acceleration spots on high-speed curves.

With Special Tool P 78

1. Remove the main jet carrier from one carburetor.
2. Install the float level gauge (Special Tool P 78) in place of the main jet carrier (see illustration).

3. Start engine and allow to idle until engine is running smoothly at operating temperature. The fuel should rise to a point between the marking rings on the gauge tube. Should the fuel level deviate (which is quite uncommon), first check the float for leaks, then the float adjustment swivel, and finally the float needle valve.

4. Should the above items appear sound, proceed to readjust the float level by resetting the externally located float level adjusting screw.

IMPORTANT: Turn the screw in to lower the fuel level, turn the screw out to raise the fuel level. Make minimal ($\frac{1}{4}$ turn) adjustments, then wait for the fuel level to stabilize. Turning the adjustment screw in causes the float to move downward which, in turn, causes the fuel level to raise. Therefore, allow the engine to use up the excess fuel before making the final adjustment.

Without Special Tool P 78

1. With the car on a level base and the engine running smoothly, remove the plug from the float inspection port (see illustration).

2. The float level is correct when fuel is seen $\frac{1}{32}$ to $\frac{1}{16}$ in. below the machined groove within the threaded part of the port.

3. Should the fuel level deviate (which is quite uncommon), first check the float for leaks, then the float adjustment swivel, and finally the float needle valve.

4. Should the above items appear sound, proceed to reset the float level by resetting the externally located float level adjusting screw.

IMPORTANT: Turn the screw in to lower the fuel level, turn the screw out to raise the fuel level. Make minimal ($\frac{1}{4}$ turn) adjustments, then wait for the fuel level to stabilize. Turning the adjustment screw in causes the float to move downward which, in turn, causes some of the fuel to run out through the inspection port. Therefore, allow the engine to use up the fuel excess before making the final adjustment.

ADJUSTING THROTTLE LINKAGE

IMPORTANT: Smooth and even closing action of the throttles can be achieved only when all throttle linkage ball joints move freely. Be sure to keep ball joints lubricated and lock nuts tightened.

The throttle linkage must be so adjusted that all throttle valves work in unison. Make sure none of the throttles bind throughout the entire extent of travel from idle to full power settings.

SERVICING THROTTLE LINKAGE

1. Detach throttle rod at ball joint of cross-shaft at air blower housing.
2. Remove passenger compartment carpeting to gain access to opening in the floorboard.
3. Remove gearshift lever base retaining screw (hex head), then withdraw gearshift lever with base.
4. Remove handbrake lever with base (see BRAKING SYSTEM for procedure).
5. Remove attaching clip of throttle rod through freed openings.
6. Detach throttle rod from rear cross-shaft ball joint (beneath transmission), then pull throttle rod rearward to withdraw.
7. To install, reverse the above procedure, making sure the ball joint lock nuts are properly tightened and the ball joints and all moving joints of the cross-shaft are well lubricated.

SERVICING FUEL LINE

1. Remove both air cleaners.
2. Disconnect fuel lines from both carburetors by removing fittings.
3. Remove attaching clip from behind the air blower housing.
4. Pull off the fuel hose from the fuel pump.
5. To install fuel line, reverse the order of the previous instructions, using a new gasket and attaching the fuel line so it does not touch the housing to cause rattles.

REMOVING AND INSTALLING CARBURETORS

Removal

1. Unsnap air cleaner fasteners, then remove air cleaners.
2. Remove air cleaner base plate.
3. Disconnect carburetor linkage from throttle arm, detach fuel line (see illustration).
4. Remove the four carburetor retaining nuts from the carburetor flange, then withdraw the carburetor.
5. Be sure to keep the intake duct covered to prevent the entry of dirt.

Installation

To install, reverse the previous order, making sure

Solex Carburetor 40 PII — 4/1+2 (1965 and later)

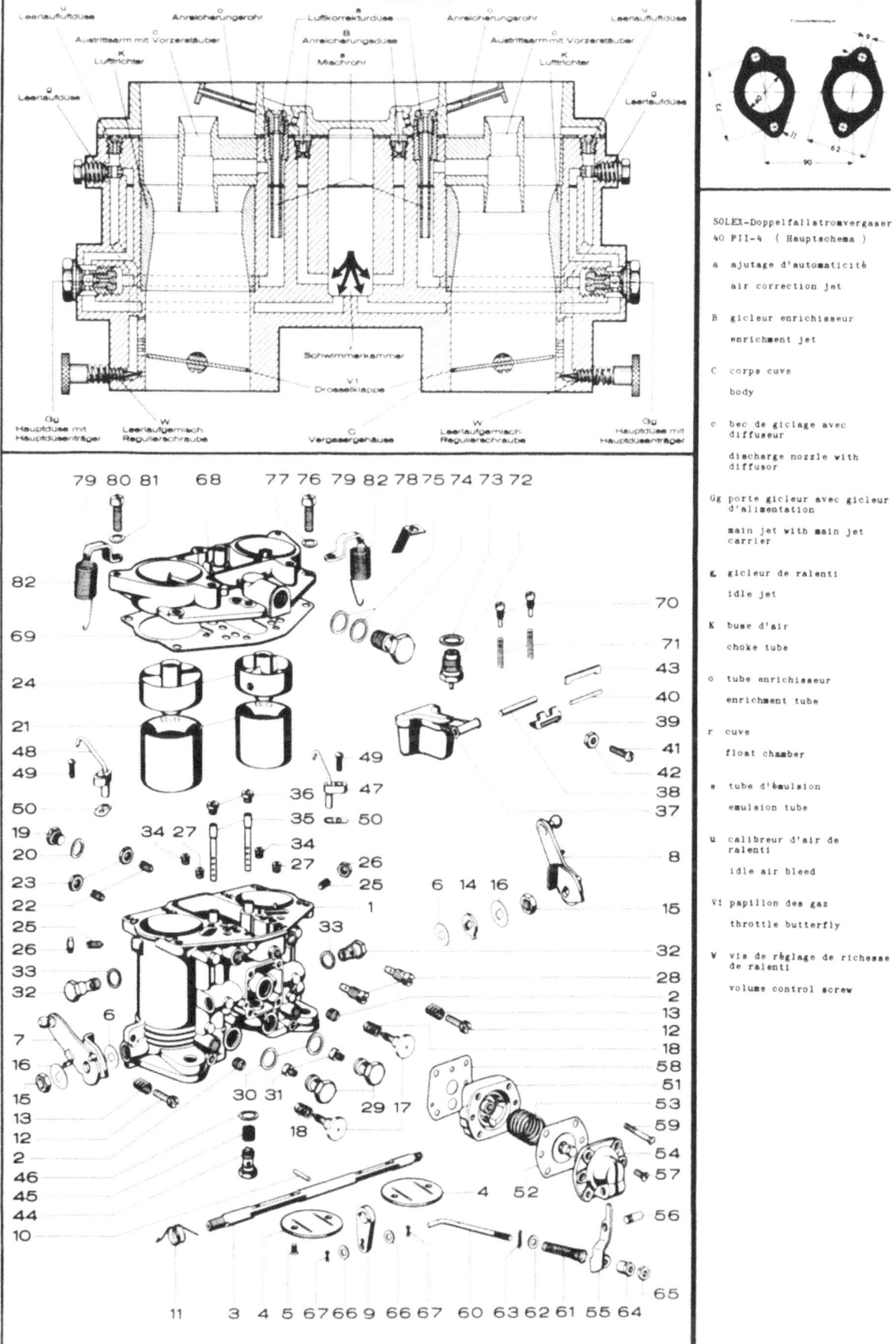

SOLEX-Doppelfallstromvergaser 40 PII-4 (Hauptschema)

a ajutage d'automaticité
   air correction jet

B gicleur enrichisseur
   enrichment jet

C corps cuve
   body

c bec de giclage avec diffuseur
   discharge nozzle with diffusor

Gg porte gicleur avec gicleur d'alimentation
   main jet with main jet carrier

g gicleur de ralenti
   idle jet

K buse d'air
   choke tube

o tube enrichisseur
   enrichment tube

r cuve
   float chamber

s tube d'émulsion
   emulsion tube

u calibreur d'air de ralenti
   idle air bleed

Vi papillon des gaz
   throttle butterfly

V vis de réglage de richesse de ralenti
   volume control screw

165

Emission Control Solex Carburetor 2 x 40 PII — 4 (1968 and later)

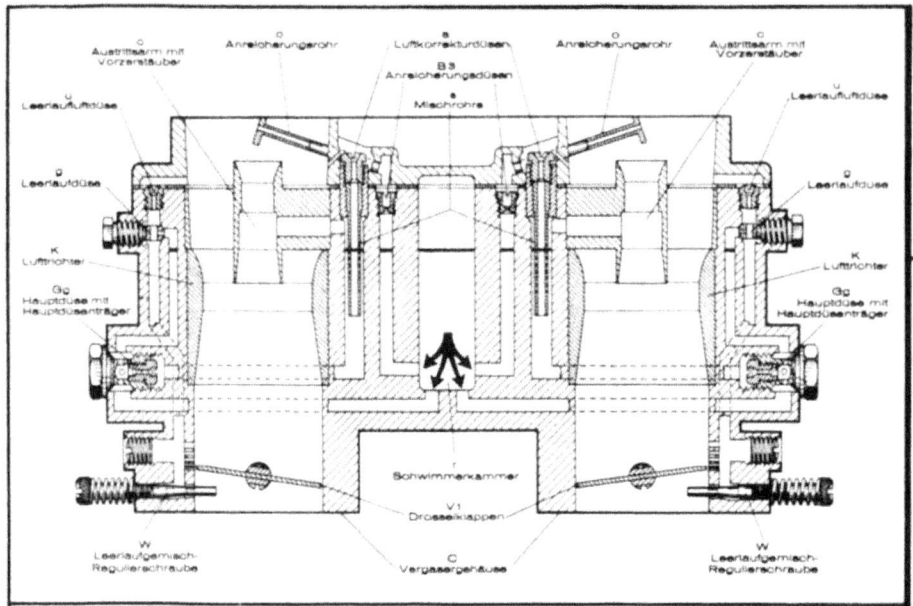

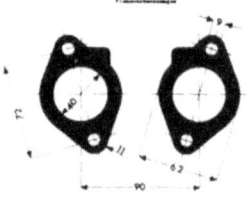

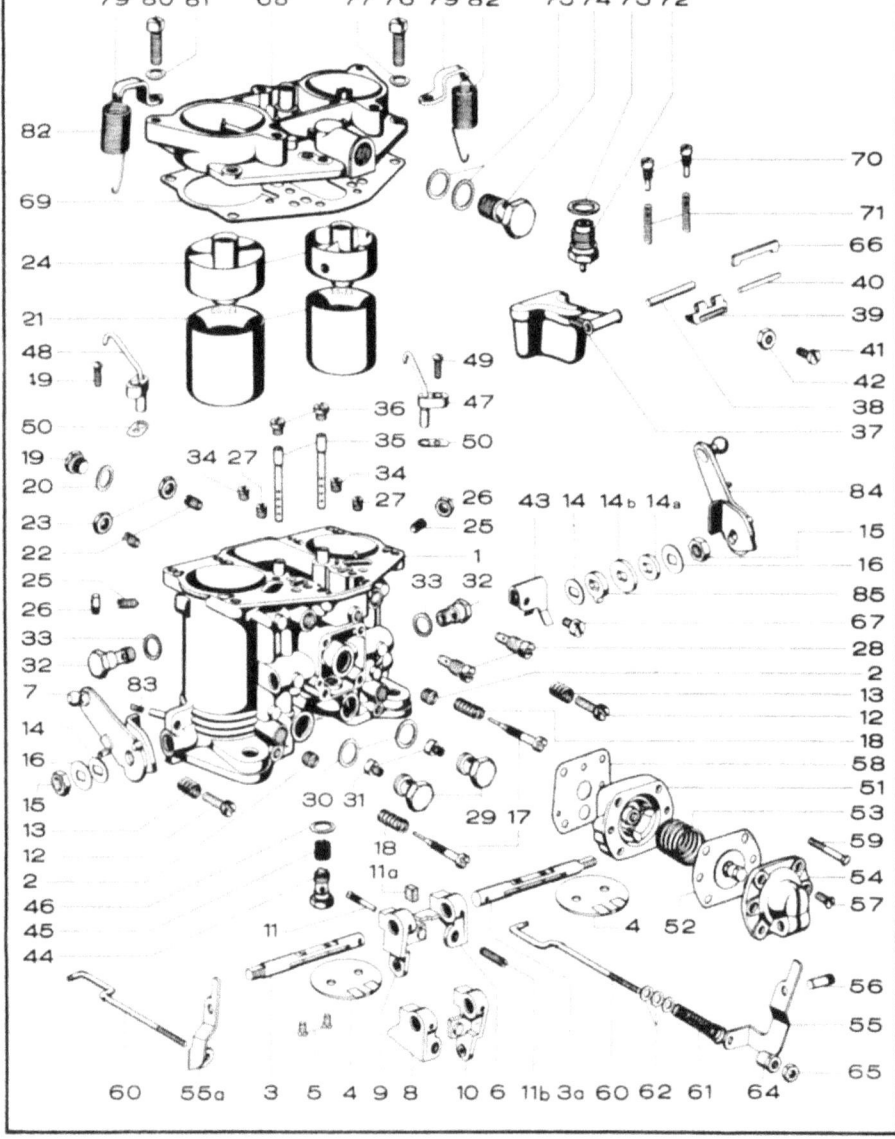

SOLEX-Doppelfallstromvergaser 40 PII-4 (Hauptschema)

- a ajutage d'automaticité
     air correction jet
- B gicleur enrichisseur
     enrichment jet
- C corps cuve
     body
- c bec de giclage avec diffuseur
     discharge nozzle with diffusor
- Gg porte gicleur avec gicleur d'alimentation
     main jet with main jet carrier
- g gicleur de ralenti
     idle jet
- k buse d'air
     choke tube
- o tube enrichisseur
     enrichment tube
- r cuve
     float chamber
- s tube d'émulsion
     emulsion tube
- u calibreur d'air de ralenti
     idle air bleed
- V1 papillon des gaz
     throttle butterfly
- W vis de réglage de richesse de ralenti
     volume control screw

that the gaskets seat properly and the linkage is free-moving.

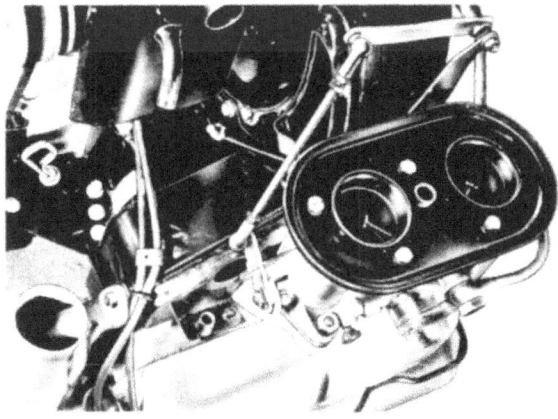

SERVICING CARBURETOR

Disassembly

With carburetor removed from intake duct and exterior washed in clean solvent, proceed as follows for reconditioning (see previous illustrations under DESCRIPTION):

1. Remove retaining screws from carburetor cover, then withdraw cover with gasket, noting location of float pin retainers.
2. Remove float with pin and intermediate swivel joint.
3. Remove four accelerating pump retaining screws, then remove pump.
4. Remove main jet carrier with jets, then remove idle air bleed and idle jets.
5. Remove air correction jets and shake out emulsion tubes.
6. Remove injection nozzle retaining screws and carefully withdraw the nozzles, making certain not to bend nozzles in the process.
7. Remove both pump jets and accelerating pump check valve.
8. Remove float needle valve assembly, then remove power enrichment jets.
9. Remove the idle mixture adjusting screws.
10. Loosen the preatomizer set screws, then pull out preatomizers by first freeing with a gentle twist (see illustration).
11. Loosen and remove venturi set screws, pull out venturis by first freeing with a gentle twist, then carefully lifting out, making sure they do not bind.
12. Carefully file off any burrs in the venturi which were caused by set screw pressure around the outside circumference only. DO NOT disturb the inside of the venturi.

Cleaning

Clean the carburetor in carburetor cleaner solution. Clear all jets and ports of casting with compressed air ONLY, and in no case use wire or other mechanical devices to clean (especially jets) because the calibrated orifices can be damaged or enlarged.

Inspection And Reassembly

To reassemble, reverse the previous disassembly procedure, noting the following points:

1. Check the float for leaks as follows:
   a. Hold near your ear and shake. Replace if there is a splashing noise.
   b. To double check, immerse it in hot water. Air bubbles rising to the surface will indicate a leak. DO NOT solder a leak, since this will change the weight, which is critical. Renew the float.
2. Check the float needle valve and seat for wear, then test it for leaks using fuel.
3. Fuel line connector threads in cover must be undamaged.
4. Check condition of gaskets, replace if necessary (usual practice is to use a whole carburetor rebuilding kit).
5. Check that the pump diaphragm is firm, flexible, and whole.
6. Check the two pump springs against each other; they should be equal in resistance.
7. Make sure that all jets are of proper size by comparing with CARBURETOR SPECIFICATION table.

NOTE: When replacing jets or check valves, make

sure that only genuine SOLEX-stamped parts are used. The parts are carefully calibrated to permit precise settings and low fuel consumption.

8. Make sure idle mixture adjustment screws have a cone tip that is tapered, not blunted, bent or burred; replace if necessary. Fully close the four idle mixture adjustment screws one at a time in both carburetors, turning very slowly (so as not to damage the cone tip) until it just touches. From this position, turn each screw two turns out.

9. Install venturis, making certain that the venturi throats face up, that is, the writing on the venturi tubes should be seen from above (see both illustrations). Firmly tighten venturi set screws but do not overtighten.

10. Check radial clearance of throttle shaft. Excessive clearance allows extra air to pass through and impairs engine starting and idling.

Replacement

To replace, reverse the removal procedure, noting the following points:

1. Use a new intake duct gasket. Make sure the gasket matches the contours of the intake port in the cylinder head.
2. Place the graphite-coated side of the gasket towards the cylinder head.
3. Inspect the manifold for cracks. If cracked at all, replace it.
4. Carefully and evenly tighten the intake duct retaining nuts and bolt.
5. Install a new gasket between the duct and carburetor.

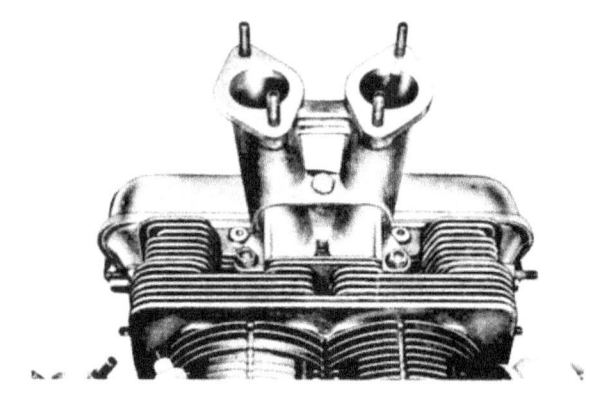

FUEL PUMP

NOTE: Should the vehicle's engine be operating roughly, check the fuel pump pressure. Insufficient pump pressure causes a lean combustion mixture and thus, a rough running engine with misfiring at high rpm and decreased power output. Excessive pump pressure causes carburetor flooding and, in almost all cases, leads to dilution of crankcase oil, causing harm to the wearing surfaces of the engine.

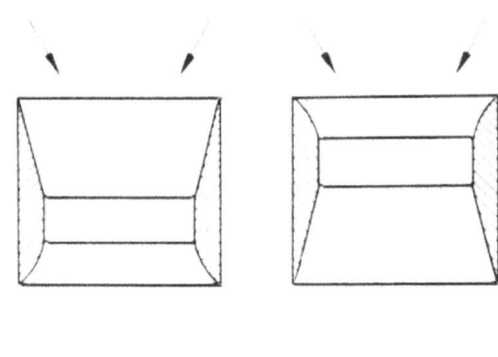

Wrong!   Correct!

SERVICING INTAKE MANIFOLD

Removal

1. Remove carburetor and spark plug connectors from spark plugs.
2. Remove the side cover plate.
3. Remove the retaining nuts and bolt from the intake manifold and withdraw the manifold.
4. Cover the intake port in the cylinder head.

DESCRIPTION

The fuel pump is mounted on the engine crankcase, and pumps fuel to the carburetors by means of a mechanically actuated diaphragm. The actuation is accomplished by an eccentric machined into the distributor pinion shaft. The quantity of fuel delivered by the pump is metered automatically in direct proportion to the amount of fuel dispensed by the carburetors. The actual fuel pump consists of an upper and lower assembly, with the upper assembly containing an inlet and outlet valve and a fuel filter. The lower assembly contains an actuating plunger, which acts upon the diaphragm and diaphragm spring located between both

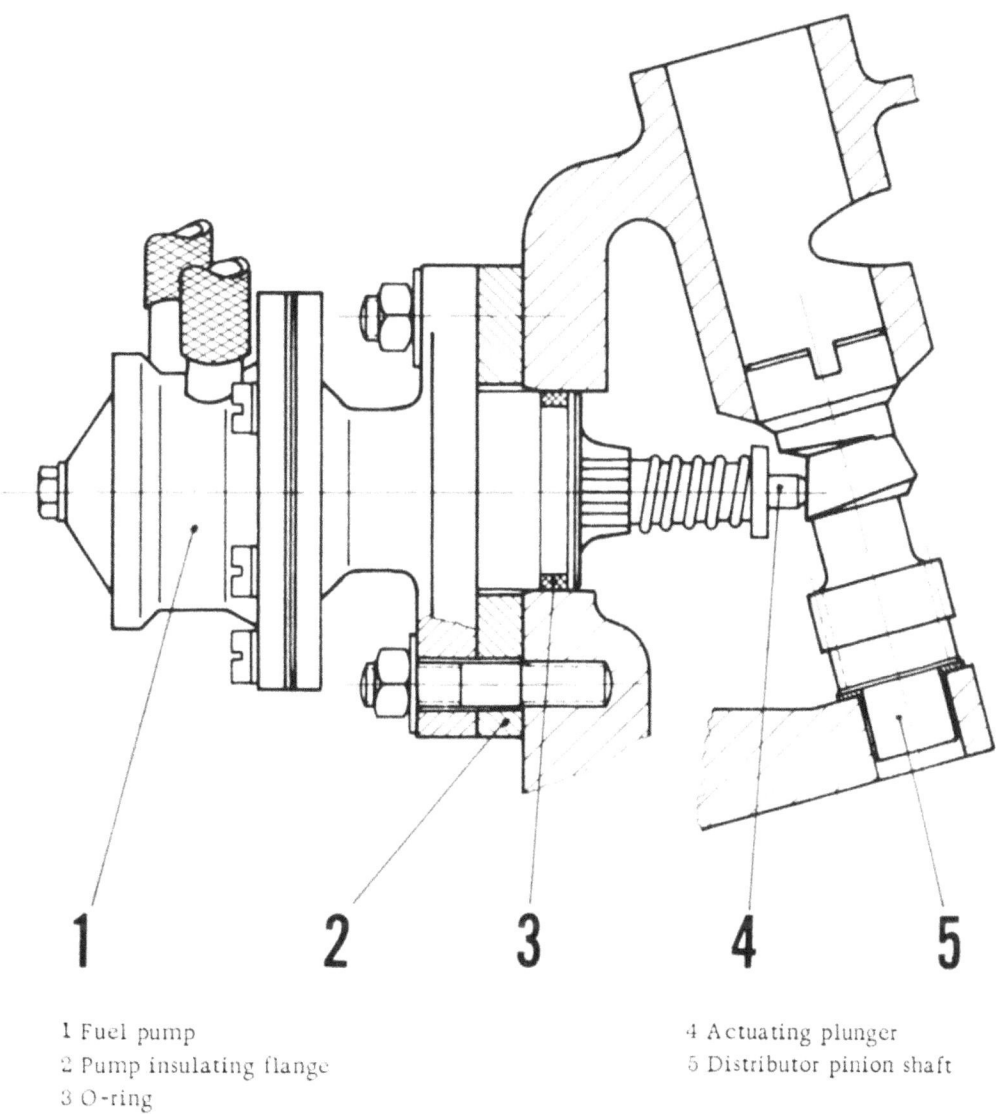

1 Fuel pump
2 Pump insulating flange
3 O-ring
4 Actuating plunger
5 Distributor pinion shaft

assemblies. The diaphragm is built up of several layers of a fuel-proof material, and is sandwiched between two supporting discs which are riveted to the plunger coupling; the diaphragm also acts as a gasket.

As the distributor pinion shaft turns, the eccentric raises the diaphragm actuating plunger. The plunger transmits the pressure to the diaphragm coupling, overcoming the pressure of the plunger return spring but with the support of the diaphragm spring. This forces the fuel contained in the pump to exit through the outlet valve up to the carburetors. As the pinion shaft continues to turn, the actuating plunger moves back to its at-rest position through its own tensioning and the help of the plunger return spring, creating a negative pressure in the chamber above the diaphragm. This opens the inlet valve and allows fresh fuel to enter into the pump chamber. This pumping action repeats with every revolution of the eccentric (once every two revolutions of the crankshaft). The amount of fuel passing through the pump is governed by the amount dispensed by the carburetors, i.e., only that amount of fuel can be pumped which is able to pass through the more or less opened float needle valves in the carburetors.

The lower assembly is vented through two orifices in the casting. Should the fuel leak into this part of the pump, it will drain through these venting holes rather than entering the crankcase. The pump pressure is determined by the degree of spring compression during the intake stroke of the pump. The spring tension is so calibrated that it allows the fuel to enter the carburetor only so long as the carburetor float needle valve is open. When the buoyancy of the float forces the float needle valve to close, pressure builds up in the fuel line and pump fuel chamber, shortening the pump stroke. In normal operation, the diaphragm stroke amounts to only a few tenths of a millimeter.

Fuel Pump Schematic

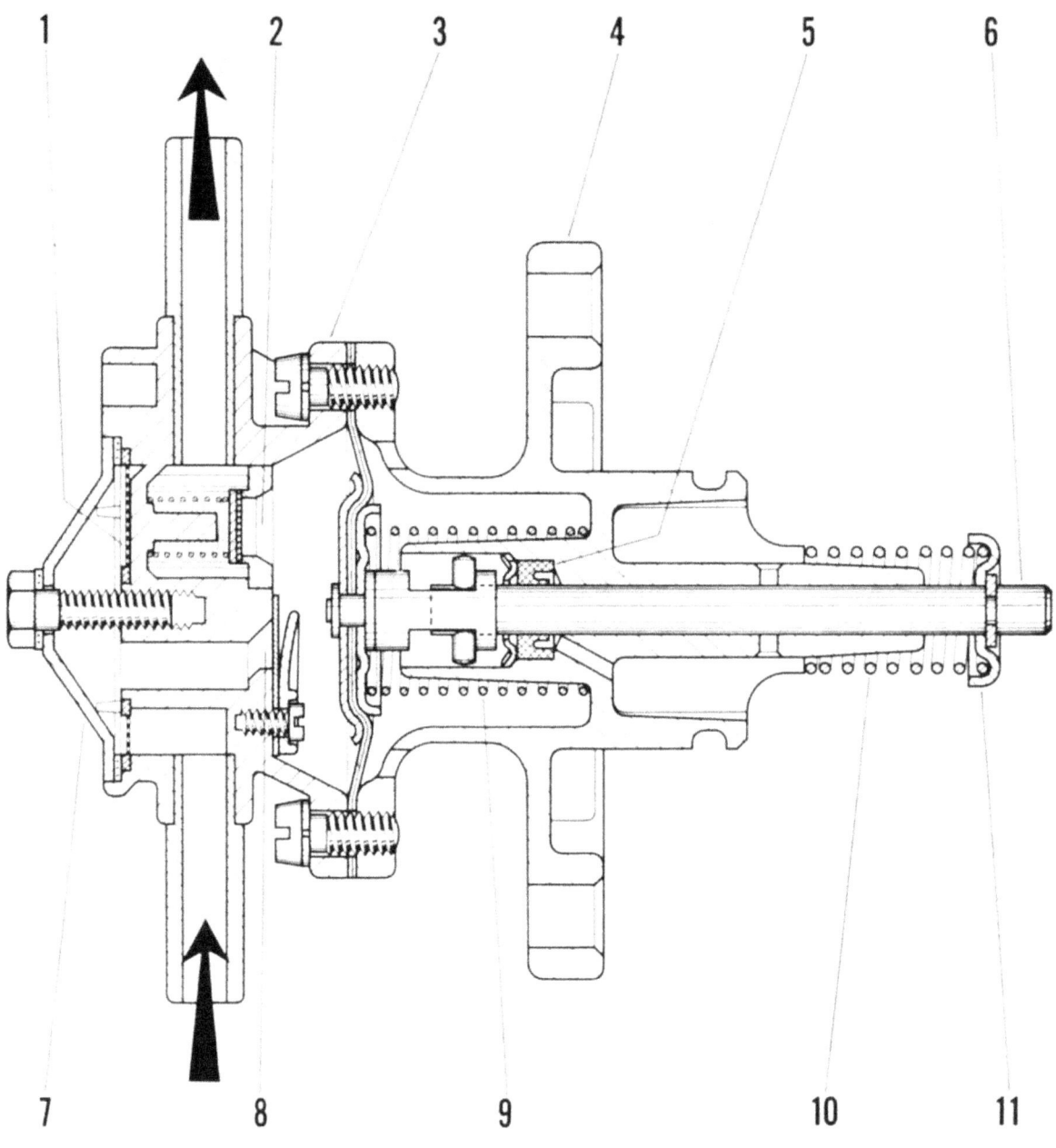

1 Fuel screen
2 Outlet valve
3 Upper assembly
4 Lower assembly
5 Oil scraper
6 Actuating plunger
7 Pump cover
8 Inlet valve
9 Diaphragm spring
10 Plunger return spring
11 Spring retainer

TESTING FUEL PUMP

Essential for proper pump pressure is correct spring tension and faultless condition of the diaphragm and control valves. The simplest way to check the fuel pump pressure is with the aid of a pressure gauge inserted into the fuel line between the pump and the carburetor by means of a T-joint. A fuel shut-off valve is incorporated in the line behind the pressure gauge.

The pump pressure should be 2.9 to 3.5 psi (0,20 to 0,24 atm) with the float needle valve closed and engine running at 1,000 to 3,000 rpm. Minimum fuel delivery should be 7.9 U.S. gallons (30 liters) per hour, which equals 16.9 U.S. fluid oz. (500 cc) per minute, at 4,500 rpm.

FUEL PUMP REMOVAL AND REPLACEMENT

Removal

1. Pull off fuel hoses from pump.
2. Remove pump shield (see illustration).

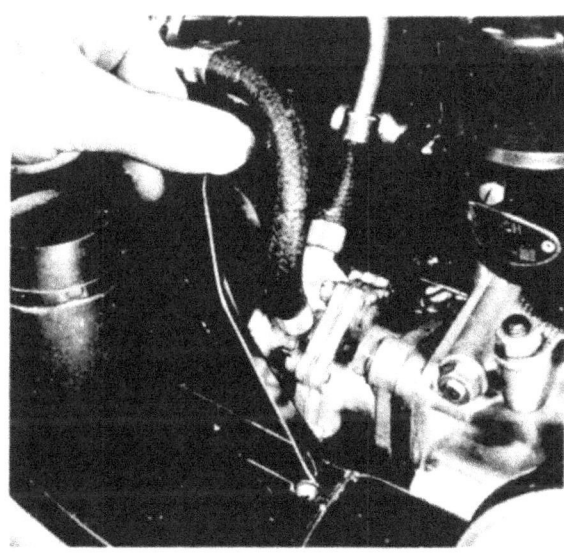

3. Remove attaching nuts from flange, then remove pump and insulating spacer (see illustration).

Replacement

To install fuel pump, reverse the removal procedure, making sure the O-ring is not damaged or aged, and replacing if necessary.

SERVICING FUEL PUMP

Disassembly

1. Remove fuel pump as previously described, then wash with gasoline or solvent.
2. Remove cover retaining hex bolt (see illustrations under FUEL SYSTEM DESCRIPTION).
3. Remove cover and fuel screen (see illustration).
4. Remove six fillister screws which secure the upper assembly, then pull off the assembly (see illustration).

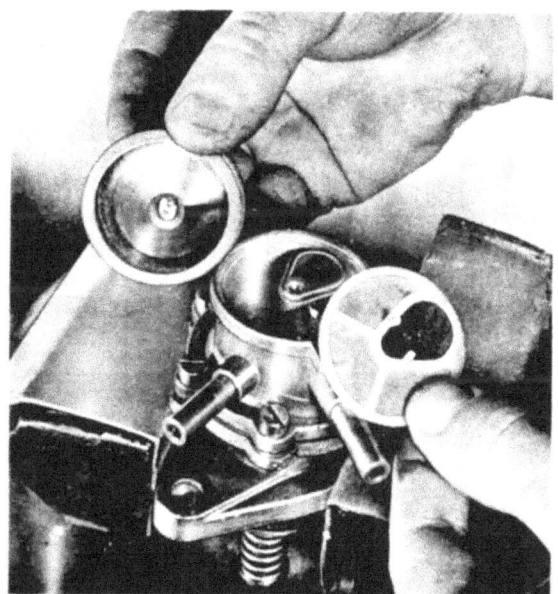

FUEL PUMP COMPONENTS

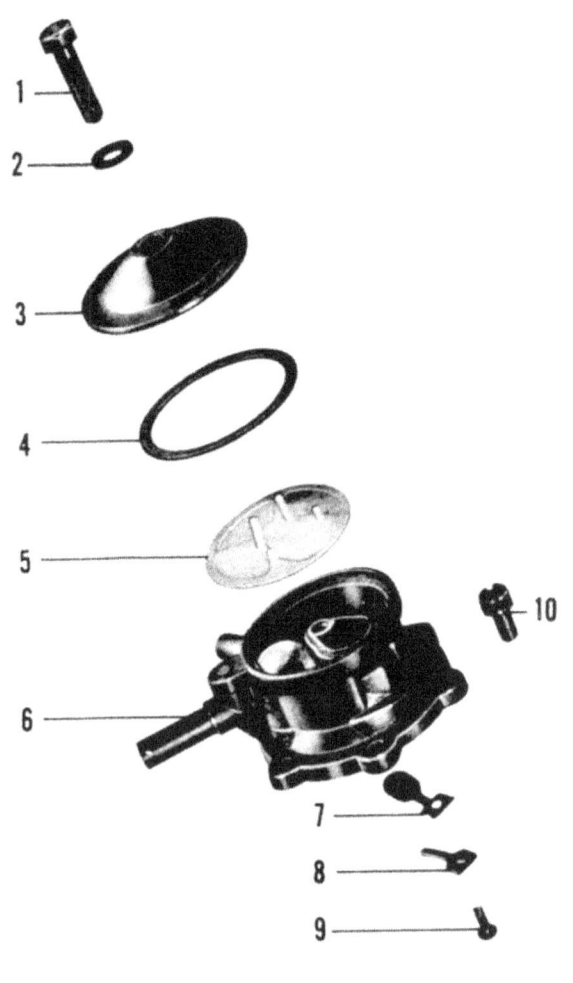

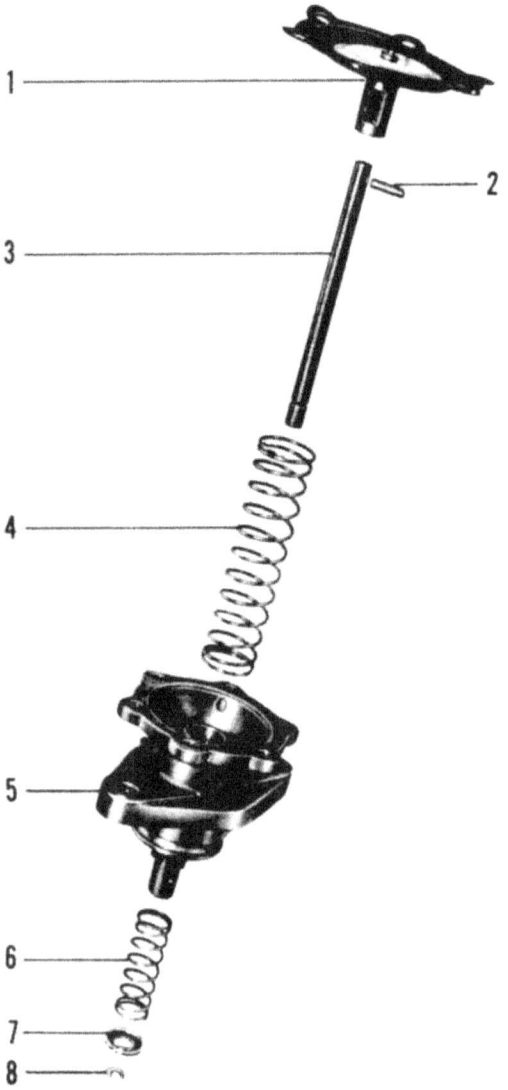

1 Hex bolt
2 Gasket
3 Cover
4 Gasket
5 Fuel screen
6 Pump, upper assembly
7 Leaf spring valve
8 Valve limiter
9 Self-threading screw M 3x8
10 Fillister screw with washer

1 Diaphragm assembly
2 Coupling pin
3 Plunger
4 Diaphragm spring
5 Pump, lower assembly
6 Plunger return spring
7 Spring retainer
8 Lock ring

5. Rest the lower assembly of the pump on the diaphragm supporting disc, push the spring retainer down with pliers, then remove the lock ring, spring retainer, and spring (see illustration).

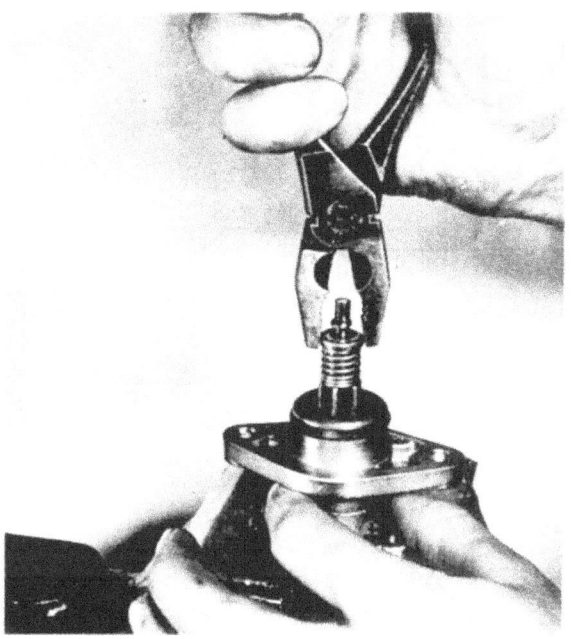

6. Pull out the diaphragm—plunger—spring assembly from the lower pump casting. Make sure there is no grit around the lock ring groove in the plunger so as to prevent damaging the oil scraper.

7. Remove the coupling pin from the actuating plunger with a punch, then detach the diaphragm from the plunger (see illustration).

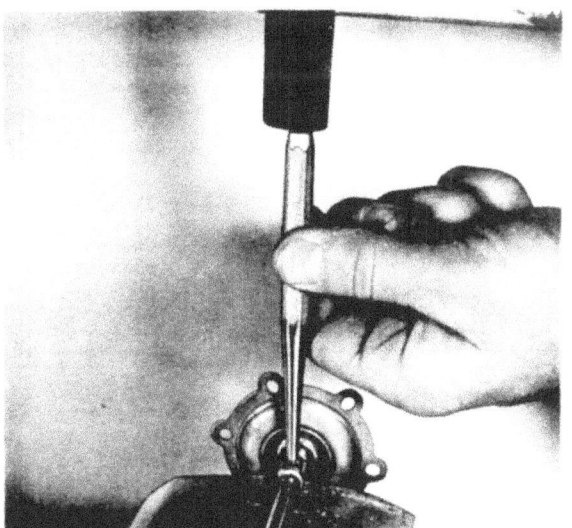

8. Remove the self-threading fillister screw from inlet valve and remove leaf spring valve and valve limiter (see illustration).

NOTE: Outlet valve cannot be removed.

9. Clean metal pump parts ONLY with carburetor cleaner solution. Clean non-metal parts ONLY with gasoline.

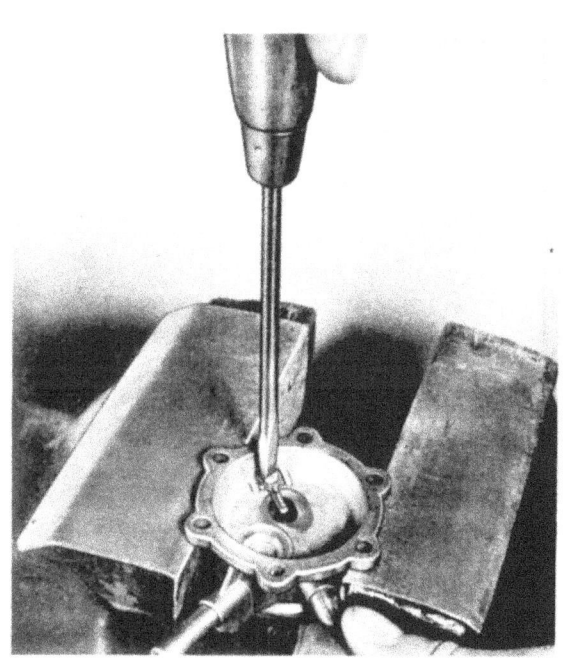

Reassembly

To reassemble the fuel pump, reverse the previous procedure, noting the following points:

1. Check the sealing surface of the inlet valve.
2. Check the outlet valve in the upper assembly for proper function (blow and inhale).
3. Install the leaf spring valve and valve limiter, then check for proper operation (blow and inhale).
4. Reconnect diaphragm to plunger with the pin, then check free movement of plunger, in diaphragm coupling. Center coupling pin in plunger.
5. When mounting pump upper assembly, make sure that the diaphragm is not creased. Evenly tighten the screws in a cross-sequence.
6. Replace pump cover gasket if at all damaged.

CARBURETOR SERVICE DIAGNOSIS

Malfunction	Possible Cause	Remedy
1. Engine does not start despite properly functioning ignition and adequate fuel in tank.	a) No fuel in fuel system	a) Clean main jets. Check fuel supply lines. Detach fuel line connecting pump with carburetor actuate starter (ignition off). If fuel flows from pump, float needle valve is plugged, if no fuel flows from pump, possibly pump check valves are stuck or pump mechanism defective.
	b) Carburetor floods.	b) Check and clean float needle valve, check gasket at float needle valve assembly. Check float, replace if defective.
2. Uneven idling.	a) Improperly adjusted idling.	a) Readjust idling.
	b) Idle jets or idle air bleed plugged.	b) Clean idle jets or idle air bleed, as required.
	c) Leak in the intake ducts.	c) Check intake ducts, flange connections, and gaskets.
	d) Defective idle mixture screws.	d) Install new idle mixture adjusting screws.

Malfunction	Possible Cause	Remedy
3. Poor power transition (flat spot).	a) Idle adjustment too lean. b) Improperly set float level. c) Omproper injection quantity. d) Intake ducts leaking.	a) Readjust idling (check jets). b) Readjust float level. c) Readjust injection quantity. d) Check intake ducts, flange connections, and gaskets.
4. Engine stalls when throttle is quickly closed.	Improper idle adjustment.	Readjust idling.
5. Engine runs unevenly, misses, backfires.	a) Mixture too rich. b) Mixture too lean. c) Intake duct leaking.	a) Check fuel pump pressure. Check float level. Check float needle valve. b) Clean main jets. Check fuel lines. Check float level. c) Check intake ducts, flange connections, and gaskets.
6. High fuel consumption.	a) High fuel pump pressure overriding float needle valve. b) Defective float (leaking). c) Float needle valve not closing.	a) Check fuel pressure. b) install new float. c) Check float needle valve.

CARBURETOR SPECIFICATIONS

Carburetor type	Solex 40 P II-4	2 per engine
Venturi (K)	32	2 per carburetor
Main jet (Gg)	0120	2 per carburetor
Air correction jet (a)	180	2 per carburetor
Idle metering jet (g)	57.5	2 per carburetor
Idle air bleed (u)	1.8	2 per carburetor
Accelerating pump	72	1 per carburetor
Pump jet (Gp)	50	2 per carburetor
Accelerating pump nozzle	high-type with 0.4 restrictor	2 per carburetor
Float needle valve (spring-loaded)	175	1 per carburetor
Float	7.4 g	1 per carburetor
Emulsion tube	Nr. 25	2 per carburetor
Main jet carrier	6	2 per carburetor
Intermediate metering ports	1.7; 1.4; 1.0	
Injection quantity (warm season)	0.45 cc (7.3 minims) from 2 strokes, each nozzle	2 nozzles per carburetor
Injection quantity (cold season)	0.65 cc (10.6 minims) from 2 strokes, each nozzle	

EXHAUST EMISSION CONTROL SYSTEM

DESCRIPTION

The Exhaust Emission Control (EEC) System is designed to reduce the expulsion of air pollutants, such as hydrocarbons and carbon monoxide, through the process of afterburning. This is accomplished with an air pump. The air is drawn from the left wet-screen air cleaner, pumped through control valves, and is finally blown into the exhaust ports in the cylinder heads where it supports the combustion of the exhaust gases.

Engine speed governs the volume of air propelled into the system since the air pump is belt-driven off the crankshaft. The single unit control valve consists of two valves, one a flow-back check valve and the other a pressure relief valve. The flow-back valve prevents exhaust gases from backing up into the air supply channels when the air pump should become inoperative, such as due to V-belt failure. The pressure relief valve releases surplus air into the open when the engine is at high rpm. On some models, a diverter valve may be fitted to the control valve. The diverter valve prevents exhaust backfire on the overrun (when there is a high degree of vacuum present in the intake manifold because of high engine speed and shut throttles). In this case, the air from the air pump is expelled briefly into the engine compartment rather than being pumped into the exhaust ports.

A throttle valve compensator also aids in the above case (such as when the car is coasting on a long downgrade). This opens the throttle valve slightly, preventing the preparation of an over-rich mixture which would be normally present.

The above devices provide a fully combustible fuel/air mixture with a highly reduced percentage of unburned air pollutants in the exhaust gases. An additional control is a vacuum control device which retards the ignition timing at idle speed. A vacuum line is connected between the ignition distributor and the carburetor, with the line so connected at the carburetor that the occurring vacuum can be effective only in the idle

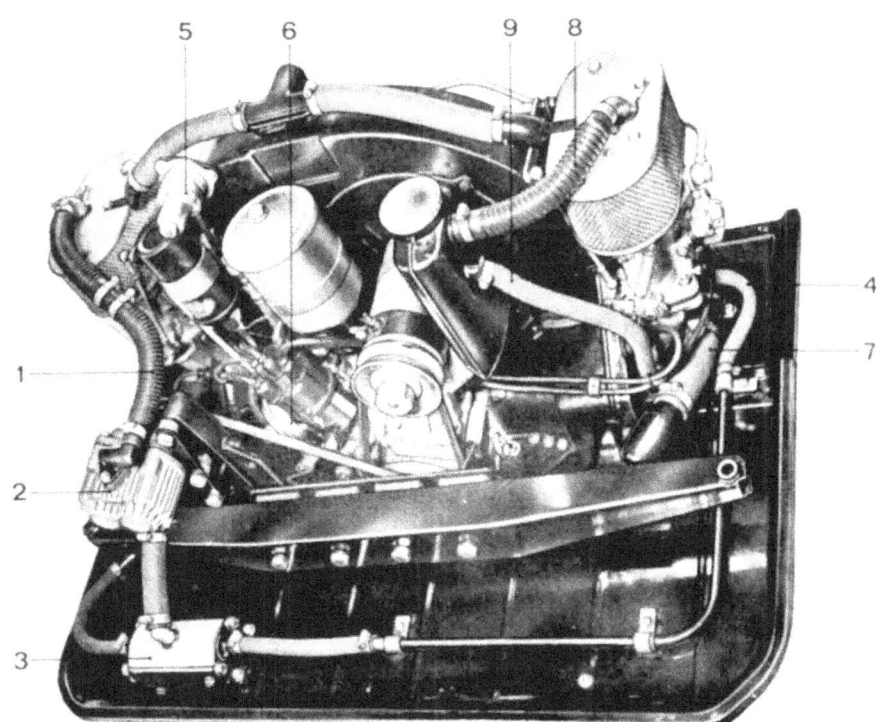

1 Air pump intake duct
2 Air pump
3 Control valve

4 Air pressure duct
5 Throttle valve compensator
6 Vacuum servo unit

7 Carburetor preheating duct
8 Crankcase breather duct
9 Crankcase breather hose

speed position. The retarded ignition timing makes it possible to have the throttle valves opened slightly wider than normal in the idle speed position. This results in better cylinder filling at idle speed position, and a more combustible mixture on deceleration. The intake manifolds are also heated with warm air to improve the preparation of the fuel/air mixture.

Only certain spark plugs may be used with the EEC System. The Porsche approved plugs as of May, 1967 are the Bosch W 200 T 35, the Bosch W 225 T 7 or the Champion G1 82 Y, all with a gap of 0,6 to 0,7 mm. Consult a Porsche dealership as to the recommended spark plugs for later models.

LUBRICATION

The oil level of the air pump gear compartment should be checked every 6,000 mi. (10,000 km). Make a dipstick, using the metric measurements in the diagram, to check the oil level.

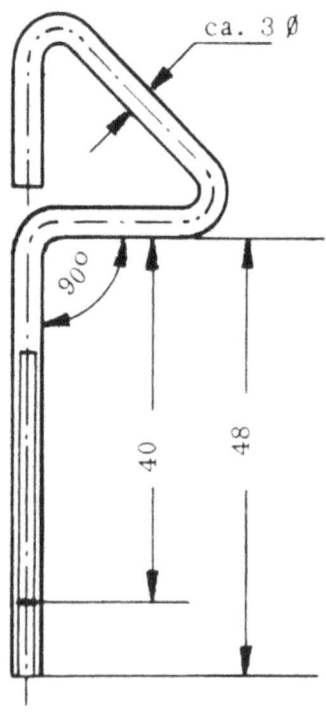

Insert the dipstick into the filler hole (see illustration) until the horizontally bent part of the handle comes to rest against the seat of the oil filler plug. The oil level must be between the dipstick mark or the lowest end of the dipstick. If necessary, replenish with Type-A Automatic Transmission Fluid. This should be done with care, since the pump should contain only about .85 fl. oz. (25 cc) of oil. In no case may the oil level be higher than the dipstick mark, so add a small amount of oil and then check the level with the dipstick. If there is excess oil added, drain some off with a syphon hose.

TESTING EEC SYSTEM

This test requires that an exhaust gas analzer be used to test for the carbon monoxide content of the exhaust. Be sure to conduct test with proper ventilation.

1. Make sure carburetors are correctly adjusted as described in the FUEL SYSTEM chapter.
2. Connect the exhaust gas analyzer to the exhaust pipe according to the manufacturer's directions.
3. With engine idling, carbon monoxide content should be about 2.5 to 3 percent.

VACUUM CONTROL UNIT TEST

Description

The firing point is 3° before top dead center (TDC) of cylinder No. 1, equivalent to about 3,8 mm on the outer circumference of the crankshaft pulley. This point should be marked with a pencil ahead of the TDC mark in the direction of crankshaft rotation. Check that this pencil mark is lined up with the notch in the crankcase housing while at the same time the distributor rotor points to the terminal for cylinder No. 1 and to the notch in the distributor housing. Make another pencil mark to the left of the TDC mark (3,8 mm or 3°) for checking the vacuum control unit. The timing should be set with the engine running and the vacuum control unit working correctly. The timing should be set 3° AFTER TDC using a stroboscope (timing light).

Ignition Timing Check

1. Check the ignition points and adjust the gap to .016 in. (0,4 mm), making dwell angle 50° ± 3°.

IMPORTANT: Be sure the above is correctly set, and

that the points are not damaged, since the whole test will be made invalid otherwise.

2. Remove distributor cap and rotor, then loosen distributor clamp screw at the distributor base.
3. Connect a 12-volt test light with one clamp to Terminal 1 at the distributor and the other clamp to ground. Switch on the ignition.
4. Turn the distributor body clockwise until the points have closed, then in the opposite direction to the point where the points open and the test light illuminates.
5. At this point tighten the distributor clamp screw.
6. Turn the crankshaft counterclockwise by about 30°, then slowly clockwise until the test light illuminates once again. Stop turning crankshaft at this point.
7. If the timing has been properly set, the test light should go on exactly at the point where the pencil mark to the right of the TDC mark has lined up with the notch in the crankcase housing. If not, loosen the distributor clamp screw and readjust the timing.
8. Replace the rotor and the distributor cap.

Vacuum Control Unit Check

NOTE: The vacuum control unit is actuated by negative pressures in the induction system, and is connected by hose to the intake manifolds of cylinders No. 2 and 4. Before continuing with the test, make sure the hose is firmly seated (see illustration).

1. Connect a stroboscope (timing light) to ignition lead of cylinder No. 1, using the manufacturer's directions.
2. With engine idling, check whether the pencil mark made to the left of the TDC mark appears in line with the notch in the crankcase housing when being flashed with the stroboscope. If not, check the hose for damage and the control unit for vacuum leakage, replacing parts as necessary.

NOTE: The lower connector on the intake manifold (actually part of the carburetor gasket) is connected to the distributor vacuum control unit. Do not confuse this connector with the upper connector.

IDLE SPEED ADJUSTMENT

IMPORTANT: Idle speed adjustment for EEC System-equipped cars is contained under IDLE SPEED ADJUSTMENT in the FUEL SYSTEM chapter. Be sure to return to the procedure following on TESTING THROTTLE VALVE COMPENSATOR after making idle speed adjustment.

TESTING THROTTLE VALVE COMPENSATOR

NOTE: Before conducting test, make sure the vacuum hoses are undamaged and properly seated on the upper connectors of the intake manifolds. Run engine until it reaches operating temperature.

1. Test by operating engine at about 3,000 rpm, then suddenly closing throttle. Engine speed should decrease to about 900 rpm or idle speed (900-950 rpm) within 3 to 5 seconds (set for lower time).
2. If test is negative, check the adjustment of the throttle compensator linkage and the vacuum control unit.
3. To test and adjust the throttle compensator linkage, follow these steps (see illustration):

a. Operate engine, then push the drag lever so far back that the stop disc of the connecting link comes to rest against the body of the throttle compensator. Engine speed should be 2,000 to 2,200 rpm at this point.

b. If a lower rpm reading is given, shorten the linkage of the compensator; if a higher rpm reading is given, lengthen the linkage.

4. To test and adjust the throttle compensator vacuum control unit, follow these steps:

 a. Loosen the set screw located on the side of the adjusting screw.
 b. Carefully turn the adjusting screw. Turning the screw clockwise lengthens the throttle return lag, while turning the screw counterclockwise shortens the lag (see illustration).

 c. Following adjustment, tighten the set screw.
 d. Be sure to check that there is minimum backfiring when the throttle is suddenly closed. If backfiring cannot be minimized, fitting a diverter valve into the system or servicing the present diverter valve may solve the problem.

SERVICING THROTTLE VALVE COMPENSATOR

Removal

1. Pull off vacuum hose from the compensator assembly.
2. Remove ball-joint socket of connecting linkage.
3. Remove bolts securing compensator to air blower housing.

Replacement

1. Replace in reverse order of removal procedure.
2. See TESTING THROTTLE VALVE COMPENSATOR for function check, adjust according to instructions if necessary.

SERVICING CONTROL VALVE

Removal

1. Loosen hose clamps at the control valve assembly and at the hose junction (optional).
2. Detach hose fasteners from the engine shield (optionally).

3. Remove the four retaining bolts, then withdraw control valve from engine rear shield (see illustration).
4. Remove the two holddown bolts and disassemble the control valve (see illustration).
5. Withdraw the air lines from the valve assembly and the hose junction (optional).

Checking

Inspect the pressure relief valve and the flow-back valve for proper sealing, replacing parts as necessary. Each valve can be individually serviced.

Replacement

To replace, reverse the removal procedure, noting the following points:

1. Use new gaskets when reassembling.
2. Be sure the hose terminal in the center of the assembly points up.
3. Note the arrows on both parts of the assembly. The flowback valve points outward, while the pressure relief valve points downward.
4. Check the hose connections for proper sealing. Check hoses for damage.
5. If replacing the air lines, check that hoses are undamaged and are sealing properly, that the fasteners are tightly installed, and that neither hoses nor lines are rubbing against anything.

SERVICING OR INSTALLING DIVERTER VALVE

NOTE: The following instructions apply to kit Part Number 616.113.904.00, which may be purchased at Porsche dealership parts outlets for installation. See TESTING THROTTLE VALVE COMPENSATOR and DESCRIPTION for operating principles and usage of the diverter valve.

Removal

1. Remove the hose from between the diverter valve through the hole in the compressor bracket to the "T" fitting (see illustration).

Replacement Or Installation

1. If a new diverter valve is being installed, the hose connector must first be turned so that it faces in the same direction as the connecting flange (see illustration under step 2 of the previous REMOVAL procedure). Clamp the valve in a vise with protective jaws, then use a bar of a suitable size to position the hose connector. The following illustration shows how to do this, with the hose connector 180° from its final position.

2. Loosen the hose clamps holding the hose between the diverter valve and the control valve (see illustration).

2. Using a soft mallet, knock the hose connector down several times so it seals firmly.

3. Permanently locate the hose connector at this new position by making 3 punch marks at new locations. Be sure to strike far enough from the edge so the part is not broken. See following illustration that shows where to locate punch, but shows hose connector 180° from its final position.

3. Remove the two M 6 x 20 mm hexagon screws, spring washers and nuts, then remove the diverter valve (see previous illustration).

4. If necessary, remove the hose section between the air pump and the diverter valve intermediate plate hose connector by loosening the hose clamps.

5. If necessary, remove the nuts from the two hold-down bolts, then remove the intermediate plate (see illustration).

4. If installing a new valve, first loosen hose clamps from control valve hoses, then withdraw hoses from connectors. Remove the four retaining bolts, then remove control valve. Perform the following operations:

a. Remove the nuts on both of the clamping screws, then replace the control valve center section with the new intermediate piece. Reassemble, slip the attachment flange on the end, then replace nuts and tighten. The assembly should be identical to the illustration under step 5 of the previous REMOVAL procedure.

b. Replace the control valve in its previous position, being sure to tighten all 4 of the retaining screws. Reinstall the hoses.

c. Push the short piece of hose (included in the kit) onto the intermediate piece hose connector, then slip the 2 hose clamps over the hose.

d. Drill a 7 mm hole in the compressor bracket (see illustration under step 2 of the previous REMOVAL procedure). The dimensions are a = 30 mm, b = 15 mm.

e. Cut the existing vacuum hose that is placed between the distributor vacuum control and the "T" fitting. Cut about 30 mm from the distributor vacuum control, then place another "T" fitting (included in the kit) between the two hose sections so that it will look like the illustration under step 1 of the previous REMOVAL procedure.

f. Using the new hose included in the kit, fit it through the newly-drilled hole in the compressor bracket and onto the new "T" fitting.

5. Push the diverter valve onto the hose from the control valve, slip the gasket into place, then install on the attachment flange using the two M 6 x 20 hexagon screws, lock washers, and nuts.

6. Put the hose clamps into place and tighten so the two valves are sealed together.

7. Connect the hose from the air pump to the attachment flange hose connector, then tighten hose clamp to seal into place.

8. Replace both hoses onto control valve ends, making sure retaining clamps seal them into place.

9. Connect the vacuum hose from the "T" piece at the distributor vacuum control to the diverter valve (see previous illustration).

SERVICING AIR PUMP

Removal

1. Loosen V-belt tensioning screw.
2. Loosen hose clamps securing both hoses to air pump, then remove both hoses.
3. Remove both air pump retaining bolts, then remove air pump and V-belt (see illustration).

Air Pump Inspection

Check the V-belt pulley for excessive drag and free rotation prior to installation; minimal drag is normal for some new air pumps. Other than this, the air pumps are service free and are replaced as a unit.

Replacement

To replace, reverse the removal procedure, noting the following points:

1. Be sure the hoses are sealed into place with the hose clamps.
2. Be sure the air pump pulley lines up with the crankshaft pulley, resetting the support if necessary. Use a straight edge as an aid to judging alignment.
3. Check that the V-belt is tensioned so that it will yield about ½ in. (10 mm) when pressed with a finger at a point half way between both pulleys (see illustration). Adjust tension by loosening the upper bolt at the air pump pivot arm, then loosening lower bolt and pulling out on air pump (see illustration). Tighten both bolts and check tension again.

SERVICING CRANKSHAFT PULLEY

NOTE: **This operation can only be performed with the engine removed.**

1. To remove, first remove air hoses from control valve assembly, then remove air line fasteners from the engine rear shield.
2. Loosen the hose clamps of the carburetor heating hoses, then remove hoses and withdraw the angular piece from the lower air duct.
3. Remove the engine transverse support and the support plate.
4. Remove the crankcase breather hose from the breather.
5. Remove the retaining screws from the engine rear shield, then remove the shield.

6. Remove the crankshaft pulley shield.
7. Remove the crankshaft pulley retaining bolt, then withdraw the pulley, using 2 screwdrivers as levers (from both sides) or a puller.
8. To replace pulley, reverse the previous procedures.

NOTE: Torque bolt to 43 ft. lb. (6 mkp).

SERVICING AIR DUCT T-JUNCTION

NOTE: This operation can only be performed with the engine removed.

Removal

1. Remove carburetors as described in the FUEL SYSTEM chapter.
2. Remove front, rear, and side cylinder shrouds as described in the ENGINE chapter.
3. Remove the air supply nozzles by unscrewing bolts (see illustration).

Replacement

To replace, use the affected replacement procedures in the FUEL SYSTEM and the ENGINE chapters, then

reverse the previous removal procedure, noting the following points:

1. Check the T-junction for leaks.
2. Install new gasket rings if necessary.

ENGINE

DESCRIPTION

Before proceeding with serious mechanical repairs or alterations, it might be well to review the design and construction of the engine.

The Porsche 912 uses a flat four cylinder, air-cooled, overhead valve (OHV) engine of 96.5 cubic inches (1,582 cubic centimeter) displacement, operating on the Otto four-stroke-cycle principle. This 102-horsepower (SAE), 90-horsepower (DIN) at 5,800 rpm version is based upon the time-tested engine that has powered Porsche vehicles from their inception (basically, the first Porsche engine was a highly-tuned Volkswagen engine, but the passage of over 15 years has made the two power plants completely different). For those who are interested in such items, the horsepower per liter is rated at 64 (SAE).

The hand-assembled, magnesium alloy engine has individual cylinders arranged in pairs horizontally opposed. The engine is efficiently air-cooled by heat-dissipating light alloy fins on each of the carbon steel cylinders, and also by an oil cooler. Ventilation is provided by a constant flow of forced air from the blower.

To prevent dry-starts (which score the pistons because they lack lubrication), the oil is sent directly to the lubrication points, bypassing the oil cooler, until the engine reaches operating temperature. The engine uses a forged one-piece crankshaft with hardened journals, running on four main lead-bronze bearing inserts, the same type of bearing used for the connecting rods. The connecting rods have bronze piston pin bushings. Valve timing is effected through a helical-gear driven camshaft, valve lifters, pushrods, and rocker arms.

The cast light-alloy crankcase consists of two crankcase sections and a timing gear cover. The engine is attached to the transmission (or "trans-axle" as the

name coiners have it) by four bolts, forming a power train which is suspended in the unitized body by four rubber-cushioned mounting points. There is a two-point forward mount at the transmission neck, and a two-

NUMERICAL DESIGNATION OF CYLINDERS AND MAIN BEARINGS

Direction of travel

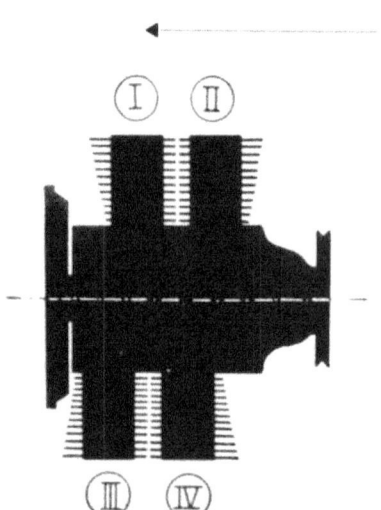

Viewed in direction of travel:

Cylinder I: Front, right side
Cylinder II: Rear, right side

Cylinder III: Front, left side
Cylinder IV: Rear, left side

Bearing 1: Inside diameter 50 mm, sleeve insert (flywheel-end)
    2:    "   "   55 mm, split insert
    3:    "   "   55 mm, split insert
    4:    "   "   40 mm, sleeve insert (at crankshaft pulley)

CROSS-SECTIONAL VIEW OF ENGINE

1 Clutch
2 Flywheel
3 Main bearing journal, Bearing 2
4 Cooling air inlet
5 Cooling blower impeller
6 Air blower housing
7 Oil filler
8 Generator
9 Generator carrier
10 V-belt
11 Spacers, adjusting V-belt tension
12 Bearing sleeve, Bearing 4
13 Pulley retaining nut
14 Flywheel gland nut
15 Cylinders and pistons
16 Camshaft
17 Oil strainer
18 Magnetic filtering element
19 Connecting rod bearing cap
20 Oil suction tube
21 Timing gear
22 Oil pump
23 Camshaft drive gear
24 Distributor drive gear
25 Crankshaft pulley

BOTTOM VIEW OF VEHICLE

1 Transmission drain plug
2 Transmission filler plug
3 Transmission
4 Clutch control lever
5 Engine drain plug
6 Oil strainer cover
7 Engine crankcase
8 Exhaust muffler

9 Forward power train carrier
10 Suspension control arm
11 Axle shaft
12 Heating air control gate
13 Shockabsorber
14 Lower air duct for heater
15 Tail pipe

point rear mount in the form of a transverse carrier situated near the crankshaft pulley.

NOTE: 1966 models had the engine mounted solidly to the body with no rubber cushions. If there is gear noise transmitted to the body, eliminate by installing the rubber cushioned mounts.

This final thought, before the uniniated begins to tear into the Porsche engine, is given in the hope that it will make him work a little slower and more carefully:

Without careful assembly, good design is sacrificed. Porsche engines are hand-constructed by craftsmen who serve a long apprenticeship before advancing to engine assembly duties. Moving parts are weighed and measured. By accurately matching tolerances of each part, an incredibly tight and balanced engine is created, often turning out more than its stated horsepower.

After bench-testing and running-in, the Porsche engine is mated to the chassis/body and undergoes thorough road testing at various speeds. This breaking-in function, which rigorously checks out the engine and its performance, usually has to be done by the owners of other autos. In this way, Porsche tests the complete car, not separate components, under severe conditions. Each car undergoes the same complete testing cycle. This is the reason Porsche's daily production rate is only 60 cars.

ENGINE
REMOVAL AND REPLACEMENT

WARNING: In spite of what other Porsche "mechanics" may tell you, it is NOT good practice for the uninitiated to remove the engine separately since it is extremely easy to ruin the clutch. With the aid of proper

equipment and knowledge, the transmission can be propped up, the engine pulled back until clear, then lowered by itself.

The engine and transmission are always removed as a single unit. Depending on the service involved, removing the engine can greatly simplify the project by providing easy access. Steam cleaning the engine while it is still in the car or after removal can make the disassembly much neater and easier, especially when one is trying to locate small bolts, etc. It is also advisable to have a helper during the engine removal. The steps involved in raising the car, placement on stands, and removal of the engine can be generalized. Use a lift, rolling stand, an assembly stand, hydraulic jack or a chain jack, if such is available. On the other hand, one can build a simple dolly on rollers to put under the engine. Build it up so it does NOT clear the engine by an inch or two when the car is in its normal position. Lift the car up and set it down gently with the dolly under the engine, supporting it. Remove all engine connections and supports, then lift the car up and pull engine to the rear. Lift car further until it clears the fan housing, then roll dolly and engine from under the car.

In any case, keep the power unit exactly centered when removing or replacing. Described below is the most convenient procedure for removing or installing the engine:

REMOVAL

1. Place car on stand, then drain the oil if necessary.
2. Disconnect the battery.
3. Detach the hot air ducts from the air gates and heat exchanger.
4. Detach both heat control cables.
5. Remove the hot air ducts from the T-joint between the air cleaners, then detach the T-joint from the blower housing.
6. Remove the tops of the air cleaners.
7. Remove the cables from the generator and blower housing, tagging the wires so they are properly reconnected (brown cable to terminal D−, black cable to terminal DF, red cable to terminal D+).
8. Remove the cable from terminal 15 and tachometer at terminal 1 at the ignition coil.
9. Remove the fuel intake line from the fuel pump, then remove the fastening clip from the engine shield.
10. Remove the cables from the oil pressure sensor and the oil temperature sensor.
11. Detach half-axles from connecting flanges.
12. Remove cables from starter motor.
13. Remove clutch cable from clutch control lever.
14. Remove the ground strap.
15. Disconnect the backup light wiring.
16. Detach the throttle linkage from the forward cross-shaft located at the transmission.
17. Remove the screws attaching the rear center-tunnel cover in the passenger compartment, then remove the cover.
18. Pull the rubber boot in the center tunnel forward, then remove the safety wire from the conical bolt and unscrew the bolt.
19. Disconnect the shift rod coupling with the shift rod off the transmission selector shift.
20. Place jack, with appropriate carrier plate attached, in the center of gravity of engine and transmission with jack under slight compression (see illustration).

21. Remove rear engine support from its base in the body, then remove the transmission support.
22. Lower engine/transmission assembly carefully, then pull to the rear.
23. If necessary as part of the repair, remove the transmission from the engine, being careful to ensure the clutch plate is not damaged in the process.

REPLACEMENT

Install the engine in reverse order, noting the following points:

1. Both the clutch throwout bearing and the transmission input shaft (runout) should be checked before the engine is attached to the transmission.
2. Fill the flywheel bushing in the gland nut with about ½ fl. oz. (2−3 cc) graphite grease.
3. Check and coat with graphite grease the transmission shaft splines and pilot journal, starter shaft bushing, and gear teeth of the starter drive pinion and flywheel gear.
4. Be sure the mating surface of the engine/transmission are clean.
5. Exercise care while guiding the transmission for attachment to the engine, or damage can be caused to the flywheel bushing, throwout bearing, or transmission input shaft. To align the clutch plate splines with those of the input shaft, slightly turn the crankshaft pulley, with the transmission in gear, until alignment is accomplished.
6. Attach the transmission by guiding it to align the lower mounting holes, inserting the lower bolts first, then pushing the transmission firmly against the engine until both flanges meet uniformly on all sides. Tighten the engine-transmission retaining bolts to a torque of 34 ft. lb. (4,7 mkp).
7. Once engine is installed, perform operation under

CLUTCH PEDAL TRAVEL LIMITER ADJUSTMENT in the CLUTCH chapter.

8. Finally, check the clutch free play, adjust if necessary, as described in the MAINTENANCE SERVICE chapter.

NOTE: If the engine is being replaced after major repairs, refer to the paragraph marked IMPORTANT in COMPONENT INSTALLATION under ENGINE DISASSEMBLY AND REASSEMBLY.

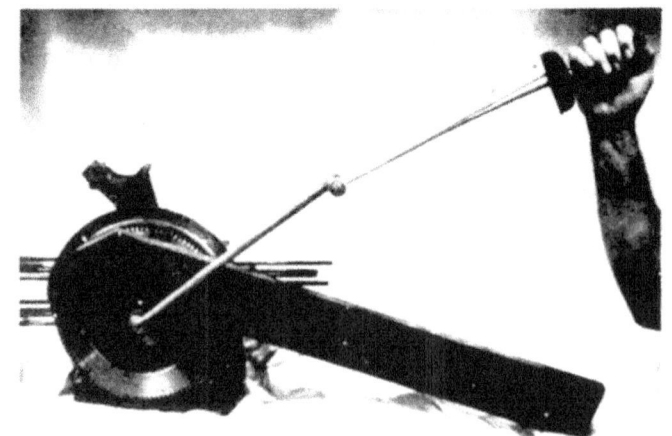

ENGINE DISASSEMBLY AND REASSEMBLY

SUMMARY

Unless one is an aircraft mechanic used to flat, horizontally opposed engines, the Porsche engine may be rather unsettling in its construction. However different, it still consists of parts assembled with nuts and bolts as is any other engine. The major differences are the cooling shrouds and ducts which effectively hide the engine, and the individual cylinders and split crankcase. Once disassembled, though, the mechanic is forced to concede that this is an extremely practical engine design, and the parts are light and easy to maneuver, unlike the typical cast-iron block engine.

If possible, use a workspace such as a large marked-off workbench on which to lay the parts, and which the kids and family dog cannot disturb. If the engine is placed in the center initially, parts can be placed at the ends of the bench, working towards the center until the crankshaft is finally removed. This way, parts can be much easier separated side-for-side. Also, carefully mark or tag cylinders, pistons, rods, valves, bearing halves, etc., as an extra safeguard so parts can be reassembled correctly.

Although there are many factory tools listed in this chapter, the home mechanic well-equipped with metric sockets, box-end wrenches, Allen socket wrenches, and screwdrivers can do most of the dismantling with these tools. If one owns a 100 to 150 ft. lb. torque wrench, he should invest in a special torque wrench extension (see illustration) since the flywheel gland nut will have to be torqued to 253–268 ft. lb. (35–37 mkp). To hold the light engine in place while removing or torquing this nut, bolt a stout 2 x 4 board to the flywheel, as shown in the illustration, about the same length as the total torque wrench, using three of the clutch pressure plate bolts and holes. Counterbore the 2 x 4 for the bolts. This added fulcrum should also aid other disassembly and torquing operations.

Once the flywheel nut is removed, repeated gentle blows with a soft hammer all around the periphery of the flywheel will loosen it, and it should come right off. Note that the pistons must be removed from the connecting rods before the crankcase can be split. Also the crankcase cannot be split until the pulley, timing gear cover, and flywheel are all removed. Regardless of how tempting it is to pound something sharp between the two halves of the crankcase, DO NOT DO IT as the soft metal can be easily damaged and scratched, resulting in oil leaks. Most likely there are still more bolts buried under the usual engine dirt (even a good steam cleaning cannot remove all grime). Firmly tap the protruding case ears with a soft hammer (leather or rubber) several times. After the crankcase is about ¼ in. apart all around, with the crankshaft and camshaft in the left case half, support the engine on its left side at about a 45° angle and lift the right crankcase half straight away, being careful that the LOOSE valve tappets in the right half of the case do not fall out into the other half of the case or onto the floor.

COMPONENT REMOVAL

To get down to the basic crankcase/crankshaft/camshaft assembly, first perform the operations under the following headings to remove all components, then note the following paragraph marked IMPORTANT:

ENGINE REMOVAL AND REPLACEMENT.
DRAINING OIL AND SERVICING OIL STRAINER and CHANGING OIL FILTER in the MAINTENANCE SERVICE chapter.
REMOVING COOLING AIR SHROUDS and SERVICING THE COOLING BLOWER AND IMPELLER under COOLING SYSTEM.
REMOVING EXHAUST MUFFLER and REMOVING HEAT EXCHANGER WITH EXHAUST PIPE under EXHAUST SYSTEM.
SERVICING OIL PRESSURE RELIEF VALVE AND BY-PASS VALVE, SERVICING OIL COOLER and SERVICING OIL PUMP under LUBRICATION SYSTEM.
CYLINDER HEAD REMOVAL under CYLINDER HEAD SERVICING.
CYLINDER REMOVAL and PISTON REMOVAL under CYLINDER AND PISTON SERVICING.
CLUTCH REMOVAL AND REPLACEMENT in the CLUTCH chapter.

IMPORTANT: Be sure to read the DESCRIPTIONS since they often contain valuable and necessary infor-

mation for the proper removal and servicing of engine components. The remainder of engine disassembly follows after the heading CRANKCASE/CRANKSHAFT/CAMSHAFT on page 212 The chapter is laid out so the more frequent component servicing (valve grinding and muffler replacement, for instance) is located in the proper order for component removal from the engine prior to complete disassembly. Engine reassembly, of course, is the reverse of the above procedures, with attention being paid to the checking and inspection instructions, and the reassembly instructions along with their assorted notes and warnings. Tables of TORQUE VALUES and TOLERANCES AND WEAR LIMITS will be found at the back of the chapter.

COMPONENT INSTALLATION

After the crankcase is completely reassembled, performing the following operations in basically the order shown will return the engine to a completed state. Then be sure to read the following paragraph marked IMPORTANT.

SERVICING DISTRIBUTOR PINION SHAFT in the POWER GENERATION AND IGNITION chapter.
CLUTCH REMOVAL AND REPLACEMENT in the CLUTCH chapter.
PISTON INSTALLATION and CYLINDER INSTALLATION under CYLINDER AND PISTON SERVICING.
CYLINDER HEAD INSTALLATION under CYLINDER HEAD SERVICING. Be sure to note the CLEANING AND INSPECTING CYLINDER HEADS and the REPLACEMENT CYLINDER HEADS instructions under the SERVICING VALVES heading.
SERVICING OIL PUMP, SERVICING OIL COOLER, and SERVICING OIL PRESSURE RELIEF VALVE AND BYPASS VALVE under LUBRICATION SYSTEM.
INSTALLING HEAT EXCHANGER WITH EXHAUST PIPE and REPLACING EXHAUST MUFFLER under EXHAUST SYSTEM.

NOTE: Be aware that the installation of some of the cooling air shrouds may be difficult with the muffler in place.

ADJUSTING LOWER DUCT WITH AIR GATE, SERVICING AIR HOSE CONNECTING DUCT, SERVICING THE COOLING BLOWER AND IMPELLER, and REPLACEMENT OF COOLING AIR SHROUDS under COOLING SYSTEM.
CHANGING OIL FILTER, DRAINING AND SERVICING OIL STRAINER, CHECKING AND ADJUSTING FAN BELT in the MAINTENANCE SERVICE chapter.

CAUTION: See the paragraphs marked IMPORTANT and NOTE in the VALVE INSTALLATION procedure under SERVICING VALVES, then see CHECKING VALVE CLEARANCE in the MAINTENANCE SERVICE chapter.

ENGINE REMOVAL AND REPLACEMENT.
POWER GENERATION AND IGNITION chapter for SERVICING SPARK PLUGS, SERVICING DISTRIBUTOR PINION SHAFT and SETTING IGNITION TIMING.
FUEL SYSTEM chapter for ADJUSTING IDLE SPEED.
EXHAUST EMISSION CONTROL SYSTEM chapter for TESTING THROTTLE VALVE COMPENSATOR.

IMPORTANT: After test running engine, recheck the engine oil level, reset the valve clearance as described above, and check for oil and fuel leakage at all fittings and gaskets. See the paragraph marked CAUTION under ADJUSTING FAN BELT in the MAINTENANCE SERVICE chapter and BREAK-IN RULES on page 7 of the DRIVER'S MANUAL.

COOLING SYSTEM

DESCRIPTION

An extension of the generator shaft drives an air blower impeller which forces air over the engine and oil cooler. The generator shaft is driven by the fan belt from the crankshaft pulley. The blower draws cooling air through an intake in the blower housing and forces it over the heavily-finned cylinders and cylinder heads. The cooling air is guided by deflector baffles in the surrounding shrouds. It is important to assemble the shroud components with care, as there must be no open areas or slits to allow the cooling air to escape. Loss of the cooling air would considerably reduce the efficiency of the cooling system.

REMOVING COOLING AIR SHROUDS

1. Remove the air cleaner and throttle control levers and linkage from both carburetors.
2. Loosen both heating hose attaching clamps (right and left), then loosen the center hose clamp and, pushing it to the right, remove from the attaching tab (see illustration).

3. Remove the bolts holding the transverse engine carrier. On cars with the later type of carrier, also remove the carrier plate.
4. Remove the crankcase breather hose from the breather (see illustration).

COOLING SYSTEM

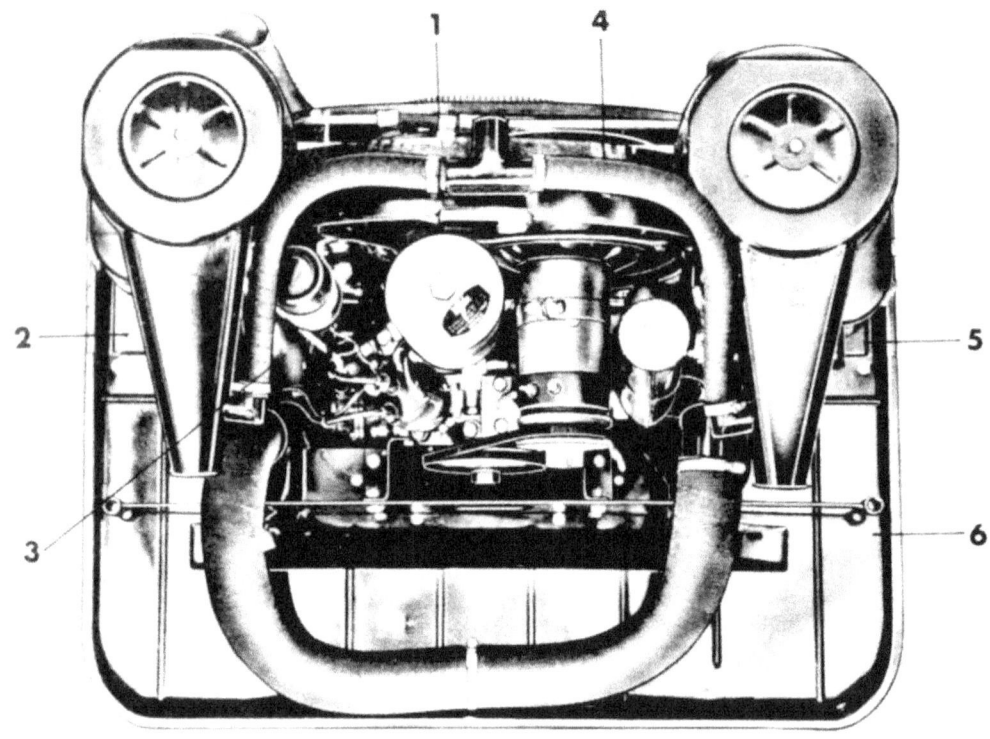

1. Engine front shield
2. Engine side shield
3. Cylinder shroud
4. Blower housing
5. Engine side shield
6. Engine rear shield

5. Remove the heating hose connecting flange from the air blower housing.
6. Remove the short connecting hose from the cover panel on the rear of the engine (see illustration).

7. Remove the retaining screws from the engine rear shield and withdraw the shield by pulling rearward, then remove both side shields, withdrawing them together with the breather (see illustration).

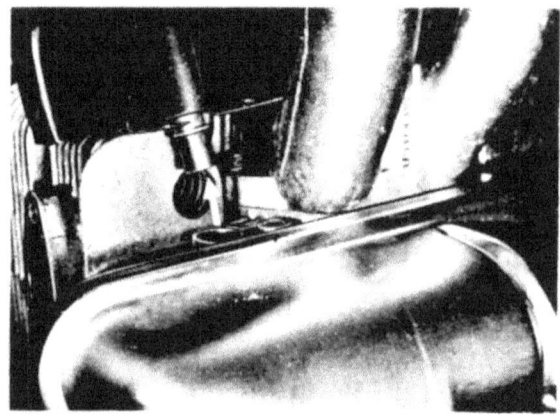

8. Remove engine front shield, then remove exhaust muffler and heat exchanger as described under EXHAUST SYSTEM (see illustration).

9. Detach cables connecting the distributor with the coil, then remove the distributor cover, spark plug cables, distributor, and (optionally) distributor pinion shaft (see POWER GENERATION AND IGNITION chapter).

NOTE: If distributor pinion shaft is to be removed and no more major repairs performed, it is best to first set Cylinder No. 1 to TDC as described under SERVICING DISTRIBUTOR PINION SHAFT in the POWER GENERATION AND IGNITION chapter. Be sure not to turn crankshaft after this setting is made. Upon reassembly, it will be simply a matter of replacing the distributor pinion shaft as described.

10. Remove the carburetor as described in the FUEL SYSTEM chapter, then remove the fan belt as described in the MAINTENANCE SERVICE chapter.
11. Remove the oil breather (see illustration), then detach the top connections from the bypass oil filter (see illustration).

12. Remove the fuel pump and shield as described in the FUEL SYSTEM chapter.
13. Remove both of the transverse carrier supports (see illustration), then remove the cover shrouds which will also come loose.

14. Unfasten the generator cables and retaining strap, then pull up on the blower housing (see illustration). Tag the cables (brown cable to terminal D−, black cable to terminal DF, red cable to terminal D+).

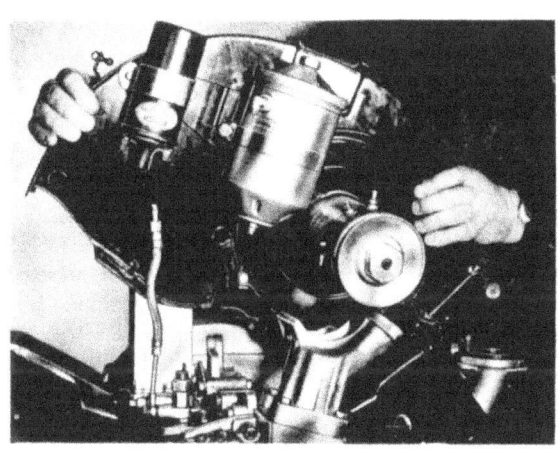

15. Remove the cylinder shrouds and lower the air duct.
16. Following removal of the cylinder heads, withdraw the deflector baffles and the supporting springs (see illustration).

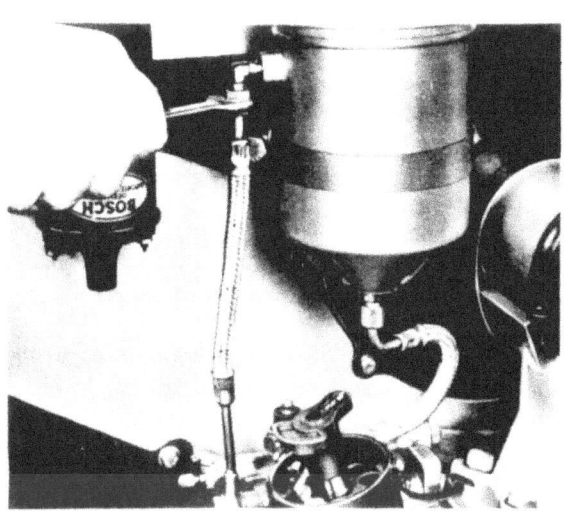

17. Following removal of the crankshaft pulley, remove the pulley shield.

REPLACEMENT OF COOLING AIR SHROUDS

NOTE: Be absolutely certain the cylinder head deflector baffles and supporting springs are in place prior to replacing the cylinder heads. These components are important to the proper cooling of the engine, and their loss could result in cylinder "hot spots". Be sure to place them in the proper location (see illustration).

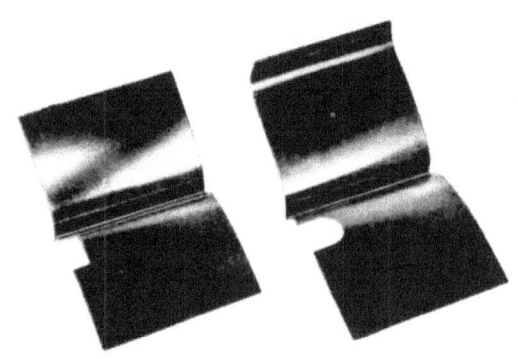

The cooling air shroud should be reinstalled in reverse order of the above, making certain that the shroud are properly fitted and the spark plug rubber covers properly seated. Replace any rubber gaskets that are torn, porous, or otherwise defective. Keep all rubber parts free of grease and oil.

Check for proper fan belt alignment between the generator and crankshaft pulleys. Correct positioning by moving the generator in its cradle. However, be sure that no tension has been created between the blower housing cover and the blower when the retaining screws are tightened. Be sure the generator cables are properly connected (brown cable to terminal D−, black cable to terminal DF, and red cable to terminal D+).

SERVICING AIR BLOWER HOUSING

NOTE: The engine must be removed from the car to remove the housing.

Use the procedure previously outlined under REMOVING COOLING AIR SHROUDS. Items concerning the specific air blower housing removal are steps (1), (5), (9) except the distributor need NOT be removed, (10), (11), and (14). However, before the housing can be withdrawn, remove the retaining screws from the cylinder end and side shrouds, and loosen the heater hose clamp. Reverse these steps to replace, being sure no gaps are left from which the cooling air can escape.

Servicing the Cooling Blower and Impeller

Use the procedure previously outlined under REMOVING COOLING AIR SHROUDS. Items concerning the specific cooling blower removal are (11) plus remove the bypass oil filter assembly, and the first part of (14). Then remove the retaining bolts from the blower housing cover (see illustration). Finally, remove the generator carrier and withdraw the generator and blower impeller assembly (see illustration). Be sure to cover the crankcase opening to prevent the entry of dirt.

Service the blower impeller as follows:

1. Mount the generator pulley spindle in a vise with soft metal jaw protectors.
2. Unscrew the impeller nut with a 36 mm hex socket, then withdraw the impeller together with its back shield (see illustration).
3. When replacing impeller, be sure the spacers are properly located, then position the impeller shield.
4. Tighten the special impeller nut to 72 ft. lb. (10 mkp).
5. When turning, the impeller should not strike the housing cover and should have about ⅛ in. (3 mm) clearance.

When the generator and blower assembly are being replaced, note the following:

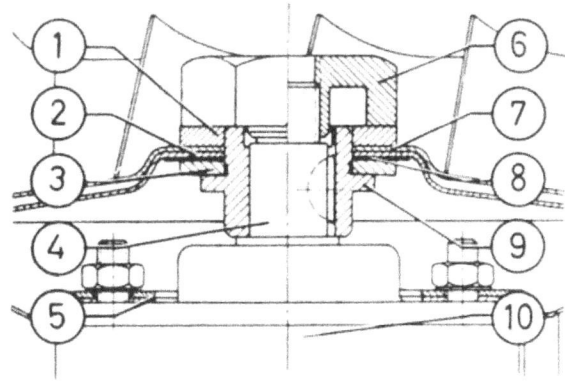

1 Thick washer
2 Impeller back shield
3 Thick washer
4 Generator shaft
5 Blower housing cover
6 Special impeller nut
7 Impeller
8 Spacers (as needed, 2-5 each)
9 Impeller hub
10 Generator

1. Insert a new gasket between the generator carrier and the timing gear cover.
2. See the third paragraph under REPLACEMENT OF COOLING AIR SHROUDS.

Servicing Air Hose Connecting Duct

Detach both the heating hose (from the connecting duct) and the breather hose. Remove the retaining nut and bolt from the connecting duct, then push the rubber hose section down and off the duct while pulling the duct diagonally upward (see illustration).

Reverse the above instructions when installing. Check the adjustment of the counternut used for fastening the connecting duct, since the nut must be screwed in deep enough to permit flush alignment of the connecting duct with the blower housing without deformation of the duct when tightened at the attaching points (see illustration). Also, check the heating hose and breather hose for air-tightness and possible damage.

Adjusting Lower Duct With Air Gate

The air gates located in the lower air duct must be so adjusted that they perform the opening and closing functions in unison. Be certain that the large air gate flaps are positioned about $\frac{13}{32}$ in. (10 mm) from the bottom of the ducts when the small air gate is fully closed. Upon mounting the lower ducts at the engine, check for proper functioning of the air gates and readjust if necessary (see illustration).

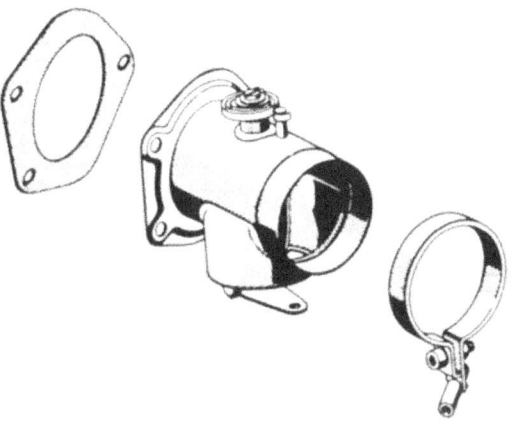

When installing the air gate assembly, check for proper seating of the cork gasket and check the heating hose attachment for air-tightness and firm seating with the help of the hose clamp (see illustration).

EXHAUST SYSTEM

SERVICING MUFFLER

Removing Exhaust Muffler

The engine NEED NOT be removed for muffler servicing. See illustration of underside of vehicle under DESCRIPTION for ENGINE chapter.

1. Remove both supports for the engine rear shield, then loosen both exhaust pipe clamps at the heat exchangers.
2. Remove the covers situated over the exhaust flange at the engine rear shield (see illustration).

3. Remove the tail pipe from the muffler.
4. Remove the exhaust flange retaining nuts from the cylinder heads and pull the muffler back to remove, loosening any jammed pipe connections by lightly tapping with a rubber mallet.
5. Remove muffler brackets (if necessary).

Replacing Exhaust Muffler

To replace, **reverse the removal procedure, noting these points:**

1. Inspect the muffler and the exhaust pipes for leaks or other damage prior to installation.
2. Straighten flattened or bent pipes.
3. Use new gaskets, and when the engine is installed, be sure the muffler does not touch the body.

HEAT EXCHANGER

Removing Heat Exchanger With Exhaust Pipe

NOTE: Engine should be removed from vehicle prior to this procedure. See DESCRIPTION for ENGINE chapter for vehicle underside full-view illustration.

1. Loosen the exhaust pipe clamps at the muffler.
2. Remove the retaining bolts from the front exhaust flange.
3. Pull off the heat exchanger with the exhaust pipe from the lower duct, loosening any jammed pipe connections by lightly tapping with a soft mallet.

Installing Heat Exchanger With Exhaust Pipe

To install, reverse the removal procedure, noting these points:

1. Check the sealing surfaces and flanges for straightness and corrosion, and use new gaskets when installing.
2. Check the heat exchanger and exhaust pipes for tightness or corrosion and damage.

LUBRICATION SYSTEM

DESCRIPTION

The Porsche engine uses a forced-feed lubrication system with provision for oil cooling. A bypass valve sends oil directly to lubrication points, bypassing the oil cooler, to prevent "dry starts". When the engine has reached operating temperature, the cooler is brought into operation, which will then maintain the correct oil temperature.

The oil pump (10) (see illustrations) is situated in the timing gear cover and is driven by the camshaft (8). When the cold engine is started, the oil pump picks up (5) cold oil from the lowest point in the crankcase sump (see illustration) and forces it to the bypass circuit valve (7), which is located in the timing gear cover. The bypass valve piston is then forced down, under the oil pressure of about 19 psi (1,3 atm), and opens the oil gallery to the lubricating points by bypassing the oil cooler (15). This ensures immediate lubrication of engine bearings and other points when the engine is started. One gallery forces oil through the main bearings (12) into the drilled oil galleries in the crankshaft and lubricates the connecting rod bearings. A second gallery brings the oil to lubricate the camshaft bearings (8), and this oil then passes through the hollow valve lifters (4) and pushrods (2) to the rocker arm (1) bearings, also lubricating the valve shafts. Cylinder walls, pistons (3), and piston pins are lubricated by oil splash.

ENGINE LUBRICATION SYSTEM

Oil Circuit Diagram

Oil Circuit in Cold Engine

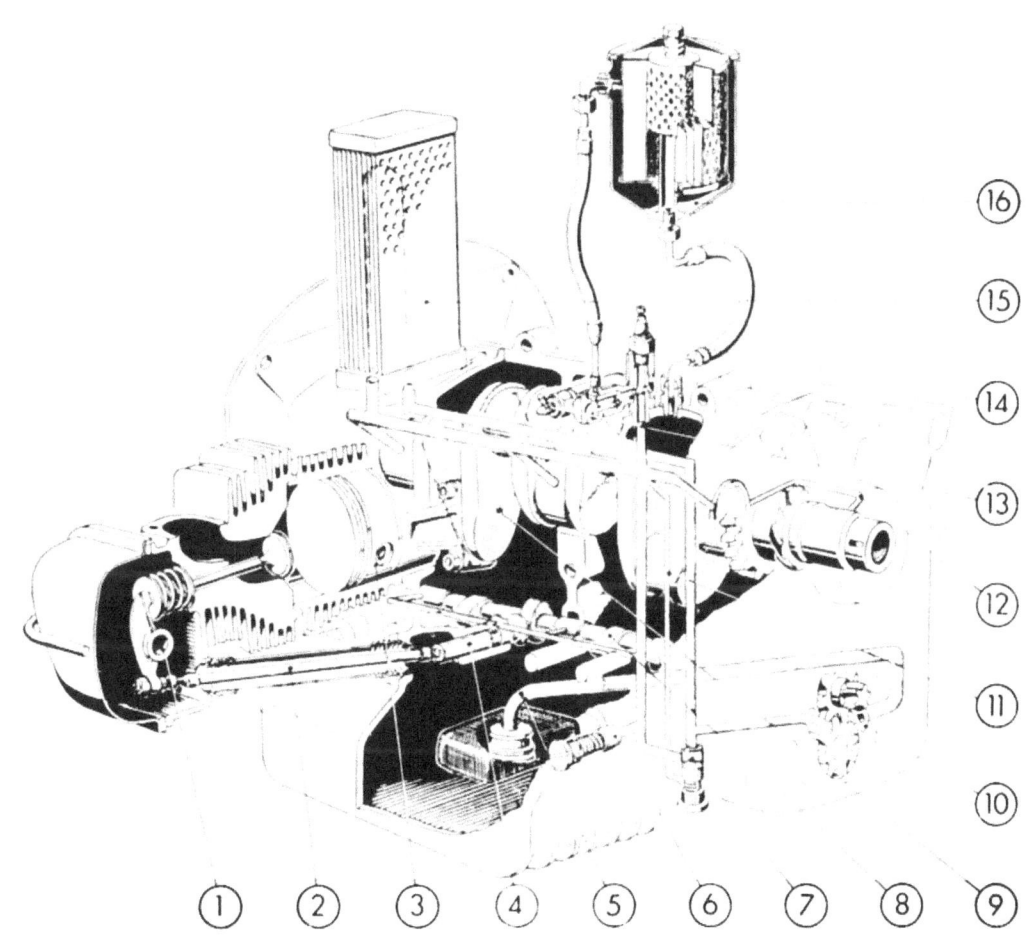

1 Rocker arm
2 Pushrod
3 Piston
4 Valve lifter
5 Oil suction tube
6 Pressure relief valve
7 Bypass valve
8 Camshaft
9 Crankshaft
10 Oil pump
11 Counter-pressure line
12 Oil line to Bearing 4
13 Oil temperature sensor
14 Oil pressure switch
15 Oil cooler (repositioned back in sketch for better view)
16 Bypass oil filter

Oil Circuit at Operating Temperature

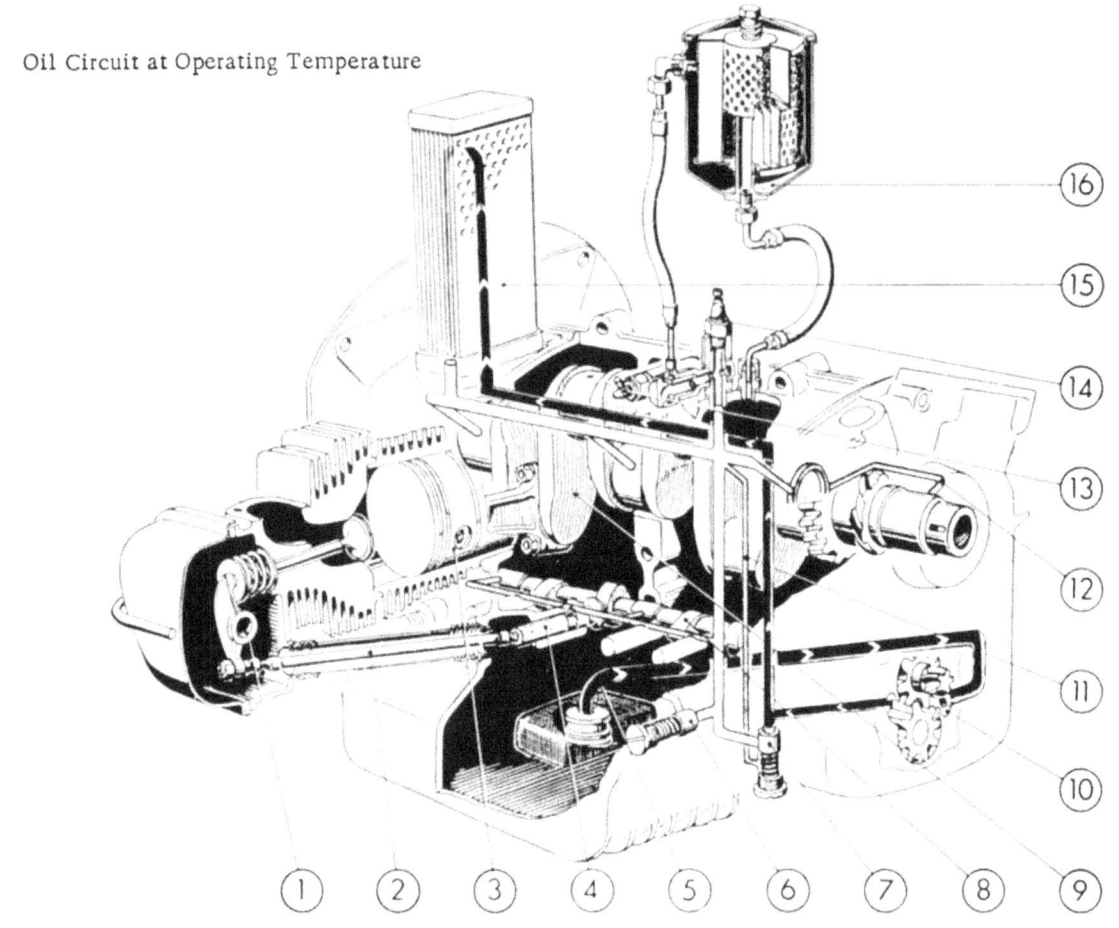

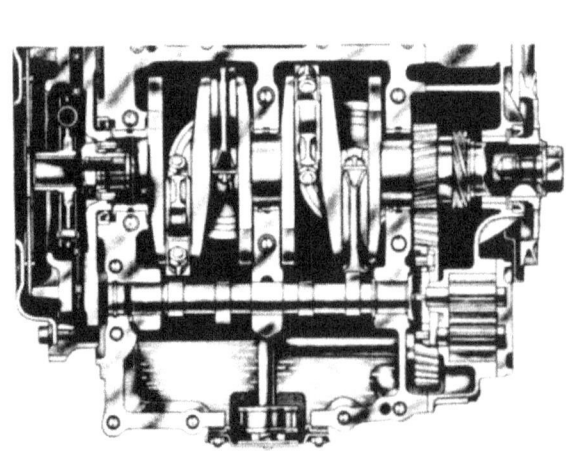
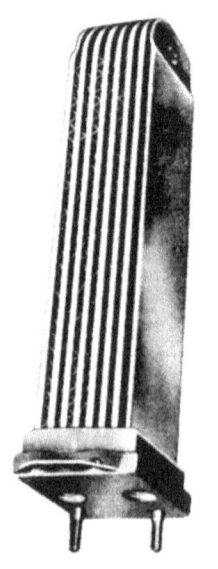

Once the oil pressure rises above 42 psi (2,9 atm), the pressure relief valve (6), located in the crankcase, is forced open and the excess oil is drained into the crankcase oil sump. When the oil galleries are full of oil and the oil pressure has stabilized, a pressure rise equivalent to the pressure in the rest of the system also occurs in the counter-pressure line (11) and under the bypass valve (7), thus equalizing the pressure exerted upon the bypass valve from the side of the pump (10).

Since the oil pressure at both ends of the bypass valve is now equal, the mechanical spring can expand and thus, push the valve plunger up to close the oil gallery of the direct lubricating circuit. This blocks the direct passage and causes the oil to flow through the oil cooler before reaching the lubricating points. The pressure relief valve (6) continues its function to limit the oil pressure in the system to 44 psi (3 atm).

The oil cooler (15) is mounted on the crankcase in the stream of cooling air forced through by the cooling blower. The oil cooler is so inserted into the oil circuit that the oil pumped by the oil pump (10) must pass through the oil cooler before it reaches the points of lubrication. Cooling of the oil ensures that it retains its full lubricating qualities even in very warm weather and under constant operating loads.

Oil draining from the points of lubrication collects in the bottom of the crankcase where it passes through an oil strainer and a magnetic filtering element, both of which will retain the foreign matter in the oil. A bypass oil filter (16) entraps the finer particles suspended in the circulating oil.

A pressure-activated switch (14) is connected to the pressure gallery between the pump and oil cooler. The switch opens the electric circuit of the oil pressure indicator lamp at a pressure between 4.5 to 8.8 psi (0,3 to 0,6 atm), causing the lamp to go out. The lamp glows when the ignition is turned on and the oil pressure is low.

NOTE: See MAINTENANCE SERVICE chapter for DRAINING OIL AND SERVICING OIL STRAINER, and for CHANGING OIL FILTER.

SERVICING OIL PRESSURE RELIEF VALVE AND BYPASS VALVE

NOTE: Servicing is the same for both assemblies. Dimensions are also similar. See illustrations below for; (1) a cut-away view without valve installed, and (2) a cut-away view with valve installed (oil cooler bypassed).

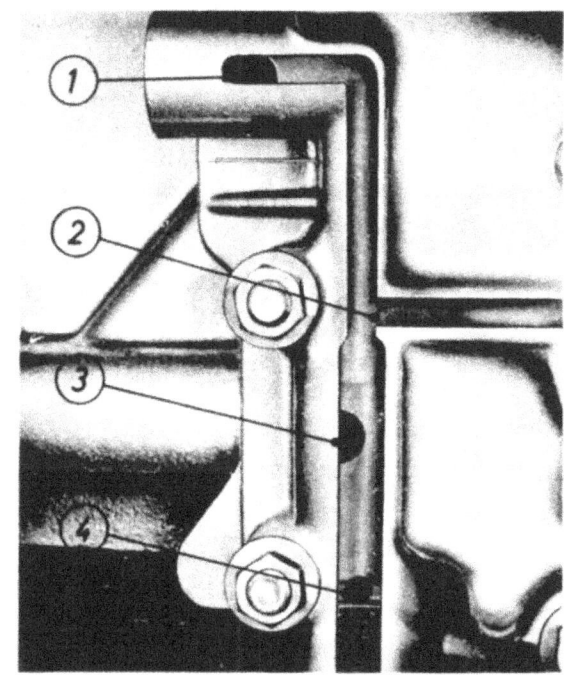

1 Oil gallery to oil cooler
2 Oil gallery from oil pump
3 Oil gallery to lubricating points by bypassing the oil cooler
4 Opening for counter-pressure oil line

Removal

1. Remove cap screw with tool P74, (see illustration), or use a very large screw driver or a chisel sharpened to fit into the screw slot. With either one, a six- to eight-inch crescent wrench probably will be needed.

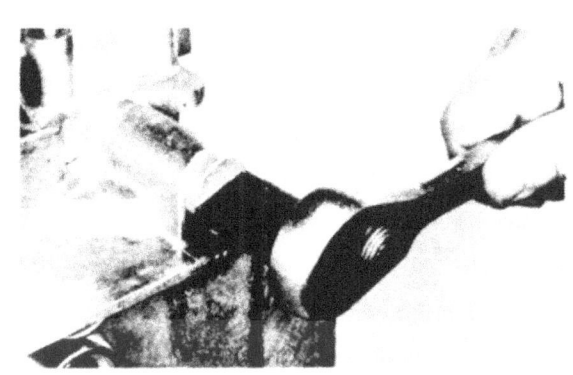

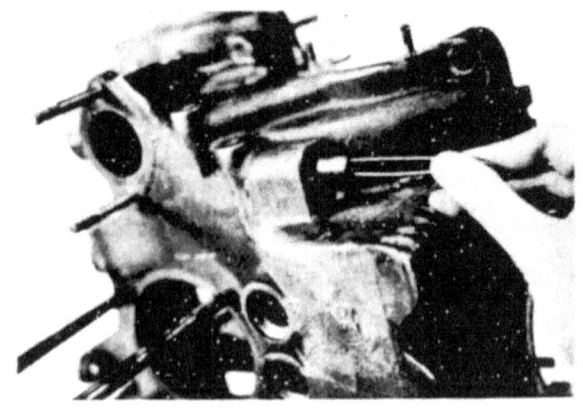

Replacement

To replace, reverse the removal procedure, noting the following:

1. Inspect valve plunger and plunger bore in the housing for traces of seizure. Carefully smoothen the bore of any scratches, replace the plunger if necessary.
2. Check the mechanical spring, using the following table:

Pressure Relief Valve and Bypass Valve Spring
Free length..............66 mm (2,6")
Wire diameter..........1,4 mm (.055")
Tension at 49 mm (1,93").....4,7 kp (10,3 lbs) ± 7%

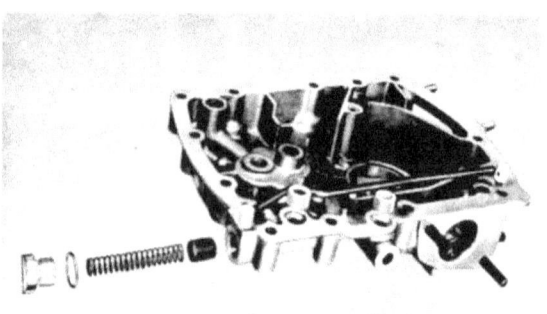

2. Withdraw spring and valve plunger; if plunger sticks, remove with an M 10 thread tap, or bend a piece of heavy wire into the shape shown in the illustration. Push the wire into the hollow valve plunger, then withdraw the plunger; should the plunger still stick, squirt some light penetrating oil into the passage (see illustration).

3. Install a new gasket washer, then insert the piston so that its hollow end faces toward the cap screw.
4. Insert the spring INTO the hollow end of the valve plunger, then place the cap screw onto the spring and tighten. Be sure the spring end has remained in the hollow end of the valve plunger, or the housing bore will be scratched (see illustration).

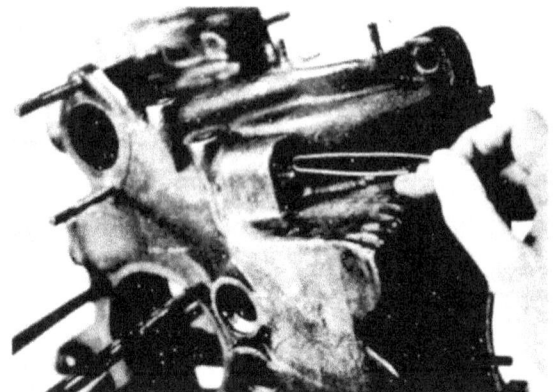

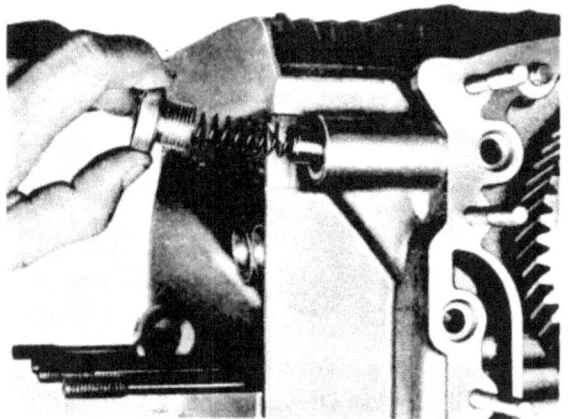

SERVICING OIL COOLER

NOTE: Should there be oil leakage from the area of the oil cooler (oil dribbling below the fan housing on the left side, straight ahead of the oil pressure indicator), suspect the rubber gaskets under the cooler FIRST before replacing the entire cooler. The cooler is fairly sturdy and is not prone to leakage, so the gaskets are usually the culprit. The cooler can only be removed with the engine out of the car, using the following and the SERVICING AIR BLOWER HOUSING procedure. If possible, warm up the engine so there will be a fresh oil leak in the area, then allow engine to cool before removing it, using the procedure under ENGINE REMOVAL AND REPLACEMENT. Then, with the air blower housing removed, closely inspect the cooler to determnie if it is leaking from the tubes or if the oil is issuing from the base.

Removal

1. Unscrew the oil cooler retaining nuts with an offset box wrench (see illustration).
2. Carefully remove the oil cooler so the gaskets may be examined (see illustration).

Inspection

1. If the cooler has no apparent leaks, check the rubber gaskets.
2. If the rubber gaskets are perfect and dry, replace the cooler.
3. If the gaskets are deteriorated, test the cooler anyway:

    a. A Porsche dealership with the proper equipment can test the cooler for leaks at 147 psi (10 atm).
    b. A crude home test is to drain and wash the cooler (use solvent, blow air through cooler, being sure to aim the outlet into a suitable container) then dunk it into hot water with both inlet and outlet holes plugged. Small air bubbles will often reveal a leak.

Installation

To install, reverse the removal procedure, noting the following:

1. Check the oil cooler for proper tightness of retaining nuts.
2. If a leak has been discovered in the unit, check the pressure relief valve valve (see SERVICING OIL PRESSURE RELIEF VALVE AND BYPASS VALVE).
3. ALWAYS replace the gaskets.

SERVICING OIL PUMP

Removal

Before the oil pump can be removed, the engine rear shield, the intermediate shield between the air ducts, the crankshaft pulley and the pulley shield must be removed. See the appropriate instructions.

1. Remove the oil pump cover retaining nuts and withdraw the cover.
2. Remove the oil pump gears (see illustration).

Inspection

1. Inspect the oil pump housing, especially gear seating areas, for wear. Such wear within the housing will decrease oil pressure.
2. Inspect the pump gears for wear, using the following table:

Gear flank clearance .001–.003 in. (0,03–0,08 mm)
Gear axial play (with gasket but without preload)....
................0014–.0039 in. (0,035–0,10 mm)
Wear limit .... .0079 in. (0,20 mm)

3. Check that the driven gear shaft is firmly seated in the housing.
4. Clean the sealing surface on the crankcase where the oil pump cover joins.
5. Place a straightedge across the face of the pump gears, then use a feeler gauge under the straightedge to measure the clearance between the cover mounting flange in the housing and face of the gears. The clearance should be .0024–.0050 in. (0,06–0,128 mm).

Replacement

1. Replace the oil pump gears.
2. Use a new, genuine Porsche part gasket, .008 in. (0,20 mm), without applying gasket paste. Gasket thickness in excess of specification will result in decreased oil pressure.
3. Replace cover and retaining nuts, torquing to specifications.

SERVICING OIL FILTER ASSEMBLY

Removal

1. Follow instructions under CHANGING OIL FILTER in the MAINTENANCE SERVICE chapter.
2. Detach oil lines from bypass oil filter.
3. Remove fittings (including oil temperature and oil pressure sending units) by unscrewing fitting below the oil pressure switch, then lift off block containing oil temperature sending unit and inlet oil line. Then remove fitting from crankcase.
4. Remove strap from filter housing, then remove housing.

Replacement

To replace oil filter assembly, reverse the removal procedure, being sure to check for leaks after running engine up to operating temperature.

CYLINDER HEAD SERVICING

DESCRIPTION

Each bank of dual cylinders has a common heavily finned, cast light-alloy cylinder head with shrunk-in steel valve seats and valve guides. Helicoil inserts are used as spark plug seats. Valves are arranged in the cylinder head in a "V" formation, the two end valves being slanted inward. No gasket is used between the cylinder head and the cylinders (see illustration).

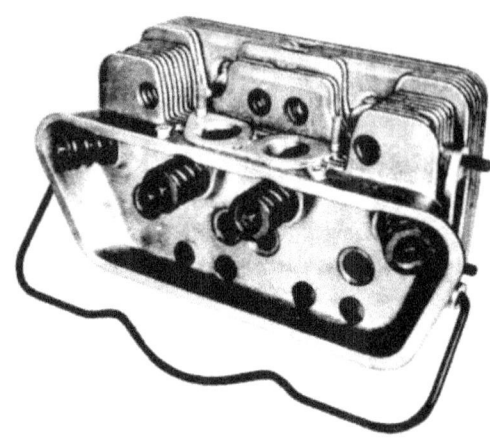

A rocker arm carrier is mounted in the "upper" part of the cylinder head, and this holds the three rocker arm shafts on which the rocker arms ride. The valve cover and its gasket are held in place with a strong spring clip.

REMOVING ROCKER ARM CARRIER

1. Unclip valve cover, carefully remove with its gasket.
2. Remove the 7 hex nuts (SW 13) from the rocker arm shafts (see illustration).

3. Withdraw the rocker arm shafts along with the arms, springs, washers and spacers, being sure to keep each set in order and separate from the other sets.
4. Remove the three rocker arm carrier retaining bolts (SW 15 mm), then withdraw the carrier (see illustration).
5. Remove valve adjusting screws (if overhauling cylinder head).
6. Remove valve pushrods, marking for proper reassembly (marking ends, also).

ROCKER ARM CARRIER INSTALLATION

To install, reverse the removal procedure, noting the following:

1. Check the rocker arm shafts and rocker arms for defects and replace any parts showing wear or damage.
2. Check the valve adjusting screws for defects, and replace any screws which show strained threads or damaged ball joint sockets.
3. Check the adjusting screws and rocker arms for unobstructed oil flow.
4. Inspect the carrier retaining bolts for defects. Coat threads and base of bolt heads with graphite oil and install new spring washers before replacing in carrier.
5. Tighten the retaining bolts to 36 ft. lb. (5 mkp) (see illustration).
6. Arrange the spacers and thrust washers as before or, in the case of new components, arrange the spacers and thrust washers in such a way that the rocker arms strike the valve shafts about in the center of the shaft

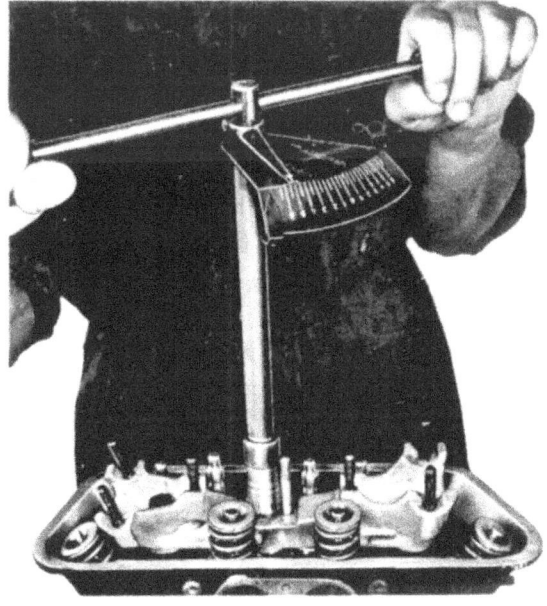

butt, and that the pushrods do not come in contact with the pushrod tubes.

7. Ensure that all other components are properly arranged (see illustration).
8. Torque the 7 rocker arm shaft retaining nuts (SW 13) to 18 ft. lb. (2.5 mkp) (see previous illustration).
9. Reoil shafts and rocker arms, then see CHECKING VALVE CLEARANCE in the MAINTENANCE SERVICE chapter.

NOTE: If valves or seats have been serviced, set valves at .010 in. (.25 mm) intake, .012 in. (.30 mm) exhaust for a one-half hour engine run, then reset as specified.

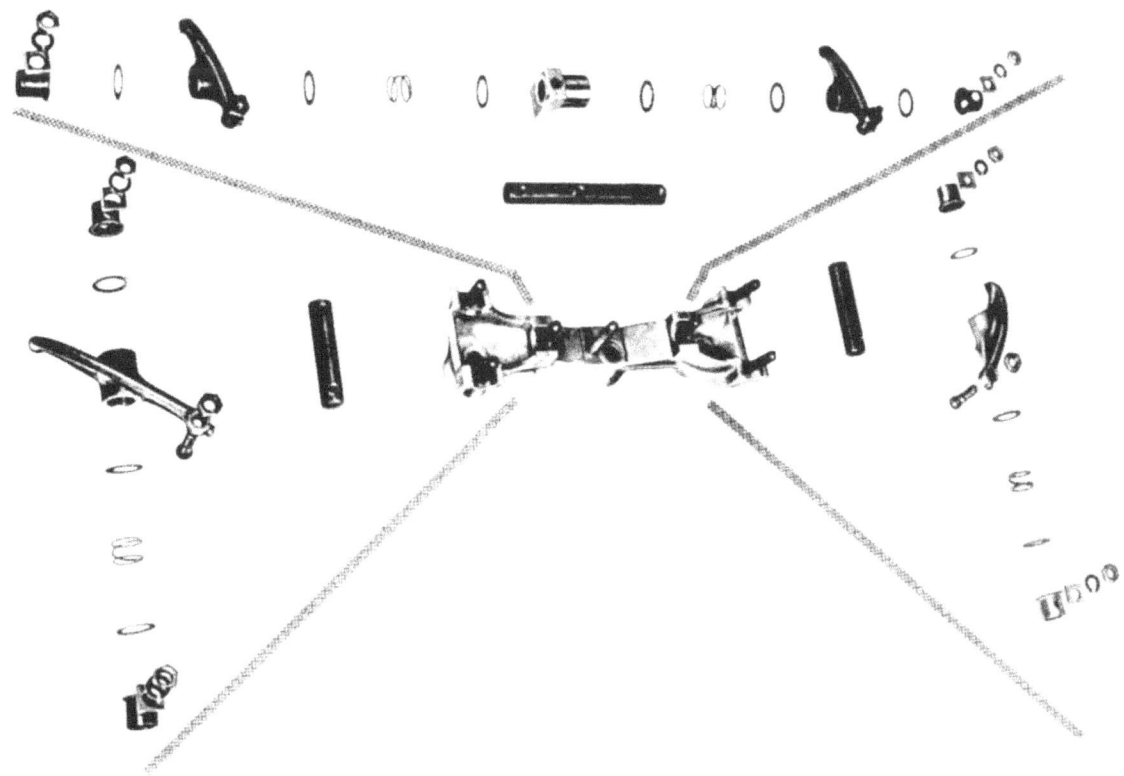

CYLINDER HEAD REMOVAL

With the engine out of the car, all shrouds, carburetors, valve covers, pushrods, spark plugs, and rocker arm carriers removed, proceed as follows:

1. Remove the intake duct retaining nuts, then remove the ducts (see illustration).

2. Remove the cylinder head retaining nuts with Allen wrench adapter (the 8 Allen nuts are shown above and below the valve stems in the illustration); remove the washers located between the nuts and the cylinder head.
3. Lift off the cylinder head, tapping lightly with a soft mallet to unstick. Retain cylinders with a holding clamp (if the cylinders are not to be immediately removed) (see illustration).

IMPORTANT: See the SERVICING VALVES procedures even if valves are to be left in place since the instructions for CLEANING AND INSPECTING CYLINDER HEADS and REPLACEMENT CYLINDER HEADS are most important.

CYLINDER HEAD REPLACEMENT

IMPORTANT: Be sure to insert the small air baffles and springs under the cylinders on each side. If necessary, write yourself a note or hang them from your wrists with a piece of string, or they'll surely be forgotten in the haste to install the shiny new heads. With valves mounted, the removal procedure is reversed, noting the following points:

1. No head gasket is needed, just be sure the mating surfaces are clean and free of burrs.
2. Be sure the small air baffles (mentioned above and illustrated) are properly positioned (compare profile of the recess for cap nut and one for hex bolt).

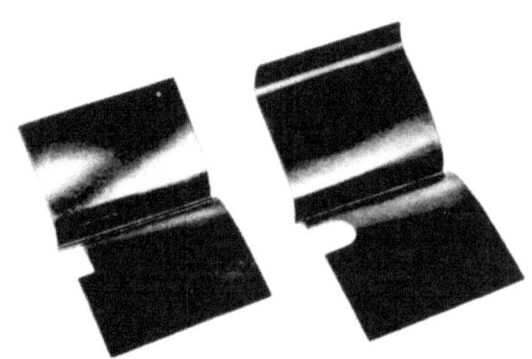

3. Insert the pushrod cover tubes. Used tubes must be slightly stretched at the bellows with box wrench or a socket drive extension (see illustration), using care to prevent possible cracking of the metal. This operation should be done at both ends, since this slight compression aids in sealing. Then install new O-rings at both ends and make sure they are properly seated in the crankcase and cylinder head; position the tube weld seams up.

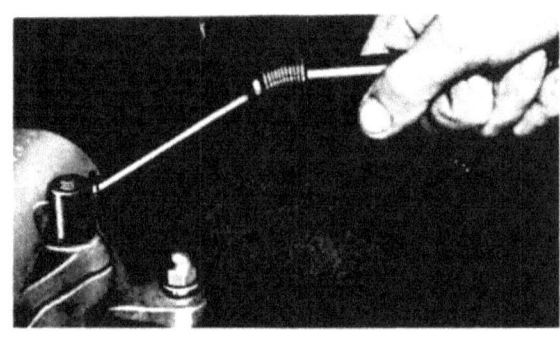

4. Oil the O-rings used under the cylinder head nuts located within the rocker box before installing (no gasket compound is needed).
5. Place one washer under each cylinder head nut located outside the rocker box (see illustration in CYLINDER HEAD REMOVAL).

NOTE: The cover tube O-rings are trapezoidal in cross-section (see illustration).

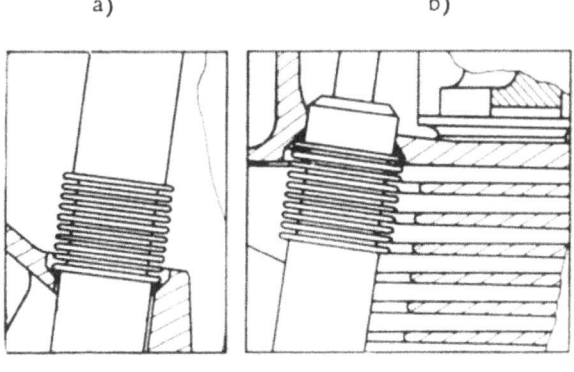

a) Sealing points in crankcase.

b) Sealing points in cylinder head.

IMPORTANT: Make absolutely sure that the cylinders are properly seated in the cylinder head. If a misaligned cylinder head is tightened, it will usually warp to the extent of being unfit for use. Then, be sure to torque in the sequence as explained to properly seal the head against the cylinders without creating warpage.

6. Coat cylinder head nuts with graphite lubricant, tighten lightly, then torque to 7 ft. lb. (1 mkp) in the sequence shown in the illustration.

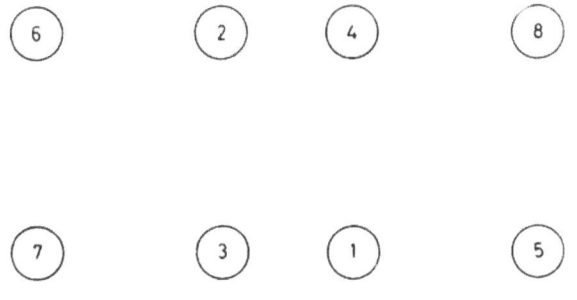

7. Retorque cylinder head nuts to 22 ft. lb. (3 mpk) in the sequence shown in the illustration. If appropriate at this time, install serviced spark plugs (see POWER GENERATION AND IGNITION chapter).

8. Pump oil into the pushrods until it runs out at the other end, then insert these pushrods (keeping the original order) into the pushrod tubes so that one end seats in the valve lifter (see illustration).

9. See ROCKER ARM CARRIER INSTALLATION for the remainder of this procedure.

SERVICING VALVES

NOTE: See MAINTENANCE SERVICE for CHECKING VALVE CLEARANCE. Use the table of TOLERANCES AND WEAR LIMITS at the back of the ENGINE chapter.

REMOVING VALVES

NOTE: There are several methods used to remove valves. The best is to use Porsche tool P-7 (see illustration). However, if the head is suitably supported, the valves can also be removed on a drill press, or just by supporting the valve head underneath and pushing down on the retaining washer by hand, using a short piece of tubing. Cut the tubing away on each side and pry in with a small screwdriver and remove the half-moon keepers.

1. With the combustion chamber side of the head on a flat, clean surface, apply pressure to the spring seat. Push it far enough down on the stem to allow removal of the keepers (see illustration), release slowly.

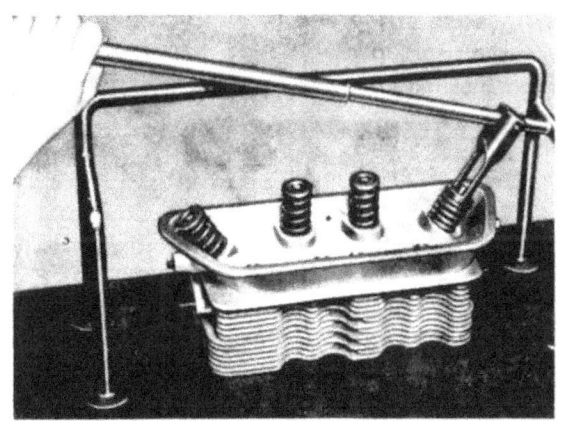

2. Remove the valve, mark it according to intake or exhaust and cylinder.
3. Remove the spring, washers, retainer, sealing cap, etc., and mark spring according to intake or exhaust and the cylinder number.

CLEANING AND INSPECTING VALVES

1. Clean carbon deposits off the valves, then examine valve head for excessive pitting, burning or warpage. Replace if necessary.

2. Examine valve stems for excessive wear (ridge formation), warpage, traces of seizure, or damaged valve keeper seats. Replace if necessary, since stems cannot be reground or straightened.

NOTE: If valves are at all doubtful, replace now that engine is disassembled.

CLEANING AND INSPECTING CYLINDER HEADS

1. Remove all carbon deposits from the cylinder side and all oil from the whole cylinder head.
2. Look for cracks in the cylinder head, ignoring small hairline cracks. Have the welding done by a cylinder head repair shop or replace the whole cylinder head.
3. Inspect the valve guides for wear and firm seating in the cylinder head. Measure guide bore with ball gauge and micrometer, or a plug gauge of .394 in. (10 mm) diameter (see TOLERANCES AND WEAR LIMITS for other dimensions). Replace valve guides if necessary, using the following procedure.
4. Check for damaged spark plug Helicoil inserts.
5. If the valve used in the particular valve location is in good condition, lap it into the seat to check the valve seating, using the following procedure. Otherwise, if the valve is worth saving, reface the valve (using the procedure that follows). In any case, valve seating is checked with machinists bluing, using the dimensions with the following illustration.

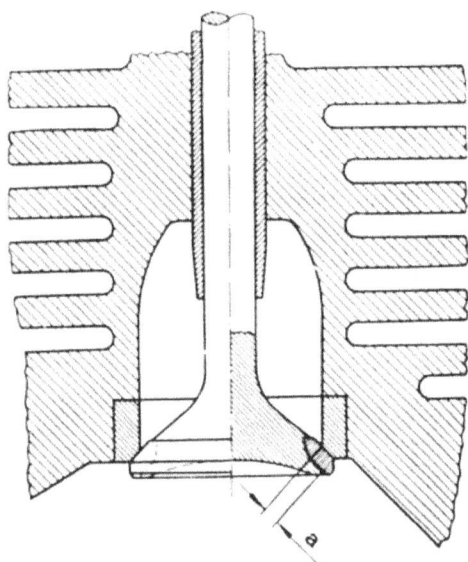

Valve seat width   Intake 1.25 ± 0.15 mm
                             (.050 ± .006 in.)

                     Exhaust 1.55 ± 0.15 mm
                             (.061 ± .006 in.).

6. If the bluing has not contacted the whole seat surface, or there is pitting, lightly rework the seat with a cutter, using the following procedure.
7. Recheck the seal using the machinists bluing. If the seal looks satisfactory, pour some gasoline into the respective port. Properly seated valves will not permit gasoline to pass through. Should the seats still need reconditioning, i.e. the valve seat must be replaced, use the procedure that follows or replace the whole head.
8. Use a straightedge to check the cylinder head for warpage. Have head milled if necessary.

INSPECTING VALVE SPRINGS

1. Clean valve springs and related components in solvent, then use the following table to check the springs.
2. Spring tension variations up to 5% are permissible, but free length must be equal since the length affects springing characteristics.

Checking valve springs:

Free length	47 mm (1.85")
Wire diameter	4.5 mm (.177")
Spring tension with spring compressed to 41 mm (1.61")	36kp(79.3lbs) ± 5kp(3.32lbs)
Spring tension with spring compressed to 30.15 mm (1.19")	97kp(213.2lbs) ± 2.5kp(5.51lbs)

CAUTION: Intake and exhaust valve springs are of the same length. The installed spring length is changed or adjusted through the addition or removal of spacers located under the springs (see illustration).

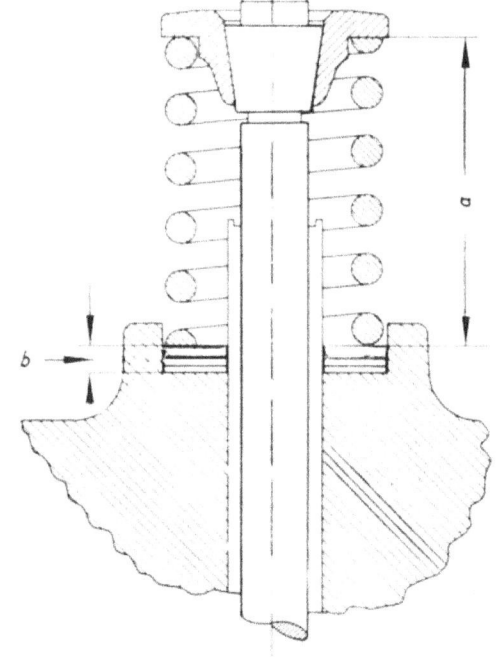

a = Installed length
b = Spacers

3. Install the special tool P 10 (gauge) with the respective spring retainer and both valve keepers.
4. Determine the indicated value and correct it, if necessary, by adding or removing spacers.
5. Install the valve springs so that the closely wound coils rest on the spacers (see illustration) and measure length (see table below).

```
Installed length of valve springs is:
Intake   = 41,0 mm (1.61")
Exhaust  = 40,5 mm (1.59")
```

LAPPING VALVES INTO SEATS

1. Smear the face of the valve with fine-grain lapping (grinding) compound (carborundum paste), then use a P 9 suction cup or equivalent to lap valve in.
2. Do not use excessive quantities of paste, and keep it in the region of the valve seat only. Placing a light coil spring under the valve head will assist considerably in the process of grinding.
3. The valve should be lapped to its seat with a semi-rotary motion and occasionally allowed to rise by the pressure of the light coil spring. This assists in spreading the paste evenly over the valve face and seat. Check surface often and make sure there is no "grooving".
4. The lapping is completed when a dull, even, matt finish, free from blemish, is produced on the valve seat and valve face.
5. Completely remove all traces of grinding compound by flushing and wiping out all involved components of the engine using water only. Be sure to clean out the valve guide bores also. Then thoroughly clean and dry out all parts with compressed air, finally oiling everything prior to reassembly.

SERVICING VALVE GUIDES

NOTE: There are two methods used to remove valve guides. The first is by drilling, but the easier method is to heat the cylinder head in an oven and then drive the guide out with a punch. Factory replacement guides are oversize externally and internally to allow for precision machining, but there are other valve guides for sale that can be chilled, coated with Led Plate compound (or both) and then easily pressed in.

Valve Guide Removal

1. Use a 10 mm tap to make a thread from the valve spring side of the valve guide; then, remove tap and install a 10 mm bolt.
2. Use a heating oven to heat the head to about 360° F. (180° C.).
3. With head still hot, use a hammer and punch to tap against the bottom of the bolt (through the valve seat area) to drive the valve guide out the top of the head.

Valve Guide Installation

NOTE: Be sure to measure the bore before the guide is purchased, unless the factory replacement guide is used, (which will have to be machined in any case). Use the following table.

1. Use a lathe to machine the oversize valve guide to bring the outside diameter matching that of the head bore. The required preload for both the intake and exhaust valve guide is .0016—.0024 in. (0,041—0,06 mm).
2. In any case, whether using the factory or other valve guides, chilling the guides in a freezer and heating the head in an oven to 400° F. (200° C.) before pressing the guide into place will make the job easier.
3. Lubricate the guide (factory recommends tallow), then press in from the rocker arm side.
4. Precision drill guide to a diameter of .394 in. (10 mm E7), or better yet, use a broach reamer. Acceptable also is a conventional reamer of this diameter.

REFACING VALVES

A valve refacing machine should be used to dress the valves only after it is determined that the wear cannot be corrected by lapping the valves into the seats with grinding compound. Naturally, the refacing procedure must be carried out in great care, particularly being sure that the valve stem has not come in contact wtih the dressing wheel; valves with stems touched by the dressing wheel must be replaced. Also be sure that only so much of the base metal is taken off as is required to produce a clean valve face. Use the accompanying table and illustration, plus the TOLERANCES AND WEAR LIMITS tables at the back of the ENGINE chapter. After refacing, be sure to lap valves in and square off the valve stem ends on the refacing machine.

Table of Dimensions for Valve Guide Installation (1mm = .03937")

Valve Guide Size	Valve Guide Outside Dia.	Diameter of Receiving Bore in Cylinder Head
Standard	14,048 - 14,059 mm	14,000 - 14,008 mm
1st oversize	14,248 - 14,259 mm	14,200 - 14,208 mm
2nd oversize	14,448 - 14,459 mm	14,400 - 14,408 mm

Valve dimensions

	Intake	Exhaust
A	37.9 - 38.1 mm (1.492 - 1.500 in.)	33.9 - 34.1 mm (1.334 - 1.342 in.)
B	117.9 mm (4.630 in.)	128.5 mm (5.060 in.)
C	9.98 - 9.99 mm (.3929 - .3933 in.)	9.96 - 9.97 mm (.3921 - .3925 in.)
b	1.7 - 2.3 mm (.067 - .091 in.)	2.0 - 2.3 mm (.079 - .091 in.)

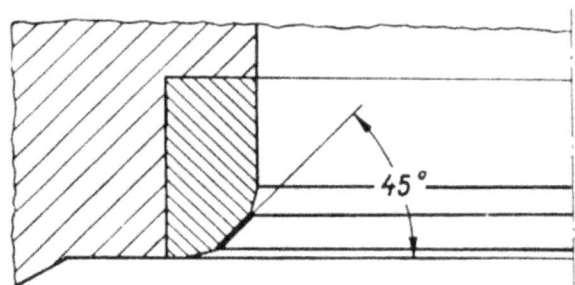

3. Perform the 75° bevel cut by lightly beveling the lower edge of the valve seat with the 75° cutter (see illustration).

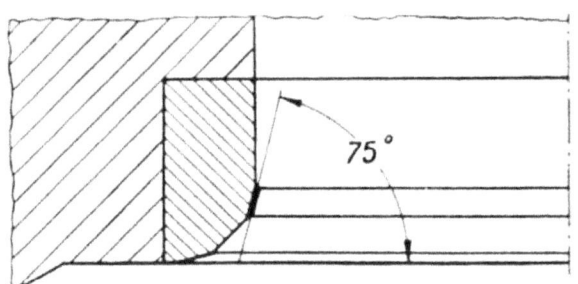

4. Finally, using the 25° cutter, perform the upper edge bevel cut until the specified seat width is obtained (see illustration).

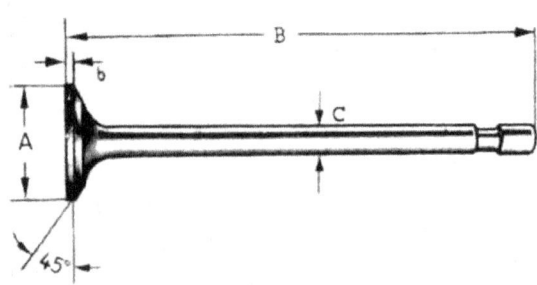

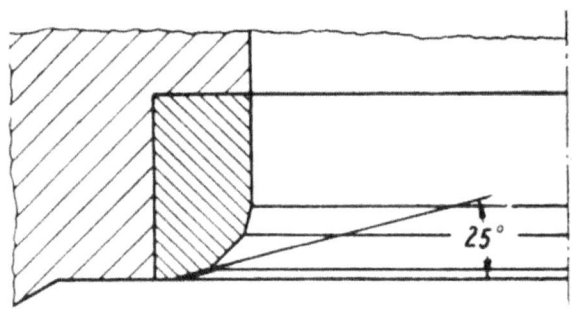

REWORKING VALVE SEATS

CAUTION: This procedure is strictly to be done by a specially equipped machine shop (Porsche dealership recommendation).

Valve seats which cannot be cleaned up by lapping the valves into the seats can be reworked providing that the permissible width of the 45° seat can be maintained, and the 25° bevel in the outer circumference does not exceed the outer diameter of the valve seat insert. If this is not possible, replace the valve seat insert or replace the whole cylinder head.

1. The tools needed are a valve seat cutter handle with a 10 mm diameter cutter guide (tool P 11) and an eight-piece valve seat cutter set (tool P 12), or equivalent. Be sure the valve guide is not worn.
2. Cut the 45° seat cut first. Apply pressure from directly above, being careful to produce a smooth surface completely free of chatter marks. Removal of base metal must be held to a minimum so as not to render the valve seat insert prematurely unusable. As soon as the entire seat area has been cleaned up by the cutter, immediately remove the cutter. Make sure no nicks or scratches have been left by the cutter teeth (see illustration).

REPLACING VALVE SEAT INSERT

CAUTION: This is a specialized and quite delicate operation, generally performed by a cylinder head rebuilding shop. The amateur should not attempt this operation unless he is properly equipped and knowledgeable.

1. Use a portable electric grinder to cut through the hardened valve seat insert so that it loosens in its seat, then drive out the old insert.
2. Precisely measure the seat receiving bore in the head, then use the following table as a reference.
3. Machine the oversize valve seat inserts on a lathe to bring to outside diameter matching that of the bore in the head. Preload as follows:

Intake valve insert ...006—.0075 in. (0,15—0,19 mm)
Exhaust valve insert ...004—.006 in. (0,10—0,15 mm)

Table of Dimensions for Valve Seat Insert Installation

Insert Size	Insert Outside Diameter	Diameter of Receiving Bore in Cylinder Head
Standard (intake)	41,182 - 41,198 mm	41,000 - 41,025 mm
1st oversize (intake)	41,502 - 41,518 mm	41,328 - 41,352 mm
Standard (exhaust)	37,120 - 37,140 mm	36,990 - 37,020 mm
1st oversize (exhaust)	37,680 - 37,700 mm	37,550 - 37,580 mm

4. Heat the cylinder head to about 400°F. (200°C.), and also chill the insert in a freezer. Lubricate contacting surfaces with HRL lubricant. This will ease the installation.
5. Using an appropriate driver, drive the valve seat insert into place.
6. Allow the cylinder head to slowly cool to room temperature.

VALVE INSTALLATION

CAUTION: Before installing valves, be sure all components are free of dirt, grinding compound, and other foreign material, then apply clean oil to metal parts. Be sure to replace parts in their original locations, and the proper thickness of spacers has been used (see INSPECTING VALVE SPRINGS).

1. Install the valve in the guide, then lubricate the sealing cap with engine oil and pull down over the valve stem and the valve guide until the base of the cap comes to rest against the valve guide (see illustration).
2. Install the spacers (see CAUTION above), then the valve spring and the valve spring retainer (see previous illustration).
3. Compress the spring as during removal and insert the keepers, being sure they are in place before releasing the valve compressor.

CAUTION: Place a cloth over the compressor just before slowly releasing spring in case the keepers are not in place and fly out.

IMPORTANT: Following engine rebuilding and valve work, the valves should be adjusted before the engine is first operated. The procedure in the MAINTENANCE SERVICE chapter is used EXCEPT that the valves are set with an additional .006 in. (0,15 mm) clearance over the specified values for a test run of at least one-half hour. This means the intake valve clearance will be .010 in. (0,25 mm), while the exhaust valve clearance will be .012 in. (0,30 mm). The reason for this setting is that lapped or refaced valves and seats seat faster than normal. After completing the test run, readjust the valve clearance to normal values as specified in the MAINTENANCE SERVICE chapter.

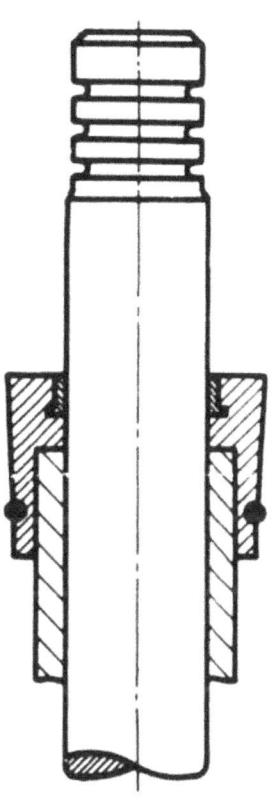

NOTE: Valve timing points are established with .394 in. (1,00 mm) clearance in a cold engine. When the timing points have been found, reset the valve clearance to the normal specifications. Following are the valve timing points:

Valve timing points:

Intake opens before	TDC	17°
Intake closes after	BDC	53°
Exhaust opens before	BDC	50°
Exhaust closes after	TDC	14°

REPLACEMENT CYLINDER HEADS

Should it become necessary to replace cylinder heads, be certain that the replacement unit has the same cubic capability as the one being traded in or replaced. The volume in ccs is stamped beside the combustion chambers. In doing any reworking such as "hop up" operations where the heads may be altered, a uniform final combustion chamber is of the utmost importance. The factory gives 1cc as the tolerance, but it is possible to come closer than this by exercising ordinary care.

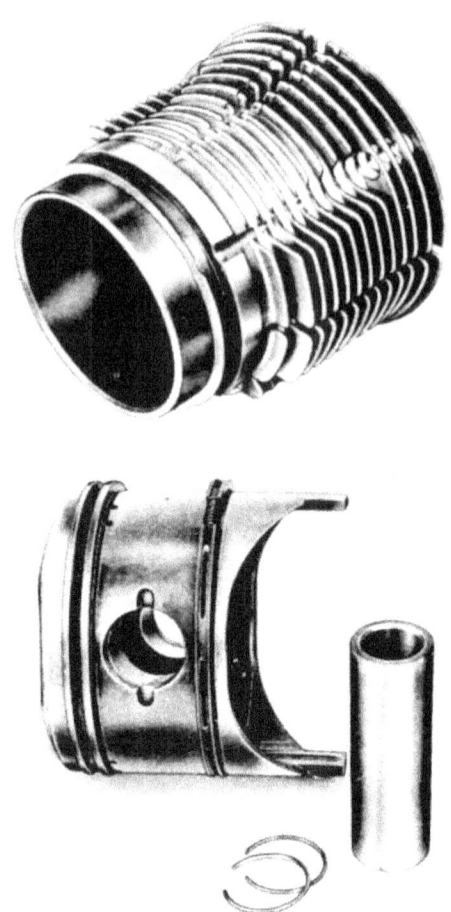

CYLINDER AND PISTON SERVICING

CYLINDER AND PISTON DESCRIPTION

The cylinders are made of carbon steel encased in light-alloy cooling fins. The Biral cylinders are available in four height groups; cylinder height is the distance between the cylinder seating flanges at the crankcase and the cylinder head.

Cylinders installed under one cylinder head must be of the same height and bear the same identifying symbols at the cylinder base. The identifying symbol is a triangle inside which the number 5, 6, 7, or 8 is stamped, depending on the actual size group.

The piston-to-cylinder clearance when new is .0008 in. (0,02 mm), and the final wear limit is .008 in. (0,2 mm). Cylinders worn close to the wear limit should be replaced together with the pistons; use cylinder/piston replacement sets falling into the appropriate size group. Cylinder/piston sets installed in one engine must not differ by more than one size group up or down (Example: if engine is equipped with size 5 cylinder/pistons, use size 4, 5 or 6 sets only).

The pistons are made of light alloy, and have 3 piston rings each, the lowest being the oil scraper. The piston pins float in the connecting rod bushings; they are contained within the pistons with a circlip at each end. There is a broad bevel around the piston top perimeter.

Piston pins are arranged in the pistons off center and it is, therefore, important to correctly install the pistons in the engine. The piston top bears an arrow mark. When installed, the arrow must point in the direction of travel, towards the engine's flywheel.

Owing to the off-centered piston pin, the connecting rod shifts its direction of attack, and so does the piston its tangential angle in relation to the cylinder wall prior to reaching the top dead center (TDC). Since combustion has not begun yet in this position, the prevailing side forces are still small, which permits the piston to shift onto the opposite cylinder wall softly rather than with a slamming impact. As a result, piston slap noise occurring at the time of the pressure point shift is kept at a minimum, especially when the piston-to-cylinder wall clearance is near the wear limit.

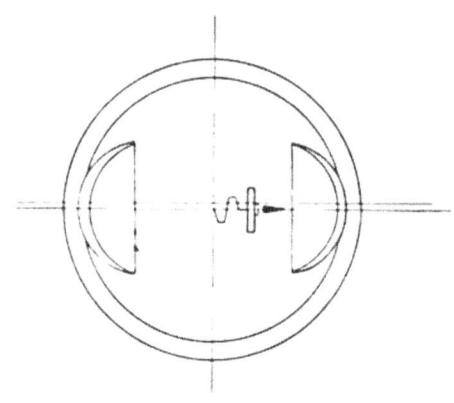

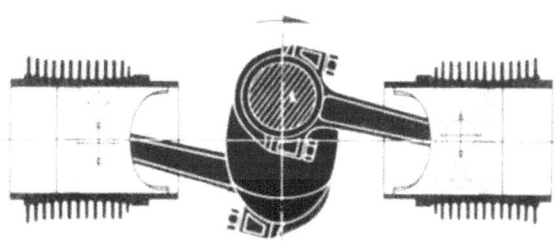

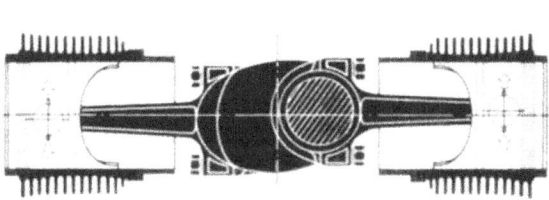

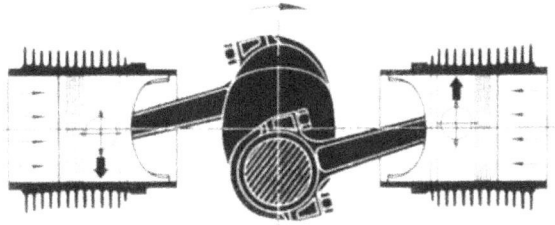

Replace cylinders (along with pistons: see PISTON INSPECTION) which are worn close to the permissible wear limit. All cylinders are marked at the base to indicate the bore diameter group, such as "O", or reconditioned units by "+KD 1", etc. The piston tops bear appropriate size values (+ 1 KD 1, etc.) (see illustration).

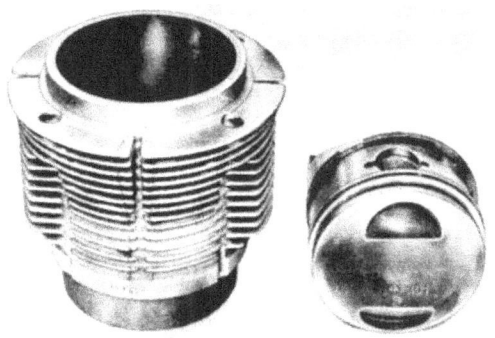

NOTE: The accompanying table shows which piston and cylinder size groups can be paired. Those sets worn close to the wear limit should be replaced by a new set; use new sets falling into the appropriate size group, but be sure sets installed in one engine do not differ by more than four size groups. See CYLINDER AND PISTON DESCRIPTION for other information.

CYLINDER REMOVAL

With engine and cylinder heads removed, proceed as follows:

1. Remove pushrod cover tubes, along with their end O-rings.
2. Withdraw the cylinders, and mark 1 through 4 using illustration at front of ENGINE chapter as a guide.

CYLINDER INSPECTION

Check cylinder for damage other than wear, replace if necessary along with piston. Wear limit is a clearance of .008 in. (0.2 mm) between piston and cylinder. Exact piston-to-cylinder clearance can be determined only by measuring each component separately. Measure cylinders at a point about ¾ in. (15 mm) below the cylinder top using a bore micrometer with setting ring P 13c or equivalent.

Standard Size

Group	Cylinder Diameter	Piston Diameter
-1	82.485 - 82.494	82.47
0	82.495 - 82.504	82.48
+1	82.505 - 82.514	82.49

1st Oversize

Group	Cylinder Diameter	Piston Diameter
-1 KD 1	82.985 - 82.994	82.97
0 KD 1	82.995 - 83.004	82.98
+1 KD 1	83.005 - 83.014	82.99

PISTON REMOVAL

CAUTION: The piston top is marked with an arrow which must point in the direction of travel, i.e. towards the flywheel, when the piston is installed. Correct installation is important since the piston pins are off-center. Remember, remove pistons before splitting crankcase (they will not fit through crankcase bores).

1. With cylinders removed, mark the pistons to ensure correct reassembly, using illustration at the front of the ENGINE chapter as a guide.
2. Remove circlips from both ends of the piston pins, making sure circlips do not fall into crankcase (place a lint-free cloth in crankcase bore).
3. Heat pistons to about 175°F. (80°C.) using an electric piston heater (see illustration). This is necessary since the piston pins are a light press fit. Use piston mandrel to drive pins out, then remove pistons.

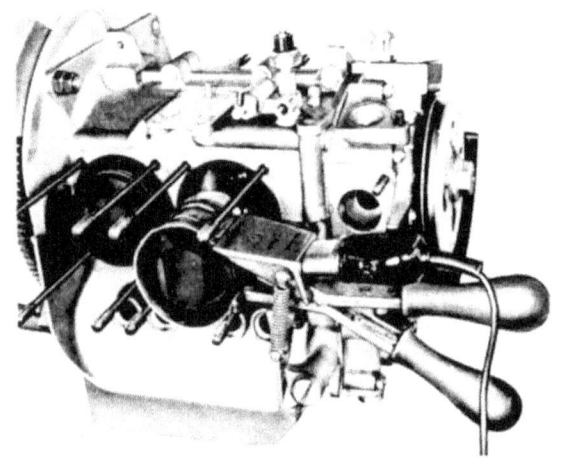

ALTERNATE METHODS: Pistons can also be heated with hot oil or water, but a better way to do it is with a small butane or propane torch with a flame spreader tip. For the price of these items, both the removal and installation of the pistons can be readily accomplished. It helps to have a special pusher for pin removal that has a pilot which fits inside the pin. Be sure to support the piston if you must pound on the pin so the connecting rod does not take the force and bend. The best method is to turn the engine so that the crankshaft is vertical while removing the pistons. The force of gravity should allow the pin to drop right out, then remove the piston. Play the torch over the whole piston for several minutes, being careful not to overheat any particular part.

CAUTION: Use wet rags to cover the oily areas near the torch so the whole engine does not go up in a huge cloud of black smoke.

4. Remove piston rings, if necessary, using a piston ring expander. If the rings are to be reused, expand them as little as possible, keeping them close to the piston body. Otherwise they will bend or snap (see illustration).

COMPETITION EQUIPMENT

Special lightweight forged aluminum pistons of extreme strength can be used in the place of normal equipment. Other kits supply both the cylinder and lightweight pistons in larger bores up to 1750 cc, and compression ratio can be changed from 9.5:1 to 10.5:1. All come equipped with rings (some with pins and circlips), and require no machining of heads or crankcase.

PISTON INSPECTION

1. Clean piston, then remove carbon deposits from piston tops and ring grooves without scratching the base metal. Evidence of uneven contact or carbon deposits on one side of the piston may indicate the connecting rod is out of alignment. Should the piston show evidence of seizure or wear, assume the piston/cylinder set is no longer serviceable. However, should the mating cylinder be in good condition, the fault can be cured by installing only a new piston/cylinder set of the same size group or letter designation.
2. Piston diameter is shown by the size group stamped into the piston top. The individual size groups are shown in the piston size table, while the piston measuring point (in millimeters) is shown in the illustration. Piston clearance at installation is .0008 in. (0,02 mm).

NOTE: Measure perpendicular to the piston pin axis (see illustration).

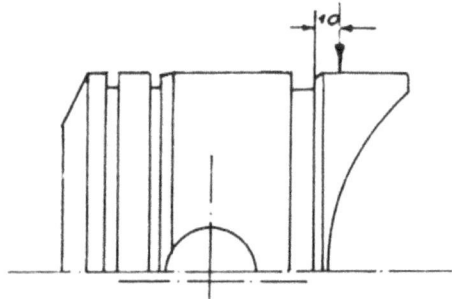

3. Precision being a prime cause with Porsche, it is recommended that a fixed dial gauge be preset with gauge blocks for the piston diameter measurement. Replace piston and cylinder as a set if near the wear limit.
4. Check piston rings for proper condition, ring gap, and ring groove clearance (see TOLERANCES AND WEAR LIMITS data at the back of this chapter). If parts are not according to tolerances, replace the piston rings or pistons, as necessary. To check piston ring gap, insert the ring into the cylinder and push it down about ¼ inch with a piston, then measure the gap with a feeler gauge, which should be .012—.018 in. (0,3—0,45 mm).
5. The piston pin is held in the piston through interference fit. Inspect for wear, discarding if necessary. If it passes the test, try pushing it into the cold piston by hand (assuming both parts are clean). If this can be done, the piston pin is worn and must be replaced with a pin of larger diameter. A color code marking inside the piston on the piston pin boss indicates the proper size of the piston pin:

WHITE	21,997 to 22,000 mm
BLUE	22,000 to 22,003 mm

See the "Piston Pin Size Groups" table to order new parts and as a reference.

PISTON SIZE TABLE

Piston Size Groups

Piston Dia. ± 0.005 mm	Stamped Marking	Size Group
82.49 82.48 82.47	+ 1 0 - 1	Standard size
82.99 82.98 82.97	+ 1 KD 1 0 KD 1 - 1 KD 1	1st oversize
83.49 83.48 83.47	+ 1 KD 2 0 KD 2 - 1 KD 2	2nd oversize

Piston Pin Size Groups

Piston Pin Tolerance Category	Color Code	Spare Part Nr.
0.000 ... -0.003 mm	White	616.103.321.01
0.000 ... +0.003 mm	Blue	616.103.321.50

6. Clearance between the connecting rod bushing and the piston pin is .0008 to .0014 in. (0,020 to 0,036 mm). If the clearance approaches the wear limit of .002 in. (0,050 mm), fit a new piston pin into a new connecting rod bushing. Use an inside and outside micrometer for this measurement, or if possible, a dial gauge preset with gauge blocks.

PISTON INSTALLATION

To install, reverse the removal procedure, noting the following:

1. Be sure the connecting rods are aligned and in proper order (correct sides facing the flywheel) and the pistons are clean.
2. Fit the compression rings and the oil scraper as follows:

    a. Use a ring expander to prevent piston damage or ring breakage. Even with this tool, use great care not to over-expand ring, or it will break and a new ring will have to be purchased.

    b. Install piston rings in the pistons so that the "TOP" or "OBEN" marking is uppermost, i.e., towards the top of the piston.

    c. Stagger piston ring gaps so that they are about 120° apart, with oil scraper gap facing toward top of engine.

3. Note which side of the piston faces the flywheel, i.e., the arrow points in the direction of vehicle travel (remember that the piston pin is off center), then install the piston pin circlip on this side. Be sure the circlip is seated in its groove and the gap is towards the crankcase.
4. Oil the piston pin, then keep it at room temperature or lower.
5. Use the procedure under PISTON REMOVAL that was previously used to heat the pistons (or, place the pistons in a Pyrex bowl or iron skillet with a lid and heat in an oven).

6. While piston is hot, place over the connecting rod and insert the oiled piston pin with light, continuous pressure until the circlip stops it. Double check to ensure the piston-top arrow points toward the flywheel.
7. Install the second circlip (open end towards the crankcase), then ensure both circlips are seated in their grooves within the piston pin boss.

CYLINDER INSTALLATION

NOTE: Be sure to install cylinder base gaskets. To install cylinders, reverse the removal procedure, noting the following:

1. After inspecting cylinders and replacing wherever needed, inspect the cylinder seat in the crankcase and the cylinder head. Burrs or dirt particles may lead to cylinder distortion. Remove as needed.
2. Check the cylinder seats in the crankcase for linear alignment of seating surfaces in relation to each other and, upon insertion of the cylinders into the crankcase, check alignment across the top of the cylinders.
3. Use new gasket rings at the base of the cylinders.
4. Before installing cylinders, be sure the piston rings are installed in the proper locations with the "TOP" markings up; also, note that the arrow mark on the piston top should be pointing towards the flywheel, i.e. in the direction of travel. If not, turn the piston around.
5. Stagger the piston ring gaps 120° apart with oil control ring gap facing up, then compress rings with a piston ring compressor. Use the type of compressor shown in the illustration, since it can be taken apart and removed after the cylinder is forced down over the rings.

6. Wipe an oil-soaked lint-free cloth around the cylinder interior, then push the cylinder onto the pistons, forcing the ring compressor down.
7. Inspect for the required clearance between the cylinder stub bores and studs, since the studs must not touch the cooling fins. Determine clearance by turning cylinders in their bases, and if necessary straighten the studs.
8. Install the pushrods cover tubes and the deflector baffles and supporting springs. These latter parts must not be omitted.
9. See CYLINDER HEAD INSTALLATION earlier in this chapter for the remainder of this procedure.

CRANKCASE/CRANKSHAFT/ CAMSHAFT

DESCRIPTION

The crankcase is assembled from three parts — the two halves and a timing gear cover. These components are cast from a magnesium alloy and are precision machined as a set. However, it is possible to replace the timing gear cover alone. Studs for bolting on the cylinder heads and the timing gear cover are screwed right into the sections. The three journals of the camshaft ride on the crankcase base metal without inserts.

The crankshaft rides on four lead-bronze insert bearings, two of which are split-sleeve inserts (bearings 2 and 3), while solid insert bearing 4 is located in the timing gear cover. Replacement of the latter bearing only involves removing the timing gear cover. Bearing 1, a solid insert bearing, also takes up the crankshaft thrust. All crankshaft journals are surface-hardened (soft nitrided), and should not be machined as the case hardening will be penetrated. The crankshaft should be replaced in this case.

The flywheel (located adjacent to bearing 1), which also carries the starter gear teeth, is attached to the crankshaft by means of a gland nut and is fixed in position by 8 aligning dowel pins. The flywheel and crankshaft are balanced as one unit, with 2 of the aligning dowel pins offset to ensure proper installation. The camshaft gear and the distributor drive gear are locked to the crankshaft through Woodruff keys and a lock ring before the gears. The crankshaft pulley is attached to the crankshaft through a hex bolt and locked with a Woodruff key. Oil seals located at the flywheel and crankshaft pulley ends seal the crankshaft in the crankcase.

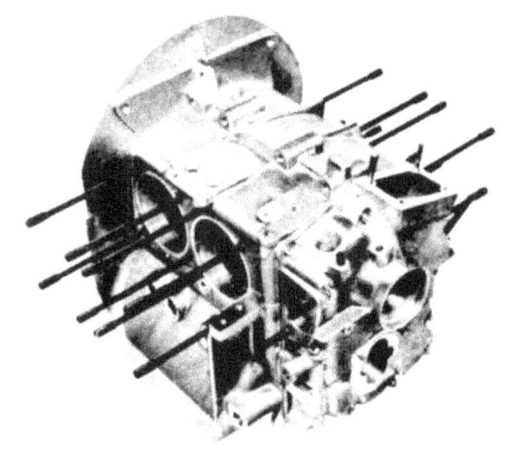

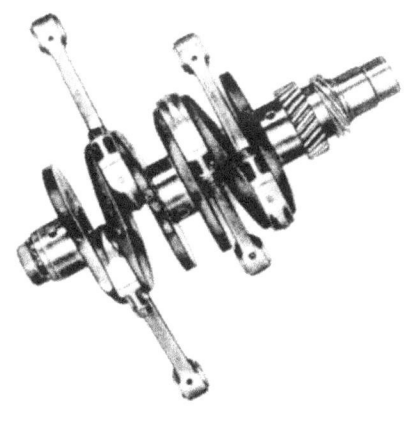

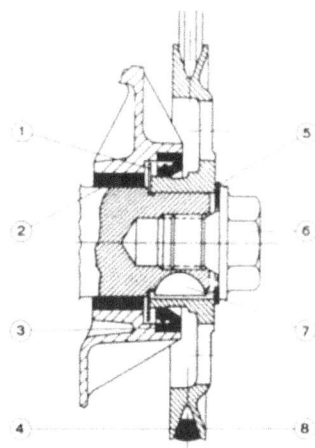

The camshaft is driven through light-alloy helical gears. The three journals of the shaft ride on the base metal of the crankcase, using no insert bearings. Valve timing is effected through cams, valve lifters, pushrods, and rocker arms. Each cam alternately actuates one valve of two opposing cylinders. The exhaust valves are cased with high-grade chrome-nickel steel.

1. Oil deflector
2. Bearing 4
3. Oil seal
4. V-belt
5. Spring washer
6. Retaining bolt
7. Woodruff key
8. Crankshaft pulley

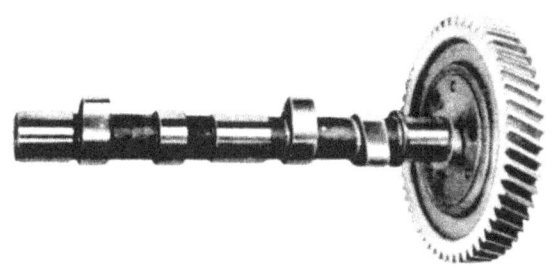

1. Inspect the crankshaft pulley, prior to installation, for good condition of its seat and belt running surfaces.
2. Check pulley runout, replace pulley if excessive.
3. Check the oil sealing surface of the pulley.
4. Check the oil seal for damage or wear, replace if necessary.

SERVICING TIMING GEAR COVER

SERVICING CRANKSHAFT PULLEY

Removal

With the engine rear shield and the fan belt removed, proceed as follows:

1. Unscrew the crankshaft pulley retaining bolt (counterclockwise).
2. Withdraw the crankshaft pulley, using a puller or two screwdrivers while tapping pulley with a plastic hammer if the pulley hangs up on the Woodruff key (one screwdriver will cause aluminum pulley to break) (see illustration).
3. Remove pulley shield and Woodruff key.

NOTE: Be sure to remove the Woodruff key from the crankshaft before withdrawing the timing gear cover to prevent damaging the cover oil seal.

Installation

To install the pulley, reverse the removal procedure, torqueing the bolt to 43 ft. lb. (6 mkp), and noting the following:

Removal

With all the above listed components removed, along with the oil pump, bypass valve, crankshaft pulley and its Woodruff key, proceed as follows:

1. Remove the retaining nuts from the timing gear cover.
2. Remove the timing gear cover.
3. Remove the counter-pressure oil line and rubber plugs.

NOTE: Be sure the Woodruff key has been removed from the crankshaft before withdrawing the timing gear cover or the cover oil seal may be damaged.

Inspection

1. Inspect bearing 4 for wear or damage, replace as described in SERVICING BEARING 4. Be sure set screw is seated firmly.
2. Inspect deflector and oil seal at the crankshaft pulley; replace if at all worn or damaged, using the SERVICING BEARING 4 OIL SEAL procedure.
3. Make sure the dowel pins are firmly seated.

Installation

To install, reverse the removal procedure, noting the following:

1. Replace all gaskets with Porsche-approved replacements, ensuring that the three O-rings (see arrows in the illustration) are in place and do not fall out when the timing gear cover is positioned on the crankcase.

2. Place one rubber plug on each end of the counter pressure oil line and install in the timing gear cover so that the upper plug open end faces the crankcase, while the lower plug open end is inside the timing gear cover (see illustration).
3. Place a new gasket under the generator carrier before installing carrier.
4. See LUBRICATION SYSTEM for oil pump and by-pass valve replacement.
5. Torque the retaining nuts of the timing gear cover to 14.5 ft. lb. (2 mkp).

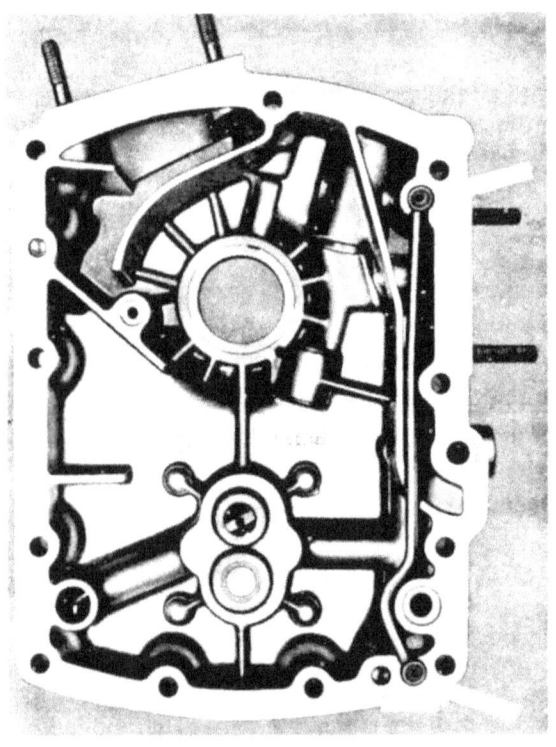

SERVICING BEARING 4 OIL SEAL

Removal

With the crankshaft pulley and Woodruff key removed, proceed as follows:

1. Deform the old oil seal by fitting a punch through the recess slot of the seal seat and striking the punch with a hammer (see illustration).

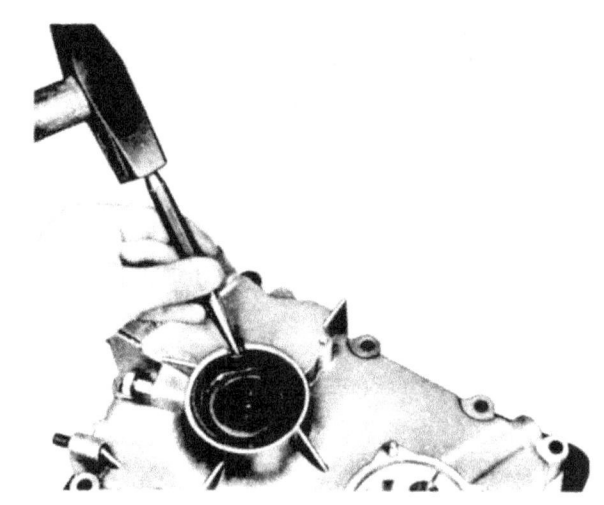

2. Withdraw the oil seal and oil deflector, prying with a screwdriver if necessary.
3. Remove any burr formed on the oil seal seat.

Installation

1. Insert the oil deflector.
2. Install the oil seal with tool P 73 or equivalent (see illustration).
3. Lubricate the oil sealing surface on the crankshaft pulley (smoothen if necessary).
4. Install the pulley as described under SERVICING CRANKSHAFT PULLEY.

SERVICING BEARING 4

Follow the above procedure to inspect the bearing and remove the seal, then proceed as follows:

Removal

1. Remove bearing set screw.
2. Remove any burr that might have been kicked up from the recess in the oil seal seat.
3. Heat the whole timing gear cover to about 140°F. (60°C.), then remove the bearing with punch P27a of the assembly plate set (or equivalent).

Installation

1. Inspect the bearing seating bore along with the rest of the timing gear cover.

2. Turn the set screw of bearing 4 until the tip of the screw projects about 1 mm into the bearing seating bore in the timing gear cover.
3. Heat the timing gear cover to about 320°F. (160°C.), then install the bearing using Special Tool P 27a.
4. Tighten the bearing set screw, making sure that the screw does not project and exert pressure on the bearing.
5. Install the oil seal as described under SERVICING BEARING 4 OIL SEAL.

SERVICING FLYWHEEL

Description

A gland nut holds the flywheel to the crankshaft, while eight dowel pins transmit the torque forces. A soft iron gasket is installed between the flywheel and the crankshaft. An oil seal, installed in the crankcase at bearing 1, prevents crankcase oil from escaping. The seal rides on the flywheel hub. The gland nut contains a pilot bushing which supports one end of the transmission input shaft (see illustration).

Removal

With the clutch pressure plate and clutch disc removed (see CLUTCH chapter), proceed as follows:

1. Remove the gland nut using a P 44 hex socket or similar tool.
2. Withdraw the flywheel.

NOTE: See the SUMMARY under ENGINE DISASSEMBLY for methods of removing the flywheel and holding the engine steady.

Inspection

1. Inspect the flywheel starter ring for serviceable condition of the gear teeth. Those teeth that are slightly flattened may be dressed with a file.
2. Check the dowel pins ni the crankshaft, replace the whole crankshaft if loose or damaged.
3. Check the dowel pin seats in the flywheel. Should the seats appear peened, replace the flywheel.
4. Inspect the oil sealing surface on the flywheel hub. It is usually advisable to replace the seal.

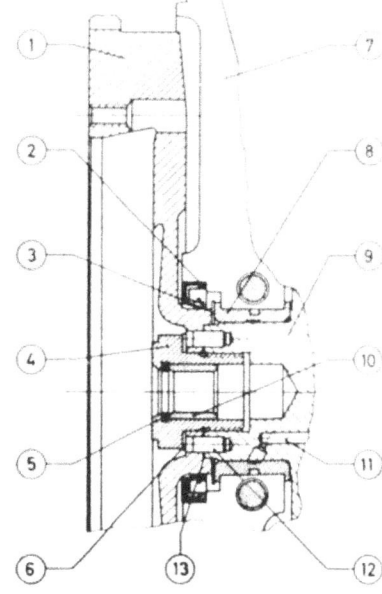

1 Flywheel
2 Oil seal
3 Spacer
4 Gland nut
5 Gasket
6 Spring washer
7 Crankcase
8 Bearing 1
9 Crankshaft
10 Pilot bushing
11 Oil gallery
12 Dowel pin
13 Soft iron gasket

5. Inspect the pilot bushing in the gland nut for wear.
6. Torque the flywheel into place on the crankshaft, then check the flywheel for runout. Maximum permissible lateral runout is .012 in. (0,3 mm), measured in the middle of the clutch plate contact area. Maximum permissible vertical runout is .004 in. (0,1 mm). Note the specifications in the TOLERANCES AND WEAR LIMITS tables.

NOTE: Use the table below to determine measurements. If flywheel reconditioning is necessary, turn slowly on a lathe. The depth from the mating surface of the flywheel-to-pressure plate and the mating surface of the flywheel-to-clutch disc must be maintained at .8858 in. (22,5 mm). In other words, be sure to cut the surface on the flywheel where it mates with the pressure plate to the same depth as the cut plus wear on the flywheel where it mates with the clutch disc.

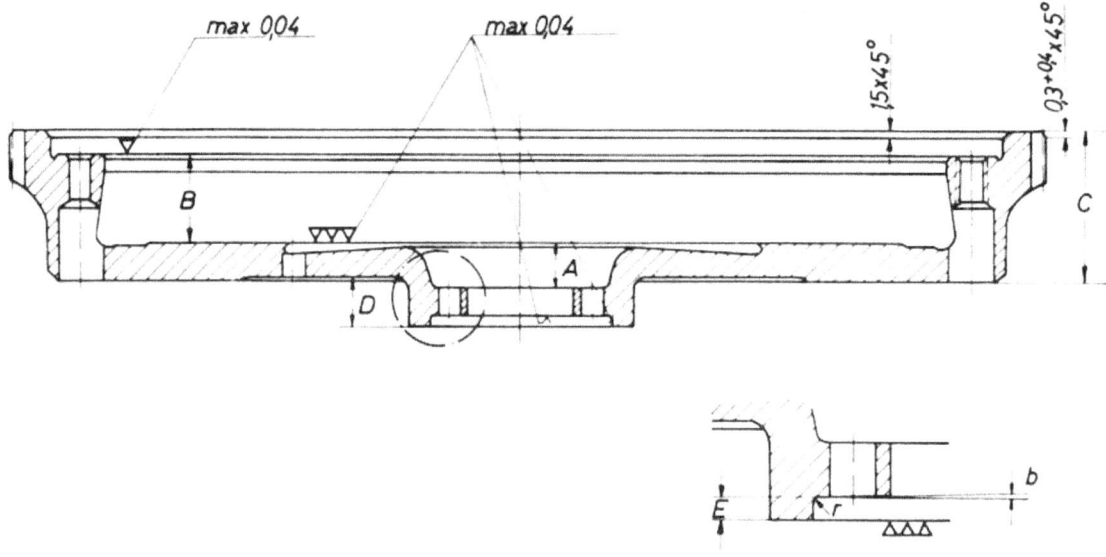

Measuring point	Original measure	Reconditioning grade			Tolerance
	mm	1	2	3	
A	12,3	11,8	11,5	11,2	± 0,1
B	22,5	-	-	-	+ 0,2
C	39,5	38,8	38,4	38,0	± 0,2
D	13,25	12,95	12,75	12,55	± 0,1
E	3,15	3,1	-	-	± 0,05
r	0,5	0,5	-	-	- 0,2
b	1°30'	-	-	-	-

NOTE: Be sure that both identifying numbers stamped on the crankshaft and flywheel are the same, since this number designates that these two components are balanced as a unit (see illustration). It should be noted that two dowel pins are positioned closer together, and the number "1" is stamped between these dowel pins on both the crankshaft and the flywheel (see illustration). In this way, proper installation is ensured. When either the flywheel or the crankshaft have to be replaced, both parts will have to be rebalanced as a unit, (competition use only). The new parts are balanced to $0°$.

Installation

To install, reverse the removal procedure, noting the following:

1. Use a new soft iron gasket.
2. If the pilot bushing (see previous illustration) requires replacement, renew its brass bushing with the gland nut.
3. Prior to installing the flywheel, lightly oil the sealing surface (hub).
4. Torque the gland nut to 326—362 ft. lb. (45—50 mkp).

NOTE: See the SUMMARY under ENGINE DISASSEMBLY for methods of installing the flywheel and holding the engine steady.

Oil Seal Removal

With flywheel removed, proceed as follows:

1. Remove old oil seal.
2. Remove all residue from the oil seal seat, then remove any sharp edges from the outer surface perimeter as may be necessary. Be sure to remove all filings, then apply a thin coat of gasket compound.

Oil Seal Installation

1. Use tool VW 240b or equivalent to install a new oil seal. To use tool, screw onto crankshaft end and tighten the guide piece which carries the oil seal. The oil seal must rest at the bottom of its seat and must not be slanted while being installed.
2. Remove installing tool, then install flywheel according to the previous instructions. Be sure to oil the hub.

SERVICING CRANKCASE

Disassembly

NOTE: With all previously mentioned components removed, proceed as follows. See the SUMMARY under ENGINE DISASSEMBLY for methods of working on the crankcase.

1. Remove crankcase retaining nuts at the camshaft end (flywheel side).
2. Remove the rest of the crankcase retaining nuts.
3. Placing crankcase on its left side, lift up on the right section of the crankcase, leaving the camshaft and the crankshaft in the left section of the crankcase.

NOTE: Once again, DO NOT try to pry apart the crankcase halves with a sharp tool. DO tap the right crankcase half with a rubber mallet to release the camshaft and crankshaft so they will remain in the left half of the crankcase, and if this fails, check and double-check under the dirt for more nuts and bolts.

4. Remove the valve lifters and place in order for replacement.
5. Carefully lift off the camshaft and the crankshaft with connecting rods.
6. Remove the camshaft end cap, then remove the crankshaft oil seal at bearing 1.
7. Remove bearing inserts 2 and 3.
8. Remove connecting rod retaining nuts, then remove connecting rods and caps complete with bearings. Mark parts so they can be kept in order, and if possible, mount crankshaft in a VW 310a bench mount or equivalent.
9. Remove the gear lock ring from the crankshaft with VW 161a lock ring pliers or equivalent.

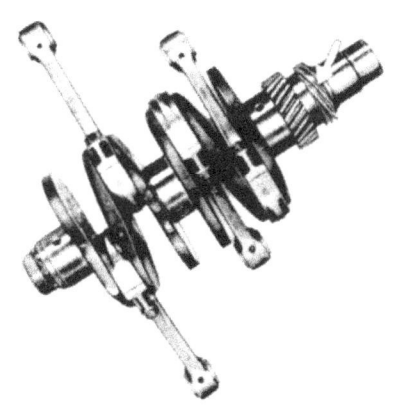

10. Remove distributor drive gear, spacer, and camshaft drive gear from crankshaft using VW 202 puller with VW 202a puller jaws and VW 202f block.

Crankcase Inspection and Cleaning

NOTE: Inspection and reassembly can be greatly simplified if all components are "boiled out" or steam-cleaned first.

1. Inspect all 3 crankcase components for cracks or damage.
2. Remove any traces of sealing compound from the crankcase mating surfaces, using solvent (such as lacquer thinner) if necessary.
3. Inspect the mating surfaces for linear alignment, burrs, scratches, or anything else which would cause oil leakage upon reassembly. Gently glide a large flat file over the mating surfaces to smoothen.
4. Assemble empty crankcase and tighten retaining nuts. Use an inside micrometer to measure the main bearing bores. If bores are especially out of round, the crankcase will have to be replaced.
5. If necessary, lightly bevel the bearing seat edges at the crankcase joint and at the bores to prevent gouging as a result of bearing preload upon reassembly of the crankcase.
6. Flush oil passages with solvent and blow through with compressed air. No sharp edges should be in evidence at the bearings or oil passages.
7. Check the oil suction tube for firm seating and tightness; use a ball end punch to tighten if necessary.
8. Check dowel pin in Bearing 1 for firm seating.
9. Check the dowel pins aligning the timing gear cover for firm seating. If a dowel is loose, making a punch indentation adjacent to the dowel should tighten it.

Crankshaft And Connecting Rod Inspection And Cleaning

1. Flush oil passages with solvent and blow through with compressed air. No sharp edges should be in evidence at the bearings or oil passages.
2. If installing a new connecting rod, check the connecting rod weight: the maximum permissible weight difference between the connecting rods of one engine is .211 oz. (6 g), although it should be possible to come much closer.
3. Check the piston pin bushing. Light finger pressure should be enough to enter the pin into the bushing. If bushing bore is too large, install a new connecting rod bushing.
4. Check the connecting rod alignment and correct if necessary. The lateral clearance between the connecting rods and the crankshaft should be .006 to .008 in. (0,15 to 0,20 mm); replace connecting rod or shaft as necessary (see illustration).

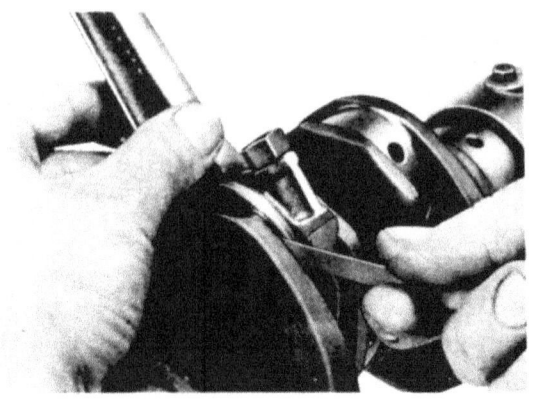

5. Check the crankshaft for scoring on the seating surfaces under the distributor drive gear, spacer, and camshaft drive gear. Minor scoring can be carefully removed with crocus cloth so long as the dressing doesn't impair the press fit of the gears.
6. Check the crankshaft for cracks (acoustical sound test; it should ring when struck), whip, and wear. Replace crankshaft if necessary, using the MAIN BEARING AND CRANKSHAFT JOURNAL DIMENSIONS found at the back of the ENGINE chapter. See illustration which shows the measuring point for establishing thickness of the bearing inserts.

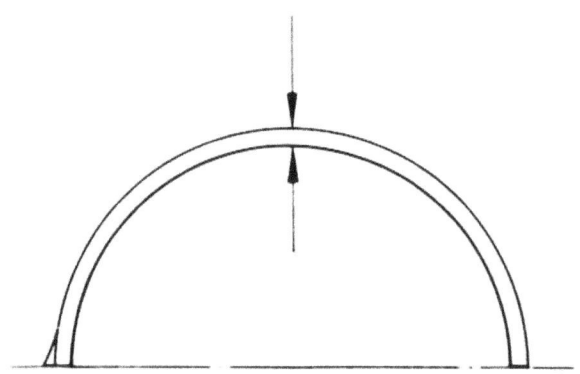

NOTE: When using undersize bearings, also determine whether the main bearing bores in the crankcase are standard or oversize. Also, having the crankshaft magnafluxed is a good precaution and a much more positive test. DO NOT grind crankshaft as case hardening will be penetrated.

7. Check the camshaft drive gear for wear and tooth contact, replace if necessary.
8. Inspect the condition of the distributor drive gear, replace if necessary.

NOTE: There are several methods of measuring the wear of bearings and camshaft and crankshaft journals. One method is to place the bearing inserts into their seats in the crankcase and torque the crankcase bolts tight. Use an inside micrometer to determine the size, and compare this with the diameter of the crankshaft journal. Be sure the insert halves have actually joined, i.e., there is no obstruction in the joint. Do the same with the connecting rods, tapping on the cap with a hammer while tightening.

An easier method is to use "Plastigage", which is put out in a kit by Perfect Circle Ring Co. The kit consists of different sizes of a plastic thread and a graduated scale. This thread, which is soft and malleable, is placed (in the direction of travel) between the journals and bearings to be measured; the respective nuts (crankcase and connecting rods) are then torqued to specifications.

After all nuts have been evenly torqued, they are removed and the components are carefully separated (especially where the Plastigage has been placed). It will be noted that the Plastigage has been squeezed flat. The graduated scale (when compared to the width of the Plastigage) will show the amount of clearance between the journal and the bearing. Be sure not to rotate the crankshaft or camshaft while the Plastigage is in place. Solid bearing inserts will have to be measured as first described. The connecting rods should not be measured at the same time as the main bearings, since there would be difficulty with keeping the crankshaft from rotating. Replacement bearings should have the smallest tolerance allowed, since they will wear to a larger tolerance in time.

Camshaft Inspection And Cleaning

1. After cleaning camshaft in solvent and blowing off with compressed air, check the shaft for wear at the bearing journals and lobes. Watch for rippled wear in the lift ramps or slanted wear, in relation to the camshaft axis, óf the cam lobes races. Replace or regrind as necessary.
2. See the table of TOLERANCES AND WEAR LIMITS for end play specifications.
3. Inspect camshaft for signs of whip.
4. Be sure the camshaft gear is firmly attached to the camshaft, that it has proper tooth contact, and is not worn or damaged.

NOTE: To align the camshaft with the crankshaft gear, the camshaft gear tooth marked "O" lies between the two crankshaft gear teeth bearing a punch mark each (see illustration).

5. As a further test, measure the gear backlash over the entire circumference of the camshaft gear by moving the gears back and forth while taking readings with a dial gauge and measuring the entire circumference of the camshaft gear. The correct backlash, in an assembled crankcase, is .0006–.0016 in. (0,015–0,04 mm).
6. Should the above test prove the camshaft gear faulty, replace gear with one of the five sizes available for such adjustment. These gears are marked on the camshaft side as follows: 0, +1, +2, −1, and −2 (see illustration). The numbers show, in hundreds of one millimeter, how much the pitch circle radius differs from the standard (O) size; "+" means an oversize gear, while "−" means an undersize gear.

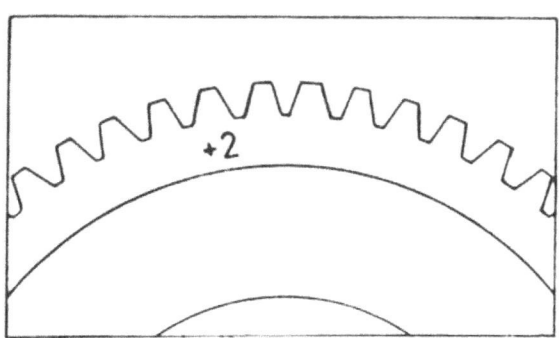

NOTE: Do not confuse the No. "0" with the timing mark "o" on the backside of the gear. The crankshaft gear is supplied in only one size, so requires no identification. If necessary, have the camshaft gear replaced by a specialty shop. If camshaft or crankcase is replaced, check the camshaft for snug but easy rotation. If necessary, check the camshaft bearings with machinist's bluing and carefully dress the bearing seats in the crankcase with a scraper.

Checking And Adjusting Crankshaft End Play

IMPORTANT: With crankshaft reassembled (see instructions following), and without the connecting rods, (they will only be in the way for now), adjust the end play to .0055 to .0067 in. (0,14 to 0,17 mm). The .0055 (0,14) figure is preferable, while the wear limit is .0087 in. (0,22 mm). This very important step of assembly requires that only one of the soft iron gaskets be used, and the spacing be adjusted with a shim of the proper thickness between the No. 1 Bearing and the flywheel. Proceed as follows:

1. Properly position Bearing 1 on Journal 1 (use the new bearing if such has been purchased as a replacement).
2. Install the soft iron gasket (which is .004–.006 in. (0,10–0,14 mm) thick) on the end of the crankshaft, then attach the flywheel and torque the gland nut to 326–362 ft. lb. (45–50 mkp).
3. Use a feeler gauge to measure the end play between the bearing flange and the flywheel shoulder (see illustration).

4. Compute the shim thickness necessary to give the preferable .0055 in. (0,14 mm) clearance. In other words, subtract .0055 in. (0,14 mm) from the feeler gauge reading. This is the amount of shimming needed.

5. Shims are available in thicknesses from .0315 to .0413 in. (0,8 to 1,05 mm) and are marked alphabetically from A through F. Use any combination to come within the required end play, but close to the lower limit.

6. Remove the flywheel from the crankshaft, install the shims selected, and replace the flywheel; retorque to the previous setting.

7. Repeat the above procedure until satisfied that the clearance is correct. Be sure to push the shaft toward the flywheel when measuring, and always use new shims. Do not use more than one of the soft iron gaskets.

8. Remove the flywheel and place it, the shims, and soft iron gasket to one side until ready for assembly onto the crankshaft.

Reassembly

Reassembly is in the reverse order of disassembly, noting the following items. Be sure parts have been properly cleaned and inspected:

1. Insert the main bearing dowel pins in No. 1 Main Bearing then install the inserts for Bearing 2 and 3, placing the insert half which has the oil passage into the left crankcase half (see illustration). Make sure the passage in the insert lines up with the passage in the crankcase bearing seat; then install the remaining insert halves in the right crankcase section. Spread an oil film over the inserts.

2. To simplify reassembly, mark the insert of Bearing 1 at the crankcase joint after placing it in its bore (this aids in locating the dowel pin seat and the oil passage). Be sure the bearing is located on its dowel pin.

CAUTION: If the bearing is NOT properly located on its dowel pin, the pin will form its own hole in the bearing shell when the two crankcase halves are torqued together, causing the bearing to bind up the crankshaft.

3. Insert the Woodruff key for the camshaft and distributor drive gears.

4. Heat the camshaft and distributor drive gears in an oven at about 350°F. (160°C.) for about half an hour. Be sure the gears are clean and free of solvent so that you do not have an explosion. Placing the gears in a clean Pyrex bowl or an iron skillet (with lids) will allow the gears to be carried to the workbench for assembly without cooling. At this temperature, no press should be needed, and the gears should simply slip into place.

5. Place the camshaft drive gear onto the crankshaft with the chamfered side facing the flywheel (No. 3 Main Bearing journal). If necessary, press into place using VW 427 guide tube.

6. Place the distributor drive gear onto the crankshaft in the proper position. If necessary, press onto the crankshaft using VW 427 guide tube or equivalent.

7. Install the gear lock ring onto the crankshaft. If possible, use VW 428 tapered guide tube to prevent damaging the bearing journal. Be sure the gears seat firmly when cooled.

8. Once again, clear the crankshaft with compressed air and flush with oil. Repeat with the connecting rods, leaving an oil film.

9. Install connecting rod inserts, wipe an oil film onto the inserts, then assemble connecting rods onto the crankshaft in the order in which they were removed.

NOTE: The identification number stamped into the side of the connecting rod and its bearing cap should be on the same side when assembled. Under no circumstances may bearings be dressed or reworked to fit.

10. Visually check to ensure that the connecting rod and its bearing cap have actually joined, i.e., there is no obstruction in the joint.

11. Relieve the minor stresses that may have built up from tightening the connecting rod retaining nuts with light hammer blows (see illustration).

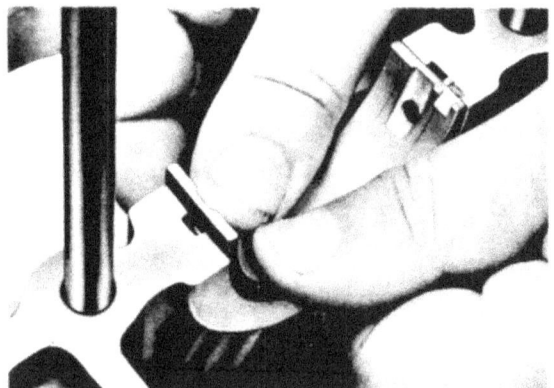
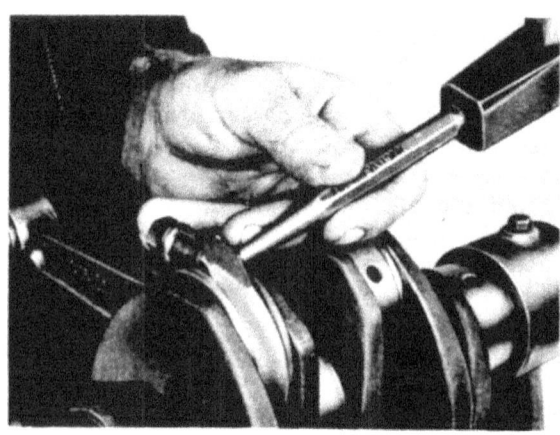

12. Torque the connecting rod retaining nuts to 32.5 ft. lb. (4,5 mkp) (see illustration). The connecting rods should fall freely by their own weight.

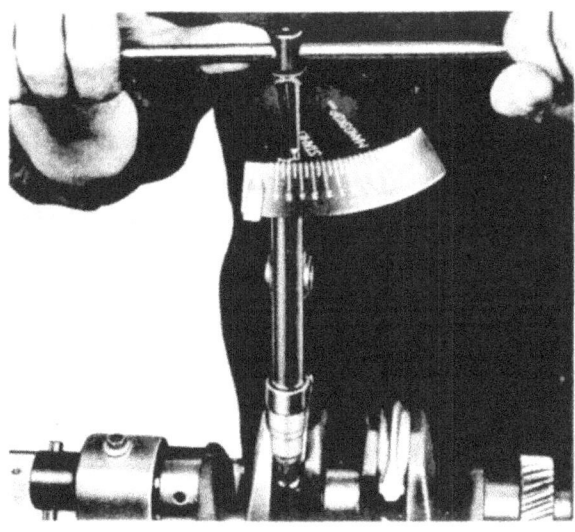

13. Install the crankshaft onto the left crankcase half, being sure to oil all bearing surfaces. (see illustration).

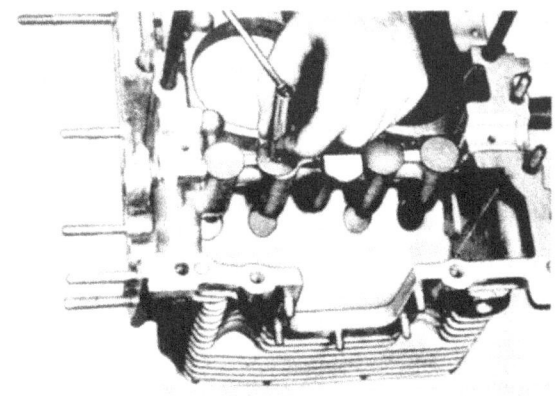

14. Install the valve lifters into place, being sure they are in the correct bores and are well lubricated with graphited oil (see illustration). Secure with P 49 retaining springs or some other clips.
15. Install the camshaft so the camshaft gear tooth marked "o" fits between the two crankshaft gear teeth bearing a punch mark each (see illustration). Be sure to lubricate camshaft with graphited oil.
16. Install thrust washer, crankshaft oil seal and Bearing 1 (see illustration).

NOTE: Be sure to install camshaft end plug as outlined following.

17. Use liquid Aviation Permatex or some other sealing compound to seal the camshaft end plug into place; be sure the plug is in its groove.

IMPORTANT: Now is the time to make certain all bearing inserts are in the correct locations with the dowels in the correct holes; that the connecting rods have emerged through their bores and are not hung up inside; rotate Bearing 1 to make sure the dowel is in its hole; be sure no parts are missing, because this is the last chance to put them in; and finally, check for free rotation of the crankshaft and the camshaft. Recheck the positioning of the crankshaft and camshaft gears (see previous illustration).

18. Use the above-mentioned sealing compound or some other to uniformly coat both crankcase mating surfaces, being sure NOT to get any in the oil passages (plug these with twisted paper if necessary while coating the surfaces). Check the crankcase mating surfaces for burrs, dirt, and chips once again while doing this.

19. Coat the oil seal surface that is squeezed between both halves of the crankcase, then coat the camshaft plug.

20. Place the right half of the crankcase onto the left half, being sure that the connecting rods are through the bores and valve lifters are in place.

21. Install the O-rings, then the beveled washers onto the stud bolts. Position the washers so that the inside bevel faces the crankcase to accommodate the O-rings. Tighten the cap nuts to 30 ft. lb. (4 mkp).

22. Install and torque the camshaft end (flywheel side) retaining nuts to 18 ft. lb. (2,5 mkp).

23. Install timing gear cover, using instructions under SERVICING TIMING GEAR COVER. Check that Bearing 4 set screw is tight but not so long as to exert pressure upon the bearing. Be sure cover has been fully serviced.

24. Tighten remaining crankcase retaining bolts to 22 ft. lb. (3 mkp).

25. See SERVICING BEARING 4 OIL SEAL to install seal in the timing gear cover.

26. Turn crankshaft to check for free rotation.

27. To replace the flywheel, shims, and soft iron gasket, see the installation procedure under SERVICING FLYWHEEL. Replace any other parts that need servicing.

28. To install the crankshaft pulley and shield see SERVICING CRANKSHAFT PULLEY.

NOTE: This completes reassembly of the crankcase with all of its parts. The remainder of the reassembly is covered in COMPONENT INSTALLATION under ENGINE DISASSEMBLY AND REASSEMBLY.

CONNECTING ROD BEARINGS

Nomenclature	Version		All Journals (mm)
Journal	Standard	Diameter	53.000-52.987
Insert	Standard	Wall thickness	1.96 - 1.97
Connecting Rod Bore	Standard	Diameter	56.980-56.999
Journal	1st undersize	Diameter	52.750-52.737
Insert	Inside undersize Outside standard	Wall thickness	2.085- 2.095
Connecting Rod Bore	Standard	Diameter	56.980-56.999

Two additional undersizes are available for the connecting rod journals and bearing inserts:

2nd Undersize:	Journal diameter	52.50 mm h5
	Wall thickness	2.215 +0.01 mm
3rd Undersize:	Journal diameter	52.25 mm h5
	Wall thickness	2.339 +0.01 mm

SPECIFICATIONS FOR PLAIN BEARING CRANKSHAFT

Stroke	mm	74 (2.913")	
Connecting rod journal diameter	mm	53 (2.0866")	
Main bearing journal diameter:	mm	Bearing 1: 50 mm (1.9685") Bearing 2: 55 mm (2.1654")	Bearing 3: 55 mm (2.1654") Bearing 4: 40 mm (1.5748")

MAIN BEARING AND CRANKSHAFT JOURNAL DIMENSIONS

MAIN BEARINGS

(1 mm = .03937")

Nomenclature	Version		Bearing 2 and 3 mm	Bearing 1 mm
Crankshaft Journal	Standard	Diameter	54.990-54.971	49.991-49.975
Bearing Insert	Inside standard	Wall thickness	2.615- 2.603	5.096- 5.108
	Outside standard	Outside diameter	-	60.29 + 0.02
Crankcase Bore	Standard	Diameter	60.24 ± 0.005	60.24 ± 0.005
Crankshaft Journal	Standard	Diameter	54.990-54.971	49.991-49.975
Bearing Insert	Inside standard	Wall thickness	2.740- 2.728	5.221- 5.233
	Outside oversize	Outside diameter	-	60.54 + 0.02
Crankcase Bore	Oversize	Diameter	60.49 ± 0.005	60.49 ± 0.005
Crankshaft Journal	1st undersize	Diameter	54.740-54.721	49.741-49.725
Bearing Insert	Inside undersize	Wall thickness	2.740- 2.728	5.221- 5.233
	Outside standard	Outside diameter	-	60.29 + 0.02
Crankcase Bore	Standard	Diameter	60.24 ± 0.005	60.24 ± 0.005
Crankshaft Journal	1st undersize	Diameter	54.740-54.721	49.741-49.725
Bearing Insert	Inside undersize	Wall thickness	2.865- 2.853	5.346- 5.358
	Outside oversize	Outside diameter	-	60.54 ± 0.02
Crankcase Bore	Oversize	Diameter	60.49 ± 0.005	60.49 ± 0.005

Nomenclature	Version		Bearing 2 and 3 mm	Bearing 1 mm
Crankshaft Journal	2nd undersize	Diameter	54.490-54.471	49.491-49.475
Bearing Insert	Inside undersize	Wall thickness	2.865- 2.853	5.346- 5.358
	Outside standard	Outside diameter	-	60.29 + 0.02
Crankcase Bore	Standard	Diameter	60.24 ± 0.005	60.24 ± 0.005
Crankshaft journal	2nd undersize	Diameter	54.490-54.471	49.491-49.475
Bearing Insert	Indise undersize	Wall thickness	2.990- 2.978	5.471- 5.483
	Outside oversize	Outside diameter	-	60.54 + 0.02
Crankcase Bore	Oversize	Diameter	60.49 ± 0.005	60.49 ± 0.005
Crankshaft Journal	3rd undersize	Diameter	54.240-54.221	49.241-49.225
Bearing Insert	Inside undersize	Wall thickness	2.990- 2.978	5.471- 5.483
	Outside standard	Outside diameter	-	60.29 + 0.02
Crankcase Bore	Standard	Diameter	60.24 ± 0.005	60.24 ± 0.005
Crankshaft Journal	3rd undersize	Diameter	54.240-54.221	49.241-49.225
Bearing Insert	Inside undersize	Wall thickness	3.115- 3.103	
	Outside oversize	Outside diameter		60.54 + 0.02
Crankcase Bore	Oversize	Diameter	60.49 ± 0.005	60.49 ± 0.005

DIMENSIONS FOR BEARING 4

Nomenclature	Version		Bearing 4 mm
Crankshaft Journal	Standard	Diameter	39.982-39.971
Bearing Insert	Inside standard	Wall thickness	4.975- 4.985
	Outside standard	Outside diameter	50.050-50.034
Crankcase Bore	Standard	Diameter	50.000-50.024
Crankshaft Journal	Standard	Diameter	39.982-39.971
Bearing Insert	Inside standard	Wall thickness	4.975- 4.985
	Outside oversize	Outside diameter	50.050-50.034
Crankcase Bore	Oversize	Diameter	No oversize provided
Crankshaft Journal	1st undersize	Diameter	39.732-39.721
Bearing Insert	Inside undersize	Wall thickness	5.100- 5.114
	Outside standard	Outside diameter	50.050-50.034
Crankcase Bore	Standard	Diameter	50.000-50.024
Crankshaft Journal	1st undersize	Diameter	39.732-39.721
Bearing Insert	Inside undersize	Wall thickness	No oversize provided
	Outside oversize	Outside diameter	
Crankcase Bore	Oversize	Diameter	No oversize provided

Two additional undersizes are available for the crankshaft journal and insert for Bearing 4:

2nd Undersize:	Crankshaft journal diameter =	39.50 mm
	Wall thickness =	5.239 mm
3rd Undersize:	Crankshaft journal diameter =	39.25 mm
	Wall thickness =	5.364 mm

TOLERANCES AND WEAR LIMITS

ENGINE

Measuring Point	Unit	Tolerance (new)	Wear Limit	
1. Cylinder seat depth in cylinder head	mm inch	9.500 - 9.600 .374 - .378	10.000 .3937	
2. Cylinder bore ovality, B minus A	mm inch	n/a n/a	0.020 .0008	
3. Piston to cylinder clearance	mm inch	0.041 - 0.059 .0016 - .0023	0.20 .008	
4. Piston ring side clearance Ring 1	mm inch	0.075 - 0.107 .0030 - .0042	0.25 - 0.30 .0098 - .0118	
Ring 2	mm inch	0.045 - 0.072 .0018 - .0028	0.25 - 0.30 .0098 - .0118	
5. Piston ring side clearance Oil ring	mm inch	0.025 - 0.052 .0010 - .0020	0.25 - 0.30 .0098 - .0118	

Measuring Point	Unit	Tolerance (new)	Wear Limit
6. Piston ring gap	mm inch	0.15 - 0.30 .0059 - .0118	0.95 .0374
7. Weight differential between pistons in one engine	g oz.	5 .176	n/a n/a
8. Weight differential between connecting rods in one engine	g oz.	15 .529	n/a n/a
9. Piston pin to connecting rod clearance	mm inch	0.012 - 0.028 .0005 - .0011	0.042 .0017
10. Crank pin to connecting rod clearance	mm inch	0.040 - 0.092 .0016 - .0036	0.130 .0051
11. Crankshaft to main bearing clearance (bearing installed)			
a. Bearing 1	mm inch	0.028 - 0.078 .0011 - .0031	0.170 .0067
b. Bearing 2 and 3	mm inch	0.046 - 0.100 .0018 - .0039	0.170 .0067
c. Bearing 4	mm inch	0.040 - 0.104 .0016 - .0041	0.170 .0067

Measuring Point	Unit	Tolerance (new)	Wear Limit
12. Crankshaft runout at Bearing 2 and 4 (Bearing 1 and 3 on V-blocks)	mm inch	max. 0.020 max. .0008	0.030 .0012
13. Crankshaft to crankshaft thrust bearing	mm inch	0.13 - 0.18 .0051 - .0071	0.3 .0118
14. Main bearing journal ovality	mm inch	n/a n/a	0.020 .0008
15. Connecting rod journal ovality	mm inch	n/a n/a	0.020 .0008
16. Crankcase bores for main bearings (dia)			
a. Bearing 1 - 3	mm inch	60.235-60.245 2.3715-2.3718	n/a n/a
b. Bearing 4	mm inch	50.000-50.025 1.9685-1.9695	n/a n/a
17. Crankshaft pulley vertical runout	mm inch	A max. 0.250 A max. .0098	n/a n/a
lateral	mm inch	B max. 0.250 B max. .0098	n/a n/a

Measuring bore for camshaft (dia.)	Unit	Tolerance (new)	Wear Limit	
18. Crankcase bore for camshaft (dia.)	mm inch	24.020 - 24.041 .9457 - .9465	24.070 .9476	
19. Camshaft: Bearing clearance	mm inch	0.020 - 0.054 .0008 - .0021	0.120 .0047	
End play, at thrust end	mm inch	0.040 - 0.080 .0016 - .0031	0.100 .0039	
Center bearing runout (camshaft mounted on centers)	mm inch	0.020 .0008	0.025 .0010	
20. Timing gear runout (gear bolted and pinned to camshaft): Lateral runout	mm inch	max. 0.100 max. .0039	n/a n/a	

Measuring Point	Unit	Tolerance (new)	Wear Limit
Timing gear runout (gear bolted and pinned to camshaft -- continued from preceding page)			
Gear blacklash	mm inch	0.015 - 0.040 .0006 - .0016	n/a n/a
Vertical runout	mm inch	0.025 .0010	0.040 .0016
21. Flywheel:			
Lateral runout, measured at starter ring (A)	mm inch	max. 0.300 max. .0118	n/a n/a
Lateral runout, measured in clutch plate recess (B)	mm inch	max. 0.040 max. .0016	n/a n/a
Vertical runout, measured at starter ring (C)	mm inch	max. 0.20 max. 0.0008	n/a n/a

Measuring Point	Unit	Tolerance (new)	Wear Limit
Vertical runout, measured in clutch disc recess (D)	mm inch	max. 0.100 max. .0039	n/a
Unbalance, measured with crankshaft	cmg oz/in.	max. 5 max. .069	n/a n/a
Diameter of oil sealing surface at hub (E)	mm inch	59.900 - 60.100 2.3583 - 2.3661	59.700 2.3504
Depth of recess to web (F)	mm inch	3.10 - 3.15 .1220 - .1240	n/a n/a
Web thickness (G)	mm inch	6.3 - 6.85 .2480 - .2697	min. 4.800 min. .1890
Width of oil sealing area (H)	mm inch	9.250 - 10.250 .3642 - .4035	n/a n/a
Machining starter ring gear teeth	mm inch	n/a n/a	max. 2.000 max. .0787
22. Valve stem diameter: Intake valve	mm inch	9.990 - 9.978 .3933 - .3928	9.940 .3701
Exhaust valve	mm inch	9.970 - 9.958 .3925 - .3920	9.940 .3701

Measuring Point	Unit	Tolerance (new)	Wear Limit
23. Valve guide to valve stem clearance:			
a) Valve guide inside diameter	mm	10.025 - 10.040	10.070
	inch	.3947 - .3953	.3965
b) Intake valve clearance in bore	mm	0.035 - 0.060	0.120
	inch	.0014 - .0024	.0047
c) Intake valve clearance in bore	mm	0.055 - 0.080	0.120
	inch	.0022 - .0031	.0047
24. Valve seat:			
Intake seat width (a)	mm	1.25 ± 0.15	n/a
	inch	.0492 ± .0059	n/a
Exhaust seat width (a)	mm	1.55 ± 0.15	n/a
	inch	.0610 ± .0059	n/a
Lateral runout of valve head to seat	mm	0.010	n/a
	inch	.0004	n/a
25. Valve springs:			
Spring length, decompressed	mm	47	n/a
	inch	1.85	n/a
Spring length, installed -- intake	mm	41	n/a
	inch	1.61	n/a
exhaust	mm	40.5	n/a
	inch	1.59	n/a
Spring pressure when compressed to 41 mm length	kp	36 ± 1.5 kp	n/a
	lbs	79 ± 3.3	n/a
Spring pressure when compressed to 30.1 mm length	kp	97 ± 2.5	n/a
	lbs	213 ± 5.5	n/a
26. Valve clearance in cold engine --- intake	mm	0.15	n/a
	inch	.006	n/a
exhaust	mm	0.10	n/a
	inch	.004	n/a

232

Measuring Point	Unit	Tolerance (new)	Wear Limit
27. Rocker arm, inside diameter	mm inch	16.000 - 16.018 .6299 - .6306	16.035 .6313
Rocker arm shaft, outside diameter	mm inch	15.984 - 15.973 .6293 - .6289	15.965 .6285
Rocker arm to shaft clearance	mm inch	0.016 - 0.045 .0006 - .0018	0.070 .0028
28. Valve lifters:			
Valve lifter bore in crankcase (dia.)	mm inch	12.000 - 12.018 .4724 - .4731	12.060 .4748
Valve lifter diameter	mm inch	11.966 - 11.984 .4711 - .4718	11.945 .4703
Valve lifter to crankcase bore clearance	mm inch	0.016 - 0.052 .0006 - .0020	0.100 .0039
29. Oil pressure:			
Warm engine, idling (pressure)	atm psi	0.5 minimum 7.3 minimum	-- --
Warm engine, at 2,500 rpm (pressure)	atm psi	3.0 minimum 44 minimum	2.0 29
30. Oil pump:			
Pump gears extend beyond (without gasket)	mm inch	0.06 - 0.125 .0024 - .0049	n/a n/a
Thickness of compressed gasket (A)	mm inch	0.16 .0063	n/a n/a
Gear end play, with gasket and cover installed (B)	mm inch	0.035 - 0.10 .0014 - .0039	0.20 .0079
Gear backlash	mm inch	0.030 - 0.080 .0012 - .0031	n/a n/a

Measuring Point	Unit	Tolerance (new)	Wear Limit	
31. Spring for pressure relief valve spring in crankcase, and Spring for bypass valve in timing gear cover:				
Free length	mm	66	n/a	
	inch	2.6	n/a	
Spring pressure when compressed to 49 mm length	kp	4.7 ± 7 %	n/a	
	lbs	10.4 ± 7 %	n/a	
Spring wire cross-section (diameter)	mm	1.4	n/a	
	inch	.055	n/a	
32. Oil pressure switch opens at pressure of	atm	0.3 - 0.6	n/a	
	psi	4.4 - 8.8	n/a	

TORQUE VALUES FOR BOLTS AND NUTS

(1 mkp = 7.233 lbs/ft)

	mkp	lbs/ft
Crankcase bolts	2.5	18
Timing gear cover nuts	2.0	14.5
Connecting rod nuts (without safety plates)	4.5	32.5
Cap nuts for through - bolts	4.0	28.9
Cylinder head nuts	3.0	21.7
Rocker arm carrier retaining bolts	5.0	36.2
Camshaft gear retaining nuts	2.5	18
Rocker arm shaft retaining nuts	2-2.5	14.5 - 18
Blower impeller retaining nut	10.0	72.3
Flywheel gland nut	45 - 50	300 - 340

DATA

SPECIFICATIONS COUPE/TARGA		912	911 T	911 E	911 S
ENGINE	Number of cylinders	4	6	6	6
	Bore	3.25 in (82.5 mm)	3.15 in (80.0 mm)	3.15 in (80.0 mm)	3.15 in (80.0 mm)
	Stroke	2.91 in (74.0 mm)	2.60 in (66.0 mm)	2.60 in (66.0 mm)	2.60 in (66.0 mm)
	Displacement, actual	96.5 cu in (1582 cc)	121.5 cu in (1991 cc)	121.5 cu in (1991 cc)	121.5 cu in (1991 cc)
	Compression ratio	9.3:1	8.6:1	9.1:1	9.9:1
	Horsepower (SAE)	102 (90 HP/DIN) at 5800 rpm	125 (110 HP/DIN) at 5800 rpm	148 (140 HP/DIN) at 6500 rpm	180 (170 HP/DIN) at 6800 rpm
	Maximum torque (SAE)	120 lbs ft (12.4 mkp) at 3500 rpm	131 lbs ft (16 mkp) at 4200 rpm	145 lbs ft (17.8 mkp) at 4500 rpm	149 lbs ft (18.5 mkp) at 5500 rpm
	Horsepower per liter	64 SAE (57 DIN)	62.5 SAE (55 DIN)	74 SAE (70 DIN)	90 SAE (85 DIN)
ENGINE DESIGN	Type	Horizontally opposed, 4-stroke cycle, air-cooled	Horizontally opposed 6, 4-stroke cycle, air-cooled	Horizontally opposed 6, 4-stroke cycle, air-cooled	Horizontally opposed 6, 4-stroke cycle, air-cooled
	Cylinders	Cast iron liner in finned light alloy jacket	Cast iron	Cast iron liner in finned light alloy jacket	Cast iron liner in finned light alloy jacket
	Cylinder heads	Light alloy			
	Number of valves	1 intake, 1 exhaust per cylinder			
	Valve arrangement	Overhead	Overhead in V	Overhead in V	Overhead in V
	Valve drive	Pushrods	1 overhead camshaft per bank of cylinders	1 overhead camshaft per bank of cylinders	1 overhead camshaft per bank of cylinders
	Camshaft drive	Gear type	By chain	By chain	By chain
	Crankshaft	Forged, 4 plain journal main bearings	Forged steel, 8 main bearings	Forged steel, 8 main bearings	Forged steel, 8 main bearings
	Connecting rod	Plain bearings			
	Blower drive	V-belt through generator			
	Lubrication	Pressure lubrication	Dry sump	Dry sump	Dry sump
	Fuel supply	1 mechanical fuel pump	1 electrical fuel pump	1 electrical fuel pump	1 electrical fuel pump
	Carburation	2 dual-throat downdraft carburetors	triple throat carburetors, one per bank of cylinders	Bosch fuel injection	Bosch fuel injection
ELECTRICAL SYSTEM	Rated Voltage	12 Volt (generator)	12 Volt (alternator)	12 Volt (alternator)	12 Volt (alternator)
	Battery	45 Ah	2 Batteries, 36 Ah each		
	Ignition	Battery coil and distributor		high capacity discharge ignition with Battery, coil and distributor	
	Firing order	1-4-3-2	1-6-2-4-3-5	1-6-2-4-3-5	1-6-2-4-3-5
DRIVE TRAIN	Location of engine	At rear, behind axle			
	Clutch	Single dry plate			
	Transmission	Porsche servo-thrust synchronization			
	Number of speeds	4 forward, 1 reverse or 5 forward, 1 reverse			
	Location of shift lever	Central floor change			
	Final drive	Spiral bevel gears and bevel gear differential			
	Axle ratio	7:31, i = 4.428			
	Power train	Through half axles to rear wheels			
CHASSIS AND SUSPENSION	Frame	Welded, pressed steel sections unitized with body			
	Front suspension	Independent, with transverse control arms and telescopic hydraulic dampers			
	Front springing	Longitudinally mounted round section torsion bar, one per wheel		Self-levelling hydro-pneumatic spring and damper	plus stabilizer bar
	Rear suspension	Independent, with longitudinal control arms. Drive through half axles			
	Rear springing	Transversely mounted round section torsion bar, one per wheel			plus stabilizer bar
	Shock absorbers	Hydraulic, double-acting telescopic shockabsorbers front and rear			
	Service brake	Dual brake system, hydraulic disc brakes on all four wheels. For 911 E and 911 S internally ventilated discs			
	Handbrake	Mechanical twin-servo drum brake, on rear wheels with control light			
	Effektive brake disk dia.	front 9.26 in (235 mm), rear 9.6 in (244 mm)		front 9.0 in (228 mm), rear 9.6 in (244 mm)	
	Braking area per wheel (service brake)	front and rear 8.14 sq in (52.5 cm²)		front 11.76 sq in (76 cm²), rear 8.14 sq in (52.5 cm²)	
	Total brake swept area (service brake)	32.5 sq in (210 cm²)		39.8 sq in (257 cm²)	
	Handbrake drum dia.	7.09 in (180 mm)			
	Total brake swept area (handbrake)	26.4 sq in (170 cm²)			
	Rims	5½ J x 15		5½ J x 14 Light alloy	6 J x 15 Light alloy
	Tires	165 HR 15		185 HR 14	185/70 VR 15
	Steering	ZF rack and pinion			
	Steering ratio	1:17.78			
TRANSMISSION GEAR RATIOS	1st gear	11:34/11:34	11:34/11:34	11:34/11:34	11:34
(5 speeds optional	2nd gear	19:32/18:34	19:31/18:34	19:31/18:34	18:34
for 912 and 911 T)	3rd gear	24:27/22:29	25:26/22:29	25:26/22:29	22:29
(no cost choice of	4th gear	28:24/25:26	29:23/25:26	29:23/25:26	25:26
4 or 5 speed for 911 E)	5th gear	28:24	29:23	29:23	29:23
	Reverse	11:16-20:43	11:16-20:43	11:16-20:43	11:16-20:43
GRADE CLIMBING	Weight of vehicle (including load)	2490 lbs (1130 kp)	2730 lbs (1240 kp)	2370 lbs (1240 kp)	2370 lbs (1240 kp)
	1st gear, max. gradient	46%/46%	60%/60%	66%/66%	66%
	2nd gear, max. gradient	21%/25%	25%/30%	28%/34%	35%
	3rd gear, max. gradient	12%/16%	14%/18%	14%/21%	21%
	4th gear, max. gradient	8%/11%	8%/13%	9%/14%	14%
	5th gear, max. gradient	8%	8%	9%	9%
CAPACITIES	Engine	approx. 4.2 qts (4 lit) HD oil	approx. 9.5 qts (9 lit) HD oil	approx. 9.5 qts (9 lit) HD oil	approx. 10.6 qts (10 lit) HD oil with oil cooler
	Transmission and differential	2.65 qts (2.5 lit)			
	Fuel tank	16.4 US gals (62 lit)			
	Brake fluid reservoir	approx. 6.8 ft oz (0.2 lit)			
	Windshield washer	approx. 2.2 qts (2.0 lit)			
DIMENSIONS	Wheelbase	89.5 in (2268 mm)			
	Track, front	53.8 in (1362 mm)	53.8 in (1362 mm)	53.8 in (1364 mm)	54.2 in (1374 mm)
	Track, rear	53.0 in (1343 mm)	53.0 in (1343 mm)	53.0 in (1345 mm)	53.5 in (1355 mm)
	Overall length	163.90 in (4163 mm)			
	Overall width	63.39 in (1610 mm)			
	Overall height (unloaded)	51.97 in (1320 mm)			
	Ground clearance	5.91 in (150 mm)			
	Turning circle	approx. 36.2 ft (10.7 m)			
WEIGHTS	Dry weight (DIN)	2095 lbs (950 kp)	2250 lbs (1020 kp)	2250 lbs (1020 kp)	2195 lbs (995 kp)
	Max. permissible weight	2870 lbs (1370 kp)	3090 lbs (1400 kp)	3090 lbs (1400 kp)	3090 lbs (1400 kp)
	Max. axle load, front	1256 lbs (570 kp)	1325 lbs (600 kp)	1325 lbs (600 kp)	1325 lbs (600 kp)
	Max. axle load, rear	1700 lbs (770 kp)	1854 lbs (840 kp)	1854 lbs (840 kp)	1854 lbs (840 kp)
PERFORMANCE	Top speed	approx. 115 mph (185 km/h)	approx. 125 mph (200 km/h)	approx. 134 mph (215 km/h)	approx. 140 mph (225 km/h)
	Power/weight ratio (1 person + dry weight DIN)	22.2 lbs/HP/SAE (11.3 kp/HP/DIN)	19.4 lbs/HP/SAE (9.9 kp/HP/DIN)	15.3 lbs/HP/SAE (7.8 kp/HP/DIN)	12.3 lbs/HP/SAE (6.3 kp/HP/DIN)
	Fuel consumption	27.6 mpg (8.5 lit/100 km)	26.2 mpg (9.0 lit/100 km)	24.5 mpg (9.6 lit/100 km)	23 mpg (10.2 lit/100 km)

Engine Type Identifying Characteristics

Designation Official	Internal	Nr. Cyl.	HP (DIN)	Design Characteristics	Remarks
912	616/36	4	90	Standard version without EECS	Mfd fm Apr 65 (1966-model)
912	616/39	4	90	Standard version with EECS	Mfd fm Jul 67 (1968-model)
2000	901/01	6	130	Standard version with SOLEX carburetors	Mfd fm Sep 64
2000 S	901/02	6	160	Super engine	Mfd fm Jul 66
2000 T	901/03	6	110	Touring engine with grey-cast iron cylinders	Mfd fm Jul 67 (1968-model)
2000	901/05	6	130	Standard version as 901/01 but with WEBER carburetors	Mfd fm Feb 66
2000	901/06	6	130	Standard version as 901/05 but changed heat exchangers and new type camshaft	Mfd fm Nov 66
2000	901/07	6	130	Standard version as 901/06 but with outfittings for Sportomatic	Mfd fm Jul 67
2000 S	901/08	6	160	Super engine as 901/02 but with outfittings for Sportomatic	Mfd fm Jul 67
2000 T	901/13	6	110	Touring engine as 901/03 but with outfittings for Sportomatic	Mfd fm Jul 67
2000	901/14	6	130	Standard version as 901/06 but with EECS for USA	Mfd fm Jul 67
2000	901/17	6	130	Standard version as 901/06 but with EECS for USA and outfittings for Sportomatic	Mfd fm Jul 67
2000 R	901/30	6	150	Rallye engine based on components from Type 901/06	Mfd fm Jul 67

Carburetor Specifications

Carburetor type		WEBER 40 IDS 3 C / 40 IDS 3 C1	WEBER 40 IDS 3 C / 40 IDS 3 C1	WEBER 40 IDAP 3 C / 40 IDAP 3 C1	WEBER 40 IDAP 3 C / 40 IDAP 3 C1	WEBER 40 IDA 3 C / 40 IDA 3 C1	WEBER 40 IDA 3 C / 40 IDA 3 C1	WEBER 40 IDT 3 C / 40 IDT 3 C1	WEBER 40 IDT 3 C / 40 IDT 3 C1	WEBER 40 IDS 3 C / 40 IDS 3 C1	SOLEX 40 PII-4	SOLEX 40 PII-4	SOLEX 40 PII-4
Vehicle and engine type		911 S 901/02 160 HP	911 S 901/08 160 HP Sportomatic	911 L USA 901/14 130 HP EECS	911 L USA 901/17 130 HP EECS Sportomatic	911 USA 901/14 130 HP EECS	911 USA 901/17 130 HP EECS Sportomatic	911 L 901/06 130 HP	911 L 901/07 130 HP Sportomatic	911 T 901/03 110 HP	911 T 901/13 110 HP Sportomatic	901/30 150 HP Rallye engine	912 616/36 90 HP New heater	912 616/36 90 HP Old heater	912 616/39 90 HP EECS
Venturi	K	32	32	30	30	30	30	30	30	27	27	34	32	32	32
Preatomizer		4.5	4.5	4.5	4.5	4.5	4.5	4.5	4.5	4.5	4.5	4.5			
Main jet	Gg	125	125	125	125	125	125	125	125	110	110	135	120*	120*	122.5
Air correction jet	a	185	185	180	180	180	180	180	180	185	185	185	180	180	180
Idle jet	g	55	55	52	52	52	52	50	50	50	50	55	57.5	57.5	55
Idle air bleed	u	110	110	110	110	110	110	110	110	110	110	110	180	180	110
Starting fuel jet	Gs														
Starting air jet	Ga														
Intermediate metering jet		50	50	50	50	50	50	50	50	50	50	50	50	50	40
Emulsion tube	s	F 5	F 5	F 26	F 26	F 26	F 26	F 26	F 26	F 2	F 2	F 3	25	25	25
Injection nozzle	i														
Injection nozzle fuel jet															
Injection nozzle air correction jet															
Pump															
Float weight	F	25.5 g	25.5 g	25.5 g	25.5 g	25.5 g	25.5 g	25.5 g	25.5 g	25.5 g	25.5 g	25.5 g	7.4 g	7.4 g	7.4 g
Float needle valve adjustment		Top edge of float to top edge of housing, w/o gasket 12.5-13.0mm	See 911 S	Top edge of float to top edge of housing, w/o gasket 12.5-13.0mm	See 911 S							See 911 S			
Fuel level in float chamber		20.75±1 mm from top edge of housing with fuel pressure of 2.5 m water column													
Float needle valve		closed	closed	closed	closed	closed	closed	closed	closed	closed	closed	closed			
Enrichment jet		adjustable	adjustable	adjustable	adjustable	adjustable	adjustable	adjustable	adjustable	adjustable	adjustable				
Pump jet type		3mm stroke	3mm stroke	3 mm stroke	3 mm stroke	3 mm stroke	3 mm stroke	closed	closed	closed	closed	3 mm stroke			
Pump cam		closed	closed	closed	closed	closed	closed					closed			
Pump suction valve															
Injection quantity	cm³	0.8cc±0.2 per stroke	0.8cc±0.2 per stroke	0.5cc±0.1 per stroke	0.5cc±0.1 per stroke	0.8cc±0.2 per stroke	0.8cc±0.2 per stroke	0.5cc±0.1 per stroke	0.5cc±0.1 per stroke	0.5cc±0.1 per stroke	0.5cc±0.1 per stroke jet stroke	See 911 S	Winter=0.65cc Summer=0.45cc with 2 strokes per nozzle		
Float chamber vent orifice		4.5 mm dia	4.5 mm dia	6.0 mm dia	6.0 mm dia	6.0 mm dia	6.0 mm dia	6.0 mm dia	6.0 mm dia	6.0 mm dia	6.0 mm dia	4.5 mm dia			
Mixture discharge orifice		5 mm	5 mm	5 mm	5 mm	5 mm	5 mm	5 mm	5 mm	5 mm	5 mm	5 mm			
Idle mixture discharge orifice		1.0 mm	1.0 mm	1.0 mm	1.0 mm	1.0 mm	1.0 mm	1.0 mm	1.0 mm	1.0 mm	1.0 mm	1.0 mm			
Bypass bores		1 = 0.8 mm 2 = 1.1 mm 3 = 1.35 mm	1 = 0.8 mm 2 = 1.1 mm 3 = 1.35 mm	1 = 0.8 mm 2 = 1.1 mm 3 = 1.35 mm	1 = 0.8 mm 2 = 1.1 mm 3 = 1.35 mm	1 = 0.8 mm 2 = 1.1 mm 3 = 1.35 mm	1 = 0.8 mm 2 = 1.1 mm 3 = 1.35 mm	1 = 0.8 mm 2 = 1.1 mm 3 = 1.35 mm	1 = 0.8 mm 2 = 1.1 mm 3 = 1.35 mm	1 = 0.8 mm 2 = 1.1 mm 3 = 1.35 mm	1 = 0.8 mm 2 = 1.1 mm 3 = 1.35 mm	1 = 0.8 mm 2 = 1.1 mm 3 = 1.35 mm	1 = 1.0 mm 2 = 1.5 mm 3 = 2.2 mm	1 = 1.0 mm 2 = 1.4 mm 3 = 1.7 mm	1 = 1.0 mm 2 = 1.4 mm 3 = 1.7 mm
Fuel pump															
Air cleaner															
Ignition adjustment specifications		30°at 6000 rpm, engine loaded or free. Basic setting at 8° BTC.	30°at 6000 rpm. In stopped engine 50 BTC. Idle speed 900/150 rpm. At idle speed, ignition timing is 2-5o ATC (compulsory setting).	30°±2 at 6000 rpm, engine loaded or free. In stopped engine 50 BTC. Idle speed 900/150 rpm. At idle speed, ignition timing is 2-5o ATC (compulsory setting).		300 at 6000 rpm, engine loaded or free. Basic setting at 50 BTC.		350 at 6000 rpm, engine loaded or free. Basic setting at 0°.				Basic setting 30 BTC.		Basic setting 38BTC. Idle speed 900±50rpm. At idle sp. ignition timing is 30ATC(compulsory setting).	
Spark plugs and distributor		Bosch W 265 P 21 Bosch WG 265 T 2 SP Beru 260/14/3 S Bosch 0231 159002	Bosch W 265 P 21 Bosch WG 265 T 2 SP Beru 260/14/3 S Bosch 0231 159002	Bosch 250 P 21 Bosch WG 265 T 2 SP Beru 260/14/3 S Champion N 6 Y Bosch 0231 169001	Bosch 250 P 21 Bosch WG 265 T 2 SP Beru 260/14/3 S Champion N 6 Y Bosch 0231 169001	Bosch 250 P 21 Bosch WG 265 T 2 SP Beru 260/14/3 S Champion N 6 Y Bosch 0231 159001	Bosch 250 P 21 Bosch WG 265 T 2 SP Beru 260/14/3 S Champion N 6 Y Bosch 0231 159001	Bosch W 230 T 30 Beru 240/14/3 Marelli S 112 AX	Bosch W 230 T 30 Beru 240/14/3 Marelli S 112 AX	Bosch W 225 T 7 Bosch W 200 T 35 Beru P 225/14 Champion UL 82 Y Bosch 0231 129022	Bosch W 225 T 7 Bosch W 200 T 35 Beru P 225/14 Champion UL 82 Y Bosch 0231 129022	See 911 S	Bosch W 200 T 35 Champion UL 82 Y Bosch 0231 115061		

*Type 912 (616/36) with wet screen air cleaner requires 115 main jet.

EECS = Exhaust Emission Control System

Transmission Type Identifying Features

S = Standard
O E = Optional at extra cost
O = Optional without price difference

Trans-mission Type	Key Nr.	Number Speeds	Gear Sets 1st	2nd	3rd	4th	5th	R&P	Transmission Numbers	From Model 1968	911 thru Model 1965	912 except USA thru Model 1965	911 USA thru Model 1965	911 except USA Model 1966 thru 1967	912 except USA Model 1966 thru 1967	911 USA Model 1966 thru 1967	912 USA Model 1966 thru 1967	911 except USA Model 1967	911 S USA Model 1967	911 S except USA from Model 1968	911 L from Model 1968	911 L except USA from Model 1968	911 T except USA from Model 1968	911 USA from Model 1968	912 except USA and Germany from Model 1968	912 USA and Germany from Model 1968	Remarks, Suggested use
901/0	-	5	12:34 AA	18:32 GA	23:28 O	26:25 U	28:23 Y	7:31 standard	100 001-102 282 (up to 26.7.65)		S	-	-	-	-	-	-	-	-	-	-	-	-	-	-	-	
901/02	42	5	11:34 A	18:34 F	22:29 M	25:26 S	29:23 Z	7:31 standard	103 001-105 191		-	-	-	-	-	-	-	S	S	S	-	-	-	-	-	-	5-speed transmission at extra cost
901/03	22	5	11:34 A	18:34 F	22:29 M	25:26 S	29:23 Z	7:31 simplified		2 280 001-2 289 999	-	-	-	O E	O E	O E	-	O E	O E	O E	-	O E	O E	O E	O E	O E	
901/10	20	4	11:34 A	18:34 F	25:26 S	29:23 Z	-	7:31 simplified		2 080 001-7 089 999	-	-	-	O E	O E	O E	-	O E	O E	O E	-	-	-	O E	O E	O E	
901/50	92	5	14:37 B	18:32 GA	22:29 M	26:26 T	28:23 Y	7:31 standard		9 280 001-9 289 999	-	-	-	O E	O E	O E	-	O E	O E	O E	S	O E	O E	O E	O E	O E	Standard special-order transmission
901/51	92	5	12:34 AA	17:34 E	20:31 I	22:29 M	23:28 O	7:31 standard		9 281 001-9 281 999	-	-	-	O E	O E	O E	-	O E	O E	O E	-	O E	O E	O E	O E	O E	For hillclimbs
901/52	92	5	12:34 AA	18:34 F	21:31 J	23:28 O	25:26 S	7:31 standard		9 282 001-9 282 999	-	-	-	O E	O E	O E	-	O E	O E	O E	-	O E	O E	O E	O E	O E	For airport races
901/53	92	5	15:36 C	20:32 HA	23:28 O	26:26 T	28:23 Y	7:31 standard		9 283 001-9 283 999	-	-	-	O E	O E	O E	-	O E	O E	O E	-	O E	O E	O E	O E	O E	For races on fast circuits
901/54	92	5	14:37 B	20:32 HA	22:29 M	25:27 R	27:25 V	7:31 standard		9 284 001-9 284 999	-	-	-	O E	O E	O E	S	O E	-	O E	-	-	-	-	O E	O E	Nuerburgring ratios
902/0	30	4	11:34 A	18:34 F	24:27 Q	28:24 X	-	7:31 standard	160 001-162 462 (up to 26.7.65) 163 001-165 214 (4-cyl. engine) 200 001-200 402 (6-cyl. engine)	3 080 001-3 089 999	-	-	O	-	-	O	-	O	-	-	-	-	-	-	-	-	
902/1	32	5	11:34 A	18:34 F	22:29 M	25:26 S	28:24 X	7:31 standard	220 001-221 721 (up to 26.7.65) 234 001-238 942 (4-cyl. engine) 130 001-131 571 (6-cyl. engine)	3 280 001-3 289 999	-	-	O	-	-	O E	S	O E	-	-	-	-	-	-	-	-	
902/01	10	4	11:34 A	19:32 H	24:27 Q	28:24 X	-	7:31 simplified		1 080 001-1 089 999	-	-	-	-	-	-	-	-	-	-	-	-	-	-	S	O E	Homologated for Type 912
902/02	12	5	11:34 A	18:34 F	22:29 M	25:26 S	28:24 X	7:31 simplified		1 280 001-1 289 999	-	-	-	-	-	-	-	-	-	-	-	-	-	-	O E	S	Homologated for Type 912
902/50	92	5	11:34 A	19:32 H	20:31 I	23:28 O	26:25 U	7:31 simplified		9 285 001-9 285 999	-	-	-	-	-	-	-	-	-	-	-	-	-	-	O E	O E	
905/00	31	4	15:36 C	19:31 HB	23:28 O	26:25 U	-	7:27 simplified		3 180 001-3 189 999	-	-	-	-	-	-	-	-	-	-	-	-	O E	O E	O E	O E	For cars with Sportomatic
905/01	41	4	15:36 C	19:31 HB	23:28 O	27:25 V	-	7:27 simplified		4 180 001-4 189 999	-	-	-	-	-	-	-	-	-	O E	-	O E	O E	O E	O E	O E	For cars with Sportomatic
-	90	4	Free choice of ratios							9 089 001-9 089 999	-	-	-	-	-	-	-	-	-	O, E	-	-	-	-	-	-	
-	92	5	Free choice of ratios							9 289 001-9 289 999	-	-	-	-	-	-	-	-	-	O E	-	O E	O E	O E	O E	O E	

APPROVED TIRES FOR 1969 MODELS

		912		911T		911E		911S	
		C	T	C	T	C	T	C	T
For 912:	165 HR 15 SEMPERIT STT	S	S						
For 911T:	165 HR 15 PIRELLI-CINTURATO	X	X	S	S				
For 911E: or	165 VR 15 DUNLOP SP	X	X	X	X	S	S		
	165 VR 15 CONTINENTAL	X	X	X	X	S	S		
For 911S: or	185 VR 15 MICHELIN X (CA4)	X	X	X	X	X	X	S	S
	185 VR 15 PIRELLI-CINTURATO HS	X	X	X	X	X	X	S	S
For comfort group : or or	185 HR 14 MICHELIN XAS	X	X	X	X	X	X		
	185 HR 14 GOODRICH GT 100*	X	X	X	X	X	X		
	185 VR 14 PIRELLI-CINTURATO*	X	X	X	X	X	X		
	* Optionally with 14" alloy wheels								
OPTIONAL TIRES:									
	165 HR-15 MICHELIN XAS	X	X						
	165 VR-15 PHOENIX-FIRESTONE P 110	X		X		X			

X = Optional   C = Coupe

S = Standard   T = Targa

On the following pages will be found a reprint of the DRIVER'S MANUAL issued with each Porsche Type 912. When using the information contained herein, please note that the balance of the publication has been authenticated for use by either the non-technician or professional mechanic, and has been updated to conform with the latest American service techniques. The DRIVER'S MANUAL has page numbering following the original publication's index which will be found on page 280 of this book (page 93 of the DRIVER'S MANUAL).

TYPE 912
Dr.-Ing. h. c. F. PORSCHE KG
STUTTGART-ZUFFENHAUSEN

The Dr. Ing. h.c.F. Porsche K.G. of Stuttgart-Zuffenhausen, Germany, a development center without precedent in the annals of automobile and engine designing, has, for some 30 years, been engaged as an independent research and development bureau with the aim of advancing the automobile and its engine. Many productions of this firm have acquired fame and reputation of international significance.

The latest creation, the Porsche Type 912 sports touring car is a product of the long experience of our construction staff and has been developed by the pick of our developing department. It has established itself an unrivalled record for performance in the fastest European class.

The Porsche torsion-bar suspension, the engine and transmission in one unit in the rear, the low center of gravity and the steering arrangement have been adopted in principle from the Auto-Union racing car, another famous Porsche creation.

The beautifully designed body is an improved version of the service-tested Auto-Union world record car which had been designed on the results of months of wind tunnel testing.

The air-cooled engine, the torsion resistant frame and the sturdy wheel suspension are backed by the abundant experience gained by the Volkswagen which was subjected to severest trials during the war in climates ranging from the glowing heat of North Africa to the ice and snow of the far north, under the worst possible conditions in regard to terrain and temperature.

With the knowledge gained from this unique background we are in a position to offer our clientele a supreme combination of speed, driving safety and high quality workmanship.

... this car has been produced in limited quantity for discriminating drivers.

Judging by the car you have chosen, one must certainly conclude that you are a motorist of a special caste. Quite likely, you are no freshman when it comes to automobiles. None the less, we have compiled much useful information in the section entitled Operating Instructions and we urge you to become familiar with the various aspects of operation before driving your Porsche 912. Likewise, the remainder of this booklet is equally important and we kindly ask of you to devote your attention to its contents at your hour of leisure. We wish you many miles of pleasure and accomplishments in your

PORSCHE

Dr.-Ing. h. c. F. Porsche KG
Stuttgart-Zuffenhausen
West Germany

Contents

OPERATING INSTRUCTIONS	7
CARE AND LUBRICATION	31
MAINTENANCE AND ADJUSTMENTS	43
GENERAL DESCRIPTION	73
TECHNICAL DATA	85
Relative Index	93

OPERATING INSTRUCTIONS

Please make it a practice to check the following items prior to starting your Porsche:

Tire pressure

Fuel level

Engine oil level

Service lights

Also, remember to test your braking action.

Starting Cold Engine

1. Shift into neutral.
2. Switch the ignition on.
3. Step on the throttle pedal, fully, two or three times.
4. While slightly touching the throttle pedal, turn the ignition key clockwise to the stop to engage the engine starter.

In cold weather it may prove advantageous to fully disengage the clutch when starting the engine to reduce the drag imposed upon the starter motor. If necessary, depress the throttle pedal a few times more than stated above to allow the accelerator pump enrich the starting mixture even more.

Starting Warm Engine

1. Shift into neutral.
2. Switch the ignition on.
3. Step on the throttle pedal, fully, and hold in that position until engine has fired up.

Note:

The engine starter should not be run longer than 15 — 20 seconds at a time. If the engine fails to start within that time, allow about 20 seconds rest before repeating the starting procedure. Once the engine has started, release the ignition key without delay, thus permitting it to return into its normal position.

Break-in Rules

Continued excellence of performance and economy depend to a great degree upon the treatment and handling given during the first 600 miles of operation. It cannot be overemphasized that not only will the engine benefit from proper break-in, but the car as a whole. During this crucial period the car must not be driven at full power over extended distances, nor should it be driven too slow. The general rules are as follows:

1. Maximum engine speed during the first 600 miles must not exceed 4500 rpm.
2. Increase the maximum applied engine speed by 500 rpm between odometer readings of 600 and 1000 miles, meaning not to exceed 5000 rpm. Drive brisqly, vary speeds frequently, and use full throttle for short spurts only.
3. Bear in mind never to lug the engine with heavy throttle at low engine speeds — a rule applicable not only during break-in but at all times.
4. Upon reaching odometer reading of 1000 miles, you can subject the car to full throttle operation, however, do not exceed 6000 rpm at any time (observe redline limit on tachometer).

Note:

Do not exceed 5000 rpm when running the engine without a load.

Instrument and Controls for Right Hand steering (Optional)

Instrument Panel for Right Hand steering (Optional)

1. Fuel spout lid
2. Glove compartment lock
3.
4. Blind switches
5. (for optional connection)
6. Ventilating air control
7. Small combination instrument
8. Combination signal and dimmer switch
9. Large combination instrument
10. Tachometer
11. Steering wheel
12. Speedometer
13. Combination wiper/washer switch
14. Clock
15. Warm air outlet for foot well
16. Front lid release knob
17. Ashtray
18. Gearshift lever
19. Heater control (engine heater)
20. Handbrake lever
21. Cigarette lighter
22. Clutch pedal
23. Brake pedal
24. Accelerator pedal
25. Starter/ignition switch and steering lock
26. Signal key
27. Light switch

Instruments and Controls for left Hand steering

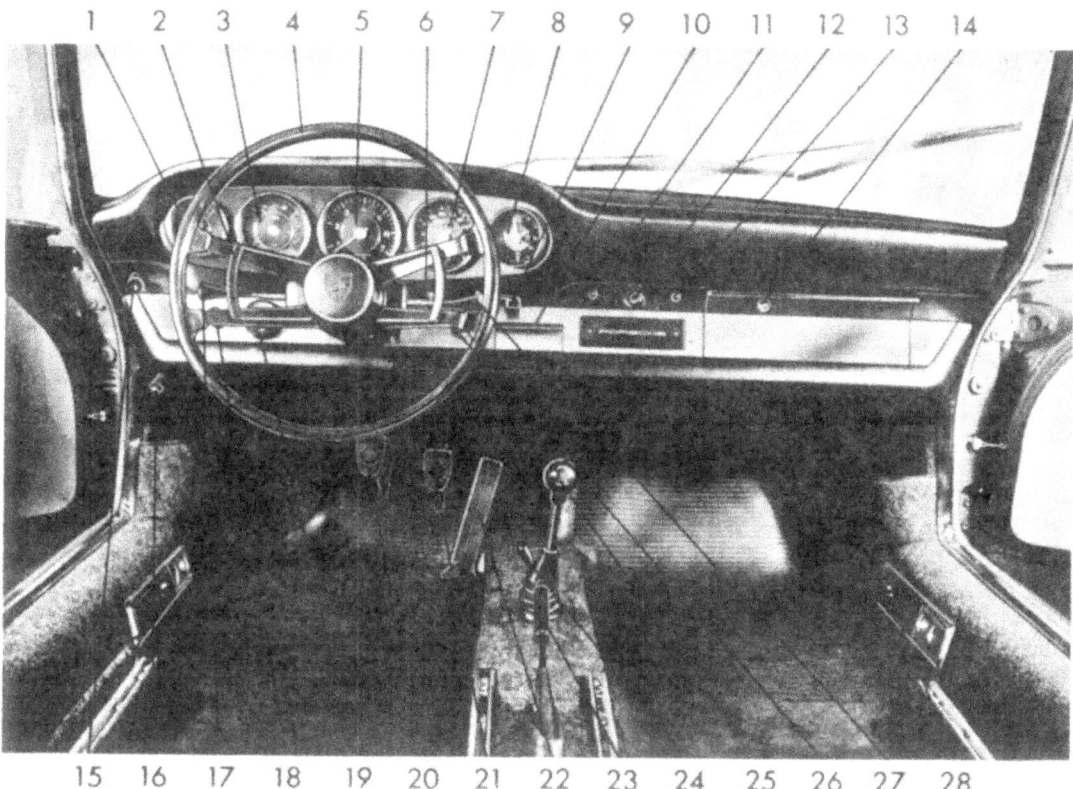

Instrument Panel

1. Small combination instrument
2. Horn ring
3. Large combination instrument
4. Steering wheel
5. Tachometer
6. Trip mileage reset control
7. Speedometer
8. Clock
9. Ventilating air control
10. Ashtray
11. Foglamp switch (optional)
12. Emergency blinker signal (USA only)
13. Auxiliary heater control (optional)
14. Glove compartment lock
15. Filler cap control
16. Front lid release knob
17. Combination turn signal, low beam and headlamp flasher switch
18. Light switch
19. Starter/ignition switch and steering lock
20. Clutch pedal
21. Brake pedal
22. Accelerator pedal
23. Hand brake lever
24. Heater control (engine heater)
25. Gearshift lever
26. Cigarette lighter
27. Combination wiper/washer switch
28. Warm air outlet for foot well

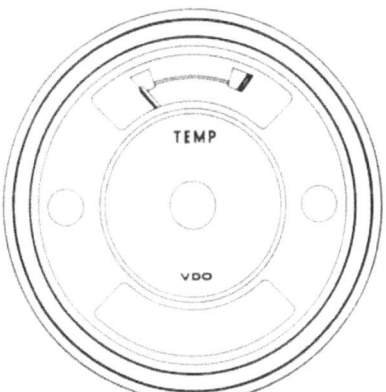

Instruments
(check regularly while driving)

Fuel gauge

The fuel gauge incorporates a red warning lamp which lights up whenever there is less than 6 litres (1.6 U.S. Gals) in the tank.

Engine oil thermometer

The engine oil temperature indicator shall not, if possible, pass over the limit of the green field. If the needle is in the red field, decelerate speed and bring the car to a workshop. A uncorrect ignition timing or a slippery V-belt may result in an anormal increase of the oil temperature.

 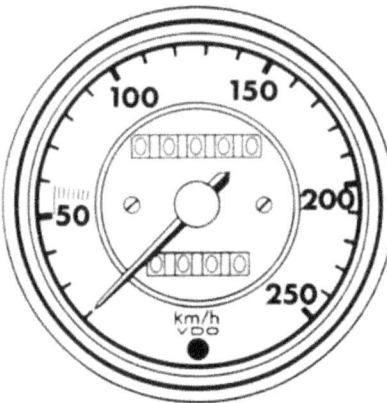 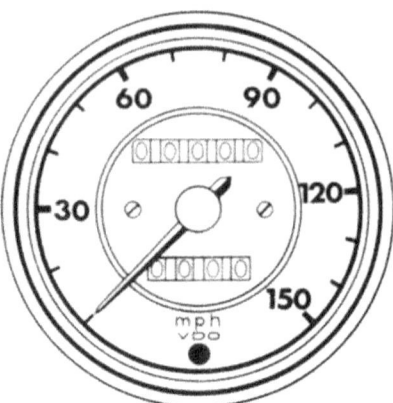

Tachometer

The transistorized tachometer operates on the impulse principle and indicates engine revolutions per minute (rpm), working only when the ignition is on. Maximum engine rpm are indicated in red on the dial face; the indicator needle should never be permitted to pass the redlined area or even enter it. Maximum speed is 6800 rpm.
Also located on the tachometer dial are control lamps for the directional signal and high beam indication.

Important

Never exceed 5000 engine rpm in neutral gear.

Speedometer

The speedometer indicates speed in miles per hour (mph) (kilometers per hour for countries using the metric system). The odometer counts total miles driven and cannot be turned back by hand. The trip mileage counter, located in the lower part of the dial, can be turned back to zero at any time through a control knob on the instrument panel. The green field in the 30 mph (50 km/h) area is provided as a convenient reminder of usual speed limits posted in populated areas. Also located on the dial face is a parking light control lamp which indicates that parking lights are on.

Clock

The electric clock is furnished as standard equipment. The clock is wound electrically as long as the battery is hooked up and in proper state of charge. The elapsed-time monitor needle (red) may be reset by turning the knob in the dial center; the time clock can be reset by first pushing the button in and then turning.

Generator Control Lamp (red)

The generator control lamp, located in the combination instrument, indicates generator operation, fan belt condition, and cooling blower operation. The lamp lights up when the ignition is switched on; as the engine is started and the rpm increase, the light intensity decreases until the lamp goes out completely. If the light should begin to flicker or go fully on while driving, it may be an indication of a loose or torn fan belt necessitating adjustment or installation of a new belt. However, the cause may also lie in a defective voltage regulator in which case the defect will have to be corrected in a reputable shop equipped for this task.

Directional Signal Control Lamp (green)

The directional signal control lamps are located on the tachometer dial and light up in unison with the selected turn indicators. The pulse of the light will speed up considerably when any of the blinker lamps in the circuit malfunctions or burns out.

High Beam Indicator (blue)

The high beam indicator lamp, located in the lower part of the tachometer dial, lights up together with the headlamp high beams and goes off when the low beam is switched on.

Oil Pressure Control Lamp (green)

The oil pressure control lamp, located in the combination instrument, goes on when the ignition is switched on; it goes off when the engine is started and the prescribed engine oil pressure reached. Should the lamp light up while driving, it is an indication of a malfunction in the lubricating system in which case the car must be stopped at once, the engine turned off, and the oil level in the crankcase checked. If the check reveals that the engine oil level is within the prescribed limits, the cause of the malfunction will have to be determined and corrected by contacting the nearest repair shop. However, an occasional flickering of the control light at idling speeds, when the engine is at operating temperature, is of no significance.

Parking Light Indicator (green)

The parking light indicator is located on the speedometer dial. The lamp lights up when the parking lights are turned on; it goes off automatically when the headlamps are switched on.

Handbrake Control Lamp (white)

When the ignition is switched on and the handbrake not fully released, the control lamp will light up to indicate this condition; it goes off only after the handbrake has been completely released.

Control Pedals and Levers

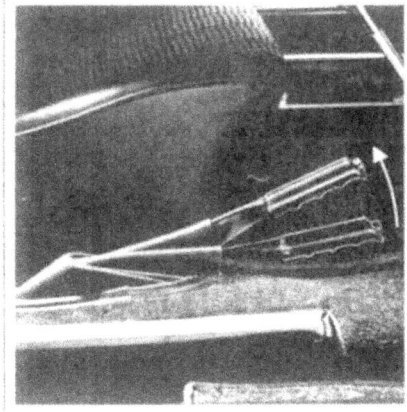

Clutch Pedal

The clutch pedal free travel is 15 to 20 mm (0.60 to 0.80 in.). To check it, the pedal must be pulled out from the floor board. See also Checking and Adjusting Pedal Free Travel, page 61.

Brake Pedal

Since the brakes are self-adjusting, the brake pedal free travel will always be constant providing that the hydraulic brake system is free of air bubbles. Pedal free travel to the point of brake actuation may be 30 – 50 % of total brake pedal travel. Whenever the brake pedal can be pushed in farther than stated above, the brakes should be checked and, possibly, bled.

Hand Brake

The handbrake is set and automatically locked in position by pulling the lever up. The handbrake can be released by first pulling the lever up a bit, pushing the release button in, and at the same time lowering the lever to the "off" position.
To prevent a possible premature wear of the handbrake linings, a control lamp has been installed within the instrument panel. The lamp goes off only after the handbrake has been fully released.

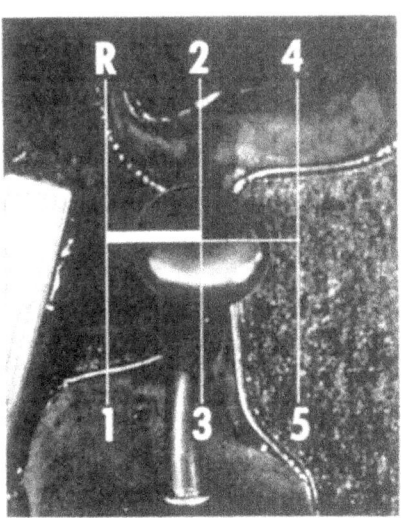

Shifting Gears

Owing to the fully synchronized transmission, it is possible to shift into any gear without "double-clutching" or intermediate throttle application. However, it should be remembered to depress the clutch pedal fully while gears are being changed.

The following maximum engine speeds (rpm) must not be exceeded when shifting down (applicable to standard gear ratios):

Five Speed Transmission
5th to 4th Gear — 4900 rpm
4th to 3rd Gear — 4800 rpm
3rd to 2nd Gear — 4200 rpm
2nd to 1st Gear — 3400 rpm

Four Speed Transmission
4th to 3rd Gear — 4500 rpm
3rd to 2nd Gear — 4000 rpm
2nd to 1st Gear — 3300 rpm

Gearshift Lever

Shift Pattern (five speed transmission)
1st Gear — To left, overcoming spring safety, then rearward
2nd Gear — Straight forward, gliding off spring safety
3rd Gear — Straight back
4th Gear — Forward right
5th Gear — Rearward right
Reverse — To left, overcoming spring safety, then forward

Shift Pattern (four speed transmission)
1st Gear — Straight forward
2nd Gear — Straight back
3rd Gear — Forward right
4th Gear — Rearward right
Reverse — To left, overcoming spring safety, then forward

Starter-Ignition Switch and Steering Lock

The five ignition key positions are as follows:

0 – "Off"

Steering locked. All electric circuits wired thru the ignition switch are turned off. When the ignition switch is in this position, overnight (one-side) parking lights can be turned on by moving the directional signal lever up or down (for left or right street side parking — see page 17).

1 – "Radio"

Steering unlocked. All electric circuits wired thru the ignition switch are switched off except the radio input.

2 – "Garage"

Steering unlocked. All electric circuits wired thru the ignition switch are off.

3 – "Ignition on"

Steering unlocked, ignition on, Accessories connected to electric circuits wired thru the ignition switch can now be put into operation. The red generator control lamp and the green oil pressure control lamp will stay on as long as the engine is not running. The parking brake control lamp is on as long as the parking brake is not fully released.

4 – "Start"

The starter motor becomes energized when the ignition key is turned fully right into Position 4. Once engine has fired up, release the key to disengage the starter (the key will jump back into Position 3).

The starter motor should not be engaged for longer than 15 – 20 seconds at a time. If necessary, engage the starter again after allowing a few moments of rest. The ignition key can be withdrawn from the lock when in Position "0" or "2".

Once unlocked with the key, the steering lock bolt will snap into the locked position only when the key is withdrawn from the lock (applies also to Position "0").

Light Switch

The two-position pull-twist light switch controls parking lights, headlights, and instrument illumination. With the knob pulled out to first stop, parking lights are turned on. Pulling the knob to second stop turns the headlights on; high and low headlamp beams are controlled thru the combination switch on the steering column. (See page 17).

Instrument Lights

The instrument lights are switched on automatically when the parking lights or the headlights are turned on. The brightness of the instrument lights can be progressively varied from completely off to fully on by turning the light switch knob left or right.

Combination Blinker, Dimmer, and Flasher Control Lever

This lever, extending to the left from the steering post, controls the directional blinkers, low and high headlamp beams, and the headlamp flasher. The directional signals are actuated in the customary way of moving the lever up for right turn, and down for left turn. In addition, overnight parking lights, which mark only the left or right side of the car, are controlled by this lever motion: when the car is parked with ignition off (switch position "0", page 16) and the blinker signal lever up (as for "right turn"), only the right front and rear parking lights will be on; with the lever down (as for "left turn"), the left front and rear lights will be on. This provision is for parking on either side of the street.

Once the main light switch is pulled out into position 2 (headlamps on), high beam is selected by moving the lever into a spring-held position away from the steering wheel, and low beam by moving the lever into the second spring-held position near the steering wheel. By moving the lever still closer to the steering wheel, overcoming a slight spring tension, the headlamps are switched on, as explained below, for as long as the lever is hand-held in that position; this provision is for signalling other drivers when passing or when otherwise desiring to attract attention. A special relay switch in this circuit provides the effect shown below:

Combination Blinker, Dimmer, and Flasher Control Lever

Position of Main Light Switch Knob	Position of Headlamp Preselector Lever	Headlamp Beam Effect
Lights off (Stop 0)	Any spring-held position	No effect
	Hand-held at steering	High beam
Parking lights on (Stop 1)	Any spring-held position	No effect
	Hand-held at steering	Low beam
Headlights on (Stop 2)	Spring-held away from steering	High beam
	Spring-held at steering	Low beam
	Hand-held at steering	High beam

Combination Switch Functions (ignition switch in position "Ignition on")

Lever moved up (to right)	Right blinkers flashing	
Lever mowed down (to left)	Left blinkers flashing	
Lever toward instruments	High beam on	(when main light switch in Pos. 2)
Lever towards steering wheel	Low beam on	

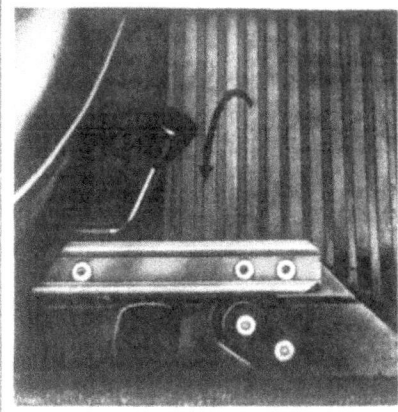

Reclining Seats

To adjust the position of the seat back rest, lean against the seat while pulling the release lever up (located at the backrest pivot). The backrest is always under spring tension and will return to the up position when the control lever is moved up.

Seat Position

The seats can be adjusted forward and back by moving the release lever up and sliding the seat into the desired position; the release lever is located on the outer side of both forward seat cushions.

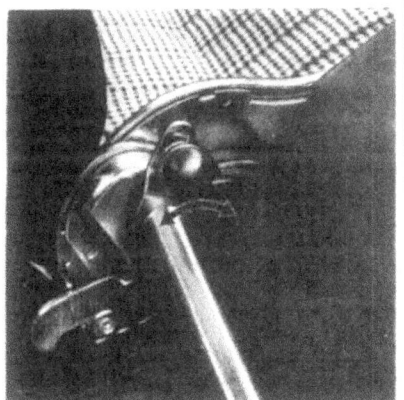

Backrest Lock

The passenger seat backrest can be tilted forward when released from the locked position. The release knob is shown in the illustration.

Armrests with Door Release

The armrests, attached to the front door panels, contain a door release button. To open the door from the inside, depress the button as shown in the illustration.
Both doors can be individually locked by depressing lock buttons in the door ledges. However, since the doors could thus not be opened from the outside, we recommend to leave these unlocked when driving for the eventuality of involvement in an accident.

Combination Wiper/Washer Switch

The control lever controls wiper motion when moved into position 0 thru 3, and the electric windshield washers when moved over two pressure stops towards the steering wheel:
0 – Wipers switched off
1 – Wipers at slow speed
2 – Wipers at medium speed
3 – Wipers at high speed

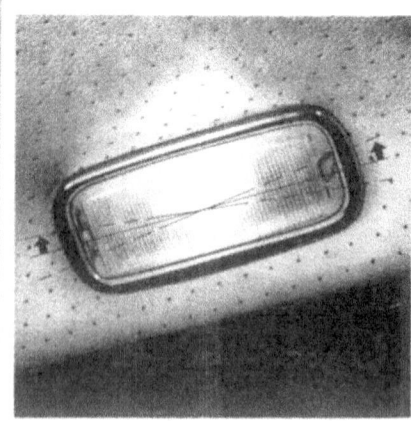

With wiper switch in Position "0", the effect is as follows:

1st stop — Windshield is sprayed with washer solution.
2nd stop — Spray continues while wiper blades clear the windshield at high wiping speed.

When the wiper switch is in Positions 1 thru 3, the washer control lever controls only the flow of the washer solution and does not affect the wiper speed. As soon as the washer control lever is released, it automatically returns into the "off" position stopping the flow of washer spray.

The washer reservoir is located in the forward luggage compartment and has a capacity of approx. 1½ quarts. Please note our instructions under the caption "Instructions for Cold Weather Operation" (Page 28).

Interior Light

The above illustration shows the right interior light. The lamp lens tilts on a pivot to serve as a three-position switch, as follows:
a) Lamps switched off.
b) Lamp switched on.
c) Lamp lights automatically when either door is opened.

Inside Rear View Mirror

The mirror can be adjusted for night driving to reduce glare from lights behind the car; the adjustment is made by tilting a small knob at the bottom of the mirror frame.

Cigarette Lighter

The heating coil in the lighter begins to heat when the lighter is pushed into its receptacle, snapping in to hold. Upon reaching proper temperature, the lighter automatically snaps away from the hold, disconnecting the flow of current, and can be withdrawn from the receptacle for use. The lighter is wired independently and can be used at all times.

Tank Filler Cover

The tank filler neck is mounted within the front fender and has a hinged cover which can be opened from the inside only by pulling the release knob located on the left side of the instrument panel.

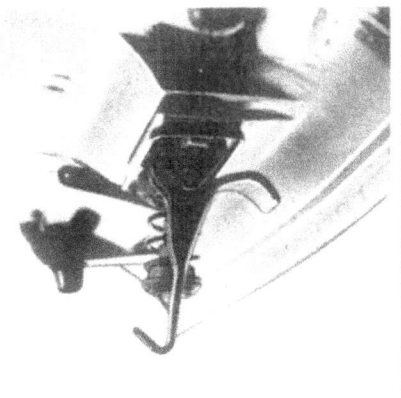
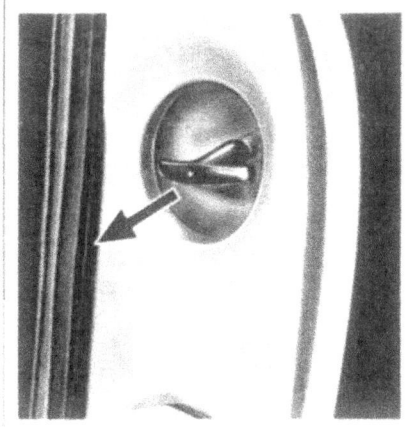

Front Lid Release

The front lid release knob is located under the left side of the instrument panel. The lid is opened by first pulling the release knob, then pushing back the safety catch under the lid. Spring tension keeps the lid in the open position.

To lock, push the lid down until the bolt snaps shut. The lock is so designed that it will open automatically if the control cable should break; the safety catch will then prevent it from drawing open while driving.

Rear Lid Release

The release knob for the rear lid is located at the left rear door post behind driver's seat. The rear lid can be opened by pulling the release knob. Spring tension keeps the lid in the open position.

To close, push the lid down until the lock bolt snaps shut. The lock is so designed that it will open automatically if the control cable should break.

SCHEMATIC VIEW OF HEATING SYSTEM

(See pages 24/25 for description)

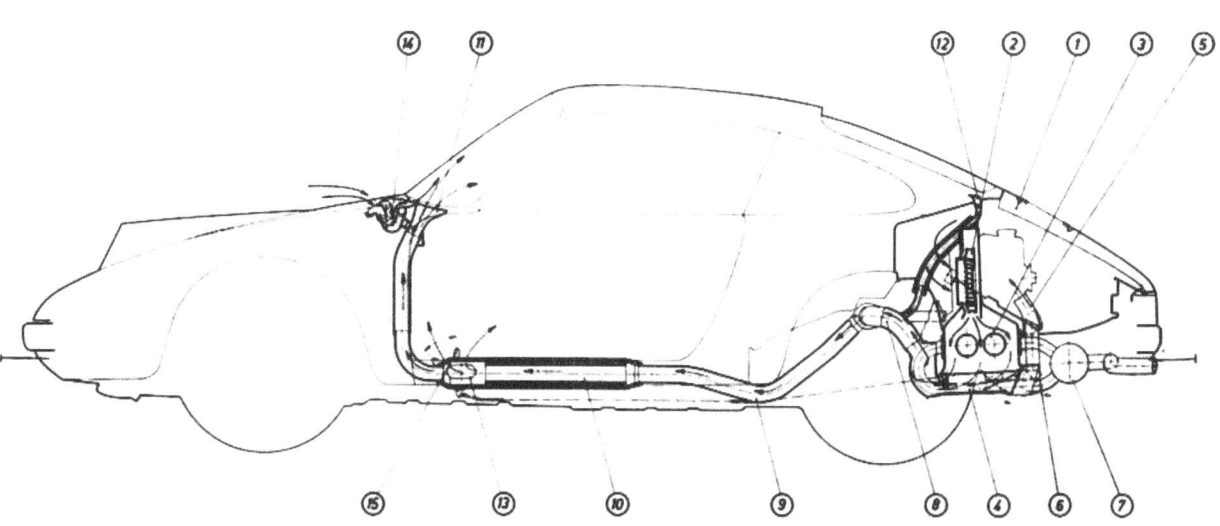

Heating and Ventilation

Description

The entire fresh air mass enters through the grill in the rear lid ① where it is drawn in by the cooling air blower. Part of the air, as required for heating the passenger compartment, is diverted from the cooling air blower ② into a separate air duct ③ and into two heat exchangers ④ at the engine exhaust manifolds. The heat exchangers consist of sheetmetal jackets which enclose the exhaust pipes ⑤. All detachable joints within the exhaust system ⑥ have been arranged outside the heat exchangers. The entire engine exhaust system as well as the main engine areas, such as the crankcase and cylinders, are located within the free air stream underneath the rear body section. The heating air flows from both heat exchangers through connecting hoses ⑦, air gates ⑧, guide ducts ⑨ and silencers (contained within the longitudinal chassis supports) ⑩, to outlets arranged in pairs within the passenger compartment. Hot air outlets are provided as follows:

For defrosting the windshield ⑪ and the rear window ⑫ by way of defroster nozzles; for the forward leg area thru sliding gates ⑬ located alongside the longitudinal chassis supports adjacent to both front seats. The air gates ⑧ are designed to permit a continuous flow of air thru the heat exchangers, regardless whether the heat controls are turned on or off.

In addition, outside air may be used in the ventilating system ⑭ by entering thru the vent in front of the windshield and bypassing the heating system completely.

Hot air needed for preheating the carburetors is taken from the heating air ducts.

Operation

The flow of heating air is controlled by a lever ⑮ located directly behind the gearshift lever. The heating air flows when the lever is moved to rear, and stops when the lever is moved forward. When the lever is moved, the action is transmitted to the air gates ⑧ thru a cable. Should the cable break, both gates will automatically stop the flow of hot air into the passenger compartment and guide it into the open.

23a

General Information – Air Conditioner

1. Car interior comfort may be selected by either selecting the fan control switch (A) or the air temperature, thermostat switch (B) or both. Turning the fan control switch clockwise decreased the air volume from the air outlet.
2. Turning the thermostat switch clockwise increases the length of time the compressor (and therefore, refrigeration) stays on. The farthest position clockwise results in the coldest air.

Operational Hints

1. If the air volume seems to get less, it is likely that the coil is freezing. To correct this, turn the thermostat counterclockwise until the condition improves.
2. If the car interior becomes too cold, even after setting the air volume on low, turn the thermostat switch counterclockwise until the desired comfort is reached.
3. The exterior of the windows are liable to fog over on warm, very muggy days, with the conditioner on maximum. Turn the thermostat switch counterclockwise.
4. The conditioner may be used to demist the interior of the windows during any weather conditions. Turn the conditioner on low and use it with the heater in the winter to dry the air while the heater warms it.
5. Operate the air conditioner for a few minutes at least twice a month, year around to keep lubricant throughout system.

"Porsche air" air conditioning, only available in USA as factory approved and dealer installed unit.

Maintenance Hints

1. The compressor belt should be tightened frequently, and especially after the first 100 miles of operation.
2. It is advisable to take a spare belt on long trips.
3. A sight glass is provided to check the refrigerant level. It is located under the left front fender. If bubbles or foam appear while the compressor is running the unit requires service by your authorized Porsche dealer.
4. Have your air conditioner serviced at your authorized Porsche dealer.

Air Conditioner Components

1. Compressor — Engine driven from the crank shaft.
2. Condenser — Primary — in engine deck lid, below grill.
3. Condenser — Secondary — Under the left front fender in front of the tire.
4. Evaporator — Slim line below fabric instrument panel board.
5. Receiver — Drier — Refrigerant storage tank and drying agent mounted in the rear section of the left fender wall.
6. The Ram Air Scoop.

All unit components are inter-connected with hoses.

Operation

The temperature and humidity control is the left hand knob on the front of the evaporator, known as the thermostat. The fan switch is a four-position switch, including off for the desired blower speed. The clutch is also controlled from the fan switch with the thermostat turned on. This allows one knob to turn the entire system off. The five vane type horizontal louvers are directional, vertically and horizontally, for desired positions.

24

Porsche Electrical Diagram Air Conditioning

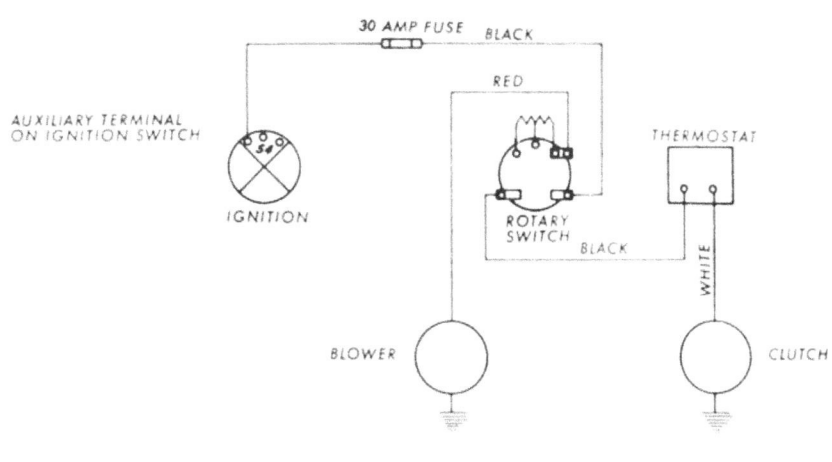

Schematic View of Air Conditioning System

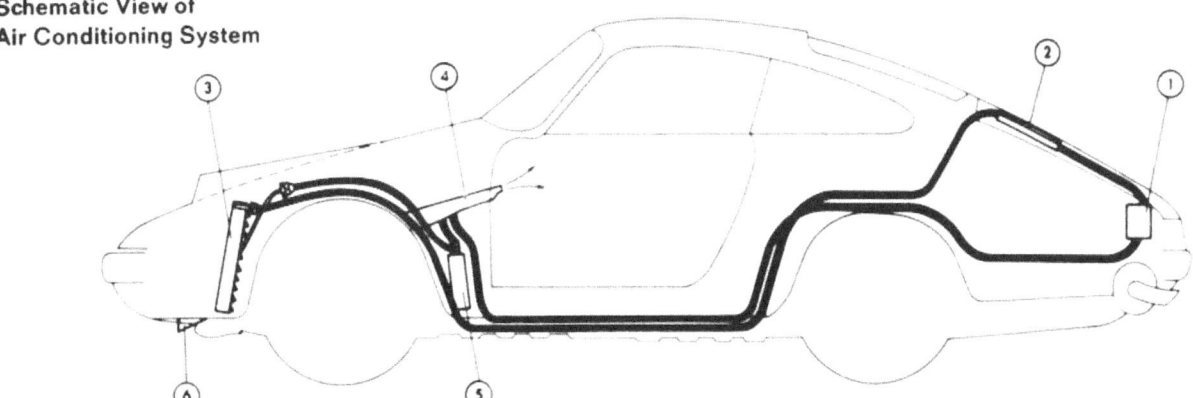

24 a

 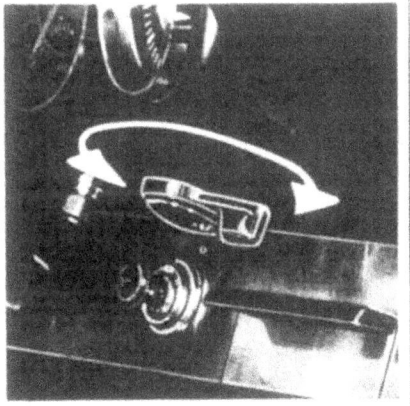

Part of the heating air can be used for heating the front leg area by adjusting the sliding air gates (13) located along the chassis members next to the front seats. Pushing the gates to the front stops the flow of air to the leg area and the entire heating air enters thru the defroster nozzles ⑪ and ⑫.

Supplemental ventilation is possible thru the ventilating system ⑭ which is controlled by levers mounted on the dashboard.
Control lever moved to the right =
Fresh air flow shut off
Control lever moved to the left =
Fresh air flow open

Electric Sunroof (Optional)

On special request, Type 912 cars can be equipped with an electric sunroof. The sunroof is controlled thru a spring-loaded toggle switch. Appropriate movement of the control lever brings the roof into the desired position. When released, the lever returns to its neutral position and roof travel ceases. The roof transport is equipped with a safety clutch which disengages the drive mechanism when certain resistance is met — an added safety feature which excludes any possibility of accidental bruising or injuries.

Manual Operation

A hand crank is provided for manual operation to cope with any unforseen malfunction within the electric transport mechanism. The transport mechanism is located above the rear window and is accessible after opening the zipper:

Remove the plastic protective cap and, using the hand crank, remove the slotted screw. Insert the forkshaped end of the crank into the appropriate recess in the manual drive coupling.

Turn the crank in either direction, as may be required, to bring the roof into the desired position. No other mechanical work is involved.

25

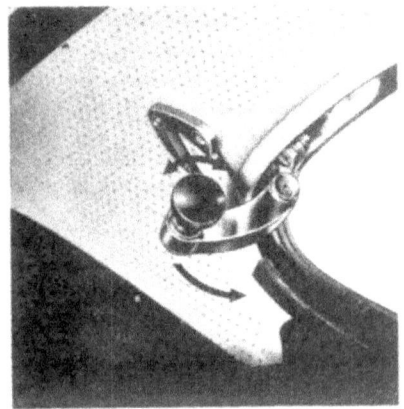

Rear Side Windows

The rear side windows are hinged and swing out for added ventilation. To open, unlock the hinge by turning the arresting knob counter-clockwise and push the window outward to the desired position.

Safety Belts

Safety belt anchoring points for attaching safety belts for both front seats have been incorporated in the body as a standard production feature. The threaded anchoring receptacles, into which the seat belt shackles are screwed in, are accessible by removing the plastic caps.

Emergency Blinker Signal (USA only)

All four directional blinkers will blink in unison when the emergency blinker control button is pulled out. This warning system has been devised to provide proper visual warning signals to approaching drivers when the car is stopped in traffic due to an emergency. A bright red control lamp included in the switch indicates that the warning system is in operation, even if only one light should be blinking. This warning system can be switched on independently and without regard to the position of the ignition switch selector.
The normal directional indicators are automatically switched off by an overrider when the emergency blinker signals are on.

Fog Lamp Switch (Optional)

On special request, two fog lamps can be installed in the Type 912 car. The fog lamps are controlled through a pull push switch and work in conjunction with the parking lights or head-lamp. A red indicator light has been incorporated in the switch knob to indicate that the fog lights are on.
USA only: The fog lamps and the indicator light go off automatically when switching from low beam to high beam.
FRANCE only: The fog lamps only work in conjunction with the park lamps.

Chassis Serial Number

Location of Identification Plates

When ordering spare parts or submitting inquiries, always include the chassis and engine serial numbers in your correspondence to ensure prompt and correct response.

Nomenclature Plate

Chassis and Color Number

Engine Serial Number

**Instructions
for Cold Weather Operation**

1. Ensure that "Winter Oil" of proper specifications is put into the crankcase at time of oil change (see Lubrication Schedule, page 31, and Filling Capacities, page 87).

2. Fill the windshield washer reservoir with an antifreeze solution of 3 parts water to 1 part denatured alcohol.

3. The paint finish, chromed and aluminum parts should be coated with an appropriate preservative (see pages 36 – 39).

4. Check regularly the state of charge of the battery and the level and specific gravity of the electrolytic solution (see page 63).

5. Protect the door locks against freezing through an application of a few drops of the lock antifreeze contained in a small dispenser which has been furnished with the car; the above should be done at regular intervals but especially after the car has been washed.

6. Coat the rubber weatherstrip, located between the body and the front lid (including areas between the profiled lips) with glycerine, to prevent the lid from freezing shut.

7. Check brake pads and handbrake linings, replace if necessary.

CARE AND LUBRICATION

LUBRICATION SCHEDULE – TYPE 912

300 to 600 mi	2800 to 3400 mi	6000 to 6500 mi	Service Required	Repeat every
●	●	●	Change engine oil Clean filtering magnet	3000 mi
●		●	Change oil filter cartridge	6000 mi
●		●	Change transmission oil	6000 mi
		●	Lubricate door and lid hinges	6000 mi

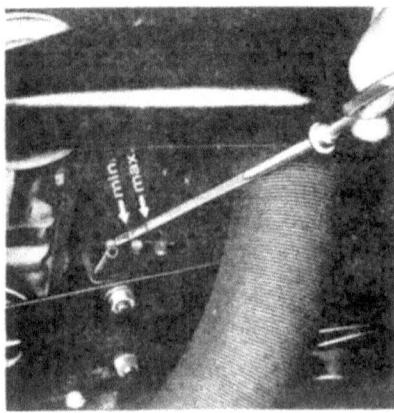

Checking Engine Oil Level

Please note:

When the engine is started, oil is pumped from the crankcase to the lubricating points through a system of oil galleries. When the engine is shut off, it takes a certain amount of time for the oil to drain and collect in the crankcase. Consequently, it is quite likely that an inspection made shortly after the engine has been shut off will reveal a lower oil level in the crankcase. Therefore, we suggest that oil level readings be made after some time, such as in the morning, prior to the engine has been out of operation for starting; at that time oil may be replenished up to the top level mark on the dipstick. When the oil level on the dipstick is approx. 10 mm ($^3/_8$ inch) below the top level mark shortly after the engine has been stopped, no oil should be added since this would result in an overfilled crankcase and cause the oil to be forced out of the engine through the engine breather.

Check oil as follows:

1. With engine at rest (see above), remove the oil dipstick and wipe off with a clean rag.
2. Push dipstick back into its receptacle.
3. After a brief pause, remove dipstick again and check the level against the markings on the dipstick. The oil level must not be higher than the top level mark nor lower than the minimum level mark.
4. If necessary, replenish with premium quality HD oil up to the top level mark on the dipstick.

Caution:

When replenishing oil in the crankcase, care must be taken to use an oil of same brand and viscosity type as the oil contained in the crankcase.

Changing Engine Oil

1. Remove drain plug from crankcase when engine is at operating temperature.
2. Drain oil completely.
3. Remove oil strainer and filtering magnet, clean and reinstall.
4. Change oil filter cartridge after every 6000 miles of operation.
5. Reinstall oil drain plug making certain that it has been properly tightened.
6. Refill crankcase with premium quality HD oil up to the top level mark on the dipstick. (See page 87 for filling capacity and oil grade.)

Bottom View of Crankcase

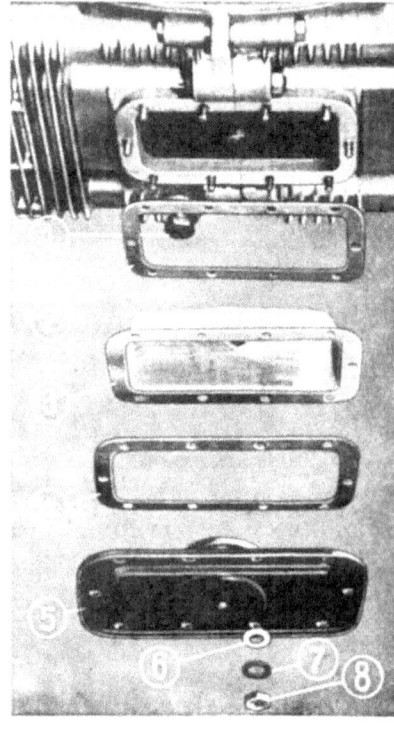

1. Oil drain plug
2. Gasket
3. Oil strainer
4. Gasket
5. Oil strainer cover with filtering magnet
6. Washer
7. Spring washer
8. Nut

Cleaning Oil Strainer and Filtering Magnet

A filtering magnet is provided in the oil circuit to ensure adequate filtration of engine oil. It is attached to the oil strainer cover in such manner that it encases the oil suction tube. The oil first passes thru the oil strainer and then flows thru the filtering magnet.

1 Crankcase
2 Oil strainer
3 Filtering magnet
4 Oil suction tube
5 Threaded stud
6 Oil strainer cover
7 Spacer
8 Rivet
9 Gasket

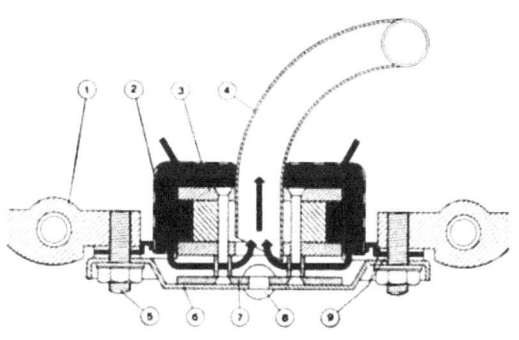

Removal

1. Remove hexagon nuts from oil strainer cover.
2. Withdraw strainer cover.
3. Withdraw oil strainer and gaskets.
4. Wash all parts in clean solvent.

Installation

The following points must be observed when installing the strainer cover and filtering magnet:

1. Check oil suction tube for tightness.
2. Clean strainer, removing all gasket remnants.
3. Use new gasket on both sides of the strainer.
4. Install the oil strainer in such way that it firmly encloses the oil suction tube.
5. Remove all gasket remnants from the oil strainer cover; straighten the cover if bent or warped.
6. Do not overtighten the hexagon nuts, especially when thicker gaskets are used, to avoid warping the cover.

Cleaning Bypass Oil Filter

The cleaning of the oil filter involves, in most part, replacement of the oil filter cartridge (accomplished after every 6000 miles of use).

1. Unscrew cover retaining nut and remove cover.
2. Remove old cartridge with a slight twist in either direction.
3. Remove old oil from filter housing.
4. Wipe the inside of housing with a clean linen cloth; do not use shredded rags.
5. Install new cartridge, guiding it in with a slight twist.
6. Position the cover in place, pressing down by hand, and tighten retaining screw. The cover gasket must be replaced whenever the cover is removed from housing.
7. Run engine at idling speed for a few moments.
8. Check filter housing and connections for absence of leaks.
9. Check engine oil level and replenish to top level mark on dipstick, using appropriate HD oil (refer to page 32, Checking Engine Oil Level).

Changing Transmission Oil

1. Remove oil drain plug from the bottom of transmission housing.
2. Allow oil to drain completely.
3. Clean the drain plug, reinstall and tighten securely.
4. Wipe dirt from oil filler plug before removing it, then remove.
5. Fill transmission with approx. $2^{1}/_{2}$ liters (2.6 US quarts) gear lubricant (see page 87 for oil type and viscosity).
6. Check transmission oil level, reinstall oil filler plug and tighten securely. Oil level in the transmission should reach the bottom of the oil filler orifice when the car is standing on level ground.

Lubricating Gearshift Lever

1. Push up the rubber dust cover on gearshift lever.
2. Depress lever and apply a few drops of engine oil to ball joint.
3. Snap dust cover in original position.

Care of Coachwork

The finish on standard production Porsches is of a high-quality, baked synthetic enamel. The color and enamel type designation is indicated on the identification plate attached to the forward door post. When corresponding with the factory in reference to the paint finish, always include the identification number.

In daily use, the car is exposed to many mechanical and chemical influencing factors, in a large part it being the weather and exposure to sun rays, during the summer season influencing even the top quality enamels. Ultra-violet rays, rapid temperature changes, rain, snow, industrial dust and chemical deposits repeatedly attack the paint surface which can withstand such abuse only through proper and regular care.

Car Washing

During the initial few weeks, the new car should be washed with clear water only. This is best accomplished by applying a fine spray of water to the entire surface to first soften the dirt deposit and remove the worst of it. After this, clean the surface using a soft sponge and plenty of water, rinse well and wipe dry with a chamois. Never attempt to wash or wax the car when the finish is hot from exposure to the sun or from engine heat. Since it is quite likely that water enters the brake components during washing, causing poor braking action or one-side pulling, it is important to test the brakes whenever the car has been washed.

Dust should never be wiped off the car with a dry rag since the dust particles are abrasive in nature and will rapidly dull the gloss, possibly causing scratches which are difficult to repair.

Road Tar

Road tar should be removed at once with tar remover since it may cause permanent stains if allowed to "soak" for any length of time. However, the finish should be treated with a wax preservative subsequent to treatment with tar removing solutions.

Care of the Finish

First it must be pointed out that oils contained in the paint structure are the most important factors contributing to the elasticity of the finish. Since these oils are gradually lost as the time goes on, due to weather and similar causes, they must be replenished thru regular and proper care of the finish. Appropriate cleaning and application of preservatives will result in high luster and provide a protective coating of lasting permanence. However, many of the marketed car "polishes" and "waxes" should be met with caution and, thus, we recommend the use of Porsche-approved products and brands which are compatible with our enamels. Given proper care, the original finish will retain its brilliance for many years. The use of polishes is recommended but only after it becomes evident that the normal preservatives no longer accomplish the job.

Caution: Keep silicone polishes off the windshield to avoid wiper smear in rain.

Spots and Stains

Road tar, grease, oil, and insects can not always be removed with soap and water alone and require special treatment. Spots of any sort should be removed without delay before they set and become difficult or impossible to remove.

Polishing

It is advisable to entrust the task of repolishing your car into the skilled hands of professionals acquainted with this work since a good degree of care and know-how is required. Briefly, the finish must be polished with clean cotton until a high luster is obtained, which should be done in small sections to ensure that the polish does not dry beforehand. A subsequent application of a wax preservative will give the finish a brilliant, long lasting gloss. Metallic finishes are especially difficult to maintain and should always be given skilled, professional care.

Protective Undercoating

The oil industry has developed undercoating and rust-proofing materials of bitumen or wax base. Contrary to the conventional so-called "spray-oil", these materials do not soften the undercoating sprayed on at the factory. Instead, they solidify and, upon drying, form a tough, pliable protective coat which has a beneficial effect on the undercarriage and various related component parts by protecting these against the effects of weather. We recommend that the undercarriage be treated with such preservative undercoating prior to the onset of the winter season as well as in spring.

Insects and Tree Sap

During the warm season, insects will accumulate on the forward areas of the body. Since these deposits are somewhat difficult to remove with sponge and water alone, a mild laundry soap solution may be applied. Tree sap accumulating thru parking under trees can also be removed with a mild soap water solution. Rinse the car throughly after cleaning and follow up with a wax preservative.

Upholstery Fabrics

Even though the upholstery fabrics in your Porsche are of topmost quality, they must be handled with proper care to prevent scuffing or bleaching in the process of cleaning, this being especially the case with fabrics of richer color shades, or when removing stains with a water solution. If a vacuum cleaner is not at hand, the upholstery may be cleaned with a soft brush. More persistent stains may be cleaned with a mild, luke warm soap and water solution. Grease and oil spots can be removed with commercial spot removers by using an undyed soft cloth and rubbing the upholstery until dry.

Leather and Leatherette

The best way to clean leather and leatherette is by using a luke warm soap water solution and a soft brush. Use sparse amounts of water to avoid soaking or drenching. Use a soft sponge to wipe each section completely dry after it has been cleaned. Clean the seams carefully, making certain that these areas have been cleaned evenly and well dried. When cleaning leather, it is advisable to follow up with a good leather conditioner.

Chrome Trim

Chromed parts should first be washed with sponge and water, then dried with a soft cloth. Road tar must be removed with tar remover rather than knives or objects of that kind. By following up with a proven chrome preservative, a high and long lasting luster will be maintained. During the winter season as well as in coastal areas it will be of advantage to cover the chromed parts with a somewhat heavier coating of the preservative as protection against salt air and extended exposure to corrosive road dirt. If necessary, coat the parts with non-corrosive vaseline or other protective compound.

Rubber Weatherstripping

Rubber weatherstripping is used around the doors and windows. Given a certain amount of care, these rubber components will remain flexible and resilient; it is normal for rubber to lose these properties thru aging which causes it to become hard and brittle. However, this condition can be effectively countered and slowed thru application of talc powder and glycerine:
Caution: Glycerine may damage the finish.

Cleaning Glass

Your Porsche is equipped with two types of glass, the windshield being of laminated safety glass and all other windows of tempered safety glass (Sekurit). The laminated glass consists of two layers of glass bonded together with a transparent layer of pliable plastic. When laminated glass is damaged, only the immediate impact area shatters leaving the rest of the surface intact to provide continued visibility thru the windshield. The tempered glass (Sekurit) is a single sheet of glass whose surface has been tempered, or hardened. This type of glass is known to withstand much abuse. However, when struck with severe force, the stresses in the glass are instantly relieved and the whole panel cracks into very small fragments rendering the glass merely translucent; in certain cases, such cracked pane may fall completely apart into small and relatively harmless pebbles. The two types of glass are utilized as both have certain advantages and their combined application in motor vehicles satisfies many aspects of the mandatory safety requirements.

The thin layer of road dirt that accumulates on the glass surface consists, to a great extent, of tire abradings and fuel or oil deposits combined with dust or dirt. The best way to clean the glass is by using luke warm water solution containing a small amount of alcohol or baking soda, and clean absorbent paper (newspaper). If a chamois is used for polishing the glass, it should be one that is used exclusively for that purpose and which has been thoroughly cleaned prior to use. Contact with the painted surfaces must definitely be avoided, especially with polishes and preservatives, to preclude the possibility of silicone transfer onto the glass.
It should be remembered not to engage the windshield wipers until the windshield has been wetted by rain or windshield washer spray.

Coachwork Cleaning Materials

Purpose	Type Material	Comments
Body washing	Water and car shampoo solution or non-caustic soap flakes; use insect remover if necessary	Rinse thoroughly
Waxing and Polishing:		
a) Preserving finish	Lechler-Kristall-Polish Glasso-Hartglanz	Contains silicone. Contact with windshield must be avoided
b) Polishing finish	Lechler-Universal-Polish Glasurit-Autoneuglanz	Should be done by paint specialists
Tar spots	Tar remover or similar preparate	Follow up with preservative
Insects	1-Z-Insekten-Entferner Auto Radil	Follow up with preservative
Polishing chrome and aluminium	Auto-Wenol, Simichrompoli, or equivalent	
Cleaning cloth upholstery and seats	Frillo-Fleckenwasser	
Rubber stripping care	Treat with talc powder or glycerine	Commercially available
Leather and leatherette	Known commercial products such as Karnol or equivalent	
Windshield leaks	National-Spezial-Zement	
Body leaks	Teroson-Tropfen und Regenleistenzement	

Known brands of commercial products other than those listed above may also be used. However, our recommendations are based on practical experience gained over many years and we can fully endorse the above listed brands as good and proper.

SERVICE SCHEDULE – TYPE 912
MAINTENANCE AND ADJUSTMENTS

300 to 600 mi	2800 to 3400 mi	6000 to 6500 mi	Service Required	Repeat every
■	■	■	Valves: Check clearance	3000 mi
		■	Spark Plugs: Check electrode gap	6000 mi
		■	Cylinders: Check compression	6000 mi
		■	Distributor: Lubricate breaker cam	6000 mi
		■	Distributor: Check breaker points	6000 mi
		■	Ignition: Check timing	6000 mi
		■	Carburetors: Lubricate linkage	6000 mi
■		■	Carburetors: Check idle speed	6000 mi
■		■	Blower Belt: Check tension	6000 mi
		■	Fuel System: Clean fuel pump strainer	6000 mi
		■	Air Cleaners: Wet screen type: Clean and coat with oil Silencer type: Replace filter cartridge	6000 mi 6000 mi
		■	Brakes: Check entire brake system for proper functioning, proper condition of components, and absence of leaks in hydraulic system	6000 mi
	■	■	Brake Pads: Remove and inspect, determine degree of wear	6000 mi
■		■	Clutch: Check pedal free travel	6000 mi
■		■	Front Axle: Check wheelbearing adjustment	6000 mi
■		■	Wheels: Check tire pressure; check wheel nuts for tightness	6000 mi
■		■	Electrical System: Check entire electrical system for proper functioning	6000 mi
		■	Battery: Check condition	6000 mi

1 Air Cleaner
2 Ignition coil
3 Bypass-oilfilter
4 Carburetor preheating system
5 Oil filler
6 Ignition distributor
7 Fanbelt
8 Generator
9 Dip-stick
10 Air duct

Cylinder Designation

Facing in direction of travel:
Cylinder I = right front
Cylinder II = right rear
Cylinder III = left front
Cylinder IV = left rear

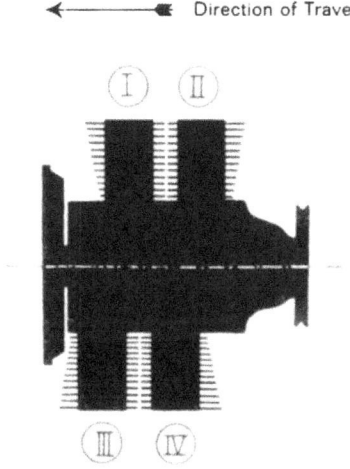

Adjusting Valve Clearance

Valve clearance (cold):
    Intake 0.10 mm (.004 in.)
    Exhaust 0.15 mm (.006 in.)

Excessive valve clearance results in a noisy engine and loss of power. Insufficient clearance reduces performance and results in burned valves; combustion flashback through an improperly closing valve can cause a carburetor fire. Consequently, we recommend that the valves be adjusted in a reputable shop. The valves should be adjusted only when the engine is cold.

The easiest way to adjust the valves is to follow the cylinder sequence 1 – 2 – 3 – 4 while turning the crankshaft counter-clockwise. To adjust the valves of any given cylinder, first bring the respective piston to its top dead center (TDC) on compression stroke because this ensures that both valves of the particular cylinder are fully closed. When the procedure is initiated with Cyl 1, turn crankshaft counter-clockwise until both valves in Cyl 1 have closed and the "OT" mark on the crankshaft pulley has lined up with the vertical mark on the crankcase housing (distributor rotor pointing to a small notch on the ridge of distributor housing = Page 47).

1. Remove rocker box cover.
2. Bring piston in Cyl 1 to TDC on compression stroke.

3. Check valve clearance with a feeler gauge.
4. Loosen hex lock nut.
5. Adjust the clearance by turning the adjusting screw with a screwdriver, holding the nut with a box wrench, and checking with a feeler gauge.
6. Hold adjusting screw firmly in place and tighten lock nut.
7. Recheck adjustment.
8. Repeat the above on all other cylinders in proper sequence.
9. Mount rocker box cover.
10. Start engine and check both covers for possible oil leaks.

Cleaning Spark Plugs

Spark plugs can be cleaned with a fine wire brush and blown clean with compressed air. The upper insulator should be wiped clean to prevent a current leakage and misfiring.

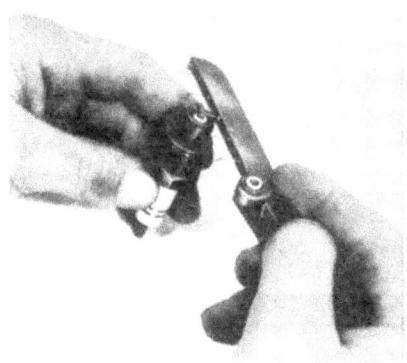

Adjusting Spark Plug Gap

1. Check gap with a wire gauge (0.6 mm or .024 in.).
2. If necessary, adjust gap by bending the ground electrode.
3. Spark plugs showing progressed erosion of electrodes must be replaced.

Checking Spark Plugs

After every 6000 miles of operation, the spark plugs must be removed and checked for proper appearance, gap, and functioning. The appearance of the electrodes and insulator is a good indicator as to the condition of the engine. In general, the tell-tales are as follows:

Medium brown:
    Proper carburetion; spark plug in good working order.

Black:
    Fuel mixture too rich; spark plug gap too wide; plug too cold.

Light grey:
    Fuel mixture too lean; spark plug loose or leaking; valves not closing fully; plug too hot.

Oil wetted:
    Oil sucked into combustion chamber due to worn cylinders or piston rings; plug misfiring.

Lubricating Distributor Cam

1. Remove distributor cap.
2. Withdraw rotor arm.
3. Lightly coat the cam with non-corrosive high temperature grease.

Note:

Do not allow grease or dirt to reach the contact breaker points. Dirty contact points will cause misfiring and quick contact erosion.

Timing Ignition

General

The firing point in Type 912 engines is 3° before top dead center (BTDC); this is equivalent to approximately 3.6 mm ($^9/_{64}$ in.) on the pulley rim. This distance should be marked on the pulley with a pencil, to the right of the "OT" designation. Turn the crankshaft clockwise until the distributor rotor points to a small notch in the distributor housing (see illustration) and, at the same time, the pencil mark lines up with the vertical marker stamped into the crankcase housing below the generator support.

Timing Procedure

1. Remove distributor cap and rotor arm.
2. Loosen clamp screw at the base of the distributor body.
3. Connect a 12 volt test lamp in series between Terminal 1 at the distributor and the ground.
4. Switch the ignition on.
5. Turn the distributor body clockwise until the light goes out (contacts closed), then turn slowly counter-clockwise until the exact moment of point opening (the instant when the light goes on again).
6. Tighten distributor clamp screw.
7. Reinstall rotor arm and distributor cap.

The ignition timing for all four cylinders is correct when the test light lights up at the precise moment when the pencil mark on the crankshaft pulley lines up with the stamped mark on the crankcase.

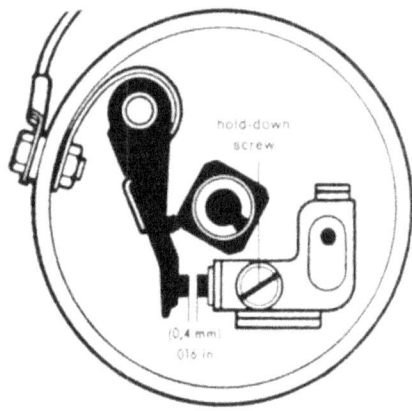

Adjusting Breaker Point Gap

The breaker points must be correctly set before an attempt is made to adjust the ignition timing. Turn the crankshaft until a cam lobe on the distributor shaft has fully raised the breaker arm.

Breaker point gap = 0.4 mm (.016 in.)

Loosen the breaker plate hold-down screw and, using a feeler gauge, adjust the breaker gap to 0.4 mm (.016 in.) by canting a screwdriver in the oval cutout, then tighten the hold-down screw.

If the points are pitted, they should first be cleaned or smoothened with a contact file although it may well be best to install a new contact set.

 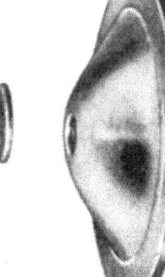  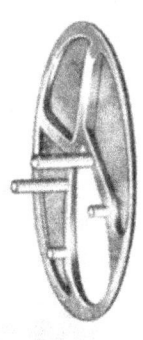 

Lubricating Carburetor Linkage

1. Lubricate all pivot points with 1 or 2 drops of engine oil while actuating the throttle controls.
2. Lubricate accelerator pump rods.
3. Disconnect all ball joints, fill cups with high temperature grease, reconnect.
4. Move linkage back and forth to check for proper functioning.

Cleaning Fuel Strainer in Pump

The fuel pump and carburetors are protected against dirt particles in the fuel by a filtering screen located in the fuel pump. The screen should be cleaned in conjunction with normal preventive maintenance.

Cleaning

1. Loosen hex retaining screw in cover and remove cover.
2. Remove strainer and wash in solvent; if necessary, install new strainer.
3. Clean pump cover.
4. Reinstall fuel screen and cover. Check gasket for serviceability and proper seating.
5. Check pump housing and connections for absence of leaks.

Cleaning Carburetors

The purpose of the carburetors is to prepare the fuel/air mixture needed for proper combustion. Carburetor condition and state of adjustment will greatly affect engine performance. Even though the fuel is carefully filtered prior to reaching the carburetors, the possibility still exists that a foreign particle clogs a jet or that dirt settles within the unit. It is, therefore, recommended that the carburetor be checked from time to time and the jets removed for cleaning.

Cleaning Jets

1. Remove air cleaners and jet carrier.
2. Remove jets and blow thru with compressed air, reinstall. Ensure that the jets are not accidentally dropped into the carburetor venturis.

Note:
To prevent a wrong placement of a jet, it is best to remove the jets individually and reinstall immediately after cleaning.
The jets should not be cleaned with sharp objects, such as wire, since this may lead to deformation of the finely drilled and calibrated jet passages resulting in impaired metering. If necessary, clogging particles may be removed from the jets by using a strong bristle.

Cleaning Air Filters

Wetted Screen Type:

The oil-wetted metal mesh air filters clean the induction air from dust and dirt. The filters should be cleaned as necessary, depending on local conditions.
Upon removal from the engine, wash the air filters in clean solvent, blow out with compressed air or let dry in the open, and oil lightly prior to installation.

Silencer Type:
Replace the filter cartridges at intervals specified in the service schedule (page 43).

1. Unsnap retaining clips and remove filter covers.
2. Replace old filter cartridge with a new one.
3. Install cover and fasten with clips, making certain that the covers are well seated and tight.

Solex 40 PJJ-4 Carburetor for Type 912 Engines

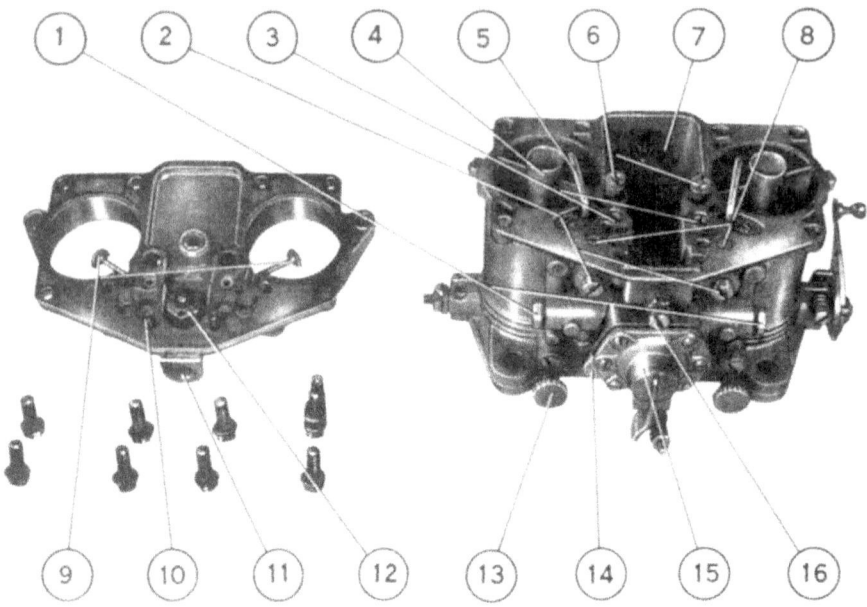

1. Accelerator pump jet
2. Idling fuel jet
3. Enriching jet
4. Pre-diffuser
5. Accelerator pump nozzle
6. Air correction jet
7. Float chamber
8. Idling air jet
9. Enricher tube
10. Float pivot retaining spring
11. Fuel line connector
12. Float needle valve
13. Idle mixture screw
14. Main jet
15. Accelerator pump
16. Float level adjustment screw

Readjusting Idle Speed

The following instructions apply only to a simple readjustment of the carburetors. We recommend that a thorough carburetor adjustment be carried out at your Porsche representative since the task requires the use of a synchronizer for achieving accurate settings on all cylinders.

1. Check spark plugs (spark plug gap is 0.6 mm or .024 in.).
2. Make sure that all throttle valves close in unison and the linkage is not binding.
3. Run engine until warm.
4. Increase engine rpm by resetting idle stop screws.
5. Adjust idle mixture on both carburetors by first fully closing the screws and reopening by 1½ turns, then closing or opening, as may be required, until reaching a point where the engine runs smoothest and fastest. However, the adjustment screws must never be left in fully closed position.
6. Back off idle speed stop screw until normal idling speed is reached. The engine should not die when depressing the clutch or quickly shutting the throttles.

Idling Speed

should be 800 to 900 rpm.

All carburetors are set at the factory and are adapted to individual engines by using premium grades of fuel. For normal use it is not permissible to modify the standard settings by installing jets or venturis of different calibrations than those specified.

When operating at greatly differing altitudes, the main jet is of special metering importance. To compensate, the following rule may be applied: Change the main jet size by 6% for every 1000 meters (3000 feet) altitude variation. For example, if the normal jet size is 120 for an altitude of 400 meters above sea level, it will require size 115 for an altitude of 1400 meters.

a. Mixture screw
b. Idling screw
c. Adjusting screw for injection pump

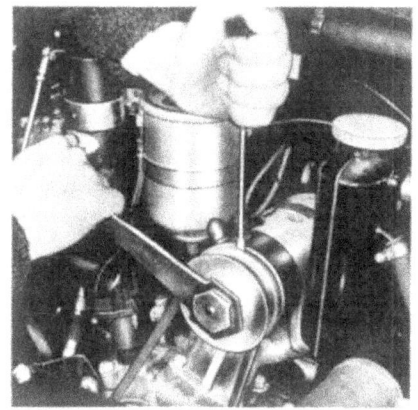 

Replacing and Adjusting Fan Belt

When adjusting or removing the fan belt, it will be necessary to remove the retaining nut and the outer half of the pulley. Insert a large screwdriver into the slot provided in the inner pulley half and brace it against the generator through bolt. Proper belt tension is obtained by moving the two pulley halves closer (to tighten tension) or farther away (to lessen tension), which is accomplished by appropriate placement of spacers between the two pulley halves. The belt is correctly adjusted when it can be depressed 15 to 20 mm ($^1/_2$ to $^3/_4$ in.) with slight thumb pressure as shown in the illustration.

New V-belts stretch somewhat after the first 50 to 100 km (30 to 60 miles) thus losing the tension required for proper functioning of the generator and cooling blower. It is, therefore, necessary to keep checking the new belt tension and readjust it when necessary.

Note:
Oiled fan belts can be easily cleaned in commercial detergents (such as the P-3 solution) and kept in further use. Do not use gasoline for cleaning purposes.
Worn belts should be replaced only with those bearing part number 999.192.006.50

Replacing Fan Belt

To change the belt, apply same procedure as that for adjusting tension. Begin assembly with 5 spacers between both pulley halves and work from there to gain proper belt adjustment by adding or withdrawing spacers.

53

Service Brakes (Disc Brakes)

When the brake pedal is depressed, hydraulic fluid transmits the pressure to brake pistons in the brake calipers, pressing brake pads against the brake discs; the brake pads are self-adjusting. Sheetmetal cover shrouds protect all discs against water spray and road dirt; however, it is still possible that the brakes are wetted when the car is washed or driven on wet roads. Consequently, when driving on expressways or other fast highways where the brakes are not frequently used, keep in mind that higher brake pedal pressures will be required for braking. It is advisable, under such conditions, to "clear" the brakes occasionally through moderate application of the brakes. Also, run the brakes dry after the car has been washed.

The virtue of disc brakes is that they retain their braking qualities at much higher operating temperatures than do the drum-type brakes. Nevertheless, use your engine for braking when descending long grades, by shifting into lower gears, to keep the brakes from overheating. Excessive brake temperatures may damage the brake seals or cause the hydraulic fluid to boil and create vapor pockets in the hydraulic system rendering the brakes very ineffective.

When participating in competition events and desiring to facilitate better cooling for the brakes, it is permissible to remove the rear brake shrouds; the front disc shrouds, however, must never be removed.

Brake Pads

Brake pad wear will depend mainly upon the severity of usage, type of driving, and condition of the roads. We recommend that the brake pads be visually inspected during the initial maintenance operations to determine if these (standard type) are adequate for the owner's way of driving. It may be expected that the pads will wear faster on dirty and wet roads (winter-serviced).

Various types of brake pads are available, such as for normal use or for competition. Competition brake pads wear slower but require higher pedal pressures. We suggest that competition brake pads be removed prior to the onset of the cold season and be replaced with pads designed for normal use. Thickness of the pads should be checked during all preventive maintenance operations or whenever the wheels are taken off the car (visual check). The pads must be thick enough between the brake pad plate and the cross spring to allow a reserve for further wear (see illustration). The permissible wear limit has been reached once the brake pad plate comes to rest against the cross spring (pad thickness approx. 2 mm or .08 in.). We also suggest that the condition of the brake pads be checked prior to departure on longer trips.

54

Replacing Brake Pads

Each car, as such, must be equipped with brake pads of identical type and brand on all wheels. Even though it is permissible to replace individual pads under certain conditions, we recommend that, in the least, the pads of a given axle be replaced altogether when the necessity to replace one pad alone should arise.

Caution:

Brake pads which were in use and are to be removed for any reason, should be appropriately marked to ensure that they are installed in their original position upon reassembly.

1. Place car on stands and remove wheels.
2. Remove safety locks and retaining pins; depress spring and remove.
3. Mark pads prior to removing these, then remove.
4. Using a piston depressor, push pistons fully back. If the special depressor is not at hand, the pistons may be pushed back with a piece of wood. Do not use other tools or improvisations for this purpose to avoid damaging the pistons or brake discs.

Note:

When the pistons are pushed back, hydraulic fluid is forced out of the cylinders and flows back into the reservoir. To prevent spillage from an overfilled or overflowing reservoir, drain it before pushing the pistons back. The scavenging tool used for this purpose should be completely clean and should not be allowed to come into contact with anything but the hydraulic brake fluid.

5. Clean the pad seating and supporting surfaces within the housing using denatured alcohol; do not use mineral solvents or sharp objects.
6. Check dust covers and safety rings for condition. Replace covers when porous or hard.
7. Clean the brake discs with fine emery cloth.
8. Install new brake pads together with retaining pins, springs, and safety locks. The brake pads should fit freely in the wells.
9. Follow the same procedure on remaining brakes.

Note:

Use only replacement brake pads offered by authorized Porsche dealers.

Before driving the car, depress the brake pedal as far as possible to bring the brake pistons and pads into normal position. Finally, check hydraulic fluid level in the reservoir and replenish if necessary.

Conditioning New Brake Pads

An inherent characteristic of new brake pads is to show effects of fading during the conditioning period, i. e., the first 125 miles subsequent to installation; this condition will not reoccur once the brake pads have become seated. If at all possible, avoid hard braking from higher speeds during the conditioning period. When new pads are installed, it will be noted that the brake pedal travel is somewhat greater than normal, the condition gradually improving as the brakes seat.

Bleeding Brake System

The brakes must be bled with great care subsequent to work performed in the brake system, when the pedal becomes soft or spongy, pedal travel abnormally long, or when the brakes pull to one side.

This procedure requires two mechanics and is always initiated at the most distant point from the brake master cylinder. All four wheels have to be taken off the car. We recommend the following sequence.

1. Left rear wheel.
2. Right rear wheel.
3. Right front wheel.
4. Left front wheel.

Note:

When the hydraulic brake system has been drained, it should be first filled, as outlined below, and then bled. Open the bleeder valve by about one-half turn, depress brake pedal, close bleeder valve, and release brake pedal. The procedure must be repeated in this sequence until brake fluid begins to flow thru the bleeder hose; this applies to all wheels and should be done in proper sequence as shown above. Having filled the hydraulic system with the brake fluid, proceed with the actual bleeding operation.

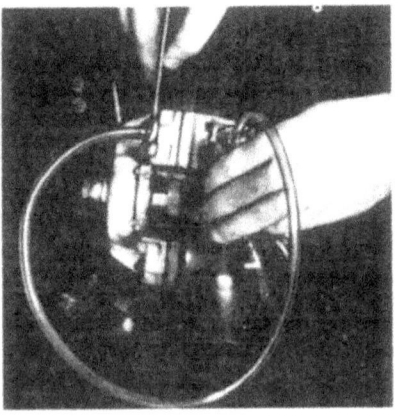

Bleeding Procedure

1. Remove dust cap from bleeder valve and attach bleeder hose.
2. Place the free end of the bleeder hose into a glass container which has some hydraulic fluid in it so that the hose can be submerged.
3. Quickly pump the brake pedal several times until pressure can be felt. Holding the pedal down, open the bleeder valve by about one-half turn and push the brake pedal all the way down. Do not release the pedal until the bleeder valve has been closed again.

Repeat this procedure until bubbles cease to appear in the fluid at the end of the hose.

4. Remove bleeder hose and install dust cap.
5. Repeat the above on all other bleeder valves in the outlined sequence. Make sure that the brake fluid reservoir does not run dry since this would allow air to enter the system again.

Caution:

Hydraulic brake fluid will damage the paint finish.

Brake fluid which has been pumped out of the brake system must not be used again.

6. Check for proper effect of bleeding and absence of leaks by holding the brake pedal under pressure.
7. Replenish brake fluid in the reservoir.

Hydraulic fluid level in the reservoir must be checked at regular intervals and replenished whenever below the top mark. Due to the relatively large cylinder cross-section in the brake calipers, the brake fluid level in the reservoir will decrease at a much faster rate, due to brake pad wear, than one is accustomed to observing in cars equipped with drum brakes.

Use only original ATE-BLAU hydraulic fluid. If the hydraulic system has been completely drained for any reason, such as complete brake overhaul, it may become necessary to bleed the brakes again after a short test drive.

Since the brakes are self-adjusting, brake pedal free travel will remain constant at all times providing that the brake system is free of air pockets. The pedal free travel represents approximately 30–50% of the total pedal travel. Subsequent to installation of new brake pads, the pedal free travel will be somewhat longer until the pads are conditioned and properly seated.

Adjusting Hand Brake

General

The hand brake is of the drum type. The action is mechanical and to rear wheels only.

1. To adjust the handbrake it is necessary to place the car on stands and remove the rear wheels.

2. Release the handbrake and free the rear brake discs by pushing all brake pads back.

3. Loosen cable lock nuts at the rear cable terminal and adjust the cable so that it has some slack.

4. Insert a screwdriver through the access hole in the parking brake drum and turn adjusting spur wheel until the brake disc no longer can be turned by hand.

5. Adjust the brake cable at the rear cable terminal so that it just begins to pull and tighten both lock nuts.

6. Turn the spur wheel to slacken the parking brake so that the disc turns without drag which normally requires backing off by about 6–8 teeth on the adjusting spur wheel.

7. Follow same procedure on the opposite brake.

8. Check free travel of parking brake lever. Road test car to ensure that parking brake works evenly. Should one-sided pulling be encountered, slacken spur wheel of the respective brake to attain even action.

9. Prior to driving, depress the brake pedal several times to bring the disc brake pistons and pads into their operating position. Check hydraulic fluid level in the reservoir.

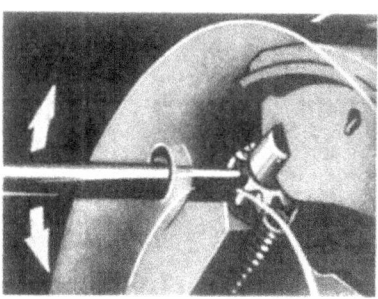

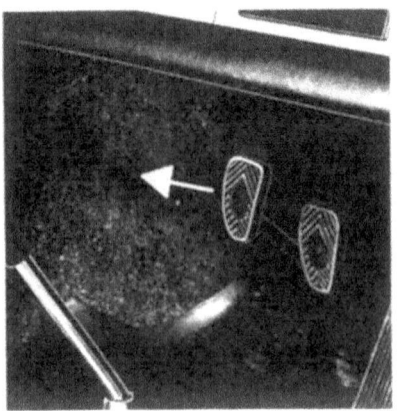

a Lock nut
b Adjusting nut

Checking and Adjusting Clutch Pedal Travel

Pedal Travel

The use of the diaphragm-type clutch pressure plate necessitates an exact limiting of clutch pedal travel. This adjustment should be checked when the transmission is warm and the engine running at idle speed. Depress clutch pedal and check ease of shifting into reverse gear. If the adjustment is correct, the reverse gear will engage practically clash-free. The pedal travel stop is a section of flat iron with an oval hole for adjustment, attached to a bracket directly in front of the clutch pedal with two 6 mm retaining bolts.

1. Unsnap forward part of floormat.
2. Loosen both stop retaining screws.
3. Move pedal stop up or down, as required, until locating the proper position, i. e., when the reverse gear will engage practically clash-free with the clutch at the point of complete disengagement.
4. Tighten pedal stop retaining screws.
5. Recheck pedal travel and fasten floormat in original position.

Checking and Adjusting Clutch

Pedal Free Travel

The correct pedal free travel is 15 to 20 mm (0.60 to 0.80 in.). It is checked by moving the clutch pedal in direction of the arrow.

Adjusting Free Travel

1. Loosen lock nut at cable rear terminal.
2. Turn adjusting nut until free travel of the clutch pedal is 15 to 20 mm (0.60 to 0.80 in.). Hold threaded cable terminal with pliers if necessary.

Adjusting Front Wheel Bearings

The front wheel bearings must be adjusted in close compliance with the following instructions to ensure long bearing life and prevent bearing failure.

Checking

Front wheel bearings are properly adjusted when the thrust washer at the outer bearing will still yield sideways with use of a screw driver as illustrated above. Prior to checking rotate wheel several times. Adjusting and checking should be done only when the hub is cold.

Adjusting

1. Remove dust cap from hub and loosen Allen screw which locks clamp nut.
2. Tighten or loosen clamp nut until adjusted so that the thrust washer will still yield sideways with use of a screw driver as illustrated above.

Adjusting Toe-In

Uneven wear found on one or more tires may be the result of improper toe-in adjustment. In such cases the car must be taken to a shop equipped with an optical wheel aligner to perform a proper check.

Note:
Toe-in can be measured only when the car is standing on its wheels on level ground since readings taken on a hoisted car will be incorrect. When measuring toe-in, the car must be empty with a full gasoline tank (empty DIN weight). See page 87, Specifications.

Wheels

Tire Pressure

The tires should be inspected for proper pressure and unusual wear or damage such as cuts, broken cords, and punctures as part of every maintenance inspection, before departure on longer trips, and at every given opportunity.

Check tire pressure when the tires are still cold.

Nominal tire pressures are as follows:
Front — 1.8 atm (26 psi)
Rear — 2.0 atm (29 psi)

Always use tires bearing the designation 6.9 H 15 or 165 HR 15.

Recommended tire pressure for snow tires:
front 2.0 atü (29 psi)
rear 2.2 atü (32 psi)

Be sure to always have your tires b a l a n c - e d. Hard breaking and uneven tire wear may necessitate rebalancing of the wheels.

Caution:
The tire pressure will increase progressively with increasing temperature; therefore, never let any air out of warm tires to meet cold tire pressure specifications.

Spare Wheel

The spare wheel is located under the front lid in the forward compartment. It should be remembered to check the spare tire pressure whenever checking other wheels. The spare tire should be inflated to the same pressure as the rear wheels.

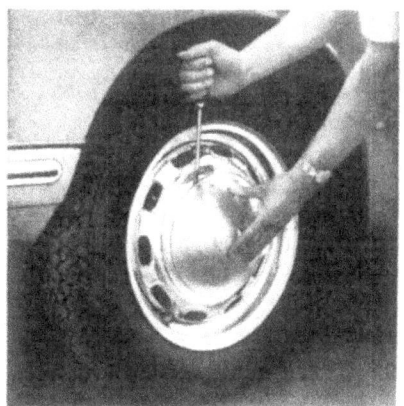  

Changing Wheels

1. Set hand brake and shift into 1st gear or reverse.
2. Remove hub cap from the respective wheel.
3. Loosen wheel lug nuts.
4. Press upper lock pawl of jack down to unlock jacking mechanism.
5. Keeping pawl down, push jacking transport all the way down.
6. Insert the square jack arm into jacking point, which is located below the body and door center, while holding the jack with the round steel pad down.
7. Push round support pipe all the way down.
8. Insert jacking lever into round socket in the jack pawl.
9. Jack the car up by moving the jacking lever up and down until the respective wheel raises off the ground.
10. Remove wheel lug nuts and pull the wheel off hub.
11. Mount spare tire and lightly tighten wheel lug nuts making certain that the cone-shaped end of each lug nut fits well into its concaved counterpart in the wheel rim.
12. Place jacking lever between both catches of the upper lock pawl and jack fork and press down to lower the car to the ground.
13. While holding the jacking lever in that position, pull round pipe of jack all the way up and withdraw jack from jacking support.
14. Tighten every other wheel lug nut (starting at the valve in sequence 1 – 3 – 5 – 2 – 4) until all nuts have been securely tightened. Mount hub cap.

Electrical System

Testing Battery

General

Good engine starting depends upon good condition of the battery. In general, battery care is confined to the addition of distilled water, testing specific gravity of the electrolyte, and testing cell voltage. The battery is located in the left forward part of the luggage compartment and is protected with a cover.

Adding Distilled Water

The level of the electrolytic solution contained in the battery decreases with time and use due to deterioration and evaporation of water contained in the electrolytic solution. Replenish only with distilled water. The liquid shall stand to the white strip or the control funnel respectively 10—15 mm (approx. $^1/_2$ inch) above the top of the battery plates.

Testing Specific Gravity of Electrolyte

Specific gravity of the electrolyte is tested with a hydrometer calibrated in degrees Beaumé or g/cm^3. The readings are interpreted as follows:

32° Bé = specific gravity 1.285 g/cm^3
= Battery fully charged
27° Bé = specific gravity 1.230 g/cm^3
= Battery half charged
18° Bé = specific gravity 1.142 g/cm^3
= Battery dead

Testing Battery Voltage

We recommend that battery voltage be tested in an auto-electric shop which will have the proper instruments for this task and provide reliable service.

Battery Care

1. The battery must be firmly attached to the car.
2. Battery terminals and cable clamps must be kept clean. Corrosion and oxydation can be prevented by coating the terminals and clamps with vaseline or terminal grease.
3. The vent caps must be securely tightened to prevent spillage.
4. Spilled electrolyte must be rinsed off at once with a solution of soda (baking soda will do the job) to neutralize the solution an prevent damage to fabrics and metal.

Automotive batteries will lose their potency when not in use; consequently, make certain that the battery is charged at intervals of approximately 6 weeks if the car is not in operation for prolonged periods. A discharged battery allows a rapid formation of sulfates on the plates leading to their deterioration.

---

1 Stoplights, directional blinkers, backup lights
2 Interior lights, cigarette lighter, electric clock
3 Auxiliary gasoline heater (optional)
4 Windshield wipers and washer pump
5 Fog lights (optional)
6 License plate light, luggage compartment light
7 Parking lights, right
8 Parking lights, left
9 Low beam, right
10 Low beam, left
11 High beam, right; high beam indicator
12 High beam, left

Replacing Fuses

The fuses are located in the left part of the luggage compartment and are protected by a plastic cover. The individual fuses can be identified by way of alphabetical symbols fuses are held by spring clamps and can be easily removed by hand.

A burnt fuse indicates an overload in the circuit. Consequently, it will not suffice to simply replace the fuse with a new one; if a fuse burns out, the circuit must be traced to determine the cause for the overload and the deficiency must be corrected.

The patching of fuses with wire or foil is not permissible since it may cause serious damage to the electrical components. It is advisable to carry an assortment of fuses in the car.

List of Bulbs (12 volt)

Headlamps	45/40 W
Foglamps	35 W
Backup light	25 W
Stop lights	18/5 W
Directional signals	18 W
Interior lights	10 W
Luggage compartment	5 W
Parking lights	4 W
License plate lights	4 W
Instrument lights	2 W
Control lamps	2 W

All fuses are 8/15 A except Fuse I (windshield wipers and washers) which is 25/40 A.

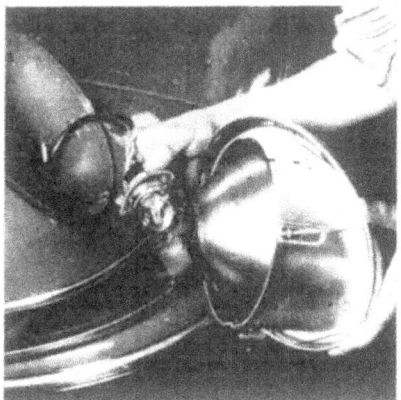
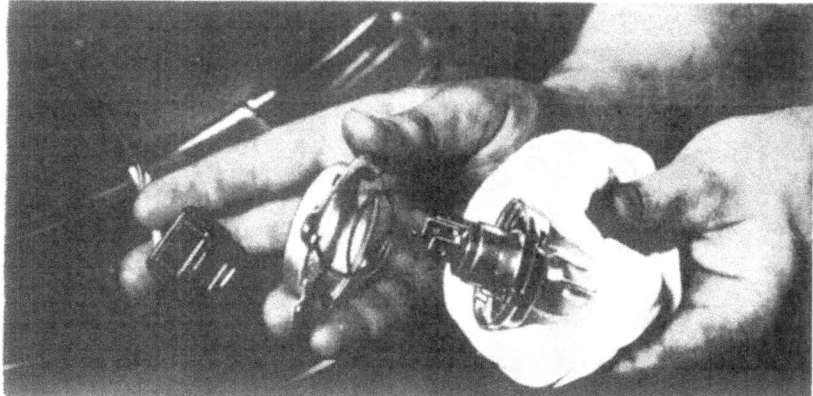

Bulb-Type Headlamps
Replacing Headlamp Bulbs

1. Unscrew retaining screw in bottom center of lamp rim and take lamp assembly out.
2. Disconnect plug from rear of lamp, depress spring-loaded bulb retainer and twist to left to remove, then pull bulb out of the base.
3. Insert new bulb. Make sure that socket guide prong of bulb is in the aligning slot in the base.
4. Place bulb retainer onto bulb socket, depress and lock with a twist to the right.
5. Connect plug to rear of bulb.
6. Install headlamp assembly and check lights for proper functioning.

Note:

Keep glass bulb free of grease or dirt, holding it only through a clean cloth or paper. When replacing the bulbs, make sure that they are well seated in the socket. Use only bulbs of brand specification and in identical pairs, i. e., of same brand and wattage.

Sealed-Beam Headlamps
Replacement

1. Unscrew retaining screw in bottom center of lamp rim and take lamp assembly out.
2. Disconnect plug from rear of lamp.
3. Remove spring clips from lamp rim by carefully pressing these down and inward with the thumb; do not use screwdrivers or similar tools since this may allow the spring clips to fly off, possibly beyond recovery, and could cause an eye injury. Pull out inner retaining ring and the sealed-beam unit.
4. Install sealed-beam unit in the reverse order of the above. Check lights for proper functioning.

65

Blink, Stop, Park, and Backup Lights
Replacing Bulbs

1. Unscrew slotted retaining screws of lamp assembly and remove assembly.
2. Using a screwdriver lift open a corner of the plastic holder and remove it.
3. Push bulb into the holder and remove with a twist to left (bayonet mount).
4. Replace bulb.

Note:

Keep glass bulb free of grease and dirt, hold it only through a clean cloth or soft paper.

5. Insert bulb by pushing it in and twisting 90° to the right to seat the retaining prongs.
6. Install holder in lamp assembly with slight pressure and allow to snap into place.
7. Install lamp assembly and tighten slotted retaining screws.
8. Check lights for proper functioning.

66

Fog Lights
Replacing Bulbs

1. Unscrew rim retaining screw and take lamp assembly off.
2. Pull out bulb holder from the lamp (snap-fit).
3. Remove bulb by pushing it into holder and turning to the left (bayonet mount).
4. Replace bulb.

Note:

Keep glass bulb free of grease and dirt, hold it only through a clean rag or soft paper.

5. Push bulb into holder and turn to the right.
6. Insert bulb holder into lamp and push in firmly.
7. Install lamp assembly into base and tighten retaining screws.
8. Check fog lights for proper functioning.

Adjusting Bulb-Type Headlamps
(Applies to asymmetric-beam design)

The following instructions are in compliance with the German Traffic Code. Cars registered outside the German Federal Republic must be handled in accordance with local laws.

If optical lamp adjusting devices are not at hand, the lights can be adjusted by projecting the light beams onto a screen. The aiming screen, or the optical device — depending on which is used — must be placed exactly in line (optical viewer) or exactly perpendicular (screen) to the longitudinal axis of the vehicle. It is most essential that: the car is standing on level ground; the tires are properly inflated; the weight conditions include a full gasoline tank without passenger or driver in the car, or a nearly empty tank with driver aboard; the car is standing 5 meters (197 inches) away from the screen. Before initiating the adjusting procedure, push the car back and forth a few times to normalize the attitude of the wheel suspension.

Headlights of the asymmetric beam design are adjusted according to the low beam projection only. Each headlamp must be adjusted separately with the other lamp covered up. Adherence to the above preliminaries is mandatory to ensure good illumination of the road without blinding oncoming drivers.

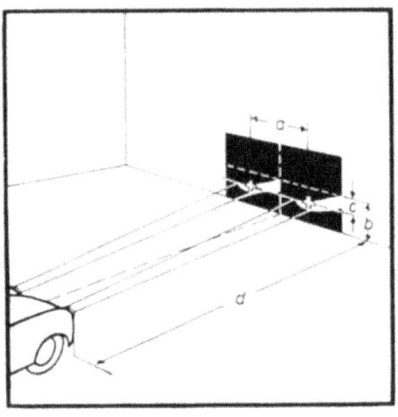

Lateral Adjustment (right/left)

The lateral aim is correct when the bisecting lines of the low beam projection and the diagonal line of the asymmetric shoulder sweep (both for upper beam perimeters) fall onto the cross marked on the screen.

Vertikal Adjustment (up/down)

The vertical adjustment is correct when the upper perimeter of the low beam projection (this is the border between the bright and dark areas) extends horizontally to the left from the cross, along the aiming line, with the diagonal projection of the asymmetric sweep falling to the right of the cross.

a = distance between headlamp centers
b = height between ground and headlamp centers
c = 1 % of the distance from the headlamps to the aiming screen (50 mm or 2 in.)
d = distance from aiming screen to headlamps (5 m or 197 in.)

If the lateral adjustment required an extensive correction, recheck the vertical adjustment since it may require correction.

To adjust the headlamps, turn the slotted screw in the lamp rim as follows:

Vertical adjustment (upper screw)
 Clockwise = lower
 Counter-clockwise = higher

Lateral adjustment (lower screw)
 Clockwise = to left
 Counter-clockwise = to right

"Right" or "Left" is as seen from the driver's seat.

a Lateral adjustment
b Vertical adjustment
c Lamp retaining screw

If your car is equipped with the asymmetric headlamps, which is a type sending a road-shoulder-sweeping beam, and you are passing through a country where driving on the left side of the road is required, cover the asymmetric light outlet in the headlamp lens with tape or other opaque material. This will block the right-side sweeping beam and, thus, prevent your blinding other drivers approaching on your right hand side of the road.

Position of standard German license plate (rear)

Adjusting Sealed-Beam Headlamps

Right screw = lateral adjustment (left/right)
    clockwise = left
    counter-clockwise = right
Left-screw = vertical adjustment (up/down)
    clockwise = up
    counter-clockwise = down

Tool Kit

The tool kit is standard equipment. It is kept in the luggage compartment under the front lid. The tool kit contains all tools needed for roadside repairs or minor adjustments. The jack is also located in the front luggage compartment, i.e., the extreme forward end under the cover mat.

Kit Contents
(Subject to changes)

Spark plug wrench
Wheel nut wrench
5 open-end wrenches
Box-end wrench
Screwdriver
Philips screwdriver
Combination pliers
V-Belt
Tire pressure gauge
Plastic bag with fuses

a Fuel tank drain
b Towing hook

Towing Hook and Fuel Tank Drain

The Type 912 is equipped with a towing hook on the body underside which should be used when towing the car.
Draining the fuel tank has been made possible by the inclusion of a drain plug (a). To drain, remove the plug and the tank filler cap. When reinstalling the drain plug, make sure that the gasket is in good condition.

GENERAL DESCRIPTION

The Type 912 is a unitized assembly (Sunroof option). The engine and transmission are located at the rear of the car. Hydraulic disc brakes and independent torsion bar wheel suspension on all wheels characterize the undercarriage. The design aspects and individual components are described in detail under appropriate title headings.

Engine Cross-Section

1 Clutch
2 Flywheel
3 Main bearing journal, Bearing 2
4 Blower intake
5 Blower impeller
6 Blower housing
7 Oil filler
8 Generator
9 Generator support
10 Fan belt
11 Spacers for fan belt adjustment
12 Bearing insert, Bearing 4
13 Retaining screw
14 Flywheel gland nut
15 Cylinder and piston
16 Camshaft
17 Oil strainer
18 Filtering magnet
19 Connecting rod bearing cap
20 Oil suction tube
21 Camshaft gear
22 Oil pump
23 Camshaft drive gear
24 Distributor drive gear
25 Crankshaft pulley

Underside View of Car

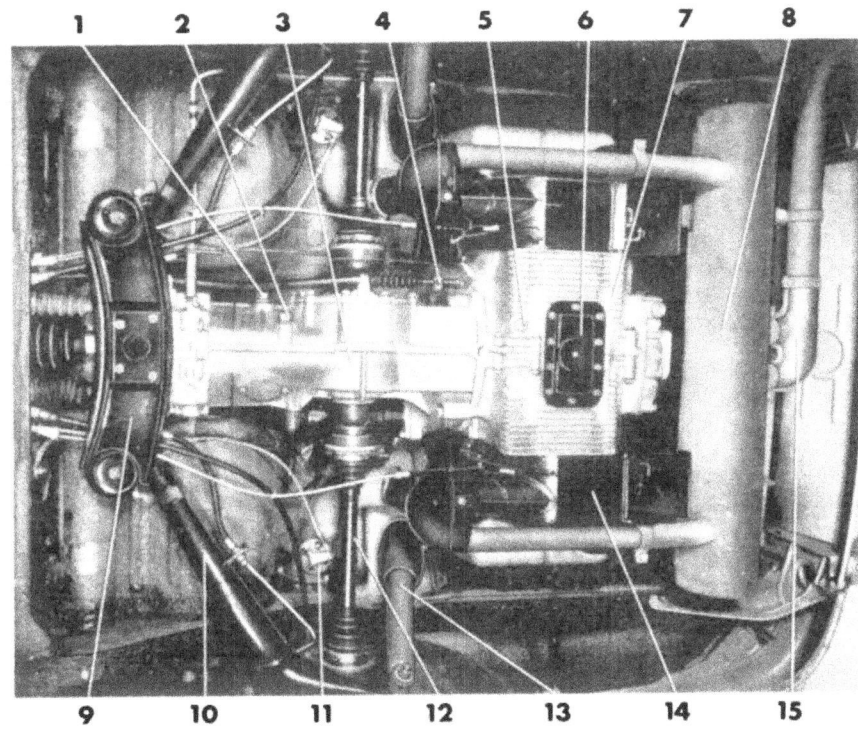

1. Transmission oil filler plug
2. Transmission oil drain plug
3. Transmission
4. Clutch release arm
5. Engine oil drain plug
6. Oil strainer cover with magnetic filter
7. Engine
8. Exhaust muffler
9. Transmission support
10. Rear axle control arm
11. Heater boxes
12. Rear axle universal shaft
13. Shock absorber
14. Hot-air guide for heating
15. Exhaust manifold

Transmission

The transmission and differential are contained in a common housing. All forward gears are synchronized. When the gears are shifted from one speed to another, a toothed sliding sleeve moves off the synchronizing ring running with the previously engaged gear, passes thru the neutral position, and slides onto the synchronizing ring of the selected gear; the servo components provide an additional thrust to the synchronizing ring permitting rapid synchronization of the differing gear speeds for easy and fast shifting of gears.

Once the speeds are synchronized, the toothed sliding sleeve moves on to engage the synchronizing drive ring, thus making a positive mechanical connection between the selected gear and the pinion shaft.

Four-Speed Transmission (Optional)

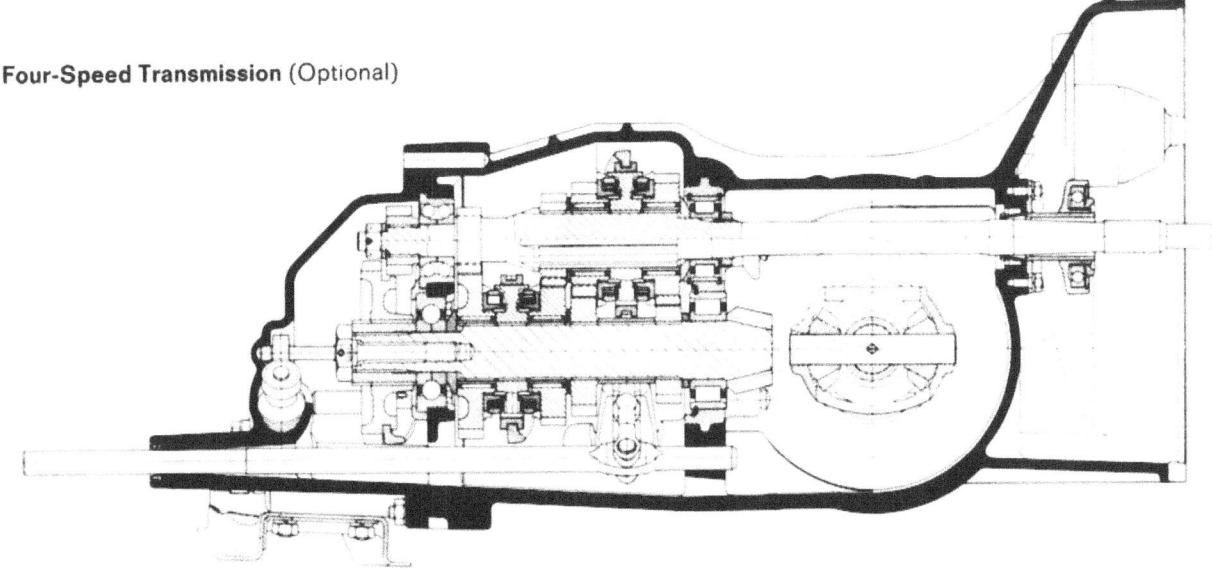

Five-Speed Transmission

1 Shift rod
2 Oil seal
3 Tachometer take-off
4 Gear shaft
5 Pinion shaft
6 Synchronizing ring
7 Spider
8 Selector fork
9 Sliding sleeve
10 Gear 1 (5th speed)
11 Input shaft
12 Differential housing
13 Differential pinion
14 Carrier shaft
15 Oil seal
16/17 Clutch release bearing

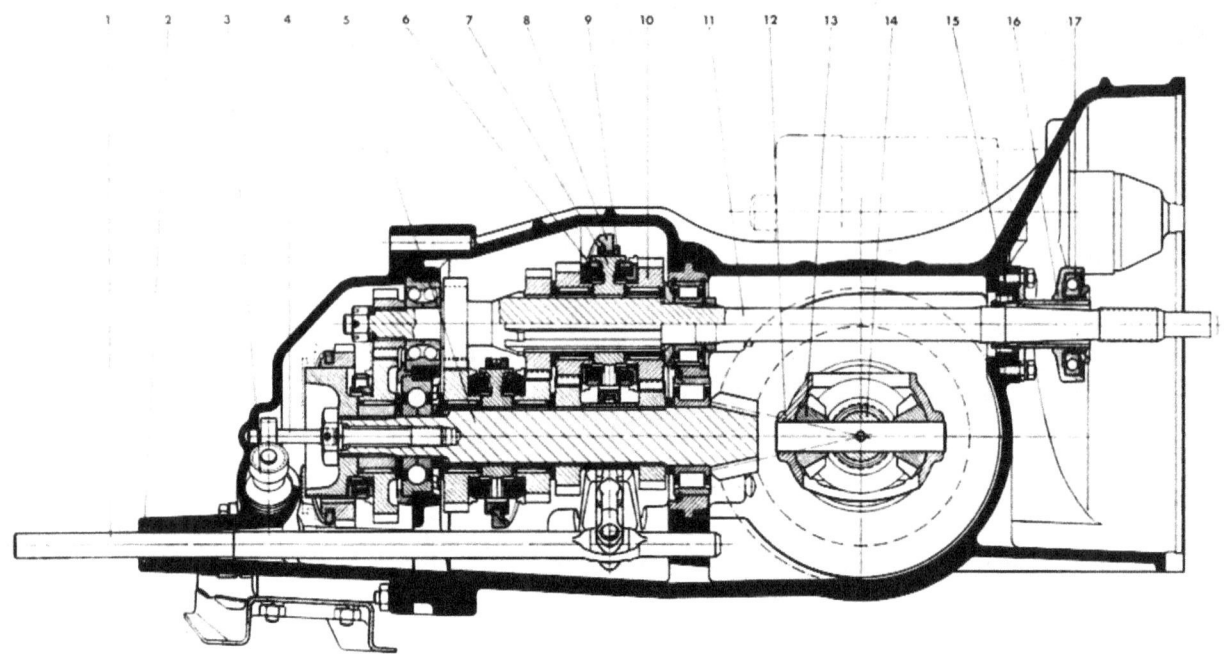

Rear Drive and Suspension

Both rear wheels are guided by triangulated control arms and driven by double-joint half axles. Each wheel is independently suspended. Springing is effected by a round transverse torsion bar on each side. A progressively acting rubber buffer is provided in each of the two telescopic shockabsorbers to supplement springing of each wheel. Both torsion bars can be accurately adjusted to specifications since the ends of each torsion bar have a different number of splines making very fine resettings possible. All joints are permanently lubricated and are service free.

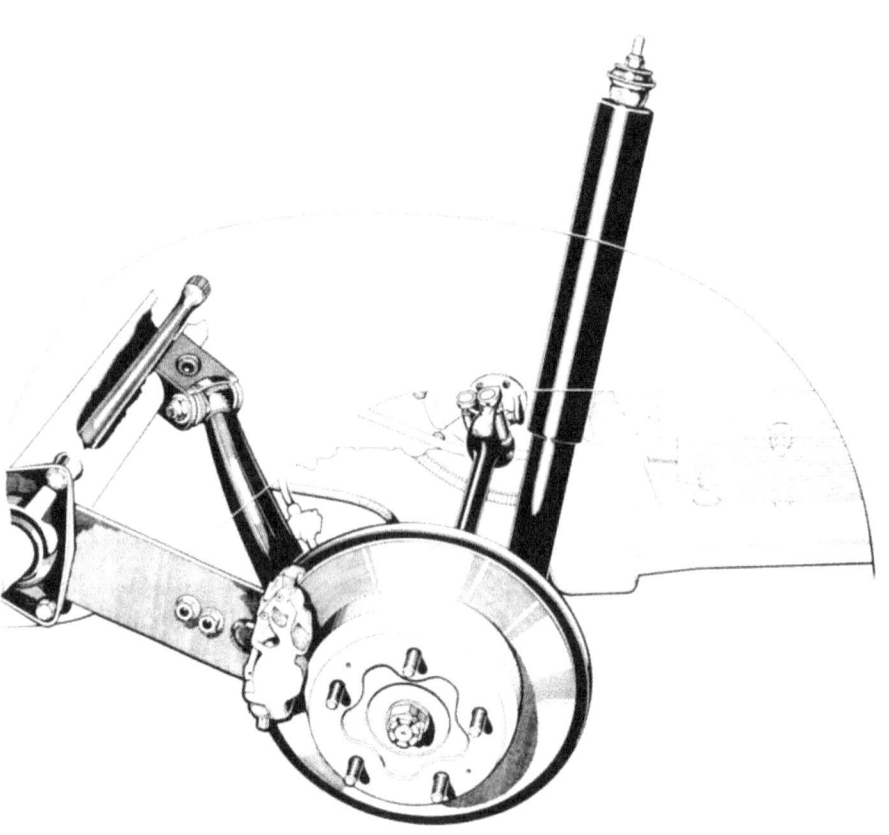

Front Axle

The independent front wheel suspension incorporates transverse control arms and shockabsorbers struts. Front wheel springing is accomplished thru longitudinal, adjustable, and service-free torsion rods on each side, each attached to a transverse control arm. A progressively acting rubber buffer has been incorporated into each of the two shockabsorber struts. A stabilizing bar complements the cornering qualities. All joints are service-free.

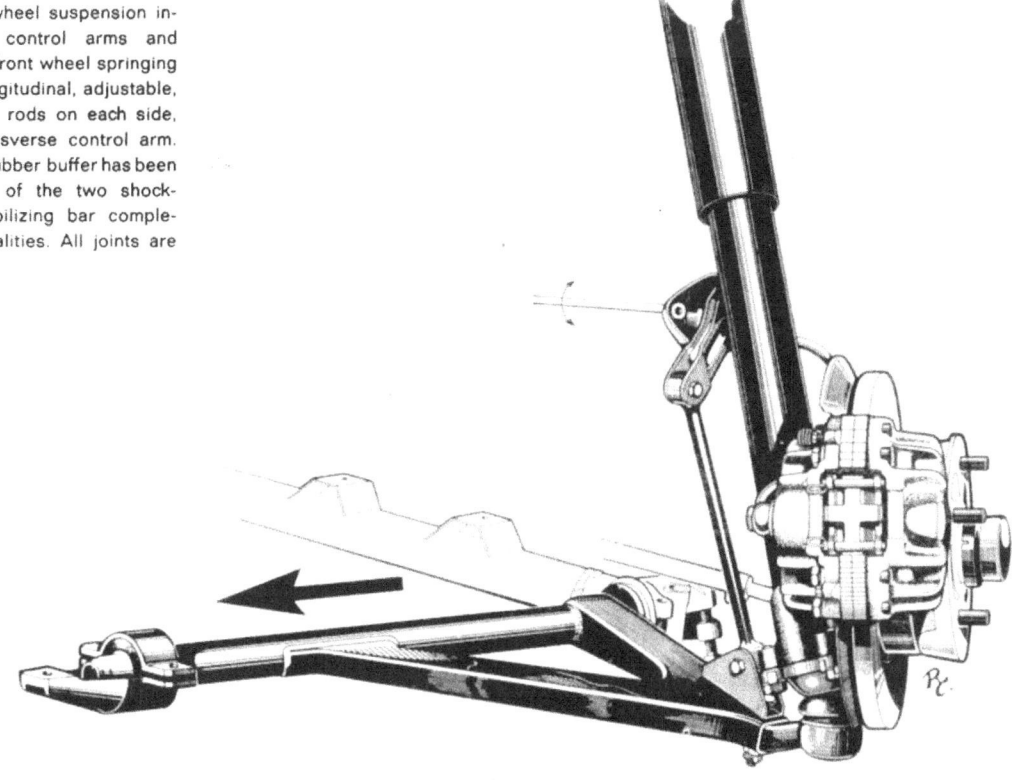

Steering

The positive action rack and pinion steering assembly lies in a symmetrical location of the front axle assembly. Movements of the steering wheel are transmitted mechanically to the steering pinion thru an offset relay shaft running in two permanently lubricated universal joints. This arrangement, as compared with that of a solid steering post, is not only of technical advantage but also offers good protection against injuries resulting from possible mishaps.

1 Threaded joint socket
2 Steering housing
3 Adjusting nut
4 Pressure block
5 Steering pinion
6 Steering rack
7 Rubber boot
8 Bushing

Brakes

The service brakes (foot brake) are of the hydraulic disc type acting on all four wheels and incorporating automatic self-adjustment. The parking brake is mechanically operated and acts on rear wheels only; the parking brake is of the drum type and represents a separate system.

Body

The all-steel body is welded to the underbody forming a unitized assembly. The doors are attached to the forward door posts on concealed hinges. The outside door locks match the ignition key.

The doors can also be locked from the inside by depressing a lock button located a top each door ledge; however, to prevent a lockout, the doors cannot be locked from the outside by depressing the lock button and slamming the door shut, locking from the outside being possible only with the key.

The windshield consists of laminated glass. All other windows are of tempered glass. The individual bucket seats are fully reclining and slide on rails attached to the floor, permitting an adjustment of the seats to individual needs. Both rear seats have folding backrests which make into a luggage platform when folded down.

The front and rear lids are mounted on concealed hinges. The front lid lock release is located on the left side of the instrument panel; the rear lid release is accomodated in the rear door-post. A safety catch in the front lid prevents an accidental wind-lifting of the lid at speed when the lid lock should malfunction for any reason.

Electrical System

A generator provides the current for the 12 Volt system. Engine starting is through a solenoid-controlled engine starter motor. A battery ignition system is utilized.

The backup lights go on automatically when reverse gear is engaged.

TECHNICAL DATA

Engine

Number of Cylinders	4
Bore	82.5 mm (3.25 in.)
Stroke	74.0 mm (2.92 in.)
Displacement, actual	1582 cc (96.5 cu.in.)
Compression Ratio	9.3:1
Horsepower Rating	90 DIN HP (102 SAE HP) @ 5800 RPM
Maximum Torque	12.4 DIN mkp; 13.5 SAE mkp; (97.6 lbs/ft) @ 3500 RPM
Specific Power Output	57 DIN HP/liter (1.06 SAE HP/cu.in.)

Engine Design Specifications

Engine Type	Horizontally opposed, four-stroke-cycle four
Cooling	Air cooled
Cylinders	Indicidual; grey cast iron liner with finned light alloy jacket
Cylinder Heads	Light alloy
Number of Valver, per cylinder	1 intake, 1 exhaust
Valve Arrangement	Overhead, in "V"
Valve Timing	Pushrods and rocker arms
Camshaft	In crankcase below crankshaft, in 3 bearings
Crankshaft	Forged, 4 plain bearings
Connecting Rod Bearings	Plain bearings, tri-metal inserts
Cooling Blower Drive	V-belt, thru generator
Crankshaft/Blower Ratio	Approx. 1.8:1
Engine Lubrication	Pressure lubrication; oil filter in by-pass circuit; oil cooler
Fuel Pump	Mechanical
Carburetors	Two dual-throat downdraft Solex 40 PJJ-4

Electrical System

Operating Voltage	12 Volts
Battery Capacity	45 Ah
Radio Noise Suppression	Remote suppression according to German requirements per VDE 0879/Part 1
Generator Output	300 W (max)
Ignition Type	Battery
Firing Order	1 – 4 – 3 – 2
Stationary Firing Point	3° BTDC
Spark Plugs	Bosch W 200 T 35, Champion UL-82 Y
	Bosch W 225 T 1, Bosch W 225 T 7, Beru P 225/14
Spark Plug Gap	0.6 mm (.024 in.)

Power Train

Engine Location	At rear, behind rear axle
Clutch	Single plate, dry disc
Transmission	Porsche, servo-lock synchronization
Number Gears	5 forward, 1 reverse; 4 forward, 1 reverse optional
Gearshift Location	On floor
Final Drive	Spiral bevel pinion and differential
Drive Ratio	7:31, i = 4.428
Rear Axle Drive	Swinging half-axles
Gear Ratios	See transmission diagram, pages 91 and 92

Chassis and Suspension

Frame	Welded assembly of sheetmetal box sections, unitized with body
Front Suspension	IFS (independent front suspension) with suspension struts and transverse arms
Front Wheel Springing	1 round, longitudinal torsion bar per wheel
Rear Suspension	IRS (independent rear suspension) half-axle drive, with trailing arms
Rear Wheel Springing	1 round, transverse torsion bar per wheel
Shockabsorbers	Double acting hydraulic, front and rear

Service Brakes	Hydraulic disc brakes on all wheels
Parking Brake	Mechanical, duo-servo, drum type, to rear wheels only
Effective Brake Disc Diameter	Front: 235 mm (9.25 in.); rear: 243 mm (9.57 in.)
Braking Area (Service Brake), per wheel	Front: 52.5 cm^2 (8.14 sq.in.); rear: 40.0 cm^2 (6.20 sq.in.)
Total Effective Braking Area (Service Brake)	185 cm^2 (28.7 sq.in.)
Parking Brake Drum Diameter	180 mm (7.09 in.)
Total Effective Braking Area (Parking Brake)	210 cm^2 (32.4 in.)
Wheel Rims	4 5 J x 15
Tire Type	6.9 H 15 or 165 HR 15
Steering	ZF rack & pinion
Steering Ratio	1:16.5 in center
Wheel Camber (DIN curb weight)	Front: 0 ± 20'; rear: −1° 15' ± 20'
Kingpin Incination (DIN curb weight)	10°56'
Toe-in (DIN curb weight)	Front: 40'; rear: 0° ± 10'
Caster (DIN curb weight)	6° 45' ± 45'

Filling Capacities

Engine	Approx. 4 liters (4.2 US qts) premium grade HD oil; summer SAE 30, winter SAE 20
Transmission and Differential	Approx. 2.5 liters (2.6 US qts) SAE 90 hypoid gear lubricant
Fuel Tank	62 liters (16.4 US gals) including approx 6 liters (1.6 US gals) reserve; required octane rating: 96 octanes (premium fuel)
Hydraulic Fluid Reservoir	Approx. 0.2 liter (7 fl.oz.)
Windshield Washer Reservoir	Approx. 2 liters (2.1 US qts)

Dimensions

Wheelbase	2211 mm (87.05 in.)
Track, front	1353 mm (53.27 in.)
Track, rear	1321 mm (52.00 in.)
Overall Length	4163 mm (163.90 in.)
Overall Width	1610 mm (63.39 in.)
Overall Height (car empty)	1320 mm (51.97 in.)
Ground Clearance (car loaded)	150 mm (5.9 in.)
Turning Circle	ca. 10.3 m (33.8 ft.)

Weights

DIN Curb Weight	970 kp (2138 lbs)
Total Permissible Weight	1290 kp (2844 lbs)
Permissible Axle Load, front	570 kp (1257 lbs)
Permissible Axle Load, rear	750 kp (1653 lbs)
Engine Weight, less oil	ca. 124 kp (274 lbs)
Transmission Weight, with oil	ca. 50 kp (110 lbs)

Performance

Maximum Speed	185 km/h (115 mph)
Power-to-Weight Ratio	10.7 kp/DIN HP (21 lbs/SAE HP)
Fuel Consumption	8.5 l/100 km (27.6 MPG-US)
Max. oil consumption	1,5 to 2,0 l/1000 km (1,32 to 1,76 quarts/ 620 miles)

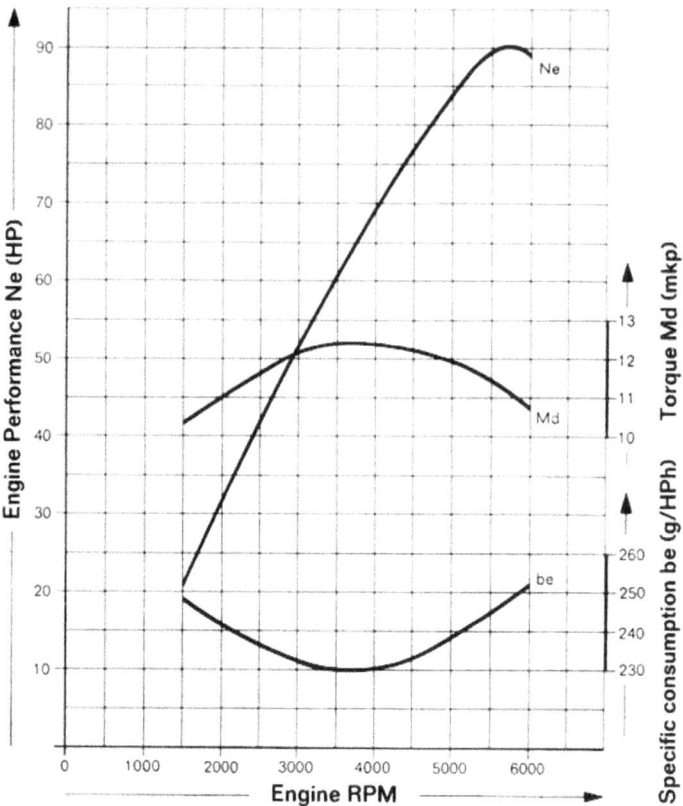

Engine Performance and Fuel Consumption Type 912

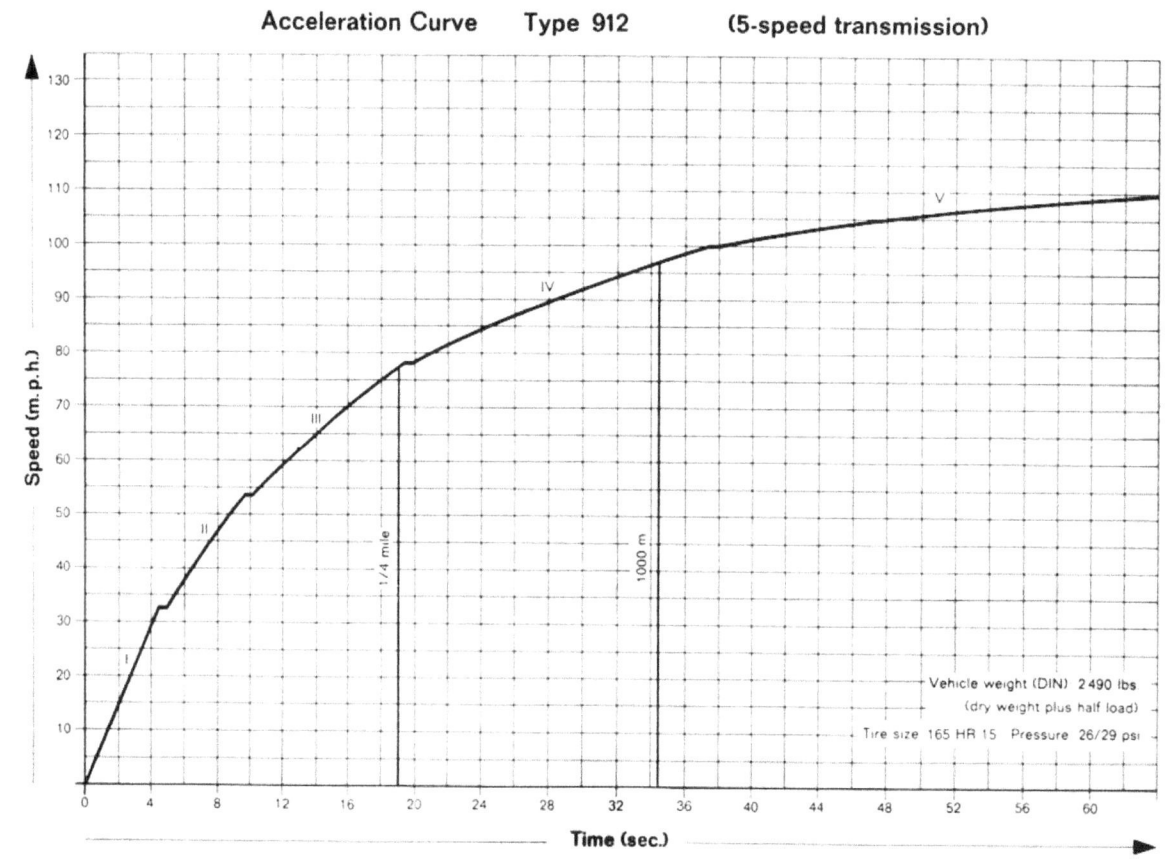

Acceleration Curve   Type 912   (5-speed transmission)

Vehicle weight (DIN) 2490 lbs (dry weight plus half load)
Tire size 165 HR 15   Pressure 26/29 psi

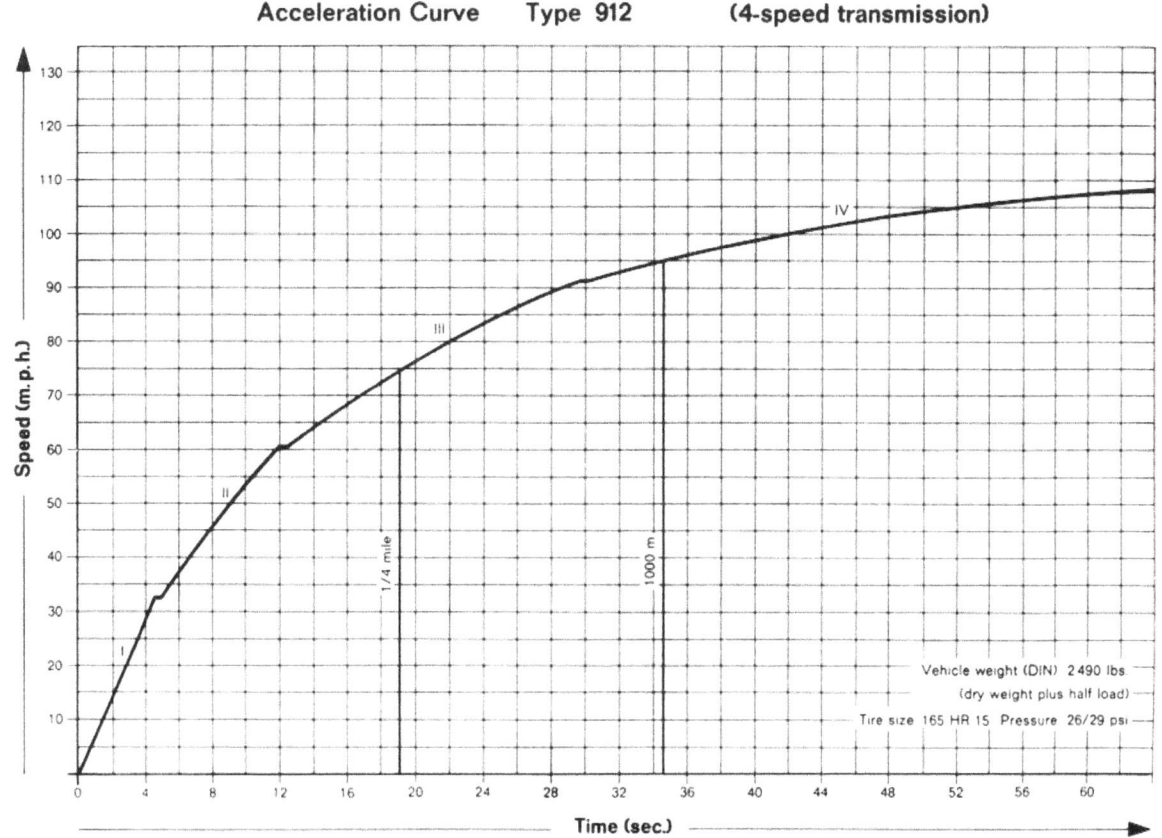

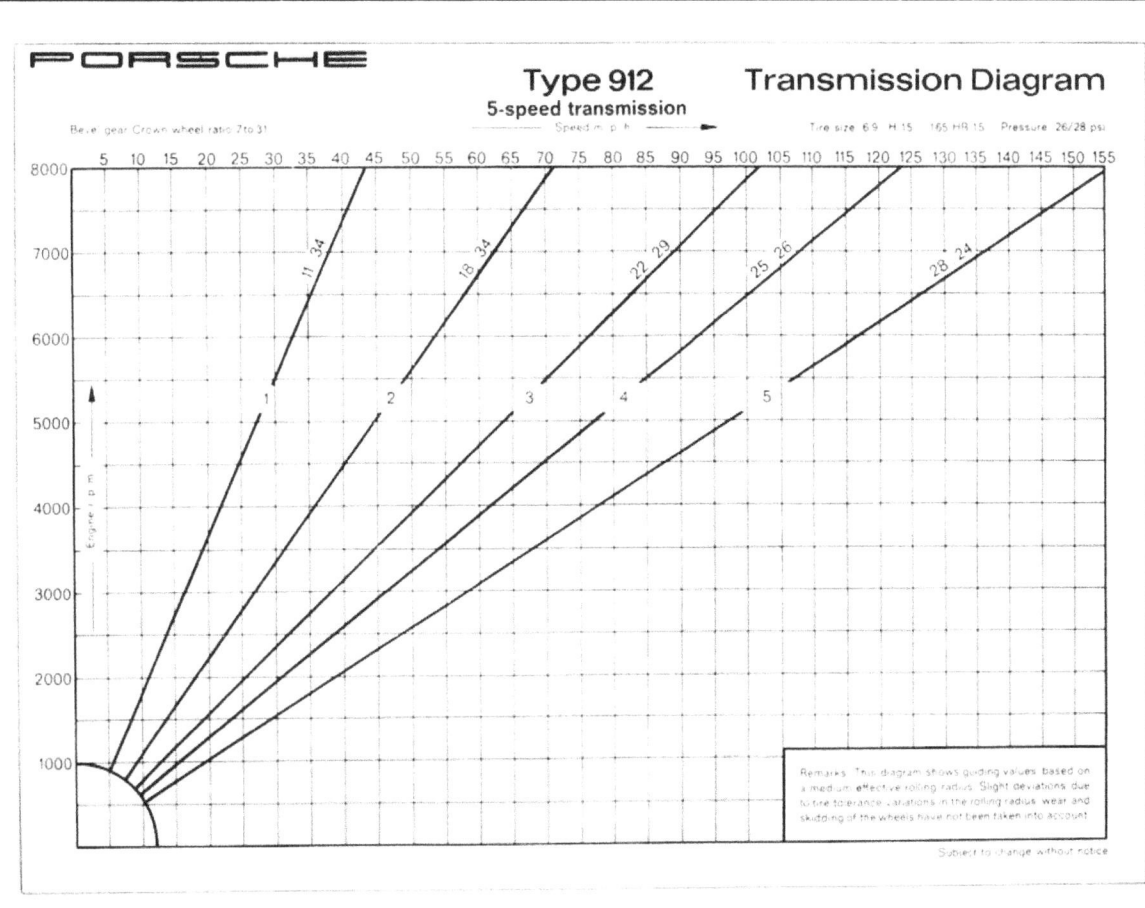

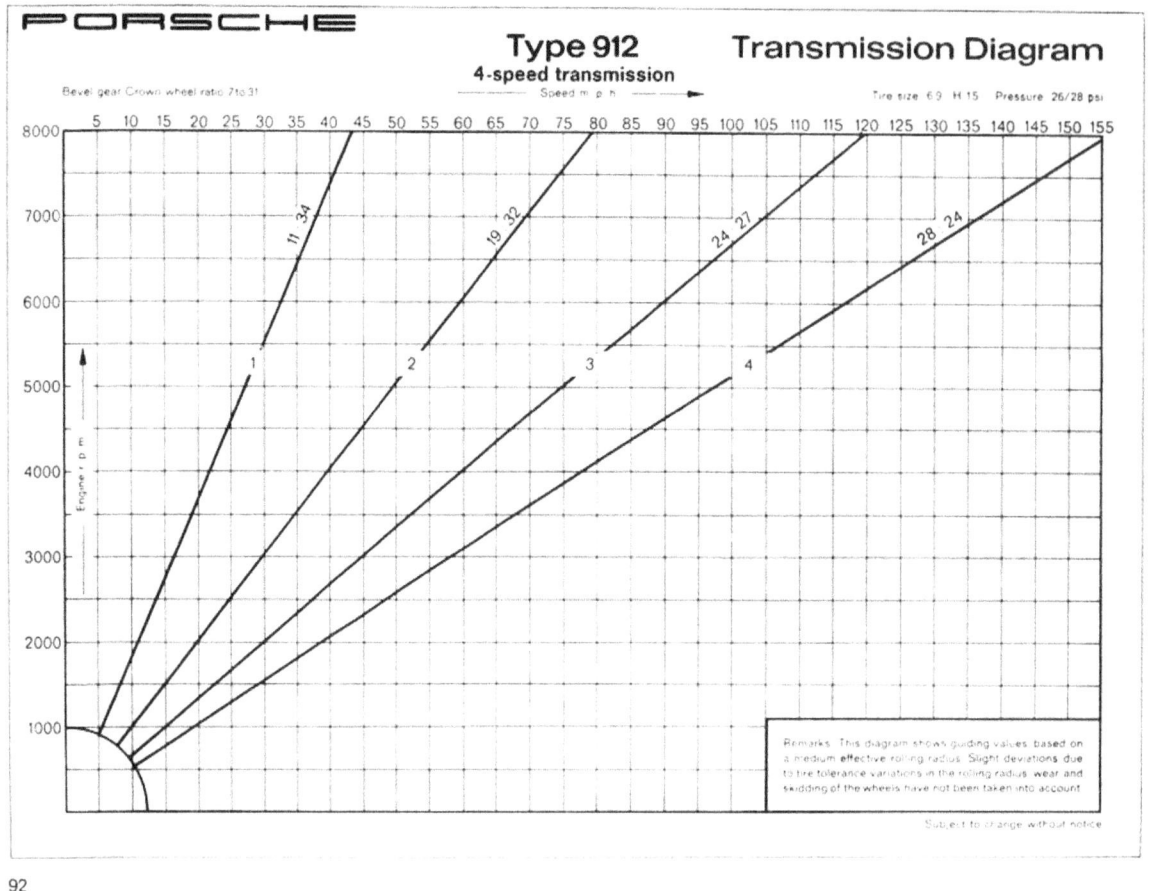

Relative Index

A

Acceleration curves	89, 90
Acid — battery	63
Adjust — blower belt	53
— breaker points	48
— carburetor idling	52
— clutch	59
— front wheel bearings	60
— hand brake	58
— headlights, bulb-type	68
— headlights, sealed-beams	69
— idling speed	52
— ignition timing	47
— parking brake	58
— spark plug gap	46
— toe-in	61
— valve clearance	45
Air cleaners	50
Air Conditioner	24, 24 a
Air pressure — tires	61
Arm rest — door button	19
Asymmetric headlamps	
— adjust	68
— replace bulbs	65

B

Backrest — adjust	18
— lock	19
Backup lights	81
Battery care	63
Belts — safety	26
Bleeding brakes	56
Blinkers — emergency signal	26
— directional signal	17
— change bulbs	66
Blower belt — cooling	53
Body — cleaning	36
— cleaning materials	39
— description	73, 81
— serial number	27
Brake pads — description	54
— conditioning	55
Brake pedal travel	14
Brake system — bleeding	56
Brakes — disc	28, 54, 80
— parking (hand)	58
Breaker points — ignition	48
Break-in rules	7
Bulb chart	64
Bulb-type headlamps	
— change bulbs	65
— adjust	68

C

Camber/caster	87
Capacities	87
Carburetors — cleaning	50
— description	51
— lubricate linkage	49
Car washing	36
Care and lubrication	29
Care of coachwork	36
Care of the finish	36
Changing — engine oil	32
— oil filter cartridge	35
— transmission oil	35
— wheels	62
Chassis — description	78
— serial number	27
Checking — clutch pedal travel	59
— engine oil level	32
— spark plugs	46
— transmission oil level	35
Chrom trim care	37
Cigarette lighter	21
Cleaning — air cleaners	50
— battery	63
— body	36
— carburetors	50
— fuel pump screen	49
— glass	38
— jets	50
— magnetic filter	34
— materials	39

— oil filter	35	
— oil strainer	34	
— spark plugs	46	
Clutch — pedal	14	
— pedal adjustment	59	
Coachwork cleaning materials	39	
Cold engine starting	7	
Cold weather operation	28	
Compression ratio	85	
Conditioning brake pads	55	
Control lamps	13	
Cylinder numbering	45	

D

Defroster	23, 24
Differential — oil capacity	87
Dimensions	88
Dimmer Switch	17
Directional signals — pilot lamp	13
— switch	17
Disc brakes	28, 54, 80
Displacement — engine	85
Distributor — contact points	48
— lubrication	47
Dome light	20
Door locks	19
Door release, inside	19
Drain plug — fuel	70

E

Electric sun roof	25
Electrical — system	63, 81
— specifications	86
— ignition	47
Electrolyte — battery	63
Emergency blinkers	26
Engine — adjust valve clearance	45
— compartment lid	22
— description	44, 74
— maximum rpm	7
— max rpm on downshift	15
— oil changing	32
— oil filter	35
— oil screen	34
— oil type and quantity	87
— serial number	27
— specifications	85
— starting	7

F

Fabrics and upholstery	37
Fan belt	53
Filling capacities	87
Filters — air	50
— fuel pump	49
oil	35
Firing order	86
Fog lamps — description	26
— changing bulbs	67

H

Hand brake — adjusting	58
— control lamp	13
— description	14
Headlights — adjusting bulb-type	68
— adjusting sealed-beam	69
— dimmer switch	17
— flasher signal	17
— replacing bulbs	65
— replacing sealed beams	65
Heating and Ventilation	23, 23 a
Heating system schematic	23
High beam indicator	13
Hood catch	22, 81
Horn — signal	4
Hydraulic brake system	28, 54, 80

I

Idle speed adjustment	52
Identification plates	27
Ignition — contact points	48
— distributor	47
— spark plugs	46
— switch	16
— timing	47
Indicator lights	13
Inside mirror	21
Instrument lights	16
Instruments	11
Interior lights	20

J

Jack	61, 62
Jets — cleaning	50
Jet size — high altitude	52

L

Lamps	64
Leather and leatherette cleaning	37
Lid locks	22
Light bulb chart	64
Light switch	16
Lighter — cigarette	21
Lubrication schedule	31
Luggage compartment lid	22

M

Magnetic oil filter	34
Maintenance and tune-up	41
Manifold heater	23, 24
Maximum engine rpm	7
Mechanical fuel pump	49
Mirror	21

N

Nomenclature plates	27

O

Octane rating	87
Oil — change (engine)	32
— change (transmission)	35

Free travel — clutch	59
Front axle	79
Front lid release	22
Front suspension	
— general	79
— toe-in	61
— wheel bearings	60
Fuel — consumption	88
— drain plug	70
— filter	49
— gauge	11
— octane rating	87
— pump cleaning	49
— reserve	87
— tank capacity	87
— tank filler neck	21
Fuses	64

G

Gasoline — octane rating	87
— filler neck	21
Gearbox description	76
Gear lubricant	87
Gearshift — pattern	15
— lubrication	35
Gear ratios	91, 92
Generator — control lamp	13
— output	86
Glass cleaning	38
Ground clearance	88

— type and viscosity	87
— filler neck	33
— filter	35
— level checking, engine	32
— level checking, transmission	35
— pressure control lamp	13
— pump	74
— strainer cleaning	34
— temperature gauge	11
Operating instructions	5
Overnight parking lights	17

P

Paint finish care	36
Parking brake — adjusting	58
— control lamp	13
Parking lights — control lamp	13
— overnight parking	17
Pedal free travel (clutch)	14, 59
Performance	88
Points — ignition	48
Polishing car	37
Pressure — oil	13
— tires	61
Preventive maintenance	43
Protective undercoating	37
Pulley — generator (V-belt adjust)	53
Pump — fuel	49
— oil	74
— windshield washer	19

281

R

Ratio — rear axle	86
— steering	87
— transmission	91, 92
Rear axle — description	78
— oil capacity	87
Rear lid lock release	22
Rear swivel windows	26
Rear drive and suspension	78
Rear view mirror	21
Reclining seats	18
RPM — maximum	7
Rubber weatherstripping	38
Running-in — engine	7
— brake pads	55

S

Safety belts	26
Sealed-beam headlamps — replace	65
— adjust	69
Seat adjustment	18
Serial numbers	27
Service and adjustments	43
Service brakes	54, 28, 80
Service schedule	43
Shifting gears	15
Shockabsorbers	78, 79
Side windows — rear	26
Signal and dimmer switch	17
Spare wheel — change	62
— location	61
Spark plugs	46, 86
Specifications	85
Speedometer	12
Spots and stains	36
Starter/ignition switch	16
Starting engine	7
Steering — description	80
— lock	16
— ratio	87
Stoplight bulb, change	66
Sunroof	25
Suspension — front and rear	78, 79
Switch — dimmer	17
— ignition/starter	16
— lights	16
— turn indicator	17
— windshield washer/wiper	19
Synthetic leather — cleaning	37

T

Tachometer	10, 12
Tail lights	66
Tank filler cover	21
Technical data	85
Temperature gauge — oil	11
Testing — battery	63
Timing — ignition	47
Tires	61
Toe-in	61
Tool kit	70
Torsion bars	78, 79
Towing hook	70
Track	88
Transmission — description	76
— diagram	91, 92
— oil capacity	87
— oil change	35
— oil type	87
— ratios	91, 92
— section view	76, 77
— serial number	27
— gear shifting	15, 76

U

Undercoating	37
Upholstery — cleaning	37
Underside view of car	75

V

Valve adjustment	45
V-belt	53
Ventilation	23, 24

W

Warm engine starting	9
Washing the car	36
Weatherstripping	38
Weights	88
Wheelbearings — front	60
Wheels — spare wheel	61, 62
— tire pressure	61
— toe-in	61, 87
Windshield — glass cleaning	38
— washers and wipers	19

A SAMPLE LIST OF OTHER BOOKS AVAILABLE FROM VELOCEPRESS

VELOCEPRESS MOTORCYCLE BOOKS & MANUALS

AJS SINGLES 1955-65 350cc & 500cc (BOOK OF)
ARIEL 1939-1960 4 STROKE SINGLES (BOOK OF)
ARIEL LEADER & ARROW 1958-1964 (BOOK OF)
ARIEL MOTORCYCLES 1933-1951 WSM
ARIEL PREWAR MODELS 1932-1939 (BOOK OF)
BMW M/CYCLES R26 R27 (1956-1967) FACTORY WSM
BMW M/CYCLES R50 R50S R60 R69S (1955-1969) FACTORY WSM
BSA BANTAM (BOOK OF)
BSA ALL FOUR-STROKE SINGLES & V-TWINS 1936-1952 (BOOK OF)
BSA OHV & SV SINGLES - 250cc 1954-1970 (BOOK OF)
BSA OHV & SV SINGLES 1945-54 250-600cc (BOOK OF)
BSA OHV SINGLES 350 & 500cc 1955-1967 (BOOK OF)
BSA PRE-WAR MODELS TO 1939 (BOOK OF)
BSA TWINS 1948-1962 (BOOK OF)
BSA TWINS 1962-1969 (SECOND BOOK OF)
DOUGLAS PRE-WAR ALL MODELS 1929-1939 (BOOK OF)
DOUGLAS POST-WAR ALL MODELS 1948-1957 FACTORY WSM
DUCATI 160cc, 250cc & 350cc OHC MODELS FACTORY WSM
HONDA 50 ALL MODELS UP TO 1970 INC MONKEY & TRAIL (BOOK OF)
HONDA 90 ALL MODELS UP TO 1966 (BOOK OF)
HONDA MOTORCYCLES 125-150 TWINS C/CS/CB/CA WSM
HONDA MOTORCYCLES 250-305 TWINS C/CS/CB WSM
HONDA MOTORCYCLES C100 SUPER CUB WSM
HONDA MOTORCYCLES C110 SPORT CUB 1962-1969 WSM
HONDA TWINS & SINGLES 50cc TO 305cc 1960-1966 (BOOK OF)
LAMBRETTA ALL 125 & 150cc MODELS 1947-1957 (BOOK OF)
LAMBRETTA LI & TV MODELS 1957-1970 (SECOND BOOK OF)
MATCHLESS 350 & 500cc SINGLES 1945-1956 (BOOK OF)
MATCHLESS 350 & 500cc SINGLES 1955-1966 (BOOK OF)
NORTON 1938-1956 (BOOK OF)
NORTON DOMINATOR TWINS 1955-1965 (BOOK OF)
NORTON MOTORCYCLES 1957-1970 FACTORY WSM
NORTON PREWAR MODELS 1932-1939 (BOOK OF)
ROYAL ENFIELD 736cc INTERCEPTOR FACTORY WSM
ROYAL ENFIELD 250cc & 350cc SINGLES 1958-1966 (SECOND BOOK OF)
SUZUKI 50cc & 80cc UP TO 1966 (BOOK OF)
SUZUKI T10 1963-1967 FACTORY WSM
SUZUKI T20 & T200 1965-1969 FACTORY WSM
TRIUMPH PRE-WAR MOTORCYCLE 1935-1939 (BOOK OF)
TRIUMPH MOTORCYCLES 1937-1951 WSM
TRIUMPH MOTORCYCLES 1945-1955 FACTORY WSM
TRIUMPH TWINS 1956-1969 (BOOK OF)
VELOCETTE ALL SINGLES & TWINS 1925-1970 (BOOK OF)
VESPA 1951-1961 (BOOK OF)
VINCENT MOTORCYCLES 1935-1955 WSM

VELOCEPRESS AUTOMOBILE BOOKS & MANUALS

ABARTH BUYERS GUIDE
AUSTIN-HEALEY 6-CYLINDER WSM
BMW 600 LIMOUSINE FACTORY WSM
BMW 600 LIMOUSINE OWNERS HAND BOOK & SERVICE MANUAL
BMW ISETTA FACTORY WSM
BOOK OF THE CARRERA PANAMERICANA - MEXICAN ROAD RACE
COMPLETE CATALOG OF JAPANESE MOTOR VEHICLES
DIALED IN - THE JAN OPPERMAN STORY
FERRARI 250/GT SERVICE AND MAINTENANCE
FERRARI 308 SERIES BUYER'S AND OWNER'S GUIDE
FERRARI BERLINETTA LUSSO
FERRARI BROCHURES AND SALES LITERATURE 1946-1967
FERRARI BROCHURES AND SALES LITERATURE 1968-1989
FERRARI GUIDE TO PERFORMANCE
FERRARI OPPERATING, MAINTENANCE & SERVICE H/BOOKS 1948-1963
FERRARI OWNER'S HANDBOOK
FERRARI SERIAL NUMBERS PART I - ODD NUMBERS TO 21399
FERRARI SERIAL NUMBERS PART II - EVEN NUMBERS TO 1050
FERRARI SPYDER CALIFORNIA
FERRARI TUNING TIPS & MAINTENANCE TECHNIQUES
HOW TO BUILD A FIBERGLASS CAR
HOW TO BUILD A RACING CAR
IF HEMINGWAY HAD WRITTEN A RACING NOVEL
JAGUAR E-TYPE 3.8 & 4.2 WSM
LE MANS 24 (THE BOOK THAT THE FILM WAS BASED ON)
MASERATI BROCHURES AND SALES LITERATURE
MASERATI OWNER'S HANDBOOK
METROPOLITAN FACTORY WSM
MGA & MGB OWNERS HANDBOOK & WSM
OBERT'S FIAT GUIDE
PERFORMANCE TUNING THE SUNBEAM TIGER
PORSCHE 356 1948-1965 WSM
PORSCHE 912 WSM
SOUPING THE VOLKSWAGEN
TRIUMPH TR2, TR3, TR4 1953-1965 WSM
VEDA ORR'S NEW REVISED HOT ROD PICTORIAL
VOLKSWAGEN TRANSPORTER, TRUCKS, STATION WAGONS WSM
VOLVO 1944-1968 ALL MODELS WSM

All VelocePress titles are available through your local independent bookseller, Amazon.com, or they may be purchased directly through our website at www.VelocePress.com. Wholesale customers may also purchase directly from us or from the Ingram Book Group.

AUTOBOOKS WORKSHOP MANUALS

ALFA ROMEO GIULIA 1300, 1600, 1750, 2000 1962-1978 WSM
AUSTIN HEALEY SPRITE, MG MIDGET 1958-1980 WSM
BMW 1600 1966-1973 WSM
BMW 2000 & 2002 1966-1976 WSM
BMW 2500, 2800, 3.0 & 3.3 1968-1977 WSM
BMW 316, 320, 320i 1975-1977 WSM
BMW 518, 520, 520i 1973-1981 WSM
FIAT 1100, 1100D, 1100R & 1200 1957-1969 WSM
FIAT 124 1966-1974 WSM
FIAT 124 SPORT 1966-1975 WSM
FIAT 125 & 125 SPECIAL 1967-1973 WSM
FIAT 126, 126L, 126 DV, 126/650 & 126/650 DV 1972-1982 WSM
FIAT 127 SALOON, SPECIAL & SPORT, 900, 1050 1971-1981 WSM
FIAT 128 1969-1982 WSM
FIAT 1300, 1500 1961-1967 WSM
FIAT 131 MIRAFIORI 1975-1982 WSM
FIAT 132 1972-1982 WSM
FIAT 500 1957-1973 WSM
FIAT 600, 600D & MULTIPLA 1955-1969 WSM
FIAT 850 1964-1972 WSM
JAGUAR E-TYPE 1961-1972 WSM
JAGUAR MK 1, 2 1955-1969 WSM
JAGUAR S TYPE, 420 1963-1968 WSM
JAGUAR XK 120, 140, 150 MK 7, 8, 9 1948-1961 WSM
LAND ROVER 1, 2 1948-1961 WSM
MERCEDES-BENZ 190 1959-1968 WSM
MERCEDES-BENZ 220/8 1968-1972 WSM
MERCEDES-BENZ 220B 1959-1965 WSM
MERCEDES-BENZ 230 1963-1968 WSM
MERCEDES-BENZ 250 1968-1972 WSM
MERCEDES-BENZ 280 1968-1972 WSM
MG MIDGET TA-TF 1936-1955 WSM
MINI 1959-1980 WSM
MORRIS MINOR 1952-1971 WSM
PEUGEOT 404 1960-1975 WSM
PORSCHE 911 1964-1973 WSM
PORSCHE 911 1970-1977 WSM
RENAULT 16 1965-1979 WSM
RENAULT 8, 10, 1100 1962-1971 WSM
ROVER 3500, 3500S 1968-1976 WSM
SUNBEAM RAPIER, ALPINE 1955-1965 WSM
TRIUMPH SPITFIRE, GT6, VITESSE 1962-1968 WSM
TRIUMPH TR2, TR3, TR3A 1952-1962 WSM
TRIUMPH TR4, TR4A 1961-1967 WSM
VOLKSWAGEN BEETLE 1968-1977 WSM

BROOKLANDS BOOKS & ROAD TEST PORTFOLIOS (RTP)

AC CARS 1904-2009
ALFA ROMEO 1920-1933 ROAD TEST PORTFOLIO
ALFA ROMEO 1934-1940 ROAD TEST PORTFOLIO
BRABHAM RALT HONDA THE RON TAURANAC STORY
BUGATTI TYPE 10 TO TYPE 40 ROAD TEST PORTFOLIO
BUGATTI TYPE 10 TO TYPE 251 ROAD TEST PORTFOLIO
BUGATTI TYPE 41 TO TYPE 55 ROAD TEST PORTFOLIO
BUGATTI TYPE 57 TO TYPE 251 ROAD TEST PORTFOLIO
DELAHAYE ROAD TEST PORTFOLIO
FERRARI ROAD CARS 1946-1956 ROAD TEST PORTFOLIO
FIAT 500 1936-1972 ROAD TEST PORTFOLIO
FIAT DINO ROAD TEST PORTFOLIO
HISPANO SUIZA ROAD TEST PORTFOLIO
HONDA ST1100/ST1300 PAN EUROPEAN 1990-2002 RTP
JAGUAR MK1 & MK2 ROAD TEST PORTFOLIO
LOTUS CORTINA ROAD TEST PORTFOLIO
MV AGUSTA F4 750 & 1000 1997-2007 ROAD TEST PORTFOLIO
TATRA CARS ROAD TEST PORTFOLIO

All VelocePress titles are available through your local independent bookseller, Amazon.com, or they may be purchased directly through our website at www.VelocePress.com. Wholesale customers may also purchase directly from us or from the Ingram Book Group.

www.ingramcontent.com/pod-product-compliance
Lightning Source LLC
Chambersburg PA
CBHW080423230426
43662CB00015B/2202